SIGNATURE SERIES

MICROSOFT® WORD 2013

Instructor's Guide

FILE   INSERT   DESIGN   PAGE LAYOUT   REFERENCES

NITA RUTKOSKY
AUDREY ROGGENKAMP

Paradigm
PUBLISHING

St. Paul

Senior Editor: Cheryl Drivdahl
Production Editor: Katherine Lee
Cover Designer: Leslie Anderson, Valerie King
Production Specialist: Sara Schmidt Boldon

Care has been taken to verify the accuracy of information presented in this book. However, the authors, editors, and publisher cannot accept responsibility for Web, email, newsgroup, or chat room subject matter or content, or for consequences from application of the information in this book, and make no warranty, expressed or implied, with respect to its content.

Trademarks: Microsoft is a trademark or registered trademark of Microsoft Corporation in the United States and/ or other countries. Some of the product names and company names included in this book have been used for identification purposes only and may be trademarks or registered trade names of their respective manufacturers and sellers. The authors, editors, and publisher disclaim any affiliation, association, or connection with, or sponsorship or endorsement by, such owners.

We have made every effort to trace the ownership of all copyrighted material and to secure permission from copyright holders. In the event of any question arising as to the use of any material, we will be pleased to make the necessary corrections in future printings. Thanks are due to the aforementioned authors, publishers, and agents for permission to use the materials indicated.

Paradigm Publishing is independent from Microsoft Corporation, and not affiliated with Microsoft in any manner. While this publication may be used in assisting individuals to prepare for a Microsoft Office Specialist (core-level or expert-level) certification exam, Microsoft, its designated program administrator, and Paradigm Publishing do not warrant that use of this publication will ensure passing a Microsoft Office Specialist (core-level or expert-level) certification exam.

ISBN 978-0-76385-196-5 (text)
ISBN 978-0-76385-204-7 (text & disc)

© Paradigm Publishing, Inc.
875 Montreal Way
St. Paul, MN 55102
Email: educate@emcp.com
Web site: www.emcp.com

Printed in the United States of America

22 21 20 19 18 17 16 15 14 13   1 2 3 4 5 6 7 8 9 10

Contents

PLANNING *Guidelines for Choosing Outcomes, Instructional Approach, Resource, and Assessments*

Note: Lesson Blueprints providing detailed lesson plans for a 16-week course are provided on the Instructor Resources disc and on the Internet Resource Center for Instructors.

ASSESSMENT *Resources for Evaluating Student Achievement*

Note: All assessment materials (including Model Answers in live file, PDF, and annotated PDF form) are provided on the Instructor Resources disc and on the Internet Resource Center for Instructors.

Planning the Course

Most educators would agree that the key to teaching a successful course is careful, thorough planning. And, as noted in *Exceptional Teaching: Ideas in Action*, published by Paradigm Publishing, "Instructors assess, plan, implement, and evaluate…repeatedly. They do this based on many of the factors that make teaching learner-centered and on several other variables. Before students even think about entering or logging into the classroom, instructors make decisions about the course. These begin with identifying the heart of the course. That is, what, exactly, are the most important outcomes that students should achieve? And what plan of action can instructors devise that will help ensure those outcomes?" Thinking through a course action plan typically includes four phases:

1. Developing the course outcomes
2. Determining the course delivery mode and structure (dividing the course into parts, each with outcomes)
3. Selecting the course's instructional approach, resources, and activities
4. Developing an assessment strategy

1. Developing Course Outcomes

In developing course outcomes, consider the following key issues:

- When this course is over, in what ways will the learner be permanently changed?
- Should instruction result in
  - building knowledge?
  - developing higher-order thinking?
  - developing independent learning skills?
  - developing technical fluency?

Considering the questions above, a set of end-of-course outcomes for a one-semester class on Microsoft Word 2013 could include the following items, stated as performances. At the conclusion of the course, the student will be able to do the following:

- Create and edit memos, letters, and reports of varying complexity
- Format and customize a range of document types and styles
- Add and modify graphics and other visual elements to enhance written communication
- Organize content into tables, lists, and other structures that promote reader understanding and efficient management in a collaborative work environment
- Plan, research, write, revise, and publish documents to meet specific information needs

2. Determining the Course Delivery Mode and Structure

Frequently, the course structure has been determined previously by your department. However, if you are in a position to develop a plan or modify an existing structure, consider these questions:

- What topics in each subject area are essential for demonstrating the course outcomes?
- Is this the only course that will address this subject and skill set?

- What do students already know about each subject? What can they learn on their own, independent of your direct instruction?
- Where in each subject area will the instruction "begin" and "end"?

Your answers to these questions will help you divide the course content into parts and identify the associated learning outcomes (also called performance objectives). Note that course outcomes are marked by higher and more challenging skill sets and typically require the integration of many skills, while module or chapter outcomes are more narrowly defined and focused.

Course Delivery Mode:
Traditional Classroom, Online (Distance Learning), or Hybrid?

The core considerations are the same whether you are planning a traditional on-campus course, an online course (also called a distance learning course), or a hybrid of the two. However, the instructional differences in these delivery modes create distinct needs you must address in the planning stage for your course. A critical challenge in teaching online courses is the issue of interacting with students. How will you communicate with them? How will you get to know them? How will they submit assignments and tests? How will you deliver feedback?

Here are some additional questions to consider when planning an online or hybrid course, as suggested in *Exceptional Teaching*:

1. What course management system will be used: Blackboard, Moodle, or some other learning management system?

2. Will you offer a Web course where everything is done online? Or will you teach a course where students work independently offline and use the course management system to review course outcomes, the syllabus, and assignment due dates; communicate with the instructor; take online quizzes; transmit completed work; and participate in chat sessions?

3. Will you have an on-campus orientation meeting with your students at the beginning of the course? In some situations, because of the distance factor, students will not be able to come to campus. However, if possible, by all means arrange for them to do so. Many students will have the same questions that can be answered at one time, and the face-to-face contact at an orientation will benefit both you and the students. If you cannot arrange an on-campus session, consider ways that you can replicate this orientation online.

4. Will the students come to the campus to take exams? If not, will students be directed to offsite locations where exams can be administered to verify that the person taking the exam is indeed the person getting credit for the course? It is critical that this step be set up before the online class begins.

5. What PC configuration and/or software requirements must a student have to participate in your online course?

Both the student and instructor resources offered with *Signature Series: Microsoft® Word 2013* can be adapted for use in an online learning environment, or a hybrid of traditional and online learning contexts. The SNAP Training and Assessment materials were developed specifically for online delivery and are well-suited for distance learning.

Course Delivery Structure: Syllabus Suggestions

A comprehensive syllabus should help you and your students prepare for each part of the class. Syllabi are useful for traditional, on-campus courses as well as for courses delivered online. Generally, the following elements are included in a syllabus:

1. Course identifying data
2. Prerequisites
3. Instructor contact information
4. Course outcomes
5. Required course resources
6. Major assignments
7. Grade composition
8. Class structure
9. Course schedule
10. College/school requirements

The following syllabus is an example for a traditional 16-week course that meets on campus three times a week and uses the *Signature Word 2013* textbook. Lesson plans that correspond to this syllabus are available on the Instructor Resources disc and on the password-protected instructor's side of the textbook's Internet Resource Center at www.ParadigmCollege.net/SignatureWord13.

Traditional 16-Week Semester Syllabus Example

Course Description

This course prepares students to work with Microsoft Word 2013 either within a career setting or for personal use. Using courseware that incorporates a step-by-step, project-based approach, students develop a mastery-level competency in Word 2013 and get an introduction to computer software and hardware. Students also develop an understanding of fundamental computer hardware and software concepts.

Prerequisites: None

Instructor Contact Information

Name:

Office Phone:

Office Email:

Office Location:

Office Hours:

Required Course Resources

- *Signature Series: Microsoft® Word 2013,* by Rutkosky and Roggenkamp, © Paradigm Publishing, Inc.
- Student Resources disc (provided with textbook)
- Internet Resource Center, at www.ParadigmCollege.net/SignatureWord13
- USB flash drive or other storage medium

Computer Time

Approximately six to eight hours per week of computer time outside of class is recommended for successful completion of course requirements.

Grading

Final grades will be calculated as follows:

Average score on...	...constitutes the following percentage of the final grade
Daily work and chapter exercises	10%
Review Key Points assignments	5%
Chapter Assessments assignments	30%
Unit Performance Assessment assignments	30%
Tests	25%

College and Course Policy Information

This college conforms to the provisions of the Americans with Disabilities Act. You are invited to report any special needs to your instructor.

- Your attendance is expected at all class sessions.
- We subscribe to the college policy on academic honesty found in the school catalog.

Course Schedule

Week	Class	Chapter	Lesson Plan File	Description
1	Class 1	Getting Started and Chapter 1	SW13-01	Introduction to course; Creating, Printing, and Editing Documents
	Class 2	Chapter 2	SW13-02	Formatting Characters
	Class 3	Chapter 3	SW13-03	Aligning and Indenting Paragraphs
2	Class 4	Chapter 4	SW13-04	Customizing Paragraphs Part I
	Class 5	Chapter 4	SW13-05	Customizing Paragraphs Part II
	Class 6	Chapter 5	SW13-06	Proofing Documents
3	Class 7	N/A	Study/Work on Unit 1 Chapters and Exercises	
	Class 8	N/A	**Unit 1 Performance Assessments**	
	Class 9	Chapter 6	SW13-07	Formatting Pages
4	Class 10	Chapter 7	SW13-08	Customizing Page Formatting
	Class 11	Chapter 8	SW13-09	Inserting Elements and Navigating in a Document
	Class 12	Chapter 9	SW13-10	Maintaining Documents
5	Class 13	Chapter 10	SW13-11	Managing and Printing Documents
	Class 14	N/A	Study/Work on Unit 2 Chapters and Exercises	
	Class 15	N/A	**Unit 2 Performance Assessments**	
6	Class 16	Chapter 11	SW13-12	Inserting Images
	Class 17	Chapter 12	SW13-13	Inserting Shapes, WordArt, and Advanced Character Formatting
	Class 18	Chapter 13	SW13-14	Creating Tables
7	Class 19	Chapter 14	SW13-15	Enhancing Tables
	Class 20	Chapter 15	SW13-16	Creating Charts
	Class 21	N/A	Study/Work on Unit 3 Chapters and Exercises	

Week	Class	Chapter	Lesson Plan File	Description
8	Class 22	N/A	**Unit 3 Performance Assessments**	
	Class 23	Chapter 16	SW13-17	Merging Documents
	Class 24	Chapter 17	SW13-18	Managing Lists
9	Class 25	Chapter 18	SW13-19	Sorting and Selecting; Finding and Replacing Data
	Class 26	Chapter 19	SW13-20	Managing Page Numbers, Headers, and Footers
	Class 27	Chapter 20	SW13-21	Managing Shared Documents
10	Class 28	N/A	Study/Work on Unit 4 Chapters and Exercises	
	Class 29	N/A	**Unit 4 Performance Assessments**	
	Class 30	Chapter 21	SW13-22	Inserting and Customizing Quick Parts
11	Class 31	Chapter 22	SW13-23	Customizing AutoCorrect and Word Options
	Class 32	Chapter 23	SW13-24	Customizing Themes
	Class 33	Chapter 24	SW13-25	Creating and Managing Styles
12	Class 34	Chapter 25	SW13-26	Protecting, Preparing, and Sharing Documents
	Class 35	N/A	Study/Work on Unit 5 Chapters and Exercises	
	Class 36	N/A	**Unit 5 Performance Assessments**	
13	Class 37	Chapter 26	SW13-27	Inserting Endnotes, Footnotes, and References
	Class 38	Chapter 27	SW13-28	Creating Indexes
	Class 39	Chapter 28	SW13-29	Creating Specialized Tables
14	Class 40	Chapter 29	SW13-30	Creating Forms Part I
	Class 41	Chapter 29	SW13-31	Creating Forms Part II
	Class 42	Chapter 30	SW13-32	Using Outline View and Formatting with Macros
15	Class 43	N/A	Study/Work on Unit 6 Chapters and Exercises	
	Class 44	N/A	**Unit 6 Performance Assessments**	
	Class 45	N/A	Begin preparing for final exam	
16	Class 46	N/A	Final Exam Signature Word 2013	

3. Selecting the Instructional Approach, Resources, and Activities

After the course outcomes and structure are determined, it is important to plan the main content of the course. This includes considering SNAP Web-based training and assessment materials, selecting student courseware, choosing instructional support materials, identifying resources for English language learners, and reviewing other resources.

SNAP Web-Based Training and Assessment

SNAP is a Web-based program offering an interactive venue for learning Microsoft Office 2013, Windows 8, and Internet Explorer 10. SNAP delivers course materials in a learning management system that includes an online grade book and course planning tools.

The following SNAP Web-based training and assessment materials are available to support *Signature Word 2013*:

- Over 175 interactive, gradable, multimedia tutorials, aligned to textbook chapters, for direct instruction or remediation
- Over 350 skill items, in which students perform tasks in Microsoft Word 2013 that are reported in the learning management system; instructors can assign predefined Skill Exams or create their own
- 30 Key Points Review matching exercises, which correspond to the Key Points Review multiple-choice exercises in the textbook
- More than 120 Grade Its, which are automatically graded versions of selected Chapter Assessments that students complete live in the Office application *Note: Chapter Assessments that are available in SNAP are indicated by a SNAP Grade It logo in the textbook margin.*
- 36 Performance Evaluations, one per chapter and one per unit, for comprehensive assessment of skills mastery
- 1,200 concept questions that can be used to monitor student understanding of computer literacy and technical knowledge; instructors can assign predefined Concept Exams or create their own

For more information and to access SNAP materials that you have purchased for this course, go to snap2013.emcp.com.

Student Resources

Selecting high-quality student courseware is an important step in the planning process. Learning materials should be engaging and accessible. The *Signature Word 2013* program offers the following valuable learning tools to help student master the course performance objectives:

- *Signature Series: Microsoft® Word 2013* textbook
- Student Resources disc provided with the textbook
- book-specific Internet Resource Center at www.ParadigmCollege.net/SignatureWord13
- online eBook
- SNAP Tutorials disc

Textbook

Signature Series: Microsoft® Word 2013 prepares students to work with Microsoft Word 2013 in a business office, an academic setting, or for personal use. Incorporating a project-based approach that organizes instruction and guided exercises around related program features, this textbook builds student competency in Word 2013 and the basics of computer software and hardware, such as identifying computer hardware, choosing commands, and customizing settings.

The textbook is divided into six units, with each unit consisting of five chapters followed by a section of end-of-unit Performance Assessments.

The opening page for each chapter presents a list of the SNAP Tutorials that support the chapter content, a list of the Performance Objectives covered in the chapter, a brief summary of the skills taught in the chapter, a disc icon that identifies the folder containing the student data files for the chapter, and a list of the documents that students will produce as they work the chapter exercises. The model answers for the chapter exercises are displayed in the several pages that follow the chapter opener.

Each chapter is organized around exercises that require using a group of related features to complete a document or build a file. The text presents instruction on the features and skills necessary to accomplish each exercise. Many of the exercises are presented in parts (e.g., Exercise 1.1A, Exercise 1.1B, etc.). Typically, a file remains open throughout all parts of the exercise. Students save their work incrementally and usually—though not always—print only at the end of the entire exercise. Model answers for the chapter exercises are provided as live files and PDF files on the Instructor Resources disc and on the password-protected Internet Resource Center for Instructors.

The textbook chapters contain the following marginal features to help students perform and remember the skills taught in the text:

- Button graphics
- Quick Steps—brief summaries for reference and review

Each chapter ends with the following review elements and exercises:

- Chapter Summary—A bulleted list captures the purpose and execution of key features.
- Commands Review—A table presents the commands taught in the chapter along with the ribbon tab, group, button, and option sequences and keyboard shortcuts for the commands.
- Key Points Review—Objective completion exercises allow students to test their recall and comprehension of program features, terminology, and functions. Answers to these items are found in the Assessments section of the *Instructor's Guide*, Instructor Resources disc, and Internet Resource Center for Instructors at www.ParadigmCollege.net/SignatureWord13. These items are also presented as matching exercises with automatic grading online in SNAP.
- Chapter Assessments—Semi-guided exercises ask students to demonstrate their mastery of the major features and program skills taught in the chapter. Three types of Chapter Assessments are included:
  - Applying Your Skills assessments invite students to demonstrate what they have learned.
  - Expanding Your Skills assessments prompt students to learn additional skills.
  - Achieving Signature Status assessments challenge students with real-world problems.

Unit Performance Assessments follow each set of five chapters and offer opportunities for cross-disciplinary, comprehensive evaluation. These are presented in two groups: Assessing Proficiencies, which are gently guided exercises, and Creating Original Documents, which ask student to apply program skills in a communications context.

Annotated model answers and grading rubrics for the Chapter Assessments and Unit Performance Assessments are displayed in the Assessment section of the *Instructor's Guide*. The Instructor Resources disc and the password-protected Internet Resource Center for Instructors at www.ParadigmCollege.net/SignatureWord13 provide these model answers as live files, PDFs, and annotated PDFs, and also supply the grading rubrics in Word documents.

Student Resources Disc

Files that serve as a starting point for completing many of the chapter exercises and end-of-chapter assessments are included on the Student Resources disc that accompanies the textbook. Typically, students are directed to open one of these files, save it with a new name, and then edit and print the file. As students begin a chapter, they should copy the folder of files for the chapter exercises and assessments to the storage medium of their choice. This folder name is displayed in a disc icon on the first page of the chapter.

Internet Resource Center for Students

The book-specific Internet Resource Center at www.ParadigmCollege.net/SignatureWord13 offers valuable information for both instructors and students. For students, the Internet Resource Center includes quick access to the student data files, informational Web links, study aids, online quizzes, and more.

eBook

For students who prefer studying with an eBook, the textbook is available in an electronic form. The Web-based, password-protected eBook features dynamic navigation tools, including bookmarking, a linked table of contents, and the ability to jump to a specific page. The eBook format also supports helpful study tools, such as highlighting and note taking.

SNAP Tutorials Disc

The SNAP tutorials are also offered on disc for use without the full SNAP program. These interactive tutorials teach the basics of Word and include self-check exercises that provide instant feedback.

Instructor Resources

Instructor support materials for *Signature Word 2013* include the *Instructor's Guide* packaged with an Instructor Resources disc, password-protected instructor materials on the Internet Resource Center, and a Blackboard Cartridge.

Instructor's Guide and Disc

Instructor support for *Signature Word 2013* includes the Instructor's Guide and Instructor Resources Disc package. This package contains course planning materials, such as syllabus suggestions and lesson plans with teaching hints; PowerPoint presentations with lecture notes; and assessment resources, including the ExamView® Assessment Suite with concepts exam question banks, an overview of available assessment venues, live-file and PDF model answers for all the exercises and assessments in the textbook, and annotated PDF model answers and grading rubrics for end-of-chapter and end-of-unit assessments.

Internet Resource Center for Instructors

With the exception of the ExamView® materials (which are available on the Instructor Resources disc only), the contents of the *Instructor's Guide* and Instructor Resources disc package are also available in the password-protected instructor area of the Internet Resource Center at www.ParadigmCollege.net/SignatureWord13.

Blackboard Cartridge

The Blackboard Cartridge provides a set of files that allows instructors to create a personalized Blackboard website for their course and provides course content, tests, and the mechanisms for establishing e-discussions and online group conferences. Available content includes a syllabus, concept exam question banks, PowerPoint presentations, and supplementary course materials. Upon request, the files can be available within 24–48 hours. Hosting the site is the responsibility of the educational institution.

Resources for English Language Learners[1]

One of the fastest growing groups of students in higher education is comprised of students whose first language is not English, and whose English is not yet equivalent to that of native English speakers in lexicon and syntax. The wide differences in fluency among limited English speakers makes your planning for meeting their needs somewhat more complex—and very important.

Chances are that you already know you will have some students whose language skills are not up to the level we expect or want. What? You're not the ESL instructor? Not your job? Think again. Your job is to help *all* the students in your course meet the intended outcomes. So plan how you're going to do this for your limited English speakers. Begin by assessing early on the language abilities of your students. Try these measures:

1. One method is a "one-minute preview." Tear some sheets of paper into four parts and give each student a piece. Ask them no more than two questions and give them one minute (okay, two) to write their answer. The question could be about their language skills, but it might be better to ask them something else. That way you get a short writing sample plus information about something else, such as why they are taking the course, something they would like to learn, the types of activities they enjoy, or what they are most worried about in the course. You don't need to be an English teacher to see which students will need help. Use your common sense.

2. If your class is small, conduct a discussion early in the course. Make sure you hear each student answer a question or ask one.

3. If you are conducting a pretest for the course, include some questions that ask students if they need to improve their English or their writing skills.

4. Tell students to e-mail you if they think they will need language help or extra exam time for reading assignments or tests.

In addition to the suggestions above, consider whether or not you need to prepare a list of terms for each session or unit that might be troublemakers for English language learners. Do you need to have students arrange for tutors to assist with completing the unguided assessments? Do you need to dedicate a session or part of one to instruction on how to prepare the work you expect?

To assist English language learners in learning computer concept terminology, the *Signature Series: Microsoft® Word 2013* Internet Resource Center at www.ParadigmCollege.net/SignatureWord13 includes a link to the *Our Digital World* glossary. This resource provides computer concepts terms and definitions in both English and Spanish.

Information about Microsoft Office 2013

Microsoft Office 2013 operates on the Windows 8 operating system, as well as on Windows 7.

Video on What's New in Office 2013

Microsoft Corporation offers its own downloadable video presentation on the new features in Office 2013 at this address: http://office.microsoft.com/en-us/support/video-whats-new-in-office-2013-VA103147615.aspx?CTT=1http.

---

[1] Excerpted from *Exceptional Teaching: Ideas in Action*, published by Paradigm Publishing, Inc.

Quick Start Guides

Microsoft provides a series of Quick Start Guides for the applications in Office 2013 at http:// office.microsoft.com/en-us/support/office-2013-quick-start-guides-HA103673669.aspx?CTT=1.

Microsoft Office 2013 Product Editions

Microsoft Office 2013 is available in the following editions:

- Microsoft Office Starter
- Office Home and Student
- Office Home and Business
- Office Professional
- Microsoft Office Professional Plus
- Microsoft Office Standard
- Microsoft Office Professional Academic

The programs included in each edition at http://office.microsoft.com/en-us/products/ FX101635841033.aspx.

Microsoft Office 2013 System Requirements

The *Signature Word 2013* textbook is designed for students to complete exercises and assessments on a computer running a standard installation of Microsoft Office 2013, Professional Edition, and the Microsoft Windows 8 operating system. *Note: Office 2013 will also operate on computers running the Windows 7 operating system.*

To effectively run the Microsoft Office suite and Windows 8 operating system, each student and instructor computer should be outfitted with the following:

- 1 gigahertz (GHz) processor or higher; 1 gigabyte (GB) of RAM (32 bit) or 2 GB of RAM (64 bit)
- 3 GB of available hard-disk space
- .NET version 3.5, 4.0, or 4.5
- DirectX 10 graphics card
- Minimum 1024×576 monitor resolution (or 1366×768 to use the Windows Snap feature)
- Computer mouse, multi-touch device, or other compatible pointing device

The screen captures in the textbook were created using a screen resolution display setting of 1600×900. *Customizing Settings* in the *Getting Started* section of the textbook presents instructions on changing a monitor's resolution. Figure G.10 on page xxv of the textbook illustrates the Microsoft Office Word ribbon at three resolutions for comparison purposes. Choose the resolution that best matches your computer; however, be aware that using a resolution other than 1600×900 means that your screens may not match the illustrations in this book.

Microsoft Office Certification

With the release of Office 2013, Microsoft has developed a new set of certification objectives, which are available at http://www.microsoft.com/learning/en/us/mos-certification.aspx. *Signature Series: Microsoft® Word 2013* has been validated and approved by ProCert Labs (www.procert.com) as courseware covering the core-level objectives in the Microsoft Office Specialist Certification and Expert Certification exams. Tables correlating the *Signature Word 2013* textbook with the objectives for those exams are provided in the *Instructor's Guide* and are also available on the Instructor Resources disc and on the password-protected Internet Resource Center for Instructors at www.ParadigmCollege.net/SignatureWord13.

4. Developing an Assessment Strategy

The final phase of planning a course is to develop an assessment strategy based on the purpose of evaluation and on your philosophy of what constitutes a high-quality assessment. The obvious purpose of assessing students' learning is to determine whether or not students have achieved the goals of the course and, if they have, to what degree. Other functions of evaluation might include motivating students, determining the overall effectiveness of your teaching, and meeting accreditation requirements.

What is your philosophy of assessment? In determining your response, consider the following suggestions from Paradigm Publishing's *Exceptional Teaching*:

1. Assessment should contribute to students' learning by asking them to apply their skills in out-of-school or workplace situations.

2. Timing, content, and form of assessments should be planned as an integral part of the course design.

3. The purpose of every assessment should be clear.

4. The type of assessment—its content and format—should be appropriate for the purpose.

5. Assessments should be scored as consistently and objectively as possible.

6. Assessments should provide students with feedback on their learning.

7. Assessments should emphasize intellectual traits of value: analytical reading, thinking, decision-making, and research skills along with individual creativity and individual intelligence.

8. Assessments should be conducted at specific, planned checkpoints.

9. Assessments should be conducted in a positive learning environment, with every effort made to lower students' test anxieties.

10. Assessments should allow students to demonstrate their accomplishment of outcomes in various ways, including ways that fit their individual learning styles.

Determining the Number, Level, and Type of Assessments

Using your philosophy of assessment as a guide, begin to formulate your evaluation and grading strategy by answering the following course-level questions, as presented in *Exceptional Teaching*:

- Do I want a course pre-assessment?

- Do I want a comprehensive course assessment—one that will determine students' mastery of the major intended outcomes for the entire course?

- Do I want a pre-assessment for each module?

- Do I want a comprehensive assessment for each module—ones that evaluates students' mastery of the major intended outcomes for that module?

- Do I want interim or checkpoint assessments that evaluate students' mastery of intended outcomes of learning chunks within modules? If so, how many? How often?

- Once my system is in place, will my students know that I value *how* and *how well* they think?

The questions above will help you establish approximately how many assessments you wish to include and their place in the course. The next decisions concern which types of assessment to use: traditional cognitive (objective) tests and/or performance-based assessments. Each of these two major categories of tests has its best uses. Traditional cognitive tests such as multiple-choice exams usually work best for testing information recall, comprehension, and analysis. They also are reliable and efficient, and relatively easy to score. On the down side, objective-type tests are criticized for not representing how students will use their new skills in an unfamiliar setting or in the real world of work. Here's where performance-based testing rises to the fore. Requiring students to demonstrate what they have learned and to apply it in a realistic context that closely approximates a real-world situation measures how well students can do what the course intended to teach them. As emphasized in *Exceptional Teaching,* "Authentic, performance-based assessments ask students to integrate what they have learned and apply it to resolve an issue, solve a problem, create something new, work collaboratively, or use their written and oral communication skills. Authentic assessments stress the process of learning as well as the outcomes of learning."

Typically, instructors develop an assessment strategy that uses the strengths of both major types of assessments. The Assessment section of the *Instructor's Guide* lists the objective and performance-based testing tools available with the textbook and also provides a grading sheet that can be customized for your assessment plan.

Creating a Grading Plan

By choosing the types of assessments that will measure students' achievement of course and program outcomes, you will already have established a schema of the major grading components. The next step is to weight the scores as preparation for entering them into a grade calculation system—for example, an Excel spreadsheet.

Will you include nonachievement factors such as effort and attendance, in students' grades? If so, consider how to measure those elements. While it is simple to track attendance, it is not so easy to objectively evaluate effort and attitude. Some experts recommend that instructors provide regular verbal and written feedback on nonachievement factors, but confine grades to academic achievement.

The following grading plan offers a starting point as you develop your comprehensive grading strategy for a course using *Signature Word 2013*:

Daily work and chapter exercises	10%
Key Points Review assignments	5%
Applying Your Skills Assessments	30%
Unit Performance Assessments	30%
Tests	25%

The Grading Sheet can be used as a resource to create your own grading plan. See also the Overview of Assessment Venues available for assessing student achievement in your course. Both of these resources are available in the *Instructor's Guide* as well as on the Instructor Resources disc and on the password-protected Internet Resource Center for Instructors at www.ParadigmCollege.net/SignatureWord13.

For More Information

Much of the content of this "Planning the Course" article is based on information found in *Exceptional Teaching: Ideas in Action*. To order a copy of this resource, please visit www.paradigmcollege.com or call or email Customer Care at 800-535-6865, educate@emcp.com.

Certification Correlation
77-418

MOS Word 2013 Objectives

Objective Domain	Textbook Location
1.0 Create and Manage Documents	
1.1 Create a Document	
1.1.1 create new blank documents	C1, pgs. 6-8
1.1.2 create new documents apply templates	C9, pgs. 287-289
1.1.3 import files	C20, pgs. 693-696
1.1.4 open non-native files directly in Word	C9, pgs. 284-287
1.1.5 open a PDF in Word for editing	C9, pgs. 286-287
1.2 Navigate through a Document	
1.2.1 search for text within document	C7, pgs. 222-227
1.2.2 insert hyperlinks	C8, pgs. 250-255
1.2.3 create bookmarks	C8, pgs. 248-250
1.2.4 demonstrate how to use Go To	C1, pgs. 17, 19
1.3 Format a Document	
1.3.1 modify page setup	C6, pgs. 178-182
1.3.2 change document themes	C2, pgs. 51-53
1.3.3 change document style sets	C2, pgs. 49-50
1.3.4 insert simple headers and footers	C7, pgs. 217-221
1.3.5 insert watermarks	C6, pgs. 193-194
1.3.6 insert page numbers	C7, pgs. 216-217
1.4 Customize Options and Views for Documents	
1.4.1 change document views	C6, pgs. 175-177
1.4.2 demonstrate how to use zoom	C6, pgs. 175-177; C10, pgs. 305-306
1.4.3 customize the Quick Access toolbar	C22, pgs. 762-767
1.4.4 customize the Ribbon	C22, pgs. 768-774
1.4.5 split the window	C10, pg. 302
1.4.6 add values to document properties	C25, pgs. 869-875
1.4.7 demonstrate how to use Show/Hide	C10, pg. 306
1.4.8 record simple macros	C30, pgs. 1070-1073
1.4.9 assign shortcut keys	C30, pgs. 1076-1078
1.4.10 manage macro security	C30, pgs. 1081-1082
1.5 Configure Documents to Print or Save	
1.5.1 configure documents to print	C1, pgs. 10-12
1.5.2 save documents in alternate file formats	C9, pgs. 281-287

Objective Domain	Textbook Location
1.5.3 print document sections	C19, pgs. 656
1.5.4 save files to remote locations	C1, pgs. 9, 12
1.5.5 protect documents with passwords	C25, pgs. 875-878
1.5.6 set print scaling	C10, pgs. 310, 312
1.5.7 maintain backward compatibility	C9, pgs. 281-284
2.0 Format Text, Paragraphs, and Sections	
2.1 Insert Text and Paragraphs	
2.1.1 append text to documents	C4, pgs. 112-120; C8, pgs. 245-246
2.1.2 find and replace text	C7, pgs. 222-227
2.1.3 copy and paste text	C4, pgs. 112-120
2.1.4 insert text via AutoCorrect	C22, pgs. 754-757
2.1.5 remove blank paragraphs	C3, pg. 65
2.1.6 insert built-in fields	C21, pgs. 739-742
2.1.7 insert special characters (©, ™, £)	C8, pgs. 241-242
2.2 Format Text and Paragraphs	
2.2.1 change font attributes	C2, pgs. 37-48
2.2.2 demonstrate how to use Find and Replace to format text	C18, pgs. 619-622
2.2.3 demonstrate how to use Format Painter	C3, pgs. 73-74
2.2.4 set paragraph spacing	C3, pgs. 72-73
2.2.5 set line spacing	C3, pgs. 75-76
2.2.6 clear existing formatting	C2, pgs. 37, 40, 43; C3, pgs. 63, 76
2.2.7 set indentation	C3, pgs. 68-71
2.2.8 highlight text selections	C2, pgs. 42, 44-45
2.2.9 add styles to text	C2, pgs. 49-50
2.2.10 change text to WordArt	C12, pgs. 402-406
2.2.11 modify existing style attributes	C2, pgs. 49-50; C24, pgs. 818-819
2.3 Order and Group Text and Paragraphs	
2.3.1 prevent paragraph orphans	C19, pgs. 657-658
2.3.2 insert breaks to create sections	C6, pgs. 183-184; C19, pgs. 643, 645
2.3.3 create multiple columns within sections	C6, pgs. 185-186; C21, pg. 715
2.3.4 add titles to sections	C19, pgs. 653-655
2.3.5 force page breaks	C7, pgs. 211-212
3.0 Create Tables and Lists	
3.1 Create a Table	
3.1.1 convert text to tables	C14, pgs. 468-469
3.1.2 convert tables to text	C14, pgs. 468-470
3.1.3 define table dimensions	C13, pgs. 428-431; C14, pgs. 464-466
3.1.4 set AutoFit options	C14, pgs. 458, 460, 465, 467, 469, 475

Objective Domain	Textbook Location
3.1.5 demonstrate how to use Quick Tables	C13, pg. 444
3.1.6 set a table title	C14, pgs. 457-458, 461-462, 469
3.2 Modify a Table	
3.2.1 apply styles to tables	C13, pgs. 435-436
3.2.2 modify fonts within tables	C13, pgs. 433-434
3.2.3 sort table data	C14, pgs. 470-471; C18, pgs. 609-610
3.2.4 configure cell margins	C14, pgs.462-464
3.2.5 demonstrate how to apply formulas to a table	C14, pgs. 471-475
3.2.6 modify table dimensions	C14, pgs. 464-466
3.2.7 merge cells	C14, pgs. 456-458
3.3 Create and Modify a List	
3.3.1 add numbering or bullets	C3, pgs. 76-81
3.3.2 create custom bullets	C17, pgs. 579-582
3.3.3 modify list indentation	C3, pgs. 68-71, 80; C17, pgs. 574-575, 582-586
3.3.4 modify line spacing	C3, pgs. 75-76
3.3.5 increase and decrease list levels	C3, pgs. 68-71, 80; C17, pgs. 574-575, 582-586
3.3.6 modify numbering	C17, pgs. 574-579
4.0 Apply References	
4.1 Create Endnotes, Footnotes, and Citations	
4.1.1 insert endnotes	C26, pgs. 921-925
4.1.2 manage footnote locations	C26, pgs. 923-925
4.1.3 configure endnote formats	C26, pgs. 923-925
4.1.4 modify footnote numbering	C26, pgs. 923-925
4.1.5 insert citation placeholders	C26, pgs. 928, 930
4.1.6 insert citations	C26, pgs. 928-930
4.1.7 insert bibliography	C26, pgs. 936-938
4.1.8 change citation styles	C26, pgs. 939
4.2 Create Captions	
4.2.1 add captions	C28, pgs. 986-988
4.2.2 set caption positions	C28, pgs. 986, 990-991
4.2.3 change caption formats	C28, pgs. 986, 990-991
4.2.4 change caption labels	C28, pgs. 986, 990-991
4.2.5 exclude labels from captions	C28, pgs. 990-991
5.0 Insert and Format Objects	
5.1 Insert and Format Building Blocks	
5.1.1 insert Quick Parts	C21, pgs. 718-721

Objective Domain	Textbook Location
5.1.2 insert textboxes	C12, pgs. 393-398
5.1.3 demonstrate how to use Building Blocks Organizer	C21, pgs. 718-721
5.1.4 customize Building Blocks	C21, pgs. 722-733
5.2 Insert and Format Shapes and SmartArt	
5.2.1 insert simple shapes	C12, pgs. 384-387
5.2.2 insert SmartArt	C11, pgs. 358-365
5.2.3 modify SmartArt properties (color, size, shape)	C11, pgs. 358-363
5.2.4 wrap text around shapes	C12, pgs. 396, 406; C11, pgs. 361-363
5.2.5 position shapes	C12, pgs. 384, 388-389, 392
5.3 Insert and Format Images	
5.3.1 insert images	C11, pgs. 341-356
5.3.2 apply artistic effects	C11, pgs. 341-342, 355-356
5.3.3 apply picture effects	C11, pgs. 341, 350, 355
5.3.4 modify image properties (color, size, shape)	C11, pgs. 341, 345, 347-348, 350, 352-355, 357
5.3.5 add Quick Styles to images	C11, pgs. 341-343, 348, 350, 354-356
5.3.6 wrap text around images	C11, pgs. 341, 344-345, 348, 350, 351-353, 356-357
5.3.7 position images	C11, pgs. 341, 344-348, 350-351, 353, 356-357

Certification Correlation
77-419

MOS Word Expert 2013 Objectives

Objective Domain	Textbook Location
1.0 Manage and Share Documents	
1.1 Manage Multiple Documents	
1.1.1 modify existing templates	C21, pgs. 722-728; C24, pgs. 826-827, 834-836
1.1.2 merge multiple documents	C20, pgs. 690-692
1.1.3 manage versions of documents	C25, pgs. 887-891
1.1.4 copy styles from templates to template	C24, pgs. 846-848
1.1.5 demonstrate how to use the style organizer	C24, pgs. 846-848
1.1.6 copy macros from document to document	C30, pgs. 1083-1085
1.1.7 link to external data	C8, pgs. 250, 252-255; C20, pgs. 693-696
1.1.8 move building blocks between documents	C21, pgs. 734-735
1.2 Prepare Documents for Review	
1.2.1 set tracking options	C20, pgs. 679-684
1.2.2 limit authors	C20, pgs. 679, 682
1.2.3 restrict editing	C25, pgs. 861-866
1.2.4 delete document draft version	C25, pgs. 889, 891
1.2.5 remove document metadata	C25, pgs. 878-881
1.2.6 mark as final	C25, pgs. 875-876
1.2.7 protect a document with a password	C25, pgs. 867-868
1.3 Manage Document Changes	
1.3.1 track changes	C20, pgs. 677-687
1.3.2 manage comments	C20, pgs. 669-677
1.3.3 demonstrate how to use markup options	C20, pgs. 677-682
1.3.4 resolve a multi-document style conflicts	C20, pgs. 690-691
1.3.5 display all changes	C20, pgs. 677-682
2.0 Design Advanced Documents	
2.1 Apply Advanced Formatting	
2.1.1 demonstrate how to use wildcards in find and replace searches	C18, pgs. 624-626
2.1.2 create custom field formats	C21, pgs. 740-742
2.1.3 set advanced layout options	C11, pgs. 351-354; C7, pgs. 227-228; C19, pgs. 653-655; C6, pgs. 185-189

Objective Domain	Textbook Location
2.1.4 set character space options	C12, pgs. 407-409
2.1.5 set advanced character attributes	C12, pgs. 407-412
2.1.6 create and break section links	C19, pgs. 653-655
2.1.7 link textboxes	C12, pgs. 399-402
2.2 Apply Advanced Styles	
2.2.1 create custom styles	C24, pgs. 818-824, 833-841
2.2.2 customize settings for existing styles	C24, pgs. 818-819, 824-825
2.2.3 create character-specific styles	C24, pgs. 819, 823
2.2.4 assign keyboard shortcuts to styles	C24, pgs. 821-824
2.3 Apply Advanced Ordering and Grouping	
2.3.1 create outline	C30, pgs. 1056-1064
2.3.2 promote sections in outlines	C30, pgs. 1057-1059
2.3.3 create master documents	C30, pgs. 1064-1070
2.3.4 insert subdocuments	C30, pgs. 1068-1070
2.3.5 link document elements	C8, pgs. 250-252, 255-257
3.0 Create Advanced References	
3.1 Create and Manage Indexes	
3.1.1 create indexes	C27, pgs. 951-963
3.1.2 update indexes	C27, pg. 963
3.1.3 mark index entries	C27, pgs. 951-954
3.1.4 demonstrate how to use index auto-mark files	C27, pgs. 960-963
3.2 Create and Manage Reference Tables	
3.2.1 create a table of contents	C28, pgs. 975-985
3.2.2 create a table of figures	C28, pgs. 985-991
3.2.3 format table of contents	C28, pgs. 978-981
3.2.4 update a table of authorities	C28, pgs. 994-996
3.2.5 set advanced reference options (captions, footnotes, citations)	C28, pgs. 990-991; C26, pgs. 923-925, 925-939
3.3 Manage Forms, Fields, and Mail Merge Operations	
3.3.1 add custom fields	C21, pgs. 740-742
3.3.2 modify field properties	C21, pgs. 740-742
3.3.3 add field controls	C29, pgs. 1007, 1011-1012, 1015-1018, 1025-1028
3.3.4 modify field control properties	C29, pgs. 1019-1024
3.3.5 perform mail merges	C16, pgs. 534-542; 552-559
3.3.6 manage recipients lists	C16, pgs. 542-547
3.3.7 insert merged fields	C16, pgs. 547-551
3.3.8 preview results	C16, pgs. 533-534

Signature Word 2013   Certification Correlation

Objective Domain	Textbook Location
4.0 Create Custom Word Elements	
4.1 Create and Modify Building Blocks	
4.1.1 create custom building blocks	C21, pgs. 722-724
4.1.2 save selections as Quick Parts	C21, pgs. 723, 725
4.1.3 edit building block properties	C21, pgs. 726-727
4.1.4 delete building blocks	C21, pgs. 736-737
4.2 Create Custom Style Sets and Templates	
4.2.1 create custom color themes	C23, pgs. 792-797
4.2.2 create custom font themes	C23, pgs. 798
4.2.3 create custom templates	C23, pgs. 799-801; C24, pgs. 826-827
4.2.4 create and manage style sets	C24, pgs. 830-832
4.3 Prepare a document for Internationalization and Accessibility	
4.3.1 configure language options in documents	C5, pgs. 148-152
4.3.2 add alt-text to document elements	C25, pgs. 882-884
4.3.3 create documents for use with accessibility tools	C25, pgs. 881-885
4.3.4 manage multiple options for +Body and +Heading fonts	C25, pgs. 883, 885
4.3.5 demonstrate how to apply global content standards	C5, pgs. 149-152
4.3.6 modify Tab order in documents elements and objects	C29, pgs. 1037-1038

Chapter Overviews

Unit 1: Preparing Documents

Chapter 1: Creating, Printing, and Editing Documents

Performance Objectives

- Open Microsoft Word
- Create, save, name, print, and close a Word document
- Create a new document
- Open a saved document
- Save a document with *Save As*
- Close Word
- Edit a document
- Select text in a document
- Use the Undo and Redo buttons
- Use the Help feature

Exercises

1.1A	Creating a Document
1.1B	Saving, Printing, and Closing a Document
1.2A	Opening and Pinning/Unpinning a Document
1.2B	Saving a Document Using *Save As*
1.3A	Scrolling in a Document
1.3B	Moving the Insertion Point in a Document
1.4	Editing a Document
1.5	Deleting and Restoring Text with the Undo Buttons
1.6A	Using the Help Feature
1.6B	Getting Help in a Dialog Box and Backstage View

Assessments

Applying Your Skills

1.1	Type a Document
1.2	Edit a Document Containing Proofreaders' Marks
1.3	Edit a Document Containing Proofreaders' Marks

Expanding Your Skills

1.4	Compose a Document on Saving a Document
1.5	Use Help to Learn about and Then Create a Document Describing Keyboard Shortcuts

Achieving Signature Status

1.6	Create a Cover Letter

Chapter 2: Formatting Characters

Performance Objectives

- Change fonts and font effects
- Apply styles from style sets
- Apply themes
- Customize style sets and themes

Exercises

2.1A Changing the Font

2.1B Applying Character Formatting to Text as You Type

2.1C Applying Font Effects

2.1D Changing the Font at the Font Dialog Box

2.2A Applying Styles and a Style Set

2.2B Applying a Theme to a Document

2.2C Customizing a Theme

Assessments

Applying Your Skills

2.1 Create and Format a Utility Program Document

2.2 Format a Memo

2.3 Format a Training Announcement

2.4 Apply Styles, a Style Set, and a Theme to a Document

Expanding Your Skills

2.5 Create and Format a Memo

2.6 Research Text Effect Button

Achieving Signature Status

2.7 Type and Format Text on Writing a Cover Letter

2.8 Type a Business Letter

Chapter 3: Aligning and Indenting Paragraphs

Performance Objectives

- Change the alignment of text in paragraphs
- Indent text in paragraphs
- Increase and decrease spacing before and after paragraphs
- Repeat the last action
- Automate formatting with Format Painter
- Change line spacing in a document
- Apply numbering and bullet formatting to text
- Reveal formatting
- Compare formatting

Exercises

Assessments

Applying Your Skills

Expanding Your Skills

Achieving Signature Status

Chapter 4: Customizing Paragraphs

Performance Objectives

- Insert paragraph borders and shading
- Sort paragraphs of text
- Set, delete, and move tabs on the horizontal ruler and at the Tabs dialog box
- Delete, cut, copy, and paste text within a document
- Copy and paste text between documents

Exercises

Assessments
Applying Your Skills

Expanding Your Skills

Achieving Signature Status

Chapter 5: Proofing Documents

Performance Objectives

- Complete a spelling check and a grammar check on text in a document
- Create a custom dictionary and change the default dictionary
- Display document word, paragraph, and character counts
- Use the thesaurus to display synonyms and antonyms for specific words
- Use the dictionary to define specific words
- Use the translation feature to translate words from English to other languages

Exercises

Assessments

Applying Your Skills

Expanding Your Skills

Achieving Signature Status

Unit 1 Performance Assessments

Assessing Proficiencies

Creating Original Documents

Unit 2: Formatting and Managing Documents

Chapter 6: Formatting Pages

Performance Objectives

- Change the document view
- Change the page setup, including the margins, page orientation, and paper size in a document

- Insert section breaks in a document
- Create and format text in columns
- Hyphenate words automatically and manually
- Insert line numbers in a document
- Format the page background using a watermark, page color, and page border

Exercises

6.1A   Changing Views

6.1B   Changing Page Orientation

6.1C   Changing Page Size

6.1D   Changing Margins and Paper Size at the Page Setup Dialog Box

6.2A   Inserting Section Breaks

6.2B   Formatting Text into Columns

6.2C   Formatting Text into Columns within a Document

6.3A   Formatting Columns at the Columns Dialog Box

6.3B   Formatting and Balancing Columns of Text

6.3C   Automatically and Manually Hyphenating Words

6.3D   Inserting Line Numbers

6.4A   Inserting a Watermark and Page Color

6.4B   Inserting a Page Border

6.4C   Changing Page Border Options

Assessments

Applying Your Skills

6.1   Apply Formatting to a Computers in Industry Report

6.2   Apply Formatting to a Data Security Training Notice

6.3   Apply Formatting to an Interface Applications Report

Expanding Your Skills

6.4   Apply a Picture Watermark

Achieving Signature Status

6.5   Create and Format an Announcement

6.6   Format a Report on Delivering a Presentation

Chapter 7: Customizing Page Formatting

Performance Objectives

- Insert a page break, blank page, and cover page
- Insert page numbering
- Insert and edit headers and footers
- Find and replace text

- Use the Click and Type feature to position the insertion point within the document
- Align text vertically

Exercises

Assessments

Applying Your Skills

Expanding Your Skills

Achieving Signature Status

Chapter 8: Inserting Elements and Navigating in a Document

Performance Objectives

- Insert symbols and special characters
- Insert a drop cap
- Insert the date and time
- Insert a file into an open document
- Navigate in a document using the Navigation pane and bookmarks
- Insert hyperlinks to a location in the same document, a different document, and a file in another program
- Create a cross-reference

Exercises

Assessments

Applying Your Skills

Expanding Your Skills

Achieving Signature Status

Chapter 9: Maintaining Documents

Performance Objectives

- Manage files by copying, moving, printing, and renaming documents; opening multiple documents; and creating new folders and renaming existing folders
- Customize the display of folders and documents
- Share documents by exporting and saving them in different formats
- Create a document using a Word template

Exercises

Chapter 10: Managing and Printing Documents

Performance Objectives

- Open, close, arrange, split, maximize, minimize, and restore documents
- Manage the list of most recently opened documents
- Preview and print pages or sections of a document
- Create and print envelopes
- Create and print labels

Exercises

Assessments

Applying Your Skills

Unit 2 Performance Assessments

Unit 3: Enhancing Documents

Chapter 11: Inserting Images

Performance Objectives

- Insert, format, size, and move pictures and clip art images
- Customize pictures and clip art images
- Create and format SmartArt graphics and organizational charts

Exercises

Chapter 12: Using Shapes, WordArt, and Advanced Character Formatting

Performance Objectives
- Insert and format screenshot images
- Draw and format shapes
- Select and align objects
- Insert and format text boxes
- Link and unlink text boxes
- Insert and format WordArt
- Apply character formatting, such as spacing, OpenType features, and text effects

Exercises

Chapter 13: Creating Tables

Performance Objectives

- Create and format a table
- Format a table by selecting specific cells
- Change the table design
- Draw a table
- Insert an Excel spreadsheet into a Word document
- Insert a predesigned table into a document

Exercises

Chapter 14: Enhancing Tables

Performance Objectives
- Change the table design and layout
- Change between table and text formats and sort text in a table
- Perform calculations on data in a table

Exercises

Assessments
Applying Your Skills

Chapter 15: Creating Charts

Performance Objectives

- Create charts
- Format charts using the chart buttons
- Change the chart design
- Format charts and chart elements

Exercises

Assessments

Applying Your Skills

Expanding Your Skills

Achieving Signature Status

Unit 3 Performance Assessments

Assessing Proficiencies

Unit 4: Managing Data

Chapter 16: Merging Documents

Performance Objectives

- Create and merge a main document and a data source file
- Merge files to create envelopes, labels, and directories
- Edit main documents and data source files
- Insert additional fields
- Merge a main document with other data sources
- Use the Mail Merge wizard to merge documents

Exercises

Assessments

Applying Your Skills

Expanding Your Skills

Achieving Signature Status

Chapter 17: Managing Lists

Performance Objectives

- Insert custom numbers and bullets
- Insert multilevel list numbering
- Insert special characters, such as symbols, hyphens, and nonbreaking spaces

Exercises

Assessments

Applying Your Skills

Chapter 18: Sorting and Selecting; Finding and Replacing Data

Performance Objectives

- Sort text in paragraphs, columns, and tables
- Sort records in a data source file
- Select specific records in a data source file for merging
- Find specific records in a data source file
- Find and replace formatting and special characters and use wildcard characters

Exercises

Assessments

Applying Your Skills

Chapter 19: Managing Page Numbers, Headers, and Footers

Performance Objectives

- Insert, format, and remove customized page numbers
- Insert, format, edit, and remove customized headers and footers
- Print specific pages or sections of a document
- Control page breaks to keep related text together

Exercises

Assessments

Applying Your Skills

Expanding Your Skills

Achieving Signature Status

Chapter 20: Managing Shared Documents

Performance Objectives

- Insert, edit, delete, display, print, and reply to comments
- Track changes made to a document and customize tracking
- Compare documents and customize compare options

- Combine documents and manage style conflicts
- Embed and link data between Excel and Word

Exercises

Assessments

Applying Your Skills

Expanding Your Skills

Achieving Signature Status

Unit 4 Performance Assessments

Assessing Proficiencies

Unit 5: Customizing Documents and Features

Chapter 21: Inserting and Customizing Quick Parts

Performance Objectives

- Sort and insert building blocks
- Create, edit, modify, and delete building blocks
- Insert document properties
- Insert, update, and customize fields

Exercises

Assessments

Applying Your Skills

Expanding Your Skills

Achieving Signature Status

Chapter 22: Customizing AutoCorrect and Word Options

Performance Objectives

- Control what kinds of corrections are made by the AutoCorrect feature
- Customize the Quick Access toolbar
- Customize the ribbon
- Import and export Quick Access toolbar and ribbon customizations
- Customize Word options

Exercises

22.1A Adding Exceptions and Text to AutoCorrect

22.1B Using the AutoCorrect Options Button

22.1C Inserting Symbols Using AutoCorrect

22.1D Changing AutoFormatting and Deleting Text from AutoCorrect

22.2A Customizing the Quick Access Toolbar

22.2B Inserting and Removing Buttons from the Quick Access Toolbar

22.2C Customizing the Ribbon

22.2D Exporting Customizations

22.3A Customizing General Options

22.3B Customizing Save Options

22.3C Returning Options to the Default

Assessments

Applying Your Skills

22.1   Insert and Format Text in a Medical Plan Document

22.2   Create a Vacation Document with AutoCorrect and Special Symbols

22.3   Create a Custom Tab and Group

Expanding Your Skills

22.4   Create a Report on Word Options and Customization Features

Achieving Signature Status

22.5   Create a Resume Document with AutoCorrect Text

Chapter 23: Customizing Themes

Performance Objectives

- Create custom themes, theme colors, and theme fonts and apply theme effects
- Save a custom theme
- Edit custom themes
- Reset a theme to the template default
- Delete custom themes and custom theme colors and fonts
- Change the default settings for the style set and theme

Exercises

Assessments

Applying Your Skills

Expanding Your Skills

Achieving Signature Status

Chapter 24: Creating and Managing Styles

Performance Objectives

- Apply styles
- Create new styles from existing formatting and styles
- Assign a keyboard shortcut to a style
- Modify styles and save styles in a template
- Display all styles
- Reveal style formatting
- Save and delete a custom style set
- Create and modify styles for multilevel lists and tables
- Investigate document styles using the Style Inspector
- Manage and organize styles

Exercises

Assessments

Applying Your Skills

Expanding Your Skills

Achieving Signature Status

Chapter 25: Protecting, Preparing, and Sharing Documents

Performance Objectives

- Protect a document by restricting formatting and editing and by controlling access and viewing
- Modify document properties by viewing and modifying document information
- Restrict access to a document and verify its authenticity
- Inspect a document for accessibility and compatibility issues and manage versions of a document
- Share documents between programs, computers, and websites and as email attachments

Exercises

25.3B Marking a Document as Final

25.3C Encrypting a Document with a Password

25.4 Inspecting a Document

25.5A Checking the Accessibility of a Document

25.5B Checking the Compatibility of Elements in a Document

25.5C Opening an Autosave Document

25.6A Optional: Inviting People to View Your Document

25.6B Optional: Sending a Document as an Email Attachment

25.6C Optional: Presenting Online

Assessments

Applying Your Skills

25.1 Restrict Formatting and Editing of a Writing Report

25.2 Restrict Editing to Comments in a Software Life Cycle Document

25.3 Insert Document Properties, Check Accessibility and Compatibility, and Save a Presentation Document in a Different Format

Expanding Your Skills

25.4 Create a Document on Inserting and Removing a Signature

Achieving Signature Status

25.5 Format, Insert Document Properties, Check Compatibility, and Save a Document in a Different Format

Unit 5 Performance Assessments

Assessing Proficiencies

U5.1 Format and Insert Fields in a Report

U5.2 Create Building Blocks and Prepare a Business Letter

U5.3 Create and Apply Custom Themes and AutoCorrect Entries to a Rental Form

U5.4 Create and Apply Building Blocks and Styles to a Business Conduct Report

U5.5 Format a Report with Styles

U5.6 Restrict Formatting in a Report

U5.7 Insert Document Properties and Save a Document in a Previous Version of Word

Creating Original Documents

U5.8 Design and Apply Building Blocks

U5.9 Create AutoCorrect Entries and Format an Agreement Document

Unit 6: Referencing Data

Chapter 26: Inserting Endnotes, Footnotes, and References

Performance Objectives

- Insert and modify footnotes and endnotes
- Insert and modify citations and bibliographies

Exercises

26.1A Creating Footnotes

26.1B Creating Endnotes

26.1C Formatting Endnotes and Converting Endnotes to Footnotes

26.2A Formatting the First Page of a Research Paper

26.2B Inserting Sources and Citations

26.2C Editing an Existing Source and Inserting a Citation with an Existing Source

26.2D Modifying Sources

26.2E Inserting a Works Cited Page

26.2F Modifying and Updating a Works Cited Page

26.2G Formatting a Works Cited Page

26.2H Changing Citation Styles

Assessments

Applying Your Skills

26.1   Insert Footnotes in a Designing Newsletters Report

26.2   Insert Sources and Citations in a Privacy Rights Report

Expanding Your Skills

26.3   Customize Footnotes/Endnotes

Achieving Signature Status

26.4   Format a Report in MLA Style

Chapter 27: Creating Indexes

Performance Objectives

- Create an index and insert it in the document
- Mark entries and subentries for an index, including cross-references
- Create a concordance file and use it to create an index
- Update and delete an index

Exercises

27.1A Marking Words for an Index

27.1B Inserting an Index

Assessments

Applying Your Skills

Expanding Your Skills

Achieving Signature Status

Chapter 28: Creating Specialized Tables

Performance Objectives

- Create, insert, and update a table of contents
- Create, insert, and update a table of figures
- Create, insert, and update a table of authorities

Exercises

Assessments

Applying Your Skills

Expanding Your Skills

Achieving Signature Status

Chapter 29: Creating Forms

Performance Objectives

- Design a form and create and protect a form template
- Insert text controls
- Fill in a form
- Edit a form template
- Insert instructional text
- Create a form using a table and insert picture and date picker content controls
- Insert a drop-down list from a data field
- Set properties for content controls
- Create a form using legacy tools
- Print a form or only the data in the form
- Customize form field options

Exercises

29.1A Creating a Mailing List Form Template

29.1B Filling in the Mailing List Form

29.1C Editing the Mailing List Form Template

29.1D Filling in the Edited Mailing List Form

29.2A Inserting Controls in a Fax Template

29.2B Inserting Picture and Date Picker Content Controls

29.2C Filling in the Fax Form

29.3A Inserting Controls in a Survey Template

29.3B Customizing Picture and Date Picker Content Control Properties

29.3C Filling in the Survey Form

29.4A Creating an Application Form Template

29.4B Inserting Check Box Form Fields

29.4C Filling in the Lifetime Annuity Form Template

29.4D Printing Only the Data in a Form Document

29.5   Inserting Drop-down Form Fields and Filling in a Form

29.6A Inserting and Customizing Check Box Form Fields

29.6B Customizing Text Form Fields

29.7   Modifying Tab Order in a Form

Assessments

Applying Your Skills

29.1   Create and Fill in a Book Order Form

29.2   Create and Fill in a Catalog Request Form

29.3   Create and Fill in an Application Form

Chapter 30: Using Outline View and Formatting with Macros

Performance Objectives

- Create an outline by assigning levels to titles, headings, and so on
- Create a master document and subdocuments
- Expand, collapse, open, close, rearrange, split, and delete subdocuments
- Record, store, and name macros
- Run, pause, and delete macros
- Assign macros to keyboard commands or toolbars
- Specify macro security settings
- Save a macro-enabled document or template
- Record and run a macro with Fill-in fields

Exercises

Assessments
Applying Your Skills

Expanding Your Skills

Achieving Signature Status

Unit 6 Performance Assessments
Assessing Proficiencies

Creating Original Documents

ASSESSMENT
Overview of Assessment Venues

The grading sheet on the following pages can be used as a resource to create your grading plan for *Signature Series: Microsoft® Word 2013.* An electronic copy of this table is provided on the Instructor Resources disc and Internet Resource Center for Instructors, and you can alter that Word file to meet your specific course needs.

As noted on the grading sheet, several venues are available for assessing student achievement in your course, including both comprehension-based and performance-based assessments.

Comprehension-Based Assessments

- Key Points Review questions appear at the end of each chapter in the textbook. These short-answer questions test student comprehension and recall of program features, terminology, and functions. Answer keys for these items are included in the *Instructor's Guide*, on the Instructor Resources disc, and in the password-protected instructor materials on the Internet Resource Center.

- The ExamView® Assessment Suite includes test-generating software plus question banks containing multiple-choice questions for each chapter in this program. Instructors can use the ExamView test generator and question banks to create web-based or printed tests.

- Online study quizzes include multiple-choice items for each chapter. Students can complete these quizzes in two modes: as a practice test with immediate feedback, and as a reported quiz with the results emailed to themselves and their instructor. These quizzes are accessed from the student materials at the Internet Resource Center.

- SNAP offers a web-based, interactive venue for learning and assessing Microsoft Word 2013 skills. SNAP includes a learning management system that creates a virtual classroom on the Web, allowing instructors to schedule multimedia tutorials, online exams, and textbook work and to employ an online grade book. SNAP online comprehension-based assessments include the following:

  o Matching-question versions of the 30 end-of-chapter Key Points Review textbook feature may be assigned evaluate student's recall and comprehension of basic chapter concepts.

  o Over 1,200 multiple-choice items (drawn from the ExamView question banks) can be used to monitor student understanding of key concepts, computer literacy, and technical knowledge. Instructors can assign predesigned end-of-chapter and final exams or create their own exams from the bank of questions. They can also create their own exam questions using an item generator that supports ten kinds of question formats.

Performance-Based Assessments

- Chapter Assessments provide additional hands-on computer practice to help reinforce learning. These assessments provide some guidance but less than is offered in the chapter exercises. Three levels of assessment are available, as listed below. Grading rubrics as well as live-file, PDF, and annotated PDF versions of the model answers for these assessments are provided on the Instructor Resources disc and the Internet Resource Center for Instructors. Copies of the grading rubrics and annotated PDF model answers are included in the *Instructor's Guide*.

  o Applying Your Skills assessments allow students to demonstrate their knowledge of the skills taught in the chapter.

- Expanding Your Skills assessments prompt students to explore new features and learn additional skills.

- Achieving Signature Status assessments challenge students to apply what they have learned while solving unique problems.

- Unit Performance Assessments present unique situations for students to apply their new skills. Two types of assessments are presented, as described below. Grading rubrics and model answers are provided these in the same forms as for the end-of-chapter assessments.

- Assessing Proficiencies assessments consist of practical computer simulation exercises that require students to make decisions about document preparation and formatting, providing ample opportunity to apply new features as well as to practice previously learned material.

- Creating Original Documents assessments are writing exercises that provide students with the opportunity to compose and format business documents, requiring problem-solving and creative abilities as well as hands-on computer skills.

- Supplemental Assessments offer additional opportunities for practice and evaluation. Five or six are provided for each unit of instruction. These assessments are similar in format to the end-of-chapter and end-of-unit assessments. They are available in the *Instructor's Guide*, on the Instructor Resources disc, and on the Internet Resource Center for Instructors. Student data files, grading rubrics, and model answers in both PDF and live application files are provided to instructors to support these assessments.

- SNAP support for *Signature Word 2013* includes the following performance-based resources:

- More than 175 interactive, gradable, multimedia tutorials, aligned to support the exercises in the textbook, can be used for direct instruction or remediation. A list of the tutorials aligned to each chapter is found on the opening page of the chapter in the textbook and marked by a SNAP icon.

- More than 350 Skill Items allow students to perform tasks in Microsoft Word 2013, evaluate their work, and report the results in the online grade book. Instructors can assign predefined skill exams or create their own exams from the item bank.

- Grade It versions of more than 120 end-of-chapter and end-of-unit assessments guide students through the steps of completing those assessments, provide immediate automatic scoring with individualized feedback of student work, and report results to the online grade book. Textbook assessments that have corresponding versions in SNAP are marked with a SNAP Grade It icon in the textbook margin.

- A total of 36 Performance Evaluations, one per chapter and one per unit, allow instructors to administer a comprehensive evaluation of skills mastery. These evaluations are unique to SNAP and provide limited guidance to students. Like the Grade It activities, they offer immediate scoring, feedback to students, and grade book entry.

Grading Sheet

Assignment Number	Assignment Title or File Name	Start from Scratch	SNAP Version Available	Date Due	Grade
UNIT 1: Preparing Documents					
Chapter 1: Creating, Printing, and Editing Documents					
Exercise 1.1	C01-E01-WebResumes.docx	✓			
Exercise 1.2	C01-E02-Email Resumes.docx				
Exercise 1.4	C01-E04-LtrKCC.docx				
Exercise 1.5	C01-E05-SoftwareSuites.docx				
Key Points Review	Chapter 1 Key Points Review		✓		
Assessment 1.1	C01-A01-CoverLtrs.docx	✓	✓		
Assessment 1.2	C01-A02-Editing.docx		✓		
Assessment 1.3	C01-A03-Format.docx				
Assessment 1.4	C01-A04-SaveAs.docx	✓			
Assessment 1.5	C01-A05-KeyboardShortcuts.docx	✓			
Assessment 1.6	C01-A06-CoverLtr.docx	✓			
IRC Study Quiz	Chapter 1 Quiz				
Concept Exam	Chapter 1 Exam		✓		
SNAP Tutorial 1.1	Creating, Saving, and Printing a Word Document		✓		
SNAP Tutorial 1.2	Opening a Document		✓		
SNAP Tutorial 1.3	Pinning a Document to the Recent List		✓		
SNAP Tutorial 1.4	Editing a Document		✓		
SNAP Tutorial 1.5	Using the Word Help Feature		✓		
SNAP Skill Exam	Chapter 1 Skill Exam		✓		
SNAP Performance Evaluation	Chapter 1 Performance Evaluation		✓		
Chapter 2: Formatting Characters					
Exercise 2.1	C02-E01-Terms.docx				
Exercise 2.2	C02-E02-CompSecurity.docx				
Key Points Review	Chapter 2 Key Points Review		✓		
Assessment 2.1	C02-A01-UtilProgs.docx	✓	✓		
Assessment 2.2	C02-A02-BookMemo.docx		✓		
Assessment 2.3	C02-A03-ManageData.docx		✓		
Assessment 2.4	C02-A04-WritingSteps.docx		✓		
Assessment 2.5	C02-A05-Memo.docx	✓			
Assessment 2.6	C02-A06-TextEffects.docx	✓			
Assessment 2.7	C02-A07-WritingCoverLtr.docx	✓			

Assignment Number	Assignment Title or File Name	Start from Scratch	SNAP Version Available	Date Due	Grade
Assessment 2.8	C02-A08-BCLtrt.docx				
IRC Study Quiz	Chapter 2 Quiz				
Concept Exam	Chapter 2 Exam		✓		
SNAP Tutorial 2.1	Modifying the Font Using the Font Group		✓		
SNAP Tutorial 2.2	Highlighting Text		✓		
SNAP Tutorial 2.3	Formatting with the Mini Toolbar		✓		
SNAP Tutorial 2.4	Applying Formatting Using the Font Dialog Box		✓		
SNAP Tutorial 2.5	Applying Styles, Style Sets, and Themes		✓		
SNAP Skill Exam	Chapter 2 Skill Exam		✓		
SNAP Performance Evaluation	Chapter 2 Performance Evaluation		✓		
Chapter 3: Aligning and Indenting Paragraphs					
Exercise 3.1	C03-E01-CompIndustry.docx				
Exercise 3.2	C03-E02-InternetSearch.docx				
Exercise 3.3	C03-E03-CompIssues.docx				
Key Points Review	Chapter 3 Key Points Review		✓		
Assessment 3.1	C03-A01-DataTraining.docx	✓	✓		
Assessment 3.2	C03-A02B-Presentation.docx		✓		
Assessment 3.3	C03-A03-Biblio.docx	✓	✓		
Assessment 3.4	C03-A04-TravelAdv.docx		✓		
Assessment 3.5	C03-A05-PlanResume.docx				
Assessment 3.6	C03-A06-ResumeStrategies.docx				
Assessment 3.7	C03-A07-PSPLetter.docx				
IRC Study Quiz	Chapter 3 Quiz				
Concept Exam	Chapter 3 Exam		✓		
SNAP Tutorial 3.1	Aligning Text in Paragraphs		✓		
SNAP Tutorial 3.2	Changing Text Indentation		✓		
SNAP Tutorial 3.3	Spacing Before and After Paragraphs		✓		
SNAP Tutorial 3.4	Using the Format Painter and Repeating a Command		✓		
SNAP Tutorial 3.5	Setting Line and Paragraph Spacing		✓		
SNAP Tutorial 3.6	Creating Bulleted and Numbered Lists		✓		
SNAP Tutorial 3.7	Revealing and Comparing Formatting		✓		

Assignment Number	Assignment Title or File Name	Start from Scratch	SNAP Version Available	Date Due	Grade
SNAP Skill Exam	Chapter 2 Skill Exam		✓		
SNAP Performance Evaluation	Chapter 2 Performance Evaluation		✓		
Chapter 4: Customizing Paragraphs					
Exercise 4.1	C04-E01-Quiz.docx				
Exercise 4.2	C04-E02-IntlCorres.docx				
Exercise 4.3	C04-E03-Tabs.docx	✓			
Exercise 4.4	C04-E04-LtrFormat.docx				
Exercise 4.5	C-4-E05-ManageData.docx				
Exercise 4.6	C04-E06-FinalAgrmnt.docx				
Key Points Review	Chapter 4 Key Points Review		✓		
Assessment 4.1	C04-A01-Abbre.docx		✓		
Assessment 4.2	C04-A02-TofC.docx	✓	✓		
Assessment 4.3	C04-A03-NewEmp.docx	✓	✓		
Assessment 4.4	C04-A04-BetaTestAgrmnt.docx				
Assessment 4.5	C04-A05-PasteOptions.docx	✓			
Assessment 4.6	C04-A06-OpenHouse.docx	✓			
Assessment 4.7	C04-A07-Ch01TofC.docx	✓			
IRC Study Quiz	Chapter 4 Quiz				
Concept Exam	Chapter 4 Exam		✓		
SNAP Tutorial 4.1	Adding a Border and Shading to Selected Text		✓		
SNAP Tutorial 4.2	Sorting Text in Paragraphs		✓		
SNAP Tutorial 4.3	Setting Tabs Using the Ruler		✓		
SNAP Tutorial 4.4	Setting Tabs Using the Tabs Dialog Box		✓		
SNAP Tutorial 4.5	Cutting, Copying, and Pasting Text		✓		
SNAP Tutorial 4.6	Using the Clipboard Task Pane		✓		
SNAP Tutorial 4.7	Using Paste Special		✓		
SNAP Skill Exam	Chapter 4 Skill Exam		✓		
SNAP Performance Evaluation	Chapter 4 Performance Evaluation		✓		
Chapter 5: Proofing Documents					
Exercise 5.1	C05-E01-VacAdeventure.docx				
Exercise 5.2	C05-E02-Interfaces.docx				
Exercise 5.3	C05-E03-Photography.docx				
Exercise 5.4	C05-E04-LetterFormat.docx C05-E04-TranslateTerms.docx				
Key Points Review	Chapter 5 Key Points Review		✓		

Assignment Number	Assignment Title or File Name	Start from Scratch	SNAP Version Available	Date Due	Grade
Assessment 5.1	C05-A01-Numbers.docx		✓		
Assessment 5.2	C05-A02-PrepareResume.docx		✓		
Assessment 5.3	C05-A03-Translations.docx	✓			
Assessment 5.4	C05-A04-OptionsTranslate.docx	✓			
Assessment 5.5	C05-A05-WriteResume.docx				
Assessment 5.6	C05-A06-MtgLtr.docx				
IRC Study Quiz	Chapter 5 Quiz				
Concept Exam	Chapter 5 Exam		✓		
SNAP Tutorial 5.1	Checking the Spelling and Grammar in a Document		✓		
SNAP Tutorial 5.2	Customizing Spelling and Grammar Checking		✓		
SNAP Tutorial 5.3	Displaying Readability Statistics		✓		
SNAP Tutorial 5.4	Creating a Custom Dictionary		✓		
SNAP Tutorial 5.5	Displaying Word Count		✓		
SNAP Tutorial 5.6	Using the Thesaurus		✓		
SNAP Tutorial 5.7	Translating Text to and From Different Languages		✓		
SNAP Skill Exam	Chapter 5 Skill Exam		✓		
SNAP Performance Evaluation	Chapter 5 Performance Evaluation		✓		
UNIT 1 Performance Assessments					
Assessment U1.1	U1-PA01-ShopOnline.docx		✓		
Assessment U1.2	U1-PA02-ComReport.docx		✓		
Assessment U1.3	U1-PA03-ManageData.docx	✓	✓		
Assessment U1.4	U1-PA04-ProdSoftware.docx		✓		
Assessment U1.5	U1-PA05-CedarMeadows.docx		✓		
Assessment U1.6	U1-PA06-TrainCosts.docx	✓	✓		
Assessment U1.7	U1-PA07-Rates.docx	✓	✓		
Assessment U1.8	U1-PA08-Activities.docx		✓		
Assessment U1.9	U1-PA09-ResumeFormat.docx	✓			
Assessment U1.10	U1-PA10-JobAnnouce.docx				
Assessment U1.11	U1-PA11-Annouce.docx	✓			
Assessment U1.12	U1-PA12-WordCommands.docx	✓			
Assessment U1.13	U1-PA13-Fonts.docx	✓			
Supplemental Assessment U1.1	U01-SA01.docx				
Supplemental Assessment U1.2	U01-SA02.docx				

Assignment Number	Assignment Title or File Name	Start from Scratch	SNAP Version Available	Date Due	Grade
Supplemental Assessment U1.3	U01-SA03.docx				
Supplemental Assessment U1.4	U01-SA04.docx				
Supplemental Assessment U1.5	U01-SA05.docx				
SNAP Performance Evaluation	Unit 1 Performance Evaluation		✓		
UNIT 2: Formatting and Managing Documents					
Chapter 6: Formatting Pages					
Exercise 6.1	C06-E01-WebReport.docx				
Exercise 6.2	C06-E02-BestFitResume.docx				
Exercise 6.3	C06-E03-CompCommunications.docx				
Exercise 6.4	C06-E04-CompAccess.docx				
Key Points Review	Chapter 6 Key Points Review		✓		
Assessment 6.1	C06-A01-CompIndustry.docx		✓		
Assessment 6.2	C06-A02-DataTraining.docx		✓		
Assessment 6.3	C06-A03-CompViruses.docx		✓		
Assessment 6.4	C06-A04-BGClientLtr.docx				
Assessment 6.5	C06-A05-Announce.docx	✓			
Assessment 6.6	C06-A06-DeliverPres.docx				
IRC Study Quiz	Chapter 6 Quiz				
Concept Exam	Chapter 6 Exam		✓		
SNAP Tutorial 6.1	Changing Document Views		✓		
SNAP Tutorial 6.2	Changing Margins, Page Orientation, and Paper Size		✓		
SNAP Tutorial 6.3	Inserting Section Breaks		✓		
SNAP Tutorial 6.4	Creating Newspaper Columns		✓		
SNAP Tutorial 6.5	Hyphenating Words		✓		
SNAP Tutorial 6.6	Inserting Line Numbers		✓		
SNAP Tutorial 6.7	Inserting a Watermark, Page Color, and Page Border		✓		
SNAP Skill Exam	Chapter 6 Skill Exam		✓		
SNAP Performance Evaluation	Chapter 6 Performance Evaluation		✓		
Chapter 7: Customizing Page Formatting					
Exercise 7.1	C07-E01-CompAccess.docx				
Exercise 7.2	C07-E02-LtrWriting.docx				
Exercise 7.3	C07-E03-Lease.docx				

Assignment Number	Assignment Title or File Name	Start from Scratch	SNAP Version Available	Date Due	Grade
Exercise 7.4	C07-E04-WordTrain.docx	✓			
Key Points Review	Chapter 7 Key Points Review		✓		
Assessment 7.1	C07-A01-Strategies.docx		✓		
Assessment 7.2	C07-A02-QuoteMarks.docx		✓		
Assessment 7.3	C07-A03-REAgrmnt.docx		✓		
Assessment 7.4	C07-A04-CoData.docx	✓			
Assessment 7.5	C07-A05-Presentation.docx				
Assessment 7.6	C07-A06-ResumeInfo.docx				
IRC Study Quiz	Chapter 7 Quiz				
Concept Exam	Chapter 7 Exam		✓		
SNAP Tutorial 7.1	Inserting a Blank Page and a Cover Page		✓		
SNAP Tutorial 7.2	Inserting Page Numbers and Page Breaks		✓		
SNAP Tutorial 7.3	Creating Headers and Footers		✓		
SNAP Tutorial 7.4	Finding and Replacing Text		✓		
SNAP Tutorial 7.5	Using Click and Type		✓		
SNAP Tutorial 7.6	Using Vertical Alignment		✓		
SNAP Skill Exam	Chapter 7 Skill Exam		✓		
SNAP Performance Evaluation	Chapter 7 Performance Evaluation		✓		
Chapter 8: Inserting Elements and Navigating in a Document					
Exercise 8.1	C08-E01-ProdSoftware.docx				
Exercise 8.2	C08-E02-VirusesSecurity.docx				
Key Points Review	Chapter 8 Key Points Review		✓		
Assessment 8.1	C08-A01-EmpAppoints.docx		✓		
Assessment 8.2	C08-A02-AuditRep.docx		✓		
Assessment 8.3	C08-A03-CompServices.docx C08-A03-DropCapMemo.docx	✓			
Assessment 8.4	C08-A04-BMCClientLtr.docx				
Assessment 8.5	C08-A05-CareerChangers.docx	✓			
IRC Study Quiz	Chapter 8 Quiz				
Concept Exam	Chapter 8 Exam		✓		
SNAP Tutorial 8.1	Inserting Symbols and Special Characters		✓		
SNAP Tutorial 8.2	Inserting a Drop Cap, Symbol, and Date and Time		✓		
SNAP Tutorial 8.3	Inserting a File		✓		
SNAP Tutorial 8.4	Navigating Using the Navigation Pane		✓		

Assignment Number	Assignment Title or File Name	Start from Scratch	SNAP Version Available	Date Due	Grade
SNAP Tutorial 8.5	Inserting and Navigating with Bookmarks		✓		
SNAP Tutorial 8.6	Creating and Editing Hyperlinks		✓		
SNAP Tutorial 8.7	Inserting Hyperlinks to Other Locations		✓		
SNAP Tutorial 8.8	Creating a Cross-Reference		✓		
SNAP Skill Exam	Chapter 8 Skill Exam		✓		
SNAP Performance Evaluation	Chapter 8 Performance Evaluation		✓		
Chapter 9: Maintaining Documents					
Exercise 9.2	C09-E02-IntlCorres.docx				
Exercise 9.2	C09-E02-IntlCorres-Word97-2003.doc				
Exercise 9.2	C09-E02-IntlCorres-PlainTxt.txt				
Exercise 9.2	C09-E02-IntlCorres-RichTxt.rtf				
Exercise 9.2	C09-E02-NSS.docx				
Exercise 9.3	C09-E03-LtrLuncheon.docx	✓			
Key Points Review	Chapter 9 Key Points Review		✓		
Assessment 9.1	C09-A01-PrintScreen.docx				
Assessment 9.2	C09-A02-Lease.docx C09-A02-Lease-PlainTxt.txt C09-A02-Lease-PDF.pdf C09-A02-Lease-PDF.docx				
Assessment 9.3	C09_A03-Fax.docx	✓	✓		
Assessment 9.4	C09_A04-Calendar.docx C09-A04-Memo.docx	✓	✓		
Assessment 9.5	C09-A05-PrintScreen.docx	✓			
Assessment 9.6	C09-A06-Invitation.docx		✓		
IRC Study Quiz	Chapter 9 Quiz				
Concept Exam	Chapter 9 Exam		✓		
SNAP Tutorial 9.1	Managing Folders on your Computer		✓		
SNAP Tutorial 9.2	Managing Documents		✓		
SNAP Tutorial 9.3	Changing Dialog Box Views		✓		
SNAP Tutorial 9.4	Saving a Document in a Different Format		✓		
SNAP Tutorial 9.5	Creating Documents Using a Word Template		✓		
SNAP Skill Exam	Chapter 9 Skill Exam		✓		
SNAP Performance Evaluation	Chapter 9 Performance Evaluation		✓		

Assignment Number	Assignment Title or File Name	Start from Scratch	SNAP Version Available	Date Due	Grade
Chapter 10: Managing and Printing Documents					
Exercise 10.1	C10-E01-CompSoftware.docx				
Exercise 10.2	C10-E02-Env.docx	✓			
Exercise 10.3	C10-E03-GSHLtr.docx				
Exercise 10.4	C10-E04-Labels.docx	✓			
Exercise 10.5	C10-E05-BGCLabels.docx	✓			
Key Points Review	Chapter 10 Key Points Review		✓		
Assessment 10.1	C10-A01-CompHardware.docx				
Assessment 10.2	C10-A02-Envelope.docx	✓	✓		
Assessment 10.3	C10-A03-Labels.docx	✓	✓		
Assessment 10.4	C10-A04-BGLabels.docx	✓			
Assessment 10.5	C10-A04-SALabels.docx	✓			
Assessment 10.6	C10-A04-PersonalLabels.docx	✓			
IRC Study Quiz	Chapter 10 Quiz				
Concept Exam	Chapter 10 Exam		✓		
SNAP Tutorial 10.1	Working with Windows		✓		
SNAP Tutorial 10.2	Changing Document Zoom and Hiding/Showing White Space		✓		
SNAP Tutorial 10.3	Managing the Recent List		✓		
SNAP Tutorial 10.4	Previewing and Printing Documents		✓		
SNAP Tutorial 10.5	Creating and Printing Envelopes		✓		
SNAP Tutorial 10.6	Creating and Printing Labels		✓		
SNAP Skill Exam	Chapter 10 Skill Exam		✓		
SNAP Performance Evaluation	Chapter 10 Performance Evaluation		✓		
UNIT 2 Performance Assessments					
Assessment U2.1	U2-PA01-Terra.docx		✓		
Assessment U2.2	U2-PA02-InvestDisc.docx	✓	✓		
Assessment U2.3	U2-PA03-CompViruses.docx		✓		
Assessment U2.4	U2-PA04-AnnualMeeting.docx	✓			
Assessment U2.5	U2-PA05-EmpAppoints.docx		✓		
Assessment U2.6	U2-PA06-Env.docx	✓	✓		
Assessment U2.7	U2-PA07-Labels.docx	✓	✓		
Assessment U2.8	U2-PA08-VisualAids.docx				
Assessment U2.9	U2-PA09-GiftCert.docx	✓			
Assessment U2.10	U2-PA10-Ltr.docx				
Assessment U2.11	U2-PA11-Calendar.docx	✓			

Assignment Number	Assignment Title or File Name	Start from Scratch	SNAP Version Available	Date Due	Grade
Assessment U2.12	U2-PA12-Netiquette.docx	✓			
Supplemental Assessment U2.1	U02-SA01.docx				
Supplemental Assessment U2.2	U02-SA02.docx				
Supplemental Assessment U2.3	U02-SA03.docx				
Supplemental Assessment U2.4	U02-SA04.docx				
Supplemental Assessment U2.5	U02-SA05.docx				
SNAP Performance Evaluation	Unit 2 Performance Evaluation		✓		
UNIT 3: Enhancing Documents					
Chapter 11: Inserting Images					
Exercise 11.1	C11-E01-EditedPictures.docx	✓			
Exercise 11.2	C11-E02-SummerRates.docx	✓			
Exercise 11.3	C11-E03-Presentation.docx				
Exercise 11.4	C11-E04-TTSMaui.docx				
Exercise 11.5	C11-E05-WritingSteps.docx				
Exercise 11.6	C11-E06-Graphics.docx	✓			
Exercise 11.7	C11-E07-OrgChart.docx	✓			
Key Points Review	Chapter 11 Key Points Review		✓		
Assessment 11.1	C11-A01-OVC.docx	✓	✓		
Assessment 11.2	C11-A02-PremPro.docx		✓		
Assessment 11.3	C11-A03-DataTraining.docx		✓		
Assessment 11.4	C11-A04-VacAdventure.docx		✓		
Assessment 11.5	C11-A05-TECGraphic.docx	✓	✓		
Assessment 11.6	C11-A06-OrgChart.docx	✓	✓		
Assessment 11.7	C11-A07-PugFlyer.docx	✓			
Assessment 11.8	C11-A05-TECLogo.docx	✓			
Assessment 11.9	C11-A06-Levels.docx	✓			
IRC Study Quiz	Chapter 11 Quiz				
Concept Exam	Chapter 11 Exam		✓		
SNAP Tutorial 11.1	Inserting and Formatting Pictures		✓		
SNAP Tutorial 11.2	Inserting, Sizing, and Moving Images		✓		
SNAP Tutorial 11.3	Customizing and Formatting an Image		✓		

Assignment Number	Assignment Title or File Name	Start from Scratch	SNAP Version Available	Date Due	Grade
SNAP Tutorial 11.4	Applying Advanced Formatting to Images		✓		
SNAP Tutorial 11.5	Creating SmartArt		✓		
SNAP Tutorial 11.6	Arranging and Moving SmartArt		✓		
SNAP Tutorial 11.7	Creating an Organizational Chart with SmartArt		✓		
SNAP Skill Exam	Chapter 11 Skill Exam		✓		
SNAP Performance Evaluation	Chapter 11 Performance Evaluation		✓		
Chapter 12: Using Shapes, WordArt, and Advanced Character Formatting					
Exercise 12.1	C12-E01-BackstageAreas.docx	✓			
Exercise 12.1	C12-E01-SFHCoverPages.docx				
Exercise 12.2	C12-E02-LelandFS.docx				
Exercise 12.3	C12-E03-Hawaii.docx				
Exercise 12.4	C12-E04-PRDonorApp.docx				
Key Points Review	Chapter 12 Key Points Review		✓		
Assessment 12.1	C12-A01-ImagesMemo.docx				
Assessment 12.2	C12-A02-BWC.docx	✓	✓		
Assessment 12.3	C12-A03-EmpofMonth.docx	✓	✓		
Assessment 12.4	C12-A04-SoftwareCycle.docx		✓		
Assessment 12.5	C12-A05-TeamBuildFlyer.docx		✓		
Assessment 12.6	C12-A06-PRDonations.docx		✓		
Assessment 12.7	C12-A07-BWC.docx				
Assessment 12.8	C12-A08-CedarMeadows.docx				
Assessment 12.9	C12-A09-FirstAidCourse.docx	✓			
Assessment 12.10	C12-A10-FirstAidMemo.docx				
IRC Study Quiz	Chapter 12 Quiz				
Concept Exam	Chapter 12 Exam		✓		
SNAP Tutorial 12.1	Creating and Inserting a Screenshot		✓		
SNAP Tutorial 12.2	Inserting and Formatting a Shape		✓		
SNAP Tutorial 12.3	Inserting and Formatting a Text Box		✓		
SNAP Tutorial 12.4	Inserting and Modifying WordArt		✓		
SNAP Tutorial 12.5	Applying Character Formatting		✓		
SNAP Tutorial 12.6	Using OpenType Features		✓		
SNAP Tutorial 12.7	Applying Text Effects		✓		
SNAP Skill Exam	Chapter 12 Skill Exam		✓		
SNAP Performance Evaluation	Chapter 12 Performance Evaluation		✓		

Assignment Number	Assignment Title or File Name	Start from Scratch	SNAP Version Available	Date Due	Grade
Chapter 13: Creating Tables					
Exercise 13.1	C13-E01-Tables.docx	✓			
Exercise 13.2	C13-E02-YrlySales.docx	✓			
Exercise 13.3	C13-E03-WMExecs.docx	✓			
Exercise 13.4	C13-E04-Worksheet.docx				
Exercise 13.5	C13-E05-Calendar.docx	✓			
Key Points Review	Chapter 13 Key Points Review		✓		
Assessment 13.1	C13-A01-LtrCofC.docx		✓		
Assessment 13.2	C13-A02-TourPkgs.docx	✓	✓		
Assessment 13.3	C13-A03-Contacts.docx	✓	✓		
Assessment 13.4	C13-A04-Jobs.docx	✓			
Assessment 13.5	C13-A05-MoCalendar.docx	✓			
Assessment 13.6	C13-A06-ResumeWords.docx	✓			
IRC Study Quiz	Chapter 13 Quiz				
Concept Exam	Chapter 13 Exam		✓		
SNAP Tutorial 13.1	Creating Tables		✓		
SNAP Tutorial 13.2	Changing the Table Design		✓		
SNAP Tutorial 13.3	Applying Shading and Borders to a Table		✓		
SNAP Tutorial 13.4	Drawing a Table		✓		
SNAP Tutorial 13.5	Inserting a Quick Table		✓		
SNAP Skill Exam	Chapter 13 Skill Exam		✓		
SNAP Performance Evaluation	Chapter 13 Performance Evaluation		✓		
Chapter 14: Enhancing Tables					
Exercise 14.1	C14-E01-LoanTables.docx				
Exercise 14.2	C14-E02-EmpTable.docx				
Exercise 14.3	C14-E03-SalesDivTable.docx				
Exercise 14.4	C14-E04-Sales&Support.docx				
Key Points Review	Chapter 14 Key Points Review		✓		
Assessment 14.1	C14-A01-SupplyForm.docx	✓	✓		
Assessment 14.2	C14-A02-Services.docx		✓		
Assessment 14.3	C14-A03-TrainCosts.docx	✓	✓		
Assessment 14.4	C14-A04-TrainDept.docx		✓		
Assessment 14.5	C14-A05-FinAnalysis.docx		✓		
Assessment 14.6	C14-A06-NSSQuizAverages.docx		✓		
Assessment 14.7	C14-A07-NSSQuizAveLtr.docx				
Assessment 14.8	C14-A08-CoverLtr.docx	✓			

Assignment Number	Assignment Title or File Name	Start from Scratch	SNAP Version Available	Date Due	Grade
IRC Study Quiz	Chapter 14 Quiz				
Concept Exam	Chapter 14 Exam		✓		
SNAP Tutorial 14.1	Changing the Table Layout		✓		
SNAP Tutorial 14.2	Merging and Splitting Cells and Tables		✓		
SNAP Tutorial 14.3	Changing Column Width and Height and Cell Margins		✓		
SNAP Tutorial 14.4	Converting Text to a Table and a Table to Text		✓		
SNAP Tutorial 14.5	Sorting Text in a Table and Performing Calculations		✓		
SNAP Skill Exam	Chapter 14 Skill Exam		✓		
SNAP Performance Evaluation	Chapter 14 Performance Evaluation		✓		
Chapter 15: Creating Charts					
Exercise 15.1	C15-E01-TECSales.docx				
Exercise 15.2	C15-E02-Singapore.docx				
Exercise 15.3	C15-E03-CIRevs.docx				
Key Points Review	Chapter 15 Key Points Review		✓		
Assessment 15.1	C15-A01-StSalesChart.docx	✓	✓		
Assessment 15.2	C15-A02-ExpChart.docx	✓	✓		
Assessment 15.3	C15-A03-CoSalesChart.docx	✓	✓		
Assessment 15.4	C15-A04-Middleton.docx		✓		
Assessment 15.5	C15-A05-TaxesChart.docx	✓			
Assessment 15.6	C15-A06-LtrtoCP.docx				
Assessment 15.7	C15-A07-NSSExpChart.docx				
IRC Study Quiz	Chapter 15 Quiz				
Concept Exam	Chapter 15 Exam		✓		
SNAP Tutorial 15.1	Creating Charts		✓		
SNAP Tutorial 15.2	Formatting with Chart Buttons		✓		
SNAP Tutorial 15.3	Changing Chart Design and Formatting		✓		
SNAP Tutorial 15.4	Applying Advanced Formatting to a Chart		✓		
SNAP Skill Exam	Chapter 15 Skill Exam		✓		
SNAP Performance Evaluation	Chapter 15 Performance Evaluation		✓		
UNIT 3 Performance Assessments					
Assessment U3.1	U3-PA01-TravelFlyer.docx	✓	✓		
Assessment U3.2	U3-PA02-OrgChart.docx	✓	✓		

Assignment Number	Assignment Title or File Name	Start from Scratch	SNAP Version Available	Date Due	Grade
Assessment U3.3	U3-PA03-ServerGraphic.docx	✓	✓		
Assessment U3.4	U3-PA04-NetworkTrain.docx	✓	✓		
Assessment U3.5	U3-PA05-RAAnnounce.docx	✓	✓		
Assessment U3.6	U3-PA06-Photography.docx		✓		
Assessment U3.7	U3-PA07-ComMembers.docx	✓	✓		
Assessment U3.8	U3-PA08-TravelPkgs.docx		✓		
Assessment U3.9	U3-PA09-EmpOrient.docx				
Assessment U3.10	U3-PA10-PurOrder.docx				
Assessment U3.11	U3-PA11-SalesChart.docx	✓	✓		
Assessment U3.12	U3-PA12-ExpendChart.docx	✓	✓		
Assessment U3.13	U3-PA13-SmartArt.docx				
Assessment U3.14	U3-PA14-EquipExpend.docx				
Assessment U3.15	U3-PA15-EquipExpChart.docx				
Assessment U3.16	U3-PA16-ESLtrhd.docx				
Supplemental Assessment U3.1	U03-SA01.docx				
Supplemental Assessment U3.2	U03-SA02.docx				
Supplemental Assessment U3.3	U03-SA03.docx				
Supplemental Assessment U3.4	U03-SA04.docx				
Supplemental Assessment U3.5	U03-SA05.docx				
SNAP Performance Evaluation	Unit 3 Performance Evaluation		✓		

UNIT 4: Managing Data

Chapter 16: Merging Documents

Exercise 16.1	C16-E01-CofELtrs.docx				
Exercise 16.2	C16-E02-CofEEnvs.docx	✓			
Exercise 16.3	C16-E03-CofELabels.docx	✓			
Exercise 16.4	C16-E04-CofEDirectory.docx	✓			
Exercise 16.5	C16-E05-Labels.docx	✓			
Exercise 16.6	C16-E06-Directory.docx				
Exercise 16.7	C16-E07-CofELetters.docx				
Exercise 16.8	C16-E08-BTTourLtrs.docx				
Exercise 16.9	C16-E09-BTTourLtrs.docx				
Exercise 16.10	C16-E10-BTTourLtrs.docx				

Assignment Number	Assignment Title or File Name	Start from Scratch	SNAP Version Available	Date Due	Grade
Exercise 16.12	C16-E12-PRLtrs.docx	✓			
Key Points Review	Chapter 16 Key Points Review		✓		
Assessment 16.1	C16-A01-BTDS.docx		✓		
Assessment 16.2	C16-A02-BTVackPkgsLetters.docx C16-A02-BTVacPkgsMD.docx		✓		
Assessment 16.3	C16-A03-BTEnvs.docx		✓		
Assessment 16.4	C16-A03-BTLabels.docx		✓		
Assessment 16.5	C16-A05-BTVacPkgsLetters.docx C16-A05-BTVacPkgsMD.docx				
Assessment 16.6	C16-A06-PREnvs.docx				
Assessment 16.7	C16-A07-PRDirectory.docx				
Assessment 16.8	C16-A08-PRLtrMD.docx				
Assessment 16.9	C16-A09-BTNameBadges.docx				
Assessment 16.10	C16-A10-CoursesLtrs.docx				
IRC Study Quiz	Chapter 16 Quiz				
Concept Exam	Chapter 16 Exam		✓		
SNAP Tutorial 16.1	Merging Documents		✓		
SNAP Tutorial 16.2	Creating a Data Source File		✓		
SNAP Tutorial 16.3	Creating a Main Document		✓		
SNAP Tutorial 16.4	Merging Envelopes and Labels		✓		
SNAP Tutorial 16.5	Merging a Directory		✓		
SNAP Tutorial 16.6	Editing a Data Source File		✓		
SNAP Tutorial 16.7	Inputting Text During a Merge		✓		
SNAP Tutorial 16.8	Merging a Main Document with Other Data Sources		✓		
SNAP Tutorial 16.9	Using the Mail Merge Wizard		✓		
SNAP Skill Exam	Chapter 16 Skill Exam		✓		
SNAP Performance Evaluation	Chapter 16 Performance Evaluation		✓		
Chapter 17: Managing Lists					
Exercise 17.1	C17-E01-TDAgenda.docx				
Exercise 17.2	C17-E02-TravelAdv.docx				
Exercise 17.3	C17-E03-CSList.docx				
Exercise 17.4	C17-E04-SpecialCharacters.docx	✓			
Key Points Review	Chapter 17 Key Points Review		✓		
Assessment 17.1	C17-A01-ElecTech.docx		✓		
Assessment 17.2	C17-A02-CorpReport.docx	✓	✓		
Assessment 17.3	C17-A03-WhiteHorses.docx	✓			

Assignment Number	Assignment Title or File Name	Start from Scratch	SNAP Version Available	Date Due	Grade
Assessment 17.4	C17-A04-TrainingLtr.docx				
IRC Study Quiz	Chapter 17 Quiz				
Concept Exam	Chapter 17 Exam		✓		
SNAP Tutorial 17.1	Inserting Custom Numbers and Bullets		✓		
SNAP Tutorial 17.2	Inserting Multilevel Lists		✓		
SNAP Tutorial 17.3	Inserting Intellectual Property Symbols		✓		
SNAP Tutorial 17.4	Inserting Hyphens and Nonbreaking Characters		✓		
SNAP Skill Exam	Chapter 17 Skill Exam		✓		
SNAP Performance Evaluation	Chapter 17 Performance Evaluation		✓		
Chapter 18: Sorting and Selecting; Finding and Replacing Data					
Exercise 18.1	C18-E01-MBSortDoc.docx				
Exercise 18.2B	C18-E02-MFLabels-01.docx				
Exercise 18.2C	C18-E02-MFLabels-02.docx				
Exercise 18.2D	C18-E02-MFLabels-03.docx				
Exercise 18.2E	C18-E02-MFLabels-04.docx				
Exercise 18.3	C18-E03-LeaseAgrmnt.docx				
Exercise 18.4	C18-E04-CompanyInfo.docx				
Exercise 18.5	C18-E05-ComLease.docx				
Key Points Review	Chapter 18 Key Points Review		✓		
Assessment 18.1	C18-A01-SFSortDoc.docx		✓		
Assessment 18.2	C18-A02-RHSSortDoc.docx		✓		
Assessment 18.3	C18-A03-KLLabels.docx	✓			
Assessment 18.4	C18-A04-KLLabelsBoston.docx	✓			
Assessment 18.5	C18-A05-EmpGuide.docx		✓		
Assessment 18.6	C18-A06-NYNameTags.docx	✓			
Assessment 18.7	C18-A07-Contacts.docx				
IRC Study Quiz	Chapter 18 Quiz				
Concept Exam	Chapter 18 Exam		✓		
SNAP Tutorial 18.1	Sorting Text in Paragraphs, Columns, and Tables		✓		
SNAP Tutorial 18.2	Sorting Records in a Data Source File		✓		
SNAP Tutorial 18.3	Selecting Specific Records for Merging		✓		
SNAP Tutorial 18.4	Finding and Replacing Formatting		✓		

Assignment Number	Assignment Title or File Name	Start from Scratch	SNAP Version Available	Date Due	Grade
SNAP Tutorial 18.5	Finding and Replacing Special Characters		✓		
SNAP Skill Exam	Chapter 18 Skill Exam		✓		
SNAP Performance Evaluation	Chapter 18 Performance Evaluation		✓		
Chapter 19: Managing Page Numbers, Headers, and Footers					
Exercise 19.1	C19-E01-CompAccess.docx				
Exercise 19.2	C19-E02-ResumeReport.docx				
Exercise 19.3	C19-E03-EmpHandbook.docx				
Exercise 19.4	C19-E04-EmpHandbook.docx				
Exercise 19.5	C19-E05-EmpHandbook.docx				
Exercise 19.6	C19-E06-EmpHandbook.docx				
Exercise 19.7	C19-E07-OnlineShop.docx				
Key Points Review	Chapter 19 Key Points Review		✓		
Assessment 19.1	C19-A01-CompSecurity.docx		✓		
Assessment 19.2	C19-A02-Robots.docx		✓		
Assessment 19.3	C19-A03-SoftwareChapters.docx		✓		
Assessment 19.4	C19-A04-OnlineShop.docx				
Assessment 19.5	C19-A05-InternetChapters.docx				
IRC Study Quiz	Chapter 19 Quiz				
Concept Exam	Chapter 19 Exam		✓		
SNAP Tutorial 19.1	Customizing Page Numbers		✓		
SNAP Tutorial 19.2	Customizing Headers and Footers		✓		
SNAP Tutorial 19.3	Print Sections of a Document		✓		
SNAP Tutorial 19.4	Keeping Text Together		✓		
SNAP Skill Exam	Chapter 19 Skill Exam		✓		
SNAP Performance Evaluation	Chapter 19 Performance Evaluation		✓		
Chapter 20: Managing Shared Documents					
Exercise 20.1	C20-E01-NDMNewEmps.docx				
Exercise 20.2	C20-E02-BldgAgrmnt.docx				
Exercise 20.3	C20-E03-ComAgrmnt.docx				
Exercise 20.4	C20-E04-CombinedLease.docx				
Exercise 20.5	C20-E05-DIRevs.docx				
Exercise 20.6	C20-E05-NSSCosts.docx				
Key Points Review	Chapter 20 Key Points Review		✓		
Assessment 20.1	C20-A01-NavigateWeb.docx		✓		
Assessment 20.2	C20-A02-CompChapters.docx		✓		

Assignment Number	Assignment Title or File Name	Start from Scratch	SNAP Version Available	Date Due	Grade
Assessment 20.3	C20-A03-Security.docx				
Assessment 20.4	C20-A04-LegalSummons.docx				
Assessment 20.5	C20-A05-WESales.docx				
Assessment 20.6	C20-A06-MBPSales.docx				
Assessment 20.7	C20-A07-NSSEmpPerf.docx				
IRC Study Quiz	Chapter 20 Quiz				
Concept Exam	Chapter 20 Exam		✓		
SNAP Tutorial 20.1	Inserting and Editing Comments		✓		
SNAP Tutorial 20.2	Inserting Comments in the Reviewing Pane; Distinguishing Comments from Other Users		✓		
SNAP Tutorial 20.3	Tracking Changes to a Document		✓		
SNAP Tutorial 20.4	Displaying Changes for Review and Showing Markup		✓		
SNAP Tutorial 20.5	Customizing Track Changes Options		✓		
SNAP Tutorial 20.6	Comparing Documents		✓		
SNAP Tutorial 20.7	Combining Documents		✓		
SNAP Tutorial 20.8	Embedding and Linking Objects		✓		
SNAP Skill Exam	Chapter 20 Skill Exam		✓		
SNAP Performance Evaluation	Chapter 20 Performance Evaluation		✓		
UNIT 4 Performance Assessments					
Assessment U4.1	U4-PA01-MALtrs.docx		✓		
Assessment U4.2	U4-PA02-MAEnvs.docx		✓		
Assessment U4.3	U4-PA03-MALtrs.docx		✓		
Assessment U4.4	U4-PA04-MALbls.docx				
Assessment U4.5	U4-PA05-MADirectory.docx				
Assessment U4.6	U4-PA06-Sort.docx		✓		
Assessment U4.7	U4-PA07-MPBStocks.docx		✓		
Assessment U4.8	U4-PA08-CompEthics.docx		✓		
Assessment U4.9	U4-PA09-CompSoftware.docx		✓		
Assessment U4.10	U4-PA10-OnlineShop.docx		✓		
Assessment U4.11	U4-PA11-Software.docx				
Assessment U4.12	U4-PA12-VolLtrs.docx				
Supplemental Assessment U4.1	U04-SA01.docx				
Supplemental Assessment U4.2	U04-SA02.docx				

Assignment Number	Assignment Title or File Name	Start from Scratch	SNAP Version Available	Date Due	Grade
Supplemental Assessment U4.3	U04-SA03.docx				
Supplemental Assessment U4.4	U04-SA04.docx				
Supplemental Assessment U4.5	U04-SA05.docx				
SNAP Performance Evaluation	Unit 4 Performance Evaluation		✓		
UNIT 5: Customizing Documents and Features					
Chapter 21: Inserting and Customizing Quick Parts					
Exercise 21.1	C21-E01-CompViruses.docx				
Exercise 21.2	C21-E02-PSltr.docx				
Exercise 21.3A	C21-E03-PSltr.docx	✓			
Exercise 21.3B	C21-E03-PacificSkyAnnounce.docx	✓			
Exercise 21.4	C21-E04-SEBetaAgrmnt.docx				
Key Points Review	Chapter 21 Key Points Review		✓		
Assessment 21.1	C21-A01-PropProIssues.docx		✓		
Assessment 21.2	C21-A02-BGRRAgmnt.docx C21-A02-PrintScreen.docx		✓		
Assessment 21.3	C21-A03-PropProIssues.docx				
Assessment 21.4	C21-A04-Equations.docx				
Assessment 21.5	C21-A05-ClientLtr.docx C21-A05-PrintScreen				
IRC Study Quiz	Chapter 21 Quiz				
Concept Exam	Chapter 21 Exam		✓		
SNAP Tutorial 21.1	Inserting and Sorting Building Blocks		✓		
SNAP Tutorial 21.2	Saving Content as Building Blocks		✓		
SNAP Tutorial 21.3	Editing Building Block Properties		✓		
SNAP Tutorial 21.4	Inserting Custom Building Blocks		✓		
SNAP Tutorial 21.5	Modifying and Deleting Building Blocks		✓		
SNAP Tutorial 21.6	Inserting and Updating Fields from Quick Parts		✓		
SNAP Tutorial 21.7	Inserting and Updating Fields from Quick Parts		✓		
SNAP Skill Exam	Chapter 21 Skill Exam		✓		
SNAP Performance Evaluation	Chapter 21 Performance Evaluation		✓		

Assignment Number	Assignment Title or File Name	Start from Scratch	SNAP Version Available	Date Due	Grade
Chapter 22: Customizing AutoCorrect and Word Options					
Exercise 22.1	C22-E01-BT-FAV.docx	✓			
Exercise 22.2	C22-E02-InterfaceApps.docx				
Exercise 22.3	C22-E03-BTAdventures.docx				
Key Points Review	Chapter 22 Key Points Review		✓		
Assessment 22.1	C22-A01-KLHPlan.docx				
Assessment 22.2	C22-A02-FAV.docx	✓			
Assessment 22.3	C22-A03-FAV-Word97-2003.doc C22-A03-PrintScreen.docx				
Assessment 22.4	C22-A04-Options.docx	✓			
Assessment 22.5	C22-A05-ResumeStyles.docx	✓			
IRC Study Quiz	Chapter 22 Quiz				
Concept Exam	Chapter 22 Exam		✓		
SNAP Tutorial 22.1	Using the AutoCorrect Feature		✓		
SNAP Tutorial 22.2	Customizing AutoCorrect and Auto Formatting		✓		
SNAP Tutorial 22.3	Customizing the Quick Access Toolbar		✓		
SNAP Tutorial 22.4	Customizing the Ribbon		✓		
SNAP Tutorial 22.5	Customizing Word Options		✓		
SNAP Skill Exam	Chapter 22 Skill Exam		✓		
SNAP Performance Evaluation	Chapter 22 Performance Evaluation		✓		
Chapter 23: Customizing Themes					
Exercise 23.1	C23-E01-Viruses.docx				
Exercise 23.2	C23-E02-NSSServices.docx				
Exercise 23.3	C23-E03-NSSSecurity.docx				
Key Points Review	Chapter 23 Key Points Review		✓		
Assessment 23.1	C23-A01-KLHPlan.docx	✓	✓		
Assessment 23.2	C23-A02-RPServices.docx	✓	✓		
Assessment 23.3	C23-A03-DevelopSoftware.docx				
Assessment 23.4	C23-A04-TECRevenues.docx C23-A04-ScreenImages.docx				
IRC Study Quiz	Chapter 23 Quiz				
Concept Exam	Chapter 23 Exam		✓		
SNAP Tutorial 23.1	Creating Custom Theme Colors and Theme Fonts		✓		
SNAP Tutorial 23.2	Applying, Editing, and Deleting a Custom Theme		✓		

Assignment Number	Assignment Title or File Name	Start from Scratch	SNAP Version Available	Date Due	Grade
SNAP Skill Exam	Chapter 23 Skill Exam		✓		
SNAP Performance Evaluation	Chapter 23 Performance Evaluation		✓		
Chapter 24: Creating and Managing Styles					
Exercise 24.1	C24-E01-AfricanAdventure.docx				
Exercise 24.2H	C24-E02-BTZenith.docx				
Exercise 24.2I	C24-E02-BTVacations.docx				
Exercise 24.3A	C24-E03-BTTours.docx				
Exercise 24.3B	C24-E03-BTTables.docx				
Exercise 24.3C	C24-E03-BTTablesModifi ed.docx				
Exercise 24.3E	C24-E03-BTZenith.docx				
Exercise 24.3F	C24-E03-BTEastAdventures.docx				
Key Points Review	Chapter 24 Key Points Review		✓		
Assessment 24.1	C24-A01-KMReport.docx		✓		
Assessment 24.2	C24-A02-KMAgendas.docx C24-A02-KMTables.docx		✓		
Assessment 24.3	C24-A03-KMSales.docx	✓			
Assessment 24.4	C24-A04-NSSTables.docx	✓			
Assessment 24.5	C24-A05-RPReport.docx C24-A05-RPTables.docx		✓		
IRC Study Quiz	Chapter 24 Quiz				
Concept Exam	Chapter 24 Exam		✓		
SNAP Tutorial 24.1	Changing the Quick Styles Set Default				
SNAP Tutorial 24.2	Creating and Modifying Styles				
SNAP Tutorial 24.3	Creating and Deleting Custom Quick Styles Sets				
SNAP Tutorial 24.4	Creating a Table Style				
SNAP Tutorial 24.5	Creating a Multilevel List Style				
SNAP Tutorial 24.6	Managing Styles				
SNAP Skill Exam	Chapter 24 Skill Exam		✓		
SNAP Performance Evaluation	Chapter 24 Performance Evaluation		✓		
Chapter 25: Protecting, Preparing, and Sharing Documents					
Exercise 25.1	C25-E01-TECAnnualReport.docx				
Exercise 25.3	C25-E03-REAgrmnt.docx				
Exercise 25.4	C25-E04-Lease.docx				
Exercise 25.5	C25-E05-BTZTAdventures.docx				
Exercise 25.6	C25-E06-BTZTAdv.docx				

Assignment Number	Assignment Title or File Name	Start from Scratch	SNAP Version Available	Date Due	Grade
Key Points Review	Chapter 25 Key Points Review		✓		
Assessment 25.1	C25-A01-Writing Process.docx		✓		
Assessment 25.2	C25-A02-CommCycle.docx		✓		
Assessment 25.3	C25-A03-PrintScreen.docx (step5d) C25-A03-Presentation.docx (step6) C25-A03-Presentation.docx C25-A03-Presentation-2003format.doc		✓		
Assessment 25.4	C25-A04-Signature.docx	✓			
Assessment 25.5	C25-A05-PrintScreen.docx C25-A05-InfoSystem.docx C25-A05-InfoSystem-2003format.doc				
IRC Study Quiz	Chapter 25 Quiz				
Concept Exam	Chapter 25 Exam		✓		
SNAP Tutorial 25.1	Restricting Formatting and Editing in a Document		✓		
SNAP Tutorial 25.2	Protecting a Document with a Password and Opening Documents in Different Views		✓		
SNAP Tutorial 25.3	Managing Document Properties		✓		
SNAP Tutorial 25.4	Restricting and Inspecting a Document		✓		
SNAP Tutorial 25.5	Checking the Accessibility and Compatibility of a Document		✓		
SNAP Tutorial 25.6	Managing Versions		✓		
SNAP Tutorial 25.7	Sharing Documents		✓		
SNAP Skill Exam	Chapter 25 Skill Exam		✓		
SNAP Performance Evaluation	Chapter 25 Performance Evaluation		✓		
UNIT 5 Performance Assessments					
Assessment U5.1	U5-PA01-Singapore.docx		✓		
Assessment U5.2	U5-PA02-TRC-CBLtr.docx		✓		
Assessment U5.3	U5-PA03-TRCRentalForm.docx U5-PA03-PrintScreen.docx		✓		
Assessment U5.4	U5-PA04-TRCBusCode.docx U5-PA04-PrintScreen.docx		✓		
Assessment U5.5	U5-PA05-NSSWebRpt.docx				
Assessment U5.6	U5-PA06-InterfaceApps.docx		✓		
Assessment U5.7	U5-PA07-KLHPHighlights.docx U5-PA07-KLHPHighlights-2003format.doc		✓		

Assignment Number	Assignment Title or File Name	Start from Scratch	SNAP Version Available	Date Due	Grade
Assessment U5.8	HCCLetterhead.docx U5-PA08-HCCLtr01.docx U5-PA08-HCCLtr02.docx				
Assessment U5.9	U5-PA09-HCCAgreement.docx				
Supplemental Assessment U5.1	U05-SA01.docx				
Supplemental Assessment U5.2	U05-SA02.docx				
Supplemental Assessment U5.3	U05-SA03.docx				
Supplemental Assessment U5.4	U05-SA04.docx				
Supplemental Assessment U5.5	U05-SA05.docx				
SNAP Performance Evaluation	Unit 5 Performance Evaluation		✓		
UNIT 6: Referencing Data					
Chapter 26: Inserting Endnotes, Footnotes, and References					
Exercise 26.1A	C26-E01-InterfaceApps.docx				
Exercise 26.1C	C26-E01-InternetFuture.docx				
Exercise 26.2	C26-E02-DevelopDTP.docx				
Key Points Review	Chapter 26 Key Points Review		✓		
Assessment 26.1	C26-A01-DesignNwsltr.docx		✓		
Assessment 26.2	C26-A02-PrivRights.docx		✓		
Assessment 26.3	C26-A03-InterfaceApps.docx				
Assessment 26.4	C26-A04-DevelopSystem.docx				
IRC Study Quiz	Chapter 26 Quiz				
Concept Exam	Chapter 26 Exam		✓		
SNAP Tutorial 26.1	Creating Footnotes and Endnotes		✓		
SNAP Tutorial 26.2	Choosing a Citation Style		✓		
SNAP Tutorial 26.3	Formatting the First Page of a Research Paper		✓		
SNAP Tutorial 26.4	Inserting and Modifying Sources and Citations		✓		
SNAP Tutorial 26.5	Inserting a Works Cited Page		✓		
SNAP Skill Exam	Chapter 26 Skill Exam		✓		
SNAP Performance Evaluation	Chapter 26 Performance Evaluation		✓		

Assignment Number	Assignment Title or File Name	Start from Scratch	SNAP Version Available	Date Due	Grade
Chapter 27: Creating Indexes					
Exercise 27.1	C27-E01-DTP.docx				
Exercise 27.2	C27-E02-Computers.docx				
Exercise 27.3	C27-E03-PlanNwsltr.docx				
Key Points Review	Chapter 27 Key Points Review		✓		
Assessment 27.1	C27-A01-InterfaceApps.docx		✓		
Assessment 27.2	C27-A02-CFile.docx C27-A02-DesignNwsltr.docx	✓	✓		
Assessment 27.3	C27-A03-DesignNwsltr.docx				
Assessment 27.4	C27-A04-SpanishDoc.docx				
Assessment 27.5	C27-A05-CFile.docx C27-A05-CompSystems.docx	✓			
IRC Study Quiz	Chapter 27 Quiz				
Concept Exam	Chapter 27 Exam		✓		
SNAP Tutorial 27.1	Marking Index Entries and Inserting an Index		✓		
SNAP Tutorial 27.2	Creating a Concordance File		✓		
SNAP Tutorial 27.3	Updating and Deleting an Index		✓		
SNAP Skill Exam	Chapter 27 Skill Exam		✓		
SNAP Performance Evaluation	Chapter 27 Performance Evaluation		✓		
Chapter 28: Creating Specialized Tables					
Exercise 28.1	C28-E01-AIReport.docx				
Exercise 28.2	C28-E02-CompEval.docx				
Exercise 28.3B	C28-E03-TechRpt.docx				
Exercise 28.3C	C28-E03-TTSAdventures.docx				
Exercise 28.4	C28-E04-LarsenBrief.docx				
Key Points Review	Chapter 28 Key Points Review		✓		
Assessment 28.1	C28-A01-PhotoRpt.docx		✓		
Assessment 28.2	C28-A02-InputDevices.docx		✓		
Assessment 28.3	C28-A03-SilversBrief.docx		✓		
Assessment 28.4	C28-A04-NavigateWeb.docx				
Assessment 28.5	C28-A05-Networks.docx				
IRC Study Quiz	Chapter 28 Quiz				
Concept Exam	Chapter 28 Exam		✓		
SNAP Tutorial 28.1	Inserting a Table of Contents		✓		
SNAP Tutorial 28.2	Customizing and Updating a Table of Contents		✓		

Assignment Number	Assignment Title or File Name	Start from Scratch	SNAP Version Available	Date Due	Grade
SNAP Tutorial 28.3	Assigning Levels to Table of Contents Entries		✓		
SNAP Tutorial 28.4	Creating and Customizing Captions		✓		
SNAP Tutorial 28.5	Inserting a Table of Figures		✓		
SNAP Tutorial 28.6	Inserting and Updating a Table of Authorities		✓		
SNAP Skill Exam	Chapter 28 Skill Exam		✓		
SNAP Performance Evaluation	Chapter 28 Performance Evaluation		✓		
Chapter 29: Creating Forms					
Exercise 29.1B	C29-E01-DesmondML.docx	✓			
Exercise 29.1D	C29-E01-PierobonML.docx				
Exercise 29.2	C29-E02-SBFax.docx				
Exercise 29.3	C29-E03-SBSurvey.docx				
Exercise 29.4	C29-E04-TrevierApp.docx				
Exercise 29.5	C29-E05-ReynoldsApp.docx				
Exercise 29.6	C29-E06-MurciaApp.docx	✓			
Exercise 29.7	C29-E07-LAAppHarris.docm				
Key Points Review	Chapter 29 Key Points Review		✓		
Assessment 29.1	C29-A01-SBRequest.docx		✓		
Assessment 29.2	C29-A02-SBHendrixCatReq.docx				
Assessment 29.3	C29-A03-FundApp.docx		✓		
Assessment 29.4	C29-A04-ESpringer.docx		✓		
Assessment 29.5	C29-A05-GC-Client.docx C29-A05-RR-Client.docx				
Assessment 29.6	C29-A06-FlightApp.docx				
Assessment 29.7	C29-A07-InsForm.docx				
IRC Study Quiz	Chapter 29 Quiz				
Concept Exam	Chapter 29 Exam		✓		
SNAP Tutorial 29.1	Creating a Form		✓		
SNAP Tutorial 29.2	Filling in a Form		✓		
SNAP Tutorial 29.3	Editing a Form Template		✓		
SNAP Tutorial 29.4	Creating a Form Using a Table		✓		
SNAP Tutorial 29.5	Creating Drop-down Lists		✓		
SNAP Tutorial 29.6	Creating a Form with Legacy Tools		✓		
SNAP Tutorial 29.7	Printing a Form		✓		
SNAP Skill Exam	Chapter 29 Skill Exam		✓		
SNAP Performance Evaluation	Chapter 29 Performance Evaluation		✓		

Assignment Number	Assignment Title or File Name	Start from Scratch	SNAP Version Available	Date Due	Grade
Chapter 30: Using Outline View and Formatting with Macros					
Exercise 30.1	C30-e01-InternetSecurity.docx				
Exercise 30.2	C30-e02-CompViruses.docx				
Exercise 30.3 (Step 11)	C30-e03-Newsletters.docx	✓			
Exercise 30.3B (Step 9)	C30-e03-Newsletters.docx				
Exercise 30.4B	C30-e04-WriteResume.docx				
Exercise 30.4C	C30-e04-ResumeStandards.docx	✓			
Exercise 30.5	C30-e05-GSHLtr.docx	✓			
Exercise 30.6	C30-e06-TofC.docx	✓			
Exercise 30.7	C30-e07-Affi davit.docx	✓			
Key Points Review	Chapter 30 Key Points Review		✓		
Assessment 30.1	C30-A01-EmpComp.docx		✓		
Assessment 30.2	C30-A02-EmpComp.docx		✓		
Assessment 30.3	C30-A03-WebContent.docx				
Assessment 30.4	C30-A04-DesignNwsltr.docx		✓		
Assessment 30.5	C30-A05-PRDept.docx	✓			
Assessment 30.6	C30-A06-Agreement.docx	✓			
Assessment 30.7	C30-A07-InterfaceApps.docx				
Assessment 30.8	C30-A08-Menu.docx C30-A08-Menu01.docx C30-A08-Menu02.docx				
IRC Study Quiz	Chapter 30 Quiz				
Concept Exam	Chapter 30 Exam		✓		
SNAP Tutorial 30.1	Creating and Organizing an Outline		✓		
SNAP Tutorial 30.2	Creating a Master Document and Subdocuments		✓		
SNAP Tutorial 30.3	Recording and Running Macros		✓		
SNAP Tutorial 30.4	Assigning a Macro to the Quick Access Toolbar		✓		
SNAP Tutorial 30.5	Recording a Macro with Fill-in Fields		✓		
SNAP Skill Exam	Chapter 30 Skill Exam		✓		
SNAP Performance Evaluation	Chapter 30 Performance Evaluation		✓		
UNIT 6 Performance Assessments					
Assessment U6.1	U6-PA01-InterfaceApps.docx		✓		
Assessment U6.2	U6-PA02-BuildWebsite.docx		✓		

Assignment Number	Assignment Title or File Name	Start from Scratch	SNAP Version Available	Date Due	Grade
Assessment U6.3	U6-PA03-CFile.docx U6-PA03-DTPDesign.docx	✓	✓		
Assessment U6.4	U6-PA04-SoftwareCareers.docx		✓		
Assessment U6.5	XXXSBPOTemplate.dotx U6-PA05-SB-JCM.docx	✓	✓		
Assessment U6.6	XXXLAProfAppTemplate.dotx U6-PA06-ProfAppHayward.docx				
Assessment U6.7	U6-PA07-CommSoftware.docx				
Assessment U6.8	U6-PA08-Lease.docx U6-PA08-REAgrmnt.docx				
Assessment U6.9	U6-PA09-BDHandbook.docx				
Assessment U6.10	U6-PA10-ERCContactInfo.docx				
Supplemental Assessment U6.1	U06-SA01.docx				
Supplemental Assessment U6.2	U06-SA02.docx				
Supplemental Assessment U6.3	U06-SA03.docx				
Supplemental Assessment U6.4	U06-SA04.docx				
Supplemental Assessment U6.5	U06-SA05.docx				
SNAP Performance Evaluation	Unit 5 Performance Evaluation		✓		
FINAL					
Concept Exam	Final Exam		✓		

Key Points Review Answers

Chapter 1; Pages 30–31

No.	Question	Answer	Page Reference
1	This is the area located near the top of the screen that contains tabs with commands and options divided into groups.	ribbon	page 6, Figure 1.1
2	This bar, located near the bottom of the screen, displays the number of pages and words, view buttons, and Zoom slider bar.	Status bar	page 6, Figure 1.1
3	This feature automatically corrects certain words as you type them.	AutoCorrect	page 7
4	This feature inserts an entire item when you type a few identifying characters and then press the Enter key or F3 key.	AutoComplete	page 8
5	This toolbar contains the Save button.	Quick Access toolbar	page 9
6	Click this tab to display the backstage area.	FILE tab	page 10
7	Use this keyboard shortcut to display the Print backstage area.	Ctrl + P	page 11
8	Use this keyboard shortcut to close a document.	Ctrl + F4	page 11
9	Use this keyboard shortcut to display a new blank document.	Ctrl + N	page 12
10	Use this keyboard command to move the insertion point to the beginning of the previous page.	Ctrl + Page Up	page 18, Table 1.2
11	Use this keyboard command to move the insertion point to the end of the document.	Ctrl + End	page 18, Table 1.2
12	Press this key on the keyboard to delete the character left of the insertion point.	Backspace key	page 20, Table 1.3
13	Using the mouse, do this to select one word.	Double-click the word	page 21, Table 1.4
14	To select various amounts of text using the mouse, click in this bar.	Selection bar	page 21, Table 1.4
15	Use this keyboard shortcut to display the Word Help window.	F1	page 25

Chapter 2; Page 56

No.	Question	Answer	Page Reference
1	Click this button in the Font group to remove all formatting from selected text.	Clear All Formatting button	page 37
2	A font consists of a typeface, typestyle, and this.	Type size	page 37
3	Proportional typefaces are divided into two main categories: serif and this.	Sans serif	page 37
4	The Bold button is located in this group on the HOME tab.	Font	page 40
5	Use this keyboard shortcut to apply italic formatting to selected text.	Ctrl + I	page 42, Table 2.2

No.	Question	Answer	Page Reference
6	This term refers to text that is raised slightly above the regular text line.	Superscript	page 42
7	This automatically displays above selected text.	Mini toolbar	page 42
8	Click this to display the Font dialog box.	Font group dialog box launcher	page 45
9	Click this button in the Paragraph group on the HOME tab to turn on the display of nonprinting characters.	Show/Hide button	page 45
10	Apply a style set by clicking the style set thumbnail in this group on the DESIGN tab.	Document Formatting	page 49
11	Apply a heading style to a title or heading in a document, hover your mouse over the left side of the title or heading, and this displays.	collapse triangle	page 49
12	Apply a theme and change theme colors, fonts, and effects with buttons in the Document Formatting group on this tab.	DESIGN tab	page 52

Chapter 3; Pages 85–86

No.	Question	Answer	Page Reference
1	This is the default paragraph alignment.	left alignment	page 63
2	Return all paragraph formatting to the default settings with this keyboard shortcut.	Ctrl + Q	page 63
3	Click this button in the Paragraph group on the HOME tab to align text at the right margin.	Align Right button	page 64, Table 3.1
4	Click this button in the Paragraph group on the HOME tab to turn on the display of nonprinting characters.	Show/Hide ¶ button	page 64
5	In this type of paragraph, the first line of text aligns at the left margin and the remaining lines of text indent to the first tab.	hanging indent	page 68
6	Repeat the last action by pressing the F4 key or using this keyboard shortcut.	Ctrl + Y	page 72
7	Use this button in the Clipboard group on the HOME tab to copy character formatting already applied to text to additional text at different locations in the document.	Format Painter button	page 73
8	Change the line spacing to 1.5 with this keyboard shortcut	Ctrl + 5	page 75, Table 3.4
9	The Numbering button is located in this group on the HOME tab.	Paragraph	page 76
10	This button displays when the AutoFormat feature inserts numbers.	AutoCorrect Options button	page 76
11	A bulleted list with a hanging indent is automatically created when you begin a paragraph with an asterisk symbol (*), a hyphen (-), or this symbol.	Greater than symbol (>)	page 79

No.	Question	Answer	Page Reference
12	Turn off automatic numbering and bulleting at the AutoCorrect dialog box with this tab selected.	AutoFormat As You Type tab	page 79
13	Automate the creation of bulleted paragraphs with this button on the HOME tab.	Bullets button	page 81
14	Press these keys to display the Reveal Formatting task pane.	Shift + F1	page 81

Chapter 4; Page 122

No.	Question	Answer	Page Reference
1	The Borders button is located in this group on the HOME tab.	Paragraph	page 95
2	Use options at this dialog box with the Borders tab selected to add a customized border to a paragraph or selected paragraphs.	Borders and Shading dialog box	page 98
3	Sort text arranged in paragraphs alphabetically by the first character in the paragraph, which can be a number, symbol, or this.	letter	page 103
4	By default, tabs are set apart from each other by this measurement.	0.5 inch	page 104
5	This is the default tab type.	left	page 104
6	When setting tabs on the horizontal ruler, choose the tab type with this button.	Alignment button	page 104
7	Press this combination of keys to end a line with the New Line command.	Shift + Enter	page 105
8	Tabs can be set on the horizontal ruler or here.	Tabs dialog box	page 108
9	This group on the HOME tab contains the Cut, Copy, and Paste buttons.	Clipboard	page 112
10	Use this keyboard shortcut to paste text.	Ctrl + V	page 112
11	To copy selected text with the mouse, hold down this key while dragging the selected text.	Ctrl	page 117
12	With this task pane, you can collect up to 24 items and then paste them in various locations in the document.	Clipboard task pane	page 118

Chapter 5; Pages 154–155

No.	Question	Answer	Page Reference
1	Click this tab to display the Proofing group.	REVIEW tab	page 133
2	Use this keyboard shortcut to begin checking the spelling and grammar in a document.	F7	page 133
3	Click this button in the Spelling task pane to skip the occurrence of the word and all other occurrences of the word when checking the document.	Ignore All button	page 134
4	Click this button in the Spelling task pane to replace the selected word in the document with the selected word in the list box.	Change button	page 134

No.	Question	Answer	Page Reference
5	This is the default setting for the *Writing Style* option at the Word Options dialog box with *Proofing* selected.	Grammar Only	page 138
6	This readability score is based on the average number of syllables per word and average number of words per sentence.	Flesch Reading Ease Score	page 140
7	When spell checking a document, Word uses this custom dictionary by default.	RoamingCustom.dic	page 141
8	Use this keyboard shortcut to display the Thesaurus task pane.	Shift + F7	page 144
9	Click the Translate button and then click the *Translate Document* option and this online service translates the text in the document.	Microsoft® Translator	page 148
10	Turn on this feature to point to a word or selected text and view a quick translation of it.	Mini translator	page 148

Chapter 6; Page 201

No.	Question	Answer	Page Reference
1	This view displays a document in a format for efficient editing and formatting.	Draft view	page 175
2	This view displays a document in a format for easy viewing and reading.	Read Mode view	page 175
3	This is the default measurement for the top, bottom, left, and right margins.	1 inch	page 178
4	This is the default page orientation.	portrait	page 178
5	Set specific margins at this dialog box with the Margins tab selected.	Page Setup dialog box	page 180
6	Balance column text on the last page of a document by inserting this type of break at the end of the text.	continuous section break	page 183
7	Use this view to display a section break.	Draft view	page 183
8	Format text into columns with the Columns button located in this group on the PAGE LAYOUT tab.	Page Setup group	page 185
9	If you hyphenate words in a document and then decide to remove the hyphens, click this button immediately.	Undo button	page 190
10	A lightened image that displays behind the text in a document is called this.	watermark	page 193
11	The Page Borders button displays in this group on the DESIGN tab.	Page Background group	page 195
12	Change the position of the page border from the edges of the page with options at this dialog box.	Border and Shading Options dialog box	page 197

Chapter 7; Pages 231–232

No.	Question	Answer	Page Reference
1	Press this combination of keys on the keyboard to insert a page break.	Ctrl + Enter	page 211
2	The Cover Page button is located in the Pages group on this tab.	INSERT tab	page 213
3	A predesigned cover page generally contains these, which are locations where you can enter specific information.	placeholders	page 213
4	The Page Number button is located in this group on the INSERT tab.	Header & Footer group	page 216
5	Text that appears at the top of every page is called this.	header	page 217
6	A footer displays in Print Layout view but not this view.	Draft view	page 219
7	Click this button in the Editing group on the HOME tab to display the Navigation pane.	Find button	page 222
8	Use this keyboard shortcut to display the Find and Replace dialog box with the Replace tab selected.	Ctrl + H	page 224
9	If you want to replace every occurrence of what you are searching for in a document, click this button at the Find and Replace dialog box.	Replace All button	page 224
10	Click this option at the Find and Replace dialog box if you are searching for a word and all of its forms.	*Find all word forms*	page 226, Table 7.1
11	Use this feature to position the insertion point at a specific location and alignment in a document.	Click and Type	page 228
12	Vertically align text with the *Vertical alignment* option at the Page Setup dialog box with this tab selected.	Layout tab	page 229

Chapter 8; Page 258–259

No.	Question	Answer	Page Reference
1	The Symbol button is located on this tab.	INSERT tab	page 241
2	Click this option at the Symbol button drop-down list to display the Symbol dialog box.	*More Symbols* option	page 241
3	The first letter of the first word of a paragraph that is set into a paragraph is called this.	drop cap	page 243
4	The Date & Time button is located in this group on the INSERT tab.	Text group	page 244
5	This is the Update Field keyboard shortcut.	key F9	page 244
6	Use this keyboard shortcut to insert the current date.	Alt + Shift + D	page 244
7	Use this keyboard shortcut to insert the current time.	Alt + Shift + T	page 244

No.	Question	Answer	Page Reference
8	Display the Insert File dialog box by clicking the Object button arrow on the INSERT tab and then clicking this option.	*Text from File* option	page 245
9	The *Navigation Pane* check box is located in the Show group on this tab.	VIEW tab	page 246
10	Turn on the display of bookmarks in a document with the *Show bookmarks* check box in this dialog box with *Advanced* selected.	Word Options dialog box	page 249
11	The Bookmark button is located in this group on the INSERT tab.	Links group	page 248
12	Navigate to a hyperlink by hovering the mouse over the hyperlink text, holding down this key, and then clicking the left mouse button.	Ctrl key	page 251
13	To link a Word document to a file in another application, click this button in the *Link to* section in the Insert Hyperlink dialog box.	Existing File or Web Page button	page 252
14	By default, cross-references are inserted in a document as this.	hyperlinks	page 255

Chapter 9; Pages 291–292

No.	Question	Answer	Page Reference
1	Create a new folder with this button in the Open or Save As dialog box.	New folder button	page 268
2	To make the previous folder active, click the folder name in this bar in the Open or Save As dialog box.	Address bar	page 268
3	Using the mouse, select adjacent documents at the Open dialog box by holding down this key while clicking the desired documents.	Shift key	page 270
4	Using the mouse, select nonadjacent documents at the Open dialog box by holding down this key while clicking the desired documents.	Ctrl key	page 270
5	Documents deleted from the hard drive are automatically sent to this bin.	Windows Recycle Bin	page 271
6	Copy a document to another folder without opening the document using the *Copy* option and this option from the Open dialog box shortcut menu.	*Paste* option	page 273
7	Use this option from the Open dialog box Organize button drop-down list to give a document a different name.	*Rename* option	page 274
8	Choose this option at the Open dialog box Change your view button drop-down list to display folders and documents alphabetized by name.	*List* option	page 276
9	Choose this option at the Open dialog box Change your view button arrow drop-down list to display information about folders and documents such as modification date, type, and size.	*Details* option	page 276

No.	Question	Answer	Page Reference
10	Saving a document in this file format removes all of the formatting.	plain text format	page 282
11	You can save a document in a different file format with this option box at the Save As dialog box.	*Save as type* option box	page 284
12	The abbreviation *PDF* stands for this.	portable document format	page 285
13	Click this button at the Export backstage area to display the Publish as PDF or XPS dialog box.	Create PDF/XPS button	page 285
14	In addition to the templates that display at the New backstage area, templates can be downloaded from this website.	Office.com	page 287

Chapter 10; Pages 321–322

No.	Question	Answer	Page Reference
1	To determine which documents are open, click the VIEW tab and then click this button in the Window group.	Switch Windows button	page 300
2	Click this button in the Window group on the VIEW tab to arrange all open documents so a portion of each document displays.	Arrange All button	page 300
3	Click this button and the active document fills the editing window.	Maximize button	page 300
4	Click this button and the active document is reduced to the Word button on the Taskbar.	Minimize button	page 300
5	To display documents side by side, click this button in the Window group on the VIEW tab.	View Side by Side button	page 303
6	If you are viewing documents side by side and decide you want to scroll in one document but not the other, click this button in the Window group on the VIEW tab.	Synchronous Scrolling button	page 303
7	When viewing documents side by side, click this button in the Window group on the VIEW tab to reset the document windows so they display equally on the divided screen.	Reset Window Position button	page 303
8	To remove white spaces from the tops and bottoms of pages, double-click this icon.	Hide White Space icon	page 306
9	Click this button, located below the Recent Documents list at the Open backstage area with *Recent Documents* selected, to display the Open dialog box with the UnsavedFiles folder active.	Recover Unsaved Documents button	page 307
10	Type this in the *Pages* text box in the *Settings* category at the Print backstage area to print pages 3 through 6 of the open document.	3-6	page 310
11	Type this in the *Pages* text box in the *Settings* category at the Print backstage area to print pages 4 and 9 of the open document.	4,9	page 310

No.	Question	Answer	Page Reference
12	The Envelopes button is located in the Create group on this tab.	MAILINGS tab	page 313
13	If you open the Envelopes and Labels dialog box in a document containing a name and address, the name and address are automatically inserted in this text box of the dialog box.	*Delivery address* text box	page 313

Chapter 11; Page 367

No.	Question	Answer	Page Reference
1	Insert an image in a document with buttons in this group on the INSERT tab.	Illustrations group	page 341
2	Click the Pictures button on the INSERT tab and this dialog box displays.	Insert Picture dialog box	page 341
3	Customize and format an image with options and buttons on this tab.	PICTURE TOOLS FORMAT tab	page 341
4	Size an image with the sizing handles that display around the selected image or with these measurement boxes on the PICTURE TOOLS FORMAT tab.	*Shape Height* and *Shape Width* measurement boxes	page 341
5	Change text wrapping with options from the Position button, the Wrap Text button, or this button, which displays just outside the upper right corner of a selected image.	Layout Options button	page 344
6	Click the Online Pictures button on the INSERT tab and this window displays.	Insert Pictures window	page 349
7	With options in the Layout dialog box with this tab selected, you can specify horizontal and vertical layout options.	Position tab	page 351
8	The Layout dialog box contains three tabs: Position, Size, and this.	Text Wrapping	page 352
9	Click this group task pane launcher on the PICTURE TOOLS FORMAT tab to display the Format Picture task pane.	Picture Styles group task pane launcher	page 354
10	If you want to edit individual components of a clip art image, you must first do this to the image.	ungroup	page 356
11	Insert a SmartArt graphic in a document and this tab is active.	SMARTART TOOLS DESIGN tab	page 358
12	To represent hierarchical data visually, consider creating this with the SmartArt feature.	organizational chart	page 363
13	The SmartArt button is located on this tab.	INSERT tab	page 363
14	Click the SmartArt button and this dialog box displays.	Choose a SmartArt Graphic dialog box	page 363

Chapter 12; Pages 414–415

No.	Question	Answer	Page Reference
1	To capture a portion of a screen, click the Screenshot button in the Illustrations group on the INSERT tab and then click this option at the drop-down list.	*Screen Clipping* option	page 382
2	The Shapes button is located on this tab.	INSERT tab	page 384
3	To draw a straight horizontal or vertical line, hold down this key while dragging in the document.	Shift key	page 384
4	To copy a selected shape, hold down this key while dragging the shape.	Ctrl key	page 388
5	Select multiple shapes by holding down the Ctrl key or this key while clicking the shapes.	Shift key	page 389
6	The Align button is located in this group on the DRAWING TOOLS FORMAT tab.	Arrange group	page 389
7	Change the shape of a selected shape by clicking this button on the DRAWING TOOLS FORMAT tab, pointing to *Change Shape*, and then clicking the desired shape at the side menu.	Edit Shape button	page 390
8	Modify a shape by dragging these points.	edit points	page 390
9	Display available predesigned pull quote text boxes by clicking the INSERT tab and then clicking this button in the Text group.	Text Box button	page 393
10	Format a pull quote text box with options on this tab.	DRAWING TOOLS FORMAT tab	page 393
11	Link text boxes with this button in the Text group on the DRAWING TOOLS FORMAT tab.	Create Link button	page 399
12	The WordArt button is located in this group on the INSERT tab.	Text group	page 402
13	Turn on kerning with the *Kerning for fonts* check box located in this section of the Font dialog box with the Advanced tab selected.	*Character Spacing* section	page 407, Figure 12.11
14	This term refers to a combination of characters joined into a single letter.	ligature	page 409
15	Use this option at the Font dialog box with the Advanced tab selected to specify if numbers should be the same height or extend above or below the baseline.	*Number forms* option	page 409
16	Click this button at the Font dialog box to display the Format Text Effects dialog box.	Text Effects button	page 411

Signature Word 2013   Key Points Review Answers

Chapter 13; Page 446

No.	Question	Answer	Page Reference
1	This term refers to the intersection between a row and a column.	cell	page 428
2	The Table button is located on this tab.	INSERT tab	page 428
3	When you hover the mouse pointer over a table, this displays in the upper left corner of the table.	table move handle	page 428
4	Press this key to move the insertion point to the next cell.	Tab key	page 429, Table 13.1
5	Press this combination of keys to move the insertion point to the previous cell.	Shift + Tab	page 429, Table 13.1
6	The space just to the left of the left edge of the table is referred to as this.	row selection bar	page 432
7	When you insert a table in a document, this tab is active.	TABLE TOOLS DESIGN tab	page 435
8	The Line Style and Line Weight buttons are located in this group on the TABLE TOOLS DESIGN tab.	Borders group	page 437
9	When you click the Borders button arrow and then click *Borders and Shading*, the Borders and Shading dialog box displays with this tab active.	Borders tab	page 437
10	To remove a border line, click this button in the Draw group on the TABLE TOOLS LAYOUT tab and then drag across the border.	Eraser button	page 440
11	Use this feature to insert a predesigned table in a document.	Quick Tables feature	page 444

Chapter 14; Pages 477–478

No.	Question	Answer	Page Reference
1	Insert and delete columns and rows with buttons in this group on the TABLE TOOLS LAYOUT tab.	Rows & Columns group	page 454
2	Click this button on the TABLE TOOLS LAYOUT tab to insert a column at the left of the column containing the insertion point.	Insert Left button	page 454
3	Click this button on the TABLE TOOLS LAYOUT tab to merge selected cells.	Merge Cells button	page 456
4	One method of changing the column width is dragging this on the horizontal ruler.	move table column marker	page 458
5	Use this measurement box on the TABLE TOOLS LAYOUT tab to increase or decrease the height of a row.	*Table Row Height* measurement box	page 458
6	When you hold down this key while dragging a table column marker, measurements display on the horizontal ruler.	Alt key	page 458
7	Use this button in the Cell Size group on the TABLE TOOLS LAYOUT tab to make the column widths automatically fit the contents.	AutoFit button	page 458

No.	Question	Answer	Page Reference
8	The left and right margins in a cell both have this default setting.	0.08 inch	page 462
9	Change the table alignment at this dialog box with the Table tab selected.	Table Properties dialog box	page 464
10	Hover the mouse pointer over a table and this displays in the lower right corner of the table.	resize handle	page 466
11	Position the mouse pointer within a table and this displays in the upper left corner.	table move handle	page 466
12	Click this button to display the *Convert Text to Table* option.	Table button	page 468
13	The Sort button is located in this group on the TABLE TOOLS LAYOUT tab.	Data group	page 470
14	When writing a formula, use this symbol to indicate multiplication.	asterisk (*)	page 474
15	When writing a formula, use this symbol to indicate division.	forward slash (/)	page 474

Chapter 15; Pages 505–506

No.	Question	Answer	Page Reference
1	This is the number of chart types available at the Insert Chart dialog box.	10	page 486
2	Use this type of chart to show trends and overall change over time.	line chart	page 486, Table 15.1
3	Use this type of chart to show proportions and relationships of the parts to the whole.	pie chart	page 486, Table 15.1
4	When creating a chart, enter the data in this.	Excel worksheet	page 486
5	Use this button, which displays at the right side of the selected chart, to apply a text wrapping option.	Layout Options button	page 489
6	Use this button, which displays at the right side of the selected chart, to isolate specific data.	Chart Filters button	page 491
7	The Quick Layout button is located on this tab.	CHART TOOLS DESIGN tab	page 493
8	Click this button to open the Excel worksheet containing the chart data.	Edit Data button	page 494
9	The Chart Elements button is located in this group on the CHART TOOLS FORMAT tab.	Current Selection group	page 496
10	Control the position of a chart in a document with options and buttons in this group on the CHART TOOLS FORMAT tab.	Arrange group	page 498
11	One method for displaying a task pane is to click the task pane launcher in this group on the CHART TOOLS FORMAT tab.	Shape Styles group	page 500
12	Display the Layout dialog box by clicking the dialog box launcher in this group on the CHART TOOLS FORMAT tab.	Size group	page 500

Chapter 16; Page 562

No.	Question	Answer	Page Reference
1	A merge generally takes two files: a data source file and this.	main document	page 528
2	This term refers to all of the information for one unit in a data source file.	record	page 528
3	Create a data source file by clicking this button on the MAILINGS tab and then clicking *Type a New List* at the drop-down list.	Select Recipient button	page 528
4	Create your own custom fields in a data source file with options at this dialog box.	New Address List dialog box	page 528
5	A data source file is saved as this type of file.	Access database	page 528
6	Use this button on the MAILINGS tab to insert all of the required fields for the inside address in a letter.	Address Block button	page 531
7	The <<*GreetingLine*>> field is considered this type of field because it includes all of the fields required for the greeting line.	composite field	page 531
8	Click this button on the MAILINGS tab to display the first record merged with the main document.	Preview Results button	page 533
9	Click this button in the Preview Results group on the MAILINGS tab to display the Find Entry dialog box.	Find Recipient button	page 533
10	Before merging a document, check for errors using this button in the Preview Results group on the MAILINGS tab.	Check for Errors button	page 534
11	To complete a merge, click this button in the Finish group on the MAILINGS tab.	Finish & Merge button	page 534
12	Select specific records in a data source file by inserting or removing check marks from the records in this dialog box.	Mail Merge Recipients dialog box	page 543
13	Use this field to insert variable information with the keyboard during a merge.	Fill-in field	page 547
14	Insert this field in a main document to insert a record number in each merged document.	Merge Record # field	page 548
15	Insert this field in a main document to tell Word to compare two values and then enter one set of text or the other.	If…Then…Else…field	page 548
16	Click this option at the Start Mail Merge button drop-down list to begin the Mail Merge wizard.	*Step by Step Mail Merge Wizard*	page 557

Chapter 17; Pages 592–593

No.	Question	Answer	Page Reference
1	The Numbering button is located in this group on the HOME tab.	Paragraph group	page 574
2	Define your own numbering format with options at this dialog box.	Define New Number Format dialog box	page 576

No.	Question	Answer	Page Reference
3	When you define a bullet at the Define New Bullet dialog box, it is automatically included in this section in the Bullets button drop-down gallery.	*Bullet Library* section	page 580
4	Click this button to number paragraphs of text at the left margin, first tab, second tab, and so on.	Multilevel List button	page 582
5	As you type a multilevel list, press this combination of keys to move to the previous level.	Shift + Tab	page 586
6	Type this sequence of characters on the keyboard to insert a copyright symbol.	(c)	page 587
7	This is the keyboard shortcut to insert the ® symbol.	Alt + Ctrl + R	page 587
8	Use this type of dash in a sentence to indicate a break in thought or to highlight a term or phrase.	em dash	page 589
9	Use this type of dash to indicate inclusive dates, times, and numbers.	en dash	page 589
10	Use this keyboard shortcut to insert a nonbreaking space.	Ctrl + Shift + spacebar	page 590

Chapter 18; Page 628–629

No.	Question	Answer	Page Reference
1	You can sort text in paragraphs, columns, or these.	tables	page 599
2	The three types of sorts you can perform in a document include text, number, and this.	date	page 603
3	The Sort button is located in this group on the HOME tab.	Paragraph group	page 603
4	Click the Sort button with paragraphs of text selected and this dialog box displays.	Sort Text dialog box	page 603
5	This is the default setting for the *Separate fields at* option at the Sort Options dialog box.	*Tabs*	page 605
6	When you sort text in columns, Word considers the left margin to be this field number.	*Field 1*	page 606
7	If you select column text, including the column headings, click this option in the *My list has* section of the Sort Text dialog box.	*Header row*	page 607
8	With the insertion point positioned in a table, clicking the Sort button displays this dialog box.	Sort dialog box	page 609
9	Click this at the Mail Merge Recipients dialog box to sort data in a specific column.	field column heading	page 610
10	Click this hyperlink at the Mail Merge Recipients dialog box and the Filter and Sort dialog box displays with the Sort Records tab selected.	Sort hyperlink	page 612
11	Click this button at the Filter and Sort dialog box with the Filter Records tab selected to clear any text from text boxes.	Clear All button	page 616

No.	Question	Answer	Page Reference
12	Click this hyperlink in the Mail Merge Recipients dialog box to search for records that match a specific criterion.	Find recipient hyperlink	page 617
13	Display the Find Font dialog box by clicking this button at the expanded Find and Replace dialog box and then clicking *Font* at the drop-down list.	Format button	page 619
14	To find the body font in a document, click this option in the *Font* list box at the Find Font dialog box.	*+Body* option	pages 620–621
15	Display a list of characters you can search for in a document by clicking this button at the Find and Replace dialog box.	Special button	page 623
16	Use this wildcard character to indicate a single character in a search to find or find and replace data.	?	page 625, Table 18.2

Chapter 19; Page 660

No.	Question	Answer	Page Reference
1	If you insert page numbers in a document, Word uses this type of number by default.	arabic	page 642
2	Customize page numbering with options at this dialog box.	Page Number Format dialog box	page 642
3	To create your own header, click the INSERT tab, click the Header button in the Header & Footer group, and then click this option at the drop-down list.	*Edit Header*	page 646
4	This group on the HEADER & FOOTER TOOLS DESIGN tab contains the Date & Time and Pictures buttons.	Insert group	page 647
5	By default, a header is positioned this distance from the top of the page.	0.5 inch	page 648
6	By default, headers and footers contain two tab settings: a center tab and this type of tab.	right tab	page 648
7	When you create a header, clicking the *Different First Page* check box causes this pane to display.	First Page Header pane	page 651
8	Type this in the *Pages* text box at the Print backstage area to print section 5.	s5	page 656
9	Type this in the *Pages* text box at the Print backstage area to print page 2 of section 4 and page 5 of section 8.	p2s4,p5s8	page 656
10	The *Keep lines together* option is available at the Paragraph dialog box with this tab selected.	Line and Page Breaks tab	page 657

Chapter 20; Page 699

No.	Question	Answer	Page Reference
1	Insert a comment into a document by clicking this button in the Comments group on the REVIEW tab.	New Comment button	page 669
2	Navigate between comments by using these two buttons in the Comments group on the REVIEW tab.	Previous button and Next button	page 672
3	Change user information with options at this dialog box.	Word Options dialog box	page 674
4	If a document contains comments, you can print only the comments by displaying the Print backstage area, clicking the first gallery in the *Settings* category, clicking this option, and then clicking the Print button.	*List of Markup* option	page 675
5	Turn on the Track Changes feature by clicking the Track Changes button on this tab.	REVIEW tab	page 677, Quick Steps
6	Use this keyboard shortcut to turn on Track Changes.	Ctrl + Shift + E	page 677, Quick Steps
7	Show all markup in a document by clicking this button arrow in the Tracking group on the REVIEW tab and then clicking *All Markup* at the drop-down list.	Display for Review	page 677
8	Display information about tracked changes in this pane.	Reviewing pane	page 679
9	When Track Changes is turned on, moved text displays in this color by default.	green	page 682
10	You can customize options for tracking changes at the Track Changes Options dialog box and this dialog box.	Advanced Track Changes Options dialog box	page 683
11	Click the *Combine* option at the Compare button drop-down list and this dialog box displays.	Combine Documents dialog box	page 690
12	Specify which source documents to display by clicking the Compare button, pointing to this option, and then clicking the desired option or options at the side menu.	*Show Source Documents* option	page 691
13	Do this to an object if you want the contents in the destination program to reflect any changes made to the object stored in the source program.	link	Page 693

Chapter 21; Pages 744–745

No.	Question	Answer	Page Reference
1	The Quick Parts button is located in the Text group on this tab.	INSERT tab	page 718
2	This dialog box provides a single location where you can view all of the predesigned and custom building blocks.	Building Blocks Organizer dialog box	page 719
3	View custom building blocks saved to the Auto Text gallery by clicking this button on the INSERT tab and then pointing to *Auto Text*.	Quick Parts button	page 723

No.	Question	Answer	Page Reference
4	With the Quick Parts button, you can save a custom building block in the *AutoText* gallery or this gallery.	*Quick Part* gallery	page 723
5	Make changes to the properties of a building block with options at this dialog box.	Modify Building Blocks dialog box	page 726
6	To make building blocks more accessible, you can insert a building block gallery as a button on this toolbar.	Quick Access toolbar	page 730
7	Delete a building block at this dialog box.	Building Blocks Organizer dialog box	page 736
8	Insert a document property placeholder by clicking the Quick Parts button on the INSERT tab, pointing to this option, and then clicking the desired option at the side menu.	*Document Property* option	page 738
9	Complete these steps to display the Field dialog box.	Click the INSERT tab, click the Quick Parts button in the Text group, and then click *Field* at the drop-down list.	page 739
10	To manually update a field, press this key on the keyboard.	F9	page 740

Chapter 22; Pages 781–782

No.	Question	Answer	Page Reference
1	This feature corrects certain words automatically as you type them.	AutoCorrect feature	page 754
2	Use this button, which displays when you hover the mouse over corrected text, to change corrected text back to the original spelling.	AutoCorrect Options button	page 757
3	Type these characters to insert the J symbol in a document.	: and) [colon and right parenthesis]; or : and - and) [colon, hyphen, and right parenthesis]	page 758, Table 22.1
4	Type these characters to insert the è symbol.	= = > [two equals signs followed by a greater-than symbol]	page 758, Table 22.1
5	When typing text, control what Word automatically formats with options at the AutoCorrect dialog box with this tab selected.	AutoFormat As You Type tab	page 760
6	Add and remove basic buttons to and from the Quick Access toolbar with options at this drop-down list.	Customize Quick Access Toolbar drop-down list	page 762
7	Add a button to the Quick Access toolbar by right-clicking the desired button and then clicking this option at the shortcut menu.	*Add to Quick Access Toolbar* option	page 762

No.	Question	Answer	Page Reference
8	If you click the Customize Quick Access Toolbar button and then click *More Commands*, this dialog box displays.	Word Options dialog box	page 765
9	This is the default setting for the *Choose commands from* option at the Word Options dialog box.	*Popular Commands* setting	page 766
10	At the Word Options dialog box with this option selected in the left panel, add a new tab by clicking the tab name in the list box that you want to precede the new tab and then clicking the New Tab button.	*Customize Ribbon* option	page 768
11	Export a file containing customizations to the ribbon and/or Quick Access toolbar with this button in the Word Options dialog box with *Customize Ribbon* or *Quick Access Toolbar* selected, respectively.	Import/Export button	page 774
12	Change the user name and initials at the Word Options dialog box with this option selected in the left panel.	*General* option	page 775

Chapter 23; Page 807

No.	Question	Answer	Page Reference
1	This is the name of the default theme.	Office	page 791
2	The Themes button is located on this tab.	DESIGN tab	page 792
3	Create custom theme colors with options at this dialog box.	Create New Theme Colors dialog box	page 792
4	Custom theme colors that you create display in this section of the Theme Colors button drop-down gallery.	*Custom* section	page 792
5	With this tab selected, the Colors dialog box displays a honeycomb of color options.	Standard	page 796
6	With this tab selected, the Colors dialog box displays the *Red, Green,* and *Blue* text boxes.	Custom	page 796
7	Create custom theme fonts with options at this dialog box.	Create New Theme Fonts dialog box	page 798
8	To edit custom theme fonts, click the Theme Fonts button, do this to the custom theme, and then click *Edit* at the shortcut menu.	right-click	page 801
9	Click this option at the Themes button drop-down gallery to set the theme back to the template default.	*Reset to Theme from Template* option	page 803
10	Delete custom themes at this dialog box.	Save Current Theme dialog box	page 804

Chapter 24; Page 851

No.	Question	Answer	Page Reference
1	Use this keyboard shortcut to display the Styles task pane.	Alt + Ctrl + Shift + S	page 815
2	Character styles display in the Styles task pane followed by this symbol.	**a**	page 815
3	If you hover the mouse pointer over a style in the Styles task pane, this displays with information about the formatting applied	ScreenTip	page 816
4	To create a style based on text with existing formatting, select the text, click the More button, and then click this option at the drop-down gallery.	*Create a Style* option	page 818
5	Assign a keyboard shortcut to a style with options at this dialog box.	Customize Keyboard dialog box	page 821
6	To modify an existing style, do this to the style in the Styles group and then click *Modify* at the shortcut menu.	right-click	page 824
7	At the Save As dialog box, save a document as a template by changing the *Save as type* option to this.	Word Template (*.dotx)	page 826
8	By default, Word saves a template document in this folder on the local hard drive.	Custom Office Templates	page 826
9	Use this keyboard shortcut to display the Reveal Formatting task pane.	Shift + F1	page 829
10	Create a multilevel list style with options at the Create New Style from Formatting dialog box with the *Style type* changed to *List* or with options at this dialog box.	Define New List Style dialog box	page 833
11	To modify a table style, click in a table, click the TABLE TOOLS DESIGN tab, right-click the table style, and then click this option at the shortcut menu.	*Modify Table Style* option	page 840
12	Use this feature to investigate the styles applied to text in a document.	Style Inspector	page 841
13	Use options at the Manage Styles dialog box with this tab selected to sort styles, select a style to edit and modify, and create a new style.	Edit tab	page 843
14	Copy a style from one template to another at this dialog box.	Organizer dialog box	page 846

Chapter 25; Page 899

No.	Question	Answer	Page Reference
1	Use options in this section of the Restrict Editing task pane to limit how users can format the text in a document.	*Formatting restrictions* section	page 861
2	Use options in this section of the Restrict Editing task pane to limit how users can revise the text in a document.	*Editing restrictions* section	page 861

No.	Question	Answer	Page Reference
3	Click this button in the Restrict Editing task pane to display the Start Enforcing Protection dialog box.	Yes, Start Enforcing Protection button	page 864
4	Protect a document with a password using options at the Start Enforcing Protection dialog box or with options at this dialog box.	General Options dialog box	page 867
5	You can add information about a document's properties at this panel.	document Information panel	page 870
6	Display the Properties dialog box by clicking the Document Properties button at the Info backstage area and then clicking this option at the drop-down list.	*Advanced Properties* option	page 871
7	Mark a document as final by clicking this button at the Info backstage area and then clicking *Mark as Final* at the drop-down list.	Protect Document button	page 875
8	Use this feature to inspect a document for personal data, hidden data, and metadata.	document inspector	page 878
9	This feature checks a document for content that people with disabilities might find difficult to read.	accessibility checker	page 881
10	Use this feature to check a document and identify elements that are not supported in previous versions of Word.	compatibility checker	page 886
11	By default, Word automatically saves a document after this number of minutes.	10 minutes	page 887
12	Word keeps backup files of unsaved files in this folder on the hard drive.	UnsavedFiles folder	page 888
13	The *Invite People* option is available at this backstage area.	Share backstage area	page 891
14	With this feature, you can share a Word document with others over the Internet.	Present Online	page 895

Chapter 26; Page 941

No.	Question	Answer	Page Reference
1	Footnotes are inserted at the bottoms of pages, whereas endnotes are inserted here.	at the end of the report or paper	page 921
2	Word numbers footnotes with this type of number.	arabic	page 921
3	Word numbers endnotes with this type of number.	lowercase roman	page 921
4	View footnotes in a document by clicking this button in the Footnotes group.	Next Footnote button	page 923
5	Three commonly used styles for providing references in a report are APA (American Psychological Association), CMS (*The Chicago Manual of Style*), and this.	MLA (Modern Language Association)	page 926
6	Insert a new citation in a document with options at this dialog box.	Create Source dialog box	page 928

No.	Question	Answer	Page Reference
7	Click this tab to display the Citations & Bibliography group.	REFERENCES tab	page 928
8	To modify a source, click this button in the Citations & Bibliography group.	Manage Sources button	page 933
9	To update a works cited page, click anywhere on the page and then click this tab.	Update Citations and Bibliography tab	page 937
10	Change the citation or reference style with this option.	*Style* option	page 939

Chapter 27; Page 965

No.	Question	Answer	Page Reference
1	Use this keyboard shortcut to display the Mark Index Entry dialog box.	Alt + Shift + X	page 951
2	When you mark a word to include in the index, the selected word displays in this text box in the Mark Index Entry dialog box.	*Main entry* text box	page 951
3	Click this button at the Mark Index Entry dialog box to mark the first occurrence of the text in each paragraph of the document.	Mark All button	page 953
4	An index generally appears at this location in a document.	at the end	page 955
5	If you want to mark more than a few words as a single index entry, consider identifying the text as this.	bookmark	page 957
6	The Mark Entry button is located in the Index group on this tab.	REFERENCES tab	page 957
7	If you want the text for an index entry to refer readers to another index entry, mark it as this.	cross-reference	page 957
8	Save time when marking text for an index by creating and using this type of file.	concordance file	page 960
9	Click this button at the Index dialog box to display the Open Index AutoMark File dialog box.	AutoMark button	page 960
10	Use this keyboard shortcut to update an index.	F9 key	page 963

Chapter 28; Page 998

No.	Question	Answer	Page Reference
1	A table of contents typically appears in this location in the document.	at the beginning	page 975
2	In a built-in table of contents, Word uses text with this heading style applied as the first level.	Heading 1 style	page 975
3	A table of contents is generally numbered with this type of numbers.	lowercase roman numerals	page 976

No.	Question	Answer	Page Reference
4	Use this keyboard shortcut to update a table of contents.	F9 key	page 979
5	Delete a table of contents by clicking the Table of Contents button on the REFERENCES tab and then clicking this option.	*Remove Table of Contents* option	page 980
6	Use this keyboard shortcut to display the Mark Table of Contents Entry dialog box.	Alt + Shift + O	page 982
7	If you mark table of contents entries as fields, you will need to activate this option at the Table of Contents Options dialog box when inserting the table in the document.	*Table entry fields* option	page 982
8	Create a table of figures with items marked with these.	captions	page 985
9	This list identifies the pages on which citations appear in a legal brief or other legal document.	table of authorities	page 991
10	Use this keyboard shortcut to display the Mark Citation dialog box.	Alt + Shift + I	page 992

Chapter 29; Page 1041

No.	Question	Answer	Page Reference
1	By default, a template is saved in this folder in the Documents folder.	Custom Office Templates folder	page 1008
2	Click the Restrict Editing button on the DEVELOPER tab and this task pane displays.	Restrict Editing task pane	page 1009
3	This group on the DEVELOPER tab contains content control buttons.	Controls group	page 1012
4	When filling in a form, press this key to move to the next data field.	Tab key	page 1012
5	Click this button on the DEVELOPER tab to insert a picture frame containing a picture icon.	Picture Content Control button	page 1017
6	Click this button on the DEVELOPER tab to insert a date picker content control.	Date Picker Content Control button	page 1017
7	Insert this type of content control in a form if you want the respondent to choose from a specific list of options.	drop-down list data field	page 1019
8	Customize a date picker content control with options at this dialog box.	Content Control Properties dialog box	page 1022
9	The Legacy Tools button is located in this group on the DEVELOPER tab.	Controls group	page 1025
10	When you insert a text form field, this is inserted in the form.	a gray shaded box	page 1025
11	Insert this type of form field if you want the respondent to choose an option by inserting an *X*.	check box form field	page 1028

No.	Question	Answer	Page Reference
12	To print only the form data, display the Word Options dialog box with this option selected and then insert a check mark in the *Print only the data from a form* check box.	*Advanced* option	page 1029
13	If you want the respondent to insert data in a data field by choosing from a list, insert this type of form field.	drop-down form field	page 1030
14	To display a check box in a form with an *X* automatically inserted in the form field, click this option at the Check Box Form Field Options dialog box.	*Checked* option	page 1034
15	With the insertion point positioned immediately right of a text form field, click this button on the DEVELOPER tab to display the Text Form Field Options dialog box.	Properties button	page 1034

Chapter 30; Pages 1091–1092

No.	Question	Answer	Page Reference
1	The Outline button is located on this tab.	VIEW tab	page 1056
2	Click this button to promote a title or heading to level 1.	Promote to Heading 1 button	page 1057
3	Promote or demote a heading in Outline view by dragging this symbol, which displays before a heading.	selection symbol	page 1058
4	Click this button on the OUTLINING tab to collapse all of the text beneath a particular heading.	Collapse button	page 1061
5	The Show Document button is located in this group on the OUTLINING tab.	Master Document group	page 1064
6	Click the Expand Subdocuments button and the name of the button changes to this.	Collapse Subdocuments button	page 1065
7	The Record Macro button is included in the Code group on this tab.	DEVELOPER tab	page 1070
9	A macro name must begin with a letter and can contain only letters and these.	numbers	page 1070
9	When macro recording is turned on, a macro icon displays on this.	Status bar	page 1071
10	Delete a macro at this dialog box.	Macros dialog box	page 1076
11	Assign a macro to a keyboard command at this dialog box.	Customize Keyboard dialog box	page 1077
12	You can add a button to this toolbar to run a recorded macro.	Quick Access toolbar	page 1078
13	Click this button in the Code group on the DEVELOPER tab to display the Trust Center.	Macro Security button	page 1081
14	Inserting this type of field in a macro requires input from the keyboard.	Fill-in field	page 1085

Model Answers

The *Signature Series: Microsoft® Word 2013* Instructor Resources disc and Internet Resource Center for Instructors provide live model answer files for all textbook exercises and assessments. The article, "Using the Microsoft Word 2013 Compare Feature," explains how to use those live files to assess student performance. In addition, the textbook displays images of the model answer files for each completed exercise and assessment so that students can check their own work.

The instructor materials also offer PDFs of the model answers for the textbook exercises and assessments. Copies of annotated versions of the PDFs for the end-of-chapter and end-of-unit assessments are provided in the *Instructor's Guide.* You can use these to perform a visual comparison of student submissions. Later in this guide you will find grading rubrics that you can use to record your evaluation of the work that students do on the end-of-chapter and end-of-unit assessments. Word documents of the grading rubrics are also provided on the Instructor Resources disc and the IRC.

Using the Microsoft Word 2013 Compare Feature

Microsoft Word 2013 offers a feature that you can use to compare students' completed files against the live model answer files provided to instructors in *Signature Series: Microsoft® Word 2013.* You can use the Compare Documents feature in Word to view two documents on the same screen and see differences between them. Word 2013 defines the two documents as the original document (the model answer document) and the revised document (the student's document). The Compare Documents feature compares the two documents and alerts you if they are identical. If the two documents differ, the feature displays the model answer document, the student's document, and a new compare document with the differences shown both as tracked changes and in a list in the Revisions pane. You can save and/or print the new compare document to show the student the differences.

Instructions for Using Word's Compare Documents Feature

1. Close all open Word documents.

2. Open a new, blank Word document.

3. Click the REVIEW tab.

4. Click the Compare button in the Compare Group and then click Compare in the drop-down list. This step opens the Compare Documents dialog box. *NOTE: By default, the Compare Documents feature is set to show differences of all types, at the word level, and in a new document. To change the default settings, click the More button in the Compare Documents dialog box.*

5. Click the browse button (looks like an open file folder) next to the Original document option box.

6. Navigate to the original document (the model answer document) and double-click to enter its name in the Original document text box.

7. Click the browse button (looks like an open file folder) next to the Revised document option box.

8. Navigate to the revised document (the student's document) and double-click to enter its name in the Revised document option box.

9. Click OK. You will now see one of two results:

   a. If the two files are identical, you will see a dialog box displaying the message "Word found no differences between the two documents."

   b. If the two files are not identical, Word will open a new Compare Results window. By default, this window displays the original document (the model answer document) and the revised document (the student's document) in stacked panes on the right, and the new compare document with differences shown both as tracked changes and in a list in the Revisions pane on the left.

10. Save the new compare document. You may want to name this document with the student's last name, the model answer document name, and -compare at the end—for example, Lastname-C01-A01-CoverLtrs-compare.

11. You can provide the student with the compare document as a Word document, a hard-copy printout, or a PDF.

1. Open **Editing.docx**.
2. Save the document with Save As and name it **C01-A02-Editing**.
3. Make the changes indicated by the proofreaders' marks in Figure 1.12.

Editing is the process of altering the contents of an existing document. Editing occurs when sometimes is inserted, deleted, or modified within a document. Editing features allow users to make changes until they are satisfied with the content. Perhaps the most valued editing feature is a spell checker, which matches each word in a document to a word list or dictionary. A spell checker is not context sensitive and will not flag words that have been spelled correctly but used incorrectly. A grammar checker checks a document for common errors in grammar, usage, and mechanics. Grammar checkers are no substitute for careful review by a knowledgeable editor, but they can be useful for identifying such problems as run-on sentences, sentence fragments, double negatives, and misused apostrophes.

*Yellow highlight - insertions
*Pink highlight - text before and after deletions

C01-A02-Editing.docx

1. At a blank document, type the text in Figure 1.11. (Correct any errors highlighted by the spelling checker as they occur and remember to space once after end-of-sentence punctuation.)

Cover letters are an essential component of your job search. During your search and transition, you will write many different letters or emails to "cover" your resume. In essence, cover letters tell your readers why you are contacting them. Often they are your very first opportunity to make an impression on a hiring decision-maker. They offer you the golden opportunity to link your unique set of skills, experiences, talents, and interests with a particular company or job opportunity. They are your formal introduction to people who can be extremely influential in your job search, and they prepare your reader for all of the details, experiences, and accomplishments you have highlighted in your resume.

C01-A01-CoverLtrs.docx

1. At a blank document, compose a paragraph explaining when you would use Save As when saving a document and what advantages this provides.

Using Save As

Using the Save As function in Word is helpful when you have made changes to a document but would not like the original document to be altered. Using Save As also allows you to change the naming of each version of document you make changes to. Save As also gives you quick access to your file management and you can easily change the location, or file type, of the document being saved.

---

1. Open **Format.docx.**
2. Save the document with Save As and name it **C01-A03-Format.**
3. Make the changes indicated by the proofreaders' marks in Figure 1.13.

Word processing programs allow many different types of formatting which is the manipulation of text to change its appearance at the word, paragraph, or document level. Many word processing programs include text, paragraph, and document formatting.

Text formatting features include the ability to change the font type, size, color, and style such as bold, italic, or underlined. A user can also adjust the leading which is the space between lines, and kerning which is the amount of space that appears between letters. Paragraph formatting changes the way a body of text flows on the page. Features related to the appearance of a paragraph include placing the text in columns or tables, aligning the text left, right, center, or justified within the margins; and double-spacing or single-spacing lines. Document formatting lets users specify the form of a document as a whole, defining page numbers, headers, footers, paper size, and margin width. Many word processing programs include a style feature that formats text in a single step. Styles allow users to apply text and paragraph formatting to a document, and then automatically apply those same attributes to other sections of text.

*Yellow highlight - insertions
*Pink highlight – deletions before and after text

1. At a blank document, click the No Spacing style thumbnail located in the Styles group on the HOME tab. (Clicking the No Spacing style changes the line spacing to single and removes the 8 points of spacing after each paragraph.)
2. Press the Enter key six times and then type the personal business letter shown in Figure 1.14. Type the current date in place of the *Current Date* text and type your first and last names in place of the *Student Name* text. Refer to Appendix B for the formatting of a block style personal business letter.

3120 Magnolia Drive
Columbia, SC 29167
Current Date

Mr. Nathaniel Jensen
Human Resources Director
Landmark Associates
4450 Seventh Avenue
Columbia, SC 29169

Dear Mr. Jensen:

In response to your advertisement on Monster.com, I would like to apply for the position of Sales Associate Trainee in the Sales and Marketing Department at your company. I have a strong interest in joining a dynamic organization such as Landmark Associates and feel I can make major contributions to the company in a short period of time.

I recently graduated from Columbia Technical College with a degree in Business Operations. For the past two years, I have been employed as an assistant in the Accounting Department at Atlantic Signs where I processed payroll and budget reports. My excellent communication skills and a strong work ethic make me a valuable asset to your training program.

I have enclosed my resume for your review. Please call me at (803) 555-3489 to schedule a meeting to discuss the Sales Associate Trainee position at Landmark Associates.

Sincerely,

Student Name

Enclosure

C01-A06-Coverltr.docx

Keyboard Shortcuts

Keyboard shortcuts are helpful in increasing the speed and efficiency in your workflow. Learning a few commonly used shortcuts will be beneficial in saving you time.

The following are common keyboard shortcuts:

F12 – launches the Save As dialog box

ESC – pressing ESC will cancel a current action

CTRL + N – opens a new Word document

CTRL + A – selects the entire document for edit or formatting

1. Click the Microsoft Word Help button, click in the search text box, type keyboard shortcuts, and then press the Enter key.
2. At the Word Help window, click the Keyboard shortcuts for Microsoft Word hyperlink.
3. At the keyboard shortcut window, click the Show All hyperlink.
4. Read through the information in the Word Help window and then close the window.
5. Create a document describing four keyboard shortcuts.

C01-A05-KeyboardShortcuts.docx

Chapter 2 Assessment Annotated Model Answers

1. At a blank document, type the document shown in Figure 2.5.

Utility Programs

A *utility program* performs a single maintenance or repair task and is useful for correcting many of the problems that computer users are likely to encounter. Some of the most popular kinds of utility programs include the following:

Antivirus software: This type of software program protects the computer system from a virus attack.

Backup utility: This utility makes a backup copy of files on a separate disk.

File compression utility: Use this utility to reduce the size of files so they take up less disk space.

Device Driver: This utility allows hardware devised, such as disk drives and printers, to work with the computer system.

Uninstaller utility: Remove programs and related system files with this utility.

An operating system typically includes several utility programs that are preinstalled at the factory. Users can also purchase and install additional utility programs of their choice. Several companies produce software suites containing a variety of utility programs.

2. Apply bold, italic, and underline formatting to the text as shown.

C02-A01-UtilProgs(Step12).docx

---

6. Select *Utility Programs*, remove the underlining, and change the case style to uppercase letters.

8. Select and then hide the text *Backup utility:* and the sentence that follows it.
10. Turn on the display of nonprinting characters and unhide the text *Backup utility:* and the sentence that follows it.

UTILITY PROGRAMS

A *utility program* performs a single maintenance or repair task and is useful for correcting many of the problems that computer users are likely to encounter. Some of the most popular kinds of utility programs include the following:

Antivirus software: This type of software program protects the computer system from a virus attack.

Backup utility: This utility makes a backup copy of files on a separate disk.

File compression utility: Use this utility to reduce the size of files so they take up less disk space.

Device Driver: This utility allows hardware devised, such as disk drives and printers, to work with the computer system.

Uninstaller utility: Remove programs and related system files with this utility.

An operating system typically includes several utility programs that are preinstalled at the factory. Users can also purchase and install additional utility programs of their choice.

7. For each of the following, remove the bold formatting from the text and apply underlining instead: *Antivirus software:*, *Backup utility:*, *File compression utility:*, *Device driver:*, and *Uninstaller utility:*. (Remove the bold formatting from the colon [:] after each utility, but do not underline the colon.)

9. Select and then hide the last sentence in the last paragraph (the sentence that begins *Several companies produce software*).

5. Select the entire document and then change the font to 12-point Cambria.
11. Turn off the display of nonprinting characters.

C02-A01-UtilProgs(Step4).docx

Top section (C02-A03-ManageData.docx):

3. Select the entire document.
4. Change the font to 16-point Candara bold and the font color to Red.

MANAGING CRUCIAL DATA

Technical Support Training

Building C, Room 250

Tuesday, April 15, 2015

9:00 a.m. to 11:30 a.m.

5. Select the title *MANAGING CRUCIAL DATA*, change the font size to 20 points, and apply the Fill - Black, Text 1, Outline - Background 1, Hard Shadow - Accent 1 text effect (second column, third row). *Hint: Use the Text Effects and Typography button to apply the text effect.*

1. Open **ManageData.docx.**
2. Save the document with Save As and name it **C02-A03-ManageData.**

C02-A03-ManageData.docx

Bottom section (C02-A02-BookMemo.docx):

3. Select the book title *Managing Network Security*, remove the underlining, and then apply italic formatting.

5. Select and apply bold formatting to the headings *TO:, FROM:, DATE:,* and *SUBJECT:.*

TO: Jim Everson, Resources Coordinator

FROM: Isabelle Brown, Training Coordinator

DATE: February 18, 2015

SUBJECT: Network and Internet Books

While attending the Southern Computer Technology Conference earlier this month, I discovered several excellent network and Internet security reference books. Two of these reference books, *Managing Network Security* by Douglas Baker (published by Evergreen Publishing House) and *Network Management* by Geraldine Kingston (published by Bonari & Jenkins), I would like you to order and make available in the business section of the library. Both books retail for approximately $65. If you have enough in your budget, please order two copies of each book.

Two other reference books, *Internet Security* by Jeong Pak (published by Meridian Publishers) and *Protecting and Securing Data* by Glenn Rowan (published by Canon Beach Publishing), I would like you to order for the technical support team training that will take place in April. I will need 15 copies of *Internet Security* and 20 copies of *Protecting and Securing Data.*

6. Insert your initials at the end of the document, replacing the *XX.* Change the document name below your initials from **BookMemo.docx** to **C02-A02-BookMemo.docx.**

XX
C02-A02-BookMemo.docx

4. Select the book title *Network Management*, remove the underlining, and then apply italic formatting.

1. Open **BookMemo.docx.**
2. Save the memo with Save As and name it **C02-A02-BookMemo.**
7. Select the entire document and then change to the Cambria font.

C02-A02-BookMemo.docx

TO: Jolie Anderson

FROM: Ronald Chen

DATE: February 18, 2015

SUBJECT: Statistical Analysis

I have been running an analysis on the areas mentioned in your February 11 memo. Completing the computations has brought up the following questions:

With smaller sector ratios of F and F (.10 to .25), what will be the yield increase?

What is the interaction effect on the scores of X_1, X_2 and X^2?

1. At a blank document, type the memo shown in Figure 2.6 in appropriate memo format. (Refer to Appendix C at the end of the textbook for information on typing a memo.) Apply italic, superscript, and subscript formatting to the text as shown in the memo.

2. After typing the memo, select the entire memo and then change the font to 12-point Constantia. (If necessary, realign the headings in the memo.)

C02-A05-Memo.docx

---

3. Apply the Heading 1 style to the title *Writing Steps*.
10. Select the title *Writing Steps*, change the font color to Dark Blue, and then apply bold formatting.

Writing Steps

A document that communicates clearly is the result of good writing and good rewriting; you can usually improve anything you have written. The writing process includes the following steps:

Define Purpose

Knowing your purpose for writing is the foundation for any written project. Before you begin writing your memo, letter, or other document, ask yourself the following questions:

- What am I trying to accomplish?
- What is my purpose for writing?
- To request information or products?
- To respond to a question or request?
- To persuade someone?
- To direct someone?

Identify Reader

As you define your purpose, you will need to develop a good picture of the person who will be reading your document. Ask yourself:

- Who is my reader?
- What do I know about my reader that will help determine the best approach?
- Is the audience one person or a group?
- Is my reader a coworker, a subordinate, a superior, or a customer?
- How is the reader likely to feel about my message?

Select and Organize Information

Once you have defined your purpose and identified your reader, decide what information you will include. Ask yourself questions such as:

- What does my reader want or need to know?
- What information must I include?
- What information will help my reader respond positively?
- What information should I not include?

Write First Draft

A first effort is rarely a final draft, even for the best writers; therefore, write something to get started. Let your purpose, reader, and organizational plan guide you, but do not let them stifle you. Keep going even if you occasionally lose your focus. Once you have a full draft, you can add or delete information, reorganize, and edit sentences.

Edit and Proofread

Editing and proofreading are essential to good writing. Planning and drafting allow you to get your information on paper; editing and proofreading help you communicate your ideas as clearly as possible to the reader.

4. Apply the Heading 2 style to the five headings in the document: *Define Purpose, Identify Reader, Select and Organize Information, Write First Draft,* and *Edit and Proofread.*

1. Open **WritingSteps.docx.**
2. Save the document with Save As and name it **C02-A04-WritingSteps.**
5. Use the Paragraph Spacing button on the DESIGN tab to change the paragraph spacing to Compact.
6. Apply the Basic (Stylish) style set.
7. Apply the Integral theme.
8. Change the theme colors to Violet II.
9. Change the theme fonts to Candara.

C02-A04-WritingSteps.docx

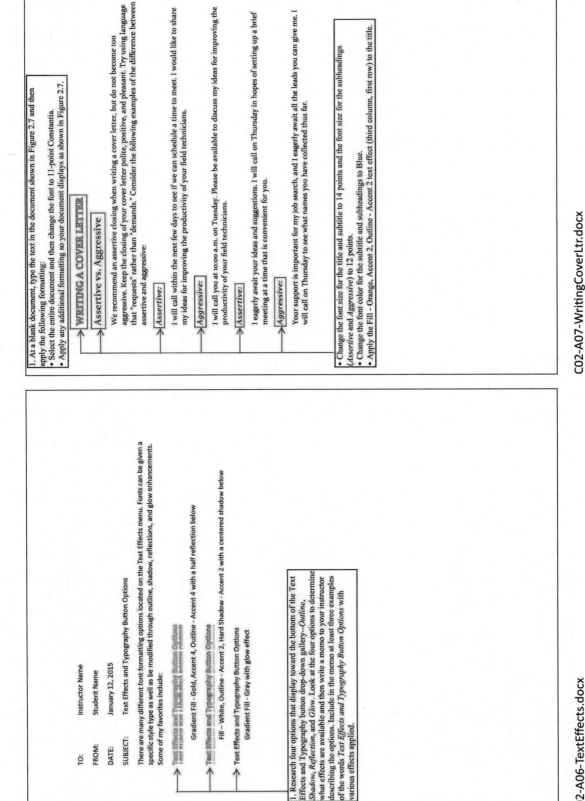

Box 1 (C02-A07-WritingCoverltr.docx):

1. At a blank document, type the text in the document shown in Figure 2.7 and then apply the following formatting:
   • Select the entire document and then change the font to 11-point Constantia.
   • Apply any additional formatting so your document displays as shown in Figure 2.7.

WRITING A COVER LETTER

Assertive vs. Aggressive

We recommend an assertive closing when writing a cover letter polite, positive, and pleasant. Try using language that "requests" rather than "demands." Consider the following examples of the difference between assertive and aggressive:

Assertive:

I will call within the next few days to see if we can schedule a time to meet. I would like to share my ideas for improving the productivity of your field technicians.

Aggressive:

I will call you at 10:00 a.m. on Tuesday. Please be available to discuss my ideas for improving the productivity of your field technicians.

Assertive:

I eagerly await your ideas and suggestions. I will call on Thursday in hopes of setting up a brief meeting at a time that is convenient for you.

Aggressive:

Your support is important for my job search, and I eagerly await all the leads you can give me. I will call on Thursday to see what names you have collected thus far.

• Change the font size for the title and subtitle to 14 points and the font size for the subheadings (*Assertive* and *Aggressive*) to 12 points.
• Change the font color for the subtitle and subheadings to Blue.
• Apply the Fill – Orange, Accent 2, Outline – Accent 2 text effect (third column, first row) to the title.

C02-A07-WritingCoverltr.docx

Box 2 (C02-A06-TextEffects.docx):

TO: Instructor Name

FROM: Student Name

DATE: January 12, 2015

SUBJECT: Text Effects and Typography Button Options

There are many different font formatting options located on the Text Effects menu. Fonts can be given a specific style type as well as be modified through outline, shadow, reflections, and glow enhancements. Some of my favorites include:

Text Effects and Typography Button Options
Gradient Fill – Gold, Accent 4, Outline – Accent 4 with a half reflection below

Text Effects and Typography Button Options
Fill – White, Outline – Accent 2, Hard Shadow - Accent 2 with a centered shadow below

Text Effects and Typography Button Options
Gradient Fill – Gray with glow effect

1. Research four options that display toward the bottom of the Text Effects and Typography button drop-down gallery—*Outline, Shadow, Reflection,* and *Glow.* Look at the four options to determine what effects are available and then write a memo to your instructor describing the options. Include in the memo at least three examples of the words *Text Effects and Typography Button Options* with various effects applied.

C02-A06-TextEffects.docx

Northland Security Systems

3200 North 22ⁿᵈ Street ♦ Springfield ♦ IL ♦ 62102

February 17, 2015

Jessie Levigne, Manager
Technical Support Department
Baldwin Corporation
1590 28ᵗʰ Street
Springfield, IL 62126

Dear Mr. Levigne:

Based on our telephone conversation about your company data security training requirements, I suggest offering three workshops to employees at Baldwin Corporation. After attending the workshops, your employees will have the skills required to secure company data. The workshops I propose include:

Rotating Backup Process: In this workshop, participants will be briefed on the rotating backup process, which involves backing up data from specific departments on specific days of the week.

Disaster Recovery: The focus of this workshop is the development of a disaster recovery plan and will include data backup procedures, remote backup locations, and redundant systems.

Data Security: The third workshop I propose is data security and data encryption. In this workshop participants will learn about encryption schemes designed to scramble information before transferring it electronically.

I am confident that these three workshops will address your security issues. I have enclosed our standard contract for you to read. Please contact me to discuss the contract as well as the location, time, and equipment requirements for each workshop.

Sincerely,

Bryce Gyverson
Vice President

XX
C02-A08-BCLtr.docx

Enclosure

1-888-555-2200 ♦ www.emcp.net/nss

> 1. Open **NSSLtrhd.docx** and then save the document and name it **C02-A08-BCLtr.**
> 2. Click the *No Spacing* style thumbnail located in the Styles group on the HOME tab and then type the text in the document shown in Figure 2.8. Refer to Appendix D at the end of the textbook for the formatting of a block style business letter with the No Spacing style applied. (Replace the *XX* with your initials near the end of the letter.)

C02-A08-BCLtr.docx

Chapter 3 Assessment Annotated Model Answers

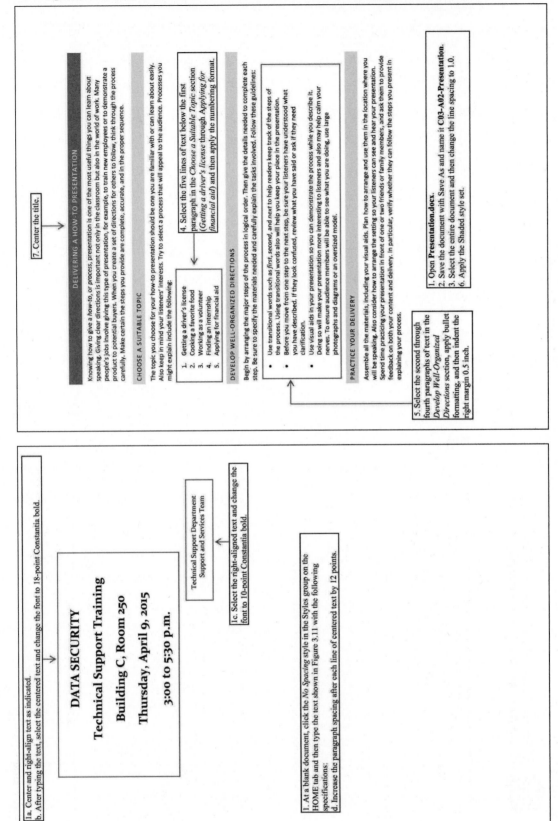

7. Center the title.

DELIVERING A HOW-TO PRESENTATION

Knowing how to give a *how-to*, or *process*, presentation is one of the most useful things you can learn about speaking. Giving clear directions is important not only in the classroom but also in the world of work. Many people's jobs involve giving this type of presentation, for example, to train new employees or to demonstrate a product to potential buyers. When you create a set of directions for others to follow, think through the process carefully. Make certain the steps you provide are complete, accurate, and in the proper sequence.

CHOOSE A SUITABLE TOPIC

The topic you choose for your how-to presentation should be one you are familiar with or can learn about easily. Also keep in mind your listeners' interests. Try to select a process that will appeal to the audience. Processes you might explain include the following:

1. Getting a driver's license
2. Cooking a favorite food
3. Working as a volunteer
4. Finding an internship
5. Applying for financial aid

4. Select the five lines of text below the first paragraph in the *Choose a Suitable Topic* section (*Getting a driver's license* through *Applying for financial aid*) and then apply the numbering format.

DEVELOP WELL-ORGANIZED DIRECTIONS

Begin by arranging the major steps of the process in logical order. Then give the details needed to complete each step. Be sure to specify the materials needed and carefully explain the tasks involved. Follow these guidelines:

- Use transitional words such as *first*, *second*, and *next* to help readers keep track of the steps of the process. Using transitional words also will help you keep your place in the presentation.
- Before you move from one step to the next step, be sure your listeners have understood what you have described. If they look confused, review what you have said or ask if they need clarification.
- Use visual aids in your presentation so you can demonstrate the process while you describe it. Doing so will make your presentation more interesting to listeners and also may help calm your nerves. To ensure audience members will be able to see what you are doing, use large photographs and diagrams or an oversized model.

PRACTICE YOUR DELIVERY

Assemble all the materials, including your visual aids. Plan how to arrange and use them in the location where you will be speaking. Also consider how to arrange the setting so your listeners can see and hear your presentation. Spend time practicing your presentation in front of one or two friends or family members, and ask them to provide feedback on both your content and delivery. In particular, verify whether they can follow the steps you present in explaining your process.

5. Select the second through fourth paragraphs of text in the *Develop Well-Organized Directions* section, apply bullet formatting, and then indent the right margin 0.5 inch.

1. Open **Presentation.docx.**
2. Save the document with Save As and name it **C03-A02-Presentation.**
3. Select the entire document and then change the line spacing to 1.0.
6. Apply the Shaded style set.

C03-A02-Presentation(Step8).docx

**1a. Center and right-align text as indicated.
b. After typing the text, select the centered text and change the font to 18-point Constantia bold.**

**DATA SECURITY
Technical Support Training
Building C, Room 250
Thursday, April 9, 2015
3:00 to 5:30 p.m.**

Technical Support Department
Support and Services Team

1c. Select the right-aligned text and change the font to 10-point Constantia bold.

1. At a blank document, click the *No Spacing* style in the Styles group on the HOME tab and then type the text shown in Figure 3.11 with the following specifications:
d. Increase the paragraph spacing after each line of centered text by 12 points.

C03-A01-DataTraining.docx

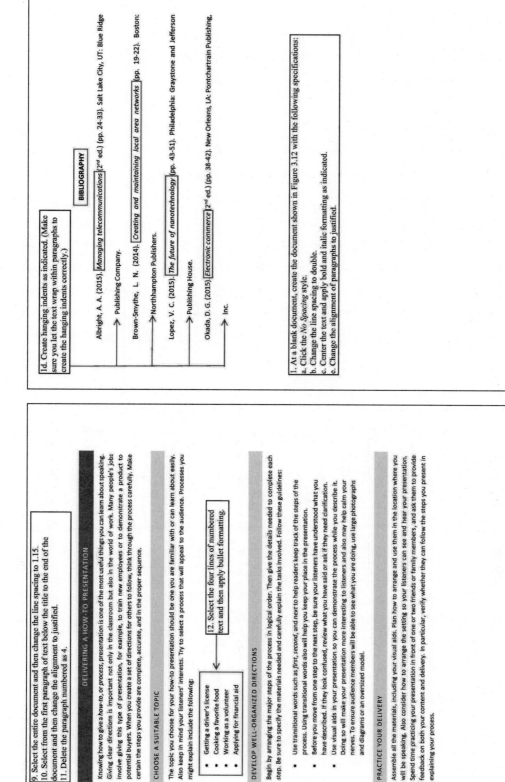

C03-A03-Biblio.docx

1d. Create hanging indents as indicated. (Make sure you let the text wrap within paragraphs to create the hanging indents correctly.)

BIBLIOGRAPHY

Albright, A. A. (2015). *Managing telecommunications* (2nd ed.) (pp. 24-33). Salt Lake City, UT: Blue Ridge Publishing Company.

Brown-Smythe, L. N. (2014). *Creating and maintaining local area networks* (pp. 19-22). Boston: Northhampton Publishers.

Lopez, V. C. (2015). *The future of nanotechnology* (pp. 43-51). Philadelphia: Graystone and Jefferson Publishing House.

Okada, D. G. (2015). *Electronic commerce* (2nd ed.) (pp. 38-42). New Orleans, LA: Pontchartrain Publishing, Inc.

1. At a blank document, create the document shown in Figure 3.12 with the following specifications:
a. Click the *No Spacing* style.
b. Change the line spacing to double.
c. Center the text and apply bold and italic formatting as indicated.
e. Change the alignment of paragraphs to justified.

C03-A02B-Presentation.docx

9. Select the entire document and then change the line spacing to 1.15.
10. Select from the first paragraph of text below the title to the end of the document and then change the alignment to justified.
11. Delete the paragraph numbered as 4.

DELIVERING A HOW-TO PRESENTATION

Knowing how to give a *how-to*, or *process*, presentation is one of the most useful things you can learn about speaking. Giving clear directions is important not only in the classroom but also in the world of work. Many people's jobs involve giving this type of presentation, for example, to train new employees or to demonstrate a product to potential buyers. When you create a set of directions for others to follow, think through the process carefully. Make certain the steps you provide are complete, accurate, and in the proper sequence.

CHOOSE A SUITABLE TOPIC

The topic you choose for your how-to presentation should be one you are familiar with or can learn about easily. Also keep in mind your listeners' interests. Try to select a process that will appeal to the audience. Processes you might explain include the following:

- Getting a driver's license
- Cooking a favorite food
- Working as a volunteer
- Applying for financial aid

12. Select the four lines of numbered text and then apply bullet formatting.

DEVELOP WELL-ORGANIZED DIRECTIONS

Begin by arranging the major steps of the process in logical order. Then give the details needed to complete each step. Be sure to specify the materials needed and carefully explain the tasks involved. Follow these guidelines:

- Use transitional words such as *first*, *second*, and *next* to help readers keep track of the steps of the process. Using transitional words also will help you keep your place in the presentation.
- Before you move from one step to the next step, be sure your listeners have understood what you have described. If they look confused, review what you have said or ask if they need clarification.
- Use visual aids in your presentation so you can demonstrate the process while you describe it. Doing so will make your presentation more interesting to listeners and also may help calm your nerves. To ensure audience members will be able to see what you are doing, use large photographs and diagrams or an oversized model.

PRACTICE YOUR DELIVERY

Assemble all the materials, including your visual aids. Plan how to arrange and use them in the location where you will be speaking. Also consider how to arrange the setting so your listeners can see and hear your presentation. Spend time practicing your presentation in front of one or two friends or family members, and ask them to provide feedback on both your content and delivery. In particular, verify whether they can follow the steps you present in explaining your process.

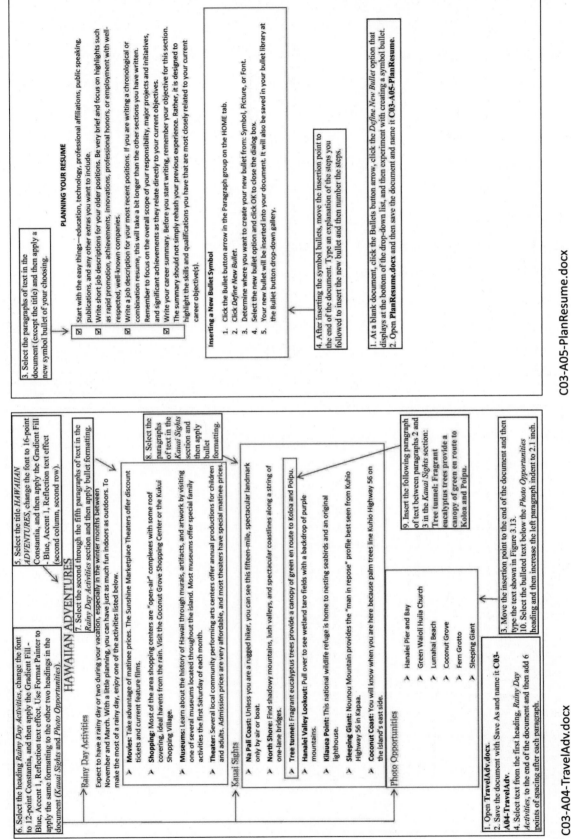

PLANNING YOUR RESUME

3. Select the paragraphs of text in the document (except the title) and then apply a new symbol bullet of your choosing.

- ☑ Start with the easy things—education, technology, professional affiliations, public speaking, publications, and any other extras you want to include.
- ☑ Write short job descriptions for your older positions. Be very brief and focus on highlights such as rapid promotion, achievements, innovations, professional honors, or employment with well-respected, well-known companies.
- ☑ Write a job description for your most recent positions. If you are writing a chronological or combination resume, this will take a bit longer than the other sections you have written. Remember to focus on the overall scope of your responsibility, major projects and initiatives, and significant achievements as they relate directly to your current objectives.
- ☑ Write your career summary. Before you start writing, remember your objective for this section. The summary should not simply rehash your previous experience. Rather, it is designed to highlight the skills and qualifications you have that are most closely related to your current career objective(s).

Inserting a New Bullet Symbol
1. Click the Bullet button arrow in the Paragraph group on the HOME tab.
2. Click *Define New Bullet*.
3. Determine where you want to create your new bullet from: Symbol, Picture, or Font.
4. Select the new bullet option and click OK to close the dialog box.
5. Your new bullet will be inserted into your document. It will also be saved in your bullet library at the Bullet button drop-down gallery.

4. After inserting the symbol bullets, move the insertion point to the end of the document. Type an explanation of the steps you followed to insert the new bullet and then number the steps.

1. At a blank document, click the Bullets button arrow, click the *Define New Bullet* option that displays at the bottom of the drop-down list, and then experiment with creating a symbol bullet.
2. Open **PlanResume.docx** and then save the document and name it **C03-A05-PlanResume**.

C03-A05-PlanResume.docx

---

6. Select the heading *Rainy Day Activities*, change the font to 12-point Constantia, and then apply the Gradient Fill - Blue, Accent 1, Reflection text effect. Use Format Painter to apply the same formatting to the other two headings in the document (*Kauai Sights* and *Photo Opportunities*).

5. Select the title *HAWAIIAN ADVENTURES*, change the font to 16-point Constantia, and then apply the Gradient Fill - Blue, Accent 1, Reflection text effect (second column, second row).

HAWAIIAN ADVENTURES

7. Select the second through the fifth paragraphs of text in the *Rainy Day Activities* section and then apply bullet formatting.

Rainy Day Activities

Expect to have a rainy day or two during your vacation, especially in the winter months between November and March. With a little planning, you can have just as much fun indoors as outdoors. To make the most of a rainy day, enjoy one of the activities listed below.

➢ **Movies:** Take advantage of matinee prices. The Sunshine Marketplace Theaters offer discount tickets and current feature films.
➢ **Shopping:** Most of the area shopping centers are "open-air" complexes with some roof covering, ideal havens from the rain. Visit the Coconut Grove Shopping Center or the Kukui Shopping Village.
➢ **Museums:** Learn about the history of Hawaii through murals, artifacts, and artwork by visiting one of several museums located throughout the island. Most museums offer special family activities the first Saturday of each month.
➢ **Theater:** Several local community performing arts centers offer annual productions for children and adults. Admission prices are very affordable, and most theaters have special matinee prices.

8. Select the paragraphs of text in the *Kauai Sights* section and then apply bullet formatting.

Kauai Sights

➢ **Na Pali Coast:** Unless you are a rugged hiker, you can see this fifteen-mile, spectacular landmark only by air or boat.
➢ **North Shore:** Find shadowy mountains, lush valleys, and spectacular coastlines along a string of one-lane bridges.
➢ **Tree tunnel:** Fragrant eucalyptus trees provide a canopy of green en route to Koloa and Poipu.
➢ **Hanalei Valley Lookout:** Pull over to see wetland taro fields with a backdrop of purple mountains.
➢ **Kilauea Point:** This national wildlife refuge is home to nesting seabirds and an original lighthouse.
➢ **Sleeping Giant:** Nounou Mountain provides the "man in repose" profile best seen from Kuhio Highway 56 in Kapaa.
➢ **Coconut Coast:** You will know when you are here because palm trees line Kuhio Highway 56 on the island's east side.

9. Insert the following paragraph of text between paragraphs 2 and 3 in the *Kauai Sights* section: **Tree tunnel:** Fragrant eucalyptus trees provide a canopy of green en route to Koloa and Poipu.

Photo Opportunities
➢ Hanalei Pier and Bay
➢ Green Waioli Huiia Church
➢ Lumahai Beach
➢ Coconut Grove
➢ Fern Grotto
➢ Sleeping Giant

3. Move the insertion point to the end of the document and then type the text shown in Figure 3.13.
10. Select the bulleted text below the *Photo Opportunities* heading and then increase the left paragraph indent to 2.1 inch.

1. Open **TravelAdv.docx**.
2. Save the document with Save As and name it **C03-A04-TravelAdv**.
4. Select text from the first heading, *Rainy Day Activities*, to the end of the document and then add 6 points of spacing after each paragraph.

C03-A04-TravelAdv.docx

NINE STRATEGIES FOR AN EFFECTIVE RESUME

Following are the nine core strategies for writing an effective and successful resume:

1. Who are you and how do you want to be perceived?
2. Sell it to me … don't tell it to me.
3. Use keywords.
4. Use the "big" and save the "little."
5. Make your resume "interviewable."
6. Eliminate confusion with structure and content.
7. Use function to demonstrate achievement.
8. Remain in the realm of reality.
9. Be confident.

Writing Style

Always write in the first person, dropping the word "I" from the front of each sentence. This style gives your resume a more aggressive and more professional tone than the passive third person voice. Here are some examples:

First Person

Manage 22-person team responsible for design and marketing of a new portfolio of PC-based applications for Landmark's consumer-sales division.

Third Person

Ms. Sanderson manages a 22-person team responsible for design and marketing of a new portfolio of PC-based application for Landmark's consumer-sales division.

REFERENCES

Kurzweil, M. J. & Middleton, C. A. (2015). Designing a sure-fire resume (pp. 6-10). Indianapolis, IN: Rushton-Jansen Publishing House.

Perreault, R. M. and Engstrom, E. L. (2014). Writing resumes and cover pages (pp. 31-34). Los Angeles: Pacific Blue Printing.

C03-A06-ResumeStrategies.docx

BARRINGTON & GATES

January 14, 2015

Ms. Cameron Silvana
Pioneer Square Properties
19332 South 122nd Street
Austin, TX 73302

Dear Ms. Silvana:

Re: Residential Lease Agreement

During our telephone conversation today, you asked me to review the standard contract your company, Pioneer Square Properties, uses for residential rental properties. I was able to download the residential lease agreement from your website and suggest that you add/change the following items:

- **Rent:** The total rent for the term is the sum of _____ DOLLARS ($_____) payable on the _____ day of each month of the term.
- **Condition of Premises:** Lessee stipulates, represents, and warrants that Lessee has examined the Premises, and that they are at the time of this Agreement in good order, repair, and in a safe, clean, and tenantable condition.
- **Damage to Premise:** In the event Premises are destroyed or rendered wholly unlivable by fire, storm, earthquake, or other casualty not caused by the negligence of Lessee, this Agreement shall terminate.

After reviewing the proposed changes, call or email me so we can schedule an appointment to finalize the agreement. During our meeting I would like to discuss the development of additional forms for your company.

Sincerely,

Grace Macintosh
Attorney at Law

XX

C03-A07-PSPLetter.docx

200 TENTH STREET • SUITE 100 • AUSTIN, TX 73341 • 512-555-2000

C03-A07-PSPLetter.docx

Chapter 4 Assessment Annotated Model Answers

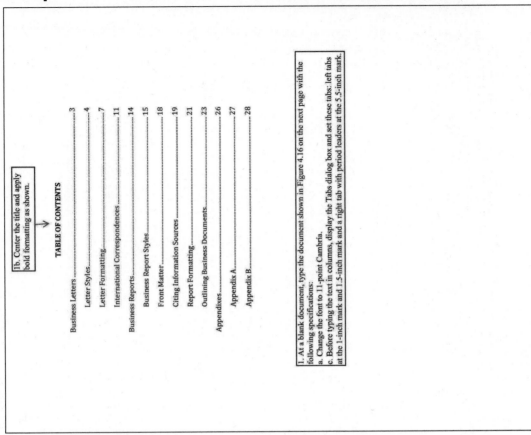

1b. Center the title and apply bold formatting as shown.

TABLE OF CONTENTS

1. At a blank document, type the document shown in Figure 4.16 on the next page with the following specifications:
   a. Change the font to 11-point Cambria.
   c. Before typing the text in columns, display the Tabs dialog box and set these tabs: left tabs at the 1-inch mark and 1.5-inch mark and a right tab with period leaders at the 5.5-inch mark.

C04-A02-TofC(Step3).docx

---

3. Apply the Heading 1 style to the title *Abbreviations* and apply the Heading 2 style to the two headings *Personal Names* and *Academic, Professional, and Religious Designations*.

8. Center the title *Abbreviations*.

9. Apply a top border to the title *Abbreviations* (in the same color as the bottom border) and apply Gold, Accent 2, Lighter 80% shading (sixth column, second row in the *Theme Colors* section).

10. Apply the same shading to the other two headings in the document.

Abbreviations

Abbreviations are selected letters (sometimes with periods) used as a shortened form of a written word or phrase. When you use abbreviations, be consistent. Abbreviate a word the same way throughout a document. Also, base your decision to abbreviate on your evaluation of the formality of the document and its intended purpose. Decide whether you will use abbreviations before you begin writing or editing.

Personal Names

Personal Titles: Always use the following abbreviations instead of the full word form:

6. Select the columns of text in the *Personal Names* section and then drag the left tab at the 1-inch mark on the horizontal ruler to the 0.5-inch mark. Also drag the left tab at the 3.5-inch mark on the horizontal ruler to the 1.5-inch mark.

Singular	Plural
Miss	Misses
Mrs.	Mmes.
Ms.	Mses.
Mr.	Messrs.
Dr.	Drs.

Academic, Professional, and Religious Designations

Attached to a Person's Name: Many abbreviations for academic, professional, and religious designations are written with periods (but no internal spacing) when attached to a person's name:

7. Select the columns of text in the *Academic, Professional, and Religious Designations* section and then complete the following:
   a. Sort the text alphabetically.
   b. Drag the left tab at the 1-inch mark on the horizontal ruler to the 0.5-inch mark.
   c. Drag the left tab at the 3.5-inch mark on the horizontal ruler to the 1.5-inch mark.

A.S.	Associate of Science
B.S.	Bachelor of Science
D.D.	Doctor of Divinity
D.D.S.	Doctor of Dental Science
Ed.D.	Doctor of Education
M.A.	Master of Arts
M.B.A.	Master of Business Administration
M.D.	Doctor of Medicine
M.S.	Master of Science
Ph.D.	Doctor of Philosophy
R.N.	Registered Nurse

General Reference to Training or Occupation: When academic, professional, or religious titles are used to designate groups of people with certain kinds of training (i.e., not attached to a person's name), the titles are often used without periods.

1. Open **Abbre.docx** and save the document with the name **C04-A01-Abbre**.
2. Type the text shown in Figure 4.15 immediately below the *R.N. Registered Nurse* text. Make sure you tab to the correct tab stop and press the Enter key to end each line.
4. Apply the Lines (Simple) style set.
5. Apply the Frame theme.

C04-A01-Abbre.docx

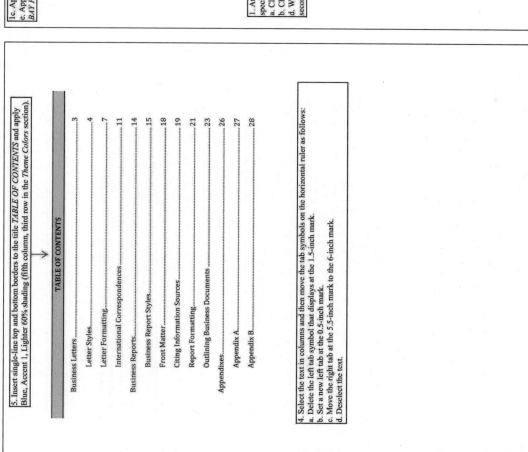

Top document (C04-A03-NewEmp.docx):

1c. Apply bold formatting to the text as shown in the figure.
e. Apply Blue, Accent 1, Lighter 60% shading (fifth column, third row in the *Theme Colors* section) to the title *MOBILE BAY PRODUCTS* and the subtitle *New Employees*. Apply the same shading to the row containing the column headings.

MOBILE BAY PRODUCTS		
New Employees		
Employee	**Hire Date**	**Department**
Smith-Larsen, Beth	07/06/2015	Public Relations
Moranski, Adam	06/22/2015	Finance
Newton, Katherine	07/06/2015	Technical Support
Oh, Soo-Yean	08/03/2015	Finance
Crowley, Nicholas	10/12/2015	Technical Support
Espinoza, Enrique	09/14/2015	Training

1f. Apply Blue, Accent 1, Lighter 80% shading (fifth column, second row in the *Theme Colors* section) to the blank line between the subtitle and column headings and then apply the same shading to the text in the columns below the column headings.

1. At a blank document, create the document shown in Figure 4.17 with the following specifications:
a. Click the *No Spacing* style in the Styles group on the HOME tab.
b. Change the font to 12-point Candara.
d. When typing the text in columns, set a left tab for the first column, a center tab for the second column, and a right tab for the third column.

Bottom document (C04-A02-TofC(Step6).docx):

5. Insert single-line top and bottom borders to the title *TABLE OF CONTENTS* and apply Blue, Accent 1, Lighter 60% shading (fifth column, third row in the *Theme Colors* section).

TABLE OF CONTENTS

4. Select the text in columns and then move the tab symbols on the horizontal ruler as follows:
a. Delete the left tab symbol that displays at the 1.5-inch mark.
b. Set a new left tab at the 0.5-inch mark.
c. Move the right tab at the 5.5-inch mark to the 6-inch mark.
d. Deselect the text.

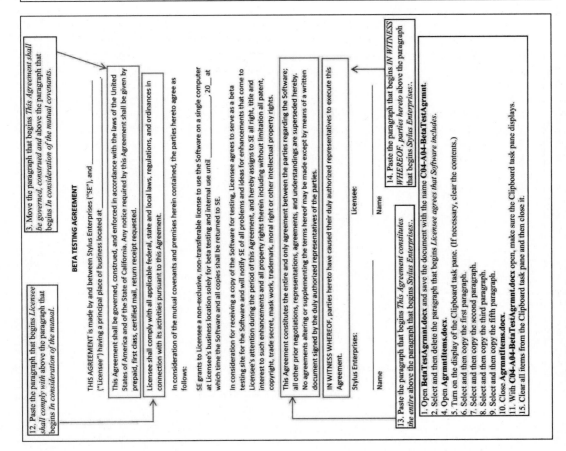

C04-A05-PasteOptions.docx

1234 Main Street
Seattle, WA 98115
February 6, 2015

Instructor Name
5754 Traffic Avenue
Kirkland, WA 98033

Dear Instructor:

After researching the Cut and Paste options in Word 2013, I have determined the following necessary steps are required to change the paste option defaults, if warranted.

The Paste Options menu includes three paste option buttons:
- Keep Source Formatting – this option keeps the original format from the text or document you are cutting from.
- Merge Formatting – this option adopts the formatting from the text or document you are pasting into.
- Keep Text Only – this option removes all formatting from the cut and pasted text.

To change the default, click the FILE tab, click Options, and then click Advanced in the left panel. Scroll through the options to the Cut, Copy and Paste section. Here you can modify the paste button options to display within your documents.

Sincerely,

Student Name

1. As you learned in this chapter, the Paste Options button displays when you paste text in a document. When you click the Paste Options button, the Paste Options gallery displays with three buttons. By default, the first button from the left (Keep Source Formatting) is active. You can change this default with options at the Word Options dialog box with *Advanced* selected in the left panel. Display this dialog box by pasting text, clicking the Paste Options button, and then clicking the *Set Default Paste* option at the bottom of the Paste Options gallery. (You can also display this dialog box by clicking the FILE tab, clicking *Options*, and then clicking the *Advanced* option in the left panel.) At a blank document, open the Word Options dialog box. Figure out how to change the default paste options when pasting text within and between documents from the default *Keep Source Formatting* to *Merge Formatting*. (Do not actually make the change.) After learning how to change the paste options default, write a letter to your instructor using the personal business letter style (refer to Appendix B). Include in the letter information on the three buttons that display in the Paste Options button gallery. In addition, include steps on how to change the options for pasting within and between documents from the defaults to *Merge Formatting*.

C04-A04-BetaTestAgrmnt.docx

12. Paste the paragraph that begins *Licensee shall comply with* above the paragraph that begins *In consideration of the mutual.*

3. Move the paragraph that begins *This Agreement shall be governed, construed and* above the paragraph that begins *In consideration of the mutual covenants.*

BETA TESTING AGREEMENT

THIS AGREEMENT is made by and between Stylus Enterprises ("SE"), and ("Licensee") having a principal place of business located at _____

This Agreement shall be governed, construed, and enforced in accordance with the laws of the United States of America and of the State of California. Any notice required by this Agreement shall be given by prepaid, first class, certified mail, return receipt requested.

Licensee shall comply with all applicable federal, state and local laws, regulations, and ordinances in connection with its activities pursuant to this Agreement.

In consideration of the mutual covenants and premises herein contained, the parties hereto agree as follows:

SE grants to Licensee a non-exclusive, non-transferable license to use the Software on a single computer at Licensee's business location solely for beta testing and internal use until _____, 20__ at which time the Software and all copies shall be returned to SE.

In consideration for receiving a copy of the Software for testing, Licensee agrees to serve as a beta testing site for the Software and will notify SE of all problems and ideas for enhancements that come to Licensee's attention during the period of this Agreement, and hereby assigns to SE all right, title and interest to such enhancements and all property rights therein including without limitation all patent, copyright, trade secret, mask work, trademark, moral right or other intellectual property rights.

This Agreement constitutes the entire and only agreement between the parties regarding the Software; all other prior negotiations, representations, agreements, and understandings are superseded hereby. No agreements altering or supplementing the terms hereof may be made except by means of a written document signed by the duly authorized representatives of the parties.

IN WITNESS WHEREOF, parties hereto have caused their duly authorized representatives to execute this Agreement.

Stylus Enterprises: Licensee:

_____ _____
Name Name

13. Paste the paragraph that begins *This Agreement constitutes the entire* above the paragraph that begins *Stylus Enterprises:.*

14. Paste the paragraph that begins *IN WITNESS WHEREOF, parties hereto* above the paragraph that begins *Stylus Enterprises:.*

1. Open **BetaTestAgrmnt.docx** and save the document with the name **C04-A04-BetaTestAgrmnt**.
2. Select and then delete the paragraph that begins *Licensee agrees that Software includes.*
4. Open **Agrmntitems.docx**.
5. Turn on the display of the Clipboard task pane. (If necessary, clear the contents.)
6. Select and then copy the first paragraph.
7. Select and then copy the second paragraph.
8. Select and then copy the third paragraph.
9. Select and then copy the fifth paragraph.
10. Close **Agrmntitems.docx**.
11. With **C04-A04-BetaTestAgrmnt.docx** open, make sure the Clipboard task pane displays.
15. Clear all items from the Clipboard task pane and then close it.

• Type the title and subtitle, press the Enter key three times, and then change the spacing after paragraphs back to 8 points.

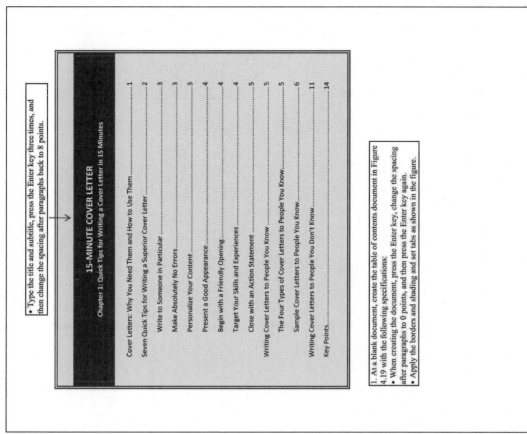

15-MINUTE COVER LETTER

Chapter 1: Quick Tips for Writing a Cover Letter in 15 Minutes

1. At a blank document, create the table of contents document in Figure 4.19 with the following specifications:
• When creating the document, press the Enter key, change the spacing after paragraphs to 0 points, and then press the Enter key again.
• Apply the borders and shading and set tabs as shown in the figure.

C04-A07-Ch01TofC.docx

• Press the Enter key once and then type the text shown in the top box in Figure 4.18.
• Apply character and paragraph formatting to the text and set tabs so the text in your document appears similar to that in Figure 4.18. Press the Enter key three times after typing the text *Refreshments available.*

OPEN HOUSE

Sponsored by the Marketing Department

Location .... Room 100
Date .... Friday, May 15
Time .... 1:00 to 3:30 p.m.

Refreshments available.

OPEN HOUSE

Sponsored by the Marketing Department

Location .... Room 100
Date .... Friday, May 15
Time .... 1:00 to 3:30 p.m.

Refreshments available.

OPEN HOUSE

Sponsored by the Marketing Department

Location .... Room 100
Date .... Friday, May 15
Time .... 1:00 to 3:30 p.m.

Refreshments available.

• Select the text in your document from the beginning of the document to the blank line below *Refreshments available.* (without including the last two blank lines in the document) and then apply the border shown in Figure 4.18 using the third line option from the bottom of the *Styles* list box, applying the Blue color in the *Standard Colors* section, and changing the width to 4 1/2 pt. Apply the Green, Accent 6, Lighter 80% paragraph shading to the text as shown in the figure.

1. At a blank document, create the document shown in Figure 4.18 with the following specifications:
• Change the font to Candara, the line spacing to single, and the spacing after paragraphs to 4 points.
• After creating the first box, copy it and paste it two times in the document so your document contains a total of three boxes, as shown in Figure 4.18.

C04-A06-OpenHouse.docx

Chapter 5 Assessment Annotated Model Answers

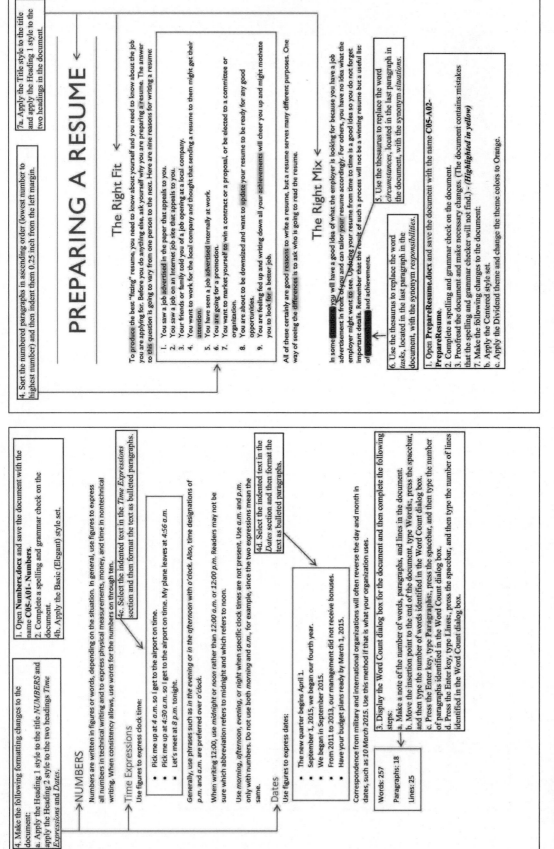

Document 1 (C05-A02-PrepareResume.docx)

7a. Apply the Title style to the title and apply the Heading 1 style to the two headings in the document.

4. Sort the numbered paragraphs in ascending order (lowest number to highest number) and then indent them 0.25 inch from the left margin.

PREPARING A RESUME

The Right Fit

To produce the best "fitting" resume, you need to know about yourself and you need to know about the job you are applying for. Before you do anything else, ask yourself why you are preparing a resume. The answer to this question is going to vary from one person to the next. Here are nine reasons for writing a resume:

1. You saw a job advertised in the paper that appeals to you.
2. You saw a job on an Internet job site that appeals to you.
3. Your friends or family told you of a job opening at a local company.
4. You want to work for the local company and thought that sending a resume to them might get their attention.
5. You have seen a job advertised internally at work.
6. You are going for a promotion.
7. You want to market yourself to win a contract or a proposal, or be elected to a committee or organization.
8. You are about to be downsized and want to update your resume to be ready for any good opportunities.
9. You are feeling fed up and writing down all your achievements will cheer you up and might motivate you to look for a better job.

All of these certainly are good reasons to write a resume, but a resume serves many different purposes. One way of seeing the differences is to ask who is going to read the resume.

The Right Mix

In some *situations*, you will have a good idea of what the employer is looking for because you have a job advertisement in front of you and can tailor your resume accordingly. For others, you have no idea what the employer might want to see. Updating your resume from time to time is a good idea so you do not forget important details. Remember that the result of such a process will not be a winning resume but a useful list of *responsibilities* and achievements.

5. Use the thesaurus to replace the word *circumstances*, located in the last paragraph in the document, with the synonym *situations*.

6. Use the thesaurus to replace the word *tasks*, located in the last paragraph in the document, with the synonym *responsibilities*.

1. Open **PrepareResume.docx** and save the document with the name C05-A02-**PrepareResume**.
2. Complete a spelling and grammar check on the document.
3. Proofread the document and make necessary changes. (The document contains mistakes that the spelling and grammar checker will not find.) – *(Highlighted in yellow)*
7. Make the following changes to the document:
  b. Apply the Centered style set.
  c. Apply the Dividend theme and change the theme colors to Orange.

Document 2 (C05-A01-Numbers.docx)

4. Make the following formatting changes to the document:
a. Apply the Heading 1 style to the title *NUMBERS* and apply the Heading 2 style to the two headings *Time Expressions* and *Dates*.

NUMBERS

Numbers are written in figures or words, depending on the situation. In general, use figures to express all numbers in technical writing and to express physical measurements, money, and time in nontechnical writing. When consistency allows, use words for the numbers on through ten.

Time Expressions

Use figures to express clock time:

- Pick me up at 4 *a.m.* so I get to the airport on time.
- Pick me up at 4:30 *a.m.* so I get to the airport on time. My plane leaves at *4:56 a.m.*
- Let's meet at 8 *p.m.* tonight.

Generally, use phrases such as *in the evening* or *in the afternoon* with *o'clock*. Also, time designations of *p.m.* and *a.m.* are preferred over *o'clock*.

When writing 12:00, use *midnight* or *noon* rather than *12:00 a.m.* or *12:00 p.m.* Readers may not be sure which abbreviation refers to midnight and which refers to noon.

Use *morning, afternoon, evening,* or *night* when specific clock times are not present. Use *a.m.* and *p.m.* only with numbers. Do not use both *morning* and *a.m.,* for example, since the two expressions mean the same.

4c. Select the indented text in the *Time Expressions* section and then format the text as bulleted paragraphs.

Dates

Use figures to express dates:

- The new quarter begins April 1.
- September 1, 2015, we began our fourth year.
- We began in September 2015.
- From 2011 to 2013, our management did not receive bonuses.
- Have your budget plans ready by March 1, 2015.

Correspondence from military and international organizations will often contain reverse the day and month in dates, such as *10 March 2015.* Use this method if that is what your organization uses.

4d. Select the indented text in the *Dates* section and then format the text as bulleted paragraphs.

3. Display the Word Count dialog box for the document and then complete the following steps:
a. Make a note of the number of words, paragraphs, and lines in the document.
b. Move the insertion point to the end of the document, type Words:, press the spacebar, and then type the number of words identified in the Word Count dialog box.
c. Press the Enter key, type Paragraphs:, press the spacebar, and then type the number of paragraphs identified in the Word Count dialog box.
d. Press the Enter key, type Lines:, press the spacebar, and then type the number of lines identified in the Word Count dialog box.

Words: 257
Paragraphs: 18
Lines: 25

1. Open **Numbers.docx** and save the document with the name C05-A01-**Numbers**.
2. Complete a spelling and grammar check on the document.
4b. Apply the Basic (Elegant) style set.

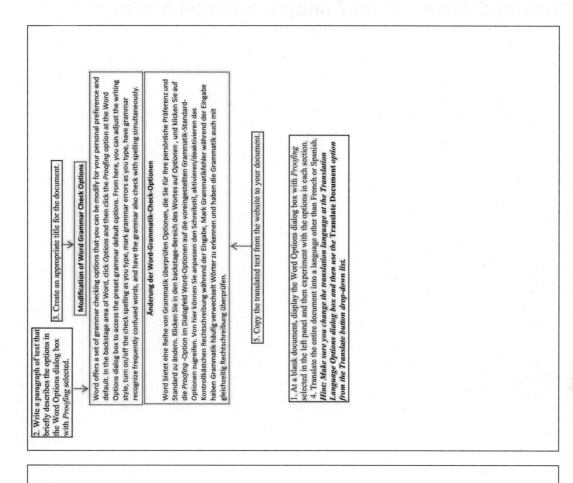

C05-A04-OptionsTranslate.docx

2. Write a paragraph of text that briefly describes the options in the Word Options dialog box with *Proofing* selected.

3. Create an appropriate title for the document.

Modification of Word Grammar Check Options

Word offers a set of grammar checking options that you can be modify for your personal preference and default. In the backstage area of Word, click *Options* and then click the *Proofing* option at the Word Options dialog box to access the preset grammar default options. From here, you can adjust the writing style, turn on/off the check spelling as you type, mark grammar errors as you type, have grammar recognize frequently confused words, and have the grammar also check with spelling simultaneously.

Änderung der Word-Grammatik-Check-Optionen

Word bietet eine Reihe von Grammatik Optionen, die Sie für Ihre persönliche Präferenz und Standard zu ändern. Klicken Sie in den backstage-Bereich des Wortes auf *Optionen*, und klicken Sie auf die *Proofing*-Option im Dialogfeld Word-Optionen auf die voreingestellten Grammatik-Standard-Optionen zugreifen. Von hier können Sie anpassen den Schreibstil, aktivieren/deaktivieren das Kontrollkästchen Rechtschreibung während der Eingabe, Mark Grammatikfehler während der Eingabe haben Grammatik häufig verwechselt Wörter zu erkennen und haben die Grammatik auch mit gleichzeitig Rechtschreibung überprüfen.

5. Copy the translated text from the website to your document.

1. At a blank document, display the Word Options dialog box with *Proofing* selected in the left panel and then experiment with the options in each section.
4. Translate the entire document into a language other than French or Spanish.
*Hint: Make sure you change the translation language at the Translation Language Options dialog box and then use the **Translate Document option** from the **Translate button drop-down list.***

C05-A03-Translations.docx

QUICK TRANSLATION GUIDE

English	Spanish	French
Memory	memoria	memoire
Logic	logica	logique
Navigate	navegar	intransitive
Register	registro	registre
System	sistema	systeme
Utility	utilidad	utilite
Voice	voz	voix

1. At a blank document, use the translation feature to find the Spanish and French translations for the following terms:
memory
logic
navigate
register
system
utility
voice
2. Type the English words followed by the Spanish and French translations. Set the text in columns and then apply formatting to enhance the appearance of the document.

Northland Security Systems

3200 North 22nd Street ♦ Springfield ♦ IL ♦ 62102

1. Open **NSSLtrhd.docx** and then save the document and name it **C05-A06-MtgLtr**.
2. Type the text in the document shown in Figure 5.10 with the following specifications:
 • Change the alignment to justify the text in the body of the letter.
3. Check the spelling and grammar in the document.

January 7, 2015

Dr. Gene Krezel
2310 North 122nd Street
Peoria, IL 61612

Dear Dr. Krezel:

RE: Shareholder's Annual General Meeting

You are cordially invited to attend the 2015 annual general meeting of shareholders of Northland Security Systems. The meeting will be held at the Evergreen Auditorium at the principal executive offices of Northland Security Systems. During the meeting, the Board will ask for your vote on the following issues:

• The election of four directors.
• The approval of an amendment to the company's long-term incentive plan to reduce the number of shares authorized for issuance under the plan.
• The ratification of the appointment by the audit committee of the company's independent auditor.
• The transaction of such other business as may be properly brought before the meeting or any adjournment or postponement of the meeting.

As an owner of shares, you can vote one of four ways. You can vote by attending the annual general meeting, by registering your vote at the company's website, by calling the company's toll-free telephone number and registering your vote, or by mailing your official ballot. If you need assistance or further information, please contact one of our support representatives available at our company website or by calling our support line.

Sincerely,

Faith Isenberg
Chief Executive Officer

XX ← Replace the XX with your initials located near the end of the letter.
C05-A06-MtgLtr.docx

• Insert bullets before the bulleted paragraphs of text as shown in the figure.

1-888-555-2200 ♦ www.emcp.net/nss

C05-A06-MtgLtr.docx

WRITING YOUR RESUME

Contact Information

Before getting into the major sections of the resume, let's briefly address the very top section: your name and contact information.

Name

You would think that writing your name would be the easiest part of writing your resume but you should consider the following factors:

• Although most people choose to use their full, formal name at the top of a resume, using the name by which you prefer to be called is becoming more acceptable.
• Keep in mind that it is to your advantage that readers feel comfortable when calling you for an interview. Their comfort level may decrease if your name is gender-neutral, difficult to pronounce, or very unusual; they don't know how to ask for you. You can make it easier for them by following these examples:

Lynn T. Cowles (Mr.)

(Ms.) Michael Murray

Tzirina (Irene) Kahn

Ndege "Nick" Vernon

Address

You should always include your home address on your resume. If you use a post office box for mail, include both your mailing address and your physical residence address. An exception to this is when you are posting your resume on the Internet. For security purposes, include just your phone and email contact as well as possibly your city and state with no street address.

Telephone Number(s)

Your home telephone number must be included so that people can pick up the phone and call you immediately. In addition, you can also include a cell phone number.

Email Address

Without question, if you have an email address, include it on your resume. Email is now often the preferred method of communication in job search, particularly in the early stages of each contact. If you do not have an email account, you can obtain a free, accessible-anywhere address from a provider such as www.yahoo.com, www.microsoft.com, or www.gmail.com.

1. Open **WriteResume.docx** and save the document with the name **C05-A05-WriteResume**.
2. Complete a spelling and grammar check and apply character and paragraph formatting so your document appears as shown in Figure 5.9. (The font used is 12-point Cambria and the title is set in 14-point Cambria.)
3. Proofread the document and make any additional edits so that your document contains the same text as the document in Figure 5.9.

C05-A05-WriteResumes.docx

Unit 1 Performance Assessment Annotated Model Answers

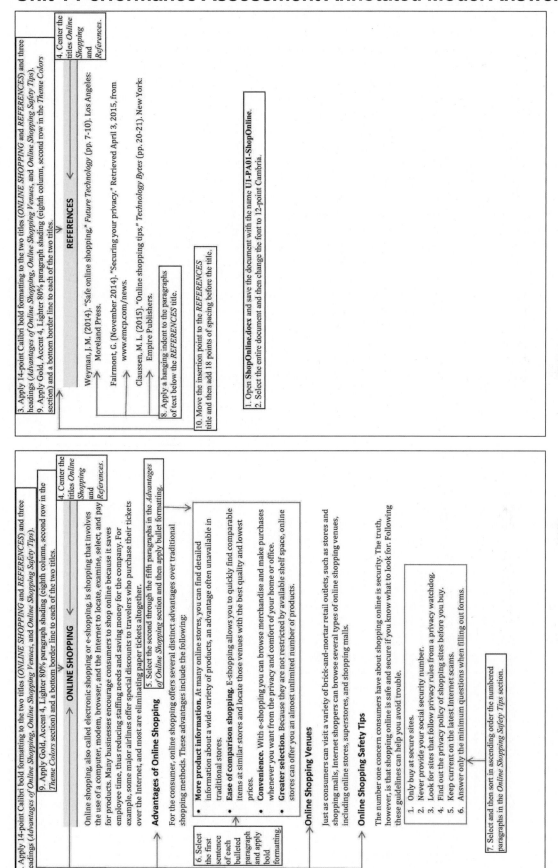

Page 1 (U1-PA01-ShopOnline.docx (page 1 of 2)):

3. Apply 14-point Calibri bold formatting to the two titles (*ONLINE SHOPPING* and *REFERENCES*) and three headings (*Advantages of Online Shopping*, *Online Shopping Venues*, and *Online Shopping Safety Tips*).

9. Apply Gold, Accent 4, Lighter 80% paragraph shading (eighth column, second row in the *Theme Colors* section) and a bottom border line to each of the two titles.

4. Center the titles *Online Shopping* and *References*.

ONLINE SHOPPING

Online shopping, also called electronic shopping or e-shopping, is shopping that involves the use of a computer, modem, browser, and the Internet to locate, examine, select, and pay for products. Many businesses encourage consumers to shop online because it saves employee time, thus reducing staffing needs and saving money for the company. For example, some major airlines offer special discounts to travelers who purchase their tickets over the Internet, and most are eliminating paper tickets altogether.

5. Select the second through the fifth paragraphs in the *Advantages of Online Shopping* section and then apply bullet formatting.

Advantages of Online Shopping

For the consumer, online shopping offers several distinct advantages over traditional shopping methods. These advantages include the following:

6. Select the first sentence of each bulleted paragraph and apply bold formatting.

- **More product information.** At many online stores, you can find detailed information about a wide variety of products, an advantage often unavailable in traditional stores.
- **Ease of comparison shopping.** E-shopping allows you to quickly find comparable items at similar stores and locate those venues with the best quality and lowest prices.
- **Convenience.** With e-shopping you can browse merchandise and make purchases whenever you want from the privacy and comfort of your home or office.
- **Greater selection.** Because they are not restricted by available shelf space, online stores can offer you an almost unlimited number of products.

Online Shopping Venues

Just as consumers can visit a variety of brick-and-mortar retail outlets, such as stores and shopping malls, Internet shoppers can browse several types of online shopping venues, including online stores, superstores, and shopping malls.

Online Shopping Safety Tips

The number one concern consumers have about shopping online is security. The truth, however, is that shopping online is safe and secure if you know what to look for. Following these guidelines can help you avoid trouble.

1. Only buy at secure sites.
2. Never provide your social security number.
3. Look for sites that follow privacy rules from a privacy watchdog.
4. Find out the privacy policy of shopping sites before you buy.
5. Keep current on the latest Internet scams.
6. Answer only the minimum questions when filling out forms.

7. Select and then sort in ascending order the numbered paragraphs in the *Online Shopping Safety Tips* section.

U1-PA01-ShopOnline.docx (page 1 of 2)

Page 2 (U1-PA01-ShopOnline.docx (page 2 of 2)):

3. Apply 14-point Calibri bold formatting to the two titles (*ONLINE SHOPPING* and *REFERENCES*) and three headings (*Advantages of Online Shopping*, *Online Shopping Venues*, and *Online Shopping Safety Tips*).

9. Apply Gold, Accent 4, Lighter 80% paragraph shading (eighth column, second row in the *Theme Colors* section) and a bottom border line to each of the two titles.

4. Center the titles *Online Shopping* and *References*.

REFERENCES

Weyman, J. M. (2014). "Safe online shopping." *Future Technology* (pp. 7-10). Los Angeles: Moreland Press.

Fairmont, G. (November 2014). "Securing your privacy." Retrieved April 3, 2015, from www.emcp.com/news.

Claussen, M. L. (2015). "Online shopping tips," *Technology Bytes* (pp. 20-21). New York: Empire Publishers.

8. Apply a hanging indent to the paragraphs of text below the *REFERENCES* title.

10. Move the insertion point to the *REFERENCES* title and then add 18 points of spacing before the title.

1. Open **ShopOnline.docx** and save the document with the name **U1-PA01-ShopOnline**.
2. Select the entire document and then change the font to 12-point Cambria.

U1-PA01-ShopOnline.docx (page 2 of 2)

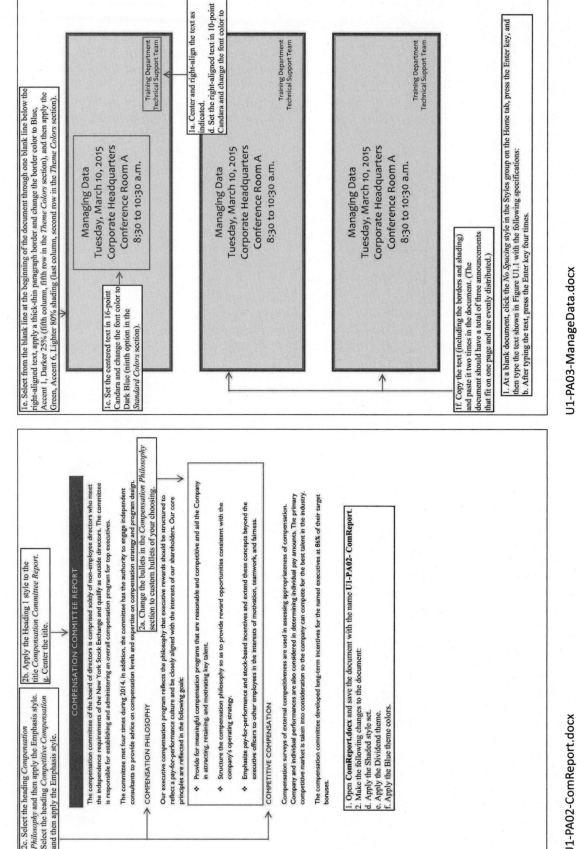

1e. Select from the blank line at the beginning of the document through one blank line below the right-aligned text, apply a thick-thin paragraph border and change the border color to Blue, Accent 1, Darker 25% (fifth column, fifth row in the *Theme Colors* section), and then apply the Green, Accent 6, Lighter 80% shading (last column, second row in the *Theme Colors* section).

1c. Set the centered text in 16-point Candara and change the font color to Dark Blue (ninth option in the *Standard Colors* section).

Managing Data
Tuesday, March 10, 2015
Corporate Headquarters
Conference Room A
8:30 to 10:30 a.m.

Training Department
Technical Support Team

1a. Center and right-align the text as indicated.
1d. Set the right-aligned text in 10-point Candara and change the font color to

Managing Data
Tuesday, March 10, 2015
Corporate Headquarters
Conference Room A
8:30 to 10:30 a.m.

Training Department
Technical Support Team

Managing Data
Tuesday, March 10, 2015
Corporate Headquarters
Conference Room A
8:30 to 10:30 a.m.

Training Department
Technical Support Team

1f. Copy the text (including the borders and shading) and paste it two times in the document. (The document should have a total of three announcements that fit on one page and are evenly distributed.)

1. At a blank document, click the *No Spacing* style in the Styles group on the Home tab, press the Enter key, and then type the text shown in Figure U1.1 with the following specifications:
b. After typing the text, press the Enter key four times.

U1-PA03-ManageData.docx

2c. Select the heading *Compensation Philosophy* and then apply the Emphasis style. Select the heading *Competitive Compensation* and then apply the Emphasis style.

2b. Apply the Heading 1 style to the title *Compensation Committee Report*.
g. Center the title.

COMPENSATION COMMITTEE REPORT

The compensation committee of the board of directors is comprised solely of non-employee directors who meet the independence requirements of the New York Stock Exchange and qualify as outside directors. The committee is responsible for establishing and administering an overall compensation program for top executives.

The committee met four times during 2014. In addition, the committee has the authority to engage independent consultants to provide advice on compensation levels and expertise on compensation strategy and program design.

COMPENSATION PHILOSOPHY

2a. Change the bullets in the *Compensation Philosophy* section to custom bullets of your choosing.

Our executive compensation program reflects the philosophy that executive rewards should be structured to reflect a pay-for-performance culture and be closely aligned with the interests of our shareholders. Our core principles are reflected in the following goals:

❖ Provide for meaningful compensation programs that are reasonable and competitive and aid the Company in attracting, retaining, and motivating key talent.

❖ Structure the compensation philosophy so as to provide reward opportunities consistent with the company's operating strategy.

❖ Emphasize pay-for-performance and stock-based incentives and extend these concepts beyond the executive officers to other employees in the interests of motivation, teamwork, and fairness.

COMPETITIVE COMPENSATION

Compensation surveys of external competitiveness are used in assessing appropriateness of compensation. Company and individual performances are also considered in determining individual pay amounts. The primary competitive market is taken into consideration so the company can compete for the best talent in the industry.

The compensation committee developed long-term incentives for the named executives at 86% of their target bonuses.

1. Open **ComReport.docx** and save the document with the name **U1-PA02-ComReport.**
2. Make the following changes to the document:
d. Apply the Shaded style set.
e. Apply the Dividend theme.
f. Apply the Blue theme colors.

U1-PA02-ComReport.docx

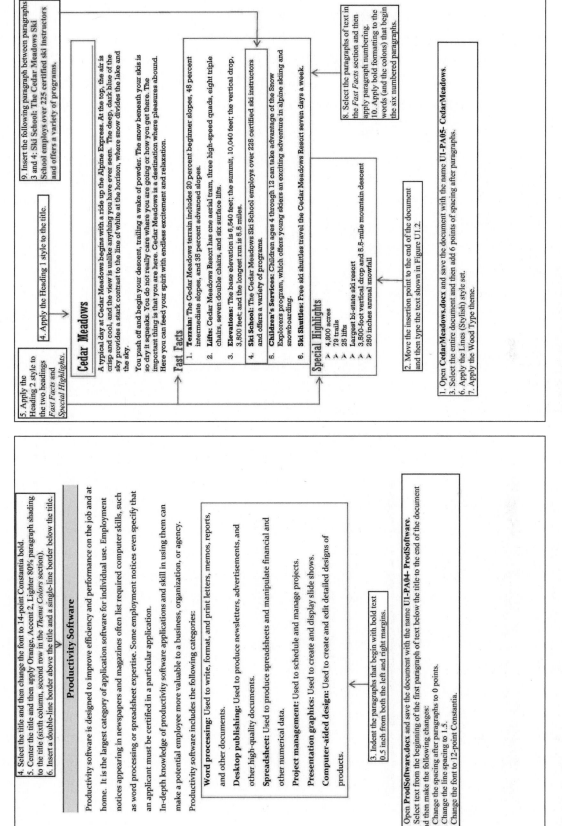

9. Insert the following paragraph between paragraphs 3 and 4: Ski School: The Cedar Meadows Ski School employs over 225 certified ski instructors and offers a variety of programs.

4. Apply the Heading 1 style to the title.

5. Apply the Heading 2 style to the two headings *Fast Facts* and *Special Highlights*.

8. Select the paragraphs of text in the *Fast Facts* section and then apply paragraph numbering.
10. Apply bold formatting to the words (and the colons) that begin the six numbered paragraphs.

Cedar Meadows

A typical day at Cedar Meadows begins with a ride up the Alpine Express. At the top, the air is crisp and cool, and the view is unlike anything you have ever seen. The deep, dark blue of the sky provides a stark contrast to the line of white at the horizon, where snow divides the lake and the sky.

You push off and begin your descent, trailing a wake of powder. The snow beneath your skis is so dry it squeaks. You do not really care where you are going or how you get there. The important thing is that you are here. Cedar Meadows is a destination where pleasures abound. Here you can feed your spirit with endless excitement and relaxation.

Fast Facts

1. **Terrain:** The Cedar Meadows terrain includes 20 percent beginner slopes, 45 percent intermediate slopes, and 35 percent advanced slopes.
2. **Lifts:** Cedar Meadows Resort has one aerial tram, three high-speed quads, eight triple chairs, seven double chairs, and six surface lifts.
3. **Elevations:** The base elevation is 6,540 feet; the summit, 10,040 feet; the vertical drop, 3,500 feet; and the longest run is 8.5 miles.
4. **Ski School:** The Cedar Meadows Ski School employs over 225 certified ski instructors and offers a variety of programs.
5. **Children's Services:** Children ages 4 through 12 can take advantage of the Snow Explorers program, which offers young skiers an exciting adventure in alpine skiing and snowboarding.
6. **Ski Shuttles:** Free ski shuttles travel the Cedar Meadows Resort seven days a week.

Special Highlights

- 4,800 acres
- 79 trails
- 28 lifts
- Largest bi-state ski resort
- 3,500-foot vertical drop and 8.5-mile mountain descent
- 280 inches annual snowfall

2. Move the insertion point to the end of the document and then type the text shown in Figure U1.2.

1. Open **CedarMeadows.docx** and then save the document with the name U1-PA05- CedarMeadows.
3. Select the entire document and then add 6 points of spacing after paragraphs.
6. Apply the Lines (Stylish) style set.
7. Apply the Wood Type theme.

U1-PA05-CedarMeadows.docx

---

4. Select the title and then change the font to 14-point Constantia bold.
5. Center the title and then apply Orange, Accent 2, Lighter 80% paragraph shading to the title (sixth column, second row in the *Theme Colors* section).
6. Insert a double-line border above the title and a single-line border below the title.

Productivity Software

Productivity software is designed to improve efficiency and performance on the job and at home. It is the largest category of application software for individual use. Employment notices appearing in newspapers and magazines often list required computer skills, such as word processing or spreadsheet expertise. Some employment notices even specify that an applicant must be certified in a particular application.

In-depth knowledge of productivity software applications and skill in using them can make a potential employee more valuable to a business, organization, or agency.

Productivity software includes the following categories:

Word processing: Used to write, format, and print letters, memos, reports, and other documents.

Desktop publishing: Used to produce newsletters, advertisements, and other high-quality documents.

Spreadsheet: Used to produce spreadsheets and manipulate financial and other numerical data.

Project management: Used to schedule and manage projects.

Presentation graphics: Used to create and display slide shows.

Computer-aided design: Used to create and edit detailed designs of products.

3. Indent the paragraphs that begin with bold text 0.5 inch from both the left and right margins.

1. Open **ProdSoftware.docx** and save the document with the name U1-PA04- ProdSoftware.
2. Select text from the beginning of the first paragraph of text below the title to the end of the document and then make the following changes:
  a. Change the spacing after paragraphs to 0 points.
  b. Change the line spacing to 1.5.
  c. Change the font to 12-point Constantia.

U1-PA04-ProdSoftware.docx

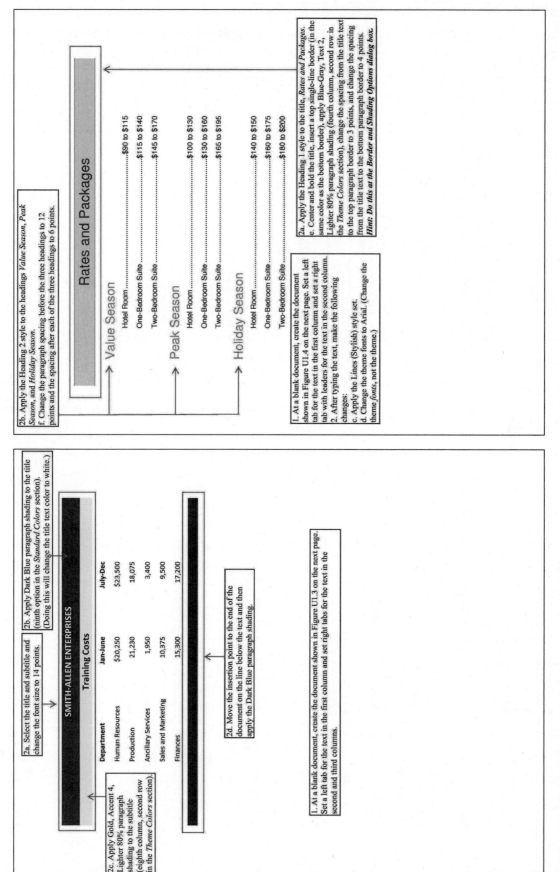

2b. Apply the Heading 2 style to the headings *Value Season, Peak Season,* and *Holiday Season.*
f. Change the paragraph spacing before the three headings to 12 points and the spacing after each of the three headings to 6 points.

Rates and Packages

Value Season

Hotel Room	$90 to $115
One-Bedroom Suite	$115 to $140
Two-Bedroom Suite	$145 to $170

Peak Season

Hotel Room	$100 to $130
One-Bedroom Suite	$130 to $160
Two-Bedroom Suite	$165 to $195

Holiday Season

Hotel Room	$140 to $150
One-Bedroom Suite	$160 to $175
Two-Bedroom Suite	$180 to $200

1. At a blank document, create the document shown in Figure U1.4 on the next page. Set a left tab for the text in the first column and set a right tab with leaders for the text in the second column.
2. After typing the text, make the following changes:
c. Apply the Lines (Stylish) style set.
d. Change the theme fonts to Arial. (Change the theme *fonts*, not the theme.)

2a. Apply the Heading 1 style to the title, *Rates and Packages.*
e. Center and bold the title, insert a top single-line border (in the same color as the bottom border), apply Blue-Gray, Text 2, Lighter 80% paragraph shading (fourth column, second row in the *Theme Colors* section), change the spacing from the title text to the top paragraph border to 3 points, and change the spacing from the title text to the bottom paragraph border to 4 points. *Hint: Do this at the Border and Shading Options dialog box.*

U1-PA07-Rates.docx

2a. Select the title and subtitle and change the font size to 14 points.

2b. Apply Dark Blue paragraph shading to the title (ninth option in the *Standard Colors* section). (Doing this will change the title text color to white.)

SMITH-ALLEN ENTERPRISES
Training Costs

Department	Jan–June	July–Dec
Human Resources	$20,250	$23,500
Production	21,230	18,075
Ancillary Services	1,950	3,400
Sales and Marketing	10,375	9,500
Finances	15,300	17,200

2c. Apply Gold, Accent 4, Lighter 80% paragraph shading to the subtitle (eighth column, second row in the *Theme Colors* section).

2d. Move the insertion point to the end of the document on the line below the text and then apply the Dark Blue paragraph shading.

1. At a blank document, create the document shown in Figure U1.3 on the next page. Set a left tab for the text in the first column and set right tabs for the text in the second and third columns.

U1-PA06-TrainCosts.docx

1. At a blank document, create the document shown in Figure U1.5. Apply character and paragraph formatting so the document appears as shown in the figure.

Executive Education Format

EDUCATION

Executive Leadership Program .... STANFORD UNIVERSITY
Executive Development Program .... NORTHWESTERN UNIVERSITY
Master of Business Administration degree .... HARVARD UNIVERSITY
Bachelor of Science degree .... UNIVERSITY OF PENNSYLVANIA

Certification Format

TECHNICAL CERTIFICATIONS & DEGREES

Registered Nurse, University of Maryland, 2014
Certified Nursing Assistant, University of Maryland, 2012
Certified Nursing Aide, State of Maryland, 2009
Bachelor of Science in Nursing, University of Maryland, 2014

---

5. Apply formatting to enhance the appearance of the document.

Research and Writing

Assume someone offered you a free personal computer system of your choice and you are to select the input, output, and storage devices you want. Create a list of uses for your new computer and then research various computer systems and components advertised in magazines and on the Internet. Choose a computer system that will meet your needs and write a paragraph explaining why you selected a particular personal computer system.

Create a table or chart for handheld computers that includes the manufacturer's name, handheld model, operating system, weight, and price. Visit a computer store in your area and examine five handhelds computers. Using the chart you prepared, record information about each model. Based upon your analysis of the handheld computers you examined, which would you prefer as your own? Are there additional features that affected your decision? Explain the reasons for your decision.

The Internet provides easy access to a wealth of information and many consider it a timesaver for busy people. Prepare a written report explaining what aspects of your life Internet use has simplified or improved. Include your predictions for additional Internet capabilities that you expect to use in the next five years.

Many projects are underway to expand the use of wearable computers in the workplace, in military applications, and for personal use. Research the uses of wearable computers. Based on your findings, write an article describing the application of wearable computers to enhance our daily lives.

Team Problem-Solving

Today's classrooms contain students that are more diverse and students with a wider range of performance capabilities compared to previous decades. In fact, some theorists claim there is a 200 percent differential in the learning rate in our classrooms today. Imagine how computers will help instructors teach so many different types of students. Consider both traditional and distance learning modes.

Artificially intelligent robots are likely to play a large role in our future. What are some possible new applications of this technology in the areas of manufacturing, health care, and home maintenance?

1. Open **Activities.docx** and save the document with the name **U1-PA08-Activities.**
2. Display the Word Options dialog box with *Proofing* selected, change the *Writing Style* option to *Grammar & Style*, and then close the dialog box.
3. Complete a spelling and grammar check on the document.
4. Proofread the document and make any necessary changes.
5. Display the Word Options dialog box with *Proofing* selected, change the *Writing Style* option to *Grammar Only*, and then close the dialog box.

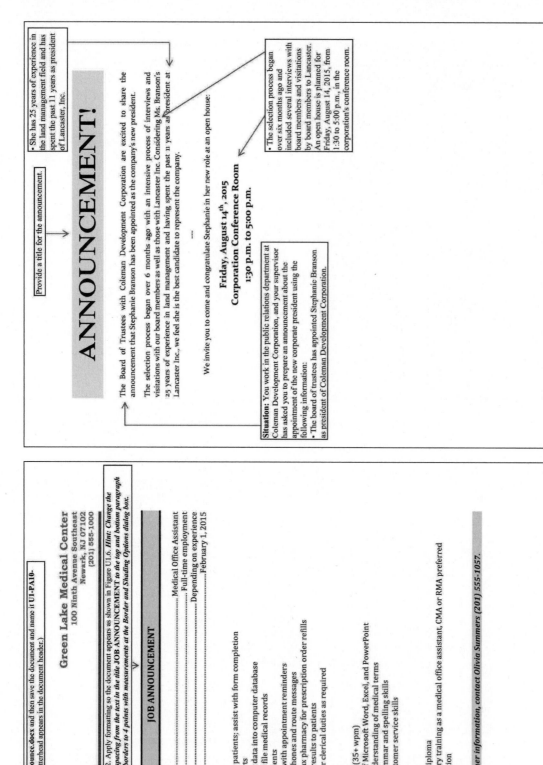

U1-PA11-Announce.docx

Provide a title for the announcement.

She has 25 years of experience in the land management field and has spent the past 11 years as president of Lancaster, Inc.

ANNOUNCEMENT!

The Board of Trustees with Coleman Development Corporation are excited to share the announcement that Stephanie Branson has been appointed as the company's new president.

The selection process began over 6 months ago with an intensive process of interviews and visitations with our board members as well as those with Lancaster Inc. Considering Ms. Branson's 25 years of experience in land management and having spent the past n years as president at Lancaster Inc., we feel she is the best candidate to represent the company.

We invite you to come and congratulate Stephanie in her new role at an open house:

Friday, August 14th, 2015
Corporation Conference Room
1:30 p.m. to 5:00 p.m.

The selection process began over six months ago and included several interviews with board members and visitations by board members to Lancaster. An open house is planned for Friday, August 14, 2015, from 1:30 to 5:00 p.m., in the corporation's conference room.

Situation: You work in the public relations department at Coleman Development Corporation, and your supervisor has asked you to prepare an announcement about the appointment of the new corporate president using the following information:
• The board of trustees has appointed Stephanie Branson as president of Coleman Development Corporation.

---

1. Open the document named **JobAnnounce.docx** and then save the document and name it **U1-PA10-JobAnnounce**. (The medical center letterhead appears in the document header.)

2. Apply formatting so the document appears as shown in Figure U1.6. *Hint: Change the spacing from the text in the title JOB ANNOUNCEMENT to the top and bottom paragraph borders to 4 points with measurements at the Border and Shading Options dialog box.*

Green Lake Medical Center
100 Ninth Avenue Southeast
Newark, NJ 07102
(201) 555-1000

JOB ANNOUNCEMENT

JOB TITLE......................................Medical Office Assistant
STATUS...Full-time employment
SALARY...Depending on experience
CLOSING..February 1, 2015

JOB SUMMARY
• Register new patients; assist with form completion
• Retrieve charts
• Enter patient data into computer database
• Maintain and file medical records
• Schedule patients
• Call patients with appointment reminders
• Answer telephones and route messages
• Call and/or fax pharmacy for prescription order refills
• Mail lab test results to patients
• Perform other clerical duties as required

REQUIRED SKILLS
• Keyboarding (35+ wpm)
• Knowledge of Microsoft Word, Excel, and PowerPoint
• Thorough understanding of medical terms
• Excellent grammar and spelling skills
• Excellent customer service skills

EDUCATION
• High school diploma
• Post-secondary training as a medical office assistant, CMA or RMA preferred
• CPR certification

For further information, contact Olivia Summers (201) 555-1057.

U1-PA10-JobAnnounce.docx

She would like you to choose two handwriting fonts, two decorative fonts, and two plain fonts and then prepare a memo to her that illustrates the use of each font. (Refer to Appendix C for information on formatting a memo.) When typing information about a font, set the text in the font you are describing.

DATE:	February 12, 2015
TO:	Makenzie Keenan, Manager
FROM:	Student Name, Public Relations Assistant
SUBJECT:	Newsletter Fonts

Standardized Fonts for Monthly Chamber Newsletter

To maintain consistency, only the following fonts are suggested to be used in the Chamber Newsletter.

For quotes, call outs and other notable text:

- *Handwriting 1 – Use font Freestyle Script in size 20*
- *Handwriting 2 – Use font MV Boli in size 16*

For titles and headings:

- DECORATIVE 1 – USE FONT COPPERPLATE GOTHIC LIGHT IN SIZES 24-36
- **Decorative 2 – Use font Broadway in sizes 24-42**

For traditional text, article use and subtitles:

- Plain 1 – Use font Gadugi in sizes 10-20
- Plain 2 – Use font Palatino Linotype in sizes 10-20

xx
U1-PA13-Fonts.docx

U1-PA13-Fonts.docx

- Commands to delete text from the insertion point to the beginning of a word and from the insertion point to the end of a word

Common Word Commands

When working in Word 2013, knowing and understanding the commands will make for a more efficient and fluent workflow. Some of the most common commands used on a regular basis include the following.

Moving the insertion point

To a specific page: To easily navigate to a specific page using keyboard shortcuts, use the command Ctrl + G to display the Find & Replace dialog box. From here, you can enter the page number to which you wish to navigate. You can also move up or down from page to page by using the Page Up and Page Down keys to move throughout the document.

To the beginning or end of a line: Move the insertion point quickly to the beginning of a line by using the Home key. Move to the end of a line by using the End key.

To the beginning or end of a document: Move the insertion point quickly to the beginning of the document by using the command Ctrl + Home. Use the command Ctrl + End to quickly move to the end of the document.

Deleting text from an insertion point

To delete an entire word: Place insertion point before the word and use the command Ctrl + Delete. If the insertion point is at the end of the word, use the command Ctrl + Backspace.

Selecting content

Select a word or paragraph using the mouse: Select a single word by double-clicking the left mouse button. Triple-click the left mouse button to select an entire paragraph.

Select the document using keyboard shortcuts: Select the entire document with the keyboard command Ctrl + A.

The ability to use these commands will allow you to better create your word documents and expand on your working knowledge of the program.

- Steps to select a word, sentence, paragraph, and entire document using the mouse
- Keyboard command to select the entire document

U1-PA12-WordCommands.docx

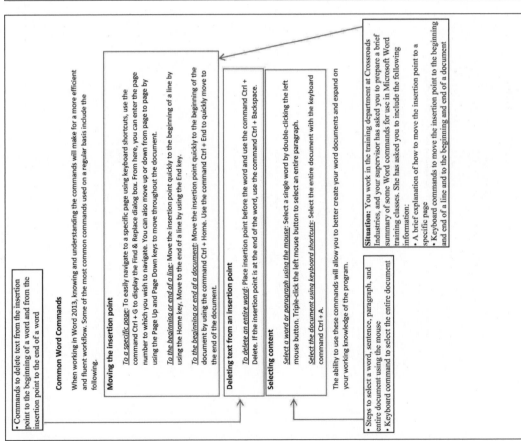

Chapter 6 Assessment Annotated Model Answers

C06-A01-CompIndustry.docx (page 1 of 2)

8. Insert the SAMPLE 1 watermark in the document. (You will need to scroll down the list box to display this watermark.)

2. Apply the Heading 1 style to the titles COMPUTERS IN INDUSTRY and REFERENCES.

3. Apply the Heading 2 style to the headings in the report.

COMPUTERS IN INDUSTRY

Computers were originally stand-alone devices, incapable of communicating with other computers. This changed in the 1970s and 1980s when the development of special telecommunications hardware and software led to the creation of the first private networks, allowing connected computers to exchange data. Exchanged data took the form of requests for information, replies to requests for information, and instructions on how to run programs stored on a network.

The linking of computers enables users to communicate and work together efficiently and effectively. Linked computers have become central to the communications and entertainment industries. They play a vital role in telecommunications, publishing, news services, and television and film.

Telecommunications

The industry that provides for communication across distances is called telecommunications. The telecommunications industry uses computers to switch and route phone calls automatically over telephone lines. Today, in addition to the spoken word, many other kinds of information move over such lines, including faxes and computer data. Data can be sent from computer to computer over telephone lines using a device known as a modem. One kind of data frequently sent by modem is electronic mail, or email, which can be sent from person to person via the Internet or an online service. A more recent innovation in telecommunications is teleconferencing, which allows people in various locations to see and hear one another and thus hold virtual meetings.

Publishing

Just twenty-five years ago, book manuscripts were typeset mechanically or on a typesetting machine and then reproduced on a printing press. Now anyone who has access to a computer and either a modem or a printer can undertake what has come to be known as electronic publishing. Writers and editors use word processing applications to produce text. Artists and designers use drawing and painting applications to create original graphics, or they use inexpensive scanners to digitize illustrations and photographs (turning them into computer-readable files). Typesetters use personal computers to combine text, illustrations, and photographs. Publishers typically send computer-generated files to printers for production of the film and plates from which books and magazines are printed.

News Services

News providers rely on reporters located worldwide. Reporters use email to send, or upload, their stories to wire services. Increasingly, individuals get daily news reports from online services. News can also be accessed from specific providers, such as the *New York Times* or *USA Today*, via the Internet. One of the most popular Internet sites provides continuously updated weather reports.

C06-A01-CompIndustry.docx (page 2 of 2)

3. Apply the Heading 2 style to the headings in the report.

2. Apply the Heading 1 style to the titles COMPUTERS IN INDUSTRY and REFERENCES.

Television and Film

Many of the spectacular graphics and special effects seen on television and in movies today are created with computers. The original *Star Wars* films, for example, relied heavily on hand-constructed models and hand-drawn graphics. Twenty years after the first release of the films, they were re-released with many new special effects, including futuristic cityscape backgrounds, new alien creatures, and new sounds that were created on computers and added to the films by means of computerized video editing. In an article on special effects, Jaclyn McFadden, an industry expert, talked about the evolution of computer simulation.

The film *Jurassic Park* brought computer simulation to a new level by combining puppetry and computer animation to simulate realistic looking dinosaurs. *Toy Story*, released in 1996, was the first wholly computer-animated commercial movie.

Software products are available that automatically format scripts of various kinds. Industry analysts predict that improvements in computer technology will continue to enhance and improve the visual appeal of television and film media.

REFERENCES

Fuller, F. & Larson, B. (2014) *Computers: Understanding technology* (pp. 121-125). St. Paul, MN: Paradigm Publishing.

McFadden, J. M. (2015) *The art of special effects* (pp. 45-48). Los Angeles: Richardson-Dryers Publishing House.

North, J. & Amundsen, R. (2014) *Computer gaming and system requirements.* Cleveland, OH: Blue Horizon Publishers.

Ziebel, K. M. & Weisenburg, H. L. (2015) *Computers and electronic publishing.* Seattle, WA: Greenlake Publishing House.

2. Apply the Heading 1 style to the titles COMPUTERS IN INDUSTRY and REFERENCES.

5. Format the paragraphs of text below the REFERENCES title using a hanging indent.

1. Open CompIndustry.docx and save the document with the name C06-A01-CompIndustry.
4. Apply the Centered style set.
6. Change the top, left, and right margins to 1.25 inches.
7. Manually hyphenate the text in the document. (Do not hyphenate proper nouns, such as names.)
9. Insert a double-line page border in Blue color with a weight of 1½ points. (Choose the first double-line border in the *Style* list box at the Borders and Shading dialog box and apply the Blue color in the *Standard Colors* section.)10. Display the Border and Shading Options dialog box and then change the top, left, bottom, and right measurements to 31 points. *Hint: Display the Border and Shading Options dialog box by clicking the Options button at the Borders and Shading dialog box with the Page Border tab selected.*

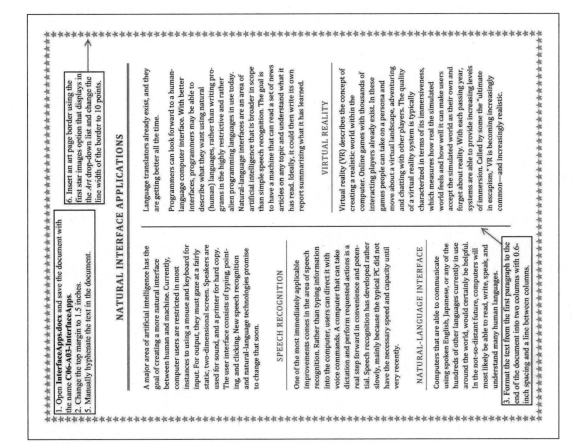

1. Open **InterfaceApps.docx** and save the document with the name **C06-A03-InterfaceApps.**
2. Change the top margin to 1.5 inches.
5. Manually hyphenate the text in the document.

6. Insert an art page border using the first star images option that displays in the *Art* drop-down list and change the line width of the border to 10 points.

NATURAL INTERFACE APPLICATIONS

A major area of artificial intelligence has the goal of creating a more natural interface between human and machine. Currently, computer users are restricted in most instances to using a mouse and keyboard for input. For output, they must gaze at a fairly static, two-dimensional screen. Speakers are used for sound, and a printer for hard copy. The user interface consists of typing, pointing, and clicking. New speech recognition and natural-language technologies promise to change that soon.

SPEECH RECOGNITION

One of the most immediately applicable improvements comes in the area of speech recognition. Rather than typing information into the computer, users can direct it with voice commands. A computer that can take dictation and perform requested actions is a real step forward in convenience and potential. Speech recognition has developed rather slowly, mainly because the typical PC did not have the necessary speed and capacity until very recently.

NATURAL-LANGUAGE INTERFACE

Computers that are able to communicate using spoken English, Japanese, or any of the hundreds of other languages currently in use around the world, would certainly be helpful. In the not-so-distant future, computers will most likely be able to read, write, speak, and understand many human languages.

3. Format the text from the first paragraph to the end of the document into two columns with 0.6-inch spacing and a line between columns.

Language translators already exist, and they are getting better all the time.

Programmers can look forward to a human-language computer interface. With better interfaces, programmers may be able to describe what they want using natural (human) languages, rather than writing programs in the highly restrictive and rather alien programming languages in use today. Natural-language interfaces are an area of artificial intelligence that is broader in scope than simple speech recognition. The goal is to have a machine that can read a set of news articles on any topic and understand what it has read. Ideally, it could then write its own report summarizing what it has learned.

VIRTUAL REALITY

Virtual reality (VR) describes the concept of creating a realistic world within the computer. Online games with thousands of interacting players already exist. In these games people can take on a persona and move about a virtual landscape, adventuring and chatting with other players. The quality of a virtual reality system is typically characterized in terms of its immersiveness, which measures how real the simulated world feels and how well it can make users accept the simulated world as their own and forget about reality. With each passing year, systems are able to provide increasing levels of immersion. Called by some the "ultimate in escapism," VR is becoming increasingly common—and increasingly realistic.

C06-A03-InterfaceApps.docx (page 1 of 2)

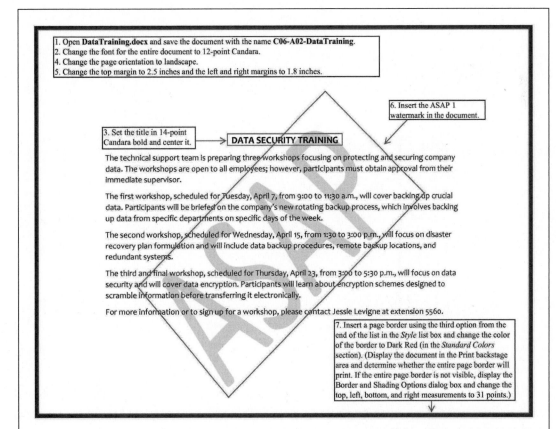

1. Open **DataTraining.docx** and save the document with the name **C06-A02-DataTraining.**
2. Change the font for the entire document to 12-point Candara.
4. Change the page orientation to landscape.
5. Change the top margin to 2.5 inches and the left and right margins to 1.8 inches.

6. Insert the ASAP 1 watermark in the document.

3. Set the title in 14-point Candara bold and center it.

DATA SECURITY TRAINING

The technical support team is preparing three workshops focusing on protecting and securing company data. The workshops are open to all employees; however, participants must obtain approval from their immediate supervisor.

The first workshop, scheduled for Tuesday, April 7, from 9:00 to 11:30 a.m., will cover backing up crucial data. Participants will be briefed on the company's new rotating backup process, which involves backing up data from specific departments on specific days of the week.

The second workshop, scheduled for Wednesday, April 15, from 1:30 to 3:00 p.m., will focus on disaster recovery plan formulation and will include data backup procedures, remote backup locations, and redundant systems.

The third and final workshop, scheduled for Thursday, April 23, from 3:00 to 5:30 p.m., will focus on data security and will cover data encryption. Participants will learn about encryption schemes designed to scramble information before transferring it electronically.

For more information or to sign up for a workshop, please contact Jessie Levigne at extension 5560.

7. Insert a page border using the third option from the end of the list in the *Style* list box and change the color of the border to Dark Red (in the *Standard Colors* section). (Display the document in the Print backstage area and determine whether the entire page border will print. If the entire page border is not visible, display the Border and Shading Options dialog box and change the top, left, bottom, and right measurements to 31 points.)

C06-A02-DataTraining.docx

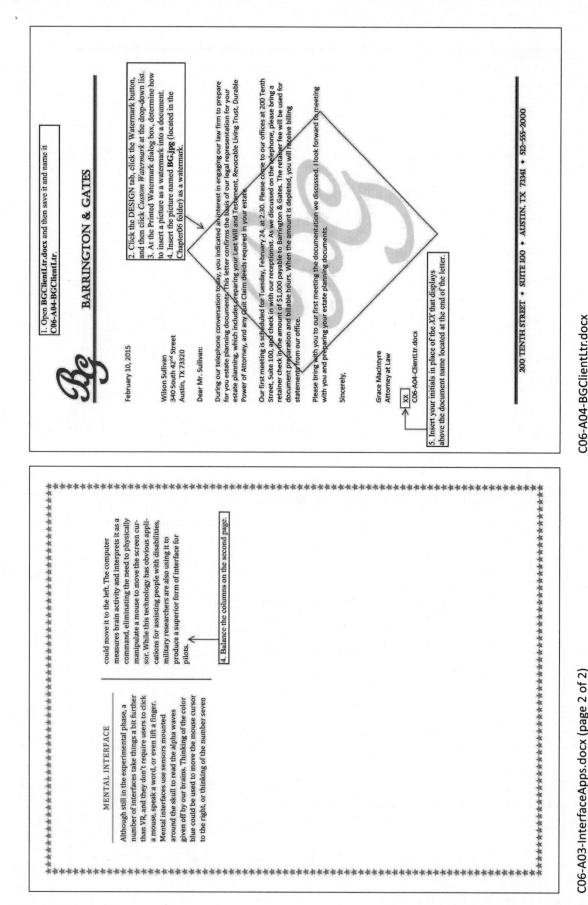

1. Open **BGClientLtr.docx** and then save it and name it **C06-A04-BGClientLtr.**

BARRINGTON & GATES

February 10, 2015

Wilson Sullivan
340 South 42ⁿᵈ Street
Austin, TX 73320

Dear Mr. Sullivan:

During our telephone conversation today, you indicated an interest in engaging our law firm to prepare for you estate planning documents. This letter confirms the basis of our legal representation for your estate planning, which includes preparing your Last Will and Testament, Revocable Living Trust, Durable Power of Attorney, and any Quit Claim deeds required in your estate.

Our first meeting is scheduled for Tuesday, February 24, at 2:30. Please come to our offices at 200 Tenth Street, Suite 100, and check in with our receptionist. As we discussed on the telephone, please bring a retainer check in the amount of $1,000 payable to Barrington & Gates. The retainer fee will be used for document preparation and billable hours. When the amount is depleted, you will receive billing statements from our office.

Please bring with you to our first meeting the documentation we discussed. I look forward to meeting with you and preparing your estate planning documents.

Sincerely,

Grace MacIntyre
Attorney at Law

XX
C06-A04-ClientLtr.docx

2. Click the DESIGN tab, click the Watermark button, and then click *Custom Watermark* at the drop-down list.
3. At the Printed Watermark dialog box, determine how to insert a picture as a watermark into a document.
4. Insert the picture named **BG.jpg** (located in the Chapter06 folder) as a watermark.

5. Insert your initials in place of the *XX* that displays above the document name located at the end of the letter.

200 TENTH STREET • SUITE 100 • AUSTIN, TX 7334l • 512-555-2000

C06-A04-BGClientLtr.docx

MENTAL INTERFACE

Although still in the experimental phase, a number of interfaces take things a bit further than VR, and they don't require users to click a mouse, speak a word, or even lift a finger. Mental interfaces use sensors mounted around the skull to read the alpha waves given off by our brains. Thinking of the color blue could be used to move the mouse cursor to the right, or thinking of the number seven could move it to the left. The computer measures brain activity and interprets it as a command, eliminating the need to physically manipulate a mouse to move the screen cursor. While this technology has obvious applications for assisting people with disabilities, military researchers are also using it to produce a superior form of interface for pilots.

4. Balance the columns on the second page.

C06-A03-InterfaceApps.docx (page 2 of 2)

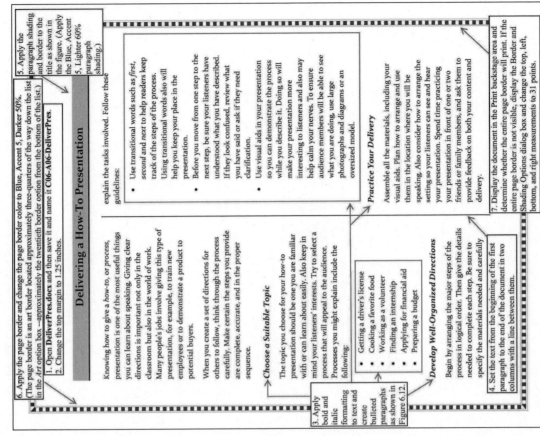

Delivering a How-To Presentation

Knowing how to give a *how-to*, or process, presentation is one of the most useful things you can learn about speaking. Giving clear directions is important not only in the classroom but also in the world of work. Many people's jobs involve giving this type of presentation, for example, to train new employees or to demonstrate a product to potential buyers.

When you create a set of directions for others to follow, think through the process carefully. Make certain the steps you provide are complete, accurate, and in the proper sequence.

Choose a Suitable Topic

The topic you choose for your how-to presentation should be one you are familiar with or can learn about easily. Also keep in mind your listeners' interests. Try to select a process that will appeal to the audience. Processes you might explain include the following:

- Getting a driver's license
- Cooking a favorite food
- Working as a volunteer
- Finding an internship
- Applying for financial aid
- Preparing a budget

Develop Well-Organized Directions

Begin by arranging the major steps of the process in logical order. Then give the details needed to complete each step. Be sure to specify the materials needed and carefully explain the tasks involved. Follow these guidelines:

- Use transitional words such as *first, second* and *next* to help readers keep track of the steps of the process. Using transitional words also will help you keep your place in the presentation.
- Before you move from one step to the next step, be sure your listeners have understood what you have described. If they look confused, review what you have said or ask if they need clarification.
- Use visual aids in your presentation so you can demonstrate the process while you describe it. Doing so will make your presentation more interesting to listeners and also may help calm your nerves. To ensure audience members will be able to see what you are doing, use large photographs and diagrams or an oversized model.

Practice Your Delivery

Assemble all the materials, including your visual aids. Plan how to arrange and use them in the location where you will be speaking. Also consider how to arrange the setting so your listeners can see and hear your presentation. Spend time practicing your presentation in front of one or two friends or family members, and ask them to provide feedback on both your content and delivery.

Callouts:

1. Open **DeliverPres.docx** and then save it and name it C06-A06-DeliverPres.
2. Change the top margin to 1.25 inches.
3. Apply bold and italic formatting to text and create bulleted paragraphs as shown in Figure 6.12.
4. Set the text from the beginning of the first paragraph to the end of the document in two columns with a line between them.
5. Apply the paragraph shading and border to the title as shown in the figure. (Apply the Blue, Accent 5, Lighter 60% paragraph shading.)
6. Apply the page border and change the page border color to Blue, Accent 5, Darker 50%. (The page border is an art border located approximately three-quarters of the way down the list in the *Art* option box --approximately the twentieth border option from the bottom of the list.)
7. Display the document in the Print backstage area and determine whether the entire page border will print. If the entire page border is not visible, display the Border and Shading Options dialog box and change the top, left, bottom, and right measurements to 31 points.

C06-A06-DeliverPres.docx

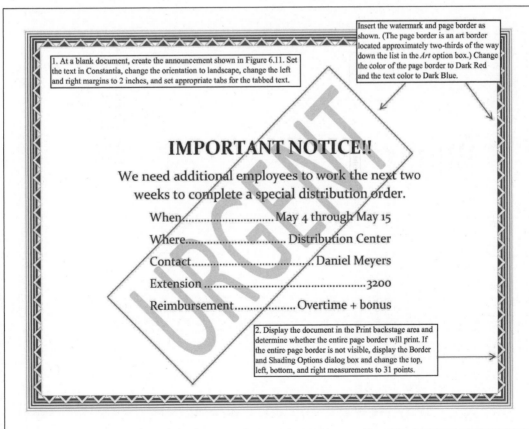

IMPORTANT NOTICE!!

We need additional employees to work the next two weeks to complete a special distribution order.

When	May 4 through May 15
Where	Distribution Center
Contact	Daniel Meyers
Extension	3200
Reimbursement	Overtime + bonus

Callouts:

1. At a blank document, create the announcement shown in Figure 6.11. Set the text in Constantia, change the orientation to landscape, change the left and right margins to 2 inches, and set appropriate tabs for the tabbed text.

Insert the watermark and page border as shown. (The page border is an art border located approximately two-thirds of the way down the list in the *Art* option box.) Change the color of the page border to Dark Red and the text color to Dark Blue.

2. Display the document in the Print backstage area and determine whether the entire page border will print. If the entire page border is not visible, display the Border and Shading Options dialog box and change the top, left, bottom, and right measurements to 31 points.

C06-A05-Announce.docx

Chapter 7 Assessment Annotated Model Answers

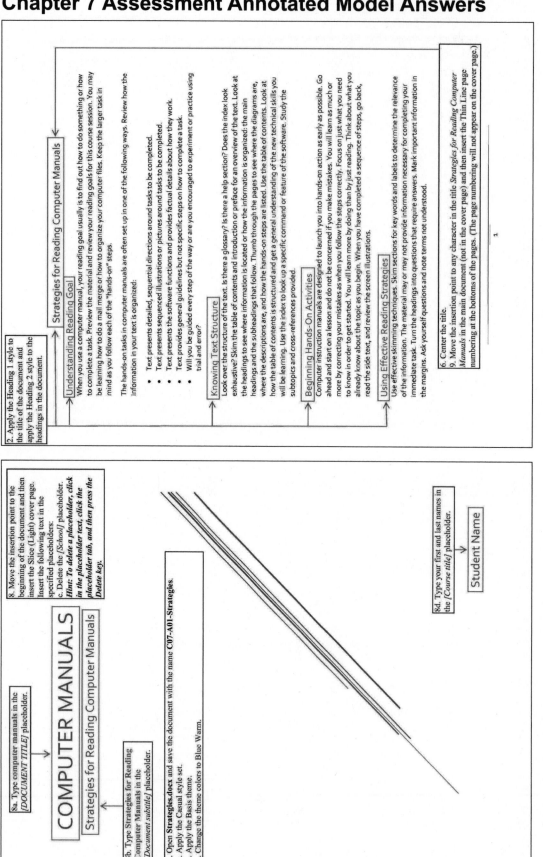

8. Move the insertion point to the beginning of the document and then insert the Slice (Light) cover page. Insert the following text in the specified placeholders:

c. Delete the *[School]* placeholder. *Hint: To delete a placeholder, click in the placeholder text, click the placeholder tab, and then press the Delete key.*

8a. Type computer manuals in the *[DOCUMENT TITLE]* placeholder.

COMPUTER MANUALS

Strategies for Reading Computer Manuals

8b. Type Strategies for Reading Computer Manuals in the *[Document subtitle]* placeholder.

1. Open **Strategies.docx** and save the document with the name **C07-A01-Strategies.**
3. Apply the Casual style set.
4. Apply the Basis theme.
5. Change the theme colors to Blue Warm.

8d. Type your first and last names in the *[Course title]* placeholder.

Student Name

C07-A01-Strategies.docx (page 1 of 3)

2. Apply the Heading 1 style to the title of the document and apply the Heading 2 style to the headings in the document.

Strategies for Reading Computer Manuals

Understanding Reading Goal

When you use a computer manual, your reading goal usually is to find out how to do something or how to complete a task. Preview the material and review your reading goals for this course session. You may be learning how to do a mail merge or how to organize your computer files. Keep the larger task in mind as you follow each of the "hands-on" steps.

The hands-on tasks in computer manuals are often set up in one of the following ways. Review how the information in your text is organized:

- Text presents detailed, sequential directions around tasks to be completed.
- Text presents sequenced illustrations or pictures around tasks to be completed.
- Text presents the software functions and provides factual details about how they work.
- Text provides general guidelines but not specific steps on how to complete a task.
- Will you be guided every step of the way or are you encouraged to experiment or practice using trial and error?

Knowing Text Structure

Look over the structure of the text. Is there a glossary? Is there a help section? Does the index look exhaustive? Skim the table of contents and introduction or preface for an overview of the text. Look at the headings to see where information is located or how the information is organized: the main headings and the subheadings that follow. Thumb through the pages to see where the diagrams are, where the descriptions are, and how the hands-on steps are listed. Use the table of contents. Look at how the table of contents is structured and get a general understanding of the new technical skills you will be learning. Use the index to look up a specific command or feature of the software. Study the subtopics and cross-references provided.

Beginning Hands-On Activities

Computer instruction manuals are designed to launch you into hands-on action as early as possible. Go ahead and start on a lesson and do not be concerned if you make mistakes. You will learn as much or more by correcting your mistakes as when you follow the steps correctly. Focus on just what you need to know in order to get started. You will learn more by doing than by just reading. Think about what you already know about the topic as you begin. When you have completed a sequence of steps, go back, read the side text, and review the screen illustrations.

Using Effective Reading Strategies

Use effective skimming techniques. Skim sections for key words and labels to determine the relevance of the information. The material may or may not provide information necessary for completing your immediate task. Turn the headings into questions that require answers. Mark important information in the margins. Ask yourself questions and note terms not understood.

6. Center the title.
9. Move the insertion point to any character in the title *Strategies for Reading Computer Manuals* in the main document (not in the cover page) and then insert the Thin Line page numbering at the bottoms of the pages. (The page numbering will not appear on the cover page.)

C07-A01-Strategies.docx (page 2 of 3)

Exact Words Spoken or Written by Someone Else

Use quotation marks to indicate that the words within are the exact words spoken or written by someone else:

She asked, "What time should I be here in the morning?"

When I asked him for a raise, he said, "I'll consider it."

"Being in business is like being in a race."

"I must say," Ryan added, "that you have all been great."

"Without you," the chairperson said, "our committee will be at a loss. But we will struggle on."

"We must not hesitate," warned Mr. Row. "The competition will not allow it."

Partial Quotation of another's Words

When you quote only part of a speaker's or writer's sentence, do not set off or separate the quotation with commas:

"An excellent meeting" is what Rachel called it.

Rachel called it "an excellent meeting."

Rachel said that the "excellent meeting" lasted a little too long.

Follow standard capitalization rules when quoted material fits into the natural sequence of the sentence, as in the examples above.

Indirect Quotations

Do not use quotation marks with indirect quotations:

Direct Quotation: She said, "I am leaving." [The writer uses the speaker's exact words.]

Indirect Quotation: She said that she was leaving. [The writer reports what the speaker said. The writer changes words and word order to refer to the speaker.]

> 5. Move the insertion point to the beginning of the document, insert the Retrospect header, and then make the following changes:
> a. Type quotation marks in the *[DOCUMENT TITLE]* placeholder.
> b. Click in the *[DATE]* placeholder, click the down-pointing arrow that displays, and then click the Today button at the drop-down calendar.

> 1. Open **QuoteMarks.docx** and save the document with the name **C07-A02-QuoteMarks**.
> 2. Change the top margin to 1.25 inches.
> 3. Apply the Banded theme.

> 6. Insert the Retrospect footer, select the name that displays at the left side of the footer, and then type your first and last names. If an *[AUTHOR]* placeholder displays, click in the placeholder and then type your first and last names.

STUDENT NAME

1

C07-A02-QuoteMarks(Step7).docx (page 1 of 2)

> 7. Insert a page break at the beginning of the heading *Using Visual Aids*.

> 2. Apply the Heading 1 style to the title of the document and apply the Heading 2 style to the headings in the document.

Using Visual Aids

Carefully read the callouts, titles, or notes that help explain the illustrations. Stop to think about why the illustration is important. Try to connect the words with the illustrations and the screen captures. Read a few steps and then examine the illustration. Then continue reading the steps, returning periodically to the illustration. Ask yourself: "What is this illustration saying that the words do not?" State the visual information in words. Illustrations provide new information. Try to state that information in your own words.

2

C07-A01-Strategies.docx (page 3 of 3)

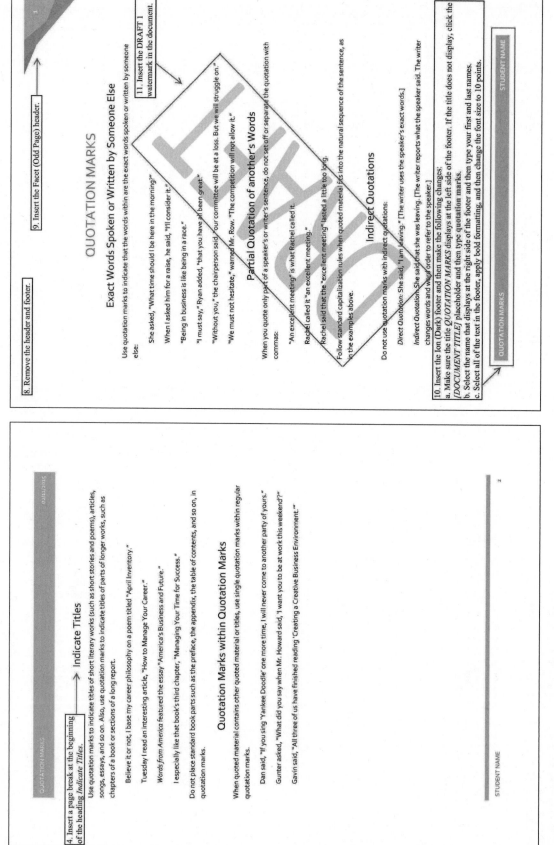

8. Remove the header and footer.

9. Insert the Facet (Odd Page) header.

11. Insert the DRAFT 1 watermark in the document.

QUOTATION MARKS

Exact Words Spoken or Written by Someone Else

Use quotation marks to indicate that the words within are the exact words spoken or written by someone else:

She asked, "What time should I be here in the morning?"

When I asked him for a raise, he said, "I'll consider it."

"Being in business is like being in a race."

"I must say," Ryan added, "that you have all been great."

"Without you," the chairperson said, "our committee will be at a loss. But we will struggle on."

"We must not hesitate," warned Mr. Row. "The competition will not allow it."

Partial Quotation of another's Words

When you quote only part of a speaker's or writer's sentence, do not set off or separate the quotation with commas:

"An excellent meeting" is what Rachel called it.

Rachel called it "an excellent meeting."

Rachel said that the "excellent meeting" lasted a little too long.

Follow standard capitalization rules when quoted material fits into the natural sequence of the sentence, as in the examples above.

Indirect Quotations

Do not use quotation marks with indirect quotations:

Direct Quotation: She said, "I am leaving." [The writer uses the speaker's exact words.]

Indirect Quotation: She said that she was leaving. [The writer reports what the speaker said. The writer changes words and word order to refer to the speaker.]

10. Insert the Ion (Dark) footer and then make the following changes:
a. Make sure the title QUOTATION MARKS displays at the left side of the footer. If the title does not display, click the [DOCUMENT TITLE] placeholder and then type quotation marks.
b. Select the name that displays at the right side of the footer and then type your first and last names.
c. Select all of the text in the footer, apply bold formatting, and then change the font size to 10 points.

QUOTATION MARKS

STUDENT NAME

C07-A02-QuoteMarks(Step12).docx (page 1 of 2)

QUOTATION MARKS   02/11/2015

4. Insert a page break at the beginning of the heading Indicate Titles.

Indicate Titles

Use quotation marks to indicate titles of short literary works (such as short stories and poems), articles, songs, essays, and so on. Also, use quotation marks to indicate titles of parts of longer works, such as chapters of a book or sections of a long report.

Believe it or not, I base my career philosophy on a poem titled "April Inventory."

Tuesday I read an interesting article, "How to Manage Your Career."

Words from America featured the essay "America's Business and Future."

I especially like that book's third chapter, "Managing Your Time for Success."

Do not place standard book parts such as the preface, the appendix, the table of contents, and so on, in quotation marks.

Quotation Marks within Quotation Marks

When quoted material contains other quoted material or titles, use single quotation marks within regular quotation marks.

Dan said, "If you sing 'Yankee Doodle' one more time, I will never come to another party of yours."

Gunter asked, "What did you say when Mr. Howard said, 'I want you to be at work this weekend?'"

Gavin said, "All three of us have finished reading 'Creating a Creative Business Environment.'"

STUDENT NAME

C07-A02-QuoteMarks(Step7).docx (page 2 of 2)

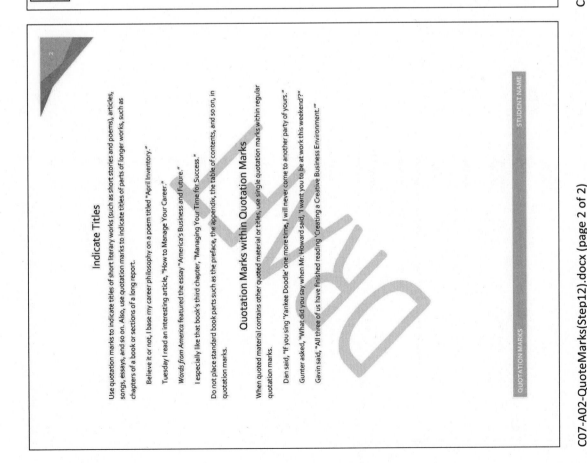

C07-A03-REAgrmnt.docx (page 1 of 2)

1. Open **REAgrmnt.docx** and save the document with the name **C07-A03-REAgrmnt**.
2. Find all occurrences of *BUYER* (matching the case) and replace with *Craig Metzner*.
3. Find all occurrences of *SELLER* (matching the case) and replace with *Carol Winters*.
4. Find all forms of the word *buy* and replace them with *purchase*.

REAL ESTATE SALE AGREEMENT

The Buyer, Craig Metzner, and Seller, Carol Winters, hereby agree that Carol Winters will sell and Craig Metzner will purchase the following property, with such improvements as are located thereon, and is described as follows: All that tract of land lying and being in Land Lot _____ of the _____ District, Section _____ of _____ County, and being known as Address: _____ City: _____ State: _____ Zip: _____, together with all light fixtures, electrical, mechanical, plumbing, air-conditioning, and any other systems or fixtures as are attached thereto; all plants, trees, and shrubbery now a part thereof, together with all the improvements thereon, and all appurtenances thereto, all being hereinafter collectively referred to as the "Property." The full legal description of said Property is the same as is recorded with the Clerk of the Superior Court of the County in which the Property is located and is made a part of this Agreement by reference.

Carol Winters will sell and Craig Metzner will purchase upon the following terms and conditions, as completed or marked. On any conflict of terms or conditions, that which is added will supersede that which is printed or marked. It is understood that the Property will be purchased by Warranty Deed, with covenants, restrictions, and easements of record.

Financing: The balance due to Carol Winters will be evidenced by a negotiable Promissory Note of Borrower, secured by a Mortgage or Deed to Secure Debt on the Property and delivered by Craig Metzner to Carol Winters dated the date of closing.

New financing: If Craig Metzner does not obtain the required financing, the earnest money deposit shall be forfeited to Carol Winters as liquidated damages. Craig Metzner will make application for financing within five days of the date of acceptance of the Agreement and in a timely manner furnish any and all credit, employment, financial and other information required by the lender.

Closing costs: Craig Metzner will pay all closing costs to include: Recording Fees, Intangibles Tax, Credit Reports, Funding Fees, Loan Origination Fee, Document Preparation Fee, Loan Insurance Premium, Title Insurance Policy, Attorney's Fees, Courier Fees, Overnight Fee, Appraisal Fee, Survey, Transfer Tax, Satisfaction and Recording Fees, Wood Destroying Organism Report and any other costs associated with the funding or closing of this Agreement.

Prorations: All taxes, rentals, condominium or association fees, monthly mortgage insurance premiums and interest on loans will be prorated as of the date of closing.

Title insurance: Within five (5) days of this Agreement Carol Winters will deliver to Craig Metzner or closing attorney: Title insurance commitment for an owner's policy in the amount of the purchase price. Any expense of securing title, including but not limited to legal fees, discharge of liens and recording fees will be paid by Carol Winters.

Survey: Within ten (10) days of acceptance of this Agreement, Craig Metzner or closing attorney, may, at Craig Metzner's expense, obtain a new staked survey showing an improvements now existing thereon and certified to Craig Metzner, lender and the title insurer.

6. Insert the Bold Numbers 2 page numbers at the bottoms of the pages.

→ Page 1 of 2

C07-A02-QuoteMarks(Step12).docx (page 2 of 2)

Indicate Titles

Use quotation marks to indicate titles of short literary works (such as short stories and poems), articles, songs, essays, and so on. Also, use quotation marks to indicate titles of parts of longer works, such as chapters of a book or sections of a long report.

Believe it or not, I base my career philosophy on a poem titled "April Inventory."

Tuesday I read an interesting article, "How to Manage Your Career."

Words from America featured the essay "America's Business and Future."

I especially like the book's third chapter, "Managing Your Time for Success."

Do not place standard book parts such as the preface, the appendix, the table of contents, and so on, in quotation marks.

Quotation Marks within Quotation Marks

When quoted material contains other quoted material or titles, use single quotation marks within regular quotation marks.

Dan said, "If you sing 'Yankee Doodle' one more time, I will never come to another party of yours."

Gunter asked, "What did you say when Mr. Howard said, 'I want you to be at work this weekend?'"

Gavin said, "All three of us have finished reading 'Creating a Creative Business Environment.'"

QUOTATION MARKS

STUDENT NAME

Document 1 (C07-A04-CoData.docx):

1. At a blank document, use the Click and Type feature to create the document shown in Figure 7.8.
2. Select the centered text and then change the font to 16-point Candara bold in Dark Blue.
4. Change the vertical alignment of the text to center alignment.

Securing Company Data

Systems for Backing up Crucial Data

Thursday, March 19, 2015

Corporate Training Center

1:30 to 4:00 p.m.

Sponsored by
Madison Security Systems

3. Select the right-aligned text and then change the font to 12-point Candara bold in Dark Blue.

C07-A04-CoData.docx

Document 2 (C07-A03-REAgrmnt.docx page 2 of 2):

5. Insert a page break at the beginning of the paragraph that begins *Default and attorney's fees:*.

Default and attorney's fees: Should Craig Metzner elect not to fulfill obligations under this Agreement, all earnest monies will be retained by Carol Winters as liquidated damages and fund settlement of any claim, whereupon Craig Metzner and Carol Winters will be relieved of all obligations under this Agreement. If Carol Winters defaults under this agreement, the Craig Metzner may seek specific performance in return of the earnest money deposit. In connection with any litigation arising out of this Agreement, the prevailing party shall be entitled to recover all costs including reasonable attorney's fees.

IN WITNESS WHEREOF, all of the parties hereto affix their hands and seals this _____ day of _____, 20____.

Page 2 of 2

C07-A03-REAgrmnt.docx (page 2 of 2)

Delivering a Presentation

DELIVERING PRESENTATIONS

Delivering a How-To Presentation

Knowing how to give a *how-to*, or *process*, presentation is one of the most useful things you can learn about speaking. Giving clear directions is important not only in the classroom but also in the world of work. Many people's jobs involve giving this type of presentation, for example, to train new employees or to demonstrate a product to potential buyers. When you create a set of directions for others to follow, think through the process carefully. Make certain the steps you provide are complete, accurate, and in the proper sequence.

Choose a Suitable Topic

The topic you choose for your how-to presentation should be one you are familiar with or can learn about easily. Also keep in mind your listeners' interests. Try to select a process that will appeal to the audience. Processes you might explain include the following:

- Getting a driver's license
- Cooking a favorite food
- Working as a volunteer
- Finding an internship
- Applying for financial aid

3. Additional headers, footers, and cover pages are available from Office.com. Click the INSERT tab, click the Header button, click the *More Headers from Office.com* option, and then choose a header from the side menu.

Develop Well-Organized Directions

Begin by arranging the major steps of the process in logical order. Then give the details needed to complete each step. Be sure to specify the materials needed and carefully explain the tasks involved. Follow these guidelines:

- Use transitional words such as *first*, *second*, and *next* to help readers keep track of the steps of the process. Using transitional words also will help you keep your place in the presentation.
- Before you move from one step to the next step, be sure your listeners have understood what you have described. If they look confused, review what you have said or ask if they need clarification.
- Use visual aids in your presentation so you can demonstrate the process while you describe it. Doing so will make your presentation more interesting to listeners and also may help calm your nerves. To ensure audience members will be able to see what you are doing, use large photographs and diagrams or an oversized model.

2b. Apply the Title style to the title in the document, the Heading 1 style to the subtitle, and the Heading 2 style to the three headings in the document.

1

---

1. Open **Presentation.docx** and then save it and name it **C07-A05-Presentation.**
2. Make the following changes to the document:
a. Change the top margin to 1.25 inches.
c. Apply the Centered style set.
d. Change the theme colors to Orange.
5. Choose a cover page from Office.com and insert the appropriate text in the cover page placeholders. (Consider deleting placeholders if they are not pertinent to the document.)

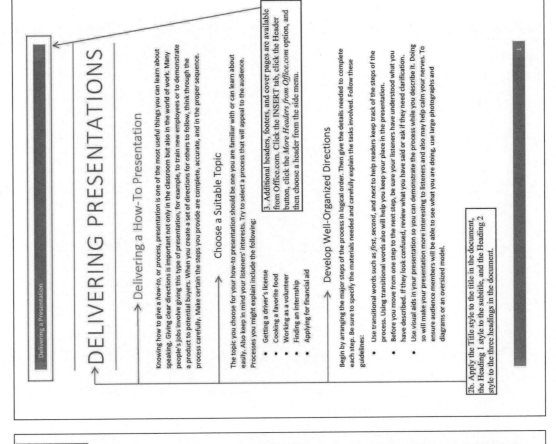

Delivering a
Presentation

Delivering a How-To Presentation

4. Choose a footer from Office.com.

Student Name   2/11/15   BTECH 210

1. Open **ResumeInfo.docx** and then save it and name it **C07-A06-ResumeInfo**.
2. Format the document so it appears as shown in Figure 7.9 with the following specifications:
b. Insert the Banded cover page and insert text in the placeholders and delete placeholders so your cover page looks like the cover page in Figure 7.9.
e. Apply any other formatting necessary so your document appears as shown in Figure 7.9.

RESUME WRITING

Student Name

C07-A06-ResumeInfo.docx (page 1 of 3)

Delivering a Presentation

Practice Your Delivery

Assemble all the materials, including your visual aids. Plan how to arrange and use them in the location where you will be speaking. Also consider how to arrange the setting so your listeners can see and hear your presentation. Spend time practicing your presentation in front of one or two friends or family members, and ask them to provide feedback on both your content and delivery. In particular, verify whether they can follow the steps you present in explaining your process.

2b. Apply the Title style to the title in the document, the Heading 1 style to the subtitle, and the Heading 2 style to the three headings in the document.

C07-A05-Presentation.docx (page 3 of 3)

2a. Apply the Heading 1 style to the title and the Heading 2 style to the headings. Also, apply the Lines (Stylish) style set and change the theme colors to Blue Green.

2c. Insert the Ion (Dark) header.

Becoming a Job Detective

Imagine the scene: an office in the city, but there is someone missing from one desk. Witnesses say the missing person is dynamic, well qualified, and pays exceptional attention to detail. Every employer has a "prime suspect" in mind when they advertise a position, and they tend to leave clues to that person's identity in their job description. In this chapter, we teach you to become a job detective, so that you can pick up all the clues and solve the mystery—what would the ideal candidate for this job look like?

To produce the best "fitting" resume, you need to know about yourself and the job you are applying for. Before you do anything else, ask yourself why you are preparing a resume. The answer to this question is going to vary from one person to the next, and here are our top ten reasons for writing a resume:

1. You have seen a job that appeals to you advertised in the newspaper.
2. You want to market yourself to win a contract or a proposal or be elected to a committee or organization.
3. You have seen a job that appeals to you on an Internet job site.
4. Your friends or family told you of a job opening at a local company.
5. You want to work for the local company and thought that sending a resume to the company might get the company's attention.
6. You have seen a job advertised internally at work.
7. You are going for a promotion.
8. You are about to be downsized and want to update your resume to be ready for any good opportunities.
9. You are feeling fed up, and writing down all your achievements will cheer you up and might motivate you to look for a better job.
10. You are thinking "Oh, so that's a resume! I've never done one. I suppose I ought to try to remember what I've been doing with my life."

All of these certainly are good reasons to write a resume, but the resume serves many different purposes. One way of understanding the differences is to ask yourself who is going to read the resume in each case.

Resumes 1 through 5 will be read by potential employers who probably do not know you. Resume 6 and 7 are likely to be read by your boss or other people who know you. Resumes 8 through 10 are really for your own benefit and should not be considered as suitable for sending out to employers.

The Right Mix

Think about the list of reasons again. How else can you divide up these reasons? A most important difference is that, in some cases, you will have a good idea of what the employer is looking for because you have a job advertisement in front of you and can tailor your resume accordingly. For others, you have no idea what the reader might want to see. Updating your resume from time to time is a good idea so you do not forget

2d. Insert the Ion (Dark) footer.

RESUME WRITING — STUDENT NAME

2a. Apply the Heading 1 style to the title and the Heading 2 style to the headings. Also, apply the Lines (Stylish) style set and change the theme colors to Blue Green.

important details, but remember that the result of such a process will not be a winning resume. It will be a useful list of tasks and achievements.

Writing a resume is like baking a cake. You need all the right ingredients: flour, butter, eggs, and so on. It is what you do with the ingredients that makes the difference between a great resume (or cake) and failure. Keeping your resume up-to-date is like keeping a stock of ingredients in the pantry—it's potentially very useful, but do not imagine that is the end of it!

Information about the Job

You should tailor the information in your resume to the main points in the job advertisement. That sounds fine, but how do you do it? Get as much information about the job and the company as you can. The main sources of information about a job are normally the following:

- A job advertisement
- A job description
- A friend in the company
- The media
- Gossip and rumor
- Someone already doing the job or something similar

There is no substitute for experience. Talking to someone who does a job similar to the one you wish to apply for in the same company may well provide you with a good picture of what the job is really like. Bear in mind, of course, that this source of information is not always reliable. You may react differently than the way that person does, and therefore his or her experience with a company may be very different than yours. However, someone with reliable information can provide a golden opportunity. Make sure you do not waste the chance to get some information.

Information about the Company

The main sources of information about an employer are normally the following:

- The media
- Annual reports/company brochures
- Industry/trade magazines or journals
- The Internet—on the company's own site or at general sites
- Industry directories
- Gossip and Rumor

Other sources of information about companies are available; if you are serious about wanting to know more about a potential employer (and you should be), it is worth a visit to your local library. Ask a reference librarian to help you with your search. It will help if you explain to the librarian that you are looking for information on a specific company to help with your job search.

RESUME WRITING — STUDENT NAME

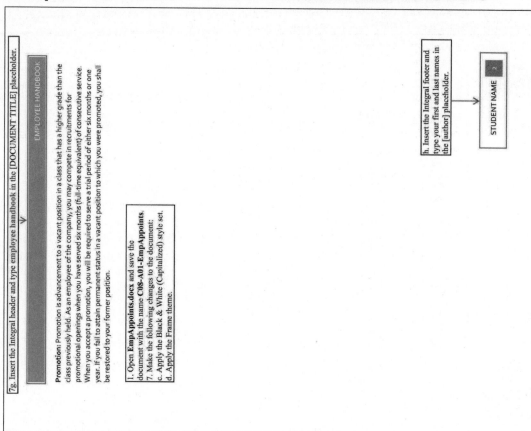

Page 2 of 3 annotations:

7g. Insert the Integral header and type employee handbook in the [DOCUMENT TITLE] placeholder.

EMPLOYEE HANDBOOK

Promotion: Promotion is advancement to a vacant position in a class that has a higher grade than the class previously held. As an employee of the company, you may compete in recruitments for promotional openings when you have served six months (full-time equivalent) of consecutive service. When you accept a promotion, you will be required to serve a trial period of either six months or one year. If you fail to attain permanent status in a vacant position to which you were promoted, you shall be restored to your former position.

1. Open **EmpAppoints.docx** and save the document with the name **C08-A01-EmpAppoints**.
7. Make the following changes to the document:
c. Apply the Black & White (Capitalized) style set.
d. Apply the Frame theme.

h. Insert the Integral footer and type your first and last names in the [author] placeholder.

STUDENT NAME   2

C08-A01-EmpAppoints.docx (page 2 of 3)

Page 1 of 3 annotations:

6. Create a drop cap with the first letter of the first paragraph of text (the word *Acceptance*) and specify that the drop cap drops two lines.

7a. Apply the Heading 1 style to the two titles in the document: *EMPLOYMENT APPOINTMENTS* and *EMPLOYEE PERFORMANCE*. f. Center the two titles.

7g. Insert the Integral header and type employee handbook in the [DOCUMENT TITLE] placeholder.

EMPLOYEE HANDBOOK

EMPLOYMENT APPOINTMENTS

TYPES OF APPOINTMENTS

A cceptance by an applicant of an offer of employment by an appointing authority and their mutual agreement to the date of hire is known as an appointment.

7b. Apply the Heading 2 style to the four headings: *Types of Appointments, Work Performance Standards, Performance Evaluation, and Employment Records.*

New Hire: When you initially accept an appointment, you are considered probationary and will be required to serve a probationary period of either six months or one year.

Reemployment: Reemployment is a type of appointment that does not result in a break in service. The types of reemployment are as follows:

1. Military reemployment: Any remaining portion of a probationary period must be completed upon return to the company.

2. Reemployment of a permanent employee who has been laid off: Completion of a new probationary period is required if the employee is reemployed in a different class or in a different department.

3. Reemployment due to reclassification of a position to a lower class.

4. Reemployment of seasonal employees.

5. Reemployment due to a permanent disability arising from an injury sustained at work.

Further information on this subject can be obtained by contacting your personnel representative or a representative in the human resources department.

Reinstatement: If you have resigned from company service as a permanent employee in good standing, you may be reinstated to the same or a similar class within a two-year period following termination.

The probationary period following reinstatement may be waived, but you will not be eligible to compete in promotional examinations until you have completed six months of permanent service. You cannot be reinstated to a position that is at grade 20 or above if the position is allocated at a higher grade level than the position you held at the time of termination.

Reappointment: You may be reappointed to a class that you formerly held or to a comparable class if you meet the current minimum qualifications and receive the appointing authority's approval. If you are a probationary employee, you must complete a new probationary period. You cannot be reappointed to a position at grade 20 or above if the position is allocated at a higher level than the position you formerly held.

Demotion: An employee may request or accept a demotion to a position in a class with a lower grade level if the employee meets the minimum qualifications and if the appointing authority approves. You may not demote through non-competitive means to a position at grade 20 or higher if the position is allocated to a higher grade level than the position you currently hold.

7h. Insert the Integral footer and type your first and last names in the [author] placeholder.

STUDENT NAME   1

C08-A01-EmpAppoints.docx (page 1 of 3)

1. Open **AuditRep.docx** and save the document with the name **C08-A02-AuditRep**.
3. Apply the following formatting:
b. Apply the Minimalist style set.
4. Turn on the display of bookmarks.
8. Navigate in the document using the bookmarks.

5. Move the insertion point to the end of the third paragraph in the document (the paragraph that begins *The audit committee selects*) and then insert a bookmark named *Audit*.

AUDIT COMMITTEE REPORT

The audit committee of the board of directors, which consists entirely of directors who meet the current independence and experience requirements of the New York Stock Exchange as determined by the board of directors, was given the following mission:

Assist the company's board of directors in fulfilling its responsibility to oversee the management's conduct of the company's financial reporting process. Such assistance includes oversight by the committee of the financial reports and other financial information provided by the company to any governmental or regulatory body, the public, or other users thereof.

The audit committee selects an independent, registered public accounting firm to be the company's independent auditor and perform the annual independent audit of the company's financial statements, the effectiveness of internal control over financial reporting.

Committee Responsibilities

The role and responsibilities of the audit committee are set forth in a written charter adopted by the board.

The audit committee reviews and reassesses the charter annually and recommends charges to the board for approval. [Audit Fees]

9. Move the insertion point to the end of the first paragraph in the *Committee Responsibilities* section and then insert a hyperlink to the *Audit Fees* bookmark.

As part of fulfilling its responsibilities for overseeing management's conduct of the company's financial reporting process for fiscal year 2014, the audit committee:

- Received management's representation that the company's consolidated financial statements for the fiscal year ended December 31, 2014, were prepared in accordance with accounting principles generally accepted in the United States.

- Monitored, reviewed, and discussed the audited financial statements for the fiscal year and the effectiveness of internal control over financial reporting and management's assessment thereof.

- Discussed with the accounting firm the matters required to be discussed by auditing standards related to the conduct of the audit.

- Received written disclosures and a letter from the accounting firm regarding its independence as required by auditing standards.

In addition, the audit committee considered the status of pending litigation, taxation matters, and other areas of oversight relating to the financial reporting and audit process that the committee determined appropriate.

Based on the audit committee's reviews, the discussions and other actions outlined above, and relying thereon, the audit committee recommended to the board that the audited financial statements be included in the company's annual report for the fiscal year for filing with the U.S. Exchange Commission.

3c. Insert the Austin footer.

[Page 1]

C08-A02-AuditRep.docx (page 1 of 3)

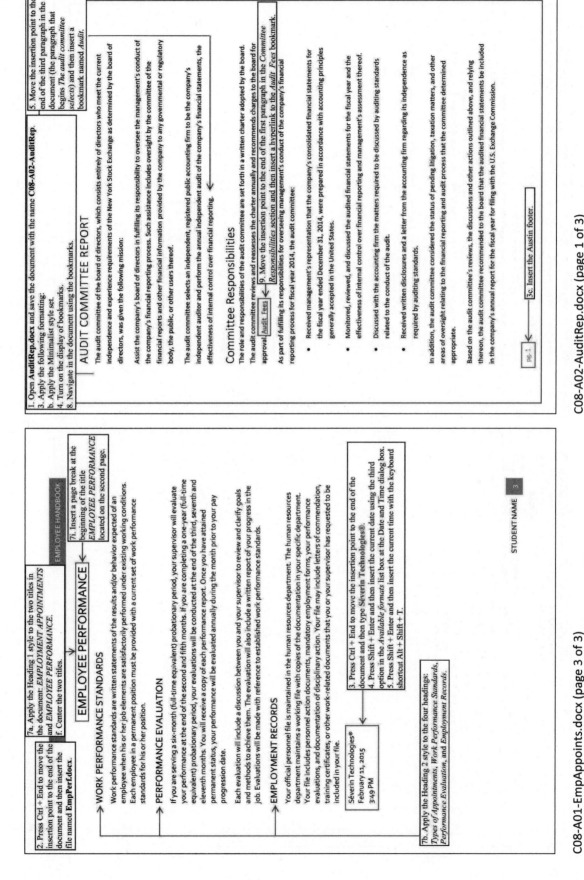

2. Press Ctrl + End to move the insertion point to the end of the document and then insert the file named **EmpPerf.docx**.

7a. Apply the Heading 1 style to the two titles in the document: *EMPLOYMENT APPOINTMENTS* and *EMPLOYEE PERFORMANCE*.
f. Center the two titles.

EMPLOYEE HANDBOOK

EMPLOYEE PERFORMANCE

7i. Insert a page break at the beginning of the title *EMPLOYEE PERFORMANCE* located on the second page.

WORK PERFORMANCE STANDARDS

Work performance standards are written statements of the results and/or behavior expected of an employee when his or her job elements are satisfactorily performed under existing working conditions. Each employee in a permanent position must be provided with a current set of work performance standards for his or her position.

PERFORMANCE EVALUATION

If you are serving a six-month (full-time equivalent) probationary period, your supervisor will evaluate your performance at the end of the second and fifth months. If you are completing a one-year (full-time equivalent) probationary period, your evaluations will be conducted at the end of the third, seventh and eleventh months. You will receive a copy of each performance report. Once you have attained permanent status, your performance will be evaluated annually during the month prior to your pay progression date.

Each evaluation will include a discussion between you and your supervisor to review and clarify goals and methods to achieve them. The evaluation will also include a written report of your progress in the job. Evaluations will be made with reference to established work performance standards.

EMPLOYMENT RECORDS

Your official personnel file is maintained in the human resources department. The human resources department maintains a working file with copies of the documentation in your specific department. Your file includes personnel action documents, mandatory employment forms, your performance evaluations, and documentation of disciplinary action. Your file may include letters of commendation, training certificates, or other work-related documents that you or your supervisor has requested to be included in your file.

Séverin Technologies®
February 11, 2015
3:49 PM

3. Press Ctrl + End to move the insertion point to the end of the document and then type Séverin Technologies®.
4. Press Shift + Enter and then insert the current date using the third option in the *Available formats* list box at the Date and Time dialog box.
5. Press Shift + Enter and then insert the current time with the keyboard shortcut Alt + Shift + T.

STUDENT NAME 3

7b. Apply the Heading 2 style to the four headings:
Types of Appointments, Work Performance Standards, Performance Evaluation, and *Employment Records.*

C08-A01-EmpAppoints.docx (page 3 of 3)

2. Move the insertion point to the end of the document and then insert the document named **CompRep.docx**.
3a. Insert a page break at the beginning of the heading *Compensation Committee Report*.

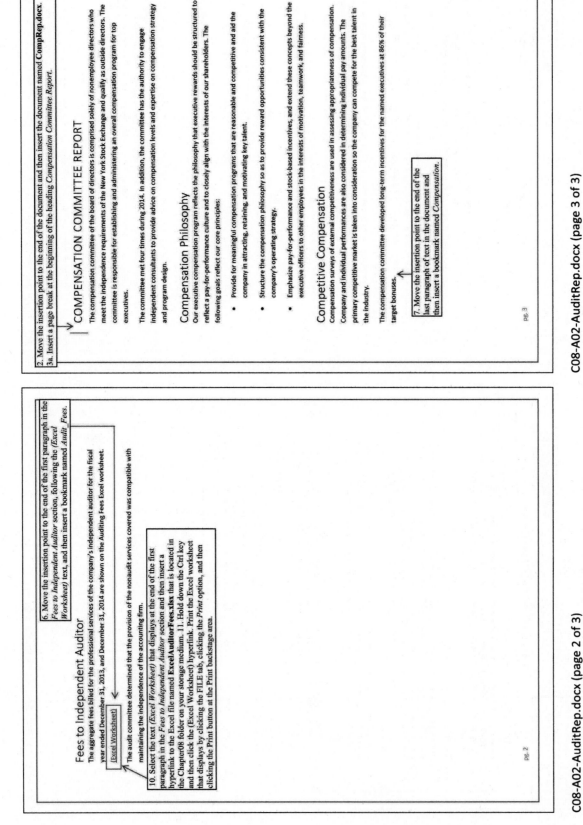

COMPENSATION COMMITTEE REPORT

The compensation committee of the board of directors is comprised solely of nonemployee directors who meet the independence requirements of the New York Stock Exchange and qualify as outside directors. The committee is responsible for establishing and administering an overall compensation program for top executives.

The committee met four times during 2014. In addition, the committee has the authority to engage independent consultants to provide advice on compensation levels and expertise on compensation strategy and program design.

Compensation Philosophy

Our executive compensation program reflects the philosophy that executive rewards should be structured to reflect a pay-for-performance culture and to closely align with the interests of our shareholders. The following goals reflect our core principles:

- Provide for meaningful compensation programs that are reasonable and competitive and aid the company in attracting, retaining, and motivating key talent.
- Structure the compensation philosophy so as to provide reward opportunities consistent with the company's operating strategy.
- Emphasize pay-for-performance and stock-based incentives, and extend these concepts beyond the executive officers to other employees in the interests of motivation, teamwork, and fairness.

Competitive Compensation

Compensation surveys of external competitiveness are used in assessing appropriateness of compensation. Company and individual performances are also considered in determining individual pay amounts. The primary competitive market is taken into consideration so the company can compete for the best talent in the industry.

The compensation committee developed long-term incentives for the named executives at 86% of their target bonuses.

7. Move the insertion point to the end of the last paragraph of text in the document and then insert a bookmark named *Compensation*.

pg. 3

C08-A02-AuditRep.docx (page 3 of 3)

---

6. Move the insertion point to the end of the first paragraph in the *Fees to Independent Auditor* section, following the *(Excel Worksheet)* text, and then insert a bookmark named *Audit_Fees*.

Fees to Independent Auditor

The aggregate fees billed for the professional services of the company's independent auditor for the fiscal year ended December 31, 2013, and December 31, 2014 are shown on the Auditing Fees Excel worksheet.

(Excel Worksheet)

The audit committee determined that the provision of the nonaudit services covered was compatible with maintaining the independence of the accounting firm.

10. Select the text *(Excel Worksheet)* that displays at the end of the first paragraph in the *Fees to Independent Auditor* section and then insert a hyperlink to the Excel file named **ExcelAuditorFees.xlsx** that is located in the Chapter08 folder on your storage medium. 11. Hold down the Ctrl key and then click the *(Excel Worksheet)* hyperlink. Print the Excel worksheet that displays by clicking the FILE tab, clicking the *Print* option, and then clicking the Print button at the Print backstage area.

pg. 2

C08-A02-AuditRep.docx (page 2 of 3)

COMPUTERS IN COMMUNICATIONS

C omputers were originally stand-alone devices, incapable of communicating with other computers. This changed in the 1970s and 1980s when the development of special telecommunications hardware and software led to the creation of the first private networks, allowing connected computers to exchange data. Exchanged data took the form of requests for information, replies to requests for information, or instructions on how to run programs stored on the network.

The ability to link computers enables users to communicate and work together efficiently and effectively. Linked computers have become central to the communications industry. They play a vital role in telecommunications, publishing, and news services.

TELECOMMUNICATIONS

T he industry that provides for communication across distances is called telecommunications. The telephone industry uses computers to switch and route phone calls automatically over telephone lines. In addition to the spoken word, many other kinds of information move over such lines, including faxes and computer data. Data can be sent from computer to computer over telephone lines using a device known as a modem. One kind of data frequently sent by modem is electronic mail, or email, which can be sent from person to person via the Internet or an online service. A more recent innovation in telecommunications is teleconferencing, which allows people

in various locations to see and hear one another and thus hold virtual meetings.

PUBLISHING

J ust twenty years ago, book manuscripts were typeset mechanically on a typesetting machine and then reproduced on a printing press. Now, anyone who has access to a computer and either a modem or a printer can undertake what has come to be known as electronic publishing. Writers and editors use word processing applications to produce text. Artists and designers use drawing and painting applications to created original graphics, or they use inexpensive scanners to digitize illustrations and photographs (turn them into computer-readable files). Typesetters use personal computers to combine text, illustrations, and photographs. Publishers typically send computer-generated files to printers for production of the film and plates from which books and magazines are printed.

NEWS SERVICES

N ews providers rely on reporters located worldwide. Reporters use email to send, or upload, their stories to wire services. Increasingly, individuals get daily news reports from online services. News can also be accessed from specific providers, such as the *New York Times* or *U.S.A. Today*, via the Internet. One of the most popular Internet sites provides continuously updated weather reports.

C08-A03-CompServices(Step4).docx

TO: Instructor

FROM: Student Name

DATE: February 11, 2015

SUBJECT: Drop Cap Steps

To create a drop cap, I simply selected the letter of the document and clicked the Drop Cap button on the INSERT tab.

To make the changes in font, size, and depth, I clicked *Drop Cap Options* from the Drop Cap button drop-down list. I selected my desired font, altered the size of the letter to 2 lines, and inserted into the text with a 0.1 indent from the text. Changing the color was done from the font group on the HOME tab.

C08-A03-DropCapMemo.docx

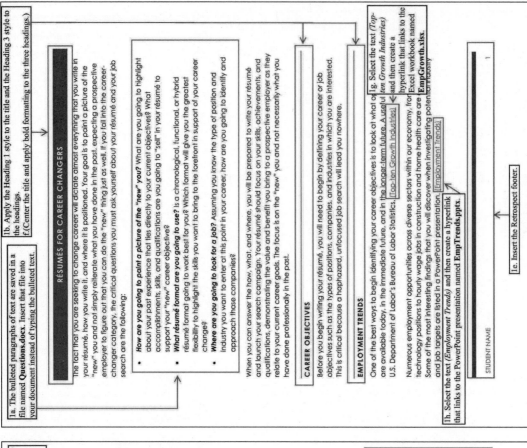

1a. The bulleted paragraphs of text are saved in a file named **Questions.docx**. Insert that file into your document instead of typing the bulleted text.

1b. Apply the Heading 1 style to the title and the Heading 3 style to the headings. *f:(Center the title and apply bold formatting to the three headings.)*

RÉSUMÉS FOR CAREER CHANGERS

The fact that you are seeking to change careers will dictate almost everything that you write in your résumé, how you write it, and where it is positioned. Your goal is to paint a picture of the "new" you and not simply reiterate what you have done in the past, expecting a prospective employer to figure out that you can do the "new" thing just as well. If you fall into the career-changer category, the critical questions you must ask yourself about your résumé and your job search are the following:

- **How are you going to paint a picture of the "new" you?** What are you going to highlight about your past experience that ties directly to your current objectives? What accomplishments, skills, and qualifications are you going to "sell" in your résumé to support your "new" career objective?

- **What résumé format are you going to use?** Is a chronological, functional, or hybrid résumé format going to work best for you? Which format will give you the greatest flexibility to highlight the skills you want to bring to the forefront in support of your career change?

- **Where are you going to look for a job?** Assuming you know the type of position and industry you want to enter at this point in your career, how are you going to identify and approach those companies?

When you can answer the how, what, and where, you will be prepared to write your résumé and launch your search campaign. Your résumé should focus on your skills, achievements, and qualifications, demonstrating the value and benefit you bring to a prospective employer as they relate to your current career goals. The focus is on the "new" you and not necessarily what you have done professionally in the past.

CAREER OBJECTIVES

Before you begin writing your résumé, you will need to begin by defining your career or job objectives such as the types of positions, companies, and industries in which you are interested. This is critical because a haphazard, unfocused job search will lead you nowhere.

EMPLOYMENT TRENDS

One of the best ways to begin identifying your career objectives is to look at what of are available today, in the immediate future, and in the longer-term future. A useful U.S. Department of Labor's Bureau of Labor Statistics... Top-Ten Growth Industries

1g. Select the text (Top-ten Growth Industries) and then create a hyperlink that links to the Excel workbook named **EmpGrowth.xlsx.**

Numerous employment opportunities across diverse sectors within our economy, from technology positions to hourly wage jobs in construction and home health care are Some of the most interesting findings that you will discover when investigating potential and job targets are listed in a PowerPoint presentation. Employment Trends

1h. Select the text (Employment Trends) and then create a hyperlink that links to the PowerPoint presentation named **EmpTrends.pptx.**

1e. Insert the Retrospect footer.

STUDENT NAME

1

C08-A05-CareerChangers.docx (page 1 of 2)

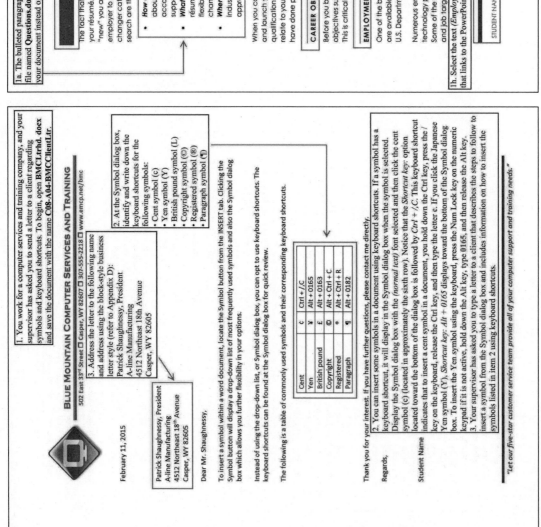

1. You work for a computer services and training company, and your supervisor has asked you to send a letter to a client regarding symbols and keyboard shortcuts. To begin, open **BMCL.rhd.docx** and save the document with the name **C08-A04-BMCClientLtr.docx**.

BLUE MOUNTAIN COMPUTER SERVICES AND TRAINING
502 East 33rd Street □ Casper, WY 82607 □ 307-555-2218 □ www.emcp.net/bmc

February 11, 2015

3. Address the letter to the following name and address using the block-style business letter style (refer to Appendix D):

Patrick Shaughnessy, President
A-line Manufacturing
4512 Northeast 18th Avenue
Casper, WY 82605

Dear Mr. Shaughnessy,

To insert a symbol within a word document, locate the Symbol button from the INSERT tab. Clicking the Symbol button will display a drop-down list of most frequently used symbols and also the Symbol dialog box which allows you further flexibility in your options.

2. At the Symbol dialog box, identify and write down the keyboard shortcuts for the following symbols:
- Cent symbol (¢)
- Yen symbol (¥)
- British pound symbol (£)
- Copyright symbol (©)
- Registered symbol (®)
- Paragraph symbol (¶)

Instead of using the drop-down list, or Symbol dialog box, you can opt to use keyboard shortcuts. The keyboard shortcuts can be found at the Symbol dialog box for quick review.

The following is a table of commonly used symbols and their corresponding keyboard shortcuts.

Cent	¢	Ctrl + /,C
Yen	¥	Alt + 0165
British pound	£	Alt + 0163
Copyright	©	Alt + Ctrl + C
Registered	®	Alt + Ctrl + R
Paragraph	¶	Alt + 0182

Thank you for your interest. If you have further questions, please contact me directly.

Regards,

Student Name

2. You can insert some symbols in a document using keyboard shortcuts. If a symbol has a keyboard shortcut, it will display in the Symbol dialog box when the symbol is selected. Display the Symbol dialog box with the *(normal text)* font selected and then click the cent symbol (¢) (located in approximately the sixth row). Notice that the *Shortcut key:* option located toward the bottom of the dialog box is followed by *Ctrl + /,C*. This keyboard shortcut indicates that to insert a cent symbol in a document, you hold down the Ctrl key, press the / key on the keyboard, release the Ctrl key, and then type the letter *c*. If you click the Japanese Yen symbol (¥), *Shortcut key: Alt + 0165* displays toward the bottom of the Symbol dialog box. To insert the Yen symbol using the keyboard, press the Num Lock key on the numeric keypad if it is not active, hold down the Alt key, type 0165, and then release the Alt key.

3. Your supervisor has asked you to type a letter to a client that describes the steps to follow to insert a symbol from the Symbol dialog box and includes information on how to insert the symbols listed in item 2 using keyboard shortcuts.

"Let our five-star customer service team provide all of your computer support and training needs."

C08-A04-BMCClientLtr.docx

1f. Apply character formatting and insert a page break as indicated in Figure 8.7. (Center the title and apply bold formatting to the three headings.)

JOB SEARCH AND YOUR CAREER

To take advantage of these opportunities, you must be an educated job seeker. This means you must know what you want in your career, where the hiring action is, what qualifications and credentials you need to attain your desired career goals, and how best to market your qualifications.

The employment market has changed dramatically from only a few years ago. According to the U.S. Department of Labor, you should expect to hold between 10 and 20 different jobs during your career. No longer is stability the status quo. Today, the norm is movement, onward and upward, in a fast-paced and intense employment market where many opportunities are available for career changers. To take advantage of all of the opportunities, every job seeker must proactively control and manage his/her career.

1b. Apply the Heading 1 style to the title and the Heading 3 style to the headings.
f. (Center the title and apply bold formatting to the three headings.)

1. At a blank document, create the document shown in Figure 8.7 on the next pages with the following specifications:
c. Apply the Shaded style set.
d. Apply the Wisp theme and change the theme colors to Violet II.
i. Apply any other formatting required to ensure that your document appears the same as the document in Figure 8.7.
2. Hold down the Ctrl key and then click the hyperlink to display the **EmpGrowth.xlsx** Excel workbook. After viewing the workbook, close Excel without saving the workbook.
3. Hold down the Ctrl key and then click the hyperlink to display the **EmpTrends.pptx** PowerPoint presentation. Run the presentation by clicking the Slide Show button that displays in the view area on the Status bar. Click the left mouse button to advance each slide. After viewing the presentation, close PowerPoint.

STUDENT NAME

2

C08-A05-CareerChangers.docx (page 2 of 2)

Chapter 9 Assessment Annotated Model Answers

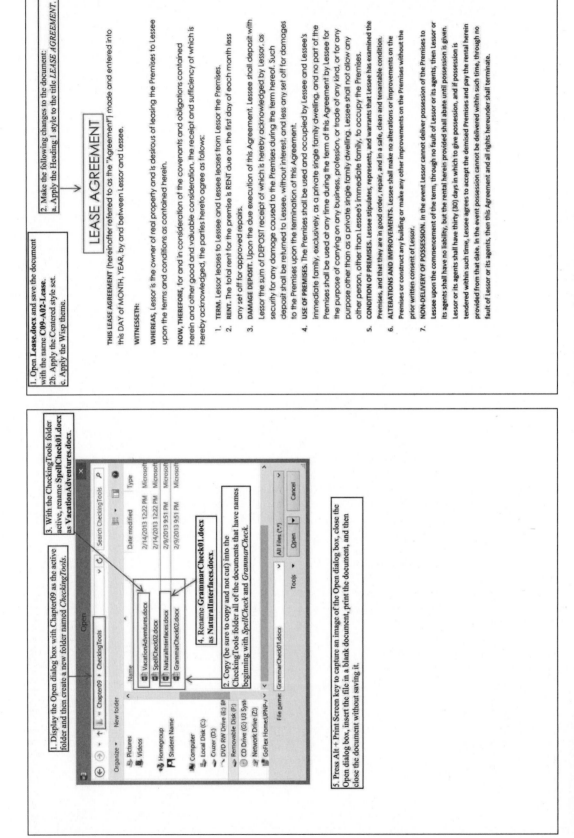

C09-A01-OpenDialogBox

1. Display the Open dialog box with Chapter09 as the active folder and then create a new folder named *CheckingTools*.

3. With the CheckingTools folder active, rename **SpellCheck01.docx** as **VacationAdventures.docx**.

4. Rename **GrammarCheck01.docx** as **NaturalInterfaces.docx**.

2. Copy (be sure to copy and not cut) into the CheckingTools folder all of the documents that have names beginning with *SpellCheck* and *GrammarCheck*.

5. Press Alt + Print Screen key to capture an image of the Open dialog box, close the Open dialog box, insert the file in a blank document, print the document, and then close the document without saving it.

C09-A02-Lease.docx (page 1 of 2)

1. Open **Lease.docx** and save the document with the name **C09-A02-Lease**.
2b. Apply the Centered style set.
c. Apply the Wisp theme.

2. Make the following changes to the document:
a. Apply the Heading 1 style to the title *LEASE AGREEMENT*.

LEASE AGREEMENT

THIS LEASE AGREEMENT (hereinafter referred to as the "Agreement") made and entered into this DAY of MONTH, YEAR, by and between Lessor and Lessee.

WITNESSETH:

WHEREAS, Lessor is the owner of real property and is desirous of leasing the Premises to Lessee upon the terms and conditions as contained herein.

NOW, THEREFORE, for and in consideration of the covenants and obligations contained herein and other good and valuable consideration, the receipt and sufficiency of which is hereby acknowledged, the parties hereto agree as follows:

1. **TERM.** Lessor leases to Lessee and Lessee leases from Lessor the Premises.

2. **RENT.** The total rent for the premise is RENT due on the first day of each month less any set off for approved repairs.

3. **DAMAGE DEPOSIT.** Upon the due execution of this Agreement, Lessee shall deposit with Lessor the sum of DEPOSIT receipt of which is hereby acknowledged by Lessor, as security for any damage caused to the Premises during the term hereof. Such deposit shall be returned to Lessee, without interest, and less any set off for damages to the Premises upon the termination of this Agreement.

4. **USE OF PREMISES.** The Premises shall be used and occupied by Lessee and Lessee's immediate family, exclusively, as a private single family dwelling, and no part of the Premises shall be used at any time during the term of this Agreement by Lessee for the purpose of carrying on any business, profession, or trade of any kind, or for any purpose other than as a private single family dwelling. Lessee shall not allow any other person, other than Lessee's immediate family, to occupy the Premises.

5. **CONDITION OF PREMISES.** Lessee stipulates, represents, and warrants that Lessee has examined the Premises, and that they are in good order, repair, and in a safe, clean and tenantable condition.

6. **ALTERATIONS AND IMPROVEMENTS.** Lessee shall make no alterations or improvements on the Premises or construct any building or make any other improvements on the Premises without the prior written consent of Lessor.

7. **NON-DELIVERY OF POSSESSION.** In the event Lessor cannot deliver possession of the Premises to Lessee upon the commencement of the term, through no fault of Lessor or its agents, then Lessor or its agents shall have no liability, but the rental herein provided shall abate until possession is given. Lessor or its agents shall have thirty (30) days in which to give possession, and if possession is tendered within such time, Lessee agrees to accept the demised Premises and pay the rental herein provided from that date. In the event possession cannot be delivered within such time, through no fault of Lessor or its agents, then this Agreement and all rights hereunder shall terminate.

LEASE AGREEMENT

THIS LEASE AGREEMENT (hereinafter referred to as the "Agreement") made and entered into this DAY of MONTH, YEAR, by and between Lessor and Lessee.

WITNESSETH:

WHEREAS, Lessor is the owner of real property and is desirous of leasing the Premises to Lessee upon the terms and conditions as contained herein.

NOW, THEREFORE, for and in consideration of the covenants and obligations contained herein and other good and valuable consideration, the receipt and sufficiency of which is hereby acknowledged, the parties hereto agree as follows:

1. **TERM.** Lessor leases to Lessee and Lessee leases from Lessor the Premises.

2. **RENT.** The total rent for the premise is RENT due on the first day of each month less any set off for approved repairs.

3. **DAMAGE DEPOSIT.** Upon the due execution of this Agreement, Lessee shall deposit with Lessor the sum of DEPOSIT receipt of which is hereby acknowledged by Lessor, as security for any damage caused to the Premises during the term hereof. Such deposit shall be returned to Lessee, without interest, and less any set off for damages to the Premises upon the termination of this Agreement.

4. **USE OF PREMISES.** The Premises shall be used and occupied by Lessee and Lessee's immediate family, exclusively, as a private single family dwelling, and no part of the Premises shall be used at any time during the term of this Agreement by Lessee for the purpose of carrying on any business, profession, or trade of any kind, or for any purpose other than as a private single family dwelling. Lessee shall not allow any other person, other than Lessee's immediate family, to occupy the Premises.

5. **CONDITION OF PREMISES.** Lessee stipulates, represents, and warrants that Lessee has examined the Premises, and that they are in good order, repair, and in a safe, clean and tenantable condition.

6. **ALTERATIONS AND IMPROVEMENTS.** Lessee shall make no alterations or improvements on the Premises or construct any building or make any other improvements on the Premises without the prior written consent of Lessor.

7. **NON-DELIVERY OF POSSESSION.** In the event Lessor cannot deliver possession of the Premises to Lessee upon the commencement of the term, through no fault of Lessor or its agents, then Lessor or its agents shall have no liability, but the rental herein provided shall abate until possession is given. Lessor or its agents shall have thirty (30) days in which to give possession, and if possession is tendered within such time, Lessee agrees to accept the demised Premises and

8. **UTILITIES.** Lessee shall be responsible for arranging for and paying for all utility services required on the Premises.

IN WITNESS WHEREOF the parties have reviewed the information above and certify, to the best of their knowledge, that the information provided by the signatory is true and accurate.

_____
Lessor

_____
Lessee

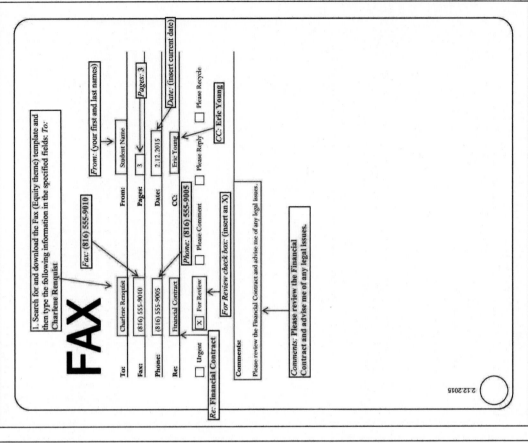

1. Search for and download the Fax (Equity theme) template and then type the following information in the specified fields: *To:* Charlene Renquist

Fax: (816) 555-9010

From: (your first and last names)

Pages: 3

Date: (insert current date)

FAX

To:	Charlene Renquist	From:	Student Name
Fax:	(816) 555-9010	Pages:	3
Phone:	(816) 555-9005	Date:	2.12.2015
Re:	Financial Contract	CC:	Eric Young

Phone: (816) 555-9005

☐ Urgent ☒ For Review ☐ Please Comment ☐ Please Reply ☐ Please Recycle

Re: Financial Contract

For Review check box: (insert an X)

CC: Eric Young

Comments:
Please review the Financial Contract and advise me of any legal issues.

Comments: Please review the Financial Contract and advise me of any legal issues.

2.12.2015

C09-A03-Fax.docx

---

pay the rental herein provided from that date. In the event possession cannot be delivered within such time, through no fault of Lessor or its agents, then this Agreement and all rights hereunder shall terminate.

8. UTILITIES. Lessee shall be responsible for arranging for and paying for all utility services required on the Premises.

IN WITNESS WHEREOF the parties have reviewed the information above and certify, to the best of their knowledge, that the information provided by the signatory is true and accurate.

_____
Lessor

_____
Lessee

8. Open **C09-A02-Lease.docx** and then save the document in PDF format with the name **C09-A02-Lease-PDF**. After viewing the document in Adobe Reader, click the Close button located in the upper right corner of the screen. (If the file opened in Windows Reader, position the mouse pointer at the top of the window, hold down the left mouse button, drag down to the bottom of the screen, and then release the mouse button.)

9. Open the **C09-A02-Lease-PDF.pdf** file in Word and click OK at the message telling you that Word will convert the PDF to an editable Word document.

10. Select the entire document and then change the font to Candara (if necessary, delete the blank page at the end of the document).

C09-A02-Lease.PDF (page 2 of 2)

5. At a blank document, write a memo to your instructor describing the steps you followed to download and create the calendar in **C09-A04-Calendar.docx**.

TO: Instructor Name

FROM: Student Name

DATE: February 12, 2015

SUBJECT: Creating a Calendar from a Template

To create a calendar from a template, simply search for a calendar option at the New backstage area. Choose a calendar based on the image, tone, and necessity it will provide. You can find weekly, monthly and yearly templates in casual, formal, and professional styles.

Double-click the template to download into a Word file. Modify any changes to the text and save the file to your computer.

C09-A04-Memo.docx

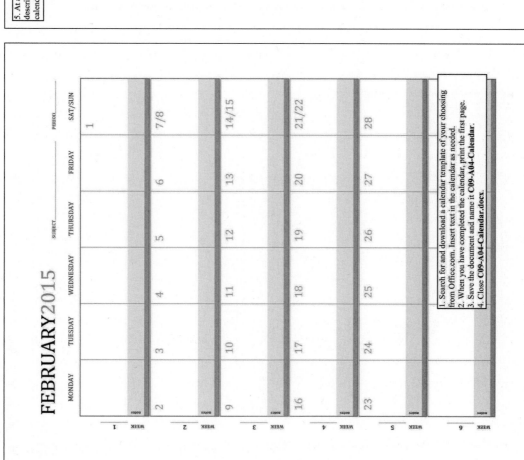

1. Search for and download a calendar template of your choosing from Office.com. Insert text in the calendar as needed.
2. When you have completed the calendar, print the first page.
3. Save the document and name it **C09-A04-Calendar.docx**.
4. Close **C09-A04-Calendar.docx**.

C09-A04-Calendar.docx

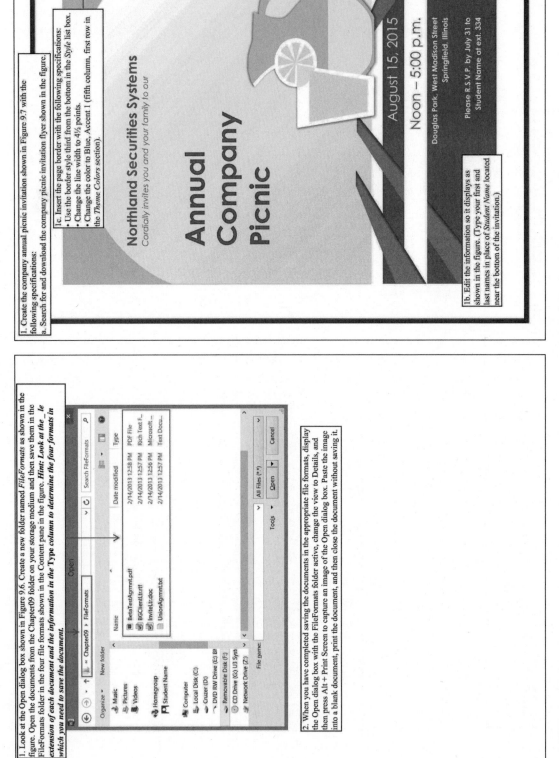

1. Create the company annual picnic invitation shown in Figure 9.7 with the following specifications:

a. Search for and download the company picnic invitation flyer shown in the figure.

1c. Insert the page border with the following specifications:
• Use the border style third from the bottom in the *Style* list box.
• Change the line width to 4½ points.
• Change the color to Blue, Accent 1 (fifth column, first row in the *Theme Colors* section).

Northland Securities Systems
Cordially invites you and your family to our

Annual Company Picnic

August 15, 2015

Noon – 5:00 p.m.

Douglas Park, West Madison Street
Springfield, Illinois

Please R.S.V.P. by July 31 to
Student Name at ext. 334

1b. Edit the information in the figure. (Type your first and last names in place of *Student Name* located near the bottom of the invitation.)

C09-A06-Invitation.docx

---

1. Look at the Open dialog box shown in Figure 9.6. Create a new folder named *FileFormats* as shown in the figure. Open the documents from the Chapter09 folder on your storage medium and then save them in the FileFormats folder in the four file formats shown in the figure. *Hint: Look at the _le extension of each document and the information in the Type column in the Content pane in the figure to determine the four formats in which you need to save the document.*

Open

← → ↑ ⧉ « Chapter09 ▶ FileFormats   ↻   Search FileFormats

Organize ▼   New folder

Name	Date modified	Type
BetaTestAgrmnt.pdf	2/14/2013 12:58 PM	PDF File
BigClientLtr.rtf	2/14/2013 12:57 PM	Rich Text F...
InviteLtr.doc	2/14/2013 12:56 PM	Microsoft...
UnionAgrmnt.txt	2/14/2013 12:57 PM	Text Docu...

★ Music
★ Pictures
★ Videos

★ Homegroup
☐ Student Name

🖥 Computer
💾 Local Disk (C:)
💿 Cruzer (D:)
💿 DVD RW Drive (E:) BP
💾 Removable Disk (F:)
💿 CD Drive (G:) U3 Syst
💾 Network Drive (Z:)

File name: All Files (*.*)

                                   Tools ▼   Open ▼   Cancel

2. When you have completed saving the documents in the appropriate file formats, display the Open dialog box with the FileFormats folder active, change the view to Details, and then press Alt + Print Screen to capture an image of the Open dialog box. Paste the image into a blank document, print the document, and then close the document without saving it.

C09-A05-OpenDialogBox

Chapter 10 Assessment Annotated Model Answers

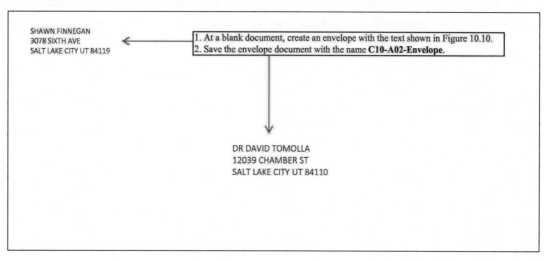

SHAWN FINNEGAN
3078 SIXTH AVE
SALT LAKE CITY UT 84119

1. At a blank document, create an envelope with the text shown in Figure 10.10.
2. Save the envelope document with the name **C10-A02-Envelope**.

DR DAVID TOMOLLA
12039 CHAMBER ST
SALT LAKE CITY UT 84110

C10-A02-Envelope.docx (page 1 of 2)

---

1. Open **BetaTestAgrmnt.docx, CompHardware.docx, and CompSecurity.docx**.
2. Make **CompHardware.docx** the active document.
3. Make **BetaTestAgrmnt.docx** the active document.
4. Arrange all of the windows.

COMPUTER HARDWARE

A computer consists of two broad categories of components: hardware and software. Computer hardware includes all of the physical components that make up the system unit plus other devices connected to it. These connected devices are referred to as *peripheral devices* because they are outside, or peripheral to, the computer. Examples include a monitor, keyboard, mouse, hard disk drive, camera, and printer. Some peripheral devices, such as the monitor and hard disk drive, are essential components of a personal computer system. Categories of hardware devices include the system unit, input devices, output devices, storage devices, and communication devices.

System Unit

The system unit is a relatively small plastic or metal cabinet that houses the electronic components, which process data into information. Inside the cabinet, the main circuit board, called the *motherboard*, provides for the installation and connection of other electronic components. Once installed on the motherboard, the components can communicate with each other, thereby allowing the processing of data into information. The motherboard has two components, the *central processing unit* (CPU), also called the *microprocessor* (or simply *processor*), and the internal memory. The processor consists of one or more electronic chips that read, interpret, and execute instructions that operate the computer and perform specific computing tasks. When a program is executed, the processor temporarily stores the program's instructions and the data needed for the instructions into the computer's memory. *Memory*, also called *primary storage*, consists of small electronic chips that provide temporary storage for instructions and data during processing.

Input Devices

An *input device* is a hardware device that allows users to enter program instructions, data, and commands into a computer. The program or application being used determines the type of input device needed. Common input devices are the keyboard, mouse, and microphone.

Output Devices

An *output device* is a device that makes information available to the user. Popular output devices include display screens (monitors), printers, television screens, and speakers. Some output devices, such as a printer, produce output in *hard copy* (tangible) form, such as on paper or plastic. Other output devices, such as a monitor, produce output in *soft copy* (intangible) form that can be viewed but not physically handled.

14. Scroll through both documents simultaneously. Notice the formatting differences between the two documents. Change the font size and paragraph shading in **C10-A01-CompHardware.docx** so they match the formatting in **Hardware.docx**.

5. Make **CompSecurity.docx** the active document and then minimize it.
6. Minimize the remaining documents.
7. Restore **BetaTestAgrmnt.docx**.
8. Restore **CompHardware.docx**.
9. Restore **CompSecurity.docx**.
10. Maximize and close **BetaTestAgrmnt.docx** and then maximize and close **CompSecurity.docx**.
11. Maximize **CompHardware.docx** and then save the document and name it C10-A01-CompHardware.
12. Open **Hardware.docx**.
13. View **C10-A01-CompHardware.docx** and **Hardware.docx** side by side.
15. Make **Hardware.docx** active and then close it.

C10-A01-CompHardware.docx

C10-A02-Envelope.docx (page 2 of 2)

LINDA GOULD 3210 CRANSTON ST PROVIDENCE RI 02903	ROBERT ALBRIGHT 10228 123 ST NE PROVIDENCE RI 02908	TRAVIS KANE 5532 S BROAD ST PROVIDENCE RI 02905
CHARLES WHITE 887 N 42 ST PROVIDENCE RI 02903	RAY PETROVICH 12309 45 AVE N PROVIDENCE RI 02904	BLAINE ISHAM 12110 141 ST SE PROVIDENCE RI 02907

1. Create mailing labels with the names and addresses shown in Figure 10.11. Use a label option of your choosing. (You may need to check with your instructor before choosing an option.)
2. Save the document with the name **C10-A03-Labels**.

C10-A03-Labels.docx

C10-A05-SALabels.docx

1. You can create a sheet of labels with the same information in each label either by typing the information in the *Address* text box at the Envelopes and Labels dialog box or by typing the desired information, selecting it, and then creating the label. Using the second technique, create the sheet of labels shown in Figure 10.12 with the following specifications:
   - At a blank document, type the company name and address (shown in the first label in Figure 10.12).
   - Set the text in 14-point Harlow Solid Italic and set the *S* in *Southland* and the *A* in *Aviation* in 20-point size. Change the font color to Blue.
   - Select the company name and address and then create the labels by displaying the Envelopes and Labels dialog box with the Labels tab selected and then clicking the New Document button. Use the Avery US Letter label, product number 5160 when creating the labels.
   - At the labels document, select the entire document and then click the Center button. (Doing this centers all of the names and addresses in each label.)

Southland Aviation
1500 Airport Way
Springdale, AR 72763

(repeated for all labels)

C10-A04-BGLabels.docx

2. Type the following name and address in the *Address* text box: Barrington & Gates 200 Tenth Street, Suite 100 Austin, TX 73341

5c. With the text in all of the labels selected, click the Align Center Left button located in the Alignment group on the TABLE TOOLS LAYOUT tab.

Barrington & Gates
200 Tenth Street, Suite 100
Austin, TX 73341

(repeated for all labels)

1. At a blank document, display the Envelopes and Labels dialog box with the Labels tab selected.
2. Click the New Document button.
3.
4. In a previous chapter, you learned how to indent paragraphs of text using the Left Indent marker on the horizontal ruler. You can also use this marker to increase the indent of text within labels. Increase the indent of the labels text by completing the following steps:
   a. Press Ctrl + A to select all of the labels.
   b. Drag the Left Indent marker on the horizontal ruler to the 0.5-inch marker.
   c. Click in any label to deselect the text.
5. With the insertion point positioned in a label, the TABLE TOOLS LAYOUT tabs display on the ribbon. With options on the TABLE TOOLS LAYOUT tab, you can adjust the vertical alignment of text within labels. You decide that the label text will look better if it is centered vertically in each label. To do this, complete the following steps:
   a. Click the TABLE TOOLS LAYOUT tab.
   b. Click the Select button at the left side of the TABLE TOOLS LAYOUT tab and then click *Select Table* at the drop-down list.
   d. Click in any label to deselect the text.

1. At a blank document, type your name and address and then apply formatting to enhance the appearance of the text. (You determine the font, font size, and font color.)
2. Create labels with your name and address. (You determine the label vendor and product number.)

STUDENT NAME
123 COLLEGE DRIVE
ANYTOWN, WA 98136

STUDENT NAME
123 COLLEGE DRIVE
ANYTOWN, WA 98136

STUDENT NAME
123 COLLEGE DRIVE
ANYTOWN, WA 98136

STUDENT NAME
123 COLLEGE DRIVE
ANYTOWN, WA 98136

STUDENT NAME
123 COLLEGE DRIVE
ANYTOWN, WA 98136

STUDENT NAME
123 COLLEGE DRIVE
ANYTOWN, WA 98136

STUDENT NAME
123 COLLEGE DRIVE
ANYTOWN, WA 98136

STUDENT NAME
123 COLLEGE DRIVE
ANYTOWN, WA 98136

STUDENT NAME
123 COLLEGE DRIVE
ANYTOWN, WA 98136

STUDENT NAME
123 COLLEGE DRIVE
ANYTOWN, WA 98136

STUDENT NAME
123 COLLEGE DRIVE
ANYTOWN, WA 98136

STUDENT NAME
123 COLLEGE DRIVE
ANYTOWN, WA 98136

STUDENT NAME
123 COLLEGE DRIVE
ANYTOWN, WA 98136

STUDENT NAME
123 COLLEGE DRIVE
ANYTOWN, WA 98136

STUDENT NAME
123 COLLEGE DRIVE
ANYTOWN, WA 98136

STUDENT NAME
123 COLLEGE DRIVE
ANYTOWN, WA 98136

STUDENT NAME
123 COLLEGE DRIVE
ANYTOWN, WA 98136

STUDENT NAME
123 COLLEGE DRIVE
ANYTOWN, WA 98136

STUDENT NAME
123 COLLEGE DRIVE
ANYTOWN, WA 98136

STUDENT NAME
123 COLLEGE DRIVE
ANYTOWN, WA 98136

STUDENT NAME
123 COLLEGE DRIVE
ANYTOWN, WA 98136

STUDENT NAME
123 COLLEGE DRIVE
ANYTOWN, WA 98136

STUDENT NAME
123 COLLEGE DRIVE
ANYTOWN, WA 98136

STUDENT NAME
123 COLLEGE DRIVE
ANYTOWN, WA 98136

STUDENT NAME
123 COLLEGE DRIVE
ANYTOWN, WA 98136

STUDENT NAME
123 COLLEGE DRIVE
ANYTOWN, WA 98136

STUDENT NAME
123 COLLEGE DRIVE
ANYTOWN, WA 98136

STUDENT NAME
123 COLLEGE DRIVE
ANYTOWN, WA 98136

STUDENT NAME
123 COLLEGE DRIVE
ANYTOWN, WA 98136

STUDENT NAME
123 COLLEGE DRIVE
ANYTOWN, WA 98136

Unit 2 Performance Assessment Annotated Model Answers

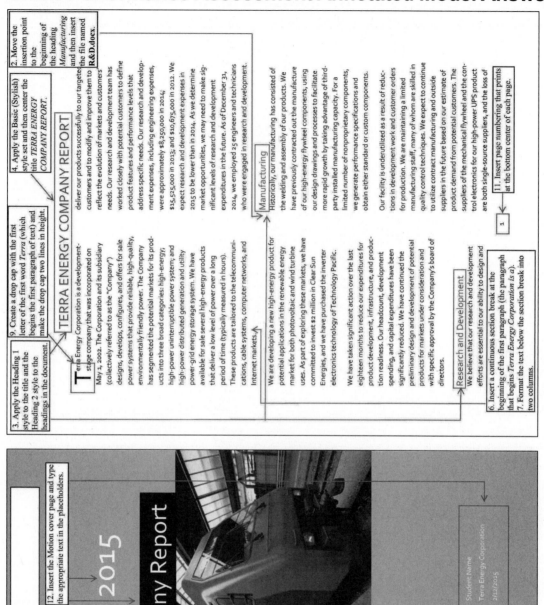

1. Open **Terra.docx** and save the document with the name **U2-PA01-Terra.**
5. Apply the Frame theme and then change the theme colors to Blue II.
10. Manually hyphenate the text in the document.

12. Insert the Motion cover page and type the appropriate text in the placeholders.

2015

Terra Energy Company Report

Student Name
Terra Energy Corporation
2/12/2015

3. Apply the Heading 1 style to the title and the Heading 2 style to the headings in the document.

9. Create a drop cap with the first letter of the first word *Terra* (which begins the first paragraph of text) and make the drop cap two lines in height.

4. Apply the Basic (Stylish) style set and then center the title *TERRA ENERGY COMPANY REPORT.*

2. Move the insertion point to the beginning of the heading *Manufacturing* and then insert the file named **R&D.docx.**

TERRA ENERGY COMPANY REPORT

Terra Energy Corporation is a development-stage company that was incorporated on May 1, 2002. The Corporation and its subsidiary (collectively referred to as the "Company") designs, develops, configures, and offers for sale power systems that provide reliable, high-quality, environmentally friendly power. The Company has segmented the potential markets for its products into three broad categories: high-energy; high-power uninterruptible power system; and high-power distributed generation and utility power-grid energy storage system. We have available for sale several high-energy products that deliver a low level of power over a long period of time (typically measured in hours). These products are tailored to the telecommunications, cable systems, computer networks, and Internet markets.

We are developing a new high-energy product for potential applications in the renewable energy market for both photovoltaic and wind turbine uses. As part of exploring these markets, we have committed to invest $2 million in Clear Sun Energies, and we have purchased the inverter electronics technology of Technology Pacific.

We have taken significant action over the last eighteen months to reduce our expenditures for product development, infrastructure, and production readiness. Our headcount, development spending, and capital expenditures have been significantly reduced. We have continued the preliminary design and development of potential products for markets under consideration and with specific approval by the Company's board of directors.

Research and Development

We believe that our research and development efforts are essential to our ability to design and

deliver our products successfully to our targeted customers and to modify and improve them to reflect the evolution of markets and customers' needs. Our research and development team has worked closely with potential customers to define product features and performance levels that address specific needs. Our research and development expenses, including engineering expenses, were approximately $8,250,000 in 2014; $15,525,000 in 2013; and $10,675,000 in 2012. We expect research and development expenses in 2015 to be lower than in 2014. As we determine market opportunities, we may need to make significant levels of research and development expenditures in the future. As of December 31, 2014, we employed 25 engineers and technicians who were engaged in research and development.

Manufacturing

Historically, our manufacturing has consisted of the welding and assembly of our products. We have previously contracted out the manufacture of our high-energy flywheel components, using our design drawings and processes to facilitate more rapid growth by taking advantage of third-party installed manufacturing capacity. For a limited number of nonproprietary components, we generate performance specifications and obtain either standard or custom components.

Our facility is underutilized as a result of reductions in development work and customer orders for production. We are maintaining a limited manufacturing staff, many of whom are skilled in quality control techniques. We expect to continue to utilize contract manufacturing and outside suppliers in the future based on our estimate of product demand from potential customers. The suppliers of the mechanical flywheel and the control electronics for our high-power UPS product are both single-source suppliers, and the loss of

6. Insert a continuous section break at the beginning of the first paragraph (the paragraph that begins *Terra Energy Corporation is a*).
7. Format the text below the section break into two columns.

11. Insert page numbering that prints at the bottom center of each page.

1

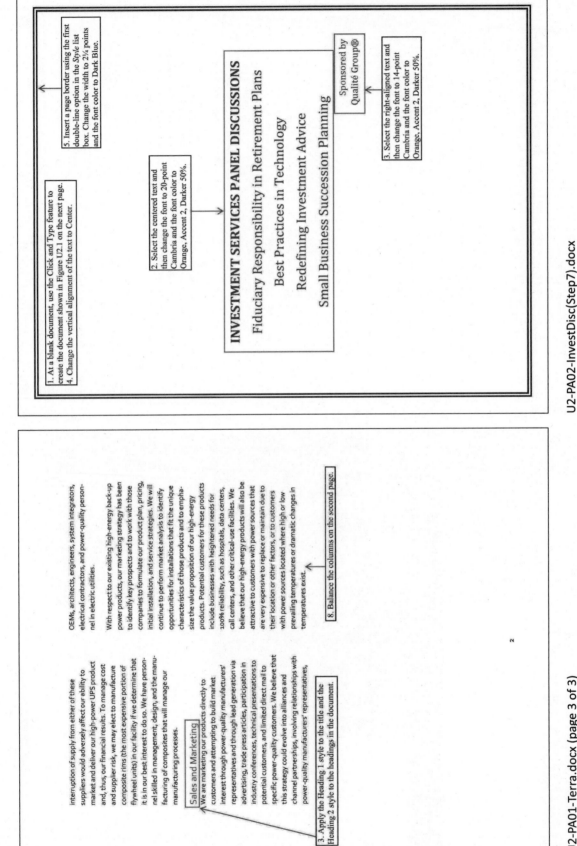

INVESTMENT SERVICES PANEL DISCUSSIONS

Fiduciary Responsibility in Retirement Plans

Best Practices in Technology

Redefining Investment Advice

Small Business Succession Planning

Sponsored by
Qualité Group®

1. At a blank document, use the Click and Type feature to create the document shown in Figure U2.1 on the next page.
4. Change the vertical alignment of the text to Center.

2. Select the centered text and then change the font to 20-point Cambria and the font color to Orange, Accent 2, Darker 50%.

3. Select the right-aligned text and then change the font to 14-point Cambria and the font color to Orange, Accent 2, Darker 50%.

5. Insert a page border using the first double-line option in the *Style* list box. Change the width to 2¼ points and the font color to Dark Blue.

U2-PA02-InvestDisc(Step7).docx

interruption of supply from either of these suppliers would adversely affect our ability to market and deliver our high-power UPS product and, thus, our financial results. To manage cost and supplier risk, we may elect to manufacture composite rims (the most expensive portion of flywheel units) in our facility if we determine that it is in our best interest to do so. We have personnel skilled in management, design, and the manufacturing of composites that will manage our manufacturing processes.

OEMs, architects, engineers, system integrators, electrical contractors, and power-quality personnel in electric utilities.

With respect to our existing high-energy back-up power products, our marketing strategy has been to identify key prospects and to work with those companies to formulate our product plan, pricing, initial installation, and service strategies. We will continue to perform market analysis to identify opportunities for installations that fit the unique characteristics of those products and to emphasize the value proposition of our high-energy products. Potential customers for these products include businesses with heightened needs for 100% reliability, such as hospitals, data centers, call centers, and other critical-use facilities. We believe that our high-energy products will also be attractive to customers with power sources that are very expensive to replace or maintain due to their location or other factors, or to customers with power sources located where high or low prevailing temperatures or dramatic changes in temperatures exist.

Sales and Marketing

We are marketing our products directly to customers and attempting to build market interest through power-quality manufacturers' representatives and through lead generation via advertising, trade press articles, participation in industry conferences, technical presentations to potential customers, and limited direct mail to specific power-quality customers. We believe that this strategy could evolve into alliances and channel partnerships, involving relationships with power-quality manufacturers' representatives,

3. Apply the Heading 1 style to the title and the Heading 2 style to the headings in the document.

8. Balance the columns on the second page.

2

U2-PA01-Terra.docx (page 3 of 3)

3. Move to the end of the paragraph in the *Types of Viruses* section, press the spacebar, and then type (Pie Chart).

5. Move the insertion point to the end of the paragraph in the *Types of Viruses* section (following the *(Pie Chart)* text), press the spacebar, and then insert a bookmark named *Types*.

10. Select the text *(Pie Chart)* that you inserted at the end of the paragraph in the *Types of Viruses* section and then insert a hyperlink to the Excel file named **Viruses.xlsx**, located in the Unit02PA folder on your storage medium.

COMPUTER VIRUSES

One of the most familiar forms of risk to computer security is the computer virus. A computer virus is a program written by a hacker or cracker designed to perform some kind of trick upon an unsuspecting victim. The trick performed in some cases is mild, such as drawing an offensive image on the screen, or changing all of the characters in a document to another language. Sometimes the trick is much more severe, such as reformatting the hard drive and erasing all the data, or damaging the motherboard so that it cannot operate properly.

Types of Viruses

Viruses can be categorized by their effect, which include nuisance, data-destructive, espionage, and hardware-destructive. A nuisance virus usually does no real damage, but is rather just an inconvenience. The most difficult part of a computer to replace is the data on the hard drive. The installed programs, the documents, databases, and saved emails form the heart of a personal computer. A data-destructive virus is designed to destroy this data. Some viruses are designed to create a backdoor into a system to bypass security. Called espionage viruses, they do no damage, but rather allow a hacker or cracker to enter the system later for the purpose of stealing data or spying on the work of the competitor. Very rarely, a virus is created that attempts to damage the hardware of the computer system itself. Called hardware-destructive viruses, these bits of programming can weaken or destroy chips, drives, and other components. (Pie Chart)

Methods of Virus Operation

Viruses can create effects that range from minor and annoying to highly destructive, and are operated and transmitted by a variety of methods. An email virus is normally transmitted as an attachment to a message sent over the Internet. Email viruses require the victim to click on the attachment and cause it to execute. Another common form of virus transmission is by a macro, a small subprogram that allows users to customize and automate certain functions. A macro virus is written specifically for one program, which then becomes infected when it opens a file with the virus stored in its macros. The boot sector of a floppy disk or hard disk contains a variety of information, including how the disk is organized and whether it is capable of loading an operating system. When a disk is left in a drive and the computer reboots, the operating system automatically reads the boot sector to learn about that disk and to attempt to start any operating system on that disk. A boot sector virus is designed to alter the boot sector of a disk, so that whenever the operating system reads the boot sector, the computer will automatically become infected.

Other methods of virus infection include the Trojan horse virus, which hides inside another legitimate program or data file, and the stealth virus, which is designed to hide itself from detection software. Polymorphic viruses alter themselves to prevent antivirus software from detecting them by examining familiar patterns. Polymorphic viruses alter themselves randomly as they move from computer to computer, making detection more difficult. Multipartite viruses alter their form of attack. Their name derives from their ability to attack in several different ways. They may first infect the boot sector and then later move on to become a Trojan horse type by infecting a disk file. These viruses are more sophisticated, and therefore more difficult to guard against. Another type of virus is the logic bomb, which generally sits dormant waiting for a specific event or set of conditions to occur. A famous logic bomb was the widely publicized Michelangelo virus, which infected personal computers and caused them to display a message on the artist's birthday.

6. Move the insertion point to the end of the first paragraph in the *Methods of Virus Operation* section and then insert a bookmark named *Effects*.

7. Move the insertion point to the end of the second paragraph in the *Methods of Virus Operation* section and then insert a bookmark named *Infection*.

STUDENT NAME

2c. Insert the Retrospect footer and type your first and last names at the left side of the footer.

U2-PA03-ComputerViruses.docx (page 1 of 2)

---

8. Change the page orientation to landscape.

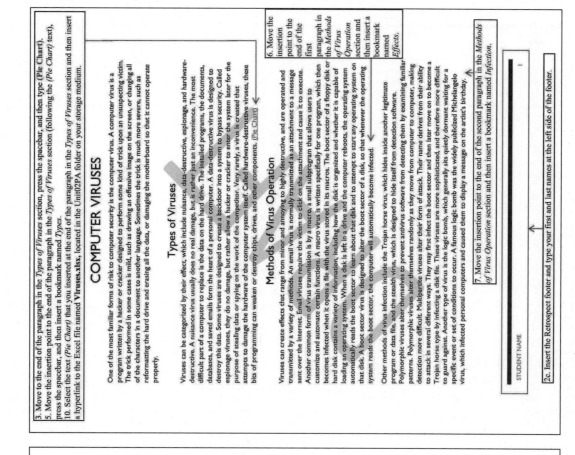

INVESTMENT SERVICES PANEL DISCUSSIONS

Fiduciary Responsibility in Retirement Plans

Best Practices in Technology

Redefining Investment Advice

Small Business Succession Planning

Sponsored by
Qualité Group®

U2-PA02-InvestDisc(Step9).docx

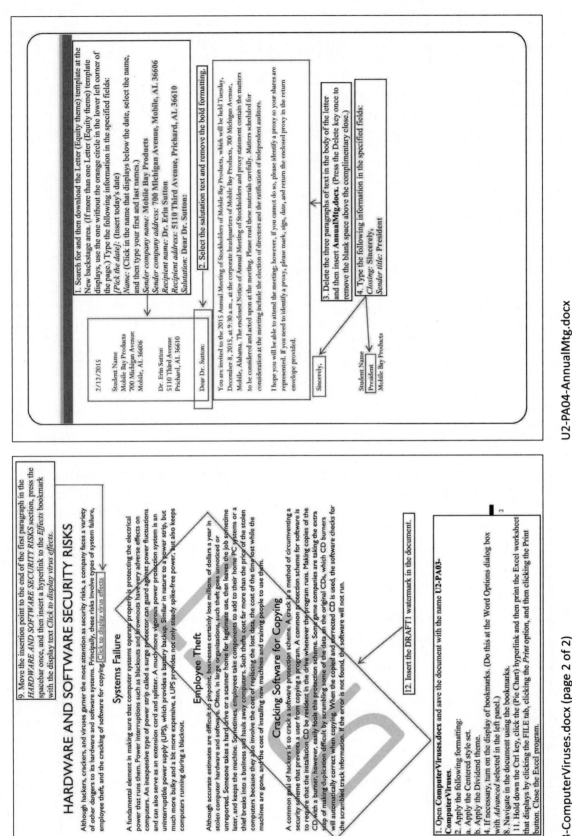

1. Search for and then download the Letter (Equity theme) template at the New backstage area. (If more than one Letter (Equity theme) template displays, use the one without the orange circle in the lower left corner of the page.) Type the following information in the specified fields:
[Pick the date]: (Insert today's date)
Name: (Click in the name that displays below the date, select the name, and then type your first and last names.)
Sender company name: Mobile Bay Products
Sender company address: 700 Michigan Avenue, Mobile, AL 36606
Recipient name: Dr. Erin Sutton
Recipient address: 5110 Third Avenue, Prichard, AL 36610
Salutation: Dear Dr. Sutton:

2. Select the salutation text and remove the bold formatting.

3. Delete the three paragraphs of text in the body of the letter and then insert **AnnualMtg.docx**. (Press the Delete key once to remove the blank space above the complimentary close.)
4. Type the following information in the specified fields:
Closing: Sincerely,
Sender title: President

2/12/2015

Student Name
Mobile Bay Products
700 Michigan Avenue
Mobile, AL 36606

Dr. Erin Sutton
5110 Third Avenue
Prichard, AL 36610

Dear Dr. Sutton:

You are invited to the 2015 Annual Meeting of Stockholders of Mobile Bay Products, which will be held Tuesday, December 8, 2015, at 9:30 a.m., at the corporate headquarters of Mobile Bay Products, 700 Michigan Avenue, Mobile, Alabama. The enclosed Notice of Annual Meeting of Stockholders and proxy statement contain the matters to be considered and acted upon at the meeting. Please read these materials carefully. Matters scheduled for consideration at the meeting include the election of directors and the ratification of independent auditors.

I hope you will be able to attend the meeting; however, if you cannot do so, please identify a proxy so your shares are represented. If you need to identify a proxy, please mark, sign, date, and return the enclosed proxy in the return envelope provided.

Sincerely,

Student Name
President
Mobile Bay Products

---

9. Move the insertion point to the end of the first paragraph in the *HARDWARE AND SOFTWARE SECURITY RISKS* section, press the spacebar once, and then insert a hyperlink to the *Effects* bookmark with the display text *Click to display virus effects*.

HARDWARE AND SOFTWARE SECURITY RISKS

Although hackers, crackers, and viruses garner the most attention as security risks, a company faces a variety of other dangers to its hardware and software systems. Principally, these risks involve types of system failure, employee theft, and the cracking of software for copying. Click to display virus effects

Systems Failure

A fundamental element in making sure that computer systems operate properly is protecting the electrical power that runs them. Power interruptions such as blackouts and brownouts have very adverse effects on computers. An inexpensive type of power strip called a surge protector can guard against power fluctuations and can also serve as an extension cord and splitter. A much more vigorous power protection system is an uninterruptible power supply (UPS), which provides a battery backup. Similar in nature to a power strip, but much more bulky and a bit more expensive, a UPS provides not only steady spike-free power, but also keeps computers running during a blackout.

Employee Theft

Although accurate estimates are difficult to pinpoint, businesses certainly lose millions of dollars a year in stolen computer hardware and software. Often, in large organizations, such theft goes unnoticed or unreported. Someone takes a hard drive or a scanner home for legitimate use, then leaves the job sometime later, and keeps the machine. Sometimes, employees take components to add to their home PC systems or a thief breaks into a business and hauls away computers. Such thefts cost far more than the price of the stolen computers because they also involve the cost of replacing the lost data, the cost of the time lost while the machines are gone, and the cost of installing new machines and training people to use them.

Cracking Software for Copying

A common goal of hackers is to crack a software protection scheme. A crack is a method of circumventing a security scheme that prevents a user from copying a program. A common protection scheme for software is to require that the installation CD be resident in the drive whenever the program runs. Making copies of the CD with a burner, however, easily fools this protection scheme. Some game companies are taking the extra step of making duplication difficult by scrambling some of the data on the original CDs, which CD burners will automatically correct when copying. When the copied and corrected CD is used, the software checks for the scrambled crack information. If the error is not found, the software will not run.

12. Insert the DRAFT1 watermark in the document.

---

1. Open **ComputerViruses.docx** and save the document with the name **U2-PA03-ComputerViruses.**
2. Apply the following formatting:
a. Apply the Centered style set.
b. Apply the Dividend theme.
4. If necessary, turn on the display of bookmarks. (Do this at the Word Options dialog box with *Advanced* selected in the left panel.)
8. Navigate in the document using the bookmarks.
11. Hold down the Ctrl key, click the (Pie Chart) hyperlink and then print the Excel worksheet that displays by clicking the FILE tab, clicking the *Print* option, and then clicking the Print button. Close the Excel program.

Page 2 of 2

Employee Handbook

6. Insert a page break at the beginning of the text *Reappointment.*

Reappointment: You may be reappointed to a class that you formerly held or to a comparable class if you meet the current minimum qualifications and receive the appointing authority's approval. If you are a probationary employee, you must complete a new probationary period. You cannot be reappointed to a position at grade 20 or above if the position is allocated at a higher level than the position you formerly held.

Demotion: An employee may request or accept a demotion to a position in a class with a lower grade level if the employee meets the minimum qualifications and if the appointing authority approves. You may not demote through non-competitive means to a position at grade 20 or higher if the position is allocated to a higher grade level than the position you currently hold.

Promotion: Promotion is advancement to a vacant position in a class that has a higher grade than the class previously held. As an employee of the company, you may compete in recruitments for promotional openings when you have served six months (full-time equivalent) of consecutive service. When you accept a promotion, you will be required to serve a trial period of either six months or one year. If you fail to attain permanent status in a vacant position to which you were promoted, you shall be restored to your former position.

2/12/2015 3:01 PM

7. Move the insertion point to the end of the document and then insert the current date and time.

1. Open **EmpAppoints.docx** and save the document with the name **U2-PA05-EmpAppoints.**
2. Change the top, left, and right margins to 1.25 inches.
3. Apply the Minimalist style set.
4. Apply the Slice theme.

pg. 2

Page 1 of 2

8. Insert the Austin header and type
Employee Handbook for the document title.

Employee Handbook

3. Apply the Heading 1 style to the title *EMPLOYMENT APPOINTMENTS* and the Heading 2 style to the heading *Types of Appointments.*

EMPLOYMENT APPOINTMENTS

Acceptance by an applicant of an offer of employment by an appointing authority and their mutual agreement to the date of hire is known as an appointment.

Types of Appointments

New Hire: When you initially accept an appointment, you are considered a new hire. As a new hire, you will be required to serve a probationary period of either six months or one year.

Reemployment: Reemployment is a type of appointment that does not result in a break in service. The types of reemployment are as follows:

1. Military reemployment: Any remaining portion of a probationary period must be completed upon return to the company.
2. Reemployment of a permanent employee who has been laid off:
   Completion of a new probationary period is required if the employee is reemployed in a different class or in a different department.
3. Reemployment due to reclassification of a position to a lower class.
4. Reemployment of seasonal employees.
5. Reemployment due to a permanent disability arising from an injury sustained at work.

Further information on this subject can be obtained by contacting your personnel representative or a representative in the human resources department.

Reinstatement: If you have resigned from company service as a permanent employee in good standing, you may be reinstated to the same or a similar class within a two-year period following termination.

The probationary period following reinstatement may be waived, but you will not be eligible to compete in promotional examinations until you have completed six months of permanent service. You cannot be reinstated to a position that is at grade 20 or above if the position is allocated at a higher grade level than the position you held at the time of termination.

pg. 1

9. Insert the Austin footer.

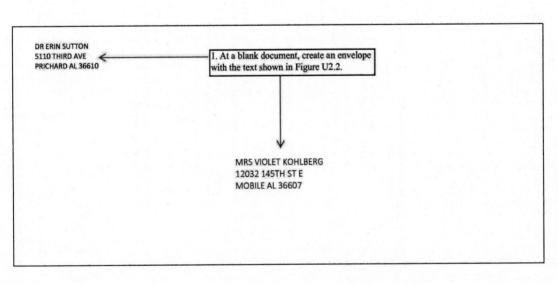

DR ERIN SUTTON
5110 THIRD AVE
PRICHARD AL 36610

I. At a blank document, create an envelope
with the text shown in Figure U2.2.

MRS VIOLET KOHLBERG
12032 145TH ST E
MOBILE AL 36607

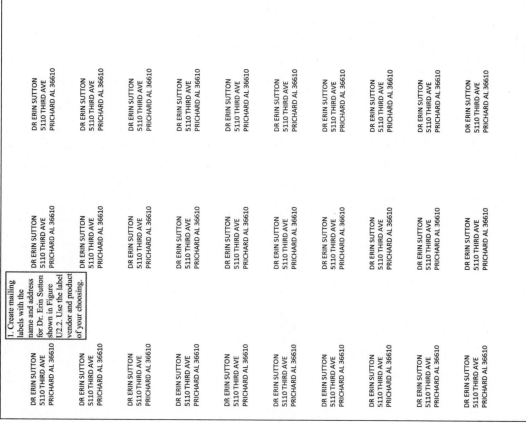

2. • Insert the Ion (Dark) header and footer.

• Set the text in 12-point Cambria and set the title in 16-point Cambria.

2. • Apply bullets to the text as shown in the figure and then decrease the indent so the bullets align at the left margin.

ENHANCING A PRESENTATION

Many oral presentations can be enhanced with the use of visual aids: illustrations, diagrams, models, and other materials listeners can see. Selecting appropriate visual aids and handling them purposefully are the keys to their effective use.

Using Visual Aids

Using visuals is a good idea if doing so will help support the audience's understanding of your message. Here are some tips on deciding whether and how to include visual aids:

- For some subjects, such as art and travel, the value of using visual aids is obvious.
- Using visuals also makes sense in a how-to speech in which you demonstrate a process.
- Visuals are useful, as well, for topics that involve statistics and other numbers, which lend themselves to charts and graphs. In any case, avoid using visual aids as filler for your presentation.
- Choose a reasonable number and variety of visual aids. What matters is the appropriateness, not the quantity, of items. In fact, having too many visuals may interfere with your delivery and make your presentation run over the allotted time.

Locating Visual Aids

There are many sources of visual aids. Photographs, reproductions of artwork, and charts and diagrams are available in magazines, newspapers, and books and on the Internet. Some libraries have folders containing pamphlets, illustrations, and similar materials. If you photocopy printed materials or download items from the Internet, be sure you follow copyright law. For assistance, check with your teacher or librarian. Another option is to create visual aids, such as charts of statistics. Prepare each chart on a large piece of cardboard or tag board using felt-tip pens. Ensure that all type and graphics are legible. At the bottom of the chart, in smaller type, provide the source of the information.

Practicing Your Presentation

If you plan to use an overhead or PowerPoint projector, make sure the display can be viewed clearly from all areas of the room. Likewise, ensure that everyone will be able to see any photograph, chart, or diagram you display. Audience members will lose interest and become distracted if you use visuals they cannot see. Passing materials among audience members may distract their attention from your presentation. If you need to distribute materials, place them on audience members' seats

ENHANCING A PRESENTATION   STUDENT NAME

2. • Insert the Ion (Dark) header and footer.

U2-PA08-VisualAids.docx (page 1 of 2)

---

1. Create mailing labels with the name and address for Dr. Erin Sutton shown in Figure U2.2. Use the label vendor and product of your choosing.

DR ERIN SUTTON
5110 THIRD AVE
PRICHARD AL 36610

(mailing labels repeated in a grid)

U2-PA07-Labels.docx

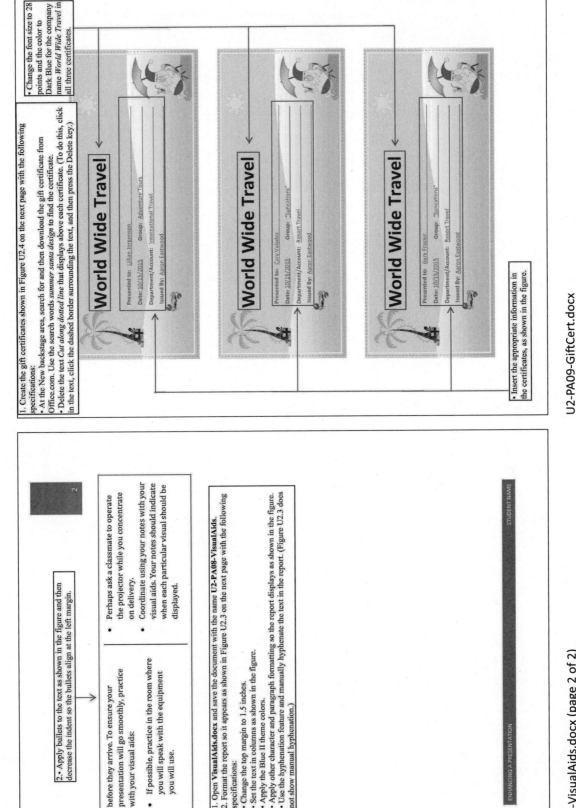

1. Create the gift certificates shown in Figure U2.4 on the next page with the following specifications:
• At the New backstage area, search for and then download the gift certificate from Office.com. Use the search words *summer santa design* to find the certificate.
• Delete the text *Cut along dotted line* that displays above each certificate. (To do this, click in the text, click the dashed border surrounding the text, and then press the Delete key.)

• Change the font size to 28 points and the color to Dark Blue for the company name *World Wide Travel* in all three certificates.

• Insert the appropriate information in the certificates, as shown in the figure.

World Wide Travel

Presented to: Lillian Jorgenson
Date: 10/15/2015   Group: Adventure Tours
Department/Account: International Travel
Issued By: Aaron Eastwood

World Wide Travel

Presented to: Cary Valadez
Date: 10/15/2015   Group: "Suncations"
Department/Account: Resort Travel
Issued By: Aaron Eastwood

World Wide Travel

Presented to: Gary Frazier
Date: 10/15/2015   Group: "Suncations"
Department/Account: Resort Travel
Issued By: Aaron Eastwood

U2-PA09-GiftCert.docx

---

2 • Apply bullets to the text as shown in the figure and then decrease the indent so the bullets align at the left margin.

before they arrive. To ensure your presentation will go smoothly, practice with your visual aids:
• If possible, practice in the room where you will speak with the equipment you will use.

• Perhaps ask a classmate to operate the projector while you concentrate on delivery.
• Coordinate using your notes with your visual aids. Your notes should indicate when each particular visual should be displayed.

1. Open **VisualAids.docx** and save the document with the name **U2-PA08-VisualAids**.
2. Format the report so it appears as shown in Figure U2.3 on the next page with the following specifications:
• Change the top margin to 1.5 inches.
• Set the text in columns as shown in the figure.
• Apply the Blue II theme colors.
• Apply other character and paragraph formatting so the report displays as shown in the figure. (Figure U2.3 does not show manual hyphenation.)
• Use the hyphenation feature and manually hyphenate the text in the report.

STUDENT NAME

ENHANCING A PRESENTATION

U2-PA08-VisualAids.docx (page 2 of 2)

COMPUTER USE GUIDELINES

1. General

MBP provides computing services to employees and contractors. This document outlines MBP's guidelines for confidentiality and privacy, copyrights, computer accounts and passwords, computer and data security, electronic communications, and networks.

2. Confidentiality and Privacy

Everyone—including managers, supervisors, and systems administrators—shall respect and protect the privacy of others. This document defines the limited conditions under which access to information and files can be obtained. Although MBP is committed to protecting individual privacy and information privacy, it cannot guarantee that correspondence and information stored and transmitted through company computer networks and systems are private. Because confidential information is often stored on desktop machines, displayed on screens, or printed on paper that could be publicly viewed, users need to control access to such information by implementing the following safeguards:

- using passwords
- turning screens away from public view
- logging out of systems when leaving the work area
- shredding reports containing private information prior to disposal
- clearing confidential information off desks in public areas

3. Copyrights

Laws that protect the owners of intellectual, textual, music, audio, photographic, artistic, and graphic property apply to all computer media such as software, electronic library material, and paid subscriptions. MBP is committed to protecting copyrights.

3.1. Software Copyrights

Commercial programs produced for use on computers are protected by copyright. Copying computer software without authorization violates federal copyright law. Payment for a software product represents a license fee to use a designated number of copies. The buyer does not own the software but merely buys a license to use it. The license is not a blanket authorization to copy.

3.1.1. Site Licenses

MBP enters into site license agreements with commercial vendors for company-wide use of certain software products. MBP currently has site licenses for products, including word-processing, spreadsheet, and database management applications software. Before buying a particular product, departments should contact the technical support department to determine whether MBP has a site license or volume purchase discounts for the software in question.

3.2. Software Developed Internally

MBP personnel may develop computer programs using company resources. Such software may be subject to the company's intellectual property policy.

1

2015

Situation: You work in the technology support department at Mobile Bay Products and your supervisor has asked you to format a document that outlines computer use guidelines. Open **CompGuidelines.docx**, save the document with the name **U2-PA10-CompGuidelines.docx**, and then format it by applying or inserting at least the following elements: a style set; a heading style; a header, footer, and/or page numbers; and a cover page. Save, print, and then close **U2-PA10-CompGuidelines.docx**. Use one of the Word letter templates and write a letter to your instructor describing how you formatted **U2-PA10-CompGuidelines.docx**, including the reasons you chose specific formats.

Computer Use Guidelines

STUDENT NAME

4. Computer Accounts and Passwords

MBP provides computer accounts to authorized users for access to various company systems. These accounts are a means of operator identification, and passwords are used as a security measure. Account use is a privilege not a right.

4.1. Account Authentication

Passwords, PINs, and other identifiers authenticate the user's identity and match the user to the privileges granted on company computer networks and systems. A password is a security measure designed to prevent unauthorized persons from logging on with another person's computer account and reading or changing data accessible to that user. Users should create passwords carefully and handle them with care and attention. For this security feature to be effective, the user must protect the secrecy of his or her password. Each user should adhere to the following safeguards:

- change his or her password regularly and at any time he or she feels the password may have been compromised
- avoid writing the password down
- not disclose or share the password with anyone
- choose a password that is easy to remember but hard to guess
- apply similar measures to all authentication methods such as PINs

4.2. Account Termination and Locking

When an individual leaves MBP, his or her account(s) will be locked and eventually deleted. If misuse or theft is detected or suspected, account(s) will be locked according to the company's procedures.

5. Computer and Data Security

Everyone at MBP shares responsibility for the security of computer equipment and information.

5.1. Physical Security

Everyone is responsible for the proper use and protection of company computer equipment. Examples of protection measures include the following:

- locking areas after business hours or at other times when not in use
- taking special precautions for high-value, portable equipment
- following company policies for taking computer equipment off campus

5.2. Information Security

Security of information is an essential responsibility of computer system managers and users alike. Users are responsible for the following:

- ensuring the routine backup of their files
- using data only for approved company purposes
- ensuring the security and validity of information transferred from company systems

5.3. Computer Viruses

Because of the proliferation of computer viruses and the damage they can cause, MBP strongly recommends that users keep current anti-viral software active and scan frequently for viruses. For example, the following should be scanned for viruses:

2

U2-PA10-CompGuidelines.docx (page 3 of 4)

- attachments
- downloaded files
- shared diskettes, CDs, and other media

6. Electronic Communications

Electronic communications include information in any form such as data, audio, video, and text that is conveyed or stored electronically, for example, by email, web pages, and in files. Electronic communications are intended to further the education, research, and public service mission of MBP and may be used for incidental personal use but may not be used for commercial purposes or profit-making. The following types of communication are prohibited:

- chain letters, pyramid schemes, and unauthorized mass mailings
- fraudulent, threatening, defamatory, obscene, harassing, or illegal materials
- nonwork- or nonclass-related information sent to an individual who requests the information not be sent
- copyright law violation
- commercial or personal advertisements, solicitations, promotions, destructive programs, or any other unauthorized use

Users should understand that electronic communications, because of their nature, can be intentionally or unintentionally viewed by others or forwarded to others and are therefore inherently not private. In addition, addressing errors, system malfunctions, and system management may result in communications being viewed and/or read by other individuals and/or system administrators.

3

U2-PA10-CompGuidelines.docx (page 4 of 4)

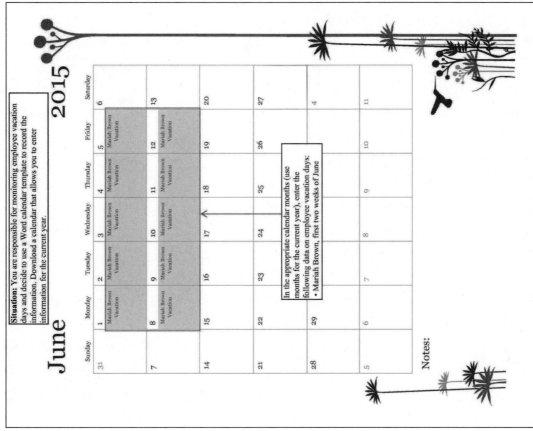

Situation: You are responsible for monitoring employee vacation days and decide to use a Word calendar template to record the information. Download a calendar that allows you to enter information for the current year.

June 2015

Sunday	Monday	Tuesday	Wednesday	Thursday	Friday	Saturday
31	1 Mariah Brown Vacation	2 Mariah Brown Vacation	3 Mariah Brown Vacation	4 Mariah Brown Vacation	5 Mariah Brown Vacation	6
7	8 Mariah Brown Vacation	9 Mariah Brown Vacation	10 Mariah Brown Vacation	11 Mariah Brown Vacation	12 Mariah Brown Vacation	13
14	15	16	17	18	19	20
21	22	23	24	25	26	27
28	29	30				4
5	6	7	8	9	10	11

In the appropriate calendar months (use months for the current year), enter the following data on employee vacation days:
• Mariah Brown, first two weeks of June

Notes:

Use one of the Word letter templates and write a letter to your instructor describing how you formatted **U2-PA10-CompGuidelines.docx,** including the reasons you chose specific formats.

February 12, 2015

Instructor Name
School Name
1234 Main Street
Seattle, WA 98115

Dear Instructor Name:

Word 2013 has several predesigned style options for formatting a report. In the Computer Use Guidelines exercise (U2-PA10-CompGuidelines.docx), I used several of the heading styles provided within the program to differentiate the various levels of information outlined therein.

The following is a list of design formats used in the Computer Use Guidelines document:

- Document is set with Simple (Basic) style set
- Document title uses the Title style
- Main document headings use the Heading 1 style
- Subheadings use the Heading 3 style to better differentiate their level of information
- Third level headings use the Heading 6 style with italics

In addition to the various heading styles, the header of the document includes the document name and the footer includes a simple page number. I chose a simple cover sheet, Ion (Light), to maintain the professional feel and tone of the document.

Sincerely,

Student Name

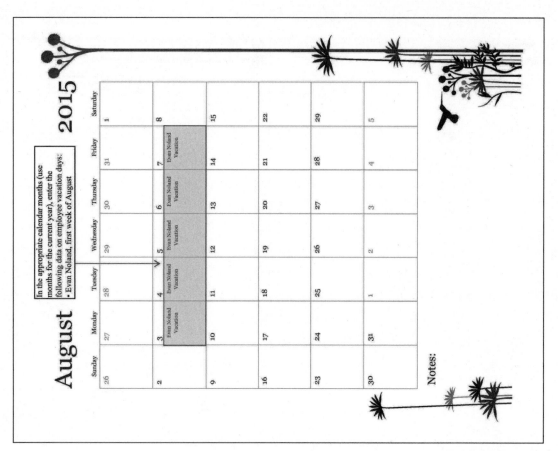

July 2015

In the appropriate calendar months (use months for the current year), enter the following data on employee vacation days:
• Jaden Holland, second week of July

Sunday	Monday	Tuesday	Wednesday	Thursday	Friday	Saturday
28	29	30	1	2	3	4
5	6 Jaden Holland Vacation	7 Jaden Holland Vacation	8 Jaden Holland Vacation	9 Jaden Holland Vacation	10 Jaden Holland Vacation	11
12	13	14	15	16	17	18
19	20 Maddie O'Hara Vacation	21 Maddie O'Hara Vacation	22 Maddie O'Hara Vacation	23 Maddie O'Hara Vacation	24 Maddie O'Hara Vacation	25
26	27 Maddie O'Hara Vacation	28 Maddie O'Hara Vacation	29 Maddie O'Hara Vacation	30 Maddie O'Hara Vacation	31 Maddie O'Hara Vacation	1
2	3	4	5	6	7	8

In the appropriate calendar months (use months for the current year), enter the following data on employee vacation days:
• Maddie O'Hara, last two weeks of July

Notes:

U2-PA11-Calendar.docx (page 2 of 3)

August 2015

In the appropriate calendar months (use months for the current year), enter the following data on employee vacation days:
• Evan Noland, first week of August

Sunday	Monday	Tuesday	Wednesday	Thursday	Friday	Saturday
26	27	28	29	30	31	1
2	3 Evan Noland Vacation	4 Evan Noland Vacation	5 Evan Noland Vacation	6 Evan Noland Vacation	7 Evan Noland Vacation	8
9	10	11	12	13	14	15
16	17	18	19	20	21	22
23	24	25	26	27	28	29
30	31	1	2	3	4	5

Notes:

U2-PA11-Calendar.docx (page 3 of 3)

who may be reading what you wrote, including employers, potential job opportunities, and other networking peers.

SOURCES:
Wiki.Answers.com - http://wiki.answers.com/Q/What_is_the_basic_rule_of_netiquette
Yahoo Voices - http://voices.yahoo.com/10-best-rules-netiquette-1952570.html?cat=15
Education.com - http://www.education.com/reference/article/netiquette-rules-behavior-internet/
Wikipedia - http://en.wikipedia.org/wiki/Etiquette_(technology)

At the end of the document, type the web addresses for the sites you used as references.

Situation: Your supervisor at Mobile Bay Products wants to provide employees with a document that describes netiquette ("Internet etiquette" rules). She has asked you to research the topic and then create a document that will be distributed to employees. Use the Internet (or other resources available to you) and search for information on "rules of netiquette." Locate at least two sources that provide information on netiquette. Using this information, create a document that describes netiquette rules and apply formatting to enhance the appearance of the document. Be sure to use your own words when describing netiquette rules; cutting and pasting text from Internet sources is plagiarism.

RULES OF NETIQUETTE

Netiquette is a term used for Network Etiquette, or Internet Etiquette. As the online social presence continues to grow, so does the need for rules of conduct to reinforce respect, kindness, and understanding in this growing platform of communication.

Many are aware with some of the basic Netiquette rules such as:

- Avoid typing in ALL CAPS: Typing in bold, all caps, or other formatting style conveys emphasis and emotion. All Caps is considered shouting. Use with caution.
- Be kind: Avoid posting comments or opinions that you would not feel comfortable speaking to someone directly and keep comments and subject matter appropriates. The Internet is a very public forum.
- Don't troll: Through forums, comments and other feedback options, it is considered bad form to hijack conversation threads for personal gain, steer conversation towards off-topic subjects, or post inflammatory controversial rants or personal attacks towards another user in effort to provoke and spur emotional responses.
- Privacy sensitivity: Always limit your audience to a need-to-know basis – don't assume Reply to All is a useful tactic – and never disrupt chain of command. While these things seems obvious, they happen frequently.
- Limiting the spread of spam: Spam is the equivalent of junk mail that clogs email inboxes and offers little professional or personal value while potentially opening up the users to hacking.
- Be mindful of copyrights: Just as copying someone's writing is considered plagiarizing, so is the act of using someone else's photo, comic, joke, or quote without giving proper credit to its creator or author.
- Write using proper spelling and grammar: Though many liberties are taken with online word use, not all can follow a comment or conversation with little or no respect to the written word. Save acronyms, web jargon, and shorthand for its prospective audience if it must be used at all.

With more social dialog taking place across the Internet on Facebook, Twitter, Instagram, Pinterest, and various other social networks, the rules are rapidly changing and while some rules apply in some settings, others may not.

For instance, many users of Twitter will hold accounts under alias to allow for some personal anonymity. The rules here are different that that when using company email to professional colleagues as well as addressing close friends on your Facebook timeline. Regardless of anonymity or not, it is always vitally important to be mindful of your comments and responses as the written word conveys a much different message and allows for greater misunderstanding.

To remedy tone, many have taken to the rampant use of emoticons, though it should be cautioned that there is rarely a place for them in a professional work setting and should be reserved for casual interactions and not be overused in any context at the risk of credibility.

While it may seem that the rules of netiquette are intense or stifle personal expression, we should be mindful that while we cannot see each other, we are still dealing with other people. In a time when more and more people use the Internet than ever before, it's a good thing to remember to be forgiving of others for their grammatical and spelling errors, misunderstandings, and opinions. You never know

Chapter 11 Assessment Annotated Model Answers

1. Open **PremPro.docx** and save the document with the name **C11-A02-PremPro.**

PREMIUM PRODUCE

3500 Fairview Drive ❧ Lincoln, NE 74932 ❧ (402) 555-8900 ❧ www.emcp.net/prempro

Farm-fresh and Organic Produce

Premium Produce is your source for local, farm-fresh produce. All of our produce is organically grown without pesticides, herbicides or other sprays. We ship our produce daily to a seven-state region in the Midwest.

Featured Product of the Month

Many fruits and vegetables are being harvested now while they are at the peak of their flavor. Featured produce this month include:

- Squash
- Potatoes
- Apples

Ordering from Premium Produce

Before ordering from Premium Produce, check our sale prices for the current month. After viewing the sale prices, call our toll-free number at 1-800-555-8900.

2. Insert a clip art image from Office.com with the following specifications:
a. At the Insert Picture window, use the word *cornucopia* to search for and then download the image shown in Figure 11.16.
b. Change the height of the clip art image to 1.4 inches.
c. Change the brightness and contrast to Brightness: 0% (Normal) Contrast: +20%.
d. Change the position to Position in Middle Right with Square Text Wrapping.
e. Apply the Offset Diagonal Bottom Left picture effect shadow. *Hint: Use the Picture Effects button in the Pictures Styles group and then point to Shadow.*

---

1. At a blank document, press the Enter key three times, type Ocean View Condominiums, press the Enter key, and then type 1-888-555-6570.
3. Select the text, change the font to 26-point Script MT Bold and the text color to White, and then center the text.

Ocean View Condominiums
1-888-555-6570

2. Press Ctrl + Home and then insert the picture **Ocean.jpg** with the following specifications:
a. Change the position to Position in Top Center with Square Text Wrapping.
b. Change the text wrapping to Behind Text.
c. Change the width to 4.5 inches.
d. Change the brightness and contrast to Brightness: -20% Contrast: +20%.

1. Open **VacAdventure.docx** and save the document with the name **C11-A04-VacAdventure**.

"FUN2016" VACATION ADVENTURES

Hurry and book now for one of our special FUN2016 vacation packages. Book within the next two weeks and you will be eligible for our special discount savings as well as earn a complimentary $100 gift card you can use at any of the resorts in our FUN2016 plan.

FUN2016 Disneyland Adventure

Roundtrip air fare to Los Angeles, California
Three-night hotel accommodations
Three-day Resort Ticket
24-hour traveler assistance

FUN2016 Florida Adventure

Roundtrip airfare to Orlando, Florida
Seven-night hotel accommodations
Four-day Resort Ticket
Two-day Bonus Ticket
Free transportation to some sites

FUN2016 Cancun Adventure

Roundtrip airfare to Cancun, Mexico
Five-night hotel accommodations and hotel taxes
Free shuttle to and from the airport
Two excursion tickets

Book a complete air/hotel FUN2016 vacation package and SAVE on fall travel! Bookings must be made by October 1, 2016, for travel October 30 through December 19, 2016 (blackout dates apply). Take advantage of these fantastic savings!

2. Insert the clip art image shown in Figure 11.18 with the following specifications:
a. Use the words *illustrations of sunglasses, mountains and the sun* to search for the clip art image.
b. Change the text wrapping of the clip art image to Square.
c. Change the shape height measurement to 2.3 inches.
d. Ungroup the clip art image.
e. Recolor individual components in the clip art so it appears as shown in Figure 11.18. (Apply the Orange shape fill color to the sun, the Green shape fill color to the mountains, and the Blue shape fill color to the water shapes.)
f. Change the position of the image to Position in Middle Right with Square Text Wrapping.

---

1. Open **DataTraining.docx** and save the document with the name **C11-A03-DataTraining**.

DATA SECURITY TRAINING

The technical support team is preparing three workshops focusing on protecting and securing company data. The workshops are open to all employees; however, participants must obtain approval from their immediate supervisor.

The first workshop, scheduled for Tuesday, April 7, from 9:00 to 11:30 a.m., will cover backing up crucial data. Participants will be briefed on the company's new rotating backup process, which involves backing up data from specific departments on specific days of the week.

The second workshop, scheduled for Wednesday, April 15, from 1:30 to 3:00 p.m., will focus on disaster recovery plan formulation and will include data backup procedures, remote backup locations, and redundant systems.

The third and final workshop, scheduled for Thursday, April 23, from 3:00 to 5:30 p.m., will focus on data security and will cover data encryption. Participants will learn about encryption schemes designed to scramble information before transferring it electronically.

For more information or to sign up for a workshop, please contact Jessie Levigne at extension 5560.

2. Insert the clip art image shown in Figure 11.17 using the search words *computer* and *padlock icon* at the Insert Pictures window.
3. Rotate the image by flipping it horizontally.
4. Click the Picture Styles group task pane launcher to display the Format Picture task pane and then make the following changes:
a. Click the Fill & Line icon located toward the top of the task pane.
b. Click *FILL* to expand the options, click the *Gradient fill* option, click the Preset gradients button, and then click the *Light Gradient – Accent 6* option (last column, first row).
c. Click the *Effects* icon.
d. Click *SHADOW* to expand the options, click the Presets button, and then click the *Offset Diagonal Bottom Right* option (first option in the *Outer* section).
e. Click *REFLECTION* to expand the options, click the Presets button, and then click the *Tight Reflection, touching* option (first option in the *Reflection Variations* section).
5. Change the text wrapping to Square.
6. Change the shape height measurement to 1.3 inches.
7. Display the Layout dialog box with the Position tab selected and then change the horizontal absolute position to 6.2 inches to the right of the left margin and the vertical absolute position to 2.2 inches below the page. *Hint: Display the Layout dialog box by clicking the Size group dialog box launcher on the PICTURE TOOLS FORMAT tab.*

1. At a blank document, create the organizational chart shown in Figure 11.20 with the following specifications:

a. Use the Hierarchy organizational chart in the *Hierarchy* section.

b. Select the top text box and insert a shape above it.

c. Select the text box at the right in the third row and then add a shape below it.

d. Apply the *Colorful Range - Accent Colors 3 to 4* option.

e. Increase the height to 4.5 inches and the width to 6.5 inches.

f. Type the text in each text box as shown in Figure 11.20.

g. Position the organizational chart in the middle of the page.

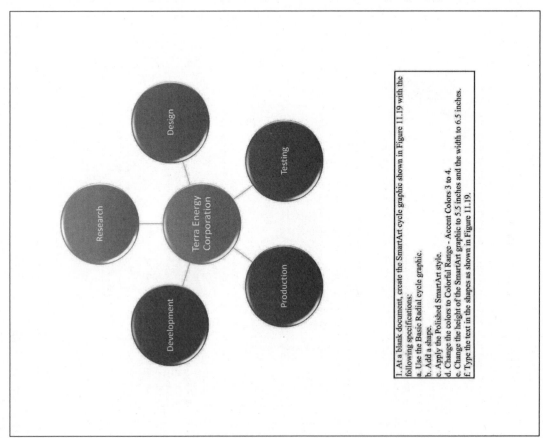

1. At a blank document, create the SmartArt cycle graphic shown in Figure 11.19 with the following specifications:

a. Use the Basic Radial cycle graphic.

b. Add a shape.

c. Apply the Polished SmartArt style.

d. Change the colors to Colorful Range - Accent Colors 3 to 4.

e. Change the height of the SmartArt graphic to 5.5 inches and the width to 6.5 inches.

f. Type the text in the shapes as shown in Figure 11.19.

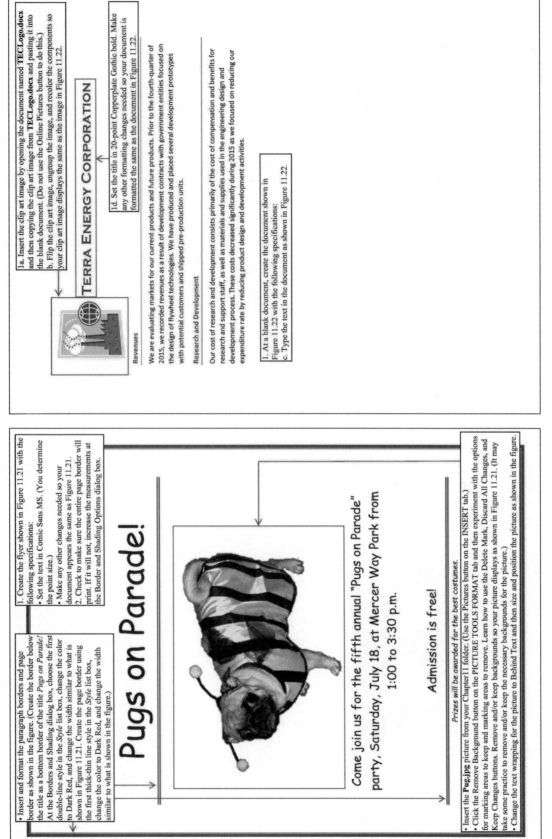

C11-A08-TECRevs.docx

1a. Insert the clip art image by opening the document named **TEC Logo.docx** and then copying the clip art image from **TEC Logo.docx** and pasting it into the blank document. (Do not use the Online Pictures button to do this.)
b. Flip the clip art image, ungroup the image, and recolor the components so your clip art image displays the same as the image in Figure 11.22.

TERRA ENERGY CORPORATION

1d. Set the title in 20-point Copperplate Gothic bold. Make any other formatting changes needed so your document is formatted the same as the document in Figure 11.22.

Revenues

We are evaluating markets for our current products and future products. Prior to the fourth-quarter of 2015, we recorded revenues as a result of development contracts with government entities focused on the design of flywheel technologies. We have produced and placed several development prototypes with potential customers and shipped pre-production units.

Research and Development

Our cost of research and development consists primarily of the cost of compensation and benefits for research and support staff, as well as materials and supplies used in the engineering design and development process. These costs decreased significantly during 2015 as we focused on reducing our expenditure rate by reducing product design and development activities.

1. At a blank document, create the document shown in Figure 11.22 with the following specifications:
c. Type the text in the document as shown in Figure 11.22.

C11-A07-PugFlyer.docx

1. Create the flyer shown in Figure 11.21 with the following specifications:
• Set the text in Comic Sans MS. (You determine the point size.)
• Make any other changes needed so your document appears the same as Figure 11.21.
2. Check to make sure the entire page border will print. If it will not, increase the measurements at the Border and Shading Options dialog box.

• Insert and format the paragraph borders and page border as shown in the figure. (Create the border below the title as a bottom border of the title *Pugs on Parade!* At the Borders and Shading dialog box, choose the first double-line style in the *Style* list box, change the color to Dark Red, and change the width similar to what is shown in Figure 11.21. Create the page border using the first thick-thin line style in the *Style* list box, change the color to Dark Red, and change the width similar to what is shown in the figure.)

Pugs on Parade!

Come join us for the fifth annual "Pugs on Parade" party, Saturday, July 18, at Mercer Way Park from 1:00 to 3:30 p.m.

Admission is free!

Prizes will be awarded for the best costumes.

• Insert the **Pug.jpg** picture from your Chapter11 folder. (Use the Pictures button on the INSERT tab.)
• Click the Remove Background button on the PICTURE TOOLS FORMAT tab and then experiment with the options for marking areas to keep and marking areas to remove. Learn how to use the Delete Mark, Discard All Changes, and Keep Changes buttons. Remove and/or keep backgrounds so your picture displays as shown in Figure 11.21. (It may take some practice to remove and/or keep the necessary backgrounds for the picture.)
• Change the text wrapping for the picture to Behind Text and then size and position the picture as shown in the figure.

Red Level
$150,000+

Blue Level
$100,000 - $149,999

Green Level
$75,000 - $99,999

1. At a blank document, create the SmartArt graphic shown in Figure 11.23 with the following specifications:
a. Use the Pyramid List graphic.
b. Apply the Inset SmartArt style.
c. Change the colors to Colorful Range - Accent Colors 5 to 6.
d. Apply Light Green shape fill color to the bottom shape, Light Blue fill color to the middle shape, and Red fill color to the top shape.
e. Type the text in each shape as shown in Figure 11.23.

C11-A09-Levels.docx

Signature Word 2013   Model Answers

Chapter 12 Assessment Annotated Model Answers

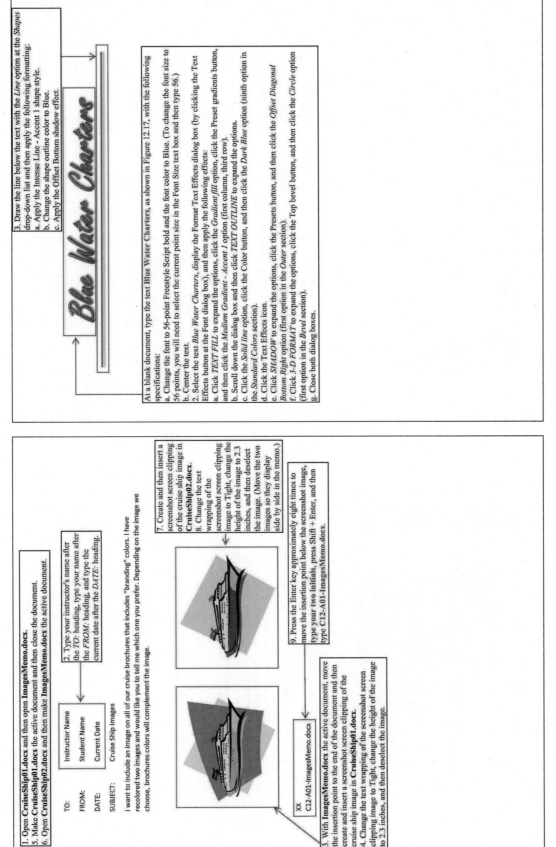

3. Draw the line below the text with the *Line* option at the *Shapes* drop-down list and then apply the following formatting:
a. Apply the Intense Line - Accent 1 shape style.
b. Change the shape outline color to Blue.
c. Apply the Offset Bottom shadow effect.

At a blank document, type the text Blue Water Charters, as shown in Figure 12.17, with the following specifications:
a. Change the font to 56-point Freestyle Script bold and the font color to Blue. (To change the font size to 56 points, you will need to select the current point size in the Font Size text box and then type 56.)
b. Center the text.
2. Select the text *Blue Water Charters*, display the Format Text Effects dialog box (by clicking the Text Effects button at the Font dialog box), and then apply the following effects:
a. Click *TEXT FILL* to expand the options, click the *Gradient fill* option, click the Preset gradients button, and then click the *Medium Gradient - Accent 1* option (first column, third row).
b. Scroll down the dialog box and then click *TEXT OUTLINE* to expand the options.
c. Click the *Solid line* option, click the Color button, and then click the *Dark Blue* option (ninth option in the *Standard Colors* section).
d. Click the Text Effects icon.
e. Click *SHADOW* to expand the options, click the Presets button, and then click the *Offset Diagonal Bottom Right* option (first option in the *Outer* section).
f. Click *3-D FORMAT* to expand the options, click the Top bevel button, and then click the *Circle* option (first option in the *Bevel* section).
g. Close both dialog boxes.

C12-A02-BWC.docx

1. Open **CruiseShip01.docx** and then open **ImagesMemo.docx**.
5. Make **CruiseShip01.docx** the active document and then close the document.
6. Open **CruiseShip02.docx** and then make **ImagesMemo.docx** the active document.

2. Type your instructor's name after the *TO:* heading, type your name after the *FROM:* heading, and type the current date after the *DATE:* heading.

TO:	Instructor Name
FROM:	Student Name
DATE:	Current Date
SUBJECT:	Cruise Ship Images

I want to include an image on all of our cruise brochures that includes "branding" colors. I have recolored two images and would like you to tell me which one you prefer. Depending on the image we choose, brochures colors will complement the image.

7. Create and then insert a screenshot screen clipping of the cruise ship image in **CruiseShip02.docx**.
8. Change the text wrapping of the screenshot screen clipping image to Tight, change the height of the image to 2.3 inches, and then deselect the image. (Move the two images so they display side by side in the memo.)

9. Press the Enter key approximately eight times to move the insertion point below the screenshot image, type your two initials, press Shift + Enter, and then type C12-A01-ImagesMemo.docx.

XX
C12-A01-ImagesMemo.docx

3. With **ImagesMemo.docx** the active document, move the insertion point to the end of the document and then create and insert a screenshot screen clipping of the cruise ship image in **CruiseShip01.docx**.
4. Change the text wrapping of the screenshot screen clipping image to Tight, change the height of the image to 2.3 inches, and then deselect the image.

C12-A01-ImagesMemo.docx

Document 1 (top)

1. Open **SoftwareCycle.docx** and save the document with the name **C12-A04- SoftwareCycle.**

COMMERCIAL LIFE CYCLE

Implementation

Software life is the term used to describe the phas... the phat 5. Select the title COMMERCIAL LIFE CYCLE and then create WordArt with the text with the testing, following specifications (see Figure 12.19):
product a. Use the Fill - Black, Text 1, Outline – Background 1, Hard Shadow - Accent 1 WordArt style
used to (second column, last row).
that the b. Apply the Blue text fill color (eighth color option in the *Standard Colors* section).
creation c. Use the Text Effects button in the WordArt Styles group to apply the Green, 5 pt glow, Accent
rather t color 6 glow text effect (last column, first row in the *Glow Variations* section).
customi d. Use the Text Effects button in the WordArt Styles group to apply the Perspective Below 3-D
commer rotation text effect (last column, first row in the *Perspective* section).
time a n e. Change the height to 1 inch and the width to 6.5 inches.
phases i f. Apply the Inflate Top transform text effect (first column, seventh row in the *Warp* section).
following...
implementation, testing, and public release.

> *"The commercial software life cycle is repeated every time a new version of a program is needed."*

Proposal and Planning

In the proposal and planning phase of a new software product, software developers describe the proposed software program and what it is supposed to accomplish. For existing software, the proposal and planning stage can be used to describe new features and improvements. Older software programs are often revised to take advantage of new hardware or software developments and to add new functions.

Design

Once a decision has been made to create or upgrade a software program, developers are ready to begin the design process. This process produces specifications that document the details of the software that will be written by programmers. Developers use problem-solving steps to determine the appropriate specifications.

Testing

A quality assurance (QA) team usually develops a testing harness, which is a scripted set of tests that a program must undergo before being considered ready for public release. These tests might cover events such as very large input loads, maximum number of users, running on several different platforms, and simulated power outages. Once testing is finished, a beta version of the software program is created for testing outside of the development group, often by a select group of knowledgeable consumers. Any suggestions this group makes can be used to improve the product before it is released to the general public. Once the beta version is finalized, the user manual can be written or updated. At this point, the software developers send the master CDs to duplicators for mass production.

Public Release and Support

When the product is deemed ready for widespread use, it is declared "gold" and released to the public. The software life cycle then begins again as software developers think of new ways to improve the product.

2. Position the insertion point at the beginning of the first paragraph of text, insert the Sideline Quote predesigned text box in the document, and then type the following text in the text box: "The commercial software life cycle is repeated every time a new version of a program is needed."
3. With the DRAWING TOOLS FORMAT tab active, change the shape width to 2.6 inches.
4. Change the position of the text box to Position in Middle Left with Square Text Wrapping.

C12-A04-SoftwareCycle.docx

Document 2 (bottom)

2. Type the text inside the shape as shown in Figure 12.18. After typing the text, select it and then change the font to 36-point Monotype Consiva bold and the color to Orange, Accent 2, Darker 50%.

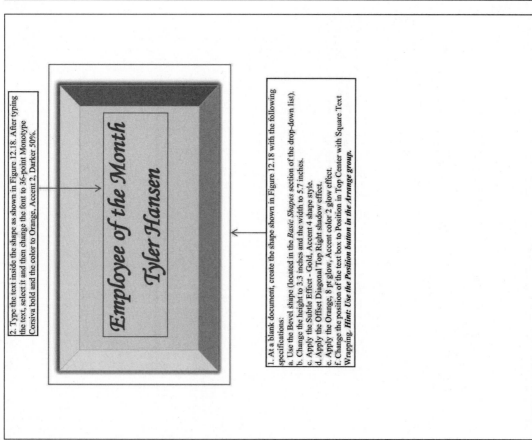

Employee of the Month
Tyler Hansen

1. At a blank document, create the shape shown in Figure 12.18 with the following specifications:
a. Use the Bevel shape (located in the *Basic Shapes* section of the drop-down list).
b. Change the height to 3.3 inches and the width to 5.7 inches.
c. Apply the Subtle Effect - Gold, Accent 4 shape style.
d. Apply the Offset Diagonal Top Right shadow effect.
e. Apply the Orange, 8 pt glow, Accent color 2 glow effect.
f. Change the position of the text box to Position in Top Center with Square Text Wrapping. **Hint: Use the Position button in the Arrange group.**

C12-A03-EmpofMonth.docx

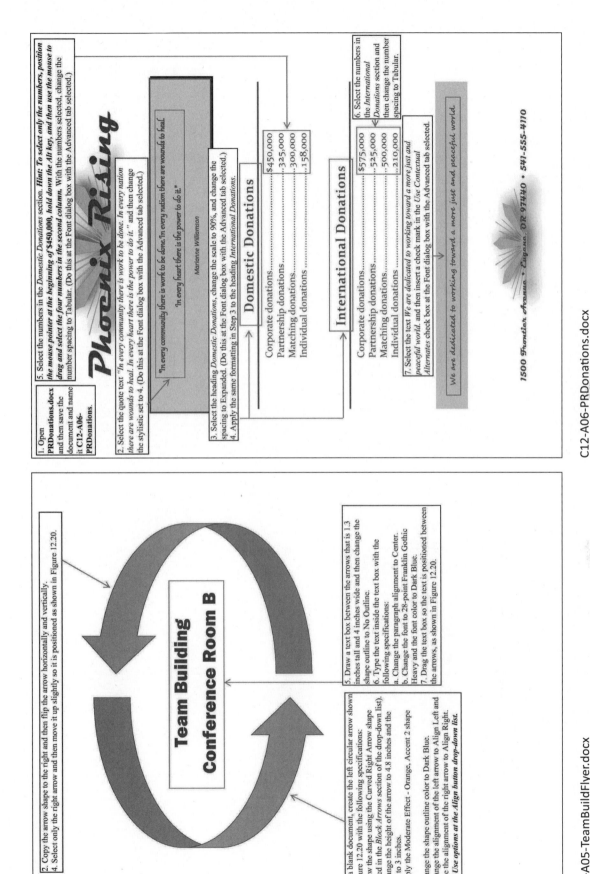

C12-A06-PRDonations.docx

1. Open **PRDonations.docx** and then save the document and name it **C12-A06-PRDonations.**

2. Select the quote text *"In every community there is work to be done. In every nation there is a wounds to heal."* and then change the stylistic set to 4. (Do this at the Font dialog box with the Advanced tab selected.)

3. Select the heading *Domestic Donations,* change the spacing to Expanded. (Do this at the Font dialog box with the Advanced tab selected.)
4. Apply the same formatting in Step 3 to the heading *International Donations.*

5. Select the numbers in the *Domestic Donations* section. *Hint: To select only the numbers, position the mouse pointer at the beginning of $450,000, hold down the Alt key, and then use the mouse to drag and select the four numbers in the second column.* With the numbers selected, change the number spacing to Tabular. (Do this at the Font dialog box with the Advanced tab selected.)

6. Select the numbers in the *International Donations* section and then change the number spacing to Tabular.

7. Select the text *We are dedicated to working toward a more just and peaceful world.* and then insert a check mark in the *Use Contextual Alternates* check box at the Font dialog box with the Advanced tab selected.

Phoenix Rising

"In every community there is work to be done. In every nation there are wounds to heal."

Marianne Williamson

"In every heart there is the power to do it."

Domestic Donations

Corporate donations	$450,000
Partnership donations	325,000
Matching donations	300,000
Individual donations	158,000

International Donations

Corporate donations	$575,000
Partnership donations	525,000
Matching donations	500,000
Individual donations	210,000

We are dedicated to working toward a more just and peaceful world.

1500 Frontier Avenue • Eugene, OR 97440 • 541-555-4110

C12-A05-TeamBuildFlyer.docx

1. At a blank document, create the left circular arrow shown in Figure 12.20 with the following specifications:
a. Draw the shape using the Curved Right Arrow shape (located in the *Block Arrows* section of the drop-down list).
b. Change the height of the arrow to 4.8 inches and the width to 3 inches.
c. Apply the Moderate Effect - Orange, Accent 2 shape style.
d. Change the shape outline color to Dark Blue.
3. Change the alignment of the left arrow to Align Left and change the alignment of the right arrow to Align Right. *Hint: Use options at the Align button drop-down list.*

2. Copy the arrow shape to the right and then flip the arrow horizontally and vertically.
4. Select only the right arrow and then move it up slightly so it is positioned as shown in Figure 12.20.

5. Draw a text box between the arrows that is 1.3 inches tall and 4 inches wide and then change the shape outline to No Outline.
6. Type the text inside the text box with the following specifications:
a. Change the paragraph alignment to Center.
b. Change the font to 28-point Franklin Gothic Heavy and the font color to Dark Blue.
7. Drag the text box so the text is positioned between the arrows, as shown in Figure 12.20.

Team Building
Conference Room B

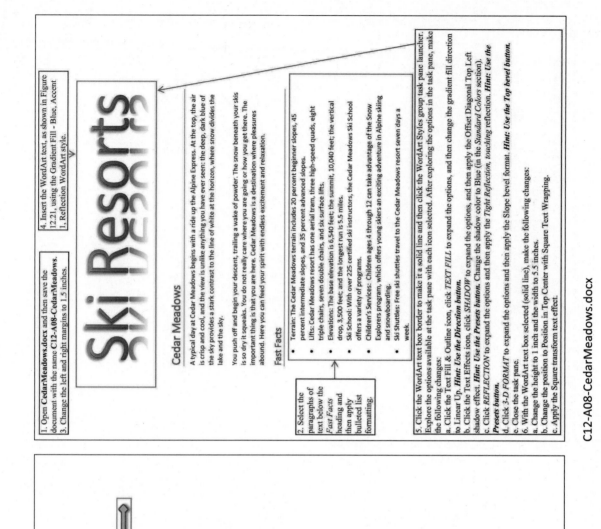

4. Insert the WordArt text, as shown in Figure 12.21, using the Gradient Fill - Blue, Accent 1, Reflection WordArt style.

Ski Resorts

Cedar Meadows

A typical day at Cedar Meadows begins with a ride up the Alpine Express. At the top, the air is crisp and cool, and the view is unlike anything you have ever seen: the deep, dark blue of the sky provides a stark contrast to the line of white at the horizon, where snow divides the lake and the sky.

You push off and begin your descent, trailing a wake of powder. The snow beneath your skis is so dry it squeaks. You do not really care where you are going or how you get there. The important thing is that you are here. Cedar Meadows is a destination where pleasures abound. Here you can feed your spirit with endless excitement and relaxation.

Fast Facts

- Terrain: The Cedar Meadows terrain includes 20 percent beginner slopes, 45 percent intermediate slopes, and 35 percent advanced slopes.
- Lifts: Cedar Meadows resort has one aerial tram, three high-speed quads, eight triple chairs, seven double chairs, and six surface lifts.
- Elevations: The base elevation is 6,540 feet; the summit, 10,040 feet; the vertical drop, 3,500 feet; and the longest run is 5.5 miles.
- Ski School: With over 225 certified ski instructors, the Cedar Meadows Ski School offers a variety of programs.
- Children's Services: Children ages 4 through 12 can take advantage of the Snow Explorers program, which offers young skiers an exciting adventure in Alpine skiing and snowboarding.
- Ski Shuttles: Free ski shuttles travel to the Cedar Meadows resort seven days a week.

2. Select the paragraphs of text below the *Fast Facts* heading and then apply bulleted list formatting.

5. Click the WordArt text box border to make it a solid line and then click the WordArt Styles group task pane launcher. Explore the options available at the task pane with each icon selected. After exploring the options in the task pane, make the following changes:
a. Click the Text Fill & Outline icon, click *TEXT FILL* to expand the options, and then change the gradient fill direction to Linear Up. **Hint: Use the Direction button.**
b. Click the Text Effects icon, click *SHADOW* to expand the options, and then apply the Offset Diagonal Top Left shadow effect. **Hint: Use the Presets button.** Change the shadow color to Blue (in the *Standard Colors* section).
c. Click *REFLECTION* to expand the options and then apply the *Tight Reflection, touching* reflection. **Hint: Use the Presets button.**
d. Click *3-D FORMAT* to expand the options and then apply the Slope bevel format. **Hint: Use the Top bevel button.**
e. Close the task pane.
6. With the WordArt text box selected (solid line), make the following changes:
a. Change the height to 1 inch and the width to 5.5 inches.
b. Change the position to Position in Top Center with Square Text Wrapping.
c. Apply the Square transform text effect.

C12-A08-CedarMeadows.docx

1. Open C12-A02-BWC.docx and save the document with the name C12-A07-BWC.

Blue Water Charters

2. Click the horizontal line to select it, click the DRAWING TOOLS FORMAT tab, and then click the Shape Styles group task pane launcher. This displays the Format Shape task pane with additional options for customizing the shape.
3. Look at the options in the Format Shape task pane with the Fill & Line icon selected. If necessary, click *LINE* to expand the options. Use options in the Format Shape task pane to change the line color to Blue, Accent 1, Lighter 40% (fifth column, fourth row in the *Theme Colors* section), change the line width to 4 points, and change the beginning arrow type and ending arrow type to Diamond Arrow. **Hint: Do this with the Begin Arrow type and End Arrow type buttons in the task pane.**
4. Click the Effects icon and then click *GLOW* to expand the options. Click the Color button and then click the *Dark Blue* color in the *Standard Colors* section. Change the size to 3 point and then close the task pane.

C12-A07-BWC.docx

1. Open **FirstAidMemo.docx** and then save it and name it **C12-A10-FirstAidMemo.**

TO: Carmen Singleton

FROM: Caleb Sullivan

DATE: Current Date

SUBJECT: FIRST AID COURSE ANNOUNCEMENTS

As you requested, I have created two announcements for the first aid course in March. Please review the two announcements shown below and let me know which one you prefer.

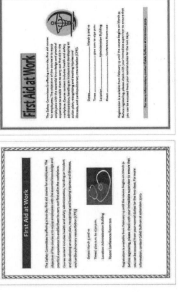

2. Insert screenshots so your document appears as shown in Figure 12.23. Use **FirstAidAnnounce.docx** to create the first screenshot and use **C12-A09-FirstAidCourse.docx** (the document you created in Assessment 12.9) for the second screenshot. Before making either screenshot, make sure the entire announcement page displays on the screen. If you cannot see the entire page, adjust the zoom.

---

1. At a blank document, create the announcement shown in Figure 12.22. Insert the WordArt text with the following specifications:
a. Use the Fill - Blue, Accent 1, Outline – Background 1, Hard Shadow - Accent 1 WordArt style.
b. Select the WordArt text box and then apply the Dark Blue text fill.
c. Apply the Blue text outline.

2. Insert the caduceus clip art image, as shown in Figure 12.22, with the following specifications:
a. Use the word *caduceus* at the Insert Pictures window to search online for the clip art image.
b. Change the text wrapping to Tight.
c. Change the clip art image color to Blue, Accent color 1 Light.
d. Change the brightness and contrast to Brightness: -20% Contrast: +40%.
e. Size and move the clip art image as shown in the figure.

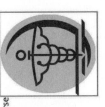

First Aid at Work

The Safety Committee is offering a two-day first aid course for employees. The objective of the course is to equip employees with the essential knowledge and practical experience to enable them to carry out first aid in the workplace. Course content includes health and safety administration, handling an incident and developing an action plan, recognizing and treating injuries and illnesses, and cardiopulmonary resuscitation (CPR).

Dates .... March 9 and 10

Times .... 9:00 a.m. to 4:30 p.m.

Location .... Administration Building

Room.................................... Conference Room 200

3. Apply character, paragraph, and page formatting so your document appears similar to the document in Figure 12.22. (Set the text in the Candara font.)

Registration is available from February 15 until the course begins on March 9. Before registering, please check with your immediate supervisor to ensure that you can be excused from your normal duties for the two days.

4. Check to make sure the entire page border will print. If it will not, increase the measurements in the Border and Shading Options dialog box.

For more information, contact Caleb Sullivan at extension 3505.

1d. Apply the Inside Diagonal Top Left shadow text effect. *Hint: Use the Text Effects button.*
e. Apply the Subtle Effect - Blue, Accent 1 shape style.
f. Apply the Offset Top shadow shape effect. *Hint: Use the Shape Effects button.*
g. Apply the Square transform text effect. *Hint: Use the Text Effects button.*

C12-A09-FirstAidCourse.docx

xx
C12-A10-FirstAidMemo.docx

Chapter 13 Assessment Annotated Model Answers

BAYSIDE TRAVEL TOUR PACKAGES

Name	Duration	Costs
Hawaiian Fun in the Sun	5 days and 4 nights	From $709 to $1049
Hawaiian Nights	8 days and 7 nights	From $1079 to $1729
Hawaiian Fun Tours	10 days and 9 nights	From $1999 to $2229
Hawaiian Island Tours	14 days and 13 nights	From $2499 to $3099

1. At a blank document, create the text and table shown in Figure 13.10 with the following specifications:
b. Use the Insert Table dialog box to create a table with three columns and five rows and choose the *Autofit to contents* option at the dialog box.
c. Type the text in the cells as shown in Figure 13.10.
d. Apply the Grid Table 4 - Accent 1 table style (second column, fourth row in the *Grid Tables* section).
e. Remove the check mark from the *First Column* check box.

C13-A02-TourPkgs.docx

---

1. Open **LtrCofC.docx** and save the document with the name **C13-A01-LtrCofC.**

2. Move the insertion point to the blank line between the two paragraphs of text in the body of the letter and then create the table shown in Figure 13.9 with the following specifications:
a. Create a table with three columns and eight rows.
b. Apply bold and italic formatting and center the text in the first row.
d. Apply Blue, Accent 5, Darker 50% shading (ninth column, bottom row in the *Theme Colors* section) to the first row.

November 5, 2015

Mr. Max Schueller
Mobile Chamber of Commerce
2400 22nd Avenue East
Mobile, AL 36602

Dear Mr. Schueller:

Thank you for alerting us to the publication deadline for the Mobile Chamber of Commerce membership pamphlet. When you update the listing for Mobile Bay Products, please include the following information:

2c. Apply bold formatting to the text in the cells below the *Name* heading.

Name	Title	Department
Shawn Kilpatrick	Chief Executive Officer	Administration
Gerald Palmer	President	Administration
Emily Higgins	Vice President	Administration
Ryan Keaton	Finances Manager	Finance
Jim Everson	Resources Coordinator	Purchasing
Isabelle Brown	Training Coordinator	Support and Training Services
Sandy Romano-Ellison	Public Relations Manager	Public Relations

2e. Apply Green, Accent 6, Lighter 80% shading (last column, second row in the *Theme Colors* section) to the second, fourth, sixth, and eighth rows.
f. Apply Blue, Accent 1, Lighter 80% shading (fifth column, second row in the *Theme Colors* section) to the third, fifth, and seventh rows.

Please note that the titles for Ryan Keaton and Isabelle Brown have changed since the last pamphlet was published. We are interested in receiving approximately 20 pamphlets from the chamber and will distribute them to contact people within our company.

Sincerely,

Angelina Ahn
Assistant Director
Public Relations Department

XX
LtrCofC.docx

C13-A01-LtrCofC.docx

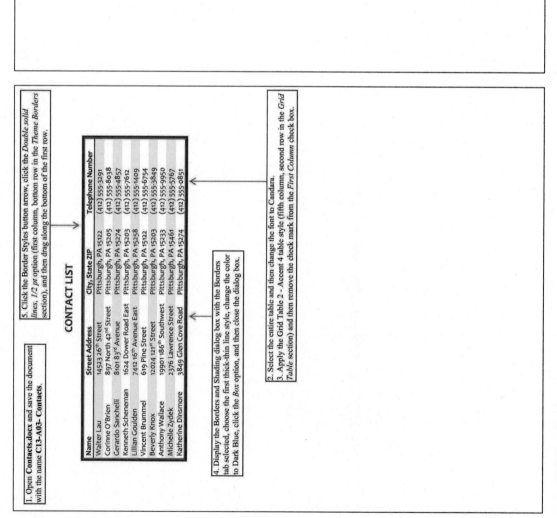

CONTACT LIST

1. Open **Contacts.docx** and save the document with the name **C13–A03– Contacts.**

Name	Street Address	City, State ZIP	Telephone Number
Walter Lau	14523 26th Street	Pittsburgh, PA 15122	(412) 555-3291
Corinne O'Brien	897 North 42nd Street	Pittsburgh, PA 15205	(412) 555-8038
Gerardo Sanchelli	8101 83rd Avenue	Pittsburgh, PA 15274	(412) 555-4857
Kenneth Scheneman	1624 Dower Road East	Pittsburgh, PA 15203	(412) 555-7612
Lillian Goulden	7412 16th Avenue East	Pittsburgh, PA 15258	(412) 555-1409
Vincent Brummel	619 Pine Street	Pittsburgh, PA 15122	(412) 555-6754
Beverly Knox	12024 121st Street	Pittsburgh, PA 15203	(412) 555-3849
Anthony Wallace	19901 186th Southwest	Pittsburgh, PA 15233	(412) 555-9950
Michelle Zydek	2376 Lawrence Street	Pittsburgh, PA 15461	(412) 555-5767
Katherine Dinsmore	3849 Glen Cove Road	Pittsburgh, PA 15274	(412) 555-0851

2. Select the entire table and then change the font to Candara.
3. Apply the Grid Table 2 – Accent 4 table style (fifth column, second row in the *Grid Table* section) and then remove the check mark from the *First Column* check box.

4. Display the Borders and Shading dialog box with the Borders tab selected, choose the first thick-thin line style, change the color to Dark Blue, click the *Box* option, and then close the dialog box.

5. Click the Border Styles button arrow, click the *Double solid lines, 1/2 pt* option (first column, bottom row in the *Theme Borders* section), and then drag along the bottom of the first row.

C13-A03-Contacts.docx

JOBS IN DEMAND

Position	Weekly Income	Yearly Openings
Accountants/Auditors	$975	852
Financial Managers	$895	343
Loan Officers	$875	301
Registered Nurses	$852	1,550
Teachers, Elementary	$780	1,112
Teachers, Secondary	$750	1,258

1. At a blank document, type the title **JOBS IN DEMAND**, press the Enter key, draw a table, and then in the table type the following text:

Position	Weekly Income	Yearly Openings
Accountants/Auditors	$975	852
Financial Managers	$895	343
Loan Officers	$875	301
Registered Nurses	$852	1,550
Teachers, Elementary	$780	1,112
Teachers, Secondary	$750	1,258

2. Apply formatting to enhance the appearance of the table.

C13-A04-Jobs.docx

1. At a blank document, create the document shown in Figure 13.11 with the following specifications:
- Use the Insert Table dialog box to create the table and choose the *AutoFit to contents* option.
- Apply to both tables the Grid Table 3 - Accent 5 table style and remove the check marks from the *Header Row* and *First Column* check boxes.
- Vertically center the text on the page.

Résumé Writing: Positive Verbs

Overcame	Achieved	Developed	Discovered	Controlled
Managed	Delivered	Reorganized	Won	Applied
Defeated	Created	Engineered	Overhauled	Presented
Founded	Instigated	Established	Succeeded	Contributed
Modified	Specialized	Expanded	Repaired	Improved
Analyzed	Coordinated	Trained	Accomplished	Investigated
Persuaded	Helped	Proved	Utilized	Simplified

Résumé Writing: Powerful Adjectives

Quickly	Successfully	Rapidly	Carefully	Decisively
Competently	Capably	Resourcefully	Efficiently	Consistently
Effectively	Positively	Cooperatively	Selectively	Creatively
Assertively	Energetically	Enthusiastically	Responsibly	Diligently

C13-A06-ResumeWords.docx

---

1. Use the Quick Tables feature to create a monthly calendar for next month.
2. Apply any additional formatting to enhance the appearance of the calendar.

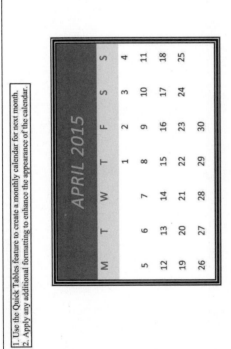

APRIL 2015						
M	T	W	T	F	S	S
5	6	7	1	2	3	4
12	13	14	8	9	10	11
19	20	21	15	16	17	18
26	27	28	22	23	24	25
			29	30		

C13-A05-MoCalendar.docx

181

Chapter 14 Assessment Annotated Model Answers

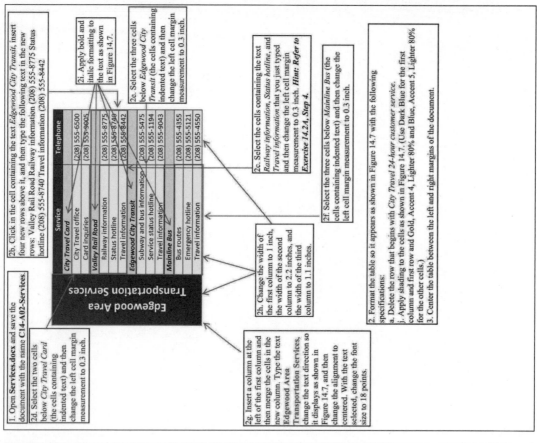

1. Open **Services.docx** and save the document with the name **C14-A02-Services**.

2b. Click in the cell containing the text *Edgewood City Transit*, insert four new rows above it, and then type the following text in the new rows: Valley Rail Road Railway information (208) 555-8775 Status hotline (208) 555-8740 Travel information (208) 555-8442

2i. Apply bold and italic formatting to the text as shown in Figure 14.7.

2e. Select the three cells below *Edgewood City Transit* (the cells containing indented text) and then change the left cell margin measurement to 0.3 inch.

2c. Select the cells containing the text *Railway information, Status hotline,* and *Travel information* that you just typed and then change the left cell margin measurement to 0.3 inch. *Hint: Refer to Exercise 14.24, Step 4.*

2f. Select the three cells below *Mainline Bus* (the cells containing indented text) and then change the left cell margin measurement to 0.3 inch.

2d. Select the two cells below *City Travel Card* (the cells containing indented text) and then change the left cell margin measurement to 0.3 inch.

2h. Change the width of the first column to 1 inch, the width of the second column to 2.2 inches, and the width of the third column to 1.1 inches.

2g. Insert a column at the left of the first column and then merge the cells in the new column. Type the text Edgewood Area Transportation Services, change the text direction so it displays as shown in Figure 14.7, and then change the alignment to centered. With the text selected, change the font size to 18 points.

2. Format the table so it appears as shown in Figure 14.7 with the following specifications:
a. Delete the row that begins with *City Travel 24-hour customer service.*
j. Apply shading to the cells as shown in Figure 14.7. (Use Dark Blue for the first column and first row and Gold, Accent 4, Lighter 80% and Blue, Accent 5, Lighter 80% for the other cells.)
3. Center the table between the left and right margins of the document.

C14-A02-Services.docx

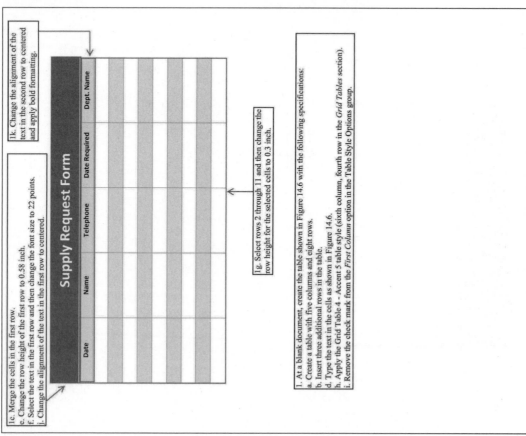

1c. Change the alignment of the text in the second row to centered and apply bold formatting.

1e. Merge the cells in the first row.
c. Change the row height of the first row to 0.58 inch.
f. Select the text in the first row and then change the font size to 22 points.
j. Change the alignment of the text in the first row to centered.

1g. Select rows 2 through 11 and then change the row height for the selected cells to 0.3 inch.

1. At a blank document, create the table shown in Figure 14.6 with the following specifications:
a. Create a table with five columns and eight rows.
b. Insert three additional rows in the table.
d. Type the text in the cells as shown in Figure 14.6.
h. Apply the Grid Table 4 - Accent 5 table style (sixth column, fourth row in the *Grid Tables* section).
i. Remove the check mark from the *First Column* option in the Table Style Options group.

C14-A01-SupplyForm.docx

Signature Word 2013   Model Answers

1. Open **TrainDept.docx** and save the document with the name C14-A04- TrainDept.
4. Apply the Grid Table 2 - Accent 4 table style (fifth column, second row in the *Grid Tables* section). Remove the check mark from the *First Column* check box in the Table Style Options group.

MOBILE BAY PRODUCTS

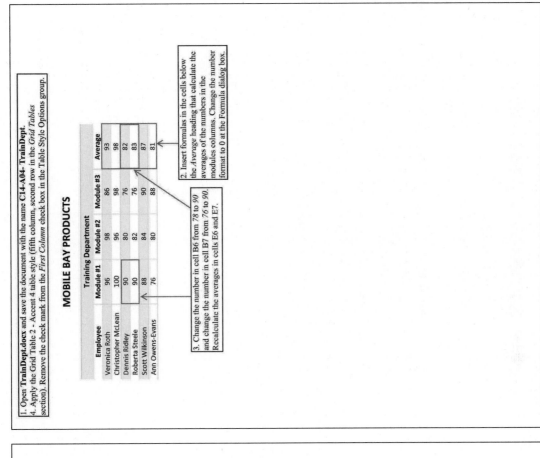

Employee	Training Department			Average
	Module #1	Module #2	Module #3	
Veronica Roth	96	98	86	93
Christopher McLean	100	96	98	98
Dennis Ridley	90	80	76	82
Roberta Steele	90	82	76	83
Scott Wilkinson	88	84	90	87
Ann Owens-Evans	76	80	88	81

2. Insert formulas in the cells below the *Average* heading that calculate the averages of the numbers in the modules columns. Change the number format to 0 at the Formula dialog box.

3. Change the number in cell B6 from *78* to *90* and change the number in cell B7 from *76* to *90*. Recalculate the averages in cells E6 and E7.

1b. Merge the cells in the top row and then change the alignment to centered.
g. Change the font size to 14 points for the text in cell A1.

1d. Change the alignment to top right for the cells containing the money amounts and the blank line below the last amount (cells B2 through B7).

TRAINING COSTS	
Human Resources	$23,150.50
Research and Development	$78,455.00
Public Relations	$10,348.20
Purchasing	$22,349.55
Administration	$64,352.00
Total	$198,655.25

2. Insert a formula in cell B7 that sums the amounts in cells B2 through B6. (Type a dollar sign before the number inserted by the formula.)

1. At a blank document, create the table shown in Figure 14.8 with the following specifications:
a. Create a table with two columns and seven rows.
c. Type the text in the cells as shown in Figure 14.8.
e. AutoFit the contents of the cells.
f. Apply the Grid Table 5 Dark - Accent 6 table style (last column, fifth row in the *Grid Tables* section).
h. Click the Cell Margins button on the TABLE TOOLS LAYOUT tab to display the Table Options dialog box and then specify that you want to allow 0.02-inch spacing between cells.

C14-A06-NSSQuizAverages.docx

1. Open **NSSQuizAverages.docx** and save the document with the name **C14-A06-NSSQuizAverages**.
4. Display the Table Options dialog box (click the Cell Margins button) and then specify that you want to allow 0.01-inch spacing between cells.

3. Move the insertion point to the empty cell below 67% and then insert a formula to calculate the averages. Click in the next empty cell in the *Average* column and then press the F4 key to repeat the last function (which was inserting the formula). Continue moving the insertion point to the next empty cell in the *Average* column and pressing the F4 key.

2. Position the insertion point in the last cell in the *Average* column containing data (the cell containing *67%*). Display the Formula dialog box, determine how the formula was written to calculate the quiz averages, determine the number format, and then close the dialog box.

Date	Course #	Employee#	Quiz 1	Quiz 2	Average
02/02/2015	A-350	A-128721	88%	92%	90%
		A-150043	68%	54%	61%
		B-234002	72%	78%	75%
		C-212859	94%	98%	96%
		C-342003	50%	48%	49%
02/04/2015	B-350	A-128721	94%	100%	97%
		A-150043	80%	76%	78%
		B-194383	74%	76%	75%
		B-234002	100%	92%	96%
		B-254406	68%	60%	64%
		C-321289	84%	88%	86%
		C-342003	90%	96%	93%
		C-351139	64%	72%	68%
		D-364055	88%	84%	86%
02/09/2015	A-415	A-103829	60%	58%	59%
		A-112390	90%	98%	94%
		B-203982	100%	100%	100%
		B-304897	82%	68%	75%
		C-331554	78%	90%	84%
		C-355778	94%	98%	96%
		D-399384	70%	64%	67%
02/11/2015	A-500	A-128721	94%	98%	96%
		A-150043	50%	56%	53%
		B-178395	100%	88%	94%
		B-234002	78%	82%	80%
		C-321289	98%	90%	94%
		C-342003	68%	60%	64%
		D-385945	84%	88%	86%

C14-A05-FinAnalysis.docx

1. Open **FinAnalysis.docx** and save the document with the name **C14-A05- FinAnalysis**.
6. Apply the Grid Table 4 - Accent 2 table style (third column, fourth row in the *Grid Tables* section). Remove the check mark from the *First Column* check box in the Table Style Options group.
7. Select the top two rows in the table and then change the alignment to centered.

2. Insert a formula in cell B13 that sums the amounts in cells B6 through B12.
3. Insert a formula in cell C13 that sums the amounts in cells C6 through C12.

4. Insert a formula in cell B14 that subtracts the amount in cell B13 from the amount in cell B4. *Hint: The formula should look like this:* **=B4-B13**.
5. Insert a formula in cell C14 that subtracts the amount in cell C13 from the amount in cell C4. *Hint: The formula should look like this:* **=C4-C13**. (Make sure you insert dollar signs before the numbers inserted by the formulas.)

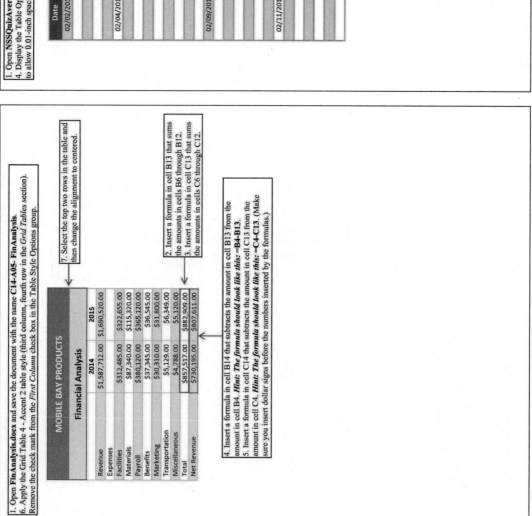

MOBILE BAY PRODUCTS		
Financial Analysis		
	2014	2015
Revenue	$1,587,712.00	$1,690,520.00
Expenses		
Facilities	$312,485.00	$322,655.00
Materials	$87,340.00	$115,320.00
Payroll	$380,120.00	$365,120.00
Benefits	$37,345.00	$36,545.00
Marketing	$30,310.00	$31,800.00
Transportation	$5,129.00	$6,349.00
Miscellaneous	$4,788.00	$5,120.00
Total	$857,517.00	$882,909.00
Net Revenue	$730,195.00	$807,611.00

Page 1 of 2

Northland Security Systems
3200 North 22nd Street ◆ Springfield ◆ IL ◆ 62102

> 1. Open NSSQuizAveLtr.docx and save the document with the name C14-A07-NSSQuizAveLtr.

March 10, 2015

Mrs. Sylvia Patterson
Human Resources Department
Rolling Hills Manufacturing
31203 33rd Street South
Springfield, IL 62133

Re: Employee Quiz Scores

Dear Mrs. Patterson:

> 2. Move the insertion point to the beginning of the second paragraph in the letter and then insert C14-A06-NSSQuizAverages.docx into the letter. *Hint: Do this with the Object button arrow in the Text group on the INSERT tab.*

Northland Security Systems offered four data security training courses during the month of February. Several employees at Rolling Hills Manufacturing have completed some or all of the data security training courses. The following table identifies the date, course number, employee number, and quiz scores as well as the average of the two quizzes for each course.

> 3. Specify that you want the first row in the table to display as a header row at the top of the table on the second page.

Date	Course #	Employee#	Quiz 1	Quiz 2	Average
02/02/2015	A-350	A-128721	88%	92%	90%
		A-150043	68%	54%	61%
		B-234002	72%	78%	75%
		C-212859	94%	98%	96%
		C-342003	50%	48%	49%
02/04/2015	B-350	A-128721	94%	100%	97%
		A-150043	80%	76%	78%
		B-194383	74%	76%	75%
		B-234002	100%	92%	96%
		B-254406	68%	60%	64%
		C-321289	84%	88%	86%
		C-342003	90%	96%	93%
		C-351139	64%	72%	68%
		D-364055	88%	84%	86%
02/09/2015	A-415	A-103829	60%	58%	59%
		A-112390	90%	98%	94%
		B-203982	100%	100%	100%
		B-304897	82%	68%	75%
		C-331154	78%	90%	84%
		C-355778	94%	98%	96%

1-888-555-2200 ◆ www.emcp.net/nss

C14-A07-NSSQuizltr.docx (page 1 of 2)

Page 2 of 2

> 3. Specify that you want the first row in the table to display as a header row at the top of the table on the second page.

Date	Course #	Employee#	Quiz 1	Quiz 2	Average
		D-399384	70%	64%	67%
02/11/2015	A-500	A-128721	94%	98%	96%
		A-150043	50%	56%	53%
		B-178395	100%	88%	94%
		B-234002	78%	82%	80%
		C-321289	98%	90%	94%
		C-342003	68%	60%	64%
		D-385945	84%	88%	86%

If you need additional information about the training, please let me know. We are currently registering people for the April data security training courses. Please contact us for registration information or visit our website to register online.

Sincerely,

Joseph Barclay
Training Coordinator

> 4. Insert your initials at the end of the letter in place of the XX.

XX
C14-A07-NSSQuizAveLtr.docx

C14-A07-NSSQuizltr.docx (page 2 of 2)

1. At a blank document, create the document shown in Figure 14.9. Create and format the table as shown in the figure.

4523 Parkland Road
Indianapolis, IN 46211
March 3, 2015

Mr. Alan Lundgren
Orion News Tribune
211 South 42nd Street
Indianapolis, IN 46204

Dear Mr. Lundgren:

Your advertised opening for a corporate communications staff writer describes interesting challenges. As you can see from the table below, my skills are excellent matches for the position.

QUALIFICATIONS AND SKILLS	
Your Requirements	**My Experience, Skills, and Value Offered**
Two years of business writing experience	Four years of experience creating diverse business messages, from corporate communications to feature articles and radio broadcast material.
Ability to complete projects on deadline	Proven project coordination skills and tight deadline focus. My current role as producer of a daily, three-hour talk-radio program requires planning, coordination, and execution of many detailed tasks, always in the face of inflexible deadlines.
Oral presentation skills	Unusually broad experience, including high-profile roles as an on-air radio presence and "the voice" for an on-hold telephone message company.
Relevant education (BA or BS)	BA in Mass Communications, one year post-graduate study in Multimedia Communications.

As you will note from the enclosed resume, my experience encompasses corporate, print media, and multimedia environments. I offer a diverse and proven skill set that can help your company create and deliver its message to various audiences to build image, market presence, and revenue. I look forward to meeting with you to discuss the value I can offer your company.

Sincerely,

Justine Brock

Enclosure: Resume

C14-A08-CoverLtr.docx

Chapter 15 Assessment Annotated Model Answers

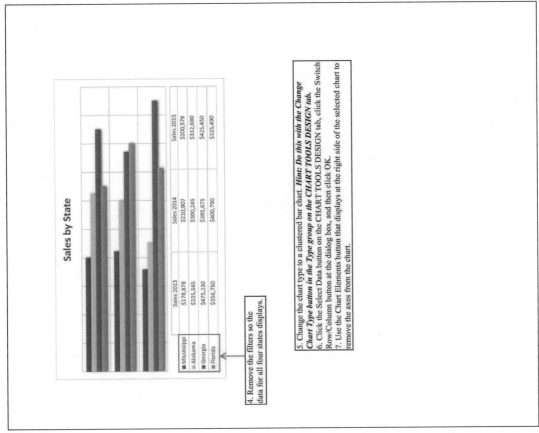

4. Remove the filters so the data for all four states displays.

5. Change the chart type to a clustered bar chart. *Hint: Do this with the Change Chart Type button in the Type group on the CHART TOOLS DESIGN tab.*
6. Click the Select Data button on the CHART TOOLS DESIGN tab, click the Switch Row/Column button at the dialog box, and then click OK.
7. Use the Chart Elements button that displays at the right side of the selected chart to remove the axes from the chart.

C15-A01-StSalesChart(Step8).docx

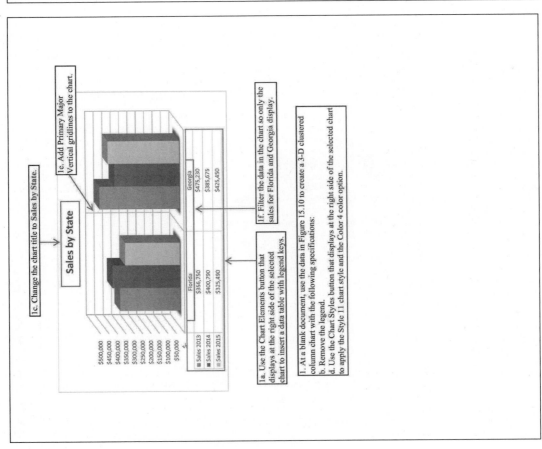

1c. Change the chart title to Sales by State.

1e. Add Primary Major Vertical gridlines to the chart.

1f. Filter the data in the chart so only the sales for Florida and Georgia display.

1a. Use the Chart Elements button that displays at the right side of the selected chart to insert a data table with legend keys.

1. At a blank document, use the data in Figure 15.10 to create a 3-D clustered column chart with the following specifications:
b. Remove the legend.
d. Use the Chart Styles button that displays at the right side of the selected chart to apply the Style 11 chart style and the Color 4 color option.

C15-A01-StSalesChart(Step3).docx

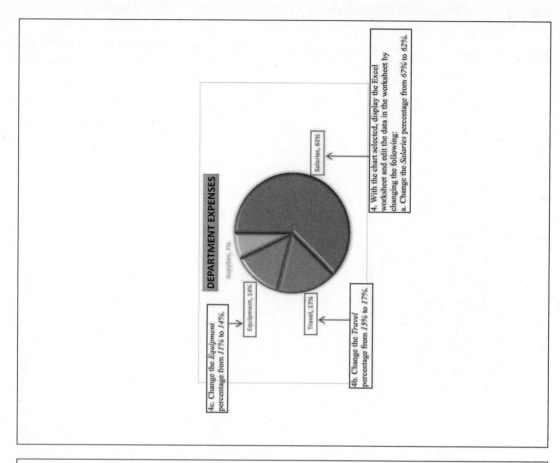

4. With the chart selected, display the Excel worksheet and edit the data in the worksheet by changing the following:
a. Change the *Salaries* percentage from *67%* to *62%*.

4c. Change the *Equipment* percentage from *11%* to *14%*.

4b. Change the *Travel* percentage from *15%* to *17%*.

C15-A02-ExpChart(Step5).docx

1. At a blank document, use the data in Figure 15.11 to create a pie chart with the following specifications:
a. Apply the Layout 4 quick layout.
b. Apply the Style 9 chart style.
d. Click a "piece" of the pie to select all of the pie pieces and then click the Shape Styles group task pane launcher. At the Format Data Series task pane, click the *Effects* icon, click *3-D FORMAT* to expand the options, and then apply the Circle top bevel.
e. Change the position of the pie chart to Position in Middle Center with Square Text Wrapping.

1c. Add the chart title *DEPARTMENT EXPENSES* above the chart and apply the Subtle Effect - Blue, Accent 1 shape style to the title.

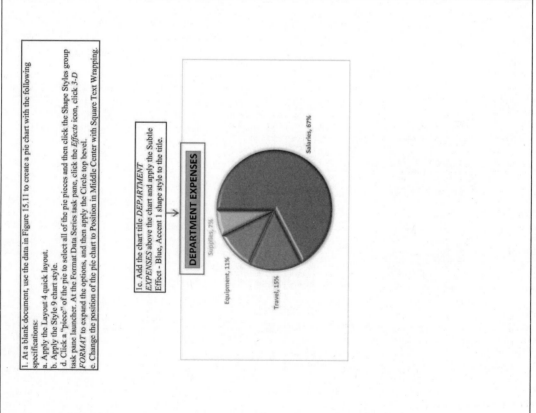

C15-A02-ExpChart(Step3).docx

1. Open **Middleton.docx** and save the document with the name **C15-A04- Middleton.**

2. Use the data in Figure 15.13 to create a line chart with the following specifications:
a. Choose the Line with Markers line chart type.
b. Switch the rows and columns.
c. Apply the Style 11 chart style.
d. Remove the chart title.

Middleton Valley

Development

Although the development of the Middleton Valley has come far, modern planners today use the ancient wisdom of the Native people when building in the area. Realizing the need to preserve the valley's beauty in the face of progress, the state formed the Middleton Valley Regional Planning Department in 1965 to oversee environmentally responsible development. The department's approach has enabled limitations to construction while devising a redevelopment plan that will improve the economy, tourist access, and the environment well into the next century. Today, the Middleton Valley retains its pioneer charm while displaying an ancient respect for nature. While hotels, casinos, and ski resorts draw millions of guests each year, the valley's main attraction continues to be the restful silence of the wilderness and the awe-inspiring beauty of the area.

Population

The year-around resident of the Middleton Valley generally live in one of the two cities in the valley—Milltown and Surrey. Over the past forty years, the building of ski resorts and casinos along with the recreational activities available in the valley, the population in both cities has increased. The following chart shows the population increase since 1970.

2e. Select the chart area, display the Format Chart Area task pane, and then apply gradient fill. f. With the chart area still selected, apply the Fill - Black, Text 1, Shadow WordArt style (first WordArt style).

Recreation

Because of the geography of the Middleton Valley and the surrounding area, summer and winter activities abound. With over 189,000 surface acres of water on or near Middleton Lake, fishing is a favorite activity. The lake is open all year for fishing for walleye, trout, bass, perch, crappie, and catfish. In the summer, people fish for some of the largest rainbow trout in the state and in the winter, ice fishing is a popular sport and easily accessible from local lodges. Other regional activities include hiking, camping, mountain biking, skiing, golf, and tennis. The valley boasts over 20 lodges and resorts and offers a full range of services for visitors, from those interested in camping to those preferring first-class amenities.

3. Display the Layout dialog box and then make the following changes:
a. With the Size tab selected, change the absolute height measurement to 2.5 inches and the absolute width measurement to 5 inches.
b. With the Text Wrapping tab selected, change the wrapping style to Top and bottom and change the distance from text bottom measurement to 0.2 inches.
c. With the Position tab selected, change the horizontal alignment to centered and change the vertical absolute position to 4.8 inches below the top margin.

c. Select the chart area and then apply the Dark Blue text fill color (ninth option in the *Standard Colors* section).

1a. Use the Chart Elements button that displays at the right side of the selected chart to remove the legend and add Primary Minor Vertical gridlines to the chart.

Sales in Millions

1b. Use the Chart Elements button on the CHART TOOLS FORMAT tab to select Series ''*Sales in Millions*'', apply the Dark Red shape fill color (first option in the *Standard Colors* section), and then apply the Light Blue shape outline color (seventh color option in the *Standard Colors* section).

1. At a blank document, use the data in Figure 15.12 to create a 3-D clustered bar chart with the following specifications:
d. Change the height of the chart to 4.5 inches and the width to 6.5 inches.

C15-A03-CoSalesChart.docx

BLUE MOUNTAIN COMPUTER SERVICES AND TRAINING

502 East 33rd Street ☐ Casper, WY 82607 ☐ 307-555-2218 ☐ www.emcp.net/bmc

July 8, 2015

Ms. Olivia Sullivan
Cashmere Products
3120 Jackson Street
Casper, WY 82645

Dear Ms. Sullivan:

We are confident that the computer training your employees have received at Blue Mountain Computer Services and Training enables them to perform their computer-related job duties more quickly and efficiently. The information below specifies the number of employees at Cashmere Products who have participated in the three sessions of training we offer on Office 2013.

2. Type the letter and insert and format the chart as shown in Figure 15.15. Apply the Style 5 chart style, change the color to Color 2, and change the font size of the title to 12 points. Size and position the chart as shown in the figure.

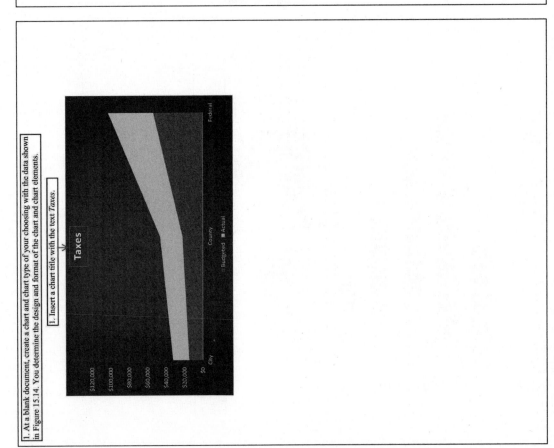

Number of Employees Participating in Office 2013 Training

We have established our computer training schedule for the second half of 2015, which is enclosed with this letter. For the second half of 2015, we are offering a number of advanced courses on Word 2013, Excel 2013, and PowerPoint 2013. If you have additional computer training needs, please let me know.

Sincerely,

Patricia Callaway
Training Coordinator

2. Insert your initials in place of the *XX* that display near the bottom of the letter.

xx
C15-A06-LtrtoCP.docx

Enclosure

"Let our five-star customer service team provide all of your computer support and training needs."

C15-A06-LtrtoCP.docx

---

1. At a blank document, create a chart and chart type of your choosing with the data shown in Figure 15.14. You determine the design and format of the chart and chart elements.

1. Insert a chart title with the text *Taxes*.

C15-A05-TaxesChart.docx

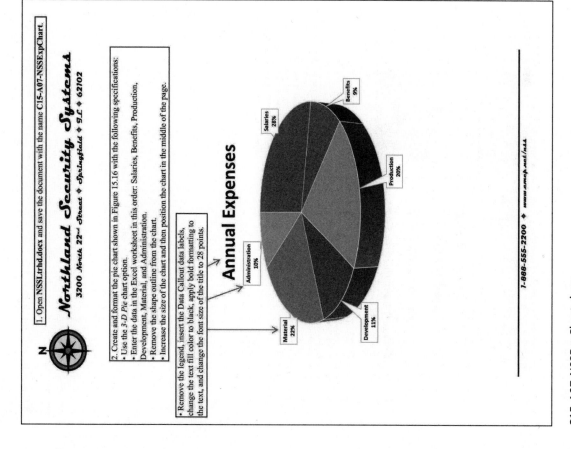

1. Open NSSLtrhd.docx and save the document with the name C15-A07-NSSExpChart.

Northland Security Systems

3200 North 22ⁿᵈ Street ✦ Springfield ✦ IL ✦ 62102

2. Create and format the pie chart shown in Figure 15.16 with the following specifications:
- Use the *3-D Pie* chart option.
- Enter the data in the Excel worksheet in this order: Salaries, Benefits, Production, Development, Material, and Administration.
- Remove the shape outline from the chart.
- Increase the size of the chart and then position the chart in the middle of the page.

- Remove the legend, insert the Data Callout data labels, change the text fill color to black, apply bold formatting to the text, and change the font size of the title to 28 points.

Annual Expenses

Administration 10%

Material 22%

Development 11%

Production 20%

Salaries 28%

Benefits 9%

1-888-555-2200 ✦ www.emcp.net/nss

C15-A07-NSSExpChart.docx

Unit 3 Performance Assessment Annotated Model Answers

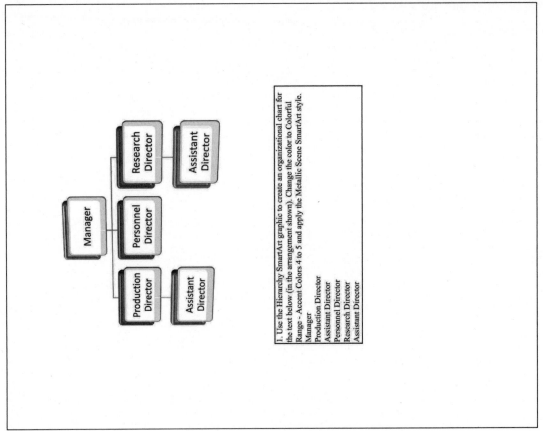

1. Use the Hierarchy SmartArt graphic to create an organizational chart for the text below (in the arrangement shown). Change the color to Colorful Range - Accent Colors 4 to 5 and apply the Metallic Scene SmartArt style.

Manager
Production Director
Assistant Director
Personnel Director
Research Director
Assistant Director

U3-PA02-OrgChart.docx

1. Create the flyer shown in Figure U3.1 with the following specifications:

b. Type the text shown in the figure set in 22-point Calibri and then apply bold formatting and center the text.

1a. Create the WordArt with the following specifications:
• Use the Fill - White, Outline - Accent 1, Shadow option (first row, fourth column) at the WordArt button drop-down gallery.
• Increase the width to 6.5 inches and the height to 1 inch.
• Apply the Deflate text effect transform shape (second column, sixth row in the *Warp* section).
• Change the text fill color to Green, Accent 6, Lighter 40%.

1c. Insert the clip art image shown in the figure (use the keywords *Eiffel Tower Paris* to find the clip art) and then change the wrapping style to Square. Change the height and width of the clip art image to 2.2 inches and position the image as shown in the figure.

U3-PA01-TravelFlier.docx

1. Create the announcement shown in Figure U3.3 with the following specifications:
a. Use the Bevel shape in the *Basic Shapes* section of the Shapes drop-down list to create the shape.
b. Apply the Moderate Effect - Green, Accent 6 style to the shape.
c. Change the shape outline color to Dark Blue.
d. Apply the Offset Diagonal Top Left shadow to the shape.
e. Change the shape height to 2.8 inches and the shape width to 6 inches.
f. Change the position of the shape to Position in Middle Center with Square Text Wrapping.

1g. Type the text inside the bevel shape as shown in the figure. Set the text in 20-point Candara with bold formatting applied and then change the font color to Dark Blue.

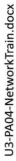
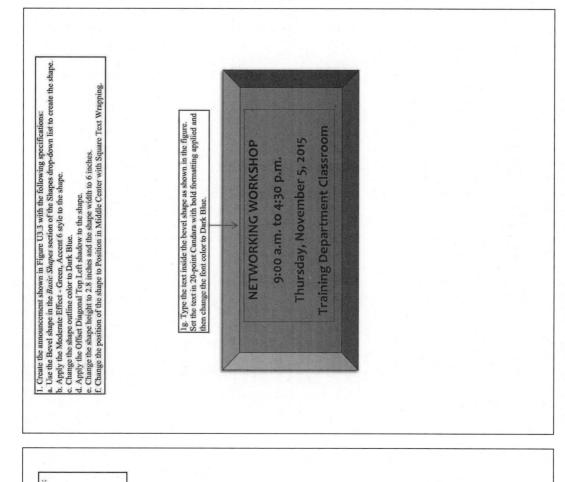

NETWORKING WORKSHOP

9:00 a.m. to 4:30 p.m.

Thursday, November 5, 2015

Training Department Classroom

1. At a blank document, create the SmartArt graphic shown in Figure U3.2 with the following specifications:
a. Create the cycle graphic using the Basic Radial SmartArt graphic, insert two additional shapes, and then type the text (applying bold formatting) in the shapes as shown in the figure.
b. Change the color to Colorful Range - Accent Colors 4 to 5.
c. Apply the Cartoon SmartArt style.
d. Increase the height to 4.5 inches and the width to 6.5 inches.
e. Change the position of the graphic to Position in Middle Center with Square Text Wrapping. Position the graphic in the middle of the page.
f. Change the text fill color to Black, Text 1.

Accounting

Shipping

Manufacturing

Intranet Server

Sales

Management

Human Resources

U3-PA06-Photography.docx

1. Open **Photography.docx** and save the document with the name U3-PA06-Photography.

2. Select the text *Photography* that displays at the beginning of the document and then create WordArt with the following specifications;
a. Use the *Fill - Black, Text 1*, Shadow WordArt option.

2b. Change the height to 0.7 inches and the width to 4 inches.
c. Change the position to Position in Top Center with Square Text Wrapping.
d. Change the text wrapping to Top and Bottom.
e. Apply the Square transform text effect (first option in the *Warp* section).

Photography

camera and then processed and printed. The camera was reloaded with film and then returned to the owner.

Camera Basics

Photographs are taken by letting light into a light-sensitive medium, which records the image. A camera consists of a light-tight box that stores a light-sensitive device and a lens that magnifies and focuses the image onto the light-sensitive device through a hole in the box called the aperture. A shutter opens and closes when the user presses the shutter release, exposing the film to the light. Cameras share some of the common features such as light-sensitive medium to capture the image, lens aperture, shutter, and viewfinder or screen.

Some additional camera features include a tripod screw of standard size to fit any tripod, a method for setting the distance, and a method for setting the film speed. Cameras vary in the amount of control a user has over the aperture, shutter, and distance settings, and whether these can be set automatically.

Photography is a method of picture making based on principles of light, optics, and chemistry. The word "photography" comes from the Greek words *photos* meaning "light" and *graphein* meaning "to draw."

History

The scientist Sir John F. W. Herschel was the first to use the word in 1839. The first fixed image was obtained by Joseph Nicephore Niepce in 1827. At about the same time, Louis Jacques Mande Daguerre was experimenting with methods for capturing an image. Approximately twelve years later, Daguerre was able to reduce the exposure time to less than 30 minutes, ushering in the age of modern photography.

In 1889, George Eastman saw the potential for mass marketing and produced a newly invented film with a flexible and unbreakable base that could be rolled. Eastman sold simple cameras that contained factory-installed film. The photographer pushed a button to produce a negative and then, when the film was used up, mailed the camera back to the Kodak factory. At the factory, the film was removed from the

"Photography, as a powerful medium of expression and communication, offers an infinite variety of perception, interpretation, and execution." Ansel Adams

"Photography can never grow up if it imitates some other medium. It has to walk alone; it has to be itself." Berenice Abbott

3. Insert the Motion Quote text box and then change the position of the text box to Position in Middle Center with Square Text Wrapping. Type "Photography, as a powerful medium of expression and communication, offers an infinite variety of perception, interpretation, and execution." Ansel Adams in the text box. Select the text in the text box, change the font size to 11 points, apply bold formatting, and then change the width of the text box to 3.1 inches.

4. Select the quote (including the author's name) that displays at the bottom of the document, display the Font dialog box with the Advanced tab selected, and then make the following changes:
a. Change the character spacing to Expanded by 0.3 points.
b. Turn on kerning for fonts 16 points and above.
c. Change the *Stylistic sets* option to 4 and then close the dialog box.

U3-PA06-Photography.docx

U3-PA05-RAAnnounce.docx

2. Crop out some of the trees at the left and right and part of the hill at the top.

2. Crop out some of the trees at the left and right and part of the hill at the top.

2. Crop out some of the trees at the left and right and part of the hill at the top.

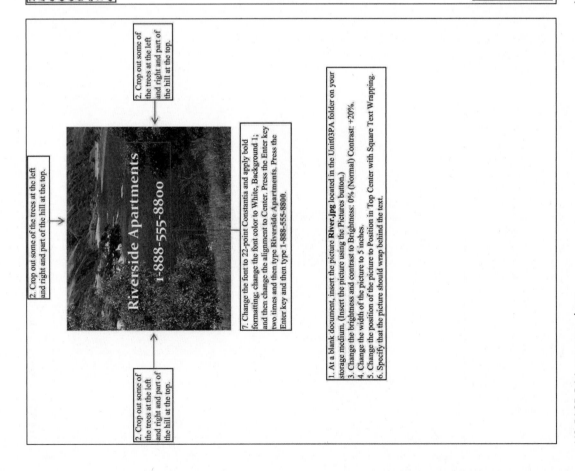

7. Change the font to 22-point Constantia and apply bold formatting; change the font color to White, Background 1; and then change the alignment to Center. Press the Enter key two times and then type Riverside Apartments. Press the Enter key and then type 1-888-555-8800.

1. At a blank document, insert the picture **River.jpg** located in the Unit03PA folder on your storage medium. (Insert the picture using the Pictures button.)
3. Change the brightness and contrast to Brightness: 0% (Normal) Contrast: +20%.
4. Change the width of the picture to 5 inches.
5. Change the position of the picture to Position in Top Center with Square Text Wrapping.
6. Specify that the picture should wrap behind the text.

U3-PA05-RAAnnounce.docx

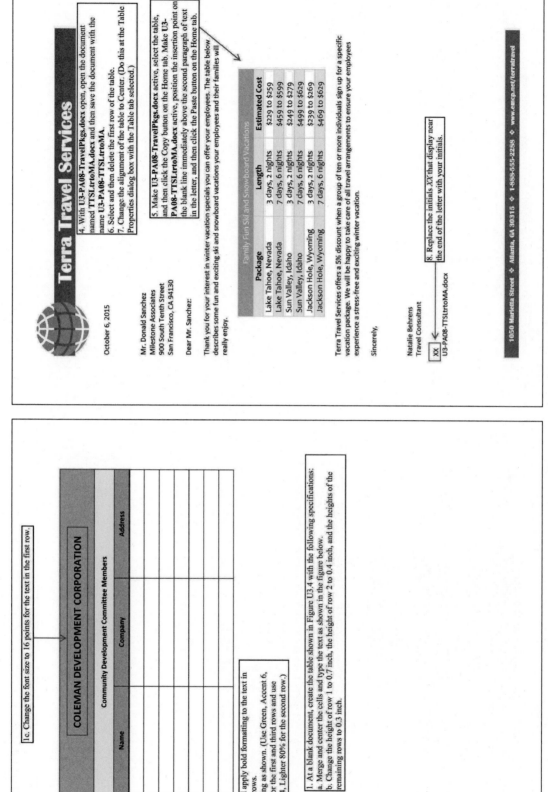

Terra Travel Services

October 6, 2015

Mr. Donald Sanchez
Milestone Associates
900 South Tenth Street
San Francisco, CA 94130

Dear Mr. Sanchez:

Thank you for your interest in winter vacation specials you can offer your employees. The table below describes some fun and exciting ski and snowboard vacations your employees and their families will really enjoy.

Family Fun Ski and Snowboard Vacations

Package	Length	Estimated Cost
Lake Tahoe, Nevada	3 days, 2 nights	$229 to $259
Lake Tahoe, Nevada	7 days, 6 nights	$459 to $599
Sun Valley, Idaho	3 days, 2 nights	$249 to $279
Sun Valley, Idaho	7 days, 6 nights	$499 to $629
Jackson Hole, Wyoming	3 days, 2 nights	$239 to $269
Jackson Hole, Wyoming	7 days, 6 nights	$469 to $629

Terra Travel Services offers a 5% discount when a group of ten or more individuals sign up for a specific vacation package. We will be happy to take care of all travel arrangements to ensure your employees experience a stress-free and exciting winter vacation.

Sincerely,

Natalie Behrens
Travel Consultant

XX
U3-PA08-TTSLrtoMA.docx

1050 Marietta Street ❖ Atlanta, GA 30315 ❖ 1-888-555-2258 ❖ www.emcp.net/terratravel

Callout boxes (Terra Travel document):

4. With U3-PA08-TravelPkgs.docx open, open the document named TTSLrtoMA.docx and then save the document with the name U3-PA08-TTSLrtoMA.

6. Select and then delete the first row of the table.

7. Change the alignment of the table to Center. (Do this at the Table Properties dialog box with the Table tab selected.)

5. Make U3-PA08-TravelPkgs.docx active, select the table, and then click the Copy button on the Home tab. Make U3-PA08-TTSLrtoMA.docx active, position the insertion point on the blank line immediately above the second paragraph of text in the letter, and then click the Paste button on the Home tab.

8. Replace the initials XX that display near the end of the letter with your initials.

U3-PA08-TravelPkgs.docx

COLEMAN DEVELOPMENT CORPORATION

Community Development Committee Members

Name	Company	Address

Callout boxes (Coleman document):

1c. Change the font size to 16 points for the text in the first row.

1d. Center and apply bold formatting to the text in the first three rows.

e. Apply shading as shown. (Use Green, Accent 6, Lighter 40% for the first and third rows and use Gold, Accent 4, Lighter 80% for the second row.)

1. At a blank document, create the table shown in Figure U3.4 with the following specifications:
a. Merge and center the cells and type the text as shown in the figure below.
b. Change the height of row 1 to 0.7 inch, the height of row 2 to 0.4 inch, and the heights of the remaining rows to 0.3 inch.

U3-PA07-ComMembers.docx

1. Open **EmpOrient.docx** and save the document with the name **U3-PA09- EmpOrient**.
3. Use the AutoFit feature to format the contents of the table.
4. Apply a table style of your choosing to the table.
5. Apply any other formatting to improve the appearance of the table.

COLEMAN DEVELOPMENT CORPORATION				
New Employee Orientation				
Name	Quiz 1	Quiz 2	Quiz 3	Average
Mary Castillo	88	74	90	84
Patrick Donahue	92	86	84	87
Angela Herron	78	66	72	72
Jason Kepler	84	76	80	80
Teresa Miroshi	76	82	78	79
Thomas Newton	96	98	94	96
Desiree Pollock	84	68	80	77

2. Insert formulas in the appropriate cells that calculate the averages of the quizzes. (Change the *Number Format* option at the Formula dialog box to 0.)

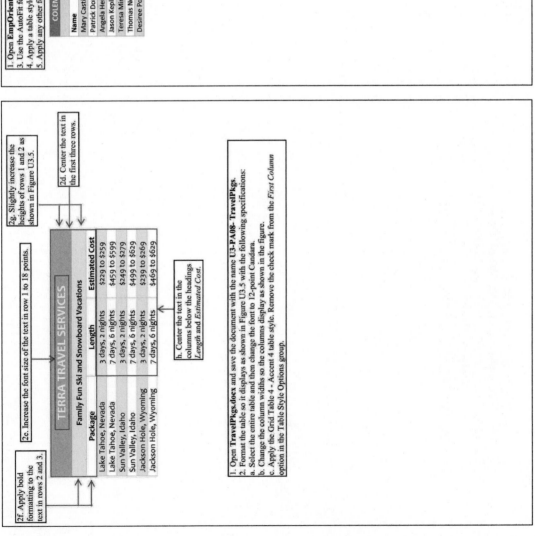

2f. Apply bold formatting to the text in rows 2 and 3.

2e. Increase the font size of the text in row 1 to 18 points.

2g. Slightly increase the heights of rows 1 and 2 as shown in Figure U3.5.

2d. Center the text in the first three rows.

TERRA TRAVEL SERVICES		
Family Fun Ski and Snowboard Vacations		
Package	Length	Estimated Cost
Lake Tahoe, Nevada	3 days, 2 nights	$229 to $259
Lake Tahoe, Nevada	7 days, 6 nights	$459 to $599
Sun Valley, Idaho	3 days, 2 nights	$249 to $279
Sun Valley, Idaho	7 days, 6 nights	$499 to $629
Jackson Hole, Wyoming	3 days, 2 nights	$239 to $269
Jackson Hole, Wyoming	7 days, 6 nights	$469 to $629

h. Center the text in the columns below the headings *Length* and *Estimated Cost*.

1. Open **TravelPkgs.docx** and save the document with the name **U3-PA08- TravelPkgs**.
2. Format the table so it displays as shown in Figure U3.5 with the following specifications:
a. Select the entire table and then change the font to 12-point Candara.
b. Change the column widths so the columns display as shown in the figure.
c. Apply the Grid Table 4 - Accent 4 table style. Remove the check mark from the *First Column* option in the Table Style Options group.

1. At a blank document, use the data in Figure U3.6 to create a column chart with the following specifications:

a. Choose the 3-D Clustered Column chart type.
b. Apply the Layout 3 chart layout.
c. Apply the Style 5 chart style.
f. Select the chart area, apply the Subtle Effect - Green, Accent 6 shape style (last column, fourth row), and apply the Offset Bottom shadow shape effect.
h. Change the chart height to 4 inches and the chart width to 6.25 inches.
i. Use the Position button in the Arrange group to position the chart in the middle of the page with square text wrapping.

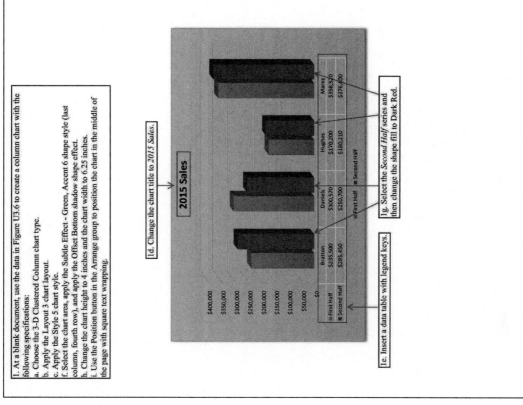

1d. Change the chart title to *2015 Sales*.

1g. Select the *Second Half* series and then change the shape fill to Dark Red.

1e. Insert a data table with legend keys.

2015 Sales

	Bratton	Daniels	Hughes	Marez
First Half	$235,500	$300,570	$170,200	$358,520
Second Half	$285,450	$250,700	$180,210	$376,600

1. Open **PurOrder.docx** and save the document with the name U3-PA10-PurOrder.

MOBILE BAY PRODUCTS

Purchase Order

Qty.	Product #	Unit Price	Total
120	TI-35L	$25.00	$3,000.00
15	0989-348	$75.00	$1,125.00
30	I-3948_LG	$59.00	$1,770.00
45	258-493-T	$29.00	$1,305.00
			$7,200.00

2. In the appropriate cells, insert formulas that multiply the quantity by the unit price. In the bottom cell in the fourth column, insert a formula that totals the amounts in the cells above.

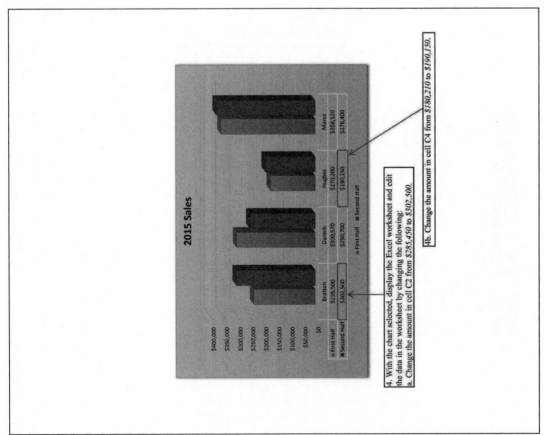

Top figure (U3-PA12-ExpendChart.docx):

1d. Move the legend to the left side of the chart.
f. Select the legend and apply the Blue shape outline color (eighth option in the *Standard Colors* section).
i. Select the legend and then move it so it is centered between the left edge of the chart border and the pie.

1c. Change the chart title to *District Expenditures*.
g. Apply the WordArt style Fill - Blue, Accent 1, Outline - Background 1, Hard Shadow - Accent 1 (third column, third row) to the chart title text.

1h. Move the data labels to the inside ends of the pie "pieces."

1. At a blank document, use the data in Figure U3.7 to create a pie chart with the following specifications:
a. Apply the Layout 6 chart layout.
b. Apply the Style 3 chart style.
e. Select the chart area, apply Gold, Accent 4, Lighter 80% shape fill (eighth column, second row in the *Theme Colors* section), and apply the Gray-50%, Accent color 3 glow shape effect (third column, third row in the *Glow Variations* section).
j. Use the Position button in the Arrange group to center the chart at the top of the page with square text wrapping.

District Expenditures pie chart — 42%, 20%, 19%, 11%, 8%; Legend: Basic Education, Special Needs, Support Services, Vocational, Compensatory

U3-PA12-ExpendChart.docx

Bottom figure (U3-PA11-SalesChart(Step5).docx):

4. With the chart selected, display the Excel worksheet and edit the data in the worksheet by changing the following:
a. Change the amount in cell C2 from *$285,450* to *$302,500*.

4b. Change the amount in cell C4 from *$180,210* to *$190,150*.

2015 Sales chart:

	Bratton	Danieb	Hughes	Marez
First Half	$235,500	$300,570	$170,200	$358,520
Second Half	$302,500	$250,700	$190,150	$376,400

U3-PA11-SalesChart(Step5).docx

Situation: You work in the training department of Coleman Development Corporation and are responsible for preparing a training document on how to use Word 2013. Create a document that describes the SmartArt feature and the types of graphics a user can create with it. Provide specific steps describing how to create an organizational chart using the Organizational Chart graphic and how to create a radial cycle graphic using the Radial Cycle graphic.

Coleman Development Corporation – Using SmartArt in Word 2013

What are SmartArt graphics?

Word 2013 includes a design feature called SmartArt. This feature allows you to insert a visual image into a document to assist in relaying information and offering a greater lasting impact.

What can you create with SmartArt?

There are several types of images that can be created in SmartArt. Choosing the correct graphic for your document is a necessary skill. You can choose from Lists, Processes, Cycles, Hierarchy, and others to contribute to the information you are choosing to include.

Creating an Organizational Chart

Organizational charts are frequently used in corporate settings and help to offer a visual understanding of an organizations chain of command.

To create an Organizational chart., you must first gather the necessary information and determine the order in which it should be displayed.

- Click the SmartArt button from the INSERT tab.
- At the Choose a SmartArt Graphic dialog box, click Hierarchy from the side menu, select the desired graphic, and then click OK.
- Click the [Text] placeholder and type the desired text.
- Delete any placeholders you don't need, or use options in the Create Graphic group on the SMARTART TOOLS DESIGN tab to add additional placeholders.

Creating a Radial Cycle

A cycle graphic is best for relaying a process or flow of something. This can be a useful image when referring to a multi-step circular process that is repetitive. A radial cycle differs in that its points of interest radiate from a center concept. It is most used to display a visual understanding of a relationship.

To create a Radial Cycle, compile your necessary information.

- Click the SmartArt button from the INSERT tab.
- At the Choose a SmartArt Graphic dialog box, click Relationship from the side menu, then click the specific radial design that best fits your document and click OK.
- Click the [Text] placeholder and type the desired text.
- Delete any placeholders you don't need, or use options in the Create Graphic group on the SMARTART TOOLS DESIGN tab to add additional placeholders.

Coleman Development Corporation
Equipment Expenditures

Department	Amount
Personnel	$20,400
Research	$58,300
Finance	$14,900
Production	$90,100
Sales	$51,000
Marketing	$52,600

Situation: You are the vice president of Coleman Development Corporation and need to prepare a table showing the equipment expenditures for each department, as shown below:

COLEMAN DEVELOPMENT CORPORATION

Equipment Expenditures

Department	Amount
Personnel	$20,400
Research	$58,300
Finance	$14,900
Production	$90,100
Sales	$51,000
Marketing	$52,600

Create a table with the data and apply appropriate formatting to it.

EVERGREEN SPORTS

4500 Lowell Avenue • Portland, OR 99821

Telephone (503) 555-8220

Situation: You work for Evergreen Sports, a sports equipment store that specializes in hiking gear. You have been asked to design a letterhead for the store. When designing the letterhead, include an appropriate clip art image along with the following information:

Evergreen Sports
4500 Lowell Avenue
Portland, OR 99821
(503) 555-8220

U3-PA16-ESLtrhd.docx

Situation: You decide that the data in the table you created in Assessment U3.14 will be easier to visualize if it is inserted in a chart. Using the information from the table, create a column chart and apply formatting to enhance the appearance of the chart.

Coleman Development Corporation
Equipment Expenditures

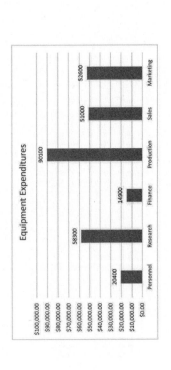

U3-PA15-EquipExpChart.docx

Signature Word 2013   Model Answers

Chapter 16 Assessment Annotated Model Answers

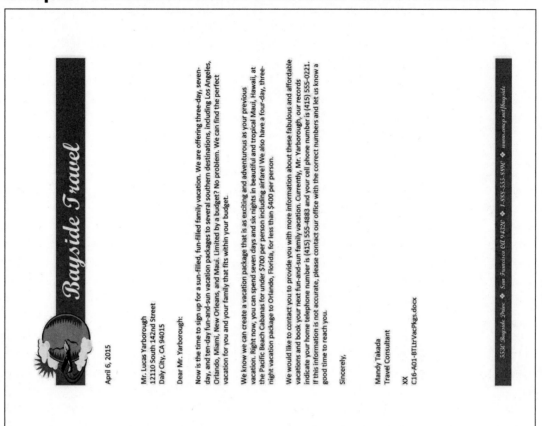

Page 2 letter:

Bayside Travel

April 6, 2015

Mr. Lucas Yarborough
12110 South 142nd Street
Daly City, CA 94015

Dear Mr. Yarborough:

Now is the time to sign up for a sun-filled, fun-filled family vacation. We are offering three-day, seven-day, and ten-day fun-and-sun vacation packages to several southern destinations, including Los Angeles, Orlando, Miami, New Orleans, and Maui. Limited by a budget? No problem. We can find the perfect vacation for you and your family that fits within your budget.

We know we can create a vacation package that is as exciting and adventurous as your previous vacation. Right now, you can spend seven days and six nights in beautiful and tropical Maui, Hawaii, at the Pacific Beach Cabanas for under $700 per person including airfare! We also have a four-day, three-night vacation package to Orlando, Florida, for less than $400 per person.

We would like to contact you to provide you with more information about these fabulous and affordable vacations and book your next fun-and-sun family vacation. Currently, Mr. Yarborough, our records indicate your home telephone number is (415) 555-4883 and your cell phone number is (415) 555-0221. If this information is not accurate, please contact our office with the correct numbers and let us know a good time to reach you.

Sincerely,

Mandy Takada
Travel Consultant

XX
C16-A02-BTVacPkgs.docx

3530 Bayside Drive ❖ San Francisco CA 94320 ❖ 1-888-555-8890 ❖ www.emcp.net/bayside

Page 1 letter (with annotations):

1. Open **BTVacPkgs.docx** and then save the document with Save As and name it **C16-A02-BTVacPkgsMD**.
2. Select **C16-A01-BTDS.mdb**, which you created in Assessment 1, as the data source file.
6. Merge the main document with all of the records in the data source file.

Bayside Travel

April 6, 2015

Mrs. Tina Cardoza
2314 Magnolia Drive
P.O. Box 231
San Francisco, CA 94120

3. Move the insertion point to the beginning of the first paragraph of text in the body of the letter, insert the «AddressBlock» field, and then press Enter twice.

Dear Mrs. Cardoza:

4. Insert the «GreetingLine» field specifying a colon rather than a comma as the greeting line format and then press Enter twice.

Now is the time to sign up for a sun-filled, fun-filled family vacation. We are offering three-day, seven-day, and ten-day fun-and-sun vacation packages to several southern destinations, including Los Angeles, Orlando, Miami, New Orleans, and Maui. Limited by a budget? No problem. We can find the perfect vacation for you and your family that fits within your budget.

We know we can create a vacation package that is as exciting and adventurous as your previous vacation. Right now, you can spend seven days and six nights in beautiful and tropical Maui, Hawaii, at the Pacific Beach Cabanas for under $700 per person including airfare! We also have a four-day, three-night vacation package to Orlando, Florida, for less than $400 per person.

We would like to contact you to provide you with more information about these fabulous and affordable vacations and book your next fun-and-sun family vacation. Currently, Mrs. Cardoza, our records indicate your home telephone number is (415) 555-2265 and your cell phone number is (415) 555-7523. If this information is not accurate, please contact our office with the correct numbers and let us know a good time to reach you.

5. Move the insertion point one space to the right of the period that ends the third paragraph of text in the body of the letter and then type the following text inserting the «Title», «Last_Name», «Home_Phone», «Cell_Phone» fields where indicated: Currently, «Title» «Last_Name», our records indicate your home telephone number is «Home_Phone» and your cell phone number is «Cell_Phone». If this information is not accurate, please contact our office with the correct numbers and let us know a good time to reach you.

Sincerely,

Mandy Takada
Travel Consultant

XX
C16-A01-BTLtrVacPkgs.docx

3530 Bayside Drive ❖ San Francisco CA 94320 ❖ 1-888-555-8890 ❖ www.emcp.net/bayside

Bayside Travel

April 6, 2015

Mr. Daryl Gillette
13181 North 42nd Street
San Francisco, CA 94128

Dear Mr. Gillette:

Now is the time to sign up for a sun-filled, fun-filled family vacation. We are offering three-day, seven-day, and ten-day fun-and-sun vacation packages to several southern destinations, including Los Angeles, Orlando, Miami, New Orleans, and Maui. Limited by a budget? No problem. We can find the perfect vacation for you and your family that fits within your budget.

We know we can create a vacation package that is as exciting and adventurous as your previous vacation. Right now, you can spend seven days and six nights in beautiful and tropical Maui, Hawaii, at the Pacific Beach Cabanas for under $700 per person including airfare! We also have a four-day, three-night vacation package to Orlando, Florida, for less than $400 per person.

We would like to contact you to provide you with more information about these fabulous and affordable vacations and book your next fun-and-sun family vacation. Currently, Mr. Gillette, our records indicate your home telephone number is (415) 555-8302 and your cell phone number is (415) 555-6455. If this information is not accurate, please contact our office with the correct numbers and let us know a good time to reach you.

Sincerely,

Mandy Takada
Travel Consultant

XX
C16-A01-BTLtrVacPkgs.docx

5538 Bayside Drive ❖ San Francisco CA 94320 ❖ 1-888-555-8890 ❖ www.emcp.net/bayside

C16-A02-BTVacPkgsLetters.docx (page 4 of 4)

Bayside Travel

April 6, 2015

Mrs. Lucille Alvarez
2542 Ranchero Drive
Apt. 115
Daly City, CA 94017

Dear Mrs. Alvarez:

Now is the time to sign up for a sun-filled, fun-filled family vacation. We are offering three-day, seven-day, and ten-day fun-and-sun vacation packages to several southern destinations, including Los Angeles, Orlando, Miami, New Orleans, and Maui. Limited by a budget? No problem. We can find the perfect vacation for you and your family that fits within your budget.

We know we can create a vacation package that is as exciting and adventurous as your previous vacation. Right now, you can spend seven days and six nights in beautiful and tropical Maui, Hawaii, at the Pacific Beach Cabanas for under $700 per person including airfare! We also have a four-day, three-night vacation package to Orlando, Florida, for less than $400 per person.

We would like to contact you to provide you with more information about these fabulous and affordable vacations and book your next fun-and-sun family vacation. Currently, Mrs. Alvarez, our records indicate your home telephone number is (415) 555-8372 and your cell phone number is (415) 555-4411. If this information is not accurate, please contact our office with the correct numbers and let us know a good time to reach you.

Sincerely,

Mandy Takada
Travel Consultant

XX
C16-A01-BTLtrVacPkgs.docx

5538 Bayside Drive ❖ San Francisco CA 94320 ❖ 1-888-555-8890 ❖ www.emcp.net/bayside

C16-A02-BTVacPkgsLetters.docx (page 3 of 4)

Mr. Lucas Yarborough
12110 South 142nd Street
Daly City, CA 94015

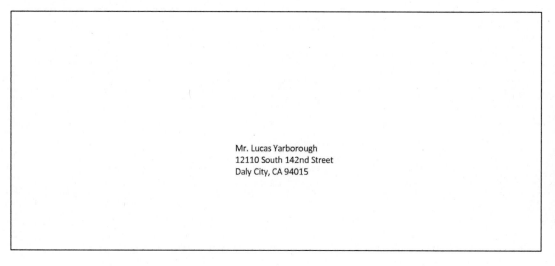

1. Create an envelope main document using the standard size 10 envelope.
2. Select **C16-A01-BTDS.mdb** as the data source file.
4. Merge the envelope main document with all of the records in the data source file.

3. Insert the «*AddressBlock*» field in the appropriate location in the envelope document.

Mrs. Tina Cardoza
2314 Magnolia Drive
P.O. Box 231
San Francisco, CA 94120

Mr. Daryl Gillette
13181 North 42nd Street
San Francisco, CA 94128

C16-A03-BTEnvs.docx (page 4 of 4)

Mrs. Lucille Alvarez
2542 Ranchero Drive
Apt. 115
Daly City, CA 94017

C16-A03-BTEnvs.docx (page 3 of 4)

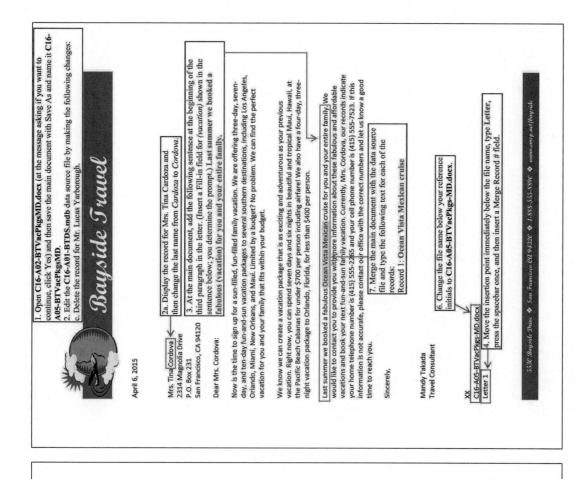

Bayside Travel

1. Open **C16-A02-BTVacPkgsMD.docx** (at the message asking if you want to continue, click Yes) and then save the main document with Save As and name it **C16-A05-BTVacPkgsMD**.
2. Edit the **C16-A01-BTDS.mdb** data source file by making the following changes:
c. Delete the record for Mr. Lucas Yarborough.

April 6, 2015

2a. Display the record for Mrs. Tina Cardoza and then change the last name from *Cardoza* to *Cordova*.

Mrs. Tina Cordova
2314 Magnolia Drive
P.O. Box 231
San Francisco, CA 94120

Dear Mrs. Cordova:

3. At the main document, add the following sentence at the beginning of the third paragraph in the letter. (Insert a Fill-in field for *(vacation)* shown in the sentence below; you determine the prompt.) Last summer we booked a fabulous *(vacation)* for you and your entire family.

Now is the time to sign up for a sun-filled, fun-filled family vacation. We are offering three-day, seven-day, and ten-day fun-and-sun vacation packages to several southern destinations, including Los Angeles, Orlando, Miami, New Orleans, and Maui. Limited by a budget? No problem. We can find the perfect vacation for you and your family that fits within your budget.

We know we can create a vacation package that is as exciting and adventurous as your previous vacation. Right now, you can spend seven days and six nights in beautiful and tropical Maui, Hawaii, at the Pacific Beach Cabanas for under $700 per person including airfare! We also have a four-day, three-night vacation package to Orlando, Florida, for less than $400 per person.

Last summer we booked a fabulous Ocean Vista Mexican cruise for you and your entire family. We would like to contact you to provide you with more information about these fabulous and affordable vacations and book your next fun-and-sun family vacation. Currently, Mrs. Cordova, our records indicate your home telephone number is (415) 555-2265 and your cell phone number is (415) 555-7523. If this information is not accurate, please contact our office with the correct numbers and let us know a good time to reach you.

7. Merge the main document with the data source file and type the following text for each of the records:
Record 1: Ocean Vista Mexican cruise

Sincerely,

Mandy Takada
Travel Consultant

6. Change the file name below your reference initials to **C16-A05-BTVacPkgs-MD.docx.**

XX

C16-A05-BTVacPkgs-MD.docx
Letter 1

4. Move the insertion point immediately below the file name, type Letter, press the spacebar once, and then insert a Merge Record # field.

5530 Bayside Drive ❖ San Francisco CA 94320 ❖ 1-888-555-8900 ❖ www.emcp.net/bayside

C16-A05-BTVacPkgsLetters.docx (page 1 of 5)

Mrs. Tina Cardoza
2314 Magnolia Drive
P.O. Box 231
San Francisco, CA 94120

Mr. Lucas Yarborough
12110 South 142nd Street
Daly City, CA 94015

Mrs. Lucille Alvarez
2542 Ranchero Drive
Apt. 115
Daly City, CA 94017

Mr. Daryl Gillette
13181 North 42nd Street
San Francisco, CA 94128

3. Insert the *«AddressBlock»* field.

1. Create a label main document using the *Avery US Letter 5160 Easy Peel Address Labels* option.
2. Select **C16-A01-BTDS.mdb** as the data source file.
4. Update the labels.
5. Merge the label main document with all of the records in the data source file.
6. Select the entire document and then apply the No Spacing style.

C16-A04-BTLabels.docx

Bayside Travel

April 6, 2015

2b. Display the record for Mr. Daryl Gillette, change the street address from *13181 North 42nd Street* to *9843 22nd Street South*, and change the zip code from *94128* to *94102*.

Mr. Daryl Gillette
9843 22nd Street South
San Francisco, CA 94102

Dear Mr. Gillette:

Now is the time to sign up for a sun-filled, fun-filled family vacation. We are offering three-day, seven-day, and ten-day fun-and-sun vacation packages to several southern destinations, including Los Angeles, Orlando, Miami, New Orleans, and Maui. Limited by a budget? No problem. We can find the perfect vacation for you and your family that fits within your budget.

We know we can create a vacation package that is as exciting and adventurous as your previous vacation. Right now, you can spend seven days and six nights in beautiful and tropical Maui, Hawaii, at the Pacific Beach Cabanas for under $700 per person including airfare! We also have a four-day, three-night vacation package to Orlando, Florida, for less than $400 per person.

Last summer we booked a fabulous Ocean Vista Caribbean cruise for you and your entire family. We would like to contact you to provide you with more information about these fabulous and affordable vacations and book your next fun-and-sun family vacation. Currently, Mr. Gillette, our records indicate your home telephone number is (415) 555-8302 and your cell phone number is (415) 555-6455. If this information is not accurate, please contact our office with the correct numbers and let us know a good time to reach you.

Sincerely,

Mandy Takada
Travel Consultant

XX
C16-A05-BTVacPkgs-MD.docx
Letter 3

7. Merge the main document with the data source file and type the following text for each of the records:
Record 3: Ocean Vista Caribbean cruise

5330 Bayside Drive ❖ San Francisco CA 94320 ❖ 1-888-555-8590 ❖ www.emcp.net/bayside

C16-A05-BTVacPkgsLetters.docx (page 3 of 5)

Bayside Travel

April 6, 2015

5. Move the insertion point immediately after the job title in the closing of the letter. Press the Enter key twice and then insert an If…Then…Else… field with the following specifications:

a. At the Insert Word Field: IF dialog box, specify the *City* field in the *Field name* option box.
b. Type Daly City in the *Compare to* text box.
c. In the *Insert this text* text box, type the text shown below and then close the dialog box: P.S. A representative from Wildlife Eco-Tours will present information on upcoming tours at our Daly City branch office the first Saturday of next month. Come by and hear about exciting and adventurous eco-tours.

Mrs. Lucille Alvarez
2542 Ranchero Drive
Apt. 115
Daly City, CA 94017

Dear Mrs. Alvarez:

Now is the time to sign up for a sun-filled, fun-filled family vacation. We are offering three-day, seven-day, and ten-day fun-and-sun vacation packages to several southern destinations, including Los Angeles, Orlando, Miami, New Orleans, and Maui. Limited by a budget? No problem. We can find the perfect vacation for you and your family that fits within your budget.

We know we can create a vacation package that is as exciting and adventurous as your previous vacation. Right now, you can spend seven days and six nights in beautiful and tropical Maui, Hawaii, at the Pacific Beach Cabanas for under $700 per person including airfare! We also have a four-day, three-night vacation package to Orlando, Florida, for less than $400 per person.

Last summer we booked a fabulous Disneyland California vacation for you and your entire family. We would like to contact you to provide you with more information about these fabulous and affordable vacations and book your next fun-and-sun family vacation. Currently, Mrs. Alvarez, our records indicate your home telephone number is (415) 555-8372 and your cell phone number is (415) 555-4411. If this information is not accurate, please contact our office with the correct numbers and let us know a good time to reach you.

Sincerely,

Mandy Takada
Travel Consultant

P.S. A representative from Wildlife Eco-Tours will present information on upcoming tours at our Daly City branch office the first Saturday of next month. Come by and hear about exciting and adventurous eco-tours.

XX
C16-A05-BTVacPkgs-MD.docx
Letter 2

7. Merge the main document with the data source file and type the following text for each of the records:
Record 2: Disneyland California vacation

5330 Bayside Drive ❖ San Francisco CA 94320 ❖ 1-888-555-8590 ❖ www.emcp.net/bayside

C16-A05-BTVacPkgsLetters.docx (page 2 of 5)

Bayside Travel

April 6, 2015

2d. Insert two new records with the following information:
Ms. Tanya Forrester
575 Taylor Street (leave blank)
Apt. 120
San Francisco, CA 94127
Home Phone: (415) 555-2211
Cell Phone: (415) 555-7913

Ms. Tanya Forrester
575 Taylor Street
Apt. 120
San Francisco, CA 94127

Dear Ms. Forrester:

Now is the time to sign up for a sun-filled, fun-filled family vacation. We are offering three-day, seven-day, and ten-day fun-and-sun vacation packages to several southern destinations, including Los Angeles, Orlando, Miami, New Orleans, and Maui. Limited by a budget? No problem. We can find the perfect vacation for you and your family that fits within your budget.

We know we can create a vacation package that is as exciting and adventurous as your previous vacation. Right now, you can spend seven days and six nights in beautiful and tropical Maui, Hawaii, at the Pacific Beach Cabanas for under $700 per person including airfare! We also have a four-day, three-night vacation package to Orlando, Florida, for less than $400 per person.

Last summer we booked a fabulous Disney World Florida vacation for you and your entire family. We would like to contact you to provide you with more information about these fabulous and affordable vacations and book your next fun-and-sun family vacation. Currently, Ms. Forrester, our records indicate your home telephone number is (415) 555-2211 and your cell phone number is (415) 555-7913. If this information is not accurate, please contact our office with the correct numbers and let us know a good time to reach you.

Sincerely,

Mandy Takada
Travel Consultant

XX
C16-A05-BTVacPkgs-MD.docx
Letter 5

7. Merge the main document with the data source file and type the following text for each of the records:
Record 5: Disney World Florida vacation

5530 Bayside Drive ❖ San Francisco CA 94320 ❖ 1-888-555-8590 ❖ www.emcp.net/bayside

---

Bayside Travel

April 6, 2015

2d. Insert two new records with the following information:
Mr. Curtis Jackson
13201 North Fourth Street
Daly City, CA 94017
Home Phone: (415) 555-9743
Cell Phone: (415) 555-1027

Mr. Curtis Jackson
13201 North Fourth Street
Daly City, CA 94017

Dear Mr. Jackson:

Now is the time to sign up for a sun-filled, fun-filled family vacation. We are offering three-day, seven-day, and ten-day fun-and-sun vacation packages to several southern destinations, including Los Angeles, Orlando, Miami, New Orleans, and Maui. Limited by a budget? No problem. We can find the perfect vacation for you and your family that fits within your budget.

We know we can create a vacation package that is as exciting and adventurous as your previous vacation. Right now, you can spend seven days and six nights in beautiful and tropical Maui, Hawaii, at the Pacific Beach Cabanas for under $700 per person including airfare! We also have a four-day, three-night vacation package to Orlando, Florida, for less than $400 per person.

Last summer we booked a fabulous River Rafting Adventure vacation for you and your entire family. We would like to contact you to provide you with more information about these fabulous and affordable vacations and book your next fun-and-sun family vacation. Currently, Mr. Jackson, our records indicate your home telephone number is (415) 555-9743 and your cell phone number is (415) 555-1027. If this information is not accurate, please contact our office with the correct numbers and let us know a good time to reach you.

Sincerely,

Mandy Takada
Travel Consultant

P.S. A representative from Wildlife Eco-Tours will present information on upcoming tours at our Daly City branch office the first Saturday of next month. Come by and hear about exciting and adventurous eco-tours.

XX
C16-A05-BTVacPkgs-MD.docx
Letter 4

7. Merge the main document with the data source file and type the following text for each of the records:
Record 4: River Rafting Adventure vacation

5530 Bayside Drive ❖ San Francisco CA 94320 ❖ 1-888-555-8590 ❖ www.emcp.net/bayside

Ms. Hannah Devereaux
9005 Fifth Street
Springfield, OR 97478

1. At a blank document, use the Mail Merge wizard to merge the records in the **PRClients.mdb** data source with an envelope main document. (Use the standard size 10 envelope.)
2. Save the merged envelope document with the name **C16-A06-PREnvs**.
3. Print only the first two envelopes in the document and then close **C16-A06-PREnvs.docx**.

Mr. Donald Reyes
14332 150th Street East
Eugene, OR 97408

C16-A07-PRDirectory(Step14).docx

12. Select the text in the document and then convert it to a table. *Hint: Use the Table button in the Tables group on the INSERT tab.*

13. With the text converted to a table, delete the first column (which is empty), format the contents of the table using the AutoFit feature, and then apply a table style of your choosing. Make other formatting changes to enhance the display of the table.

Name	Telephone
Reyes, Donald	(541) 555-3904
Devereaux, Hannah	(541) 555-6675
Heaton, Delores	(541) 555-4982
LeBlanc, Keith	(541) 555-0012
Seydell, Lynn	(541) 555-6599
Pena, Ramon	(541) 555-2189
Morrisey, Faith	(541) 555-9922
Parker, Greg	(541) 555-4188
Takahara, Jane	(541) 555-9441
Jennings, Karen	(541) 555-6717
Martinez, Chris	(541) 555-4045

C16-A07-PRDirectory(Step11).docx

9. Insert the heading *Name* with bold formatting applied above the column containing the last and first names. Insert the heading *Telephone* with bold formatting applied above the column containing the telephone numbers.

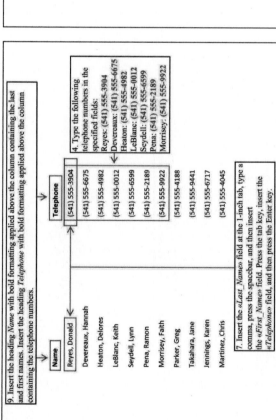

Name	Telephone
Reyes, Donald	(541) 555-3904
Devereaux, Hannah	(541) 555-6675
Heaton, Delores	(541) 555-4982
LeBlanc, Keith	(541) 555-0012
Seydell, Lynn	(541) 555-6599
Pena, Ramon	(541) 555-2189
Morrisey, Faith	(541) 555-9922
Parker, Greg	(541) 555-4188
Takahara, Jane	(541) 555-9441
Jennings, Karen	(541) 555-6717
Martinez, Chris	(541) 555-4045

4. Type the following telephone numbers in the specified fields:
Reyes: (541) 555-3904
Devereaux: (541) 555-6675
Heaton: (541) 555-4982
LeBlanc: (541) 555-0012
Seydell: (541) 555-6599
Pena: (541) 555-2189
Morrisey: (541) 555-9922

7. Insert the *«Last_Name»* field at the 1-inch tab, type a comma, press the spacebar, and then insert the *«First_Name»* field. Press the tab key, insert the *«Telephone»* field, and then press the Enter key.

1. Make a copy of the **PRClients.mdb** file located in your Chapter16 folder and insert the copy into the same folder. Rename the copied file **C16-A07-PRClients.mdb**.

2. At a blank document, create a directory main document and specify **C16-A07-PRClients.mdb** as the data source file.

3. Add a new field named *Telephone* to the **C16-A07-PRClients.mdb** data source file. *Hint: To do this, click the Edit Recipient List button, click the C16-A07-PRClients.mdb file name in the Data Source list box, and then click the Edit button. At the Edit Data Source dialog box, click the Customize Columns button. Add the new Telephone field and then move it so it displays after the ZIP Code field.*

5. Add the following records to the data source file (in the appropriate fields):

Mr. Greg Parker
3411 45th Street
Eugene, OR 97405
(541) 555-4188

Dr. Jane Takahara
10293 Mountain Drive
Springfield, OR 97477
(541) 555-9441

Mrs. Karen Jennings
1302 Washington
Eugene, OR 97402
(541) 555-6817

Mr. Chris Martinez
109 Voss Drive
Springfield, OR 97478
(541) 555-4045

6. At the blank directory document, set left tabs at the 1-inch mark and 4-inch mark.

8. Merge the directory main document with the data source file.

10. Save the directory and name it **C16-A07-PRDirectory**. (If the merge is missing a field of information, close the merged document without saving changes and then complete the merge again.)

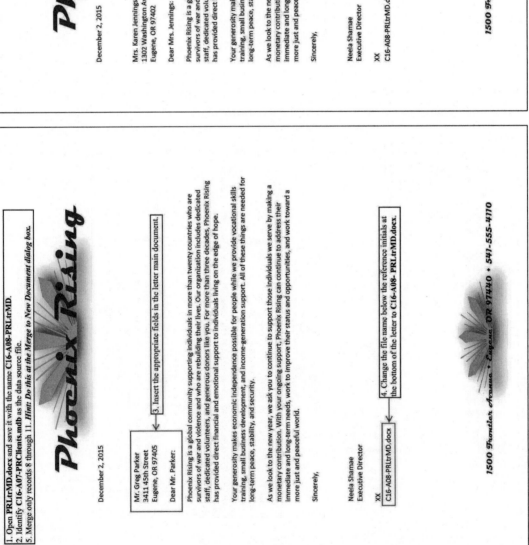

Phoenix Rising

1. Open **PRLtrMD.docx** and save it with the name **C16-A08-PRLtrMD.**
2. Identify **C16-A07-PRClients.mdb** as the data source file.
5. Merge only records 8 through 11. *Hint: Do this at the Merge to New Document dialog box.*

December 2, 2015

Mr. Greg Parker
3411 45th Street
Eugene, OR 97405

Dear Mr. Parker:

3. Insert the appropriate fields in the letter main document.

Phoenix Rising is a global community supporting individuals in more than twenty countries who are survivors of war and violence and who are rebuilding their lives. Our organization includes dedicated staff, dedicated volunteers, and generous donors like you. For more than three decades, Phoenix Rising has provided direct financial and emotional support to individuals living on the edge of hope.

Your generosity makes economic independence possible for people while we provide vocational skills training, small business development, and income-generation support. All of these things are needed for long-term peace, stability, and security.

As we look to the new year, we ask you to continue to support those individuals we serve by making a monetary contribution. With your ongoing support, Phoenix Rising can continue to address their immediate and long-term needs, work to improve their status and opportunities, and work toward a more just and peaceful world.

Sincerely,

Neela Shamae
Executive Director

XX
C16-A08-PRLtrMD.docx

4. Change the file name below the reference initials at the bottom of the letter to **C16-A08- PRLtrMD.docx.**

1500 Frontier Avenue • Eugene, OR 97440 • 541-555-4110

C16-A08-PRLtrs8-11.docx (page 1 of 4)

Phoenix Rising

December 2, 2015

Mrs. Karen Jennings
1302 Washington Avenue
Eugene, OR 97402

Dear Mrs. Jennings:

Phoenix Rising is a global community supporting individuals in more than twenty countries who are survivors of war and violence and who are rebuilding their lives. Our organization includes dedicated staff, dedicated volunteers, and generous donors like you. For more than three decades, Phoenix Rising has provided direct financial and emotional support to individuals living on the edge of hope.

Your generosity makes economic independence possible for people while we provide vocational skills training, small business development, and income-generation support. All of these things are needed for long-term peace, stability, and security.

As we look to the new year, we ask you to continue to support those individuals we serve by making a monetary contribution. With your ongoing support, Phoenix Rising can continue to address their immediate and long-term needs, work to improve their status and opportunities, and work toward a more just and peaceful world.

Sincerely,

Neela Shamae
Executive Director

XX
C16-A08-PRLtrMD.docx

1500 Frontier Avenue • Eugene, OR 97440 • 541-555-4110

C16-A08-PRLtrs8-11.docx (page 2 of 4)

Phoenix Rising

December 2, 2015

Dr. Jane Takahara
10293 Mountain Drive
Springfield, OR 97477

Dear Dr. Takahara:

Phoenix Rising is a global community supporting individuals in more than twenty countries who are survivors of war and violence and who are rebuilding their lives. Our organization includes dedicated staff, dedicated volunteers, and generous donors like you. For more than three decades, Phoenix Rising has provided direct financial and emotional support to individuals living on the edge of hope.

Your generosity makes economic independence possible for people while we provide vocational skills training, small business development, and income-generation support. All of these things are needed for long-term peace, stability, and security.

As we look to the new year, we ask you to continue to support those individuals we serve by making a monetary contribution. With your ongoing support, Phoenix Rising can continue to address their immediate and long-term needs, work to improve their status and opportunities, and work toward a more just and peaceful world.

Sincerely,

Neela Shamae
Executive Director

XX
C16-A08-PRLtrMD.docx

1500 Frontier Avenue • Eugene, OR 97440 • 541-555-4110

C16-A08-PRLtrs8-11.docx (page 3 of 4)

Phoenix Rising

December 2, 2015

Mr. Chris Martinez
109 Voss Drive
Springfield, OR 97478

Dear Mr. Martinez:

Phoenix Rising is a global community supporting individuals in more than twenty countries who are survivors of war and violence and who are rebuilding their lives. Our organization includes dedicated staff, dedicated volunteers, and generous donors like you. For more than three decades, Phoenix Rising has provided direct financial and emotional support to individuals living on the edge of hope.

Your generosity makes economic independence possible for people while we provide vocational skills training, small business development, and income-generation support. All of these things are needed for long-term peace, stability, and security.

As we look to the new year, we ask you to continue to support those individuals we serve by making a monetary contribution. With your ongoing support, Phoenix Rising can continue to address their immediate and long-term needs, work to improve their status and opportunities, and work toward a more just and peaceful world.

Sincerely,

Neela Shamae
Executive Director

XX
C16-A08-PRLtrMD.docx

1500 Frontier Avenue • Eugene, OR 97440 • 541-555-4110

C16-A08-PRLtrs8-11.docx (page 4 of 4)

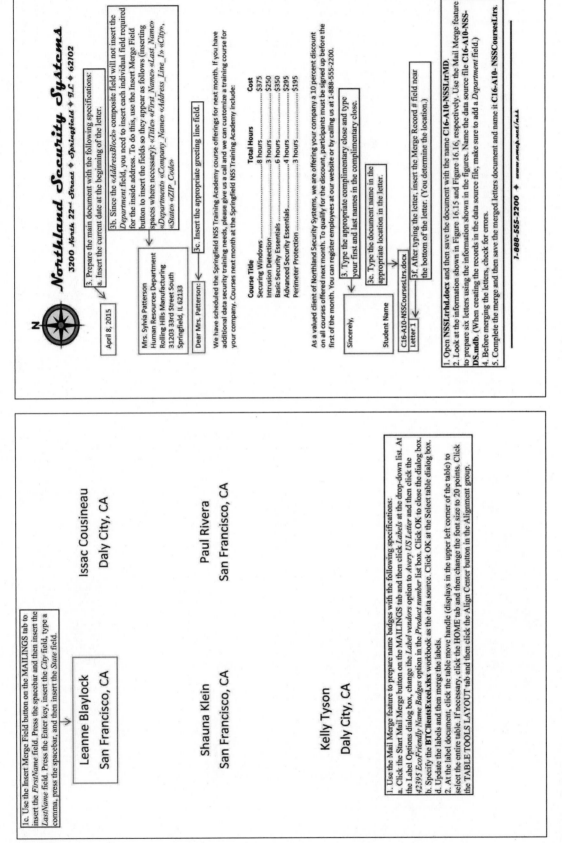

Northland Security Systems

3200 North 22ⁿᵈ Street ♦ Springfield ♦ IL ♦ 62102

3. Prepare the main document with the following specifications:
a. Insert the current date at the beginning of the letter.

April 8, 2015

3b. Since the «AddressBlock» composite field will not insert the Department field, you need to insert each individual field required for the inside address. To do this, use the Insert Merge Field button to insert the fields so they appear as follows (inserting spaces where necessary): «Title» «First_Name» «Last_Name» «Department» «Company_Name» «Address_Line_1» «City», «State» «ZIP_Code»

Mrs. Sylvia Patterson
Human Resources Department
Rolling Hills Manufacturing
31203 33rd Street South
Springfield, IL 62133

3c. Insert the appropriate greeting line field.

Dear Mrs. Patterson:

We have scheduled the Springfield NSS Training Academy course offerings for next month. If you have additional data security training needs, please give us a call and we can customize a training course for your company. Courses next month at the Springfield NSS Training Academy include:

Course Title	Total Hours	Cost
Securing Windows	8 hours	$375
Intrusion Detection	3 hours	$250
Basic Security Essentials	6 hours	$350
Advanced Security Essentials	4 hours	$295
Perimeter Protection	3 hours	$195

As a valued client of Northland Security Systems, we are offering your company a 10 percent discount on all courses offered next month. To qualify for the discount, participants must be signed up before the first of the month. You can register employees at our website or by calling us at 1-888-555-2200.

3. Type the appropriate complimentary close and type your first and last names in the complimentary close.

Sincerely,

3e. Type the document name in the appropriate location in the letter.

Student Name

C16-A10-NSSCoursesLtrs.docx

Letter 1

3f. After typing the letter, insert the Merge Record # field near the bottom of the letter. (You determine the location.)

1. Open **NSSLtrhd.docx** and then save the document with the name **C16-A10-NSSLtrMD**.
2. Look at the information shown in Figure 16.15 and Figure 16.16, respectively. Use the Mail Merge feature to prepare six letters using the information in the figures. Name the data source file **C16-A10-NSS-DS.mdb**. (When creating the records in the data source file, make sure to add a *Department* field.)
4. Before merging the letters, check for errors.
5. Complete the merge and then save the merged letters document and name it **C16-A10- NSSCoursesLtrs**.

1-888-555-2200 ♦ www.emcp.net/nss

C16-A10-NSSCoursesLtrs.docx (page 1 of 6)

1c. Use the Insert Merge Field button on the MAILINGS tab to insert the *FirstName* field. Press the spacebar and then insert the *LastName* field. Press the Enter key, insert the *City* field, type a comma, press the spacebar, and then insert the *State* field.

Leanne Blaylock
San Francisco, CA

Issac Cousineau
Daly City, CA

Shauna Klein
San Francisco, CA

Paul Rivera
San Francisco, CA

Kelly Tyson
Daly City, CA

1. Use the Mail Merge feature to prepare name badges with the following specifications:
a. Click the Start Mail Merge button on the MAILINGS tab and then click *Labels* at the drop-down list. At the Label Options dialog box, change the *Label vendors* option to *Avery US Letter* and then click the *42395 EcoFriendly Name Badges* option in the *Product number* list box. Click OK to close the dialog box.
b. Specify the **BTClientsExcel.xlsx** workbook as the data source. Click OK at the Select table dialog box.
d. Update the labels and then merge the labels.
2. At the label document, click the table move handle (displays in the upper left corner of the table) to select the entire table. If necessary, click the HOME tab and then change the font size to 20 points. Click the TABLE TOOLS LAYOUT tab and then click the Align Center button in the Alignment group.

C16-A09-BTNameBadges.docx

N

Northland Security Systems
3200 North 22nd Street ✦ Springfield ✦ IL ✦ 62102

April 8, 2015

Mr. Russell Navarro
Technology Department
Woodmark Products
8844 South 24th Street
Peoria, IL 61623

Dear Mr. Navarro:

We have scheduled the Springfield NSS Training Academy course offerings for next month. If you have additional data security training needs, please give us a call and we can customize a training course for your company. Courses next month at the Springfield NSS Training Academy include:

Course Title	Total Hours	Cost
Securing Windows	8 hours	$375
Intrusion Detection	3 hours	$250
Basic Security Essentials	6 hours	$350
Advanced Security Essentials	4 hours	$295
Perimeter Protection	3 hours	$195

At our Peoria NSS Training Academy, we are offering two additional courses including *Network Security* and *Web Applications Security*. Please call for more information about these courses. As a valued client of Northland Security Systems, we are offering your company a 10 percent discount on all courses offered next month. To qualify for the discount, participants must be signed up before the first of the month. You can register employees at our website or by calling us at 1-888-555-2200.

Sincerely,

Student Name

C16-A10-NSSCoursesLtrs.docx
Letter 3

1-888-555-2200 ✦ www.emcp.net/nss

N

Northland Security Systems
3200 North 22nd Street ✦ Springfield ✦ IL ✦ 62102

April 8, 2015

Mr. Dale Marshall
Training Department
Providence Care
2712 Martin Luther King, Jr. Way
Peoria, IL 61636

Dear Mr. Marshall:

We have scheduled the Springfield NSS Training Academy course offerings for next month. If you have additional data security training needs, please give us a call and we can customize a training course for your company. Courses next month at the Springfield NSS Training Academy include:

Course Title	Total Hours	Cost
Securing Windows	8 hours	$375
Intrusion Detection	3 hours	$250
Basic Security Essentials	6 hours	$350
Advanced Security Essentials	4 hours	$295
Perimeter Protection	3 hours	$195

At our Peoria NSS Training Academy, we are offering two additional courses including *Network Security* and *Web Applications Security*. Please call for more information about these courses. As a valued client of Northland Security Systems, we are offering your company a 10 percent discount on all courses offered next month. To qualify for the discount, participants must be signed up before the first of the month. You can register employees at our website or by calling us at 1-888-555-2200.

Sincerely,

Student Name

C16-A10-NSSCoursesLtrs.docx
Letter 2

> 3g. Insert an If…Then…Else field at the beginning of the last paragraph of text in the letter (the paragraph that begins *As a valued client...*). Specify the *City* field in the *Field name* option box, type Peoria in the *Compare to* text box, and then type the following information in the *Insert this text* text box. (Make sure you press the spacebar once after typing the text.) At our Peoria NSS Training Academy, we are offering two additional courses including *Network Security* and *Web Applications Security*. Please call for more information about these courses.

1-888-555-2200 ✦ www.emcp.net/nss

Northland Security Systems
3200 North 22ⁿᵈ Street ◆ Springfield ◆ IL ◆ 62102

April 8, 2015

Ms. Amanda Sperring
Human Resources Department
Frontier Steel
310 Riddell Avenue
Decatur, IL 62524

Dear Ms. Sperring:

We have scheduled the Springfield NSS Training Academy course offerings for next month. If you have additional data security training needs, please give us a call and we can customize a training course for your company. Courses next month at the Springfield NSS Training Academy include:

Course Title	Total Hours	Cost
Securing Windows	8 hours	$375
Intrusion Detection	3 hours	$250
Basic Security Essentials	6 hours	$350
Advanced Security Essentials	4 hours	$295
Perimeter Protection	3 hours	$195

As a valued client of Northland Security Systems, we are offering your company a 10 percent discount on all courses offered next month. To qualify for the discount, participants must be signed up before the first of the month. You can register employees at our website or by calling us at 1-888-555-2200.

Sincerely,

Student Name

C16-A10-NSSCoursesLtrs.docx
Letter 4

1-888-555-2200 ◆ www.emcp.net/nss

C16-A10-NSSCoursesLtrs.docx (page 4 of 6)

Northland Security Systems
3200 North 22ⁿᵈ Street ◆ Springfield ◆ IL ◆ 62102

April 8, 2015

Mr. Wade Townsend
IT Department
Keystone Technologies
145 South 95th Street
Springfield, IL 62129

Dear Mr. Townsend:

We have scheduled the Springfield NSS Training Academy course offerings for next month. If you have additional data security training needs, please give us a call and we can customize a training course for your company. Courses next month at the Springfield NSS Training Academy include:

Course Title	Total Hours	Cost
Securing Windows	8 hours	$375
Intrusion Detection	3 hours	$250
Basic Security Essentials	6 hours	$350
Advanced Security Essentials	4 hours	$295
Perimeter Protection	3 hours	$195

As a valued client of Northland Security Systems, we are offering your company a 10 percent discount on all courses offered next month. To qualify for the discount, participants must be signed up before the first of the month. You can register employees at our website or by calling us at 1-888-555-2200.

Sincerely,

Student Name

C16-A10-NSSCoursesLtrs.docx
Letter 5

1-888-555-2200 ◆ www.emcp.net/nss

C16-A10-NSSCoursesLtrs.docx (page 5 of 6)

Northland Security Systems

3200 North 22nd Street ✦ Springfield ✦ IL ✦ 62102

April 8, 2015

Mrs. Emma Battner
Training Department
Franklin Services
2010 Patterson Court East
Peoria, IL 61618

Dear Mrs. Battner:

We have scheduled the Springfield NSS Training Academy course offerings for next month. If you have additional data security training needs, please give us a call and we can customize a training course for your company. Courses next month at the Springfield NSS Training Academy include:

Course Title	Total Hours	Cost
Securing Windows	8 hours	$375
Intrusion Detection	3 hours	$250
Basic Security Essentials	6 hours	$350
Advanced Security Essentials	4 hours	$295
Perimeter Protection	3 hours	$195

At our Peoria NSS Training Academy, we are offering two additional courses including *Network Security* and *Web Applications Security*. Please call for more information about these courses. As a valued client of Northland Security Systems, we are offering your company a 10 percent discount on all courses offered next month. To qualify for the discount, participants must be signed up before the first of the month. You can register employees at our website or by calling us at 1-888-555-2200.

Sincerely,

Student Name

C16-A10-NSSCoursesLtrs.docx
Letter 6

1-888-555-2200 ✦ www.emcp.net/nss

C16-A10-NSSCoursesLtrs.docx (page 6 of 6)

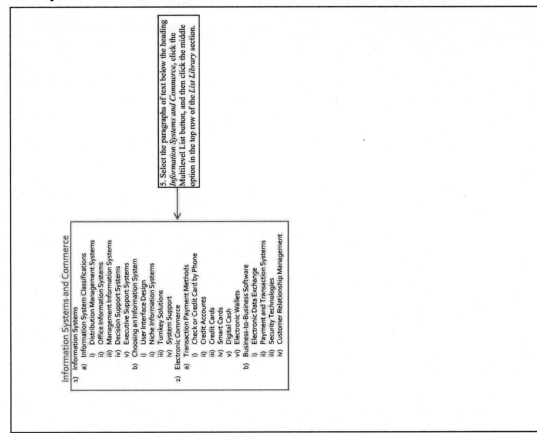

5. Select the paragraphs of text below the heading *Information Systems and Commerce*, click the Multilevel List button, and then click the middle option in the top row of the *List Library* section.

Information Systems and Commerce
1) Information Systems
   a) Information System Classifications
      i) Distribution Management Systems
      ii) Office Information Systems
      iii) Management Information Systems
      iv) Decision Support Systems
      v) Executive Support Systems
   b) Choosing an Information System
      i) User Interface Design
      ii) Niche Information Systems
      iii) Turnkey Solutions
      iv) System Support
2) Electronic Commerce
   a) Transaction Payment Methods
      i) Check or Credit Card by Phone
      ii) Credit Accounts
      iii) Credit Cards
      iv) Smart Cards
      v) Digital Cash
      vi) Electronic Wallets
   b) Business-to-Business Software
      i) Electronic Data Exchange
      ii) Payment and Transaction Systems
      iii) Security Technologies
      iv) Customer Relationship Management

C17-A01-ElecTech(Step7).docx (page 2 of 3)

---

1. Open **ElecTech.docx** and save the document with the name **C17-A01-ElecTech**.
2. Apply the following formatting to the document:
a. Apply the Lines (Simple) style set.
b. Apply the Frame theme.

ELECTRONIC TECHNOLOGY

Technology Information Questions

3. Select the questions below the heading *Technology Information Questions* and then insert check mark (✓) bullets.

✓ What is inside the printer?
✓ How many ways can a user output data?
✓ Which features should be considered when you purchase a printer?
✓ Which storage device meets your needs?

Technology Timeline: Storage Devices and Media

1956: IBM unveils the 350 Disk Storage Unit, the first random-access (direct-access) hard disk.
1973: IBM releases the 3340, the first Winchester hard disk with a capacity of 70 megabytes (MB) spread over four disk platters.
1985: The first CD-ROM drives make their debut on personal computers.
1998: The DVD-ROM drive debuts with 5.2 gigabytes (GB) of rewritable capacity on a double-sided cartridge—enough to hold a two-hour movie.
2001: Constellation 3D Inc. introduces a new type of optical disc storage called FMD-ROM, which holds up to 140 GB of data.
2003: USB flash drives (also called keychain drives because they are about the size of a key fob) hit the consumer market.
2006: Sony introduces Blu-ray disc technology that makes use of the shorter blue-violet wave lengths in the light spectrum allowing for up to 50 GB on a single disc.
2008: Solid-state drives (SSD) using flash memory that does not employ any moving mechanical components became available to consumers.

4. Create a computer disc symbol bullet in 14-point font size and then apply the symbol bullet to the eight paragraphs of text below the heading *Technology Timeline: Storage Devices and Media*. **Hint: You can find the disc symbol in the Wingdings font (located in approximately the second row).**

C17-A01-ElecTech(Step7).docx (page 1 of 3)

ELECTRONIC TECHNOLOGY

Technology Information Questions

✓ What is inside the printer?
✓ How many ways can a user output data?
✓ Which features should be considered when you purchase a printer?
✓ Which storage device meets your needs?

Technology Timeline: Storage Devices and Media

🔳 1956: IBM unveils the 350 Disk Storage Unit, the first random-access (direct-access) hard disk.

🔳 1973: IBM releases the 3340, the first Winchester hard disk with a capacity of 70 megabytes (MB) spread over four disk platters.

🔳 1985: The first CD-ROM drives make their debut on personal computers.

🔳 1998: The DVD-ROM drive debuts with 5.2 gigabytes (GB) of rewritable capacity on a double-sided cartridge—enough to hold a two-hour movie.

🔳 2001: Constellation 3D Inc. introduces a new type of optical disc storage called FMD-ROM, which holds up to 140 GB of data.

🔳 2003: USB flash drives (also called keychain drives because they are about the size of a key fob) hit the consumer market.

🔳 2006: Sony introduces Blu-ray disc technology that makes use of the shorter blue-violet wave lengths in the light spectrum allowing for up to 50 GB on a single disc.

🔳 2008: Solid-state drives (SSD) using flash memory that does not employ any moving mechanical components became available to consumers.

6. Select the paragraphs of text below the heading *Internet* and then apply the same multilevel list numbering.

Internet
1) Global Network
   a) Communications
   b) Research
   c) Distance Learning
   d) Entertainment
2) Connecting to the Internet
   a) Hardware Requirements
   b) Software Requirements
3) Navigating the Internet
4) Inter Community Issues
   a) Privacy Issues
   b) Security Protection
   c) Viruses
   d) Copyright Infringement

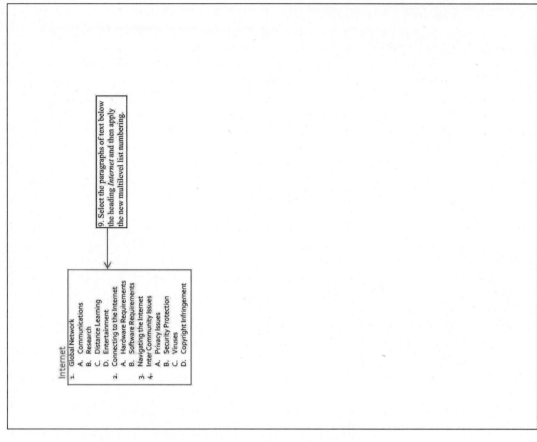

Internet

1. Global Network
   A. Communications
   B. Research
   C. Distance Learning
   D. Entertainment
2. Connecting to the Internet
   A. Hardware Requirements
   B. Software Requirements
3. Navigating the Internet
4. Inter Community Issues
   A. Privacy Issues
   B. Security Protection
   C. Viruses
   D. Copyright Infringement

9. Select the paragraphs of text below the heading *Internet* and then apply the new multilevel list numbering.

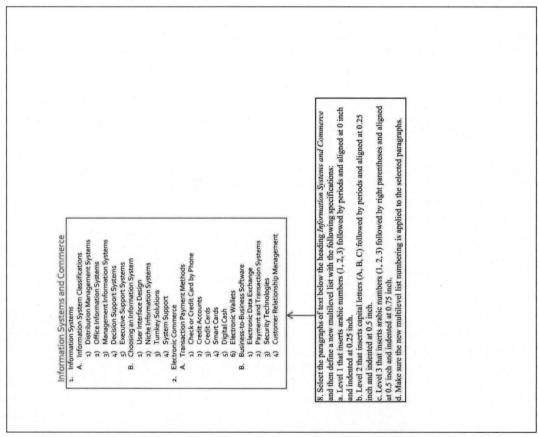

Information Systems and Commerce

1. Information Systems
   A. Information System Classifications
      1) Distribution Management Systems
      2) Office Information Systems
      3) Management Information Systems
      4) Decision Support Systems
      5) Executive Support Systems
   B. Choosing an Information System
      1) User Interface Design
      2) Niche Information Systems
      3) Turnkey Solutions
      4) System Support
2. Electronic Commerce
   A. Transaction Payment Methods
      1) Check or Credit Card by Phone
      2) Credit Accounts
      3) Credit Cards
      4) Smart Cards
      5) Digital Cash
      6) Electronic Wallets
   B. Business-to-Business Software
      1) Electronic Data Exchange
      2) Payment and Transaction Systems
      3) Security Technologies
      4) Customer Relationship Management

8. Select the paragraphs of text below the heading *Information Systems and Commerce* and then define a new multilevel list with the following specifications:
   a. Level 1 that inserts arabic numbers (1, 2, 3) followed by periods and aligned at 0 inch and indented at 0.25 inch.
   b. Level 2 that inserts capital letters (A, B, C) followed by periods and aligned at 0.25 inch and indented at 0.5 inch.
   c. Level 3 that inserts arabic numbers (1, 2, 3) followed by right parentheses and aligned at 0.5 inch and indented at 0.75 inch.
   d. Make sure the new multilevel list numbering is applied to the selected paragraphs.

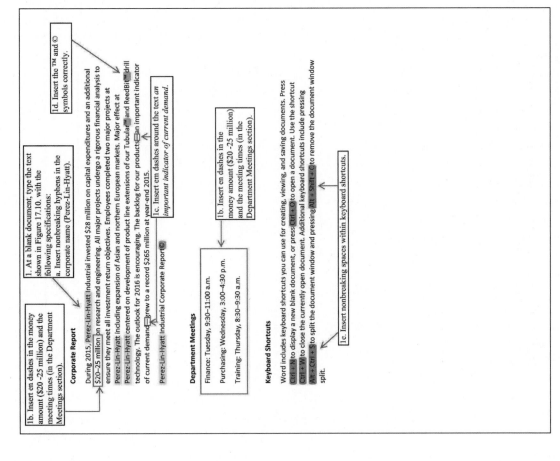

C17-A03-WhiteHorses.docx

1. Create the document shown in Figure 17.11 with the following specifications:
a. Change the left and right margins to 1.5 inches.

1d. As shown in the figure, apply Green, Accent 6, Darker 25% shading to the title, change the title text font color to White, Background 1, and apply bold formatting.

WHITE HORSES OF
WILTSHIRE COUNTY, ENGLAND

1c. In addition to symbols and pictures provided by Microsoft, you can create bullets with your own pictures. Use the Picture button in the Define New Bullet dialog box to insert the **WhiteHorse.jpg** image located in your Chapter17 folder as the picture bullets. After inserting the picture bullets, click the first bullet (which selects all of the bullets) and then change the font size to 36 points.

- Broad Town White Horse
- Hackspen White Horse
- Marlborough White Horse
- Alton Barnes White Horse
- Cherhill White Horse
- Devizes Millennium White Horse
- Pewsey White Horse
- Westburt/Bratton White Horse

1b. Set the text in 36-point Angsana New. (If this typeface is not available, choose a similar typeface.)
f. Make any other formatting changes so your document appears as shown in Figure 17.11.

1e. Insert the page border as shown in the figure. *Hint: Use the third option from the bottom in the Style list box at the Borders and Shading dialog box with the Page Border tab selected and change the color to Green, Accent 6, Darker 25%.*

C17-A02-CorpReport.docx

1b. Insert en dashes in the money amount ($20 -25 million) and the meeting times (in the Department Meetings section).

1. At a blank document, type the text shown in Figure 17.10. with the following specifications:
a. Insert nonbreaking hyphens in the corporate name (Perez-Lin-Hyatt).

1d. Insert the ™ and © symbols correctly.

Corporate Report

During 2015, Perez-Lin-Hyatt Industrial invested $28 million on capital expenditures and an additional $20–25 million on research and engineering. All major projects undergo a rigorous financial analysis to ensure they meet all investment return objectives. Employees completed two major projects at Perez-Lin-Hyatt including expansion of Asian and northern European markets. Major effect at Perez-Lin-Hyatt centered on development of product line extensions of our Tubular™ and ReedBit™ drill technology. The outlook for 2016 is encouraging. The backlog for our products—an important indicator of current demand—grew to a record $265 million at year-end 2015.

Perez-Lin-Hyatt Industrial Corporate Report©

1c. Insert em dashes around the text *an important indicator of current demand.*

Department Meetings

Finance: Tuesday, 9:30–11:00 a.m.

Purchasing: Wednesday, 3:00–4:30 p.m.

Training: Thursday, 8:30–9:30 a.m.

1b. Insert en dashes in the money amount ($20 -25 million) and the meeting times (in the Department Meetings section).

Keyboard Shortcuts

Word includes keyboard shortcuts you can use for creating, viewing, and saving documents. Press Ctrl + N to display a new blank document, or press Ctrl + O to open a document. Use the shortcut Ctrl + W to close the currently open document. Additional keyboard shortcuts include pressing Alt + Ctrl + S to split the document window and pressing Alt + Shift + C to remove the document window split.

1e. Insert nonbreaking spaces within keyboard shortcuts.

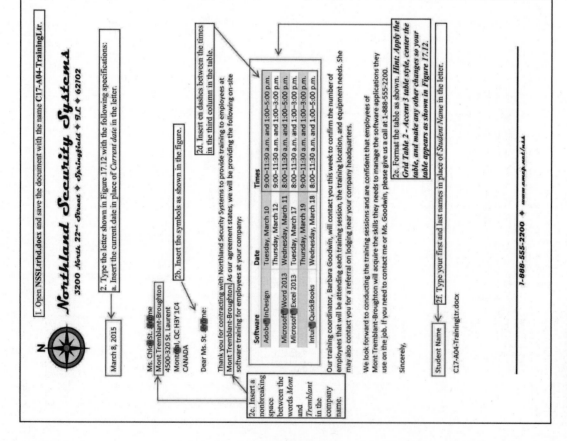

1. Open NSSLtrhd.docx and save the document with the name C17-A04-TrainingLtr.

Northland Security Systems
3200 North 22nd Street ◆ Springfield ◆ IL ◆ 62702

2. Type the letter shown in Figure 17.12 with the following specifications:
a. Insert the current date in place of *Current date* in the letter.

March 8, 2015

Ms. Chloé St. Jérôme
Mont Tremblant-Broughton
4500-320 St. Laurent
Montréal, QC H3Y 1C4
CANADA

2b. Insert the symbols as shown in the figure.

Dear Ms. St. Jérôme:

Thank you for contracting with Northland Security Systems to provide training to employees at Mont Tremblant-Broughton] As our agreement states, we will be providing the following on-site software training for employees at your company:

2c. Insert a nonbreaking space between the words *Mont* and *Tremblant* in the company name.

2d. Insert en dashes between the times in the third column in the table.

Software	Date	Times
Adobe InDesign	Tuesday, March 10	9:00–11:30 a.m. and 1:00–5:00 p.m.
	Thursday, March 12	9:00–11:30 a.m. and 1:00–5:00 p.m.
Microsoft Word 2013	Wednesday, March 11	8:00–11:30 a.m. and 1:00–5:00 p.m.
Microsoft Excel 2013	Tuesday, March 17	8:00–11:30 a.m. and 1:00–3:00 p.m.
	Thursday, March 19	9:00–11:30 a.m. and 1:00–3:00 p.m.
Intuit QuickBooks	Wednesday, March 18	8:00–11:30 a.m. and 1:00–5:00 p.m.

Our training coordinator, Barbara Goodwin, will contact you this week to confirm the number of employees that will be attending each training session, the training location, and equipment needs. She may also contact you for a referral on lodging near your company headquarters.

We look forward to conducting the training sessions and are confident that employees of Mont Tremblant-Broughton will acquire the skills they needs to manage the software applications they use on the job. If you need to contact me or Ms. Goodwin, please give us a call at 1-888-555-2200.

2e. Format the table as shown. *Hint: Apply the Grid Table 2 - Accent 3 table style, center the table, and make any other changes so your table appears as shown in Figure 17.12.*

Sincerely,

Student Name

2f. Type your first and last names in place of *Student Name* in the letter.

C17-A04-TrainingLtr.docx

1-888-555-2200 ◆ www.emcp.net/nss

C17-A04-TrainingLtr.docx

Chapter 18 Assessment Annotated Model Answers

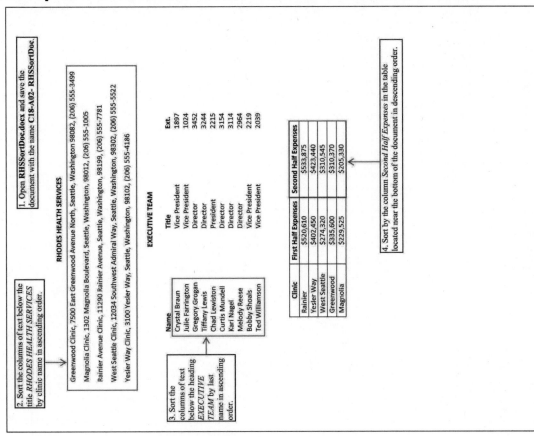

C18-A02-RHSSortDoc.docx

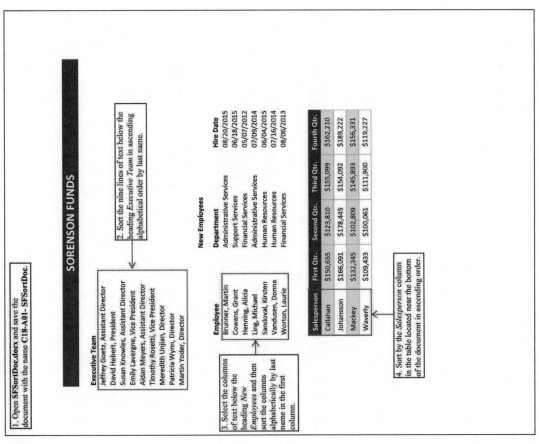

C18-A01-SFSortDoc.docx

C18-A04-KLLabelsBoston.docx

Mr. Marshall Hedges
14311 207th Avenue
Boston, MA 02113

Mr. and Mrs. William Brown
14824 North 151st
P.O. Box 3329
Boston, MA 02118

Dr. and Mrs. Lewis McKenzie
13502 159th Court East
P.O. Box 3109
Boston, MA 02126

Mrs. Blair Walters
21431 East 52nd
P.O. Box 1002
Boston, MA 02129

Mr. and Mrs. Joseph Perez
14413 South 32nd
Boston, MA 02128

1. At a blank document, use the Mail Merge feature to create mailing labels with the Avery US Letter 5360 label product. Use the existing data source **C18-A03- KLCustomersDS.mdb** for the labels.

2. Display the Mail Merge Recipients dialog box, display the Filter and Sort dialog box with the Filter Records tab selected, and then select those customers living in Boston.

3. Complete the merge and then save the labels document with the name **C18-A04-KLLabelsBoston.**

C18-A03-KLLabels.docx

Mr. Marshall Hedges
14311 207th Avenue
Boston, MA 02113

Mr. and Mrs. William Brown
14824 North 151st
P.O. Box 3329
Boston, MA 02118

Dr. and Mrs. Lewis McKenzie
13502 159th Court East
P.O. Box 3109
Boston, MA 02126

Mr. and Mrs. Joseph Perez
14413 South 32nd
Boston, MA 02128

Mrs. Blair Walters
21431 East 52nd
P.O. Box 1002
Boston, MA 02129

Mr. and Mrs. Duane Leonard
835 Harmon Way
Everett, MA 02149

Mr. Keith Shafer
407 Traffic Avenue
Everett, MA 02149

Dr. Josephine Springer
1405 Tubbs Road
Everett, MA 02149

Mr. and Mrs. Adam Zander
513 Warner Road
Everett, MA 02149

Ms. Emma Piper
2103 Ridge Street
Apt. C-105
Chelsea, MA 02150

Mrs. Corinna Trevier
5820 236th Avenue East
Chelsea, MA 02150

Mrs. Brianne Darby
410 Wilson Street
Apt. 10
Chelsea, MA 02150

3. Display the Mail Merge Recipients dialog box and sort the records first by zip code in ascending order and then by last name in ascending order.

1. Make a copy of the **KLCustomers.mdb** file by completing the following steps:
a. Display the Open dialog box and make Chapter18 the active folder.
b. If necessary, change the file type button to *All Files (*.*).*
c. Right-click on the **KLCustomers.mdb** file and then click *Copy* at the shortcut menu.
d. Position the mouse pointer in a white portion of the Open dialog box Content pane (outside any file name), click the *right* mouse button, and then click *Paste* at the shortcut menu. (This inserts a copy of the file in the dialog box Content pane and names the file **KLCustomers - Copy.mdb.**)
e. Right-click on the file name **KLCustomers - Copy.mdb** and rename it **C18-A03- KLCustomersDS** and then press the Enter key.
f. Close the Open dialog box.
2. At a blank document, use the Mail Merge feature to create mailing labels with the Avery US Letter 5360 label product using the existing data source **C18-A03-KLCustomersDS.mdb.**
4. Complete the merge and then save the label document with the name **C18-A03-KLLabels.**

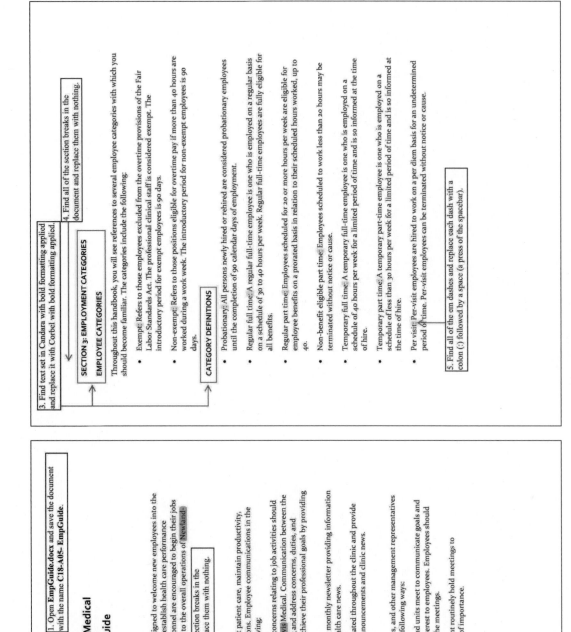

6. Using a wildcard character, find all of the occurrences of *Ne?land??Davis* and replace them with *Newland-Davis*.

1. Open **EmpGuide.docx** and save the document with the name **C18-A05- EmpGuide**.

Newland-Davis Medical

Employee Guide

3. Find text set in Candara with bold formatting applied and replace it with Corbel with bold formatting applied.

SECTION 1: GENERAL INFORMATION

NEW EMPLOYEE ORIENTATION

The Newland-Davis Medical orientation program is designed to welcome new employees into the spirit and culture of Newland-Davis Medical, to clearly establish health care performance expectations, and to set the stage for success. New personnel are encouraged to begin their jobs with the monthly orientation in order to be introduced to the overall operations of Newland-Davis Medical.

4. Find all of the section breaks in the document and replace them with nothing.

SECTION 2: COMMUNICATION

EMPLOYEE COMMUNICATION

Effective communication is essential to provide the best patient care, maintain productivity, sustain morale, and foster constructive employee relations. Employee communications in the Newland-Davis Medical environment include the following:

- Employee/supervisor meetings: Questions and concerns relating to job activities should first be presented to supervisors at Newland-Davis Medical. Communication between the supervisor and the employee should be ongoing and address concerns, duties, and expectations. Supervisors can help employees achieve their professional goals by providing career development information.
- Newsletter: Newland-Davis Medical publishes a monthly newsletter providing information on new hires, benefit updates, and the latest health care news.
- Bulletins board postings: Bulletin boards are located throughout the clinic and provide information to keep employees up to date on announcements and clinic news.

EMPLOYER COMMUNICATION

Newland-Davis Medical supervisors, department leaders, and other management representatives maintain open and constructive communication in the following ways:

- Department and unit meetings: Departments and units meet to communicate goals and objectives and to discuss workplace issues of interest to employees. Employees should check with supervisors to obtain a schedule of the meetings.
- Management meetings: All levels of management routinely hold meetings to communicate information and discuss matters of importance.

3. Find text set in Candara with bold formatting applied and replace it with Corbel with bold formatting applied.

C18-A05-EmpGuide.docx (page 1 of 2)

3. Find text set in Candara with bold formatting applied and replace it with Corbel with bold formatting applied.

4. Find all of the section breaks in the document and replace them with nothing.

SECTION 3: EMPLOYMENT CATEGORIES

EMPLOYEE CATEGORIES

Throughout this handbook, you will see references to several employee categories with which you should become familiar. The categories include the following:

- Exempt: Refers to those employees excluded from the overtime provisions of the Fair Labor Standards Act. The professional clinical staff is considered exempt. The introductory period for exempt employees is 90 days.
- Non-exempt: Refers to those positions eligible for overtime pay if more than 40 hours are worked during a work week. The introductory period for non-exempt employees is 90 days.

CATEGORY DEFINITIONS

- Probationary: All persons newly hired or rehired are considered probationary employees until the completion of 90 calendar days of employment.
- Regular full time: A regular full-time employee is one who is employed on a regular basis on a schedule of 30 to 40 hours per week. Regular full-time employees are fully eligible for all benefits.
- Regular part time: Employees scheduled for 20 or more hours per week are eligible for employee benefits on a prorated basis in relation to their scheduled hours worked, up to 40.
- Non-benefit eligible part time: Employees scheduled to work less than 20 hours may be terminated without notice or cause.
- Temporary full time: A temporary full-time employee is one who is employed on a schedule of 40 hours per week for a limited period of time and is so informed at the time of hire.
- Temporary part time: A temporary part-time employee is one who is employed on a schedule of less than 30 hours per week for a limited period of time and is so informed at the time of hire.
- Per visit: Per-visit employees are hired to work on a per diem basis for an undetermined period of time. Per-visit employees can be terminated without notice or cause.

5. Find all of the em dashes and replace each dash with a colon (:) followed by a space (a press of the spacebar).

C18-A05-EmpGuide.docx (page 2 of 2)

1. Open **Contacts.docx** and save the document with the name **C18-A07-Contacts**.
4. Apply formatting so your document and tables display as shown in Figure 18.8.

CORPORATE CONTACTS

2. Sort the text in ascending order by state and then by company name.

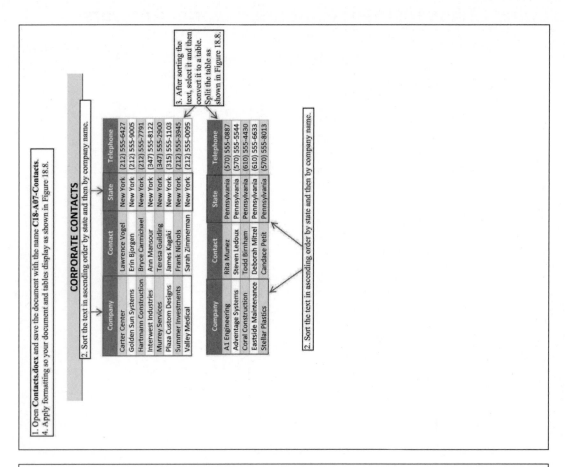

Company	Contact	State	Telephone
Carter Center	Lawrence Vogel	New York	(212) 555-6427
Golden Sun Systems	Erin Bjorgen	New York	(212) 555-9005
Hartmann Construction	Bryce Carmichael	New York	(212) 555-7791
Interwest Industries	Ann Mansour	New York	(347) 555-8122
Murrey Services	Teresa Guilding	New York	(347) 555-2900
Plaza Custom Designs	James Kagaki	New York	(315) 555-1103
Summer Investments	Frank Nichols	New York	(212) 555-3945
Valley Medical	Sarah Zimmerman	New York	(212) 555-0095

Company	Contact	State	Telephone
A1 Engineering	Rita Munez	Pennsylvania	(570) 555-0887
Advantage Systems	Steven Ledoux	Pennsylvania	(570) 555-5544
Coral Construction	Todd Birnham	Pennsylvania	(610) 555-4430
Eastside Maintenance	Deborah Mitzel	Pennsylvania	(610) 555-6633
Stellar Plastics	Candace Petit	Pennsylvania	(570) 555-8013

3. After sorting the text, select it and then convert it to a table as shown in Figure 18.8. Split the table as shown in Figure 18.8.

2. Sort the text in ascending order by state and then by company name.

C18-A07-Contacts.docx

---

8. Edit **ContactsDS.mdb** and then sort by company name in ascending order and filter by the state of New York.

Lawrence Vogel
Carter Center
New York
(212) 555-6427

Erin Bjorgen
Golden Sun Systems
New York
(212) 555-9005

1. At a blank document, click the Mailings tab, click the Start Mail Merge button, and then click *Labels* at the drop-down list.
2. At the Label Options dialog box, make sure the *Label vendors* option displays with *Avery US Letter*, click *45395 EcoFriendly Name Badges* in the list box (scroll up or down the list box to find this label), and then click OK.
3. Click the Select Recipients button, and then click *Type a New List* at the drop-down list.
4. Create and customize a data source file for the 14 records shown in Figure 18.7. Type the information in the appropriate fields for the 14 records shown in the figure.

Hartmann Construction   *Interwest Industries*
New York   *New York*

10. With the name tag labels displayed, complete the following steps:
a. Click in any label in the document and then click the Table Tools Layout tab.
b. Select the entire table. *Hint: Use the Select button on the Table Tools Layout tab.*
c. Click the Table Tools Design tab and then apply the Grid Table 3 - Accent 3 table style.
d. Click the Table Tools Layout tab and then change the alignment to center aligned.
e. With the table selected, change the font to 16-point Lucida Calligraphy with bold formatting applied.

Teresa Guilding   *James Kagaki*
Murrey Services   Plaza Custom Designs
New York   *New York*
(347) 555-2900   (315) 555-1103

Frank Nichols   *Sarah Zimmerman*
Summer Investments   Valley Medical
New York   *New York*
(212) 555-3945   (212) 555-0095

5. Name the data source file **ContactsDS**.
6. At the main document, insert the fields in the first label as shown below: «First_Name» «Last_Name» «Company_Name» «State» «Work_Phone»
7. Update the labels.
9. Merge the name tag labels.

C18-A06-NYNameTags.docx

Chapter 19 Assessment Annotated Model Answers

software. Polymorphic viruses alter themselves to prevent detection by antivirus software, which operates by examining familiar patterns. Polymorphic viruses alter themselves randomly as they move from computer to computer, making detection more difficult. Multipartite viruses alter their their form of attack. Their name reflects their ability to attack in several different ways. They may first infect the boot sector and then later act like a Trojan horse virus by infecting a disk file. These viruses are more sophisticated and therefore more difficult to guard against. Another type of virus is the logic bomb, which generally sits quietly dormant waiting for a specific event or set of conditions to occur. A well-known example of a logic bomb was the widely publicized Michelangelo virus, which infected personal computers and caused them to display a message on the artist's birthday.

1-2

C19-A01-CompSecurity.docx (page 2 of 3)

---

1. Open CompSecurity.docx and save the document with the name C19-A01- CompSecurity. 2. Make the following changes to the document: c. Apply the Centered style set.

2a. Apply the Heading 1 style to the two titles, *Computer Viruses* and *Security Risks*, and apply the Heading 2 style to the five headings.

2d. Apply chapter multilevel list numbering.

Chapter 1 Computer Viruses

One of the most familiar forms of risk to computer security is the computer virus. A computer virus is a program written by a hacker or a cracker, designed to perform some kind of trick upon an unsuspecting victim's computer. In some cases, the trick performed is mild, such as drawing an offensive image on the victim's screen or changing all of the characters in a document to another language. Sometimes the trick is much more severe, such as reformatting the hard drive and erasing all the data or damaging the motherboard so that it cannot operate properly.

Types of Viruses

Viruses can be categorized by their effects, which include being a nuisance, destroying data, facilitating espionage, and destroying hardware. A nuisance virus usually does no real damage but is an inconvenience. The most difficult part of a computer to replace is the data on the hard drive. The installed programs, documents, databases, and saved emails form the heart of a personal computer. A data-destructive virus is designed to destroy this data. Some viruses are designed to create a backdoor into a system to bypass security. Called espionage viruses, they do no damage but allow a hacker or cracker to enter the system later for the purpose of stealing data or spying on the work of the competitor. Very rarely, a virus is created to damage the hardware of the computer system itself. Called hardware-destructive viruses, these bits of programming can weaken or destroy chips, drives, and other components.

Methods of Virus Operation

Viruses operate and are transmitted in a variety of ways. An email virus is normally transmitted as an attachment to a message sent over the Internet. Email viruses require the victim to click on the attachment, which causes the virus to execute. Another common mode of virus transmission is via a macro, a small subprogram that allows users to customize and automate certain functions. A macro virus is written for a specific program, which then becomes infected when it opens a file with the virus stored in its macros. The boot sector of a compact disc or hard drive contains a variety of information, including how the disk is organized and whether it is capable of loading an operating system. When a disc is left in a drive and the computer reboots, the operating system automatically reads the boot sector to learn about that disk and to attempt to start any operating system on it. A boot sector virus is designed to alter the boot sector of a disk so that whenever the operating system reads the boot sector, the computer will automatically become infected.

Other types of viruses and methods of infection include the Trojan horse virus, which hides inside another legitimate program or data file, and the stealth virus, which is designed to hide itself from detection

2c. Insert page numbers that include chapter numbers on all of the pages in the document. Position the page number at the bottom center of each page. *Hint: Refer to Exercise 19.2, Step 9.*

1-1

C19-A01-CompSecurity.docx (page 1 of 3)

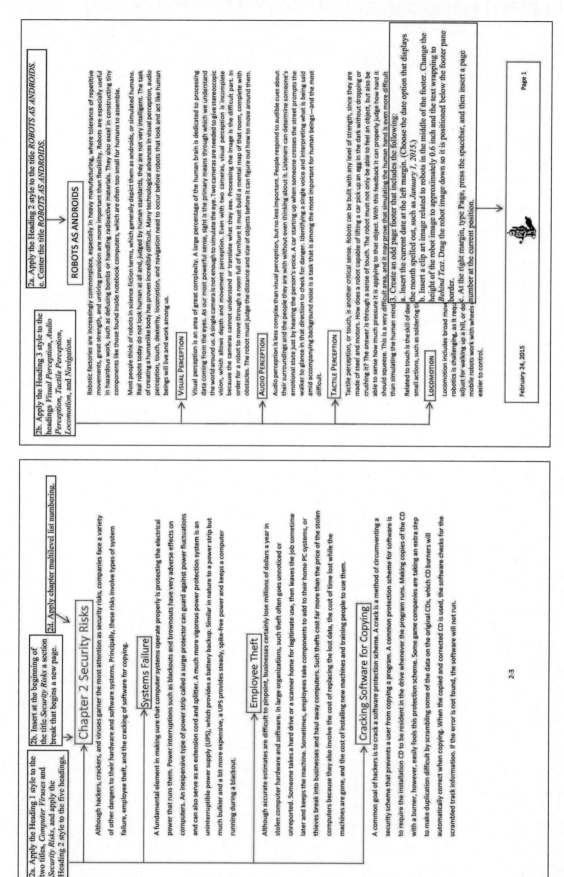

Left document — C19-A01-CompSecurity.docx (page 3 of 3):

2a. Apply the Heading 1 style to the two titles, *Computer Viruses* and *Security Risks*, and apply the Heading 2 style to the five headings.

2b. Insert at the beginning of the title *Security Risks* a section break that begins a new page.

2d. Apply chapter multilevel list numbering.

Chapter 2 Security Risks

Although hackers, crackers, and viruses garner the most attention as security risks, companies face a variety of other dangers to their hardware and software systems. Principally, these risks involve types of system failure, employee theft, and the cracking of software for copying.

Systems Failure

A fundamental element in making sure that computer systems operate properly is protecting the electrical power that runs them. Power interruptions such as blackouts and brownouts have very adverse effects on computers. An inexpensive type of power strip called a surge protector can guard against power fluctuations and can also serve as an extension cord and splitter. A much more vigorous power protection system is an uninterruptible power supply (UPS), which provides a battery backup. Similar in nature to a power strip but much bulkier and a bit more expensive, a UPS provides steady, spike-free power and keeps a computer running during a blackout.

Employee Theft

Although accurate estimates are difficult to pinpoint, businesses certainly lose millions of dollars a year in stolen computer hardware and software. In large organizations, such theft often goes unnoticed or unreported. Someone takes a hard drive or a scanner home for legitimate use, then leaves the job sometime later and keeps the machine. Sometimes, employees take components to add to their home PC systems, or thieves break into businesses and haul away computers. Such thefts cost far more than the price of the stolen computers because they also involve the cost of replacing the lost data, the cost of time lost while the machines are gone, and the cost of installing new machines and training people to use them.

Cracking Software for Copying

A common goal of hackers is to crack a software protection scheme. A crack is a method of circumventing a security scheme that prevents a user from copying a program. A common protection scheme for software is to require the installation CD to be resident in the drive whenever the program runs. Making copies of the CD with a burner, however, easily fools this protection scheme. Some game companies are taking an extra step to make duplication difficult by scrambling some of the data on the original CDs, which CD burners will automatically correct when copying. When the copied and corrected CD is used, the software checks for the scrambled track information. If the error is not found, the software will not run.

2-3

C19-A01-CompSecurity.docx (page 3 of 3)

Right document — C19-A02-Robots.docx (page 1 of 2):

2a.e. Center the title *ROBOTS AS ANDROIDS*.

2a. Apply the Heading 2 style to the title *ROBOTS AS ANDROIDS*.

2b. Apply the Heading 3 style to the headings *Visual Perception, Audio Perception, Tactile Perception, Locomotion,* and *Navigation*.

ROBOTS AS ANDROIDS

Robotic factories are increasingly commonplace, especially in heavy manufacturing, where tolerance of repetitive movements, great strength, and untiring precision are more important than flexibility. Robots are especially useful in hazardous work, such as defusing bombs or handling radioactive materials. They also excel in constructing tiny components like those found inside notebook computers, which are often too small for humans to assemble.

Most people think of robots in science fiction terms, which generally depict them as androids, or simulated humans. Real robots today do not look human at all and, judged by human standards, they are not very intelligent. The task of creating a humanlike body has proven incredibly difficult. Many technological advances in visual perception, audio perception, touch, dexterity, locomotion, and navigation need to occur before robots that look and act like human beings will live and work among us.

VISUAL PERCEPTION

Visual perception is an area of great complexity. A large percentage of the human brain is dedicated to processing data coming from the eyes. As our most powerful sense, sight is the primary means through which we understand the world around us. A single camera is not enough to simulate the eye. Two cameras are needed to give stereoscopic vision, which allows depth and movement perception. Even with two cameras, visual perception is incomplete because the cameras cannot understand or translate what they see. Processing the image is the difficult part. In order for a robot to move through a room full of furniture it must build a mental map of that room, complete with obstacles. The robot must judge the distance and size of objects before it can figure out how to move around them.

AUDIO PERCEPTION

Audio perception is less complex than visual perception, but no less important. People respond to audible cues about their surroundings and the people they are with without even thinking about it. Listeners can determine someone's emotional state just by hearing the person's voice. A car starting up when someone crosses the street prompts the walker to glance in that direction to check for danger. Identifying a single voice and interpreting what is being said amid accompanying background noise is a task that is among the most important for human beings—and the most difficult.

TACTILE PERCEPTION

Tactile perception, or touch, is another critical sense. Robots can be built with any level of strength, since they are made of steel and motors. How does a robot capable of lifting a car pick up an egg in the dark without dropping or crushing it? The answer is through a sense of touch. The robot must not only be able to feel an object, but also be able to sense how much pressure it is applying to that object. With this feedback it can properly judge how hard it should squeeze. This is a very difficult area, and it may prove that simulating the human hand is even more difficult than simulating the human mind.

Related to touch is the skill of dexterity... small actions, such as soldering th...

LOCOMOTION

Locomotion includes broad mov... robotics is challenging, as it requ... adjust for walking up a hill, or do... mobile robots work with wheels... easier to control.

3. Create an odd page footer that includes the following:

a. Insert the current date at the left margin. (Choose the date option that displays the month spelled out, such as *January 1, 2015*.)

b. Insert a clip art image related to robots in the middle of the footer. Change the height of the robot image to approximately 0.6 inch and the text wrapping to *Behind Text*. Drag the robot image down so it is positioned below the footer pane border.

c. At the right margin, type Page, press the spacebar, and then insert a page number at the current position.

February 24, 2015

Page 1

C19-A02-Robots.docx (page 1 of 2)

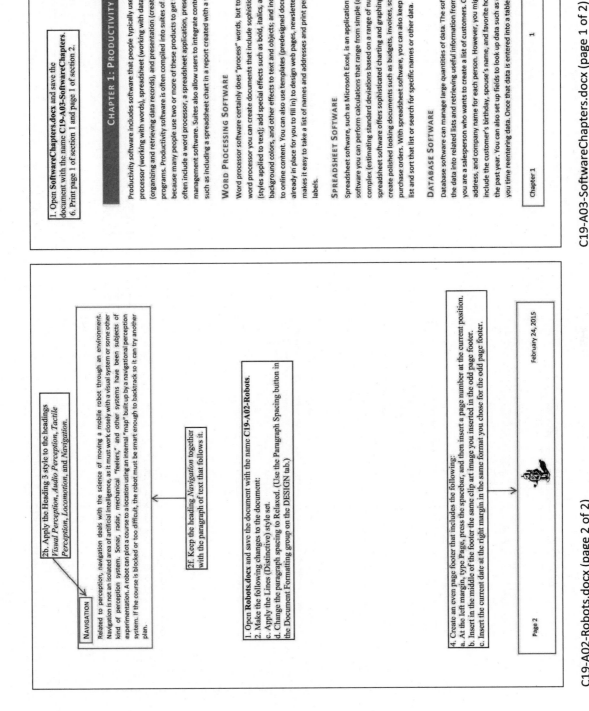

CHAPTER 1: PRODUCTIVITY SOFTWARE

Productivity software includes software that people typically use to complete work, such as a word processor (working with words), spreadsheet (working with data, numbers, and calculations), database (organizing and retrieving data records), and presentation (creating slideshows with text and graphics) programs. Productivity software is often compiled into suites of applications, such as Microsoft Office, because many people use two or more of these products to get their work completed. Office suites often include a word processor, a spreadsheet application, presentation software, and database management software. Suites also allow users to integrate content from one program into another, such as including a spreadsheet chart in a report created with a word processor.

WORD PROCESSING SOFTWARE

Word processor software certainly does "process" words, but today it does a great deal more. With a word processor you can create documents that include sophisticated formatting: change text fonts (styles applied to text); add special effects such as bold, italics, and underlining; add shadows, background colors, and other effects to text and objects; and include tables, photos, drawings, and links to online content. You can also use templates (predesigned documents with formatting and graphics already in place for you to fill in) to design web pages, newsletters, and more. A mail merge feature makes it easy to take a list of names and addresses and print personalized letters and envelopes or labels.

SPREADSHEET SOFTWARE

Spreadsheet software, such as Microsoft Excel, is an application where numbers rule. Using spreadsheet software you can perform calculations that range from simple (adding, averaging, and multiplying) to complex (estimating standard deviations based on a range of numbers, for example). In addition, spreadsheet software offers sophisticated charting and graphing capabilities. Formatting tools help you create polished looking documents such as budgets, invoices, schedules, attendance records, and purchase orders. With spreadsheet software, you can also keep track of data such as your holiday card list and sort that list or search for specific names or other data.

DATABASE SOFTWARE

Database software can manage large quantities of data. The software provides functions for organizing the data into related lists and retrieving useful information from these lists. For example, imagine that you are a salesperson who wants to create a list of customers. Of course you want to include the name, address, and company name for each person. However, you might also want each customer record to include the customer's birthday, spouse's name, and favorite hobby as well as a record of purchases in the past year. You can also set up fields to look up data such as city names based on a ZIP code, saving you time reentering data. Once that data is entered into a table you can view information in a

Chapter 1   1   Student Name

C19-A03-SoftwareChapters.docx (page 1 of 2)

NAVIGATION

Related to perception, navigation deals with the science of moving a mobile robot through an environment. Navigation is not an isolated area of artificial intelligence, as it must work closely with a visual system or some other kind of perception system. Sonar, radar, mechanical "feelers," and other systems have been subjects of experimentation. A robot can plot a course to a location using an internal "map" built up by a navigational perception system. If the course is blocked or too difficult, the robot must be smart enough to backtrack so it can try another plan.

Page 2   February 24, 2015

C19-A02-Robots.docx (page 2 of 2)

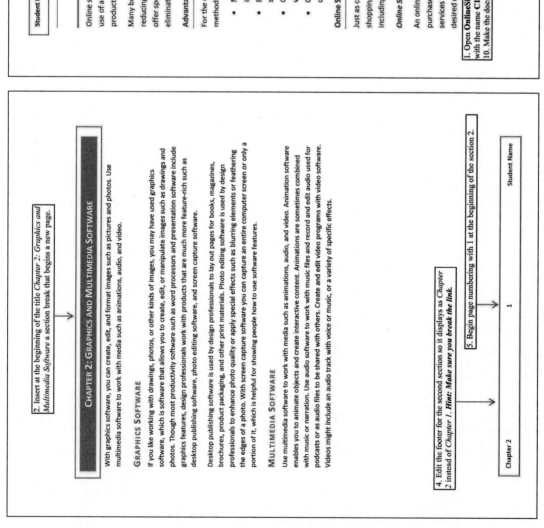

Top document:

ONLINE SHOPPING

Online shopping, also called electronic shopping or e-shopping, is shopping that involves the use of a computer, modem, browser, an... products.

Many businesses encourage consumers reducing staffing needs and saving mon... offer special discounts to travelers who... eliminating paper tickets altogether.

Advantages of Online Shopping

For the consumer, online shopping offer... methods. These advantages include the...

- More product information. At m... about a wide variety of products, an advantage often unavailable in traditional stores.
- Ease of comparison shopping. E-shopping allows you to quickly find comparable items at similar stores and locate those venues with the best quality and lowest prices.
- Convenience. With e-shopping you can browse merchandise and make purchases whenever you want from the privacy and comfort of your home or office.
- Greater selection. Because they are not restricted by available shelf space, online stores can offer you an almost unlimited number of products.

Online Shopping Venues

Just as consumers can visit a variety of brick-and-mortar retail outlets, such as stores and shopping malls, Internet shoppers can browse several types of online shopping venues, including online stores, superstores, and shopping malls.

Online Stores

An online store, also called a virtual store, is a seller's website where customers can view and purchase a merchant's products and services. The site, or storefront, groups its products or services in categories that link to a list of merchandise within each category. The user clicks a desired category to view pictures, descriptions, and prices of available products.

February 24, 2015

1. Open **OnlineShop.docx** and save the document with the name **C19-A04-OnlineShop**.
10. Make the document active.

Annotation (right margin):

7. Create a header that inserts an author document property. To do this, display the header pane, click the Quick Parts button, point to *Document Property*, and then click *Author* at the side menu. This inserts the *Author* placeholder, which contains a name. If the name is not your name, click the *Author* placeholder tab (which selects the text in the placeholder) and then type your first and last names.
8. Press the Right Arrow key to move the insertion point to the right of the *Author* placeholder and then press the Tab key twice.
9. Insert the file name as a field. To do this, click the Quick Parts button and then click *Field* at the drop-down list. At the Field dialog box, click *FileName* in the *Field names* list box and then click OK. (You will need to scroll down the list box to find the *FileName* option.) Select your name and the file name, apply bold formatting, and change the font color to Dark Blue.

C19-A04-OnlineShop.docx (page 1 of 2)

Bottom document:

2. Insert at the beginning of the title *Chapter 2: Graphics and Multimedia Software* a section break that begins a new page.

CHAPTER 2: GRAPHICS AND MULTIMEDIA SOFTWARE

With graphics software, you can create, edit, and format images such as pictures and photos. Use multimedia software to work with media such as animations, audio, and video.

GRAPHICS SOFTWARE

If you like working with drawings, photos, or other kinds of images, you may have used graphics software, which is software that allows you to create, edit, or manipulate images such as drawings and photos. Though most productivity software such as word processors and presentation software include graphics features, design professionals work with products that are much more feature-rich such as desktop publishing software, photo editing software, and screen capture software.

Desktop publishing software is used by design professionals to lay out pages for books, magazines, brochures, product packaging, and other print materials. Photo editing software is used by design professionals to enhance photo quality or apply special effects such as blurring elements or feathering the edges of a photo. With screen capture software you can capture an entire computer screen or only a portion of it, which is helpful for showing people how to use software features.

MULTIMEDIA SOFTWARE

Use multimedia software to work with media such as animations, audio, and video. Animation software enables you to animate objects and create interactive content. Animations are sometimes combined with music or narration. Use audio software to work with music files and record and edit audio used for podcasts or as audio files to be shared with others. Create and edit video programs with video software. Videos might include an audio track with voice or music, or a variety of specific effects.

4. Edit the footer for the second section so it displays as *Chapter 2* instead of *Chapter 1*. **Hint: Make sure you break the link.**

5. Begin page numbering with 1 at the beginning of the section 2.

Chapter 2   1   Student Name

C19-A03-SoftwareChapters.docx (page 2 of 2)

February 24, 2015

2b. Apply chapter multilevel list numbering. (This will insert the word *Chapter* followed by the chapter number before each of the three titles with the Heading 1 style applied.)

e. Move the insertion point to the chapter 1 title and then change the page numbering so it includes the chapter number.

Chapter 1 Navigating and Searching the Web

1. Open **InternetChapters.docx** and save the document with the name **C19-A05-InternetChapters**.

4. Save **C19-A05-InternetChapters.docx**.

5. Print only the first pages of sections 1, 2, and 3.

Since so many people create web pages, the Web should be chaotic. However, underlying systems are in place specifying how pages are organized on the Web and how they are delivered... system involves unique addresses used to access each web page, a unique address... browser features for locating and retrieving online content.

IPs and URLs

An *Internet Protocol (IP) address* is a series of numbers that uniquely identifies a lo[cal]... IP address consists of four groups of numbers separated by periods; for example: 2... nonprofit organization called ICANN keeps track of IP numbers around the world.

Because numbers would be difficult to remember for retrieving pages, we use a text-based address referred to as a *uniform resource locator (URL)* to go to a website. A URL, also called a *web address*, has several parts separated by a colon (:), slashes (/), and dots (.). The first part of a URL is called a *protocol* and identifies a certain way for interpreting computer information in the transmission process. *Http*, which stands for *hypertext transfer protocol*, and *ftp*, for *file transfer protocol*, are examples of protocols. Some sites use a secondary identifier for the type of site being contacted, such as *www* for *World Wide Web* site, but this is often optional.

The next part of the URL is the *domain name*, which identifies the group of servers (the domain) to which the site belongs and the particular company or organization name. A suffix, such as *.com* or *.edu*, further identifies the domain. For example, the *.com* in the URL http://www.emcp.com is a top-level domain (TLD). Several TLDs exists such as *.com*, *.net*, *.org*, *.edu*, and *.gov*. Table 1.1 provides a rundown of TLDs being used today.

Table 1.1 Common Top-Level Domain Suffixes Used in URLs

Suffix	Type of Organization	Example
.biz	business site	Billboard: http://www.billboard.biz
.com	company or commercial institution	Intel: http://www.intel.com
.edu	educational institution	Harvard University: http://www.harvard.edu
.gov	government site	Internal Revenue Service: http://www.irs.gov
.int	international organizations endorsed by treaty	World Health Organization: http://www.who.int
.mil	military site	U.S. Department of Defense: http://www.defenselink.net
.net	administrative site for ISPs	Earthlink: http://www.earthlink.net
.org	nonprofit or private organization	Red Cross: http://www.redcross.org

Browsing Web Pages

3. Scroll through the document. Each odd page should have your name displayed at the top of the page at the left margin and the current date at the right margin with a border line below it, along with the page number (including the chapter number) at the bottom of the page at the right margin with a border line above it. Each even page should have the current date displayed at the top of the page at the left margin and your name at the right margin with a border line below it, along with the page number (including the chapter number) at the bottom of the page at the left margin with a border line above it. The page numbers for the first two pages should display as *1-1* and *1-2*.

...pondered how ...hic, audio, or video) ...n a web document ...d is called

1-1

C19-A04-OnlineShop.docx

2. Keep the heading *Online Superstores* together with the paragraph following it.

Online Superstores

Like brick-and-mortar superstores, online superstores offer an extensive array of products, from candy bars to household appliances. Some popular superstores also have online superstores. E-tailer superstores have proved especially popular with shoppers.

Online Shopping Malls

When shopping malls were introduced in the 1950s, consumers were delighted by the convenience of being able to shop in a wide variety of stores physically connected under one roof. Similar in concept, an online shopping mall connects its stores by hyperlinks on the mall's home page. Some businesses, in fact, do not have individual online stores but instead offer their products and services only at an online shopping mall.

Online Shopping Safety Tips

The number one concern consumers have about shopping online is security. The truth, however, is that shopping online is safe and secure if you know what to look for. Following these guidelines can help you avoid trouble.

- Never provide your social security number.
- Find out the privacy policy of shopping sites before you buy.
- Keep current on the latest Internet scams.
- Look for sites that follow privacy rules from a privacy watchdog such as TRUSTe.
- Answer only the minimum questions when filling out forms.
- Only buy at secure sites.

3. Open the footer pane. Office.com provides a number of horizontal line images that you can insert in a document or in the header and/or footer in a document. Display horizontal line images by clicking the Online Pictures button in the Insert group to open the Insert Pictures window, typing horizontal line in the search text box, and then pressing the Enter key. Insert a horizontal line of your choosing in the footer pane. (To get a better view of the horizontal line options at the Insert Pictures window, hover your mouse over an option and then click the magnifying glass image that displays in the lower right corner of the option.) With the horizontal line selected, press Ctrl + E to center the line in the footer pane. Use the Color button on the PICTURE TOOLS FORMAT tab to apply a color that matches the colors in the document.

4. After inserting the horizontal line, press the Enter key and then insert the current date. Select the date, apply bold formatting, and change the font color to Dark Blue.

5. The Header & Footer Tools Design tab contains a number of buttons for inserting data in a header or footer. With the Quick Parts button in the Insert group, you can insert pieces of content such as fields and document properties. To determine what options are available, click the Quick Parts button and then hover your mouse over or click the options at the drop-down list.

6. Close the footer pane.

February 24, 2015

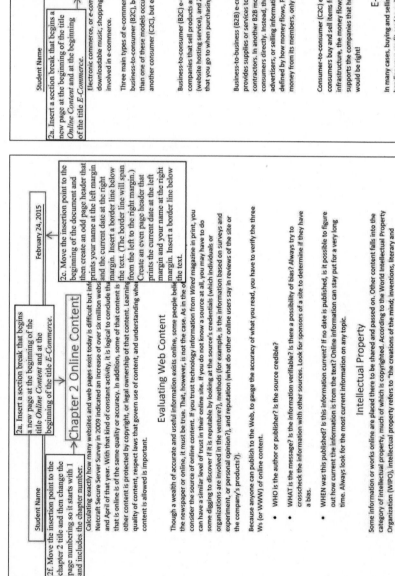

Document — C19-A05-InternetChapters.docx (page 2 of 3)

2f. Move the insertion point to the chapter 2 title and then change the page numbering so it starts with 1 and includes the chapter number.

2a. Insert a section break that begins a new page at the beginning of the title Online Content and at the beginning of the title E-Commerce.

2c. Move the insertion point to the beginning of the document and then create an odd page header that prints your name at the left margin and the current date at the right margin. Insert a border line below the text. (The border line will span from the left to the right margin.) Create an even page header that prints the current date at the left margin and your name at the right margin. Insert a border line below the text.

Chapter 2 Online Content

Calculating exactly how many websites and web pages exist today is difficult but inf[...] Netcraft Secure Server Survey in 2009 indicated an increase of over six million websit[es] and April of that year. With that kind of constant activity, it is logical to conclude tha[t] that is online is of the same quality or accuracy. In addition, some of that content is other content is protected by copyright, or legal ownership of that content. Learning quality of content, respect laws that govern use of content, and understanding whe[n] content is allowed is important.

Evaluating Web Content

Though a wealth of accurate and useful information exists online, some people beli[eve] the newspaper or online, it must be true. That, however, is not the case. As in the case consider the source of online content. If you trust technology information from *Wired* magazine in print, you can have a similar level of trust in their online site. If you do not know a source at all, you may have to do some digging to discover if it is reputable by looking at the source's credentials (which individuals or organizations are involved in the venture?), methods (for example, is the information based on surveys and experiment, or personal opinion?), and reputation (what do other online users say in reviews of the site or the company's products?).

Because anyone can publish to the Web, to gauge the accuracy of what you read, you have to verify the three Ws (or WWW) of online content.

- WHO is the author or publisher? Is the source credible?

- WHAT is the message? Is the information verifiable? Is there a possibility of bias? Always try to crosscheck the information with other sources. Look for sponsors of a site to determine if they have a bias.

- WHEN was this published? Is this information current? If no date is published, is it possible to figure out how current the information is from the text? Online information can stay put for a very long time. Always look for the most current information on any topic.

Intellectual Property

Some information or works online are placed there to be shared and passed on. Other content falls into the category of intellectual property, much of which is copyrighted. According to the World Intellectual Property Organization (WIPO), intellectual property refers to "the creations of the mind; inventions; literary and artistic works; and symbols, names, images, and designs used in commerce." Copying or distributing intellectual property without appropriate permission is illegal.

The Internet has brought the issue of illegal treatment of intellectual property front and center. Because copying and pasting content online is so simple, many people who would never dream of stealing a CD from a music store or a book from a bookstore download music illegally or plagiarize by using text or images from a website and representing that content as their own work.

Peer-to-peer (P2P) file sharing programs, such as BearShare, are used by millions of people to share music, video, and other types of files. File sharing allows people to download content from another user's hard drive. This type of sharing is ripe for copyright abuse because materials that might be downloaded from a

3. The third and fourth pages should display as 2-1 and 2-2. (The pages are numbered like this because you specified to include chapter numbers with the page numbers and to start numbering each chapter with page 1.)

2-1

C19-A05-InternetChapters.docx (page 2 of 3)

Document — C19-A05-InternetChapters.docx (page 3 of 3)

2g. Move the insertion point to the chapter 3 title and then change the page numbering so it starts with 1 and includes the chapter number.

2a. Insert a section break that begins a new page at the beginning of the title Online Content and at the beginning of the title E-Commerce.

Chapter 3 E-Commerce

Electronic commerce, or *e-commerce*, involves using the Internet to transact business. When you are buying downloadable music, shopping for shoes, or paying to access your credit report, for example, you are involved in e-commerce.

Three main types of e-commerce describe how money flows in an online business. Money can flow from business-to-consumer (B2C), business-to-business (B2B), or consumer-to-consumer (C2C). Sometimes more than one of these models occurs on a single site (for example, when a consumer on eBay buys a product from another consumer (C2C), but eBay makes money from advertisers (B2B).

B2C E-Commerce

Business-to-consumer (B2C) e-commerce is probably the kind with which you are most familiar. It involves companies that sell products and services to individual consumers, such as Amazon.com, JustHost.com (website hosting service), and Zappos.com. This is the model that most resembles those stores in the mall that you go to when purchasing books, obtaining tax return help, or finding shoes.

B2B E-Commerce

Business-to-business (B2B) e-commerce involves businesses selling to businesses. In some cases, a business provides supplies or services to another business, such as a plumbing supply site that caters to building contractors. In another B2B model, businesses provide a service to consumers but do not charge those consumers directly. Instead, their business model involves making money from selling ad space to advertisers, or selling information about their customers to advertisers. Given that e-commerce models are defined by how money flows, Facebook is an example of this second kind of B2B site because it gets no money from its members, only from advertisers (or other businesses).

C2C E-Commerce

Consumer-to-consumer (C2C) e-commerce activity occurs on sites such as Craigslist or eBay where consumers buy and sell items from each other over the Internet. Though the host site provides the infrastructure, the money flows from one consumer to another. What e-commerce model do you think supports the companies that host C2C sites? If you guessed B2B (they get their money from advertisers) you would be right!

E-Commerce and Consumer Safety

In many cases, buying and selling items online is safer than doing so offline. That's because rather than handing your credit card to a clerk in a store, you are performing a transaction over a secure connection, providing payment information to a system rather than an individual. Of course, every system has its problems, and online stores, banks, and investment sites are hacked into now and then. Still, if you use care in choosing trusted shopping sites, pay by a third-party payment service such as PayPal or by credit card (these purchases are protected from theft, while a check or debit card purchase is not), and make sure that while performing a transaction the URL prefix reads *https* (which indicates a secure connection), you can be confident that you will have a safe shopping experience.

2d. Create an odd page footer that inserts a page number at the bottom right margin of each page that includes the chapter number. Insert a border line above the page number. Create an even page footer that inserts a page number at the bottom left margin of each page that includes the chapter number. Insert a border line above the page number.

3. The fifth page should display 3-1.

3-1

C19-A05-InternetChapters.docx (page 3 of 3)

Chapter 20 Assessment Annotated Model Answers

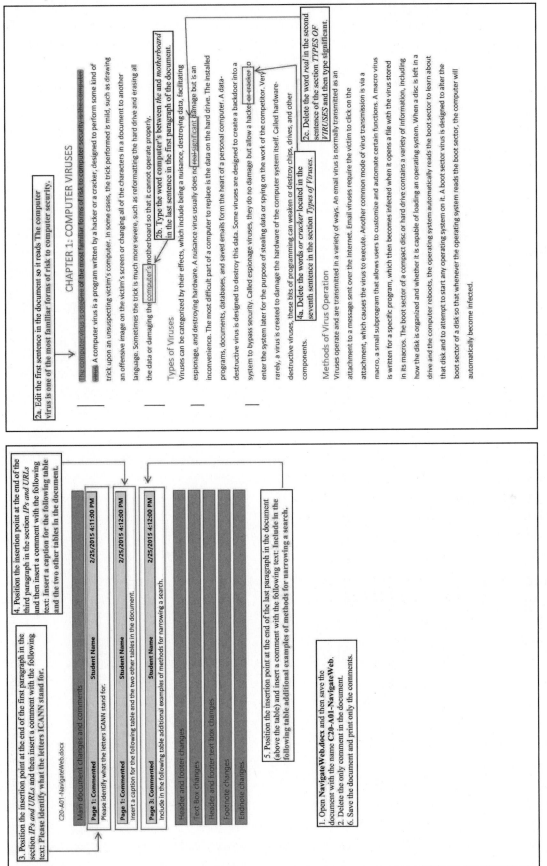

C20-A02-CompChapters(Step6).docx (page 1 of 3)

C20-A01-NavigateWeb.docx

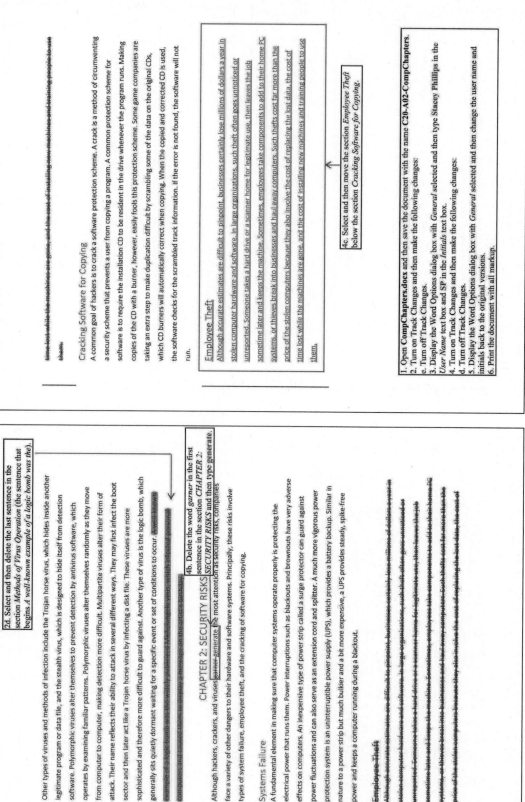

~~time lost while the machines are gone, and the cost of installing new machines and training people to use them.~~

Cracking Software for Copying

A common goal of hackers is to crack a software protection scheme. A crack is a method of circumventing a security scheme that prevents a user from copying a program. A common protection scheme for software is to require the installation CD to be resident in the drive whenever the program runs. Making copies of the CD with a burner, however, easily fools this protection scheme. Some game companies are taking an extra step to make duplication difficult by scrambling some of the data on the original CDs, which CD burners will automatically correct when copying. When the copied and corrected CD is used, the software checks for the scrambled track information. If the error is not found, the software will not run.

Employee Theft

Although accurate estimates are difficult to pinpoint, businesses certainly lose millions of dollars a year in stolen computer hardware and software. In large organizations, such theft often goes unnoticed or unreported. Someone takes a hard drive or a scanner home for legitimate use, then leaves the job sometime later and keeps the machine. Sometimes, employees take components to add to their home PC systems, or thieves break into businesses and haul away computers. Such thefts cost far more than the price of the stolen computers because they also involve the cost of replacing the lost data, the cost of time lost while the machines are gone, and the cost of installing new machines and training people to use them.

> **4c.** Select and then move the section *Employee Theft* below the section *Cracking Software for Copying.*

1. Open **CompChapters.docx** and then save the document with the name C20-A02-CompChapters.
2. Turn on Track Changes and then make the following changes:
c. Turn off Track Changes.
3. Display the Word Options dialog box with *General* selected and then type Stacey Phillips in the *User Name* text box and SP in the *Initials* text box.
4. Turn on Track Changes and then make the following changes:
d. Turn off Track Changes.
5. Display the Word Options dialog box with *General* selected and then change the user name and initials back to the original versions.
6. Print the document with all markup.

C20-A02-CompChapters(Step6).docx (page 3 of 3)

> **2d.** Select and then delete the last sentence in the section *Methods of Virus Operation* (the sentence that begins *A well-known example of a logic bomb was the*).

Other types of viruses and methods of infection include the Trojan horse virus, which hides inside another legitimate program or data file, and the stealth virus, which is designed to hide itself from detection software. Polymorphic viruses alter themselves to prevent detection by antivirus software, which operates by examining familiar patterns. Polymorphic viruses alter themselves randomly as they move from computer to computer, making detection more difficult. Multipartite viruses alter their form of attack. Their name reflects their ability to attack in several different ways. They may first infect the boot sector and then later act like a Trojan horse virus by infecting a disk file. These viruses are more sophisticated and therefore more difficult to guard against. Another type of virus is the logic bomb, which generally sits quietly dormant waiting for a specific event or set of conditions to occur. ~~A well-known example of a logic bomb was the widely publicized Michelangelo virus, which infected personal computers and instructed them to display a message on the artist's birthday.~~

CHAPTER 2: SECURITY RISKS

> **4b.** Delete the word *garner* in the first sentence in the section *CHAPTER 2: SECURITY RISKS* and then type generate.

Although hackers, crackers, and viruses ~~garner~~ generate the most attention as security risks, companies face a variety of other dangers to their hardware and software systems. Principally, these risks involve types of system failure, employee theft, and the cracking of software for copying.

Systems Failure

A fundamental element in making sure that computer systems operate properly is protecting the electrical power that runs them. Power interruptions such as blackouts and brownouts have very adverse effects on computers. An inexpensive type of power strip called a surge protector can guard against power fluctuations and can also serve as an extension cord and splitter. A much more vigorous power protection system is an uninterruptible power supply (UPS), which provides a battery backup. Similar in nature to a power strip but much bulkier and a bit more expensive, a UPS provides steady, spike-free power and keeps a computer running during a blackout.

~~Employee Theft~~

~~Although accurate estimates are difficult to pinpoint, businesses certainly lose millions of dollars a year in stolen computer hardware and software. In large organizations, such theft often goes unnoticed or unreported. Someone takes a hard drive or a scanner home for legitimate use, then leaves the job sometime later and keeps the machine. Sometimes, employees take components to add to their home PC systems, or thieves break into businesses and haul away computers. Such thefts cost far more than the price of the stolen computers because they also involve the cost of replacing the lost data, the cost of~~

C20-A02-CompChapters(Step6).docx (page 2 of 3)

CHAPTER 1: COMPUTER VIRUSES

The computer virus is one of the most familiar forms of risk to computer security. A computer virus is a program written by a hacker or a cracker, designed to perform some kind of trick upon an unsuspecting victim's computer. In some cases, the trick performed is mild, such as drawing an offensive image on the victim's screen or changing all of the characters in a document to another language. Sometimes the trick is much more severe, such as reformatting the hard drive and erasing all the data or damaging the computer's motherboard so that it cannot operate properly.

Types of Viruses

Viruses can be categorized by their effects, which include being a nuisance, destroying data, facilitating espionage, and destroying hardware. A nuisance virus usually does no significant damage but is an inconvenience. The most difficult part of a computer to replace is the data on the hard drive. The installed programs, documents, databases, and saved emails form the heart of a personal computer. A data-destructive virus is designed to destroy this data. Some viruses are designed to create a backdoor into a system to bypass security. Called espionage viruses, they do no damage but allow a hacker to enter the system later for the purpose of stealing data or spying on the work of the competitor. Very rarely, a virus is created to damage the hardware of the computer system itself. Called hardware-destructive viruses, these bits of programming can weaken or destroy chips, drives, and other components.

Methods of Virus Operation

Viruses operate and are transmitted in a variety of ways. An email virus is normally transmitted as an attachment to a message sent over the Internet. Email viruses require the victim to click on the attachment, which causes the virus to execute. Another common mode of virus transmission is via a macro, a small subprogram that allows users to customize and automate certain functions. A macro virus is written for a specific program, which then becomes infected when it opens a file with the virus stored in its macros. The boot sector of a compact disc or hard drive contains a variety of information, including how the disk is organized and whether it is capable of loading an operating system. When a disc is left in a drive and the computer reboots, the operating system automatically reads the boot sector to learn about that disk and to attempt to start any operating system on it. A boot sector virus is designed to alter the boot sector of a disk so that whenever the operating system reads the boot sector, the computer will automatically become infected.

Other types of viruses and methods of infection include the Trojan horse virus, which hides inside another legitimate program or data file, and the stealth virus, which is designed to hide itself from detection software. Polymorphic viruses alter themselves to prevent detection by antivirus software, which operates by examining familiar patterns. Polymorphic viruses alter themselves randomly as they move from computer to computer, making detection more difficult. Multipartite viruses alter their form of attack. Their name reflects their ability to attack in several different ways. They may first infect the boot sector and then later act like a Trojan horse virus by infecting a disk file. These viruses are more sophisticated and therefore more difficult to guard against. Another type of virus is the logic bomb, which generally sits quietly dormant waiting for a specific event or set of conditions to occur.

CHAPTER 2: SECURITY RISKS

Although hackers, crackers, and viruses generate the most attention as security risks, companies face a variety of other dangers to their hardware and software systems. Principally, these risks involve types of system failure, employee theft, and the cracking of software for copying.

Systems Failure

A fundamental element in making sure that computer systems operate properly is protecting the electrical power that runs them. Power interruptions such as blackouts and brownouts have very adverse effects on computers. An inexpensive type of power strip called a surge protector can guard against power fluctuations and can also serve as an extension cord and splitter. A much more vigorous power protection system is an uninterruptible power supply (UPS), which provides a battery backup. Similar in nature to a power strip but much bulkier and a bit more expensive, a UPS provides steady, spike-free power and keeps a computer running during a blackout.

Employee Theft

Although accurate estimates are difficult to pinpoint, businesses certainly lose millions of dollars a year in stolen computer hardware and software. In large organizations, such theft often goes unnoticed or unreported. Someone takes a hard drive or a scanner home for legitimate use, then leaves the job sometime later and keeps the machine. Sometimes, employees take components to add to their home PC systems, or thieves break into businesses and haul away computers. Such thefts cost far more than the price of the stolen computers because they also involve the cost of replacing the lost data, the cost of time lost while the machines are gone, and the cost of installing new machines and training people to use them.

1. Compare **Security.docx** with **EditedSecurity.docx** and insert the changes into a new document. *Hint: Choose New document at the expanded Compare Documents dialog box.*
2. Save the compared document and name it **C20-A03-Security.docx**.
3. Print only the list of markup (not the document).

CHAPTER ~~3~~ SECURITY STRATEGIES

As the Internet has evolved and computer technology has become more sophisticated, IT managers, computer experts, and security specialists have developed a set of security strategies to prevent damage and losses. ~~Including,~~ These strategies include the following:

- Data backups
- Disaster recovery plan
- Data encryption
- Firewalls
- User IDs and passwords
- Network sniffers
- ~~Mini webcams~~
- Biometric authentication
- Virus detection and removal

Data Backups

One of the crucial elements of any prevention scheme is to be prepared for the worst. What if a fire ~~burned up~~destroyed your company's offices and computers? Do all employees have recent backups on hand to replace ~~their~~ critical files? Backing up data and placing the backup in a safe ~~spot~~location is a necessary chore, because if antivirus software misses a bug or if a disaster occurs, you do not want to be left with nothing.

Organizations can choose from many backup schemes. Besides the obvious move of having a complete copy of programs and data in a safe place, companies tend to take additional measures, particularly concerning a primary database. If something goes wrong with the backup, a company could find itself out of business quickly. Organizations normally keep more than one backup of important databases and usually update them ~~on a~~ daily or weekly ~~basis~~.

A variation of the backup strategy is to create rotating backups of perhaps seven copies of company data, one for each day of the week. When it comes around to the eighth day, the administrator takes the previous backup and overwrites it, saving the new backup ~~on an old tape~~ and erasing the oldest copy. This scheme has several advantages. It saves time, as only one backup is made each day. It allows for multiple disasters to strike simultaneously, as you always have the original and seven copies of the data available, ~~making it unlikely that all are damaged and destroyed at once~~. If the database is lost or corrupted, many copies exist, some of which may predate the beginning of the problem.

Disaster Recovery Plan

A disaster recovery plan is a safety system that allows a company to restore its systems after a complete loss of data. The elements of a typical disaster recovery plan include the following:

- Data backup procedures
- Remotely located backup copies

Cracking Software for Copying

A common goal of hackers is to crack a software protection scheme. A crack is a method of circumventing a security scheme that prevents a user from copying a program. A common protection scheme for software is to require the installation CD to be resident in the drive whenever the program runs. Making copies of the CD with a burner, however, easily fools this protection scheme. Some game companies are taking an extra step to make duplication difficult by scrambling some of the data on the original CDs, which CD burners will automatically correct when copying. When the copied and corrected CD is used, the software checks for the scrambled track information. If the error is not found, the software will not run.

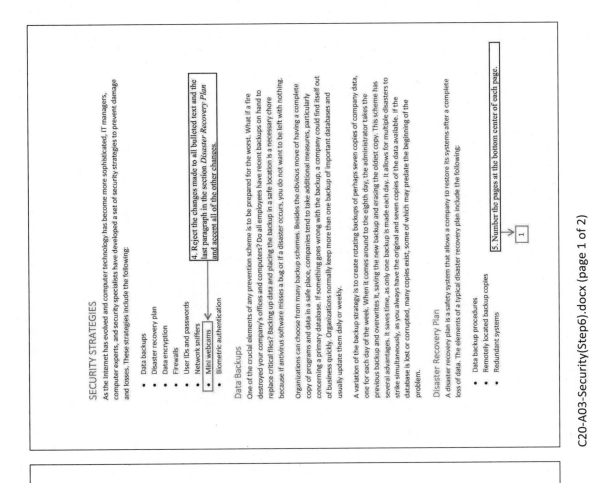

SECURITY STRATEGIES

As the Internet has evolved and computer technology has become more sophisticated, IT managers, computer experts, and security specialists have developed a set of security strategies to prevent damage and losses. These strategies include the following:

- Data backups
- Disaster recovery plan
- Data encryption
- Firewalls
- User IDs and passwords
- Network sniffers
- Mini webcams
- Biometric authentication

4. Reject the changes made to all bulleted text and the last paragraph in the section *Disaster Recovery Plan* and accent all of the other changes.

Data Backups

One of the crucial elements of any prevention scheme is to be prepared for the worst. What if a fire destroyed your company's offices and computers? Do all employees have recent backups on hand to replace critical files? Backing up data and placing the backup in a safe location is a necessary chore because if antivirus software misses a bug or if a disaster occurs, you do not want to be left with nothing.

Organizations can choose from many backup schemes. Besides the obvious move of having a complete copy of programs and data in a safe place, companies tend to take additional measures, particularly concerning a primary database. If something goes wrong with the backup, a company could find itself out of business quickly. Organizations normally keep more than one backup of important databases and usually update them daily or weekly.

A variation of the backup strategy is to create rotating backups of perhaps seven copies of company data, one for each day of the week. When it comes around to the eighth day, the administrator takes the previous backup and overwrites it, saving the new backup and erasing the oldest copy. This scheme has several advantages. It saves time, as only one backup is made each day. It allows for multiple disasters to strike simultaneously, as you always have the original and seven copies of the data available. If the database is lost or corrupted, many copies exist, some of which may predate the beginning of the problem.

Disaster Recovery Plan

A disaster recovery plan is a safety system that allows a company to restore its systems after a complete loss of data. The elements of a typical disaster recovery plan include the following:

- Data backup procedures
- Remotely located backup copies
- Redundant systems

5. Number the pages at the bottom center of each page.

1

C20-A03-Security(Step6).docx (page 1 of 2)

- Redundant systems

Besides backing up the data multiple times and storing backup copies in a different building, other precautions can be a big benefit when ~~everything goes horribly~~ things go wrong. These precautions include keeping extra pieces of critical hardware that can be quickly replaced in the damaged machines. Another safeguard is establishing redundant systems. One part of a redundant system might include having a fully mirrored hard drive that can be swapped with a damaged or corrupted hard drive thereby keeping downtime to a minimum. A mirrored hard drive is one that contains exactly the same data as the original and is updated automatically every time the original is updated. ~~That way if~~ one disk fails, the other can keep going with no loss of data. Many corporations have safeguards of this type to protect ~~their~~ critical databases.

Data Encryption

To prevent people from spying on sensitive transactions, such as the transmission of a user name and password across the Internet, companies use data encryption to scramble the information before it is transmitted. Data encryption schemes include an encryption key that is generated automatically and shared between the two computers that wish to communicate. This security can also work with cell phones and other forms of communication devices. Without this key, breaking the encryption code is very difficult.

C20-A03-Security(Step3).docx (page 2 of 2)

IN THE SUPERIOR COURT OF THE STATE OF WASHINGTON

IN AND FOR THE COUNTY OF KING

NAME1,

Plaintiff,

NO. NUMBER

SUMMONS

NAME2,

Defendant,

TO THE DEFENDANT, NAME2: A lawsuit has been started against you in the above entitled court by NAME1, plaintiff. Plaintiff's claim is stated in the written complaint, ~~two copies a copy~~ of which ~~are~~ is served upon you with this Summons.

This Summons is issued pursuant to Rule 12 of the Superior Court Civil Rules of the State of Washington.

In order to defend against this lawsuit, you must respond to the complaint by stating your defense in writing, and by serving a copy upon the person signing this Summons within twenty (20) days after the service of this Summons, excluding the day of service, or default judgment may be entered against you, NAME2, without ~~written notice~~. A default judgment is one where the plaintiff, NAME1, is entitled to what plaintiff asks for because you have not responded ~~notice~~.

You may demand that the plaintiff, NAME1, file his lawsuit with the court. If you do so, the demand must be in writing and must be served upon the person signing this Summons. Within fourteen (14) days after you serve the demand, the plaintiff, NAME1, must file this lawsuit with the court, or the service on you of this Summons will be ~~null and~~ void.

~~This Summons is issued pursuant to Rule 12 of the Superior Court Civil Rules of the State of Washington.~~

DATED this _____ day of _____, 2015.

_____
MARCIA DONOVAN
of Garcetti & Donovan

Besides backing up the data multiple times and storing backup copies in a different building, other precautions can be a big benefit when everything goes horribly wrong. These precautions include keeping extra pieces of critical hardware that can be quickly replaced in the damaged machines. Another safeguard is establishing redundant systems. One part of a redundant system might include having a fully mirrored hard drive that can be swapped with a damaged or corrupted hard drive thereby keeping downtime to a minimum. A mirrored hard drive is one that contains exactly the same data as the original and is updated automatically every time the original is updated. That way if one disk fails, the other can keep going with no loss of data. Many corporations have safeguards of this type to protect their critical databases.

Data Encryption

To prevent people from spying on sensitive transactions, such as the transmission of a user name and password across the Internet, companies use data encryption to scramble the information before it is transmitted. Data encryption schemes include an encryption key that is generated automatically and shared between the two computers that wish to communicate. This security can also work with cell phones and other forms of communication devices. Without this key, breaking the encryption code is very difficult.

4. Reject the changes made to all bulleted text and the last paragraph in the section *Disaster Recovery Plan* and accept all of the other changes.

2

8. Accept all of the changes to the document.
9. Save, print only the document, and then close C20-A04-LegalSummons.docx

IN THE SUPERIOR COURT OF THE STATE OF WASHINGTON

IN AND FOR THE COUNTY OF KING

NAME1,

    Plaintiff,   NO. NUMBER

                 SUMMONS

NAME2,

    Defendant,

TO THE DEFENDANT, NAME2: A lawsuit has been started against you in the above entitled court by NAME1, plaintiff. Plaintiff's claim is stated in the written complaint, two copies of which are served upon you with this Summons.

This Summons is issued pursuant to Rule 12 of the Superior Court Civil Rules of the State of Washington.

In order to defend against this lawsuit, you must respond to the complaint by stating your defense in writing, and by serving a copy upon the person signing this Summons within twenty (20) days after the service of this Summons, excluding the day of service, or default judgment may be entered against you, NAME2, without written notice. A default judgment is one where the plaintiff, NAME1, is entitled to what plaintiff asks for because you have not responded.

You may demand that the plaintiff, NAME1, file his lawsuit with the court. If you do so, the demand must be in writing and must be served upon the person signing this Summons. Within fourteen (14) days after you serve the demand, the plaintiff, NAME1, must file this lawsuit with the court, or the service on you of this Summons will be void.

    DATED this _____ day of _____, 2015.

_____

MARCIA DONOVAN
of Garcetti & Donovan
Attorneys for Plaintiff

Attorneys for Plaintiff

1. Open **LegalSummons.docx** and save the document with the name **C20-A04-LegalSummons.**
2. Close **C20-A04-LegalSummons.docx.**
3. At a blank screen, combine **C20-A04-LegalSummons** (the original document) with **Review1-LegalSummons.docx** (the revised document) into the original document. *Hint: Choose* **Original document** *at the* **Combine Documents expanded** *dialog box.*
4. Accept all of the changes to the document.
5. Save and then close **C20-A04-LegalSummons.docx.**
6. At a blank screen, combine **C20-A04-LegalSummons.docx** (the original document) with **Review2-LegalSummons.docx** (the revised document) into the original document.
7. Print only the list of markup.

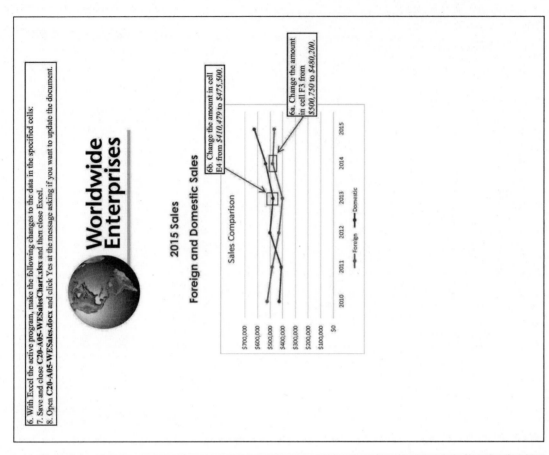

6. With Excel the active program, make the following changes to the data in the specified cells:
7. Save and close C20-A05-WESalesChart.xlsx and then close Excel.
8. Open C20-A05-WESales.docx and click Yes at the message asking if you want to update the document.

6b. Change the amount in cell E4 from *$410,479 to $475,500.*

6a. Change the amount in cell F3 from *$500,750 to $480,200.*

C20-A05-WESales(Step9).docx

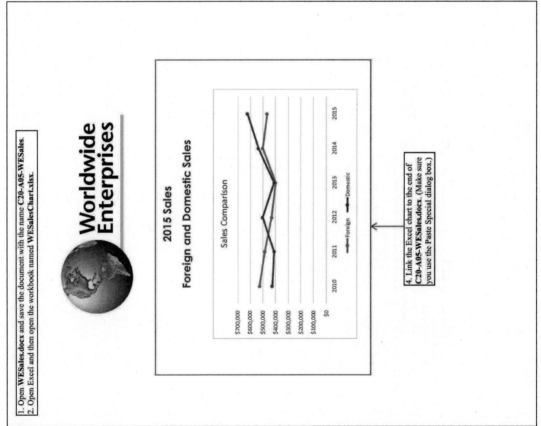

1. Open **WESales.docx** and save the document with the name **C20-A05-WESales.**
2. Open Excel and then open the workbook named **WESalesChart.xlsx.**

4. Link the Excel chart to the end of **C20-A05-WESales.docx.** (Make sure you use the Paste Special dialog box.)

C20-A05-WESales(Step5).docx

Signature Word 2013 Model Answers

5. Accept all of the changes.
6. Display the Advanced Track Changes Options dialog box and then return the inserted cells color back to Light Blue and the deleted cells color back to Pink.

Mobile Bay Products		
Salesperson	Sales, First Half	Sales, Second Half
Tanaka, Diana	$543,230	$559,988
Caswell, Martin	$495,678	$475,850
Coulter, Jolene	$312,675	$401,210
Kohler, Roger	$653,987	$623,457
Owens, Kendra	$239,223	$258,110

3a. Insert a new row at the beginning of the table.
b. Merge the cells in the new row. (At the message telling you the action will not be marked as a change, click OK.)
c. Type Mobile Bay Products in the merged cell.

3e. Insert a new row below *Tanaka, Diana* and then type Caswell, Martin in the first cell, $495,678 in the second cell, and $475,850 in the third cell.

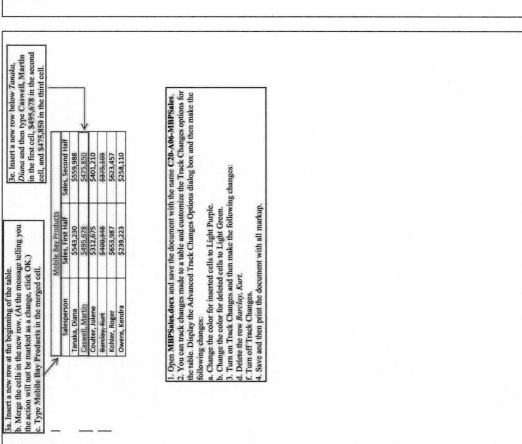

Mobile Bay Products		
Salesperson	Sales, First Half	Sales, Second Half
Tanaka, Diana	$543,230	$559,988
Caswell, Martin	$495,678	$475,850
Coulter, Jolene	$312,675	$401,210
~~Barclay, Kurt~~	~~$400,348~~	~~$375,109~~
Kohler, Roger	$653,987	$623,457
Owens, Kendra	$239,223	$258,110

1. Open **MBPSales.docx** and save the document with the name **C20-A06-MBPSales.**
2. You can track changes made to a table and customize the Track Changes options for the table. Display the Advanced Track Changes Options dialog box and then make the following changes:
a. Change the color for inserted cells to Light Purple.
b. Change the color for deleted cells to Light Green.
3. Turn on Track Changes and then make the following changes:
d. Delete the row *Barclay, Kurt.*
f. Turn off Track Changes.
4. Save and then print the document with all markup.

training certificates, or other work-related documents that your supervisor has requested to be included in your file.

1. Open **NSSEmpPerf.docx** and then save the document and name it **C20-A07-NSSEmpPerf**. 2. Turn on Track Changes and then make the changes shown in Figure 20.10. (Make the editing changes before you move the *Employment Records* information below the *Performance Evaluation* information.) 3. Turn off Track Changes and then print only the list of markup.

C20-A07-NSSEmpPerf(Step3).docx (page 2 of 2)

Northland Security Systems
3200 North 22nd Street ✦ Springfield ✦ IL ✦ 62102

EMPLOYEE PERFORMANCE

Work Performance Standards

~~Some w~~Work performance standards are written statements of the results and/or behavior expected of an employee when his or her job elements are satisfactorily performed under existing working conditions. Each employee in a permanent position must be provided with a current set of work performance standards for his or her position.

~~Employment Records~~

~~Your personnel file is maintained in the human resources department at the main office of Northland Security Systems. The human resources department maintains a file with copies of the documentation in your specific department. Your file includes personnel action documents, mandatory employment forms, your performance evaluations, and documentation of disciplinary action. Your file may include letters of commendation, training certificates, or other work-related documents that your supervisor has requested to be included in your file.~~

Performance Evaluation

If you are serving a six-month (full-time equivalent) probationary period, your supervisor will evaluate your performance at the end of the second and fifth months. If you are completing a one-year probationary period, your evaluations will be conducted at the end of the third, seventh, and eleventh month. You will receive a copy of each performance report. Once you have attained permanent employee status, your performance will be evaluated annually during the month prior to your pay progression date. Each evaluation will include a discussion between you and your supervisor to review and clarify goals and methods to achieve them. The evaluation will also include a written report of your progress on the job. Evaluations will be made with reference to established work performance standards.

Employment Records

Your personnel file is maintained in the human resources department. The human resources department maintains a working file with copies of the documentation in your specific department. Your file includes personnel action documents, mandatory employment forms, your performance evaluations, and documentation of disciplinary action. Your file may include letters of commendation,

1-888-555-2200 ✦ www.emcp.net/nss

C20-A07-NSSEmpPerf(Step3).docx (page 1 of 2)

Northland Security Systems
3200 North 22nd Street ✦ Springfield ✦ IL ✦ 62102

EMPLOYEE PERFORMANCE

Work Performance Standards

Work performance standards are written statements of the results and/or behavior expected of an employee when his or her job elements are satisfactorily performed under existing working conditions. Each employee in a permanent position must be provided with a current set of work performance standards for his or her position.

Performance Evaluation

If you are serving a six-month (full-time equivalent) probationary period, your supervisor will evaluate your performance at the end of the second and fifth months. If you are completing a one-year probationary period, your evaluations will be conducted at the end of the third, seventh, and eleventh month. You will receive a copy of each performance report. Once you have attained permanent employee status, your performance will be evaluated annually during the month prior to your pay progression date. Each evaluation will include a discussion between you and your supervisor to review and clarify goals and methods to achieve them. The evaluation will also include a written report of your progress on the job. Evaluations will be made with reference to established work performance standards:

Employment Records

Your personnel file is maintained in the human resources department. The human resources department maintains a working file with copies of the documentation in your specific department. Your file includes personnel action documents, mandatory employment forms, your performance evaluations, and documentation of disciplinary action. Your file may include letters of commendation, training certificates, or other work-related documents that your supervisor has requested to be included in your file.

1-888-555-2200 ✦ www.emcp.net/nss

C20-A07-NSSEmpPerf(Step5).docx

Northland Security Systems
3200 North 22nd Street ✦ Springfield ✦ IL ✦ 62102

EMPLOYEE PERFORMANCE

Work Performance Standards

Work performance standards are written statements of the results expected of an employee when his or her job elements are satisfactorily performed under existing working conditions. Each employee in a permanent full-time position must be provided with a current set of work performance standards for his or her position.

Performance Evaluation

If you are serving a six-month probationary period, your supervisor or manager will evaluate your performance at the end of the second and fifth months. If you are completing a one-year probationary period, your evaluations will be conducted at the end of the third, seventh, and eleventh month. You will receive a copy of each performance report. Once you have attained permanent employee status, your performance will be evaluated annually during the month prior to your pay progression date.

Each evaluation will include a discussion between you and your supervisor to review and clarify goals and methods to achieve them. The evaluation will also include a written report of your progress on the job. Evaluations will be made with reference to established work performance standards.

Employment Records

Your personnel file is maintained in the human resources department. The human resources department maintains a file with copies of the documentation in your specific department. Your file includes personnel action documents, mandatory employment forms, your performance evaluations, and documentation of disciplinary action. Your personnel file may include letters of commendation, training certificates, or other work-related documents that your supervisor has requested to be included in your file.

1-888-555-2200 ✦ www.emcp.net/nss

C20-A07-NSSEmpPerf(Step8).docx

Unit 4 Performance Assessment Annotated Model Answers

Motorway Autos

1250 Motorway Boulevard ◆ Grand Rapids, MI 49500 ◆ 616.555.1250

September 20, 2015

Mr. and Mrs. Lawrence Nesbitt
11023 South 32nd Street
Kentwood, MI 49506

Dear Mr. and Mrs. Nesbitt:

Because you are a valued customer of Motorway Autos, we are offering you a free oil change with your next 15,000-mile, 36,000-mile, or 60,000-mile car service appointment. Mention the free offer the next time you schedule a service appointment and the oil change is on us!

For the entire month of October, we are offering fantastic deals on new 2015 models. If you buy a new car from us, we will offer you top trade-in dollars for your used car. Along with our low, low prices, we are also offering low-interest and, in some cases, no-interest loans. Come in and talk with one of our sales representatives to see if you qualify for these special loans.

Please come down to visit our showroom and check out the best-priced automobiles in the region. We are open for your convenience Monday through Friday from 8:00 a.m. to 8:00 p.m., Saturday from 9:00 a.m. to 6:00 p.m., and Sunday from 9:00 a.m. to 5:00 p.m.

Sincerely,

Dusty Powell
Director of Sales

XX
U4-PA01-MA-MD.docx

Motorway Autos

1250 Motorway Boulevard ◆ Grand Rapids, MI 49500 ◆ 616.555.1250

1. Open **MALtrhd.docx** and save the document with the name **U4-PA01-MA-MD.**
2. Look at the information shown in Figure U4.1 and Figure U4.2. Use the Mail Merge feature to prepare six letters using the information shown in the figures.

September 20, 2015

Mr. Roy Heitzman
5043 Pleasant Street
Grand Rapids, MI 49518

Dear Mr. Heitzman:

Because you are a valued customer of Motorway Autos, we are offering you a free oil change with your next 15,000-mile, 36,000-mile, or 60,000-mile car service appointment. Mention the free offer the next time you schedule a service appointment and the oil change is on us!

For the entire month of October, we are offering fantastic deals on new 2015 models. If you buy a new car from us, we will offer you top trade-in dollars for your used car. Along with our low, low prices, we are also offering low-interest and, in some cases, no-interest loans. Come in and talk with one of our sales representatives to see if you qualify for these special loans.

Please come down to visit our showroom and check out the best-priced automobiles in the region. We are open for your convenience Monday through Friday from 8:00 a.m. to 8:00 p.m., Saturday from 9:00 a.m. to 6:00 p.m., and Sunday from 9:00 a.m. to 5:00 p.m.

Sincerely,

Dusty Powell
Director of Sales

XX
U4-PA01-MA-MD.docx

Motorway Autos
1250 Motorway Boulevard ● Grand Rapids, MI 49500 ● 616.555.1250

September 20, 2015

Ms. Julia Quintero
905 Randall Road
Kentwood, MI 49509

Dear Ms. Quintero:

Because you are a valued customer of Motorway Autos, we are offering you a free oil change with your next 15,000-mile, 36,000-mile, or 60,000-mile car service appointment. Mention the free offer the next time you schedule a service appointment and the oil change is on us!

For the entire month of October, we are offering fantastic deals on new 2015 models. If you buy a new car from us, we will offer you top trade-in dollars for your used car. Along with our low, low prices, we are also offering low-interest and, in some cases, no-interest loans. Come in and talk with one of our sales representatives to see if you qualify for these special loans.

Please come down to visit our showroom and check out the best-priced automobiles in the region. We are open for your convenience Monday through Friday from 8:00 a.m. to 8:00 p.m., Saturday from 9:00 a.m. to 6:00 p.m., and Sunday from 9:00 a.m. to 5:00 p.m.

Sincerely,

Dusty Powell
Director of Sales

XX
U4-PA01-MA-MD.docx

Motorway Autos
1250 Motorway Boulevard ● Grand Rapids, MI 49500 ● 616.555.1250

September 20, 2015

Mr. Darren Butler
23103 East Avenue
Grand Rapids, MI 49523

Dear Mr. Butler:

Because you are a valued customer of Motorway Autos, we are offering you a free oil change with your next 15,000-mile, 36,000-mile, or 60,000-mile car service appointment. Mention the free offer the next time you schedule a service appointment and the oil change is on us!

For the entire month of October, we are offering fantastic deals on new 2015 models. If you buy a new car from us, we will offer you top trade-in dollars for your used car. Along with our low, low prices, we are also offering low-interest and, in some cases, no-interest loans. Come in and talk with one of our sales representatives to see if you qualify for these special loans.

Please come down to visit our showroom and check out the best-priced automobiles in the region. We are open for your convenience Monday through Friday from 8:00 a.m. to 8:00 p.m., Saturday from 9:00 a.m. to 6:00 p.m., and Sunday from 9:00 a.m. to 5:00 p.m.

Sincerely,

Dusty Powell
Director of Sales

XX
U4-PA01-MA-MD.docx

Motorway Autos

1250 Motorway Boulevard ● Grand Rapids, MI 49500 ● 616.555.1250

September 20, 2015

Ms. Lola Rose-Simmons
3312 South Meridian
Grand Rapids, MI 49510

Dear Ms. Rose-Simmons:

Because you are a valued customer of Motorway Autos, we are offering you a free oil change with your next 15,000-mile, 36,000-mile, or 60,000-mile car service appointment. Mention the free offer the next time you schedule a service appointment and the oil change is on us!

For the entire month of October, we are offering fantastic deals on new 2015 models. If you buy a new car from us, we will offer you top trade-in dollars for your used car. Along with our low, low prices, we are also offering low-interest and, in some cases, no-interest loans. Come in and talk with one of our sales representatives to see if you qualify for these special loans.

Please come down to visit our showroom and check out the best-priced automobiles in the region. We are open for your convenience Monday through Friday from 8:00 a.m. to 8:00 p.m., Saturday from 9:00 a.m. to 6:00 p.m., and Sunday from 9:00 a.m. to 5:00 p.m.

Sincerely,

Dusty Powell
Director of Sales

XX
U4-PA01-MA-MD.docx

U4-PA01-MALtrs.docx (page 5 of 6)

Motorway Autos

1250 Motorway Boulevard ● Grand Rapids, MI 49500 ● 616.555.1250

September 20, 2015

Mr. Samuel McClelland
660 Grove Street
Grand Rapids, MI 49507

Dear Mr. McClelland:

Because you are a valued customer of Motorway Autos, we are offering you a free oil change with your next 15,000-mile, 36,000-mile, or 60,000-mile car service appointment. Mention the free offer the next time you schedule a service appointment and the oil change is on us!

For the entire month of October, we are offering fantastic deals on new 2015 models. If you buy a new car from us, we will offer you top trade-in dollars for your used car. Along with our low, low prices, we are also offering low-interest and, in some cases, no-interest loans. Come in and talk with one of our sales representatives to see if you qualify for these special loans.

Please come down to visit our showroom and check out the best-priced automobiles in the region. We are open for your convenience Monday through Friday from 8:00 a.m. to 8:00 p.m., Saturday from 9:00 a.m. to 6:00 p.m., and Sunday from 9:00 a.m. to 5:00 p.m.

Sincerely,

Dusty Powell
Director of Sales

XX
U4-PA01-MA-MD.docx

U4-PA01-MALtrs.docx (page 6 of 6)

Mr. and Mrs. Lawrence Nesbitt
11023 South 32nd Street
Kentwood, MI 49506

U4-PA02-MAEnvs.docx (page 2 of 6)

1. Use the Mail Merge feature to prepare envelopes for the letters you created in Assessment U4.1.
2. Specify **U4-PA01-MA-DS.mdb** as the data source document.

Mr. Roy Heitzman
5043 Pleasant Street
Grand Rapids, MI 49518

U4-PA02-MAEnvs.docx (page 1 of 6)

Mr. Darren Butler
23103 East Avenue
Grand Rapids, MI 49523

U4-PA02-MAEnvs.docx (page 4 of 6)

Ms. Julia Quintero
905 Randall Road
Kentwood, MI 49509

U4-PA02-MAEnvs.docx (page 3 of 6)

U4-PA02-MAEnvs.docx (page 6 of 6)

Mr. Samuel McClelland
660 Grove Street
Grand Rapids, MI 49507

U4-PA02-MAEnvs.docx (page 5 of 6)

Ms. Lola Rose-Simmons
3312 South Meridian
Grand Rapids, MI 49510

Motorway Autos

1250 Motorway Boulevard ● Grand Rapids, MI 49500 ● 616.555.1250

September 20, 2015

Mr. Roy Heitzman
5043 Pleasant Street
Grand Rapids, MI 49518

Dear Mr. Heitzman:

Because you are a valued customer of Motorway Autos, we are offering you a free oil change with your next 15,000-mile, 36,000-mile, or 60,000-mile car service appointment. Mention the free offer the next time you schedule a service appointment and the oil change is on us!

For the entire month of October, we are offering fantastic deals on new 2015 models. If you buy a new car from us, we will offer you top trade-in dollars for your used car. Along with our low, low prices, we are also offering low-interest and, in some cases, no-interest loans. Come in and talk with one of our sales representatives to see if you qualify for these special loans.

Please come down to visit our showroom and check out the best-priced automobiles in the region. We are open for your convenience Monday through Friday from 8:00 a.m. to 8:00 p.m., Saturday from 9:00 a.m. to 6:00 p.m., and Sunday from 9:00 a.m. to 5:00 p.m. According to our records, you have purchased two automobiles from us. This qualifies you for a special bonus of up to 2% off the purchase of a new automobile.

Sincerely,

Dusty Powell
Director of Sales

xx
U4-PA01-MA-MD.docx

3. At the main document, add the sentence shown in Figure U4.3 to the end of the third paragraph in the body of the letter and include fill-in fields as shown in parentheses in the figure.

1. Open **U4-PA01-MA-MD.docx** (at the SQL message, click Yes) and save the main document with the name **U4-PA03-MA-MD.**
2. Edit the **U4-PA01-MA-DS.mdb** data source file by making the following changes:
   c. Delete the record for Ms. Lola Rose-Simmons.
4. Save **U4-PA03-MA-MD.docx.**
5. Merge the records to a new document. At the dialog boxes asking for the number of automobiles and percentages, type the following:
   Record 1: Number: **two** automobiles Percent: **2%**
   Record 2: Number: **one** automobile Percent: **1%**
   Record 3: Number: **one** automobile Percent: **1%**
   Record 4: Number: **three** automobiles Percent: **3%**
   Record 5: Number: **two** automobiles Percent: **2%**
   Record 6: Number: **one** automobile Percent: **1%**

Motorway Autos

1250 Motorway Boulevard ● Grand Rapids, MI 49500 ● 616.555.1250

September 20, 2015

Mr. and Mrs. Lawrence Nesbitt
11023 South 32nd Street
Kentwood, MI 49506

Dear Mr. and Mrs. Nesbitt:

Because you are a valued customer of Motorway Autos, we are offering you a free oil change with your next 15,000-mile, 36,000-mile, or 60,000-mile car service appointment. Mention the free offer the next time you schedule a service appointment and the oil change is on us!

For the entire month of October, we are offering fantastic deals on new 2015 models. If you buy a new car from us, we will offer you top trade-in dollars for your used car. Along with our low, low prices, we are also offering low-interest and, in some cases, no-interest loans. Come in and talk with one of our sales representatives to see if you qualify for these special loans.

Please come down to visit our showroom and check out the best-priced automobiles in the region. We are open for your convenience Monday through Friday from 8:00 a.m. to 8:00 p.m., Saturday from 9:00 a.m. to 6:00 p.m., and Sunday from 9:00 a.m. to 5:00 p.m. According to our records, you have purchased one automobile from us. This qualifies you for a special bonus of up to 1% off the purchase of a new automobile.

Sincerely,

Dusty Powell
Director of Sales

xx
U4-PA01-MA-MD.docx

Motorway Autos

1250 Motorway Boulevard ◊ Grand Rapids, MI 49500 ◊ 616.555.1250

September 20, 2015

Mr. Darren Butler
715 South Fifth Street
Grand Rapids, MI 49523

Dear Mr. Butler:

Because you are a valued customer of Motorway Autos, we are offering you a free oil change with your next 15,000-mile, 36,000-mile, or 60,000-mile car service appointment. Mention the free offer the next time you schedule a service appointment and the oil change is on us!

For the entire month of October, we are offering fantastic deals on new 2015 models. If you buy a new car from us, we will offer you top trade-in dollars for your used car. Along with our low, low prices, we are also offering low-interest and, in some cases, no-interest loans. Come in and talk with one of our sales representatives to see if you qualify for these special loans.

Please come down to visit our showroom and check out the best-priced automobiles in the region. We are open for your convenience Monday through Friday from 8:00 a.m. to 8:00 p.m., Saturday from 9:00 a.m. to 6:00 p.m., and Sunday from 9:00 a.m. to 5:00 p.m. According to our records, you have purchased three automobiles from us. This qualifies you for a special bonus of up to 3% off the purchase of a new automobile.

Sincerely,

Dusty Powell
Director of Sales

XX
U4-PA01-MA-MD.docx

2a. Display the record for Mr. Darren Butler and then change the street address from *23103 East Avenue to 715 South Fifth Street.*

Motorway Autos

1250 Motorway Boulevard ◊ Grand Rapids, MI 49500 ◊ 616.555.1250

September 20, 2015

Ms. Julia Quintero
905 Randall Road
Kentwood, MI 49509

Dear Ms. Quintero:

Because you are a valued customer of Motorway Autos, we are offering you a free oil change with your next 15,000-mile, 36,000-mile, or 60,000-mile car service appointment. Mention the free offer the next time you schedule a service appointment and the oil change is on us!

For the entire month of October, we are offering fantastic deals on new 2015 models. If you buy a new car from us, we will offer you top trade-in dollars for your used car. Along with our low, low prices, we are also offering low-interest and, in some cases, no-interest loans. Come in and talk with one of our sales representatives to see if you qualify for these special loans.

Please come down to visit our showroom and check out the best-priced automobiles in the region. We are open for your convenience Monday through Friday from 8:00 a.m. to 8:00 p.m., Saturday from 9:00 a.m. to 6:00 p.m., and Sunday from 9:00 a.m. to 5:00 p.m. According to our records, you have purchased one automobile from us. This qualifies you for a special bonus of up to 1% off the purchase of a new automobile.

Sincerely,

Dusty Powell
Director of Sales

XX
U4-PA01-MA-MD.docx

Motorway Autos
1250 Motorway Boulevard ● Grand Rapids, MI 49500 ● 616.555.1250

2b. Add *and Mrs.* in the title for Mr. Samuel McClelland. (The *Title* field should display as *Mr. and Mrs.*).

September 20, 2015

Mr. and Mrs. Samuel McClelland
660 Grove Street
Grand Rapids, MI 49507

Dear Mr. and Mrs. McClelland:

Because you are a valued customer of Motorway Autos, we are offering you a free oil change with your next 15,000-mile, 36,000-mile, or 60,000-mile car service appointment. Mention the free offer the next time you schedule a service appointment and the oil change is on us!

For the entire month of October, we are offering fantastic deals on new 2015 models. If you buy a new car from us, we will offer you top trade-in dollars for your used car. Along with our low, low prices, we are also offering low-interest and, in some cases, no-interest loans. Come in and talk with one of our sales representatives to see if you qualify for these special loans.

Please come down to visit our showroom and check out the best-priced automobiles in the region. We are open for your convenience Monday through Friday from 8:00 a.m. to 8:00 p.m., Saturday from 9:00 a.m. to 6:00 p.m., and Sunday from 9:00 a.m. to 5:00 p.m. According to our records, you have purchased two automobiles from us. This qualifies you for a special bonus of up to 2% off the purchase of a new automobile.

Sincerely,

Dusty Powell
Director of Sales

XX
U4-PA01-MA-MD.docx

U4-PA03-MALtrs.docx (page 5 of 6)

Motorway Autos
1250 Motorway Boulevard ● Grand Rapids, MI 49500 ● 616.555.1250

September 20, 2015

2d. Insert a new record with the following information:
Ms. Glenda Jefferson
5048 Burton Street
Grand Rapids, MI 49503

Ms. Glenda Jefferson
5048 Burton Street
Grand Rapids, MI 49503

Dear Ms. Jefferson:

Because you are a valued customer of Motorway Autos, we are offering you a free oil change with your next 15,000-mile, 36,000-mile, or 60,000-mile car service appointment. Mention the free offer the next time you schedule a service appointment and the oil change is on us!

For the entire month of October, we are offering fantastic deals on new 2015 models. If you buy a new car from us, we will offer you top trade-in dollars for your used car. Along with our low, low prices, we are also offering low-interest and, in some cases, no-interest loans. Come in and talk with one of our sales representatives to see if you qualify for these special loans.

Please come down to visit our showroom and check out the best-priced automobiles in the region. We are open for your convenience Monday through Friday from 8:00 a.m. to 8:00 p.m., Saturday from 9:00 a.m. to 6:00 p.m., and Sunday from 9:00 a.m. to 5:00 p.m. According to our records, you have purchased one automobile from us. This qualifies you for a special bonus of up to 1% off the purchase of a new automobile.

Sincerely,

Dusty Powell
Director of Sales

XX
U4-PA01-MA-MD.docx

U4-PA03-MALtrs.docx (page 6 of 6)

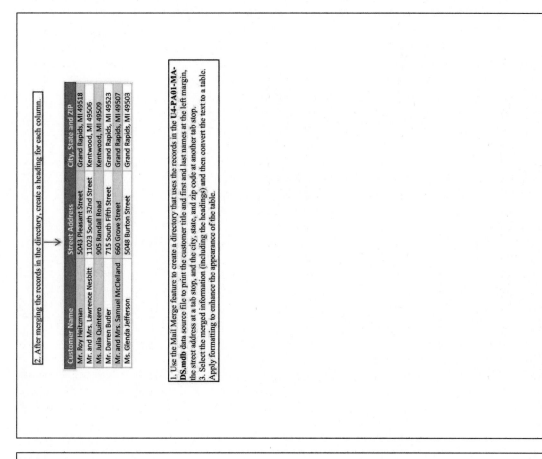

2. After merging the records in the directory, create a heading for each column.

Customer Name	Street Address	City, State and ZIP
Mr. Roy Heitzman	5043 Pleasant Street	Grand Rapids, MI 49518
Mr. and Mrs. Lawrence Nesbitt	11023 South 32nd Street	Kentwood, MI 49506
Ms. Julia Quintero	905 Randall Road	Kentwood, MI 49509
Mr. Darren Butler	715 South Fifth Street	Grand Rapids, MI 49523
Mr. and Mrs. Samuel McClelland	660 Grove Street	Grand Rapids, MI 49507
Ms. Glenda Jefferson	5048 Burton Street	Grand Rapids, MI 49503

1. Use the Mail Merge feature to create a directory that uses the records in the **U4-PA01-MA-DS.mdb** data source file to print the customer title and first and last names at the left margin, the street address at a tab stop, and the city, state, and zip code at another tab stop.
3. Select the merged information (including the headings) and then convert the text to a table. Apply formatting to enhance the appearance of the table.

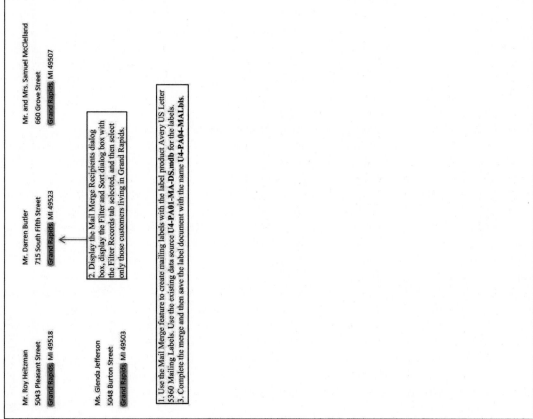

Mr. Roy Heitzman
5043 Pleasant Street
Grand Rapids, MI 49518

Mr. Darren Butler
715 South Fifth Street
Grand Rapids, MI 49523

Mr. and Mrs. Samuel McClelland
660 Grove Street
Grand Rapids, MI 49507

Ms. Glenda Jefferson
5048 Burton Street
Grand Rapids, MI 49503

2. Display the Mail Merge Recipients dialog box, display the Filter and Sort dialog box with the **Filter Records** tab selected, and then select only those customers living in Grand Rapids.

1. Use the Mail Merge feature to create mailing labels with the label product Avery US Letter 5360 Mailing Labels. Use the existing data source **U4-PA01-MA-DS.mdb** for the labels.
3. Complete the merge and then save the label document with the name **U4-PA04-MALbls**.

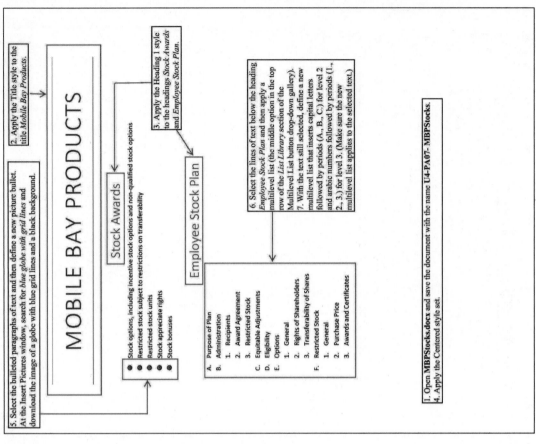

U4-PA07-MBPStocks.docx

2. Apply the Title style to the title *Mobile Bay Products*.

MOBILE BAY PRODUCTS

Stock Awards

3. Apply the Heading 1 style to the headings *Stock Awards* and *Employee Stock Plan*.

5. Select the bulleted paragraphs of text and then define a new picture bullet. At the Insert Pictures window, search for *blue globe with grid lines* and download the image of a globe with blue grid lines and a black background.

- Stock options, including incentive stock options and non-qualified stock options
- Restricted stock subject to restrictions on transferability
- Restricted stock units
- Stock appreciate rights
- Stock bonuses

Employee Stock Plan

6. Select the lines of text below the heading *Employee Stock Plan* and then apply a multilevel list (the middle option in the top row of the *List Library* section of the Multilevel List button drop-down gallery).
7. With the text still selected, define a new multilevel list that inserts capital letters followed by periods (A., B., C.) for level 2 and arabic numbers followed by periods (1., 2., 3.) for level 3. (Make sure the new multilevel list applies to the selected text.)

A. Purpose of Plan
B. Administration
   1. Recipients
   2. Award Agreement
   3. Restricted Stock
C. Equitable Adjustments
D. Eligibility
E. Options
   1. General
   2. Rights of Shareholders
   3. Transferability of Shares
F. Restricted Stock
   1. General
   2. Purchase Price
   3. Awards and Certificates

1. Open **MBPStocks.docx** and save the document with the name **U4-PA07- MBPStocks**.
4. Apply the Centered style set.

U4-PA06-Sort.docx

1. Open **Sort.docx** and save the document with the name **U4-PA06-Sort**.

CONTACTS

Contact Name	Financial Institution	Telephone
Kevin Boone	Valley Trust	(412) 555-4837
Crystal Darby	Horizon Bank	(403) 555-3319
Kimberly Gibson	First Financial Trust	(412) 555-3948
Neville Lewis	Prime One Savings	(503) 555-9986
Julio Rivas	Mountain Bank	(206) 555-1048
Ivy Talmadge	United Fidelity Trust	(206) 555-6410

2. Sort the columns of text below the *CONTACTS* title in ascending order by last name.

Mortgage Banker	Mortgage Loans	Home Equity Loans
William Morrisette	$2,409,822	$1,539,588
Marilyn Luo	$1,058,394	$1,429,554
Joseph Lundeen	$2,315,380	$1,320,341
Brittany Stevens	$2,490,520	$1,101,340
Vernon Rosenfeld	$1,905,348	$1,003,265

3. Sort the amounts in the *Home Equity Loans* column in the table in descending order.

FUTURE OF COMPUTER ETHICS

Computers and the transformations they engender have only recently entered into most people's lives. Large mainframes used by the government and businesses made their debut only 50 years ago, and the personal computer began appearing in small businesses and homes as recently as the early 1980s. While the precursor of the Internet was created almost 30 years ago, widespread use of the Internet and the creation of the World Wide Web occurred during the past ten years. The field of computer ethics has been developed to address ethical problems arising from new technologies. While accurately predicting the direction of such ethical considerations in the future is impossible, some general speculations can be made on emerging trends.

New Computer Ethics Laws

Legislation is often slow to catch up to the reality of everyday life. Eventually it does catch up and this will prove true for many of the computer ethics issues we face today. For example, many attempts have already been made in the United States to draft laws increasing personal privacy protection.

Artificial Intelligence and Avatars

The first generation of avatars, digital representations that look and talk like ordinary people, has already appeared. Given the rapid advances in technological capabilities and artificial intelligence, predicting that avatars in the future will be indistinguishable from real human beings is not farfetched. This eventuality will pose a rash of ethical dilemmas. For example, should computer users necessarily be warned that they are dealing with an avatar and not a human being? Should avatars be prevented from emulating certain behaviors? In what ways might avatars be used by some for criminal activities, and how can such behavior be prevented? These are just a few of the numerous ethical questions arising from future developments in artificial intelligence.

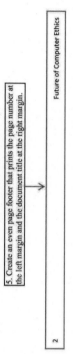

Self-Replicating Robots

We already know that robots can be created that, in turn, create other robots. Such self-replication of technology has great potential to get out of hand, and it thus poses numerous ethical concerns. For instance, have we created a technology that might someday displace, dominate, or even eliminate human beings? How can we know? These are some of the ethical questions concerning robots that will be debated in the future.

Narrowing the Digital Divide

While the digital divide between developed countries is narrowing, the gulf between developed and underdeveloped nations is still vast. Debate over how this gap is to be narrowed will continue. Should poorer nations be encouraged to concentrate on gaining basic needs, such as adequate electricity, communications, and health care infrastructures, or should they be encouraged to use available resources to develop digital technologies in order to "catch up" with developed nations? Will computer technologies truly benefit less developed societies and, if so, how? What role should developed nations play in providing and monitoring the dispersal of such technology?

Governmental Control of Internet Content

Many people today are concerned about some of the content available on the Internet. Some governments, worried about losing control over what information their citizens can access, have already placed severe restrictions on Internet access and content. The question of whether or not the government should control Internet content remains a topic of lively debate. The truth is that even if government controls of some type are enforced, rapid changes in technology will probably allow their circumvention. In the future, the questions of what should be done to control unacceptable Internet content and who should undertake such control will continue to be widely discussed.

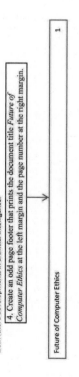

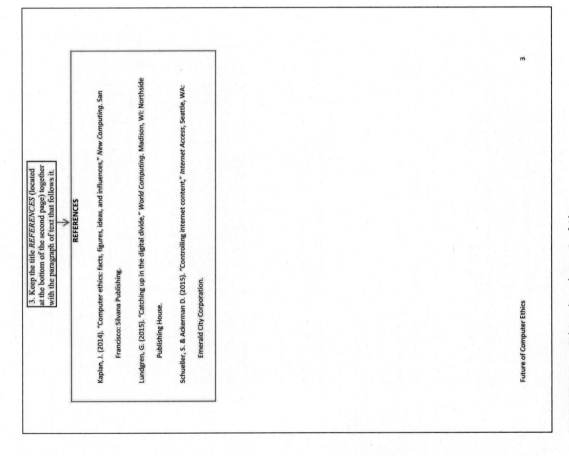

3. Keep the title *REFERENCES* (located at the bottom of the second page) together with the paragraph of text that follows it.

REFERENCES

Kaplan, J. (2014). "Computer ethics: facts, figures, ideas, and influences," *New Computing.* San

Francisco: Silvana Publishing.

Lundgren, G. (2015). "Catching up in the digital divide," *World Computing.* Madison, WI: Northside

Publishing House.

Schueller, S. & Ackerman D. (2015). "Controlling internet content," *Internet Access,* Seattle, WA:

Emerald City Corporation.

3

Future of Computer Ethics

U4-PA08-FutureEthics.docx (page 3 of 3)

Signature Word 2013   Model Answers

Chapter 21 Assessment Annotated Model Answers

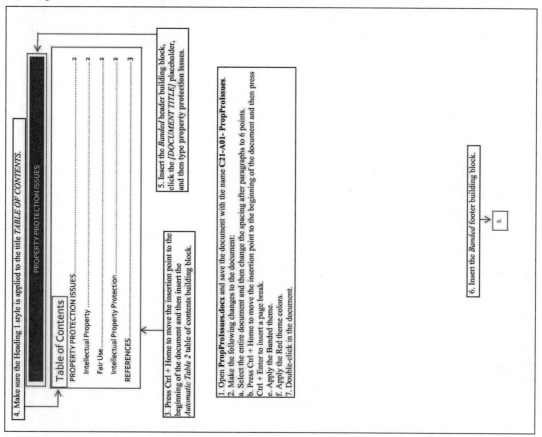

4. Make sure the Heading 1 style is applied to the title *TABLE OF CONTENTS*.

PROPERTY PROTECTION ISSUES

Table of Contents

3. Press Ctrl + Home to move the insertion point to the beginning of the document and then insert the *Automatic Table 2* table of contents building block.

5. Insert the *Banded* header building block, click the *[DOCUMENT TITLE]* placeholder, and then type property protection issues.

1. Open **PropProIssues.docx** and save the document with the name **C21-A01- PropProIssues.**
2. Make the following changes to the document:
a. Select the entire document and then change the spacing after paragraphs to 6 points.
b. Press Ctrl + Home to move the insertion point to the beginning of the document and then press Ctrl + Enter to insert a page break.
e. Apply the Banded theme.
f. Apply the Red theme colors.
7. Double-click in the document.

6. Insert the *Banded* footer building block.

1

8. Press Ctrl + Home and then insert the *Banded* cover page with the following specifications:
d. Select and then delete the *[Company address]* placeholder.

8a. Select the title *PROPERTY PROTECTION ISSUES* and then change the font size to 28 points.

PROPERTY PROTECTION ISSUES

8b. Select the name that displays near the bottom of the cover page above the *[COMPANY NAME]* placeholder and then type your first and last names.

Student Name

BARRINGTON & GATES

8c. Click the *[COMPANY NAME]* placeholder and then type barrington & gates.

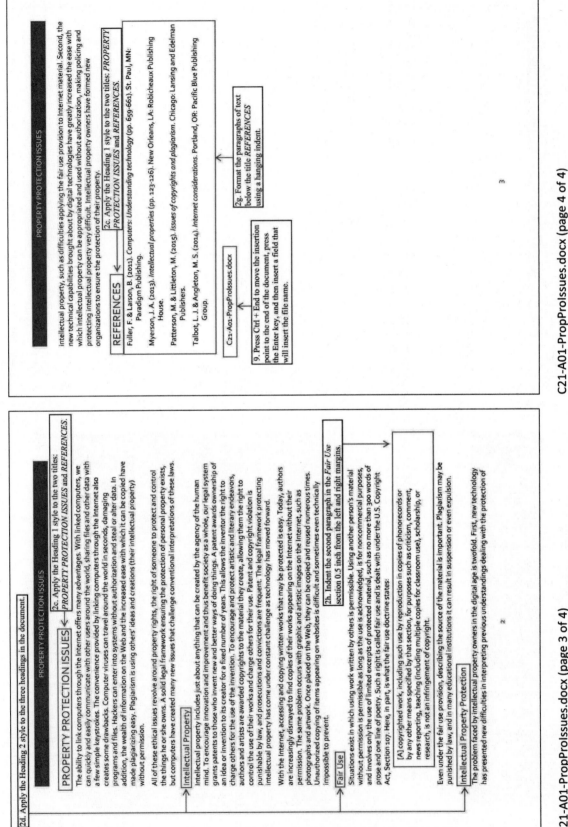

20. Click the AutoText button on the Quick Access toolbar, press the Print Screen button on your keyboard, and then click in the document to remove the drop-down list.
21. At the blank document, click the Paste button. (This pastes the screen capture in your document.)

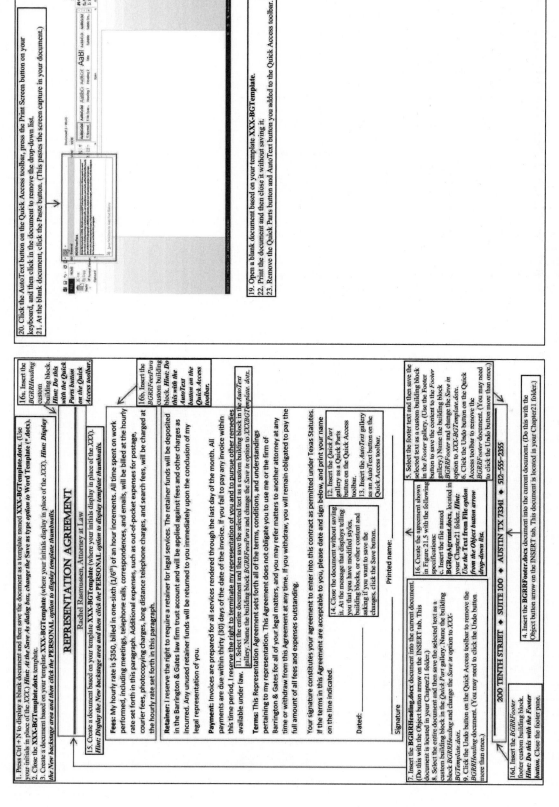

19. Open a blank document based on your template XXX-BGTemplate.
22. Print the document and then close it without saving it.
23. Remove the Quick Parts button and AutoText button you added to the Quick Access toolbar.

---

1. Press Ctrl + N to display a blank document and then save the document as a template named XXX-BGTemplate.dotx. (Use your initials in place of the XXX.) *Hint: At the Save As dialog box, change the Save as type option to Word Template (*.dotx).*
2. Close the **XXX-BGTemplate.dotx** template.
3. Create a document based on your template **XXX-BGTemplate** (where your initials display in place of the XXX). *Hint: Display the New backstage area and then click the PERSONAL option to display template thumbnails.*

REPRESENTATION AGREEMENT

Rachel Rasmussen, Attorney at Law

15. Create a document based on your template **XXX-BGTemplate** (where your initials display in place of the XXX). *Hint: Display the New backstage area and then click the PERSONAL option to display template thumbnails.*

Fees: My hourly rate is $350, billed in one-sixth (1/6th) of an hour increments. All time spent on work performed, including meetings, telephone calls, correspondences, and emails, will be billed at the hourly rate set forth in this paragraph. Additional expenses, such as out-of-pocket expenses for postage, courier fees, photocopying charges, long distance telephone charges, and search fees, will be charged at the hourly rate set forth in this paragraph.

Retainer: I reserve the right to require a retainer for legal services. The retainer funds will be deposited in the Barrington & Gates law firm trust account and will be applied against fees and other charges as incurred. Any unused retainer funds will be returned to you immediately upon the conclusion of my legal representation of you.

Payment: Invoices are prepared for all services rendered through the last day of the month. All payments are due within thirty (30) days of the date of the invoice. If you fail to pay any invoice within this time period, I reserve the right to terminate my representation of you and to pursue other remedies available under law.

Terms: This Representation Agreement sets forth all of the terms, conditions, and understandings pertaining to my representation. This Agreement does not obligate you to use me or the firm of Barrington & Gates for all of your legal matters, and you may refer matters to another attorney at any time or withdraw from this Agreement at any time. If you withdraw, you will remain obligated to pay the full amount of all fees and expenses outstanding.

Your signature constitutes your agreement to enter into this contract as permitted under Texas Statutes. If the terms in this Agreement are acceptable to you, please date and sign below, and print your name on the line indicated.

Dated:

Printed name:

Signature

200 TENTH STREET ◆ SUITE 100 ◆ AUSTIN TX 73341 ◆ 512-555-2355

16a. Insert the *BGRRHeading* custom building block. *Hint: Do this with the Quick Parts button on the Quick Access toolbar.*

16b. Insert the *BGRRFeesPara* custom building block. *Hint: Do this with the AutoText button on the Quick Access toolbar.*

11. Select the entire document and then save the selected text as a custom building block in the *AutoText* gallery. Name the building block *BGRRFeesPara* and change the *Save In* option to *XXXBGTemplate.dotx.*

12. Insert the *Quick Part* gallery as a Quick Parts button on the Quick Access toolbar.

13. Insert the *AutoText* gallery as an AutoText button on the Quick Access toolbar.

14. Close the document without saving it. At the message that displays telling you that you have modified styles, building blocks, or other content and asking if you want to save the changes, click the Save button.

7. Insert the **BGRRHeading.docx** document into the current document. (Do this with the Object button arrow on the INSERT tab. This document is located in your Chapter21 folder.)

8. Select the entire document and then save the selected text as a custom building block in the *Quick Part* gallery. Name the building block *BGRRHeading* and change the *Save in* option to *XXX-BGTemplate.dotx.*

9. Click the Undo button on the Quick Access toolbar to remove the *BGRRHeading* document. (You may need to click the Undo button more than once.)

5. Select the footer text and then save the selected text as a custom building block in the *Footer* gallery. (Use the Footer button to save the content to the *Footer* gallery.) Name the building block *BGRRFooter* and change the *Save in* option to *XXX-BGTemplate.dotx.*

6. Click the Undo button on the Quick Access toolbar to remove the *BGRRFooter* document. (You may need to click the Undo button more than once.)

16. Create the agreement shown in Figure 21.5 with the following specifications:
c. Insert the file named **BGRepAgrmnt.docx**, located in your Chapter21 folder. *Hint: Use the Text from File option from the Object button arrow drop-down list.*

16d. Insert the **BGRRFooter.docx** document into the current document. (Do this with the Object button arrow on the INSERT tab. This document is located in your Chapter21 folder.)

4. Insert the *BGRRFooter* custom building block.

16d. Insert the *BGRRFooter* footer custom building block. *Hint: Do this with the Footer button.* Close the footer pane.

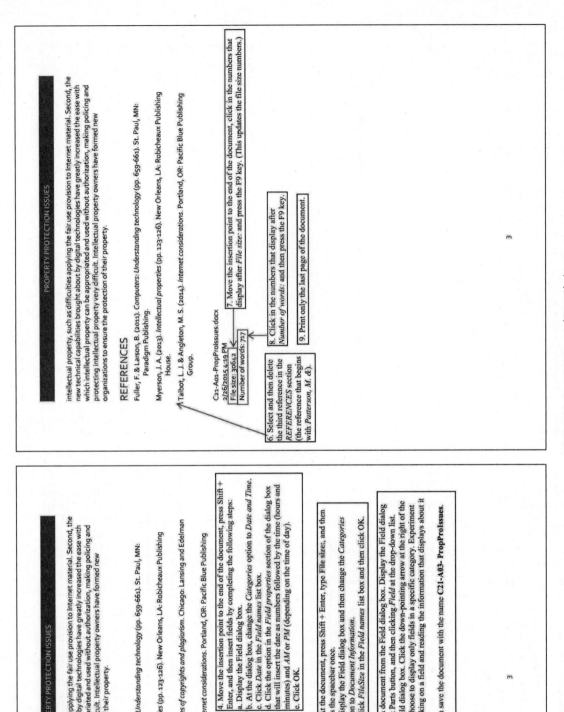

Top document (C21-A03-PropProIssues(Step9).docx)

PROPERTY PROTECTION ISSUES

intellectual property, such as difficulties applying the fair use provision to Internet material. Second, the new technical capabilities brought about by digital technologies have greatly increased the ease with which intellectual property can be appropriated and used without authorization, making policing and protecting intellectual property very difficult. Intellectual property owners have formed new organizations to ensure the protection of their property.

REFERENCES

Fuller, F. & Larson, B. (2011). *Computers: Understanding technology* (pp. 659-661). St. Paul, MN: Paradigm Publishing.

Myerson, J. A. (2013). *Intellectual properties* (pp. 123-126). New Orleans, LA: Robicheaux Publishing House.

Talbot, L. J. & Angleton, M. S. (2014). *Internet considerations.* Portland, OR: Pacific Blue Publishing Group.

C21-A01-PropProIssues.docx
2/26/2015 4:19 PM
File size: 306,42
Number of words: 717

6. Select and then delete the third reference in the *REFERENCES* section (the reference that begins with *Patterson, M. &*).

7. Move the insertion point to the end of the document, click in the numbers that display after *File size:* and press the F9 key. (This updates the file size numbers.)

8. Click in the numbers that display after *Number of words:* and then press the F9 key.

9. Print only the last page of the document.

3

C21-A03-PropProIssues(Step9).docx

Bottom document (C21-A03-PropProIssues(Step5).docx)

PROPERTY PROTECTION ISSUES

intellectual property, such as difficulties applying the fair use provision to Internet material. Second, the new technical capabilities brought about by digital technologies have greatly increased the ease with which intellectual property can be appropriated and used without authorization, making policing and protecting intellectual property very difficult. Intellectual property owners have formed new organizations to ensure the protection of their property.

REFERENCES

Fuller, F. & Larson, B. (2011). *Computers: Understanding technology* (pp. 659-661). St. Paul, MN: Paradigm Publishing.

Myerson, J. A. (2013). *Intellectual properties* (pp. 123-126). New Orleans, LA: Robicheaux Publishing House.

Patterson, M. & Littleton, M. (2015). *Issues of copyrights and plagiarism.* Chicago: Lansing and Edelman Publishers.

Talbot, L. J. & Angleton, M. S. (2014). *Internet considerations.* Portland, OR: Pacific Blue Publishing Group.

C21-A01-PropProIssues.docx
2/26/2015 4:16 PM
File size: 30,428
Number of words: 732

4. Move the insertion point to the end of the document, press Shift + Enter, and then insert fields by completing the following steps:
a. Display the Field dialog box.
b. At the dialog box, change the *Categories* option to *Date and Time.*
c. Click *Date* in the *Field names* list box.
d. Click the option in the *Field properties* section of the dialog box that will insert the date as numbers followed by the time (hours and minutes) and *AM* or *PM* (depending on the time of day).
e. Click OK.

4f. At the document, press Shift + Enter, type File size, and then press the spacebar once.
g. Display the Field dialog box and then change the *Categories* option to *Document Information.*
h. Click *FileSize* in the *Field names* list box and then click OK.

4i. At the document, press Shift + Enter, type Number of words:, and then press the spacebar once.
j. Display the Field dialog box, make sure the *Categories* option is *Document Information,* and then click *NumWords* in the *Field names* list box.
k. Click OK.

1. In this chapter, you learned to insert fields in a document from the Field dialog box. Display the Field dialog box by clicking the Insert tab, clicking the Quick Parts button, and then clicking *Field* at the drop-down list.
2. Experiment with the various options at the Field dialog box. Click the down-pointing arrow at the right of the *Categories* option box and notice how you can choose to display only fields in a specific category. Experiment with other options in the dialog box, such as clicking on a field and reading the information that displays about it in the dialog box.
3. Open **C21-A01-PropProIssues.docx** and then save the document with the name **C21-A03- PropProIssues.**
5. Print only the last page of the document.

3

C21-A03-PropProIssues(Step5).docx

INSERTING EQUATIONS INTO A WORD DOCUMENT

To insert an equation into a Word document, click the INSERT tab, click the Quick Parts button, and then click *Building Blocks Organizer* at the drop-down list to access the Building Blocks Organizer dialog box.

From the Building Blocks Organizer dialog box, click the desired equation from the gallery options.

Once an equation is inserted, you can modify and format the equation from the EQUATION TOOLS DESIGN tab.

The EQUATION TOOLS DESIGN tab includes the following groups:

- Tools
- Symbols
- Structures

1. The Building Blocks Organizer dialog box contains a number of predesigned equations that you can insert in a document. At a blank document, display the Building Blocks Organizer dialog box and then insert one of the predesigned equations.
2. Select the equation and then click the Equation Tools Design tab. Notice that several groups of commands are available for editing an equation.
3. Delete the equation and then type the steps you followed to insert it in the document. Also type a list of the groups available in the Equation Tools Design tab.

C21-A04-Equations.docx

---

12. Select the entire document and then save the selected text as a custom building block in the *AutoText* gallery. Name the building block *BGRRIntroPara* and change the *Save In* option to *XXX-BGTemplate.docx*.

BARRINGTON & GATES

Rachel Rasmussen, Associate

February 26, 2015

Mr. Evan Markham
310 South 44th Street
Austin, TX 73348

Dear Mr. Markham:

Thank you for your interest in hiring me as your attorney. At Barrington & Gates, we pride ourselves on providing the highest-quality legal counsel and advice to our clients. Please read the enclosed *Representation Agreement*, sign in the appropriate location, and then return the agreement to me by fax, as an email attachment, or by mail to the address listed below.

As I mentioned during our telephone conversation, I will review the information you are returning and then send my responses, suggestions, and questions to you in an email. After reading my email, please call me so we can schedule a meeting to further discuss your legal concerns.

Very truly yours,

Rachel Rasmussen
Attorney at Law

XX
C21-A05-ClientLtr.docx

Enclosure

2. Insert the **BGRRLtrhd.docx** document into the current document. (Do this with the Object button arrow on the INSERT tab. This document is located in your Chapter21 folder.)
3. Select the entire document and then save the selected text as a custom building block in the *Quick Part* gallery. Name the building block *BGRRLetterhead* and change the *Save In* option to *XXX-BGTemplate.docx*.
4. Click the Undo button on the Quick Access toolbar to remove the *BGRRLtrhd* document. (You may need to click the Undo button more than once.)

1. Open a blank document based on your template **XXX-BGTemplate** (where your initials display in place of the *XXX*) that you created in Assessment 21.2. *Hint: Display the New backstage area and then click the **PERSONAL** option to display template thumbnails.*

6. Type Very truly yours, and then press the Enter key four times.
7. Type Rachel Rasmussen and then press the Enter key.
8. Type Attorney at Law and then press the Enter key.

11. Click the *No Spacing* style in the Styles group on the Home tab and then type the following paragraph of text: Thank you for your interest in hiring me as your attorney and in having the firm of Barrington & Gates represent you. At Barrington & Gates, we pride ourselves on providing the highest-quality legal counsel and advice to our clients. Please read the enclosed *Representation Agreement*, sign in the appropriate location, and then return the agreement to me by fax, as an email attachment, or by mail to the address listed below.

5. Click the HOME tab and then click the *No Spacing* style in the Styles group.
9. Press Ctrl + A to select the entire document and then save the selected text as a custom building block in the *AutoText* gallery. Name the building block *BGRRClose* and change the *Save In* option to *XXX-BGTemplate.docx*.
10. With the entire document selected, press the Delete key.

13. Close the document without saving it. At the message that displays asking if you want to save the changes to **XXX-BGTemplate.docx**, click the Save button.
14. Open a blank document based on the **XXX-BGTemplate.dotx** template.
15. Click the *No Spacing* style in the Styles group on the Home tab and then create the business letter shown in Figure 21.6. Use the building blocks you created to insert the letterhead (insert as a header), footer (insert as a footer), first paragraph of text, and complimentary close (the text that begins *Very truly yours.*). Type the additional text shown in the figure. (Type your initials in place of the *XX* located near the end of the letter.)

C21-A05-ClientLtr.docx

19. Click the Insert tab, click the Quick Parts button, point to *AutoText* (to display the side menu with your custom building block), and then press the Print Screen button on your keyboard.

20. Click in the document to remove the side menu and then click the Paste button. (This pastes the screen capture of your document with the AutoText side menu displayed.)

18. Open a blank document based on your template **XXX-BGTemplate**.

21. Print the document and then close it without saving it.

22. Delete your template **XXX-BGTemplate.dotx** by completing the following steps:

a. Press Ctrl + F12 to display the Open dialog box.

b. Click the *Documents* folder in the Navigation pane.

c. Double-click the *Custom Office Templates* folder in the Open dialog box Content pane.

d. Click **XXX-BGTemplate.dotx** (where your initials display in place of the *XXX*).

e. Click the Organize button and then click *Delete* at the drop-down list.

f. Close the Open dialog box.

C21-A05-PrintScreen.docx

Chapter 22 Assessment Annotated Model Answers

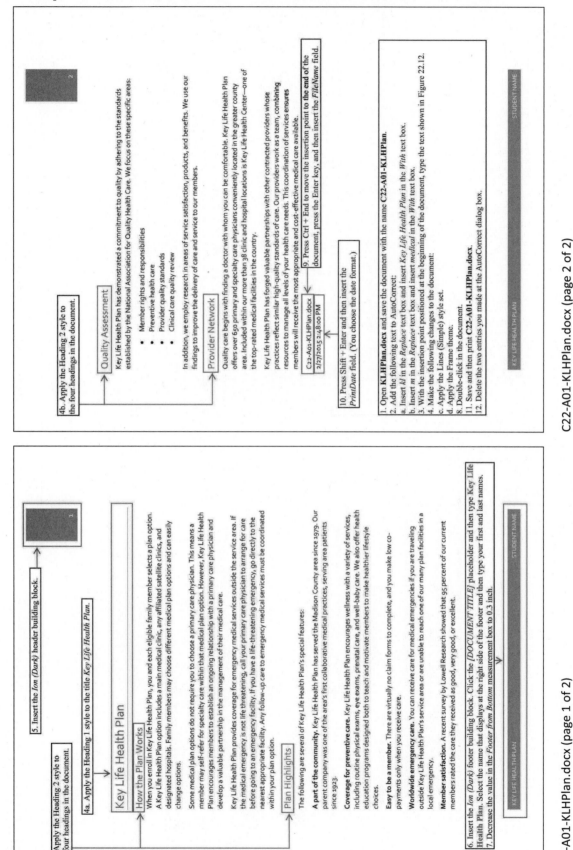

Page 2 annotations:

4b. Apply the Heading 2 style to the four headings in the document.

Quality Assessment

Key Life Health Plan has demonstrated a commitment to quality by adhering to the standards established by the National Association for Quality Health Care. We focus on these specific areas:

- Member rights and responsibilities
- Preventive health care
- Provider quality standards
- Clinical care quality review

In addition, we employ research in areas of service satisfaction, products, and benefits. We use our findings to improve the delivery of care and service to our members.

Provider Network

Quality care begins with finding a doctor with whom you can be comfortable. Key Life Health Plan offers over 650 primary and specialty care physicians conveniently located in the greater county area. Included within our more than 38 clinic and hospital locations is Key Life Health Center—one of the top-rated medical facilities in the country.

Key Life Health Plan has forged valuable partnerships with other contracted providers whose practices reflect similar high-quality standards of care. Our providers work as a team, combining resources to manage all levels of your health care needs. This coordination of services ensures members will receive the most appropriate and cost-effective medical care available.

C22-A01-KLHPlan.docx
2/27/2015 2:48:00 PM

9. Press Ctrl + End to move the insertion point to **the end of the** document, press the Enter key, and then insert the *FileName* field.

10. Press Shift + Enter and then insert the *PrintDate* field. (You choose the date format.)

1. Open **KLHPlan.docx** and save the document with the name **C22-A01-KLHPlan.**
2. Add the following text to AutoCorrect:
   a. Insert *kl* in the *Replace* text box and insert *Key Life Health Plan* in the *With* text box.
   b. Insert *m* in the *Replace* text box and insert *medical* in the *With* text box.
3. With the insertion point positioned at the beginning of the document, type the text shown in Figure 22.12.
4. Make the following changes to the document:
   c. Apply the Lines (Simple) style set.
   d. Apply the Frame theme.
8. Double-click in the document.
11. Save and then print **C22-A01-KLHPlan.docx.**
12. Delete the two entries you made at the AutoCorrect dialog box.

STUDENT NAME

KEY LIFE HEALTH PLAN

C22-A01-KLHPlan.docx (page 2 of 2)

Page 1 annotations:

5. Insert the *Ion (Dark)* header building block.

4b. Apply the Heading 2 style to the four headings in the document.

4a. Apply the Heading 1 style to the title *Key Life Health Plan.*

Key Life Health Plan

How the Plan Works

When you enroll in Key Life Health Plan, you and each eligible family member selects a plan option. A Key Life Health Plan option includes a main medical clinic, any affiliated satellite clinics, and designated hospitals. Family members may choose different medical plan options and can easily change options.

Some medical plan options do not require you to choose a primary care physician. This means a member may self-refer for specialty care within that medical plan option. However, Key Life Health Plan encourages members to establish an ongoing relationship with a primary care physician and develop a valuable partnership in the management of their medical care.

Key Life Health Plan provides coverage for emergency medical services outside the service area. If the medical emergency is not life threatening, call your primary care physician to arrange for care before going to an emergency facility. If you have a life-threatening emergency, go directly to the nearest appropriate facility. Any follow-up care to emergency medical services must be coordinated within your plan option.

Plan Highlights

The following are several of Key Life Health Plan's special features:

A part of the community. Key Life Health Plan has served the Madison County area since 1979. Our parent company was one of the area's first collaborative medical practices, serving area patients since 1923.

Coverage for preventive care. Key Life Health Plan encourages wellness with a variety of services, including routine physical exams, eye exams, prenatal care, and well-baby care. We also offer health education programs designed both to teach and motivate members to make healthier lifestyle choices.

Easy to be a member. There are virtually no claim forms to complete, and you make low co-payments only when you receive care.

Worldwide emergency care. You can receive care for medical emergencies if you are traveling outside Key Life Health Plan's service area or are unable to reach one of our many plan facilities in a local emergency.

Member satisfaction. A recent survey by Lowell Research showed that 95 percent of our current members rated the care they received as good, very good, or excellent.

6. Insert the *Ion (Dark)* footer building block. Click the *[DOCUMENT TITLE]* placeholder and then type **Key Life Health Plan.** Select the name that displays at the right side of the footer and then type your first and last names.

7. Decrease the value in the *Footer from Bottom* measurement box to 0.3 inch.

STUDENT NAME

KEY LIFE HEALTH PLAN

C22-A01-KLHPlan.docx (page 1 of 2)

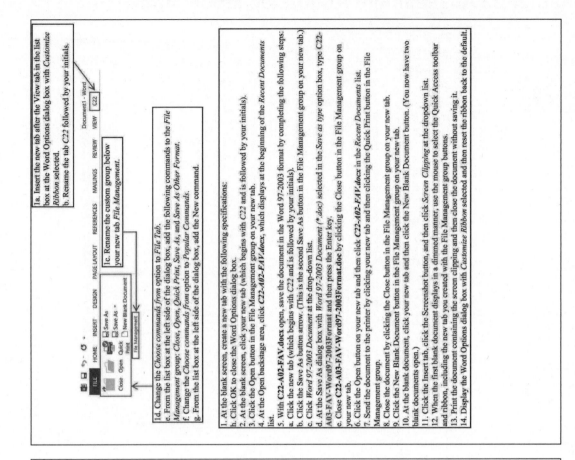

1a. Insert the new tab after the View tab in the list box at the Word Options dialog box with *Customize Ribbon* selected.
b. Rename the tab *C22* followed by your initials.

1c. Rename the custom group below your new tab *File Management*.

FILE HOME INSERT DESIGN PAGE LAYOUT REFERENCES MAILINGS REVIEW VIEW C22

Document1 - Word

Close Open Quick Print Save As Save As * New Blank Document File Management

1d. Change the *Choose commands from* option to *File Tab*.
e. From the list box at the left side of the dialog box, add the following commands to the *File Management* group: *Close, Open, Quick Print, Save As,* and *Save As Other Format*.
f. Change the *Choose commands from* option to *Popular Commands*.
g. From the list box at the left side of the dialog box, add the New command.

1. At the blank screen, create a new tab with the following specifications:
h. Click OK to close the Word Options dialog box.
2. At the blank screen, click your new tab (which begins with C22 and is followed by your initials).
3. Click the Open button in the File Management group on your new tab.
4. At the Open backstage area, click *C22-A02-FAV.docx*, which displays at the beginning of the *Recent Documents* list.
5. With *C22-A02-FAV.docx* open, save the document in the Word 97-2003 format by completing the following steps:
a. Click the new tab (which begins with C22 and is followed by your initials).
b. Click the Save As button arrow. (This is the second Save As button in the File Management group on your new tab.)
c. Click *Word 97-2003 Document* at the drop-down list.
d. At the Save As dialog box with *Word 97-2003 Document (*.doc)* selected in the *Save as type* option box, type *C22-A03-FAV-Word97-2003Format* and then press the Enter key.
e. Close *C22-A03-FAV-Word97-2003Format.doc* by clicking the Close button in the File Management group on your new tab.
6. Click the Open button on your new tab and then click *C22-A02-FAV.docx* in the *Recent Documents* list.
7. Send the document to the printer by clicking your new tab and then clicking the Quick Print button in the File Management group.
8. Close the document by clicking the Close button in the File Management group on your new tab.
9. Click the New Blank Document button in the File Management group on your new tab.
10. At the blank document, click your new tab and then click the New Blank Document button. (You now have two blank documents open.)
11. Click the Insert tab, click the Screenshot button, and then click *Screen Clipping* at the dropdown list.
12. When the first blank document displays in a dimmed manner, use the mouse to select the Quick Access toolbar and ribbon, including the new tab you created with the File Management group buttons.
13. Print the document containing the screen clipping and then close the document without saving it.
14. Display the Word Options dialog box with *Customize Ribbon* selected and then reset the ribbon back to the default.

C22-A03-Screenshot(Step13).docx

LUXURY FAMILY ADVENTURE VACATIONS

Sign up today for one of our exciting luxury family adventure vacations, created for families who enjoy a multitude of outdoor activities and a bit of luxury. Our Chile luxury vacation combines whitewater rafting, hiking, kayaking, and horseback riding into one fun-filled week of adventure travel in beautiful Patagonia, Chile.

More than a family rafting trip, we'll make sure you are exposed to all that the Futaleufú Valley has to offer including whitewater rafting on the Futaleufú River, which contains sections for all levels of ability and experience; hiking up some of the beautiful tributaries of the Futaleufú River; and horseback riding across beautiful valleys at the base of snow-peaked mountains.

Patagonia, Chile, provides a wide variety of opportunities for active travel that the whole family can enjoy. You can feel confident that we will take care of all the details so that your experience is a mix of fun, comfort, and relaxation.☺

Price for single occupancy:
$2,899
€2,675

Price for double occupancy:
$2,699
€2,450

Price for triple occupancy:
$2,499
€2,100

2. Type the text shown in Figure 22.13. Create the smiley face icon by typing :) and then pressing the spacebar. (To insert the euro currency symbol, type eu and then press the spacebar. Press the Backspace key once and then type the amount.)

1. At a blank document, add the following text to AutoCorrect:
a. Insert *Pt* in the *Replace* text box and insert *Patagonia* in the *With* text box.
b. Insert *Ft* in the *Replace* text box and insert *Futaleufú* in the *With* text box.
c. Insert the euro (€) currency symbol in the *With* text box (using the Symbol dialog box) and type eu in the *Replace* text box. (The euro currency symbol is located near the bottom of the Symbol dialog box list box with *(normal text)* selected.)
2. Save the document with the name **C22-A02-FAV**.
3. Print and then close **C22-A02-FAV.docx**.
4. Delete the *eu, Ft,* and *Pt* AutoCorrect entries.

C22-A02-FAV.docx

CHANGING WORD OPTIONS

1. Display the Word Options dialog box and determine how to do the following:
a. Change the Office theme. (General)
b. Change the number of minutes for saving AutoRecover information. (Save)
c. Change the number of recent documents that display in the Recent Documents list at the Open backstage area. (Advanced)

2. At a blank document, create a report that describes how to do the following:
a. Steps to change the Office theme to Dark Gray.

4. Format your document to improve its appearance.

Word allows modification change to many of the options included in the program. You can change the program theme, adjust the time for saving as AutoRecover, and adjust the number of documents that display in your Recent Documents, among many other variables.

Below are the instructions to make the suggested changes and adjustments.

Change the Office theme
- From the backstage area, click *Options*.
- With *General* selected in the left panel, click the *Office Theme* option arrow and then click *Dark Gray* at the drop-down list.
- Click OK to close the Word Options dialog box and apply your change.

Change number of minutes for saving AutoRecover information
- From the backstage area, click *Options*.
- With *Save* selected in the left panel, click the up-pointing arrow at the right of the *Save AutoRecover information every* measurement box until 5 displays.
- Although not recommended, you can also turn this feature off.
- Click OK to close the Word Options dialog box and apply your change.

Change the number of documents displayed in Recent Documents
- From the backstage area, click *Options*.
- With *Advanced* selected in the left panel, scroll down to the *Display* section
- Click the up- or down-pointing arrow at the right of the *Show this number of Recent Documents* measurement box until 15 displays.
- Click OK to close the Word Options dialog box and apply your change.

ADDING FUNCTIONS TO THE STATUS BAR

Word also allows modification to the Status bar. To do this, right click in any blank space on the Status bar to see the features that can be included and turned on or off.

To add the Track Changes feature and the caps lock notification to the Status bar, complete the following steps:
- Right-click in a blank area of the Status bar.
- At the shortcut menu, click *Track Changes*.
- Right-click in a blank area of the Status bar and then click *Caps Lock*.

Some features, like the CAPS Lock feature, do not appear on the Status bar until the item is engaged in the program. Turning on the CAPS Lock with your keyboard will add CAPS to the Status bar. Track Changes remains on the Status bar to advise if the feature is on or off.

2b. Steps to change the minutes for saving AutoRecover information to 5 minutes.

2c. Steps to change the number of recent documents that display in the *Recent Documents* list at the Open backstage area to 15.

3. Right-click on a blank location on the Status bar and then look at the options that display in the shortcut menu. Determine how to add the Track Changes feature and caps lock notification to the Status bar, and then add to your report steps that describe how to add these functions.

C22-A04-Options.docx

1b. Set the body text in 11-point Constantia and the title in 26-point Constantia. Change the font color to Dark Blue.

1e. Format the clip art by changing the text wrapping to Tight, flipping the image horizontally, and changing the color to Blue, Accent color 1 Light. (If you did not use the clip art image shown in Figure 22.14, choose your own formatting for the clip art image you insert in the document.) Size and position the clip art image as shown in the figure.

RESUME STYLES

You can write a resume in a variety of ways since different approaches work for different people. The three most popular resume styles include: chronological resume, functional resume, and hybrid resume.

CHRONOLOGICAL RESUME

The chronological resume is the one many people use without thinking. It lists your training and jobs in order of the dates you started each of them. Typically, people list their most recent training and jobs first and proceed backwards to the first things they did in the past. This is called reverse chronological order. The components of this resume include:

- Personal contact information
- Employment history, including employers, dates of employment, positions held, and achievements
- Educational qualifications
- Professional development

FUNCTIONAL RESUME

The functional resume emphasizes the skills of the individual and his or her achievements. It is often used when the applicant lacks formal education, or his or her educational qualifications are judged obsolete or irrelevant. If you have had many different jobs with no clear pattern or progression, or a lot of gaps in your work history, some people recommend this approach.

HYBRID RESUME

The hybrid resume is an increasingly popular resume style that combines the best of both the chronological resume and the functional resume. A hybrid resume retains much of the fixed order of the chronological resume, but more emphasis is placed on skills and achievements – sometimes in a separate section. The hybrid resume is the one that we recommend to most people, in that it produces an excellent clear structure but requires the person to really think hard about his or her achievements and what he or she has to offer. If you decide to use a hybrid resume, you may wish to leave out the detailed responsibilities section and just emphasize the skills, knowledge, and abilities you have.

1c. Insert the page border, paragraph border, and paragraph shading as shown in Figure 22.14. Make sure you change the paragraph and page border color to Dark Blue and change the page border width to 1½ pt.

1f. Insert the five symbols at the end of the document as shown in the figure. (The symbol is located in the Wingdings font.) Change the color of the symbols to Dark Blue.

1d. Insert the clip art image shown in the figure. *Hint: Look for this clip art image by typing document office papers in the search text box at the Insert Pictures window. If this clip art image is not available, choose a similar image.*

1. At a blank document, create the document shown in Figure 22.14 on page 786 with the following specifications:
a. Create AutoCorrect entries for *chronological resume, functional resume,* and *hybrid resume.* You determine the replacement text. *Hint: When typing the headings, type the replacement text in all caps and Word will insert the AutoCorrect text in all capital letters.*

C22-A05-ResumeStyles.docx

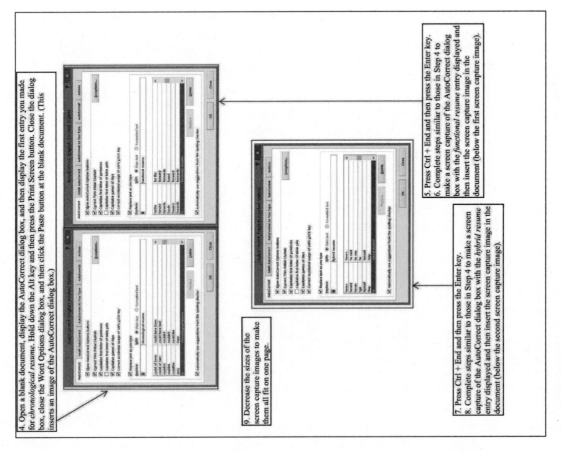

4. Open a blank document, display the AutoCorrect dialog box, and then display the first entry you made for *chronological resume*. Hold down the Alt key and then press the Print Screen button. Close the dialog box, close the Word Options dialog box, and then click the Paste button at the blank document. (This inserts an image of the AutoCorrect dialog box.)

5. Press Ctrl + End and then press the Enter key.
6. Complete steps similar to those in Step 4 to make a screen capture of the AutoCorrect dialog box with the *functional resume* entry displayed and then insert the screen capture image in the document (below the first screen capture image).

9. Decrease the sizes of the screen capture images to make them all fit on one page.

7. Press Ctrl + End and then press the Enter key.
8. Complete steps similar to those in Step 4 to make a screen capture of the AutoCorrect dialog box with the *hybrid resume* entry displayed and then insert the screen capture image in the document (below the second screen capture image).

C22-A05-ScreenCaps.docx

Chapter 23 Assessment Annotated Model Answers

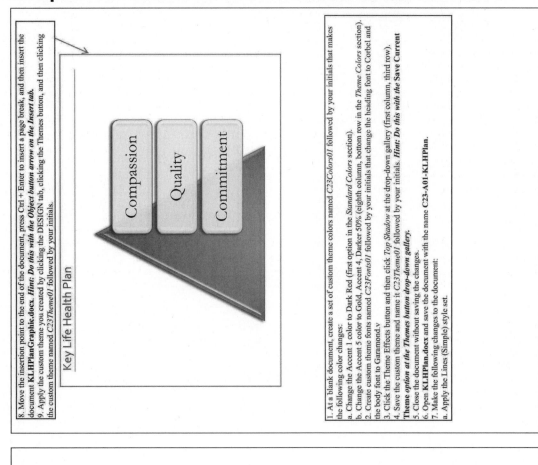

8. Move the insertion point to the end of the document, press Ctrl + Enter to insert a page break, and then insert the document **KLHPlanGraphic.docx**. *Hint: Do this with the Object button arrow on the Insert tab.*
9. Apply the custom theme you created by clicking the DESIGN tab, clicking the Themes button, and then clicking the custom theme named *C23Theme01* followed by your initials.

Key Life Health Plan

Compassion

Quality

Commitment

1. At a blank document, create a set of custom theme colors named *C23Colors01* followed by your initials that makes the following color changes:
a. Change the Accent 1 color to Dark Red (first option in the *Standard Colors* section).
b. Change the Accent 5 color to Gold, Accent 4, Darker 50% (eighth column, bottom row in the *Theme Colors* section).
2. Create custom theme fonts named *C23Fonts01* followed by your initials that change the heading font to Corbel and the body font to Garamond.v
3. Click the Theme Effects button and then click *Top Shadow* at the drop-down gallery (first column, third row).
4. Save the custom theme and name it *C23Theme01* followed by your initials. *Hint: Do this with the Save Current Theme option at the Themes button drop-down gallery.*
5. Close the document without saving the changes.
6. Open **KLHPlan.docx** and save the document with the name **C23-A01-KLHPlan.**
7. Make the following changes to the document:
a. Apply the Lines (Simple) style set.

7b. With the insertion point positioned at the beginning of the document, type the title Key Life Health Plan.
c. Apply the Heading 1 style to the title.

Key Life Health Plan

Plan Highlights

The following are several of Key Life Health Plan's special features:

A part of the community. Key Life Health Plan has served the Madison County area since 1979. Our parent company was one of the area's first collaborative medical practices, serving area patients since 1923.

Coverage for preventive care. Key Life Health Plan encourages wellness with a variety of services, including routine physical exams, eye exams, prenatal care, and well-baby care. We also offer health education programs designed both to reach and motivate members to make healthier lifestyle choices.

Easy to be a member. There are virtually no claim forms to complete, and you make low co-payments only when you receive care.

Worldwide emergency care. You can receive care for medical emergencies if you are traveling outside Key Life Health Plan's service area or are unable to reach one of our many plan facilities in a local emergency.

Member satisfaction. A recent survey by Lowell Research showed that 95 percent of our current members rated the care they received as good, very good, or excellent.

Quality Assessment

Key Life Health Plan has demonstrated a commitment to quality by adhering to the standards established by the National Association for Quality Health Care. We focus on these specific areas:

- Member rights and responsibilities
- Preventive health care
- Provider quality standards
- Clinical care quality review

In addition, we employ research in areas of service satisfaction, products, and benefits. We use our findings to improve the delivery of care and service to our members.

Provider Network

Quality care begins with finding a doctor with whom you can be comfortable. Key Life Health Plan offers over 650 primary and specialty care physicians conveniently located in the greater county area. Included within our more than 38 clinic and hospital locations is Key Life Health Center—one of the top-rated medical facilities in the country.

Key Life Health Plan has forged valuable partnerships with other contracted providers whose practices reflect similar high-quality standards of care. Our providers work as a team, combining resources to manage all levels of your health care needs. This coordination of services ensures members will receive the most appropriate and cost-effective medical care available.

7d. Apply the Heading 2 style to the three headings in the document.

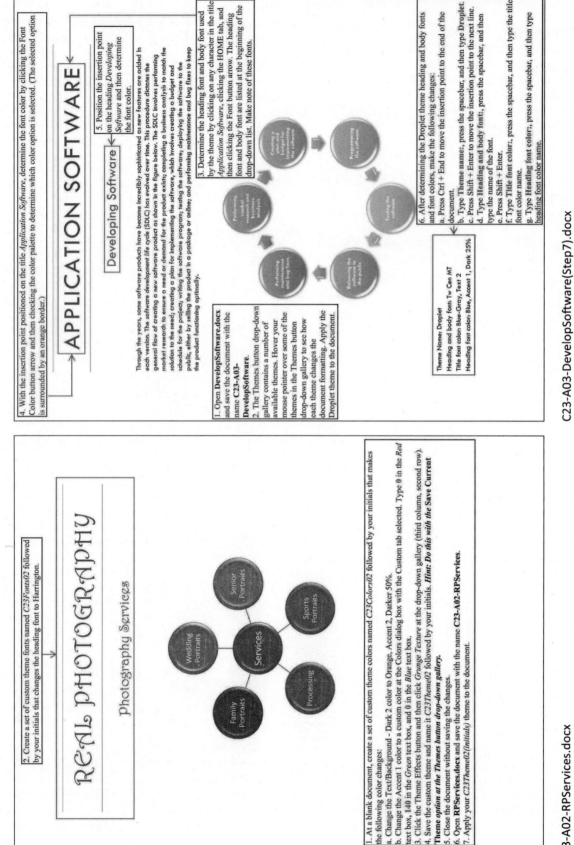

APPLICATION SOFTWARE

Developing Software

4. With the insertion point positioned on the title *Application Software*, determine the font color by clicking the Font Color button arrow and then checking the color palette to determine which color option is selected. (The selected option is surrounded by an orange border.)

5. Position the insertion point on the heading *Developing Software* and then determine the font color.

Through the years, some software products have become incredibly sophisticated as new features are added in each version. The software development life cycle (SDLC) has evolved over time. This procedure dictates the general flow of creating a new software product as shown in the figure below. The SDLC involves performing market research to ensure a need or demand for the product exists; completing a business analysis to match the solution to the need; creating a plan for implementing the software, which involves creating a budget and schedule for the project; writing the software program; testing the software; deploying the software to the public, either by selling the product in a package or online; and performing maintenance and bug fixes to keep the product functioning optimally.

1. Open DevelopSoftware.docx and save the document with the name C23-A03-DevelopSoftware.

2. The Themes button drop-down gallery contains a number of available themes. Hover your mouse pointer over some of the themes in the Themes button drop-down gallery to see how each theme changes the document formatting. Apply the Droplet theme to the document.

3. Determine the heading font and body font used by the theme by clicking on any character in the title *Application Software*, clicking the HOME tab, and then clicking the Font button arrow. The heading font and body font are listed at the beginning of the drop-down list. Make note of these fonts.

6. After determining the Droplet theme heading and body fonts and font colors, make the following changes:
a. Press Ctrl + End to move the insertion point to the end of the document.
b. Type Theme name, press the spacebar, and then type Droplet.
c. Press Shift + Enter to move the insertion point to the next line.
d. Type Heading and body font:, press the spacebar, and then type the name of the font.
e. Press Shift + Enter.
f. Type Title font color:, press the spacebar, and then type the title font color name.
g. Type Heading font color:, press the spacebar, and then type heading font color name.

Theme Name: Droplet
Heading and body font: Tw Cen MT
Title font color: Blue-Gray, Text 2
Heading font color: Blue, Accent 1, Dark 25%

C23-A03-DevelopSoftware(Step7).docx

REAL PHOTOGRAPHY

Photography Services

2. Create a set of custom theme fonts named C23Fonts02 followed by your initials that changes the heading font to Harrington.

1. At a blank document, create a set of custom theme colors named C23Colors02 followed by your initials that makes the following color changes:
a. Change the Text/Background - Dark 2 color to Orange, Accent 2, Darker 50%.
b. Change the Accent 1 color to a custom color at the Colors dialog box with the Custom tab selected. Type 0 in the *Red* text box, 140 in the *Green* text box, and 0 in the *Blue* text box.
3. Click the Theme Effects button and then click *Grunge Texture* at the drop-down gallery (third column, second row).
4. Save the custom theme and name it *C23Theme02* followed by your initials. *Hint: Do this with the Save Current Theme option at the Themes button drop-down gallery.*
5. Close the document without saving the changes.
6. Open RPServices.docx and save the document with the name C23-A02-RPServices.
7. Apply your *C23Theme02(Initials)* theme to the document.

C23-A02-RPServices.docx

10. At a blank document, use the Print Screen button to make a screen capture of the Theme Colors button drop-down gallery (make sure your custom theme colors display), a screen capture of the Theme Fonts button drop-down gallery (make sure your custom theme fonts display), and a screen capture of the Save Current Theme dialog box (make sure your custom themes are visible). Insert all three screen capture images on the same page. (You will need to size the images.)

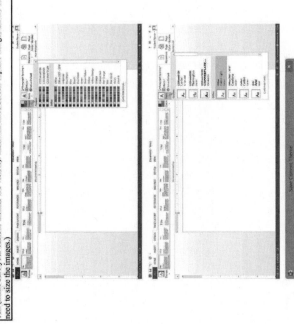

11. Save the document and name it **C23-A04-ScreenImages.**
12. Print and then close **C23-A04-ScreenImages.docx.**
13. At a blank document, delete the custom color themes, custom font themes, and custom themes that you created in this chapter.

C23-A04-ScreenImages.docx

APPLICATION SOFTWARE

Developing Software

Through the years, some software products have become incredibly sophisticated as new features are added in each version. The *software development life cycle* (SDLC) has evolved over time. This procedure dictates the general flow of creating a new software product as shown in the figure below. The SDLC involves performing market research to ensure a need or demand for the product exists; completing a business analysis to match the solution to the need; creating a plan for implementing the software, which involves creating a budget and schedule for the project; writing the software program; testing the software; deploying the software to the public, either by selling the product in a package or online; and performing maintenance and bug fixes to keep the product functioning optimally.

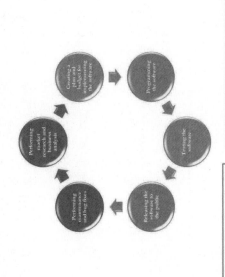

Theme Name: Organic
Heading and body font: Garamond
Title font color: Gray-80%, Text 2
Heading font color: Green, Accent 1, Dark 25%

8. Apply the Organic theme to the document and then determine the heading and body font, the title font color, and the heading font color. Change the information that displays at the bottom of the document to reflect the new theme.

C23-A03-DevelopSoftware(Step9).docx

TANDEM ENERGY CORPORATION

CORPORATE VISION

Tandem Energy Corporation will be the leading developer of clean and environmentally friendly products. Building on strong leadership, development, and resources, we will provide superior-quality products and services to our customers and consumers around the world.

CORPORATE VALUES

We value the environment in which we live, and we will work to produce and maintain energy-efficient and environmentally safe products and strive to reduce our carbon footprint on the environment.

CORPORATE LEADERSHIP

Tandem Energy Corporation employees conduct business under the leadership of the chief executive officer, who is subject to the oversight and direction of the board of directors. Four vice presidents work with the chief executive officer to manage and direct business.

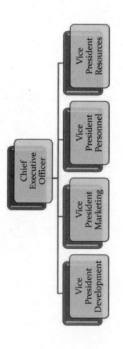

C23-A04-TECCorporate.docx (page 1 of 2)

TANDEM ENERGY CORPORATION

REVENUES

We are evaluating markets for our current and future products. Prior to the fourth quarter of 2015, we recorded revenues as a result of development contracts with government entities focused on the design of flywheel technologies. We have produced and placed several development prototypes with potential customers and shipped preproduction units.

RESEARCH AND DEVELOPMENT

Our cost of research and development consists primarily of the cost of compensation and benefits for research and support staff, as well as materials and supplies used in the engineering design and development process. These costs decreased significantly during 2015 as we focused on reducing our expenditure rate by reducing product design and development activities.

PREFERRED STOCK DIVIDENDS

Prior to our initial public offering of our common stock, we had various classes of preferred stock outstanding, each of which was entitled to receive dividends. We accrued dividend expenses monthly according to the requirements of each class of preferred stock.

1. Open **TECRevenues.docx** and save the document and name it **C23-A04-TECRevenues**.
2. Create the following custom theme colors named *C23ColorsTEC* followed by your initials with the following changes:
a. Change the Text/Background - Dark 2 color to Orange, Accent 2, Darker 50% (sixth column, last row in the *Theme Colors* section).
b. Change the Accent 1 color to Green, Accent 6, Darker 50% (tenth column, last row in the *Theme Colors* section)
c. Change the Accent 4 color to Orange, Accent 2, Darker 50%.
d. Change the Accent 6 color to Green, Accent 6, Darker 25%.
3. Create the following custom theme fonts named *C23FontsTEC* followed by your initials with the following changes:
b. Change the body font to Constantia.
4. Apply the Riblet theme effect (last column, third row).
5. Save the custom theme and name it *C23ThemeTEC* followed by your initials. **Hint: *Do this with the Save Current Theme option at the Themes button drop-down gallery.***

C23-A04-TECCorporate.docx (page 2 of 2)

C24-A01-KMReport.docx (page 1 of 2)

9. Apply the KodiakTitle style to the two titles in the document: *Audit Committee Report* and *Compensation Committee Report*. 12. Edit the KodiakTitle style by changing the font color to Dark Blue and underlining the text.

1. Open **KMStyles.docx** and save the document with the name **C24-A01- KMStyles.**

10. Apply the KodiakHeading style to the four headings in the report: *Committee Responsibilities, Fees to Independent Auditor, Compensation Philosophy,* and *Competitive Compensation.* 13. Edit the KodiakHeading style by changing the font color to Dark Blue.

11. Apply the KodiakQuote style to the second paragraph of text in the document (the paragraph that begins *Assist the company's board of directors*).

KODIAK MANUFACTURING

AUDIT COMMITTEE REPORT

The audit committee of the board of directors, which consists entirely of directors who meet the current independence and experience requirements of the New York Stock Exchange as determined by the board of directors, was given the following mission:

Assist the company's board of directors in fulfilling its responsibility to oversee the management's conduct of the company's financial reporting process. Such assistance includes oversight by the committee of the financial reports and other financial information provided by the company to any governmental or regulatory body, the public, or other users thereof.

The audit committee selects an independent, registered public accounting firm to be the company's independent auditor and to perform the annual independent audit of the company's financial statements and measure the effectiveness of internal control over financial reporting.

COMMITTEE RESPONSIBILITIES

The role and responsibilities of the audit committee are set forth in a written charter adopted by the board. The audit committee reviews and reassesses the charter annually and recommends changes to the board for approval.

As part of fulfilling its responsibilities for overseeing management's conduct of the company's financial reporting process for fiscal year 2014, the audit committee:

Received management's representation that the company's consolidated financial statements for the fiscal year ended December 31, 2014, were prepared in accordance with accounting principles generally accepted in the United States.

Monitored, reviewed, and discussed the audited financial statements for the fiscal year and the effectiveness of internal control over financial reporting and management's assessment thereof.

Discussed with the accounting firm the matters required to be discussed by auditing standards related to the conduct of the audit.

Received written disclosures and a letter from the account firm regarding its independence as required by auditing standards.

In addition, the audit committee considered the status of pending litigation, taxation matters, and other areas of oversight relating to the financial reporting and audit process that the committee determined appropriate.

15. Select the bulleted text in the *Committee Responsibilities* section and then apply the Block Text style. With the text still selected, click the Font Color button on the HOME tab and then click the *Dark Blue* color.

2. Create a style based on the formatting of the *KodiakTitle* text and name it *KodiakTitle.* (Make sure you select the paragraph symbol with the text.)

3. Press Ctrl + End to move the insertion point to the end of the document and then create a new style named *KodiakQuote.* Apply the following formatting at the Create New Style from Formatting expanded dialog box: a. Change the left and right indents to 0.5 inch and the spacing after paragraphs to 12 points. *Hint: Display these formatting options by clicking the Format button in the lower left corner of the dialog box and then clicking **Paragraph**.*
b. Click the Italic button. c. Change the font color to Dark Blue. d. Insert a blue, single-line top border and a blue, single-line bottom border. *Hint: Display these formatting options by clicking the Format button and then clicking **Border**.*

C24-A01-KMReport.docx (page 1 of 2)

C24-A01-KMReport.docx (page 2 of 2)

9. Apply the KodiakTitle style to the two titles in the document: *Audit Committee Report* and *Compensation Committee Report.*

Based on the audit committee's reviews, the discussions and other actions outlined above, and relying thereon, the audit committee recommended to the board that the audited financial statements be included in the company's annual report for the fiscal year for filing with the U.S. Exchange Commission.

FEES TO INDEPENDENT AUDITOR

The aggregate fees billed for the professional services of the company's independent auditor for the fiscal year ended December 31, 2013, and December 31, 2014, are shown on the Auditing Fees Excel worksheet

The audit committee determined that the provision of the nonaudit services covered was compatible with maintaining the independence of the accounting firm.

COMPENSATION COMMITTEE REPORT

The compensation committee of the board of directors is comprised solely of nonemployee directors who meet the independence requirements of the New York Stock Exchange and qualify as outside director. The committee is responsible for establishing and administering an overall compensation program for top executives.

The committee met four times during 2014. In addition, the committee has the authority to engage independent consultants to provide advice on compensation levels and expertise on compensation strategy and program design.

COMPENSATION PHILOSOPHY

Our executive compensation program reflects the philosophy that executive rewards should be structured to reflect a pay-for-performance culture and to closely align with the interests of our shareholders. Our core principles include the following:

Provide for meaningful compensation programs that are reasonable and competitive and aid the company in attracting, retaining, and motivating key talent.

Structure the compensation philosophy so as to provide reward opportunities consistent with the company's operating strategy.

Emphasize pay-for-performance and stock-based incentives, and extend these concepts beyond the executive officers to other employees in the interests of motivation, teamwork, and fairness.

COMPETITIVE COMPENSATION

Compensation surveys of external competitiveness are used in assessing appropriateness of compensation. Company and individual performances are also considered in determining individual pay amounts. The primary competitive market is taken into consideration so the company can compete for the best talent in the industry.

The compensation committee developed long-term incentives for the named executives at 86% of their target bonuses.

8. Change to the style set named with your initials followed by *Kodiak.*

5. Save the styles you created in a style set named with your three initials followed by *Kodiak.*

16. Select the bulleted text in the *Compensation Philosophy* section, apply the Block Text style, and then change the font color to Dark Blue.

6. Save and then close **C24-A01-KMStyles.docx.**

17. Save the modified styles as a style set with the same name (your initials followed by *Kodiak*). (At the Save as a New Style Set dialog box, click your style set name in the Content pane and then click the Save button. At the message asking if you want to replace the existing file, click Yes.)

7. Open **KMReport.docx** and then save the document with the name **C24-A01- KMReport.**

14. Turn on the display of the Styles task pane and then display all of the styles in alphabetical order. *Hint: Do this at the Style Pane Options dialog box.*

4. At the document, press the Up Arrow key once and then create a style named *KodiakHeading* and apply the following formatting:
a. Change the font to Copperplate Gothic Bold.
b. Change the font color to Blue.

C24-A01-KMReport.docx (page 2 of 2)

KODIAK MANUFACTURING

5. Open a document based on the XXX-KMStyles.dotx template. *Hint: Do this at the New backstage area.*
6. Insert the file named **KMSales.docx** and then save the document with the name C24-A03- KMSales.

7. Apply the KodiakTitle style to the title *Quarterly Sales.*

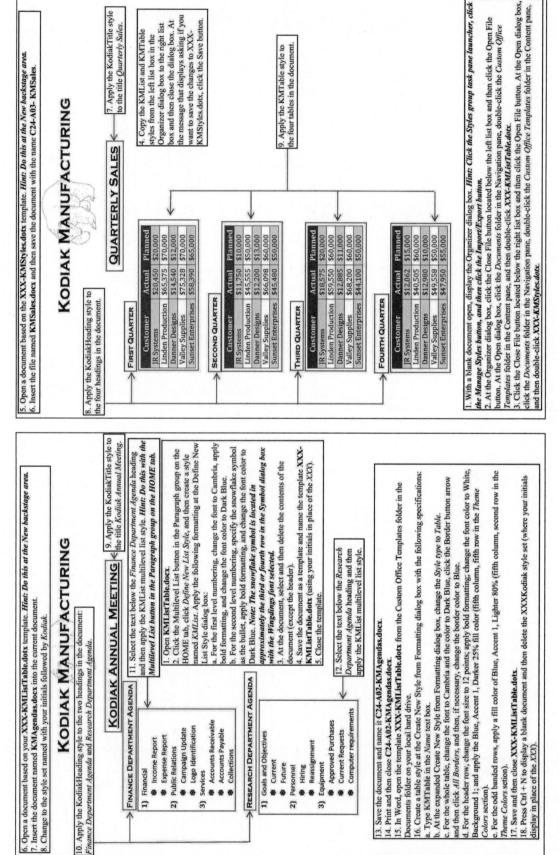

8. Apply the KodiakHeading style to the four headings in the document.

4. Copy the KMList and KMTable styles from the left list box to the right list box in the Organizer dialog box and then close the dialog box. At the message that displays asking if you want to save the changes to XXX-KMStyles.docx, click the Save button.

9. Apply the KMTable style to the four tables in the document.

QUARTERLY SALES

FIRST QUARTER

Customer	Actual	Planned
JR Systems	$20,450	$20,000
Linden Production	$65,375	$70,000
Danner Designs	$14,540	$12,000
Valley Supplies	$75,328	$70,000
Sunset Enterprises	$58,390	$65,000

SECOND QUARTER

Customer	Actual	Planned
JR Systems	$11,750	$10,000
Linden Production	$45,555	$50,000
Danner Designs	$12,200	$13,000
Valley Supplies	$66,098	$60,000
Sunset Enterprises	$45,480	$50,000

THIRD QUARTER

Customer	Actual	Planned
JR Systems	$18,575	$20,000
Linden Production	$59,550	$60,000
Danner Designs	$12,885	$11,000
Valley Supplies	$68,200	$60,000
Sunset Enterprises	$44,100	$50,000

FOURTH QUARTER

Customer	Actual	Planned
JR Systems	$12,062	$15,000
Linden Production	$40,505	$60,000
Danner Designs	$12,980	$10,000
Valley Supplies	$49,558	$50,000
Sunset Enterprises	$47,950	$55,000

1. With a blank document open, display the Organizer dialog box. *Hint: Click the Styles group task pane launcher, click the Manage Styles button, and then click the Import/Export button.*
2. At the Organizer dialog box, click the Close File button located below the left list box and then click the Open File button. At the Open dialog box, click the *Documents* folder in the Navigation pane, double-click the *Custom Office Templates* folder in the Content pane, and then double-click **XXX-KMListTable.docx**.
3. Click the Close File button located below the right list box and then click the Open File button. At the Open dialog box, click the *Documents* folder in the Navigation pane, double-click the *Custom Office Templates* folder in the Content pane, and then double-click **XXX-KMStyles.dotx**.

C24-A03-KMSales.docx

KODIAK MANUFACTURING

6. Open a document based on your XXX-KMListTable.dotx template. *Hint: Do this at the New backstage area.*
7. Insert the document named **KMAgendas.docx** into the current document.
8. Change to the style set named with your initials followed by *Kodiak.*

10. Apply the KodiakHeading style to the two headings in the document: *Finance Department Agenda* and *Research Department Agenda.*

KODIAK ANNUAL MEETING

9. Apply the KodiakTitle style to the title *Kodiak Annual Meeting.*

FINANCE DEPARTMENT AGENDA

11. Select the text below the *Finance Department Agenda* heading and then apply the KMList multilevel list style. *Hint: Do this with the Multilevel List button in the Paragraph group on the HOME tab.*

1. Open KMListTable.docx.
2. Click the Multilevel List button in the Paragraph group on the HOME tab, click *Define New List Style,* and then create a style named *KMList.* Apply the following formatting at the Define New List Style dialog box:
   a. For the first level numbering, change the font to Cambria, apply bold formatting, and change the font color to Dark Blue.
   b. For the second level numbering, specify the snowflake symbol as the bullet, apply bold formatting, and change the font color to Dark Blue. *Note: The snowflake symbol is located in approximately the third or fourth row in the Symbol dialog box with the Wingdings font selected.*
3. At the document, select and then delete the contents of the document (except the header).
4. Save the document as a template and name the template **XXX-KMListTable.dotx** (using your initials in place of the *XXX*).
5. Close the template.

RESEARCH DEPARTMENT AGENDA

12. Select the text below the *Research Department Agenda* heading and then apply the KMList multilevel list style.

FINANCE DEPARTMENT AGENDA

1) Financial
   * Income Report
   * Expense Report
2) Public Relations
   * Campaign Update
   * Logo Identification
3) Services
   * Accounts Receivable
   * Accounts Payable
   * Collections

RESEARCH DEPARTMENT AGENDA

1) Goals and Objectives
   * Current
   * Future
2) Personnel
   * Hiring
   * Reassignment
3) Equipment
   * Approved Purchases
   * Current Requests
   * Computer requirements

13. Save the document and name it C24-A02-KMAgendas.docx.
14. Print and then close C24-A02-KMAgendas.docx.
15. In Word, open the template **XXX-KMListTable.dotx** from the Custom Office Templates folder on your local hard drive.
16. Create a table style at the Create New Style from Formatting dialog box with the following specifications:
   a. Type KMTable in the *Name* text box.
   b. At the expanded Create New Style from Formatting dialog box, change the *Style type* to *Table.*
   c. For the whole table, change the font to Cambria and the color to Dark Blue, click the Border button arrow and then click *All Borders,* and then, if necessary, change the border color to Blue.
   d. For the header row, change the font size to 12 points; apply bold formatting; change the font color to White, Background 1; and apply the Blue, Accent 1, Darker 25% fill color (fifth column, fifth row in the *Theme Colors* section).
   e. For the odd banded rows, apply a fill color of Blue, Accent 1, Lighter 80% (fifth column, second row in the *Theme Colors* section).
17. Save and then close **XXX-KMListTable.dotx**.
18. Press Ctrl + N to display a blank document and then delete the XXXKodiak style set (where your initials display in place of the *XXX*).

C24-A02-KMAgendas.docx

13. At a blank document, write a memo to your instructor that describes the three styles you created, including the name of each style and the formatting you applied to it. Save the completed document and name it **C24-A05-MemotoInstructor**.

TO: Instructor Name

FROM: Student Name

DATE: March 2, 2015

SUBJECT: Creating Styles

I created three styles for Real Photography documents as described below.

1. **RPTitle** – This is a title style. I applied 12-point Papyrus font, center alignment, bold formatting, 6 points of spacing after paragraphs, a bottom single green border line, and a light green shading to the title text.
2. **RPHeading** – This is a heading style. I applied Papyrus font, bold formatting, and a green font color.
3. **RPQuote** – This is a quote style. I applied Corbel font, italic formatting, center alignment, a green border around the text, and indented the text 0.5 inch from the left and right margins.

Northland Security Systems

1. In this chapter, you learned how to create a table style and apply all of the formatting to the style. You can also create a style based on an existing predesigned table style. At a blank document, insert a table with a couple of rows and columns and then determine how to modify an existing table style. After experimenting with modifying a table style, close the document without saving it.
2. Open **NSSTables.docx** and save the document with the name **C24-A04-NSSTables**.
3. Click in any cell in the top table and then click the Table Tools Design tab.

4. Modify the List Table 1 Light - Accent 1 table style (second column, first row in *List Tables* section) by changing the name to *NSSTable* and then apply the following formatting:
a. For the whole table, change the font to Candara and change the alignment to Align Center. *Hint: The alignment button is located to the right of the Fill Color button.*

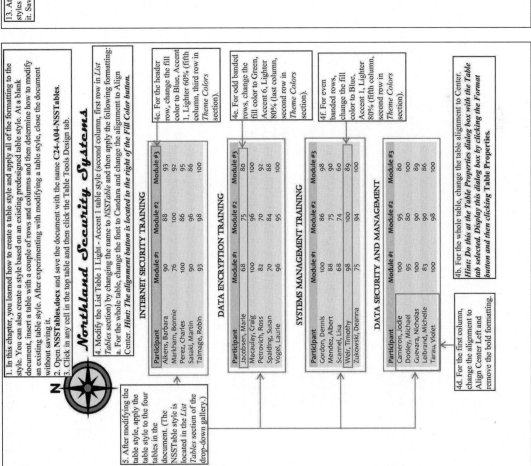

INTERNET SECURITY TRAINING

Participant	Module #1	Module #2	Module #3
Aikens, Barbara	90	88	93
Markham, Bonnie	76	100	92
Perez, Charles	100	86	95
Sasaki, Martin	90	96	86
Talmage, Robin	93	98	100

4c. For the header row, change the fill color to Blue, Accent 1, Lighter 60% (fifth column, third row in *Theme Colors* section).

DATA ENCRYPTION TRAINING

Participant	Module #1	Module #2	Module #3
Jacobsen, Marie	68	75	80
Macaulay, Craig	100	96	100
Petrovich, Ross	82	70	92
Spalding, Susan	70	84	88
Vogel, Laurie	96	95	100

4d. For odd banded rows, change the fill color to Green, Accent 6, Lighter 80% (last column, second row in *Theme Colors* section).

SYSTEMS MANAGEMENT TRAINING

Participant	Module #1	Module #2	Module #3
Gordon, Dennis	100	86	98
Mendez, Albert	88	75	90
Scannel, Lisa	68	74	60
Weir, Timothy	98	100	89
Zukowski, Deanna	75	94	100

4f. For even banded rows, change the fill color to Blue, Accent 1, Lighter 80% (fifth column, second row in *Theme Colors* section).

DATA SECURITY AND MANAGEMENT

Participant	Module #1	Module #2	Module #3
Cameron, Jodie	100	95	80
Dooley, Michael	95	80	100
Guevara, Nicholas	100	89	89
Leibrand, Michelle	83	90	86
Tarau, Violet	100	98	100

4b. For the whole table, change the table alignment to Center. *Hint: Do this at the Table Properties dialog box with the Table tab selected. Display this dialog box by clicking the Format button and then clicking **Table Properties**.*

4d. For the first column, change the alignment to Align Center Left and remove the bold formatting.

5. After modifying the table style, apply the table style to the four tables in the document. (The NSSTable style is located in the *List Tables* section of the *List Tables* drop-down gallery.)

closes when the user presses the shutter release, exposing the film to the light. Cameras share some of the following common features:

- Light-tight body
- Lens
- Lens aperture, which controls the amount of light reaching the medium
- Light-sensitive medium to capture the image
- Shutter, which opens and closes to allow light to act for a specified time
- Viewfinder or screen

Some additional camera features include a tripod screw of standard size to fit any tripod, a method for setting the distance, and a method for setting the film speed. Cameras vary in the amount of control a user has over the aperture, shutter and distance settings, and whether these can be set automatically.

Digital Cameras

A digital camera is a camera equipped with an electronic photosensitive sensor that stores photographs in a digital format directly in the camera's memory. The photographs can be downloaded to a computer. Some digital camera terminology includes white balance, pixel, ppi, and dpi.

Pixels

The word *pixel* is a contraction of the term *picture element.* Digital images are made up of small squares. Each pixel in an image has a numerical value of 0 to 255 and is made up of three colors—red, green and blue. Over 16 million combinations of colors are available with each one presenting a different color. A common method for categorizing digital cameras is in the number of pixel count. This represents the number of individual pixels that go into making each image. This number can range from approximately one million to 14 million or more. One million pixels equal one megapixel, which is written as MP. So, a 1MP digital camera has one million pixels and a 5MP camera has five million pixels.

Aspect Ratio

Most digital cameras have an aspect ratio of 3:2. The aspect ratio is the width divided by the height of an image and is usually expressed as two integers. For example, width/height = 1.5 is expressed as width:height = 3:2.

White Balance

White balance is the process of removing unrealistic color casts so that objects appearing white in person appear white in a photograph. Camera white balance takes into account the "color temperature" of a light source, which is the relative warmth or coolness of white light. Our eyes are good at judging what is white under different light sources; however, digital cameras often have difficulty with auto white balance. With a digital camera, the user can pick the *white balance* to suit the light source, so that white looks white, not yellow or blue. Normally, a camera automatically determines the white balance

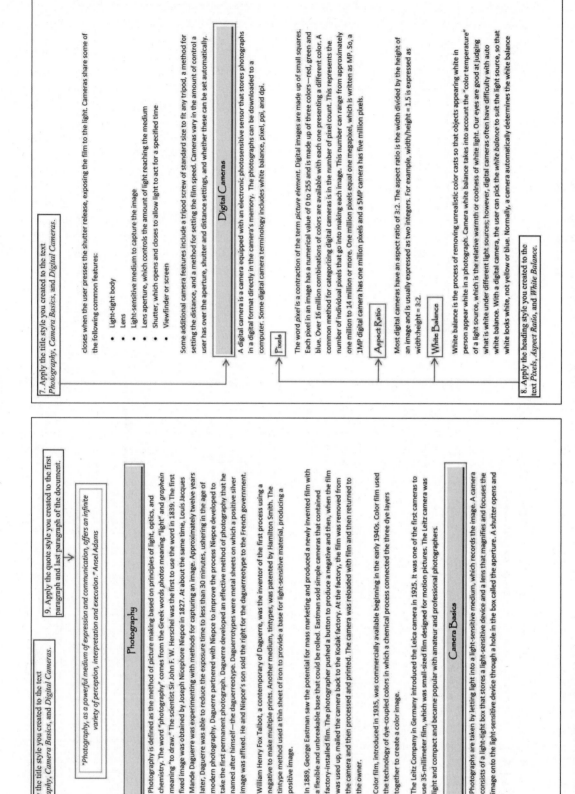

"Photography, as a powerful medium of expression and communication, offers an infinite variety of perception, interpretation and execution." Ansel Adams

Photography

Photography is defined as the method of picture making based on principles of light, optics, and chemistry. The word "photography" comes from the Greek words *photos* meaning "light" and *graphein* meaning "to draw." The scientist Sir John F. W. Herschel was the first to use the word in 1839. The first fixed image was obtained by Joseph Nicephore Niepce in 1827. At about the same time, Louis Jacques Mande Daguerre was experimenting with methods for capturing an image. Approximately twelve years later, Daguerre was able to reduce the exposure time to less than 30 minutes, ushering in the age of modern photography. Daguerre partnered with Niepce to improve the process Niepce developed to take the first permanent photograph. Daguerre developed an effective method of photography that he named after himself—the daguerreotype. Daguerreotypes were metal sheets on which a positive silver image was affixed. He and Niepce's son sold the right for the daguerreotype to the French government.

William Henry Fox Talbot, a contemporary of Daguerre, was the inventor of the first process using a negative to make multiple prints. Another medium, tintypes, was patented by Hamilton Smith. The tintype method used a thin sheet of iron to provide a base for light-sensitive material, producing a positive image.

In 1889, George Eastman saw the potential for mass marketing and produced a newly invented film with a flexible and unbreakable base that could be rolled. Eastman sold simple cameras that contained factory-installed film. The photographer pushed a button to produce a negative and then, when the film was used up, mailed the camera back to the Kodak factory. At the factory, the film was removed from the camera and then processed and printed. The camera was reloaded with film and then returned to the owner.

Color film, introduced in 1935, was commercially available beginning in the early 1940s. Color film used the technology of dye-coupled colors in which a chemical process connected the three dye layers together to create a color image.

The Leitz Company in Germany introduced the Leica camera in 1925. It was one of the first cameras to use 35-millimeter film, which was small-sized film designed for motion pictures. The Leitz camera was light and compact and became popular with amateur and professional photographers.

Camera Basics

Photographs are taken by letting light into a light-sensitive medium, which records the image. A camera consists of a light-tight box that stores a light-sensitive device and a lens that magnifies and focuses the image onto the light-sensitive device through a hole in the box called the aperture. A shutter opens and

14. At a blank document, create a table style for Real Photography. (You determine the name and formatting.) Save the document and name it **C24-A05-TableStyle**.

15. Open the Manage Styles dialog box from the Styles task pane and display the Organizer dialog box. Copy the table style you created to the **XXX-RPStyles.dotx** template and then close the document.

July Weekly Invoices

18. Apply your title style to the text *July Weekly Invoices*, apply your heading style to the four headings, and apply your table style to the four tables.

Week Ending August 7

Invoice #	Client #	Service	Date	Amount
1010	10-788	Family Portraits	08/04/2015	$450.00
1011	11-279	Wedding Portraits	08/05/2015	$995.00
1012	11-279	Development	08/06/2015	$225.00
1013	11-279	Development	08/06/2015	$225.00

Week Ending August 14

Invoice #	Client #	Service	Date	Amount
1014	04-325	Sports Pictures	08/11/2015	$750.00
1015	06-411	Studio Sitting Fee	08/12/2015	$150.00
1016	02-988	Senior Portraits	08/12/2015	$875.00
1017	04-325	Development	08/13/2015	$200.00
1018	10-788	Portraits	08/14/2015	$175.00

Week Ending August 21

Invoice #	Client #	Service	Date	Amount
1019	11-005	Studio Sitting Fee	08/17/2015	$150.00
1020	11-279	Development	08/18/2015	$275.00
1021	04-325	Development	08/19/2015	$125.00
1022	38-539	Consultation	08/20/2015	$100.00

Week Ending August 28

Invoice #	Client #	Service	Date	Amount
1023	11-005	Development	08/25/2015	$250.00
1024	20-549	Wedding Deposit	08/25/2015	$350.00
1025	11-279	Development	08/26/2015	$400.00
1026	10-586	Business Pictures	08/27/2015	$225.00
1027	02-988	Development	08/28/2015	$175.00

16. Create a document based on the **XXX-RPStyles.dotx** template.

17. Insert the document named **RPTables.docx**.

19. Save the document and name it **C24-A05-RPTables**.

20. Make sure all of the tables display on one page. You may need to delete blank lines between headings and tables or remove blank lines at the end of the document.

21. Print and then close **C24-A05-RPTables.docx**.

22. At a blank document, delete the style set you created.

C24-A05-RPTables.docx

---

setting to use. Most digital cameras have settings for sunlight, shade, electronic flash, fluorescent lighting, and tungsten lighting. Some have a *manual* or custom setting where the user points the camera at a white card and lets the camera figure out what setting to use to make it white.

> "Photography can never grow up if it imitates some other medium. It has to walk alone; it has to be itself." Berenice Abbott

9. Apply the quote style you created to the first paragraph and last paragraph of the document.

1. Open **RPLtrhd.docx** and save the document with the name **C24-A05-RPStyles**.

2. Looking at the letterhead font and colors, create a title style, heading style, and quote style. You determine the formatting and names of the styles.

3. Save the styles in a style set and name it *XXXRPPhoto* (using your initials in place of the *XXX*).

4. Save and then close **C24-A05-RPStyles.docx**.

5. Open **RPReport.docx** and save the document with the name **C24-A05-RPReport**.

6. Apply the *XXXRPPhoto* style set.

10. Save and then print **C24-A05-RPReport.docx** and then select all of the report content and delete it.

11. Save **C24-A05-RPReport.docx** as a template in the Custom Office Templates folder and name it **XXX-RPStyles** (using your initials in place of the *XXX*).

12. Close the template.

Chapter 25 Assessment Annotated Model Answers

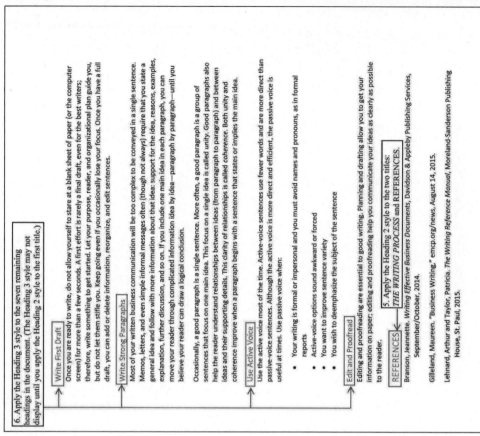

6. Apply the Heading 3 style to the seven remaining headings in the document. (The Heading 3 style may not display until you apply the Heading 2 style to the first title.)

5. Apply the Heading 2 style to the two titles: *THE WRITING PROCESS* and REFERENCES.

THE WRITING PROCESS

An effective letter or memo does not simply appear on your paper or computer screen. Instead, it begins to take shape when you think carefully about the situation within which you must write, when you define your purpose for writing. It continues to develop as you consider your reader, the information you must communicate, and the way in which you plan to present that information. Finally, a document that communicates clearly is the result of good writing and good rewriting; you can usually improve anything you have written. This document represents a process for approaching any writing task.

Define Purpose

Knowing your purpose for writing is the foundation for any written project. Before you begin writing your memo, letter, or other document, ask yourself the following questions:

- What am I trying to accomplish?
- What is my purpose for writing?
- To request information or products?
- To respond to a question or request?
- To persuade someone?
- To direct someone?

Identify Reader

As you define your purpose, you will need to develop a good picture of the person who will be reading your document. Ask yourself:

- Who is my reader?
- What do I know about my reader that will help determine the best approach?
- Is the audience one person or a group?
- Is my reader a coworker, a subordinate, a superior, or a customer?
- How is the reader likely to feel about my message?

Select and Organize Information

Once you have defined your purpose and identified your reader, decide what information you will include. Ask yourself questions such as:

- What does my reader want or need to know?
- What information must I include?
- What information will help my reader respond positively?
- What information should I not include?

To answer these questions, you may find it helpful to spend a few minutes listing all the information you could include in your document. You may also find it helpful to write a rough draft of your document. Write the draft quickly, including any information that comes to you. Once you have it all on paper, you can work with it, deciding what to include and what to leave out.

1. Open **WritingProcess.docx** and save the document with the name **C25-A01- WritingProcess.**
2. Display the Restrict Editing task pane and then restrict formatting to Heading 2 and Heading 3 styles. (At the message that displays asking if you want to remove formatting or styles that are not allowed, click No.)
3. Enforce the protection and provide the password *writing.*
4. Click the Available styles hyperlink in the Restrict Editing task pane.
7. Close the Styles task pane and then close the Restrict Editing task pane.
8. Save the document and then print only page 1.

6. Apply the Heading 3 style to the seven remaining headings in the document. (The Heading 3 style may not display until you apply the Heading 2 style to the first title.)

Write First Draft

Once you are ready to write, do not allow yourself to stare at a blank sheet of paper (or the computer screen) for more than a few seconds. A first effort is rarely a final draft, even for the best writers; therefore, write something to get started. Let your purpose, reader, and organizational plan guide you, but do not let them stifle you. Keep going even if you occasionally lose your focus. Once you have a full draft, you can add or delete information, reorganize, and edit sentences.

Write Strong Paragraphs

Most of your written business communication will be too complex to be conveyed in a single sentence. Memos, letters, and even simple informal messages often (though not always) require that you state a general idea and follow with more information about that idea: support for the idea, reasons, examples, explanation, further discussion, and so on. If you include one main idea in each paragraph, you can move your reader through complicated information idea by idea—paragraph by paragraph—until you believe your reader can draw a logical conclusion.

Occasionally, a good paragraph is a single sentence. More often, a good paragraph is a group of sentences that focus on one main idea. This focus on a single idea is called *unity*. Good paragraphs also help the reader understand relationships between ideas (from paragraph to paragraph) and between ideas and their supporting details. This clarity of relationships is called *coherence*. Both unity and coherence improve when a paragraph begins with a sentence that states or implies the main idea.

Use Active Voice

Use the active voice most of the time. Active-voice sentences use fewer words and are more direct than passive-voice sentences. Although the active voice is more direct and efficient, the passive voice is useful at times. Use passive voice when:

- Your writing is formal or impersonal and you must avoid names and pronouns, as in formal reports
- Active-voice options sound awkward or forced
- You want to improve sentence variety
- You wish to deemphasize the subject of the sentence

Edit and Proofread

Editing and proofreading are essential to good writing. Planning and drafting allow you to get your information on paper; editing and proofreading help you communicate your ideas as clearly as possible to the reader.

5. Apply the Heading 2 style to the two titles: *THE WRITING PROCESS* and REFERENCES.

REFERENCES

Branson, Jeannette. *Writing Effective Business Documents,* Davidson & Appleby Publishing Services, September/October, 2014.

Gilleland, Maureen. "Business Writing." emcp.org/news, August 14, 2015.

Lenhard, Arthur and Taylor, Patricia. *The Writing Reference Manual,* Moreland-Sanderson Publishing House, St. Paul, 2015.

9. Run the compatibility checker to determine what features are not supported by earlier versions of Word.
10. Save the document in the *Word 97-2003 Document (*.doc)* format and name it **C25-A03-Presentation-2003format.**

Delivering a How-To Presentation

Knowing how to give a *how-to*, or *process*, presentation is one of the most useful things you can learn about speaking. Giving clear directions is important not only in the classroom but also in the world of work. Many people's jobs involve giving this type of presentation, for example, to train new employees or to demonstrate a product to potential buyers. When you create a set of directions for others to follow, think through the process carefully. Make certain the steps you provide are complete, accurate, and in the proper sequence.

Choose a Suitable Topic

The topic you choose for your how-to presentation should be one you are familiar with or can learn about easily. Also keep in mind your listeners' interests. Try to select a process that will appeal to the audience. Processes you might explain include the following:

- Getting a driver's license
- Cooking a favorite food
- Working as a volunteer
- Finding an internship
- Applying for financial aid

Develop Well-Organized Directions

Begin by arranging the major steps of the process in logical order. Then give the details needed to complete each step. Be sure to specify the materials needed and carefully explain the tasks involved. Follow these guidelines:

- Use transitional words such as *first*, *second*, and *next* to help readers keep track of the steps of the process. Using transitional words also will help you keep your place in the presentation.
- Before you move from one step to the next step, be sure your listeners have understood what you have described. If they look confused, review what you have said or ask if they need clarification.
- Use visual aids in your presentation so you can demonstrate the process while you describe it. Doing so will make your presentation more interesting to listeners and also may help calm your nerves. To ensure audience members will be able to see what you are doing, use large photographs and diagrams or an oversized model.

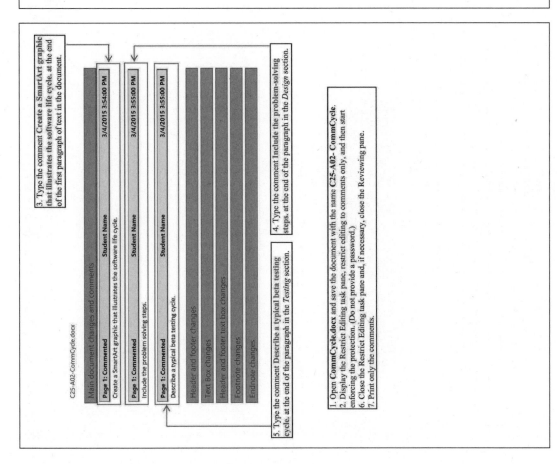

3. Type the comment **Create a SmartArt graphic that illustrates the software life cycle.** at the end of the first paragraph of text in the document.

C25-A02-CommCycle.docx

Main document changes and comments

| Page 1: Commented | Student Name | 3/4/2015 3:54:00 PM |

Create a SmartArt graphic that illustrates the software life cycle.

| Page 1: Commented | Student Name | 3/4/2015 3:55:00 PM |

Include the problem solving steps.

| Page 1: Commented | Student Name | 3/4/2015 3:55:00 PM |

Describe a typical beta testing cycle.

Header and footer changes

Text Box changes

Header and footer text box changes

Footnote changes

Endnote changes

4. Type the comment **Include the problem-solving steps.** at the end of the paragraph in the *Design* section.

5. Type the comment **Describe a typical beta testing cycle.** at the end of the paragraph in the *Testing* section.

1. Open **CommCycle.docx** and save the document with the name **C25-A02- CommCycle.**
2. Display the Restrict Editing task pane, restrict editing to comments only, and then start enforcing the protection. (Do not provide a password.)
6. Close the Restrict Editing task pane and, if necessary, close the Reviewing pane.
7. Print only the comments.

C25-A02-CommCycle(Comments).docx

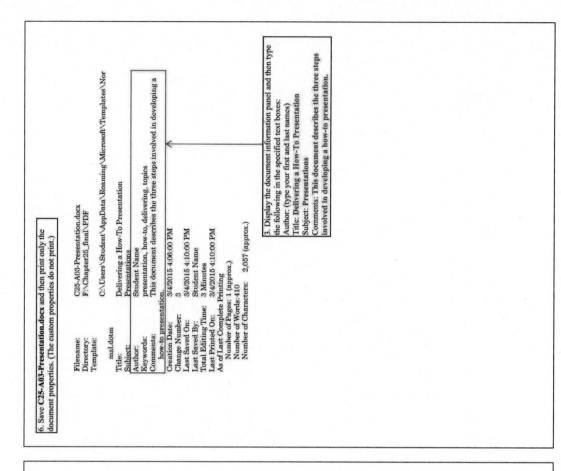

6. Save **C25-A03-Presentation.docx** and then print only the document properties. (The custom properties do not print.)

Filename: C25-A03-Presentation.docx
Directory: F:\Chapter25_final\PDF
Template: C:\Users\Student\AppData\Roaming\Microsoft\Templates\Nor
mal.dotm
Title: Delivering a How-To Presentation
Subject: Presentations
Author: Student Name
Keywords: presentation, how-to, delivering, topics
Comments: This document describes the three steps involved in developing a
how-to presentation.
Creation Date: 3/4/2015 4:06:00 PM
Change Number: 3
Last Saved On: 3/4/2015 4:10:00 PM
Last Saved By: Student Name
Total Editing Time: 3 Minutes
Last Printed On: 3/4/2015 4:10:00 PM
As of Last Complete Printing
  Number of Pages: 1 (approx.)
  Number of Words: 410
  Number of Characters: 2,057 (approx.)

3. Display the document information panel and then type the following in the specified text boxes:
Author: (type your first and last names)
Title: **Delivering a How-To Presentation**
Subject: **Presentations**
Comments: **This document describes the three steps involved in developing a how-to presentation.**

C25-A03-Presentation(Properties).docx

Practice Your Delivery

Assemble all the materials, including your visual aids. Plan how to arrange and use them in the location where you will be speaking. Also consider how to arrange the setting so your listeners can see and hear your presentation. Spend time practicing your presentation in front of one or two friends or family members, and ask them to provide feedback on both your content and delivery. In particular, verify whether they can follow the steps you present in explaining your process.

Choose a topic → Develop directions → Practice delivery

C25-A03-Presentation-2003format.doc (page 2 of 2)

2b. Apply the Heading 2 style to the three headings in the document.

Practice Your Delivery

Assemble all the materials, including your visual aids. Plan how to arrange and use them in the location where you will be speaking. Also consider how to arrange the setting so your listeners can see and hear your presentation. Spend time practicing your presentation in front of one or two friends or family members, and ask them to provide feedback on both your content and delivery. In particular, verify whether they can follow the steps you present in explaining your process.

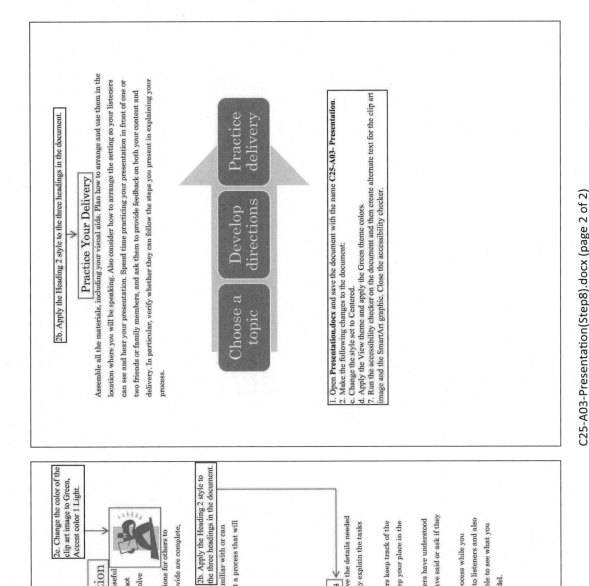

1. Open **Presentation.docx** and save the document with the name **C25-A03- Presentation.**
2. Make the following changes to the document:
c. Change the style set to Centered.
d. Apply the View theme and apply the Green theme colors.
7. Run the accessibility checker on the document and then create alternate text for the clip art image and the SmartArt graphic. Close the accessibility checker.

C25-A03-Presentation(Step8).docx (page 2 of 2)

2c. Change the color of the clip art image to Green, Accent color 1 Light.

2a. Apply the Heading 1 style to the title *Delivering a How-To Presentation.*

Delivering a How-To Presentation

Knowing how to give a *how-to*, or *process*, presentation is one of the most useful things you can learn about speaking. Giving clear directions is important not only in the classroom but also in the world of work. Many people's jobs involve giving this type of presentation, for example, to train new employees or to demonstrate a product to potential buyers. When you create a set of directions for others to follow, think through the process carefully. Make certain the steps you provide are complete, accurate, and in the proper sequence.

2b. Apply the Heading 2 style to the three headings in the document.

Choose a Suitable Topic

The topic you choose for your how-to presentation should be one you are familiar with or can learn about easily. Also keep in mind your listeners' interests. Try to select a process that will appeal to the audience. Processes you might explain include the following:

- Getting a driver's license
- Cooking a favorite food
- Working as a volunteer
- Finding an internship
- Applying for financial aid

Develop Well-Organized Directions

Begin by arranging the major steps of the process in logical order. Then give the details needed to complete each step. Be sure to specify the materials needed and carefully explain the tasks involved. Follow these guidelines:

- Use transitional words such as *first, second,* and *next* to help readers keep track of the steps of the process. Using transitional words also will help you keep your place in the presentation.
- Before you move from one step to the next step, be sure your listeners have understood what you have described. If they look confused, review what you have said or ask if they need clarification.
- Use visual aids in your presentation so you can demonstrate the process while you describe it. Doing so will make your presentation more interesting to listeners and also may help calm your nerves. To ensure audience members will be able to see what you are doing, use large photographs and diagrams or an oversized model.

C25-A03-Presentation(Step8).docx (page 1 of 2)

Using Signature Lines

How to Create Signature Lines

Create a signature line by placing your insertion point where you want the feature. Click the INSERT tab, click the Signature Line button, and then choose Microsoft Office Signature Line.

How to Sign a Signature Line

To sign a signature line, right-click in the signature line box and choose *Sign* from the menu. Type your name or insert an image of your written signature.

How to Remove Signature Lines

To remove a signature line, right-click the signature line box and choose *Remove Signature* from the menu. Confirm the removal by clicking Yes at the dialog box that displays.

Adding Invisible Digital Signatures

Invisible digital signatures can be added from the Info backstage area. Click the Protect Document button and click *Add a Digital Signature* from the drop-down menu. Click OK to the pop-up message and type the purpose for signing in the appropriate Sign box. Click Sign.

---

1. The Text group on the INSERT tab contains a Signature Line button for inserting a signature in a document. Use Word's Help feature to learn about inserting and removing a signature by typing add or remove a digital signature at the Word Help window and then clicking the Add or remove a digital signature in Office files hyperlink. Read the information in the article and then prepare a Word document with the following information:

- An appropriate title
- How to create a signature line in Word
- How to sign a signature line in Word
- How to remove a signature from Word
- How to add an invisible digital signature in Word

2. Apply formatting to enhance the appearance of the document.

C25-A04-Signature.docx

---

5. At the document, complete the following steps:
a. Close the document information panel.
b. Press Ctrl + N to open a blank document.
c. Click the Paste button to insert the screen capture image.

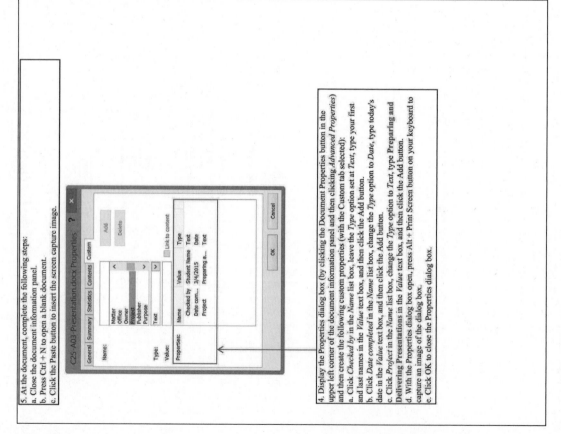

4. Display the Properties dialog box (by clicking the Document Properties button in the upper left corner of the document information panel and then clicking *Advanced Properties*) and then create the following custom properties (with the Custom tab selected):
a. Click *Checked by* in the *Name* list box, leave the *Type* option set at *Text*, type your first and last names in the *Value* text box, and then click the Add button.
b. Click *Date completed* in the *Name* list box, change the *Type* option to *Date*, type today's date in the *Value* text box, and then click the Add button.
c. Click *Project* in the *Name* list box, change the *Type* option to *Text*, type Preparing and Delivering Presentations in the *Value* text box, and then click the Add button.
d. With the Properties dialog box open, press Alt + Print Screen button on your keyboard to capture an image of the dialog box.
e. Click OK to close the Properties dialog box.

C25-A03-Step5_PrintScreen.docx

278   *Signature Word 2013*   Model Answers

Support Stage

A system goes into the support stage after it has been accepted and approved. A support contract normally allows users to contact the systems house for technical support, training, and sometimes on-site troubleshooting. Even if the system was designed in-house, the responsible department often operates as an independent entity—sometimes even charging the department acquiring the system. The support stage continues until a new information system is proposed and developed, usually years later. At that point, the existing system is retired and no longer used.

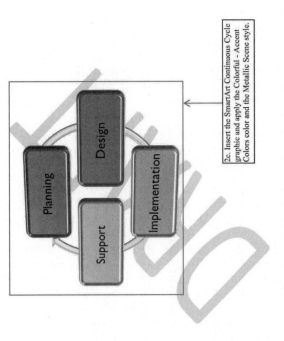

2c. Insert the SmartArt Continuous Cycle graphic and apply the Colorful – Accent Colors color and the Metallic Scene style.

6. Inspect the document and remove any hidden text.
7. Run the accessibility checker and then create alternate text for the clip art image.
8. Save **C25-A05-InfoSystem.docx**.
9. Run the compatibility checker to determine what features are not supported by earlier versions of Word.

STUDENT NAME 2

---

1. Open **InfoSystem.docx** and save the document with the name **C25-A05-InfoSystem**.
2. Format the document so it appears as shown in Figure 25.13 with the following specifications:
a. Apply the Lines (Stylish) style set and then apply the Dividend theme.
c. Make any other changes necessary so your document displays as shown in Figure 25.13.

Developing an Information System

Identifying and assembling a team of employees with the required skills and expertise is a necessary first step in developing a new in-house information system. A management group may be involved in answering questions and providing information in the early planning phases of the project, but programmers and/or software engineers handle the design and implementation of any new system.

Programmers specialize in the development of new software, while software engineers are highly skilled professionals with programming and teamwork training. Their organized, professional application of the software development process is called software engineering.

Project Plan

The first step in the system development life cycle is planning. The planning step involves preparing a needs analysis and conducting feasibility studies. During this step, a company usually establishes a project team, and the team creates a project plan. The project plan includes an estimate of how long the project will take to complete, an outline of the steps involved, and a list of deliverables. Deliverables are documents, services, hardware, and software that must be finished and delivered by a certain time and date.

Project Team

Because of their large size, information systems require the creation of a project team. A project team usually includes a project manager, who acts as the team leader. Sometimes the project manager also functions as a systems analyst, responsible for completing the systems analysis and making design recommendations. Other project team members include software engineers and technicians. The software engineers deal with programming software, while technicians handle hardware issues. The comprehensive process software engineers initiate is called the system development life cycle (SDLC), a series of steps culminating in a completed information system.

2d. Recolor the clip art image as shown in the figure.

Designing the System

A project is ready to move into the design stage once the project team has approved the plan, including the budget. The design process begins with the writing of the documentation, which covers functional and design specifications. In most cases, the project team creates the functional specifications, describing what the system must be able to do.

Implementation

The project can move into the next phase, implementation, once the development team and the systems house develop the design specification and approve the plans. This step is where the actual work of putting the system together is completed, including creating a prototype and completing the programming. In most cases, implementing the new system is the longest, most difficult step in the process.

2b. Insert the Integral footer and type your name as the author.

STUDENT NAME 1

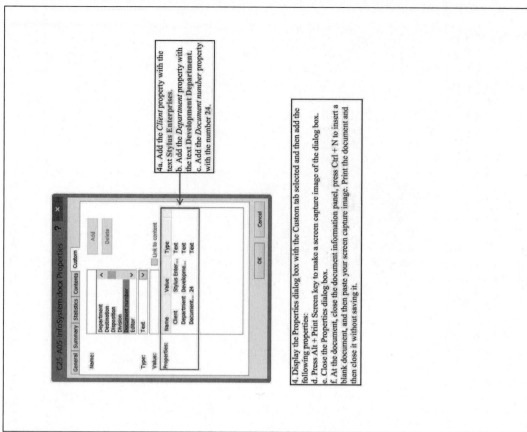

4a. Add the *Client* property with the text Stylus Enterprises.
b. Add the *Department* property with the text Development Department.
c. Add the *Document number* property with the number 24.

4. Display the Properties dialog box with the Custom tab selected and then add the following properties:
d. Press Alt + Print Screen key to make a screen capture image of the dialog box.
e. Close the Properties dialog box.
f. At the document, close the document information panel, press Ctrl + N to insert a blank document, and then paste your screen capture image. Print the document and then close it without saving it.

C25-A05-Step4_PrintScreen.docx

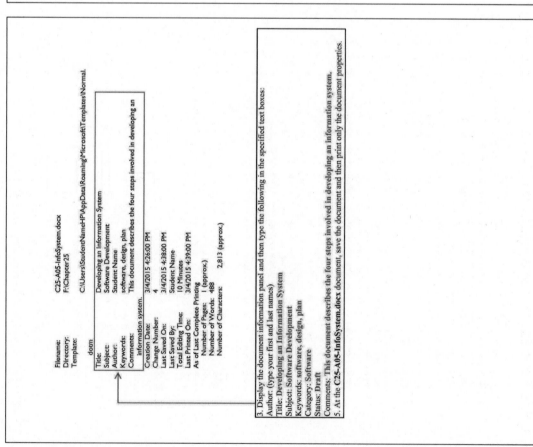

3. Display the document information panel and then type the following in the specified text boxes:
Author: (type your first and last names)
Title: Developing an Information System
Subject: Software Development
Keywords: software, design, plan
Category: Software
Status: Draft
Comments: This document describes the four steps involved in developing an information system.
5. At the **C25-A05-InfoSystem.docx** document, save the document and then print only the document properties.

C25-A05-InfoSystem(Step5,Properties).docx

Unit 5 Performance Assessment Annotated Model Answers

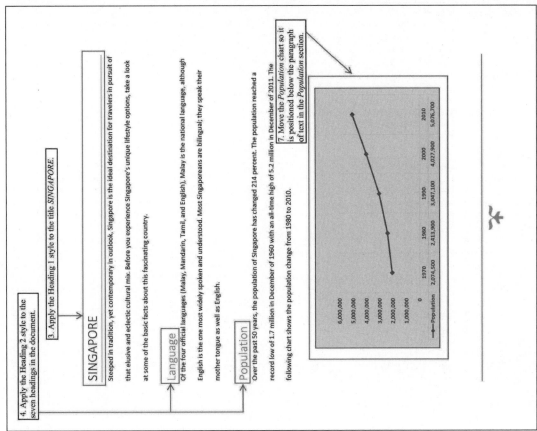

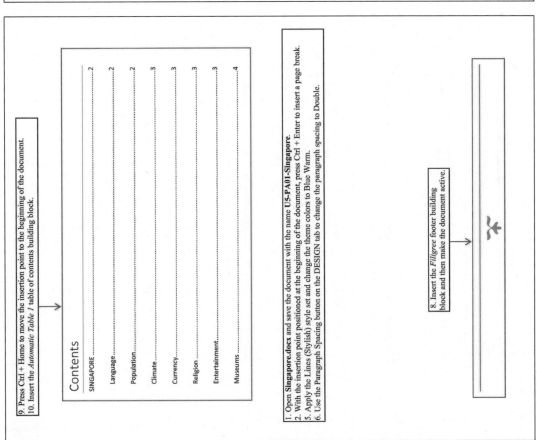

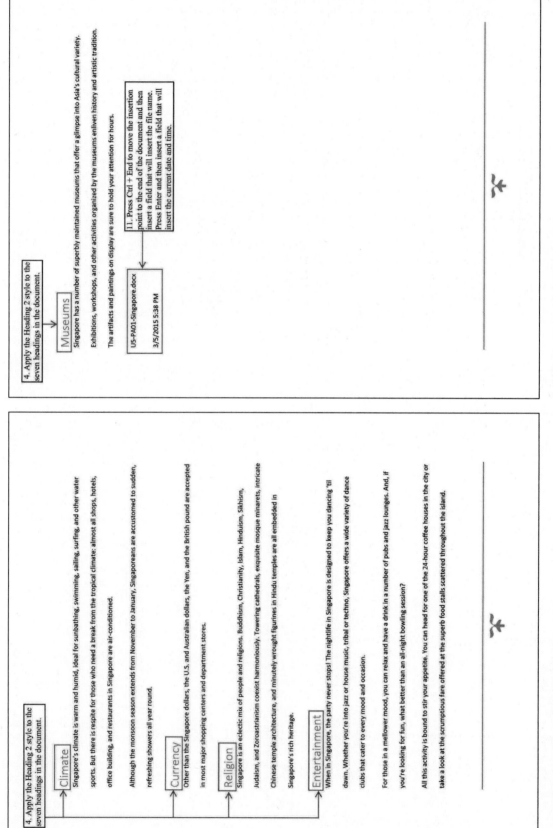

4. Apply the Heading 2 style to the seven headings in the document.

Museums

Singapore has a number of superbly maintained museums that offer a glimpse into Asia's cultural variety.

Exhibitions, workshops, and other activities organized by the museums enliven history and artistic tradition.

The artifacts and paintings on display are sure to hold your attention for hours.

U5-PA01-Singapore.docx

3/5/2015 5:38 PM

11. Press Ctrl + End to move the insertion point to the end of the document and then insert a field that will insert the file name. Press Enter and then insert a field that will insert the current date and time.

U5-PA01-Singapore.docx (page 4 of 4)

---

4. Apply the Heading 2 style to the seven headings in the document.

Climate

Singapore's climate is warm and humid, ideal for sunbathing, swimming, sailing, surfing, and other water sports. But there is respite for those who need a break from the tropical climate: almost all shops, hotels, office building, and restaurants in Singapore are air-conditioned.

Although the monsoon season extends from November to January, Singaporeans are accustomed to sudden, refreshing showers all year round.

Currency

Other than the Singapore dollars, the U.S. and Australian dollars, the Yen, and the British pound are accepted in most major shopping centers and department stores.

Religion

Singapore is an eclectic mix of people and religions. Buddhism, Christianity, Islam, Hinduism, Sikhism, Judaism, and Zoroastrianism coexist harmoniously. Towering cathedrals, exquisite mosque minarets, intricate Chinese temple architecture, and minutely wrought figurines in Hindu temples are all embedded in Singapore's rich heritage.

Entertainment

When in Singapore, the party never stops! The nightlife in Singapore is designed to keep you dancing 'til dawn. Whether you're into jazz or house music, tribal or techno, Singapore offers a wide variety of dance clubs that cater to every mood and occasion.

For those in a mellower mood, you can relax and have a drink in a number of pubs and jazz lounges. And, if you're looking for fun, what better than an all-night bowling session?

All this activity is bound to stir your appetite. You can head for one of the 24-hour coffee houses in the city or take a look at the scrumptious fare offered at the superb food stalls scattered throughout the island.

U5-PA01-Singapore.docx (page 3 of 4)

Signature Word 2013   Model Answers

Tennison Rental Company

Council Bluffs Location

11a. Insert as a page header the custom building block that is named with your initials followed by *TRC-CBLrhd*. **Hint: To do this, click the *Quick Parts* button on the *Quick Access toolbar*, right-click the custom building block, and then click the Insert at Page Header option.**

Current Date

1. Open **TRC-CBFooter.docx.**
2. Select the entire document, save the selected text in a custom building block with your initials followed by *TRC-CBFooter.*
3. Close **TRC-CBFooter.docx.**
4. Open **TRC-CBLrhd.docx.**
5. Select the entire document, save the selected text in a custom building block with your initials followed by *TRC-CBLrhd.*
6. Close **TRC-CBLrhd.docx.**

Mr. Harold Nesbitt
Nesbitt Construction
3102 South 32nd Street
Council Bluffs, IA 51053

Dear Mr. Nesbitt:

Thank you for your interest in renting equipment from our company, Tennison Rental Company. We pride ourselves on maintaining the most extensive and well-maintained equipment in the greater Nebraska-Iowa region.

We carry a variety of earth-moving equipment for heavy construction including backhoes, dozers, excavators (including hydraulic excavators and mini-excavators), skid-steer loaders (including compact skid-steer, track skid-steer, and wheeled skid-steer loaders), tractors, cable locators, trenchers (including ride-on and walk-behind trenchers), and wheel loaders.

Come to our Council Bluffs site or visit our Omaha location and check out our inventory of earth-moving equipment. We are confident that we have the machinery you need.

Sincerely,

Kelsey Sanderson
General Manager

xx
U5-PA02-TRC-CBLtr.docx

7. At a blank document, click the *No Spacing* style in the Styles group on the Home tab and then type the following text: We carry a variety of earth-moving equipment for heavy construction including backhoes, dozers, excavators (including hydraulic excavators and mini-excavators), skid-steer loaders (including compact skid-steer, track skid-steer, and wheeled skid-steer loaders), tractors, cable locators, trenchers (including ride-on and walk-behind trenchers), and wheel loaders.

8. Select the entire document, save the selected text in a custom building block in the *Quick Part* gallery, and name the building block with your initials followed by *TRC-CBEquipPara.*

11c. Insert the custom building block that is named with your initials followed by *TRC-CBEquipPara.*

9. Save each custom building block in the *Quick Part* gallery as a Quick Parts button on the Quick Access toolbar.
10. Close the document without saving it.
11. At a blank document, click the *No Spacing* style and then create the business letter shown in Figure U5.1 with the following specifications:
d. Type the remaining text in the letter.

11e. Insert as a page footer the custom building block that is named with your initials followed by *TRCC-CBFooter*. **Hint: Refer to Step 11a.**

4410 West Broadway ✕ Council Bluffs, IA 51052 ✕ 712.555.8800

U5-PA02-TRC-CBLtr.docx

---

15. Click the Quick Parts button on the Quick Access toolbar, press the Print Screen button on your keyboard, and then click in the document.

14. Press Ctrl + N to open a new blank document.
16. At the blank document, click the Paste button. (This pastes the screen capture into your document.)
17. Print the document and then close it without saving it.
18. Remove the Quick Parts button from the Quick Access toolbar and then delete your custom building blocks.

U5-PA02-PrintScreen(Step17).docx

9. Apply the Heading 1 style to the title *Construction Equipment Rental Agreement* and apply the Heading 2 style to the headings in the document (*Lease, Rent, Use and Operation of Equipment, Insurance, Risk of Loss, Maintenance, Return of Equipment, Warranties of Lessee, Default,* and *Further Assurances*).

6. Search for all occurrences of *rc* and replace them with *Tennison Rental Company*.

7. Add the following text to AutoCorrect:
a. Insert *trc* in the *Replace* text box and insert *Tennison Rental Company* in the *With* text box.

13. Center the title and change the spacing after the title to 12 points.

Construction Equipment Rental Agreement

A Construction Equipment Rental Agreement entered into this ___ day of _____, 20__ by and between Tennison Rental Company and _____ ("Lessee").

Lessee desires to lease from Tennison Rental Company and Tennison Rental Company desires to lease to Lessee all the items of equipment and personal property described in Exhibit A on the terms and conditions stated herein.

Therefore, in consideration of the premises and mutual covenants and agreements set forth herein, the parties agree as follows:

Lease

Tennison Rental Company leases to Lessee and Lessee rents from Tennison Rental Company the Equipment from the date of this Construction Equipment Rental Agreement to _____ (the "Term").

Rent

The rent for the leasing of the Equipment ("Rental") shall be $____ per month, payable in advance on the first day of each month during the term, except that the Rental for the month of ____ shall be an appropriate fraction of the monthly Rental and shall be payable on the date of execution of this Construction Equipment Rental Agreement. Rentals and any and all other payments due Tennison Rental Company shall be paid to Tennison Rental Company at Tennison Rental Company's office at ____.

Use and Operation of Equipment

Lessee agrees that it will use the Equipment in accordance with this Construction Equipment Rental Agreement, provided that any such use is in conformity with all applicable laws and regulations, any insurance policies, and any warranties of the manufacturer and any maintenance agreements with respect to the Equipment. Lessee shall not permit anyone other than its authorized agents or employees to operate the Equipment.

Insurance

Lessee will, at its own expense, insure the Equipment at all times against all hazards requested by Tennison Rental Company including, but not limited to, fire, theft and extended coverage insurance, and such policies shall be payable to Tennison Rental Company as its interest may appear. Such policies of insurance shall be reasonably satisfactory to Tennison Rental Company as to form, amount and insurer, and shall provide for at least ten days written notice of cancellation to Tennison Rental Company. Lessee shall furnish certificates, policies or endorsements to Tennison Rental Company as proof of such insurance.

Risk of Loss

Lessee assumes all risk of loss, damage, theft or destruction of the Equipment. No loss, damage, theft or destruction of the Equipment, in whole or in part, shall impair the obligations of Lessee under this Construction Equipment Rental Agreement, all of which shall continue in full force and effect. Lessee, at Tennison Rental Company's option, shall either:

12. Insert the Semaphore footer.

Page 1 of 3

15b. With the Save Current Theme dialog box open, press Alt + Print Screen.

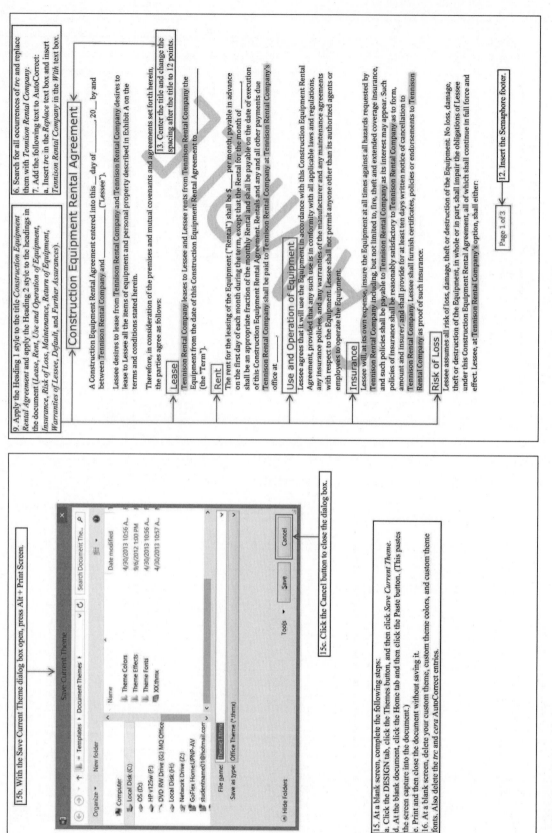

15c. Click the Cancel button to close the dialog box.

15. At a blank screen, complete the following steps:
a. Click the DESIGN tab, click the Themes button, and then click *Save Current Theme.*
d. At the blank document, click the Home tab and then click the Paste button. (This pastes the screen capture into the document.)
e. Print and then close the document without saving it.

16. At a blank screen, delete your custom theme, custom theme colors, and custom theme fonts. Also delete the *trc* and *cera* AutoCorrect entries.

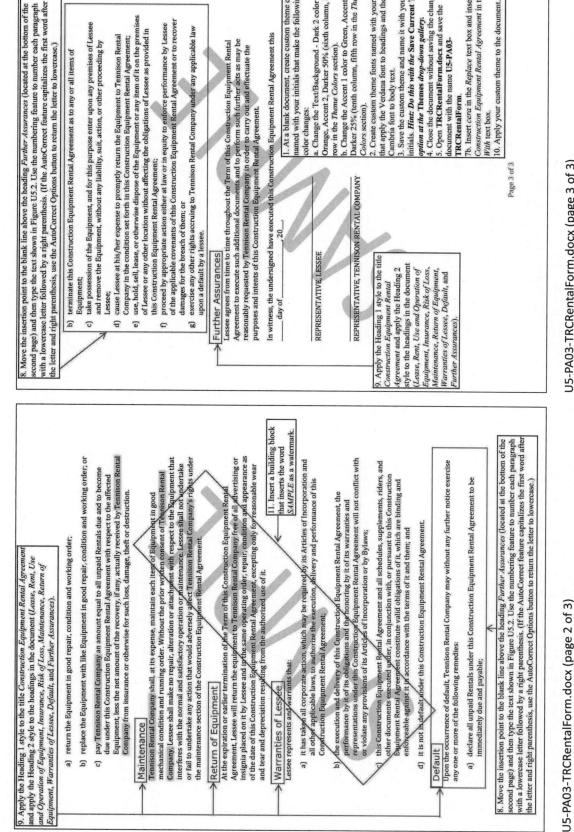

8. Move the insertion point to the blank line above the heading *Further Assurances* (located at the bottom of the second page) and then type the text shown in Figure U5.2. Use the numbering feature to number each paragraph with a lowercase letter followed by a right parenthesis. (If the AutoCorrect feature capitalizes the first word after the letter and right parenthesis, use the AutoCorrect Options button to return the letter to lowercase.)

b) terminate this Construction Equipment Rental Agreement as to any or all items of Equipment;
c) take possession of the Equipment, and for this purpose enter upon any premises of Lessee and remove the Equipment, without any liability, suit, action, or other proceeding by Lessee;
d) cause Lessee at his/her expense to promptly return the Equipment to Tennison Rental Company in the condition set forth in this Construction Equipment Rental Agreement;
e) use, hold, sell, lease, or otherwise dispose of the Equipment or any item of it on the premises of Lessee or any other location without affecting the obligations of Lessee as provided in this Construction Equipment Rental Agreement;
f) proceed by appropriate action either at law or in equity to enforce performance by Lessee of the applicable covenants of this Construction Equipment Rental Agreement or to recover damages for the breach of them; or
g) exercise any other rights accruing to Tennison Rental Company under any applicable law upon a default by a lessee.

Further Assurances

Lessee agrees from time to time throughout the Term of this Construction Equipment Rental Agreement to execute such additional documents and to perform such further acts as may be reasonably requested by Tennison Rental Company in order to carry out and effectuate the purposes and intents of this Construction Equipment Rental Agreement.

In witness, the undersigned have executed this Construction Equipment Rental Agreement this _____ day of _____, 20___.

REPRESENTATIVE, LESSEE

REPRESENTATIVE, TENNISON RENTAL COMPANY

9. Apply the Heading 1 style to the title *Construction Equipment Rental Agreement* and apply the Heading 2 style to the headings in the document (*Lease, Rent, Use and Operation of Equipment, Insurance, Risk of Loss, Maintenance, Return of Equipment, Warranties of Lessee, Default, and Further Assurances*).

1. At a blank document, create custom theme colors named with your initials that make the following color changes:
   a. Change the Text/Background - Dark 2 color to Orange, Accent 2, Darker 50% (sixth column, last row in the *Theme Colors* section).
   b. Change the Accent 1 color to Green, Accent 6, Darker 25% (tenth column, fifth row in the *Theme Colors* section).
2. Create custom theme fonts named with your initials that apply the Verdana font to headings and the Cambria font to body text.
3. Save the custom theme and name it with your initials. *Hint: Do this with the Save Current Theme option at the Themes drop-down gallery.*
4. Close the document without saving the changes.
5. Open **TRCRentalForm.docx** and save the document with the name **U5-PA03-TRCRentalForm**.
7b. Insert *cera* in the *Replace* text box and insert *Construction Equipment Rental Agreement* in the *With* text box.
10. Apply your custom theme to the document.

Page 3 of 3

U5-PA03-TRCRentalForm.docx (page 3 of 3)

---

9. Apply the Heading 1 style to the title *Construction Equipment Rental Agreement* and apply the Heading 2 style to the headings in the document (*Lease, Rent, Use and Operation of Equipment, Insurance, Risk of Loss, Maintenance, Return of Equipment, Warranties of Lessee, Default, and Further Assurances*).

a) return the Equipment in good repair, condition and working order;
b) replace the Equipment with like Equipment in good repair, condition and working order; or
c) pay Tennison Rental Company an amount equal to all unpaid Rentals due and to become due under this Construction Equipment Rental Agreement with respect to the affected Equipment, less the net amount of the recovery, if any, actually received by Tennison Rental Company from insurance or otherwise for such loss, damage, theft or destruction.

Maintenance

Tennison Rental Company shall, at its expense, maintain each item of Equipment in good mechanical condition and running order. Without the prior written consent of Tennison Rental Company, Lessee shall make no repair, alteration or attachment with respect to the Equipment that interferes with the normal and satisfactory operation or maintenance. Lessee shall not undertake or fail to undertake any action that would adversely affect Tennison Rental Company's rights under the maintenance section of the Construction Equipment Rental Agreement.

Return of Equipment

At the expiration or earlier termination of the Term of this Construction Equipment Rental Agreement, Lessee will return the equipment to Tennison Rental Company free of all advertising or insignia placed on it by Lessee and in the same operating order, repair, condition and appearance as of the date of this Construction Equipment Rental Agreement, excepting only for reasonable wear and tear and depreciation resulting from the authorized use of it.

Warranties of Lessee

Lessee represents and warrants that:

a) it has taken all corporate action, which may be required by its Articles of Incorporation and all other applicable laws, to authorize the execution, delivery and performance of this Construction Equipment Rental Agreement;
b) the execution and delivery of this Construction Equipment Rental Agreement, the performance by it of its obligations and the honoring by it of its warranties and representations under this Construction Equipment Rental Agreement will not conflict with or violate any provisions of its Articles of Incorporation or by Bylaws;
c) this Construction Equipment Rental Agreement and all schedules, supplements, riders, and other documents executed under, in conjunction with, or pursuant to this Construction Equipment Rental Agreement constitute valid obligations of it, which are binding and enforceable against it in accordance with the terms of it and them; and
d) it is not in default under this Construction Equipment Rental Agreement.

Default

Upon the occurrence of default, Tennison Rental Company may without any further notice exercise any one or more of the following remedies:

a) declare all unpaid Rentals under this Construction Equipment Rental Agreement to be immediately due and payable;

11. Insert a building block that inserts the word *SAMPLE* as a watermark.

8. Move the insertion point to the blank line above the heading *Further Assurances* (located at the bottom of the second page) and then type the text shown in Figure U5.2. Use the numbering feature to number each paragraph with a lowercase letter followed by a right parenthesis. (If the AutoCorrect feature capitalizes the first word after the letter and right parenthesis, use the AutoCorrect Options button to return the letter to lowercase.)

U5-PA03-TRCRentalForm.docx (page 2 of 3)

Tennison Rental Company

Omaha Location

Business Conduct Code

POLICY STATEMENT

The policy of Tennison Rental Company is to conduct its affairs in accordance with all applicable laws and regulations of the counties in which it does business. The code is designed to promote:

- honest and ethical conduct, including the ethical handling of actual and apparent conflicts of interest between personal and professional relationships;
- compliance with applicable governmental laws, rules, and regulations;
- the prompt reporting to the appropriate person of violations of laws, rules, regulations, and this code and other company policies; and
- accountability for adherence to this code.

Tennison Rental Company promotes ethical behavior and encourages employees to talk to supervisors, managers, or other appropriate personnel when in doubt of the best course of action in a particular situation. Employees should report violations of laws, rules, regulations and policies to appropriate personnel. Employees reporting such violations in good faith will not be subject to retaliation.

APPROVALS AND WAIVERS

Certain provisions of this code require you to act, or refrain from acting, unless prior approval is received from the appropriate person. Employees requesting approval pursuant to this code should request such approval in writing to the Compliance Officer. Other provisions of this code require you to act, or refrain from acting, in a particular manner and do not permit exceptions based on obtaining approval. Waiver of those provisions may only be granted by the Audit Committee, and changes in this code may only be made by the board of directors.

CONFLICTS OF INTEREST

Conflicts of interest are strictly prohibited. A conflict of interest arises any time your personal interests or activities interfere with your ability to act in the best interests of the company. Employees must discharge their responsibilities solely on the basis of what is in the best interest of the company and independent of personal consideration or relationships. Although Tennison Rental Company has no interest in preventing employees from engaging in lawful activities during nonworking hours, employees must make sure that their outside activities do not conflict or interfere with their responsibilities to the company. For example, without approval by the company, a Tennison Rental Company employee generally may not:

- engage in self-employment or perform paid or unpaid work for others in a field of interest similar to Tennison Rental Company;
- use proprietary or confidential company information for personal gain or to the company's detriment;

1002 Tenth Street ✦ Omaha NE 68107 ✆ 402.555.9522

U5-PA04-TRCBusCode.docx (page 1 of 3)

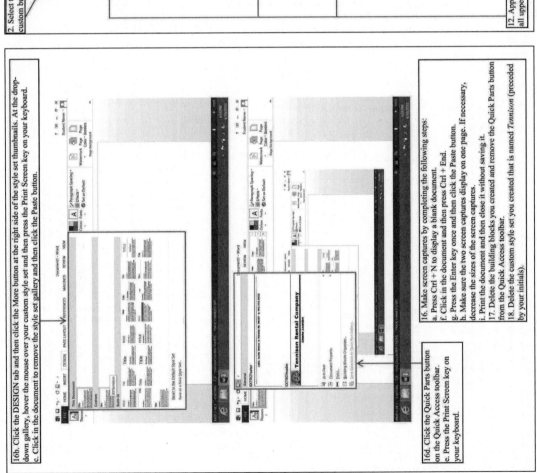

U5-PA04-PrintScreen(Step16).docx

Page 3 of 3

Tennison Rental Company

Omaha Location

13. Insert the *TRCHeader* building block (preceded by your initials) as a

- if a potential customer has a contract with a competitor, or has placed a firm rental order with a competitor, do not try to convince the customer to breach that contract or order; and
- maintaining the company's valuable reputation, compliance with its quality processes and safety requirements is essential.

Suppliers

Suppliers that sell products and services to our company are important to our business. Company employees should always treat suppliers and potential suppliers in accordance with the highest standards of business conduct. Suppliers should be selected on the basis of objective criteria, such as value, price, technical excellence, service reputation, and production/service capacity.

Contracts and Commitments

No employee may enter into any agreement binding Tennison Rental Company without express authorization. The company has instituted contract and signature approval policies, which identify those individuals who have the authority to approve and sign certain contracts. Employees involved in proposals, bid preparations, or contract regulations should strive to ensure that all statements, communications, and representations to prospective customers are truthful and accurate.

FAIR COMPETITION

Fair competition laws limit what Tennison Rental Company can do with another company and what the Tennison Rental Company can do on its own. Generally, the laws are designed to prohibit agreements or actions that reduce competition and hard consumers. You may not enter into agreements or discussions with competitors that have the effect of fixing or controlling prices, dividing and allocating markets or territories, or boycotting suppliers or customers.

INQUIRIES

Questions regarding the policies in this code may be directed to the Compliance Officer. Managers and supervisors provide timely advice and guidance to employees on ethics and compliance concerns and are expected to take a leadership role in promoting ethical business conduct. This code is intended to clarify your existing obligation for proper conduct. The standards and supporting policies and procedures may change from time to time at the company's discretion.

12. Apply your custom title style to the title *Business Conduct Code*; apply your custom Heading 1 style to the headings in all uppercase letters; and apply your custom Heading 2 style to the headings with only the first letter in uppercase.

1. Open **TRCStyles.docx**.
4. Insert each custom building block in the *Quick Part* gallery as a Quick Parts button on the Quick Access toolbar.
8. Save the styles you created as a style set named with your initials followed by *Tennison*.
9. Close **TRCStyles.docx** without saving the changes.
10. Open **TRCBusCode.docx** and save the document with the name U5-PA04- TRCBusCode.
11. Change to the style set named *Tennison* (preceded by your initials).

1002 Tenth Street ✱ Omaha NE 68107 ✱ 402.555.9522

3. Select the horizontal line and the address and telephone number below, save the selected text in a custom building block in the *Quick Part* gallery, and name the building block with your initials followed by *TRCFooter*.

U5-PA04-TRCBusCode.docx (page 3 of 3)

Page 2 of 3

12. Apply your custom title style to the title *Business Conduct Code*; apply your custom Heading 1 style to the headings in all uppercase letters; and apply your custom Heading 2 style to the headings with only the first letter in uppercase.

Tennison Rental Company

Omaha Location

- use company assets or labor for personal use, except for incidental use permitted under the company's policies; or
- acquire any interest in property or assets of any kind for the purpose of selling or leasing it to the company.

7. Select the *Heading 2* text and then create a style named with your initials followed by *TRCHeading2*.

Community Activities

Tennison Rental Company encourages you to be actively involved in your community through volunteer service to charitable, civic, and public service organizations and through participation in the political process and trade associations. Employees must make sure, however, that their service is consistent with their employment with Tennison Rental Company and does not pose a conflict of interest.

Competitor Relationships

Employees must avoid even the appearance of a conflict of interest in their relationships with competitors. Without approval, employees may not:

- provide compensated or uncompensated services to a competitor, except for services rendered under a valid Tennison Rental Company contract with the competitor;
- disclose any company proprietary information to a competitor, unless a nondisclosure agreement is in place; or
- utilize for any unauthorized purposes or disclose to a competitor or other third-party any proprietary data that has been entrusted to the company by a customer or supplier.

6. Select the *Heading 1* text and then create a style named with your initials followed by *TRCHeading1*.

BUSINESS RELATIONSHIPS

Tennison Rental Company seeks to outperform its competition fairly and honestly. The company seeks competitive advantages through superior performance, not unethical or illegal business practices. Each employee should endeavor to deal fairly with the company's customers, suppliers, competitors, and employees and should not take advantage of them through manipulation, concealment, abuse of privileged information, misrepresentation of material facts, or any unfair dealing practices.

Customer Relationships

Our customers are of the utmost important to Tennison Rental Company. Employees should always treat customers and potential customers according to the highest standards of business conduct. Company policy is to market our products and services on their merits and to avoid making disparaging comments about the products and services of competitors unless they can be substantiated. Employees should be careful in commenting upon the character, financial condition, or potential legal or regulatory problems of competitors. Employees should consider the following guidelines when marketing our products and services:

- sell on the strength of our company and our products and services;
- do not make claims about our products or services unless the claims can be made in good faith;

1002 Tenth Street ✱ Omaha NE 68107 ✱ 402.555.9522

14. Insert the *TRCFooter* building block (preceded by your initials) as a footer.

U5-PA04-TRCBusCode.docx (page 2 of 3)

Page 1

> 7b. Apply the NSSHeading1 style to the three headings in the document.

Northland Security Systems

> 1. At a blank screen, create a new tab with the following specifications:
> a. Insert the new tab after the View tab in the list box in the Word Options dialog box with the *Customize Ribbon* option selected.
> b. Rename the tab *NSS* followed by your initials.
> c. Rename the custom group below your new tab as *Building Blocks*.

> 7. Apply the following styles:
> a. Apply the NSSTitle style to the title *Navigating and Searching the Web.*

NAVIGATING AND SEARCHING THE WEB

Since so many people create web pages, the Web should be chaotic. However, underlying systems are in place specifying how pages are organized on the Web and how they are delivered to your computer. This system involves unique addresses used to access each web page, a unique address for each computer, and browser features for locating and retrieving online content.

IPs and URLs

An *Internet Protocol (IP) address* is a series of numbers that uniquely identifies a location on the Internet. An IP address consists of four groups of numbers separated by periods. For example: 225.73.110.102. A nonprofit organization called ICANN keeps track of IP numbers around the world.

Because numbers would be difficult to remember for retrieving pages, we use a text-based address referred to as a *uniform resource locator (URL)* to go to a website. A URL, also called a *web address*, has several parts separated by a colon (:), slashes (/), and dots (.). The first part of a URL is called a *protocol* and identifies a certain way for interpreting computer information in the transmission process. *Http,* which stands for *hypertext transfer protocol,* and *ftp,* for *file transfer protocol,* are examples of protocols. Some sites use a secondary identifier for the type of site being contacted, such as www for *World Wide Web* site, but this is often optional.

The next part of the URL is the *domain name,* which identifies the group of servers (the domain) to which the site belongs and the particular company or organization name. A suffix, such as *.com* or *.edu,* further identifies the domain. For example, the *.com* in the URL http://www.emcp.com is a top-level domain (TLD). Several TLDs exists such as *.com, .net, .org, .edu,* and *.gov.* Table A provides a rundown of TLDs being used today.

Suffix	Type of Organization	Example
biz	business site	Billboard: http://www.billboard.biz
.com	company or commercial site	Intel: http://www.intel.com
.edu	educational institution	Harvard University: http://www.harvard.edu
.gov	government site	Internal Revenue Service: http://www.irs.gov
.int	international organizations endorsed by treaty	World Health Organization: http://www.who.int
.mil	military site	U.S. Department of Defense: http://www.defenselink.mil
.net	administrative site for ISPs	Earthlink: http://www.earthlink.net
.org	nonprofit or private organization	Red Cross: http://www.redcross.org

Navigating and Searching the Web

> 7c. Apply the NSSTable style to the three tables in the document. *Hint: Do this at the Table Tools Design tab.*

U5-PA05-NSSWebRpt(Step10).docx (page 1 of 3)

Page 2

> 7b. Apply the NSSHeading1 style to the three headings in the document.

Browsing Web Pages

You may already be quite comfortable with browsing the Internet, but you may not have pondered how browsers move around the Web and retrieve data. Any element of a web page (text, graphic, audio, or video) can be linked to another page using a hyperlink. A hyperlink describes a destination within a web document and can be inserted in text or a graphical object such as a company logo. Text that is linked is called *hypertext.*

A website is a series of related web pages that are linked together. You get to a website by entering the URL, such as www.amazon.com, in your browser. Every website has a starting page, called the *home page,* which is displayed when you enter the site URL. You can also enter a URL to jump to a specific page on a site, such as the Video-On-Demand page at Amazon's site, www.amazon.com/Video-On-Demand.

Searching for Content Online

A search engine, such as Google.com, Ask.com, and Yahoo.com, catalogs and indexes web pages for you. A type of search engine, called a search directory, can also catalog pages into topics such as *finance, health, news, shopping,* and so on. Search engines may seem to be free services, but in reality they are typically financed by selling advertising. Some also make money by selling information about your online activities and interests to advertisers.

The newest wave of search engines, including Microsoft Bing and Google Squared, not only search for content but also make choices among content to deliver more targeted results. Such search engines allow you, for example, to ask for a list of female tennis stars from 1900, on and they then assemble a table of them for you. Table B shows some common search tools with their URLs and an indication of whether they offer the ability to catalog pages in directories.

Search Tool	URL	Type
Ask	www.ask.com	engine
Bing	www.bing.com	engine
Dogpile	www.dogpile.com	engine
Google	www.google.com	engine/directory
MSN	www.msn.com	engine/directory
Yahoo!	www.yahoo.com	engine/directory

> 9e. Insert the *Title* document property using the Document Property button on your custom tab. (When you insert the document property, it automatically inserts the title you typed earlier.)

So how do search engines work? You can search for information by going to the search engine's website and typing your search text, which is comprised of one or more keywords or keyword phrases. For example, to find information about the international space station, you could type *space station* in the search engine's search text box and press the Enter key. You can narrow your search by specifying that you want to view links to certain types of results such as images, maps, or videos.

You can get more targeted search results by honing your searching technique. Effective searching is a skill that you gain through practice. For example, typing *space station* in a search engine's web page could easily return more than eighty million results. If what you really need is the cost to build the station, consider a more targeted keyword phrase like "space station cost." Search engines provide

> 9f. Double-click in the document to make it active.

Navigating and Searching the Web

> 9. Insert a footer by completing the following steps:
> a. Click the Building Blocks Organizer button in the Building Blocks group on your tab. b. At the Building Blocks Organizer, click the *Name* column heading to sort the building blocks by name. c. Insert the *Blank* column building block and not the *Blank (Three Columns)* footer. (Make sure you insert the *Blank* footer and not the *Blank (Three Columns)* footer.) d. Select and then delete the *[Type here]* placeholder in the footer pane.

> 7c. Apply the NSSTable style to the three tables in the document. *Hint: Do this at the Table Tools Design tab.*

U5-PA05-NSSWebRpt(Step10).docx (page 2 of 3)

Northland Security Systems

I1. Make the following modifications to the styles:
a. Modify the font color of the NSSHeading1 style to Dark Blue.

NAVIGATING AND SEARCHING THE WEB

Since so many people create web pages, the Web should be chaotic. However, underlying systems are in place specifying how pages are organized on the Web and how they are delivered to your computer. This system involves unique addresses used to access each web page, a unique address for each computer, and browser features for locating and retrieving online content.

IPs and URLs

An *Internet Protocol (IP) address* is a series of numbers that uniquely identifies a location on the Internet. An IP address consists of four groups of numbers separated by periods. For example: 225.73.110.102. A nonprofit organization called ICANN keeps track of IP numbers around the world.

Because numbers would be difficult to remember for retrieving pages, we use a text-based address referred to as a *uniform resource locator (URL)* to go to a website. A URL, also called a *web address*, has several parts separated by a colon (:), slashes (/), and dots (.). The first part of a URL is called a *protocol* and identifies a certain way for interpreting computer information in the transmission process. *Http*, which stands for *hypertext transfer protocol*, and *ftp*, for *file transfer protocol*, are examples of protocols. Some sites use a secondary identifier for the type of site being contacted, such as *www* for *World Wide Web* site, but this is often optional.

The next part of the URL is the *domain name*, which identifies the group of servers (the domain) to which the site belongs and the particular company or organization name. A suffix, such as *.com* or *.edu*, further identifies the domain. For example, the *.com* in the URL http://www.emcp.com is a top-level domain (TLD). Several TLDs exists such as *.com*, *.net*, *.org*, *.edu*, and *.gov*. Table A provides a rundown of TLDs being used today.

Suffix	Type of Organization	Example
.biz	business site	Billboard: http://www.billboard.biz
.com	company or commercial institution	intel: http://www.intel.com
.edu	educational institution	Harvard University: http://www.harvard.edu
.gov	government site	Internal Revenue Service: http://www.irs.gov
.int	international organizations endorsed by treaty	World Health Organization: http://www.who.int
.mil	military site	U.S. Department of Defense: http://www.defenselink.mil
.net	administrative site for ISPs	Earthlink: http://www.earthlink.net
.org	nonprofit or private organization	Red Cross: http://www.redcross.org

I1b. Modify the NSSTable style so it aligns the entire table data at the left margin and applies Blue, Accent 1, Lighter 80% shading to the even banded rows.

Navigating and Searching the Web

1d. Change the *Choose commands from* option to *All Commands*.
e. From the list box at the left side of the dialog box, add the following commands to the Building Blocks group in the new tab: *Building Blocks Organizer, Document Property, Field,* and *Organizer*.
f. Click OK to close the Word Options dialog box.

2. Close the document without saving it.

advanced search options, which you can use to include or exclude certain results. For example, you can exclude pages with certain domain suffixes (such as .com and .net) to limit your search results to educational and government sites. Table C offers some ways you can narrow your search by entering your keywords in various ways.

7c. Apply the NSSTable style to the three tables in the document. **Hint: Do this at the Table Tools Design tab.**

Item	What It Does	Example
Quotes ("")	Instruction to use exact word or words in the exact order given	"Pearl Harbor"
Minus symbol (-)	Excludes words preceded by the minus symbol from the search	jaguar –car
Wildcard (*)	Treat the asterisk as a placeholder for any possible word	*bird for bluebird, redbird, etc.
Or	Allow either one word or the other	Economy 2014 or Economy 2015

A metasearch engine, such as dogpile.com, searches keywords across several websites at the same time. For example, imagine you need to fly from Atlanta to Seattle. Instead of checking available flights on three different airline websites, you can use a metasearch engine to check all of the airline sites at once.

Navigating and Searching the Web
Student Name

8. Insert a document property by completing the following steps:
a. Move the insertion point to the end of the document.
b. Click the Document Property button in the Building Blocks group on your tab and then click *Title* at the drop-down list.
c. Type Navigating and Searching the Web in the *[Title]* placeholder and then press the Right Arrow key to deselect the placeholder.
d. Press Shift + Enter and then insert the *Author* document property. Select the name that appears in the *[Author]* placeholder, type your first and last names, and then press the Right Arrow key to deselect the placeholder.

3. Open the document named **NSSStyles.docx**.
4. Copy styles by completing the following steps:
a. Click your new NSS tab (the one that begins with *NSS* followed by your initials).
b. Click the Organizer button in the Building Blocks group.
c. At the Organizer dialog box, click the Close File button located below the right list box and then click the Open File button. (Make sure you click the Close File button below the right list box and not the left list box.)
d. At the Open dialog box, display all file types. (Do this with the option box that displays to the right of the *File name* text box.)
e. Navigate to your Unit05PA folder and then double-click *NSSWebRpt.docx*.
f. Copy from the left list box to the right list box the following styles: NSSHeading1, NSSTable, and NSSTitle.
g. Close the Organizer dialog box. At the message that displays asking if you want to save the changes to **NSSWebRpt.docx**, click the Save button.
5. Close **NSSStyles.docx**.
6. Open **NSSWebRpt.docx** and save the document with the name **U5-PA05- NSSWebRpt**.

Navigating and Searching the Web

Browsing Web Pages

You may already be quite comfortable with browsing the Internet, but you may not have pondered how browsers move around the Web and retrieve data. Any element of a web page (text, graphic, audio, or video) can be linked to another page using a hyperlink. A hyperlink describes a destination within a web document and can be inserted in text or a graphical object such as a company logo. Text that is linked is called *hypertext*.

A website is a series of related web pages that are linked together. You get to a website by entering the URL, such as www.amazon.com, in your browser. Every website has a starting page, called the *home page*, which is displayed when you enter the site URL. You can also enter a URL to jump to a specific page on a site, such as the Video-On-Demand page at Amazon's site, www.amazon.com/Video-On-Demand.

Searching for Content Online

A search engine, such as Google.com, Ask.com, and Yahoo.com, catalogs and indexes web pages for you. A type of search engine, called a search directory, can also catalog pages into topics such as *finance, health, news, shopping,* and so on. Search engines may seem to be free services, but in reality they are typically financed by selling advertising. Some also make money by selling information about your online activities and interests to advertisers.

The newest wave of search engines, including Microsoft Bing and Google Squared, not only search for content but also make choices among content to deliver more targeted results. Such search engines allow you, for example, to ask for a list of female tennis stars from 1900, on and they then assemble a table of them for you. Table B shows some common search tools with their URLs and an indication of whether they offer the ability to catalog pages in directories.

Search Tool	URL	Type
Ask	www.ask.com	engine
Bing	www.bing.com	engine
Dogpile	www.dogpile.com	engine
Google	www.google.com	engine/directory
MSN	www.msn.com	engine/directory
Yahoo!	www.yahoo.com	engine/directory

> 11b. Modify the NSSTable style so it aligns the entire table data at the left margin and applies Blue, Accent 1, Lighter 80% shading to the even banded rows.

So how do search engines work? You can search for information by going to the search engine's website and typing your search text, which is comprised of one or more keywords or keyword phrases. For example, to find information about the international space station, you could type *space station* in the search engine's search text box and press the Enter key. You can narrow your search by specifying that you want to view links to certain types of results such as images, maps, or videos.

You can get more targeted search results by honing your searching technique. Effective searching is a skill that you gain through practice. For example, typing *space station* in a search engine's web page could easily return more than eighty million results. If what you really need is the cost to build the station, consider a more targeted keyword phrase like "space station cost." Search engines provide

---

advanced search options, which you can use to include or exclude certain results. For example, you can exclude pages with certain domain suffixes (such as .com and .net) to limit your search results to educational and government sites. Table C offers some ways you can narrow your search by entering your keywords in various ways.

Item	What It Does	Example
Quotes ("")	Instruction to use exact word or words in the exact order given	"Pearl Harbor"
Minus symbol (-)	Excludes words preceded by the minus symbol from the search	jaguar –car
Wildcard (*)	Treat the asterisk as a placeholder for any possible word	*bird for bluebird, redbird, etc.
Or	Allow either one word or the other	Economy 2014 or Economy 2015

> 11b. Modify the NSSTable style so it aligns the entire table data at the left margin and applies Blue, Accent 1, Lighter 80% shading to the even banded rows.

A metasearch engine, such as dogpile.com, searches keywords across several websites at the same time. For example, imagine you need to fly from Atlanta to Seattle. Instead of checking available flights on three different airline websites, you can use a metasearch engine to check all of the airline sites at once.

Navigating and Searching the Web
Student Name

12. Save, print, and then close **U5-PA05-NSSWebRpt.docx.**
13. At the blank document, reset your ribbon. *Hint: Do this at the Word Options dialog box with Customize Ribbon selected in the left panel.*

7. Apply the Heading 1 style to the title of the report and apply the Heading 2 style to four headings in the report.

1. Open InterfaceApps.docx and save the document with the name U5-PA06-InterfaceApps.
2. Display the Restrict Editing task pane and then restrict formatting to the Heading 1 and Heading 2 styles. (At the message that displays asking if you want to remove formatting or styles that are not allowed, click No.)
3. Enforce the protection and provide the password *report*.

NATURAL INTERFACE APPLICATIONS

Creating a more natural interface between human and machine is the goal in a major area of artificial intelligence. Currently, computer users are restricted in most instances to using a mouse and keyboard for input. For output, they must gaze at a fairly static, two-dimensional screen. Speakers are used for sound, and a printer for hard copy. The user interface consists of typing, pointing, and clicking. New speech recognition and natural-language technologies promise to change that soon.

Speech Recognition

One of the most immediately applicable improvements in technology comes in the area of speech recognition. Rather than typing information in the computer, users can direct the computer with voice commands. A computer that can take dictation and perform requested actions is a real step forward in convenience and potential. Speech recognition technology has developed rather slowly, mainly because the typical PC did not have the necessary speed and capacity until very recently.

Natural-Language Interface

Computers that are able to communicate using spoken English or Japanese, or any of the hundreds of other languages currently in use around the world, would certainly be helpful. Computers, in the not-so-distant future, will most likely be able to read, write, speak, and understand many human languages. Language translators already exist, and they are getting better all the time.

Programmers can look forward to a human-language computer interface. With better interfaces, programmers may be able to describe what they want using natural (human) language rather than writing programs in the highly restrictive (and rather alien) programming languages in use today. Natural-language interfaces are an area of artificial intelligence that is broader in scope than simple speech recognition. The goal is to have a machine that can read a set of news articles on any topic and understand what it has read. Ideally, it could then write its own report summarizing what it has learned.

Virtual Reality

Virtual reality (VR) describes the concept of creating a realistic world within the computer. Online games with thousands of interacting players already exist. In these games, people can take on a persona and move about a virtual landscape, adventuring and chatting with other players. The quality of a virtual reality system is typically characterized in terms of its *immersiveness*, which measures how real the simulated world feels and how well it can make users accept the simulated world as their own and forget about reality. With each passing year, systems are able to provide increasing levels of immersion. Called by some the "ultimate in escapism," VR is becoming increasingly common — and increasingly real.

Mental Interface

Although still in the experimental phase, a number of interfaces take things a bit further than VR, and they don't require users to click a mouse, speak a word, or even lift a finger. Mental interfaces use sensors mounted around the skull to read the alpha waves given off by our brains. Thinking of the color blue could be used to move the mouse cursor to the right, or thinking of the number seven could move it to the left. The computer measures brain activity and interprets it as a command, eliminating the need to physically manipulate a mouse to move the screen cursor. While this technology has obvious

5. Open U5-PA06-InterfaceApps.docx.
6. Make sure the Restrict Editing task pane displays and then click the Available styles hyperlink.
8. Close the Styles task pane.
9. Close the Restrict Editing task pane.
10. Save the document and then print only page 1.

U5-PA06-InterfaceApps.docx

---

9. Assume that the document will be read by a colleague with Word 2003. Run the compatibility checker to determine what features are not supported by earlier versions of Word.
10. Save the document in the *Word 97-2003 Document (*.doc)* format and name it **U5-PA07-KLHHighlights-2003format.**

Plan Highlights

The following are several of Key Life Health Plan's special features:

A part of the community. Key Life Health Plan has served the Madison County area since 1979. Our parent company was one of the area's first collaborative medical practices, serving area patients since 1923.

Coverage for preventive care. Key Life Health Plan encourages wellness with a variety of services, including routine physical exams, eye exams, prenatal care, and well-baby care. We also offer health education programs designed both to teach and motivate members to make healthier lifestyle choices.

Easy to be a member. There are virtually no claim forms to complete, and you make low co-payments only when you receive care.

Worldwide emergency care. You can receive care for medical emergencies if you are traveling outside Key Life Health Plan's service area or are unable to reach one of our many plan facilities in a local emergency.

Member satisfaction. A recent survey by Lowell Research showed that 95 percent of our current members rated the care they received as good, very good, or excellent.

Quality Assessment

Key Life Health Plan has demonstrated a commitment to quality by adhering to the standards established by the National Association for Quality Health Care. We focus on these specific areas:

- Member rights and responsibilities
- Preventive health care
- Provider quality standards
- Clinical care quality review

In addition, we employ research in areas of service satisfaction, products, and benefits. We use our findings to improve the delivery of care and service to our members.

Provider Network

Quality care begins with finding a doctor with whom you can be comfortable. Key Life Health Plan offers over 650 primary and specialty care physicians conveniently located in the greater county

U5-PA07-KLHHighlights-2003format.doc (page 1 of 2)

5. Close the document information panel.
6. Save the document and then print only the document properties.

Filename: U5-PA07-KLHHighlights.docx
Directory: F:\Unit05PA
Template: C:\Users\Student\AppData\Roaming\Microsoft\Templates\Normal.dotm
Title: Key Life Health Plan
Subject: Company Health Plan
Author: Student Name
Keywords: health, plan, network
Comments: This document describes highlights of the Key Life Health Plan.
Creation Date: 3/5/2015 10:20:00 PM
Change Number: 6
Last Saved On: 3/5/2015 10:26:00 PM
Last Saved By: Student Name
Total Editing Time: 5 Minutes
Last Printed On: 3/5/2015 10:27:00 PM
As of Last Complete Printing
Number of Pages: 1 (approx.)
Number of Words: 366
Number of Characters: 2,016 (approx.)

4. Display the document information panel and then type the following information in the specified text boxes:
Author: (Type your first and last names.)
Title: **Key Life Health Plan**
Subject: Company Health Plan
Keywords: health, plan, network
Category: Health Plan
Comments: **This document describes highlights of the Key Life Health Plan.**

---

area. Included within our more than 38 clinic and hospital locations is Key Life Health Center—one of the top-rated medical facilities in the country.

Key Life Health Plan has forged valuable partnerships with other contracted providers whose practices reflect similar high-quality standards of care. Our providers work as a team, combining resources to manage all levels of your health care needs. This coordination of services ensures members will receive the most appropriate and cost-effective medical care available.

Key Life Health Plan

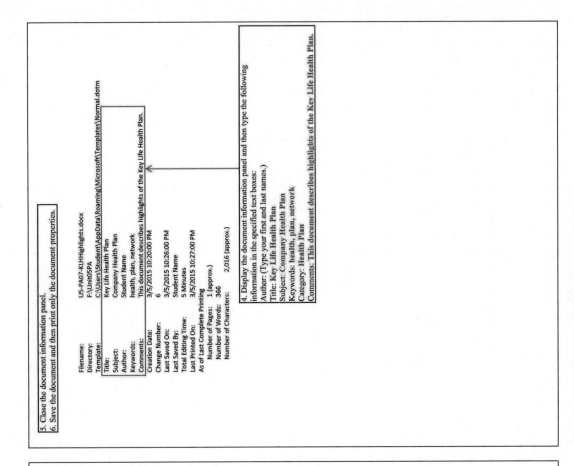

U5-PA07-KLHHighlights-2003format.doc (page 2 of 2)

Signature Word 2013   Model Answers

2a. Apply the Heading 1 style to the three headings in the document (*Plan Highlights*, *Quality Assessment*, and *Provider Network*).

1. Open **KLHHighlights.docx** and save the document with the name **U5-PA07-KLHHighlights**.
2. Make the following changes to the document:
   b. Change the style set to Centered.
   c. Apply the Blue II theme colors.
7. Inspect the document and remove any hidden text.

Plan Highlights

The following are several of Key Life Health Plan's special features:

A part of the community. Key Life Health Plan has served the Madison County area since 1979. Our parent company was one of the area's first collaborative medical practices, serving area patients since 1923.

Coverage for preventive care. Key Life Health Plan encourages wellness with a variety of services, including routine physical exams, eye exams, prenatal care, and well-baby care. We also offer health education programs designed both to teach and motivate members to make healthier lifestyle choices.

Easy to be a member. There are virtually no claim forms to complete, and you make low co-payments only when you receive care.

Worldwide emergency care. You can receive care for medical emergencies if you are traveling outside Key Life Health Plan's service area or are unable to reach one of our many plan facilities in a local emergency.

Member satisfaction. A recent survey by Lowell Research showed that 95 percent of our current members rated the care they received as good, very good, or excellent.

Quality Assessment

Key Life Health Plan has demonstrated a commitment to quality by adhering to the standards established by the National Association for Quality Health Care. We focus on these specific areas:

- Member rights and responsibilities
- Preventive health care
- Provider quality standards
- Clinical care quality review

In addition, we employ research in areas of service satisfaction, products, and benefits. We use our findings to improve the delivery of care and service to our members.

Provider Network

Quality care begins with finding a doctor with whom you can be comfortable. Key Life Health Plan offers over 650 primary and specialty care physicians conveniently located in the greater county

area. Included within our more than 38 clinic and hospital locations is Key Life Health Center—one of the top-rated medical facilities in the country.

Key Life Health Plan has forged valuable partnerships with other contracted providers whose practices reflect similar high-quality standards of care. Our providers work as a team, combining resources to manage all levels of your health care needs. This coordination of services ensures members will receive the most appropriate and cost-effective medical care available.

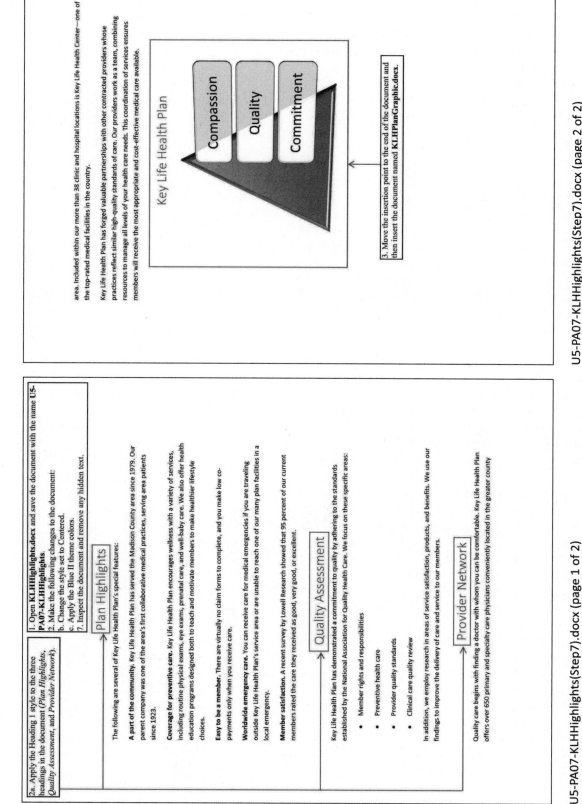

Key Life Health Plan

- Compassion
- Quality
- Commitment

3. Move the insertion point to the end of the document and then insert the document named **KLHPlanGraphic.docx**.

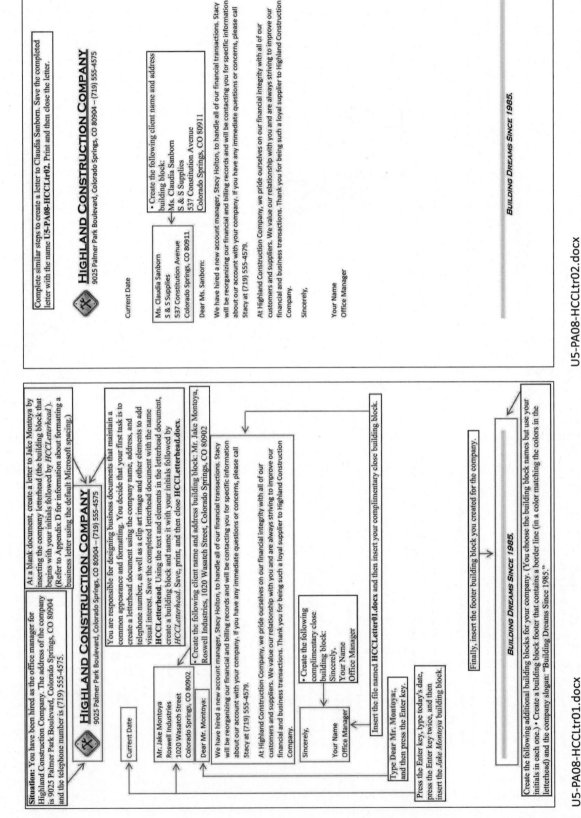

Situation: You have been hired as the office manager for Highland Construction Company. The address of the company is 9025 Palmer Park Boulevard, Colorado Springs, CO 80904 and the telephone number is (719) 555-4575.

At a blank document, create a letter to Jake Montoya by inserting the company letterhead (the building block that begins with your initials followed by *HCCLetterhead*). (Refer to Appendix D for information about formatting a business letter using the default Microsoft spacing.)

HIGHLAND CONSTRUCTION COMPANY
9025 Palmer Park Boulevard, Colorado Springs, CO 80904 – (719) 555-4575

You are responsible for designing business documents that maintain a common appearance and formatting. You decide that your first task is to create a letterhead document using the company name, address, and telephone number, as well as a clip art image and other elements to add visual interest. Save the completed letterhead document with the name **HCCLetterhead**. Using the text and elements in the letterhead document, create a building block and name it with your initials followed by *HCCLetterhead*. Save, print, and then close **HCCLetterhead.docx**.

Current Date

Mr. Jake Montoya
Roswell Industries
1020 Wasatch Street
Colorado Springs, CO 80902

Dear Mr. Montoya:

• Create the following client name and address building block: Mr. Jake Montoya, Roswell Industries, 1020 Wasatch Street, Colorado Springs, CO 80902

We have hired a new account manager, Stacy Holton, to handle all of our financial transactions. Stacy will be reorganizing our financial and billing records and will be contacting you for specific information about our account with your company. If you have any immediate questions or concerns, please call Stacy at (719) 555-4579.

At Highland Construction Company, we pride ourselves on our financial integrity with all of our customers and suppliers. We value our relationship with you and are always striving to improve our financial and business transactions. Thank you for being such a loyal supplier to Highland Construction Company.

Sincerely,

Your Name
Office Manager

• Create the following complimentary close building block:
Sincerely,
Your Name
Office Manager

Type Dear Mr. Montoya:, and then press the Enter key.

Press the Enter key, type today's date, press the Enter key twice, and then insert the *Jake Montoya* building block.

Insert the file named **HCCLetter01.docx** and then insert your complimentary close building block.

Finally, insert the footer building block you created for the company.

BUILDING DREAMS SINCE 1985.

Create the following additional building blocks for your company. (You choose the building block names but use your initials in each one.) • Create a building block footer that contains a border line (in a color matching the colors in the letterhead) and the company slogan: "Building Dreams Since 1985."

U5-PA08-HCCLtr01.docx

Complete similar steps to create a letter to Claudia Sanborn. Save the completed letter with the name **U5-PA08-HCCLtr02**. Print and then close the letter.

HIGHLAND CONSTRUCTION COMPANY
9025 Palmer Park Boulevard, Colorado Springs, CO 80904 – (719) 555-4575

• Create the following client name and address building block:
Ms. Claudia Sanborn
S & S Supplies
537 Constitution Avenue
Colorado Springs, CO 80911

Current Date

Ms. Claudia Sanborn
S & S Supplies
537 Constitution Avenue
Colorado Springs, CO 80911

Dear Ms. Sanborn:

We have hired a new account manager, Stacy Holton, to handle all of our financial transactions. Stacy will be reorganizing our financial and billing records and will be contacting you for specific information about our account with your company. If you have any immediate questions or concerns, please call Stacy at (719) 555-4579.

At Highland Construction Company, we pride ourselves on our financial integrity with all of our customers and suppliers. We value our relationship with you and are always striving to improve our financial and business transactions. Thank you for being such a loyal supplier to Highland Construction Company.

Sincerely,

Your Name
Office Manager

BUILDING DREAMS SINCE 1985.

U5-PA08-HCCLtr02.docx

Page 1 of 3

BUILDING CONSTRUCTION AGREEMENT

Situation: As the office manager at Highland Construction Company, you are responsible for preparing construction agreements.

Create an AutoCorrect entry that will replace *hcc* with *Highland Construction Company* and *bca* with *Building Construction Agreement.*

Open **HCCAgreement.docx** and then type the text shown in Figure U5.3 at the beginning of the document. Insert the following in the document:

• Insert a cover page.

Add or apply any other elements or formats to improve the appearance of the document and then save the document with the name **U5-PA09-HCCAgreement.docx.**

Print and then close the document.

Delete the building blocks you created and then delete the AutoCorrect entries *hcc* and *bca.*

STUDENT NAME

HIGHLAND CONSTRUCTION COMPANY

U5-PA09-HCCAgreement.docx (page 1 of 3)

Page 2 of 3

Building Construction Agreement

THIS Building Construction Agreement made this _____ day of _____, 20 _____, by and between Highland Construction Company and _____, hereinafter referred to as "owner," for the considerations hereinafter named, Highland Construction Company and owner agree as follows:

Financing Agreements: The owner will obtain a construction loan to finance construction under this Building Construction Agreement. If adequate financing has not been arranged within thirty days of the date of this Building Construction Agreement, or the owner cannot provide evidence to Highland Construction Company of other financial ability to pay the full amount, then Highland Construction Company may treat this Building Construction Agreement as null and void and retain the down payment made on the execution of this Building Construction Agreement.

Supervision of Work: Owner agrees that the direction and supervision of the working force including subcontractor, rests exclusively with Highland Construction Company, or his/her duly designated agent, and owner agrees not to issue any instructions to, or otherwise interfere with, same.

Changes, Alterations, and Extras: All changes in or departures from the plans and/or specifications shall be in writing. Where changes in or departure from plans and specifications requested in writing by owner will result in furnishing of additional labor and materials, the owner shall pay Highland Construction Company for such extras at a price agreed upon in writing before commencement of said changes. Where such changes result in the omitting of any labor or materials, Highland Construction Company shall allow the owner a credit therefore at a price agreed to in writing before commencement of said changes.

Possession of Residence Upon Completion: On final payment by owner and upon owner's request, Highland Construction Company will provide owner with affidavit stating that all labor, materials, and equipment used in the construction have been paid for, or will be paid for, in full by Highland Construction Company unless otherwise noted. Highland Construction Company shall not be required to give possession of the residence to the owner before final payment by owner. Final payment constitutes acceptance of the residence as being satisfactorily completed unless a separate escrow agreement is executed between the parties stipulating the unfinished items.

Exclusions: The owner is solely responsible for the purchase and installation of any septic tank or other individual subsurface sewage disposal system that may be required on the property.

Builder's Right to Terminate the Contract: Should the work be stopped by any public authority for a period of thirty days or more through no fault of Highland Construction Company, or should the work be stopped through act or neglect of the owner for a period of seven days, or should the owner fail to pay Highland Construction Company any payment within seven days after it is due, then Highland Construction Company, upon seven days' written notice to the owner, may stop work or terminate the agreement and recover from the owner payment for all work executed and any loss sustained and reasonable profit and damages.

The Owner acknowledges that she/he has read and fully understands the provisions of this Building Construction Agreement.

BUILDING DREAMS SINCE 1985.

• Insert your footer building block as a footer.

U5-PA09-HCCAgreement.docx (page 2 of 3)

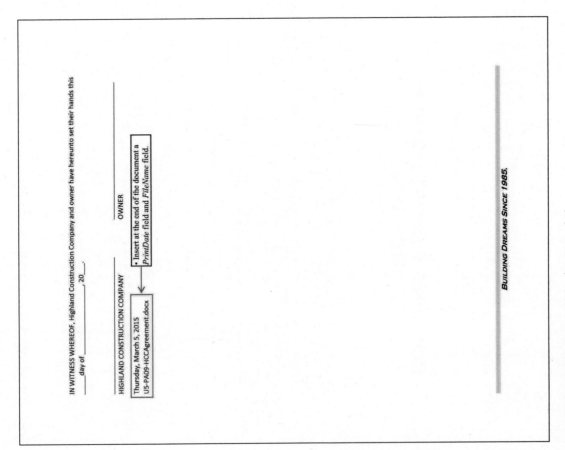

IN WITNESS WHEREOF, Highland Construction Company and owner have hereunto set their hands this _____ day of _____, 20___

OWNER

HIGHLAND CONSTRUCTION COMPANY

Thursday, March 5, 2015
U5-PA09-HCCAgreement.docx

- Insert at the end of the document a *PrintDate* field and *FileName* field.

BUILDING DREAMS SINCE 1985.

U5-PA09-HCCAgreement.docx (page 3 of 3)

Chapter 26 Assessment Annotated Model Answers

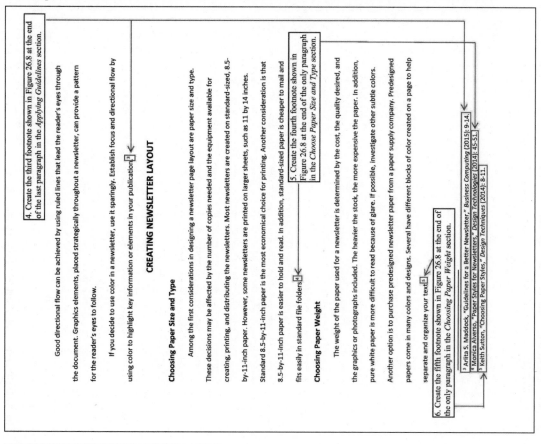

Page 2 of 3 (top):

4. Create the third footnote shown in Figure 26.8 at the end of the last paragraph in the *Applying Guidelines* section.

5. Create the fourth footnote shown in Figure 26.8 at the end of the only paragraph in the *Choose Paper Size and Type* section.

6. Create the fifth footnote shown in Figure 26.8 at the end of the only paragraph in the *Choosing Paper Weight* section.

Good directional flow can be achieved by using ruled lines that lead the reader's eyes through the document. Graphics elements, placed strategically throughout a newsletter, can provide a pattern for the reader's eyes to follow.

If you decide to use color in a newsletter, use it sparingly. Establish focus and directional flow by using color to highlight key information or elements in your publication.[3]

CREATING NEWSLETTER LAYOUT

Choosing Paper Size and Type

Among the first considerations in designing a newsletter page layout are paper size and type. These decisions may be affected by the number of copies needed and the equipment available for creating, printing, and distributing the newsletters. Most newsletters are created on standard-sized, 8.5-by-11-inch paper. However, some newsletters are printed on larger sheets, such as 11 by 14 inches. Standard 8.5-by-11-inch paper is the most economical choice for printing. Another consideration is that 8.5-by-11-inch paper is easier to hold and read. In addition, standard-sized paper is cheaper to mail and fits easily in standard file folders.[4]

Choosing Paper Weight

The weight of the paper used for a newsletter is determined by the cost, the quality desired, and the graphics or photographs included. The heavier the stock, the more expensive the paper. In addition, pure white paper is more difficult to read because of glare. If possible, investigate other subtle colors. Another option is to purchase predesigned newsletter paper from a paper supply company. Predesigned papers come in many colors and designs. Several have different blocks of color created on a page to help separate and organize your text.[5]

[3] Arita S. Maddock, "Guidelines for a Better Newsletter," *Business Computing* (2015): 9-14.
[4] Monica Alverso, "Paper Styles for Newsletters," *Design Technologies* (2014): 45-51.
[5] Keith Sutton, "Choosing Paper Styles," *Design Techniques* (2014): 8-11.

C26-A01-DesignNwsltr(Step7).docx (page 2 of 3)

Page 1 of 3 (bottom):

1. Open **DesignNwsltr.docx** and save the document with the name **C26-A01- DesignNwsltr.**

2. Create the first footnote shown in Figure 26.8 at the end of the first paragraph in the *Applying Guidelines* section.

3. Create the second footnote shown in Figure 26.8 at the end of the third paragraph in the *Applying Guidelines* section.

DESIGNING A NEWSLETTER

Applying Guidelines

One of the biggest challenges in creating a newsletter is balancing change with consistency. A newsletter is a document that is typically reproduced regularly, whether monthly, bimonthly, or quarterly. Each issue features new content—new ideas, new text, and new graphics or photos. However, for your newsletter to be effective, each issue must also maintain a consistent appearance. Consistency contributes to your publication's identity and gives your readers a feeling of familiarity.[1]

As you design your newsletter, think about the elements that should remain consistent from issue to issue. Consistent newsletter features and elements may include: margin size, column layout, nameplate formatting and location, logo, color, ruled lines, and formatting of headlines, subheads, and body text.

Focus and balance can be achieved in a newsletter through the design and size of the nameplate, the arrangement of text on the page, the use of graphics images or scanned photographs, and the careful use of lines, borders, and backgrounds. When you choose graphics, images, or photos, use restraint and consider the appropriateness of the image. A single, large illustration is usually more effective than many small images scattered throughout the document. Size graphics, images, or photos according to their relative importance to the content. Headlines and subheads can serve as secondary focal points as well as provide balance to the total document.[2]

White space around a headline creates contrast and attracts the reader's eyes to the headline. Surround text with white space if you want the text to stand out. If you want to draw attention to the nameplate or headline of the newsletter, you may want to choose a bold type style and a larger type size.

[1] James Habermann, "Designing a Newsletter," *Desktop Designs* (2015): 23-29.
[2] Shirley G. Pilante, "Adding Pizzazz to Your Newsletter," *Desktop Publisher* (2014): 32-37.

C26-A01-DesignNwsltr(Step7).docx (page 1 of 3)

8. Select the entire document and then change the font to Constantia.
9. Select all of the footnotes and change the font to Constantia.
10. Delete the third footnote.

DESIGNING A NEWSLETTER

Applying Guidelines

One of the biggest challenges in creating a newsletter is balancing change with consistency. A newsletter is a document that is typically reproduced regularly, whether monthly, bimonthly, or quarterly. Each issue features new content—new text, new ideas, new text, and new graphics or photos. However, for your newsletter to be effective, each issue must also maintain a consistent appearance. Consistency contributes to your publication's identity and gives your readers a feeling of familiarity.[1]

As you design your newsletter, think about the elements that should remain consistent from issue to issue. Consistent newsletter features and elements may include: margin size, column layout, nameplate formatting and location, logo, color, ruled lines, and formatting of headlines, subheads, and body text.

Focus and balance can be achieved in a newsletter through the design and size of the nameplate, the arrangement of text on the page, the use of graphics images or scanned photographs, and the careful use of lines, borders, and backgrounds. When you choose graphics, images, or photos, use restraint and consider the appropriateness of the image. A single, large illustration is usually more effective than many small images scattered throughout the document. Size graphics, images, or photos according to their relative importance to the content. Headlines and subheads can serve as secondary focal points as well as provide balance to the total document.[2]

White space around a headline creates contrast and attracts the reader's eyes to the headline. Surround text with white space if you want the text to stand out. If you want to draw

---

[1] James Habermann, "Designing a Newsletter," *Desktop Designs* (2015): 23-29.
[2] Shirley G. Plante, "Adding Pizzazz to Your Newsletter," *Desktop Publisher* (2014): 32-37.

Creating Margins

After considering paper size, type, and weight, determine the margins of your newsletter pages. Margin size is linked to the number of columns used, the formality desired, the visual elements used, and the amount of text available. Keep all margins consistent throughout your newsletter. Listed here are a few generalizations about margins in newsletters:

- A wide right margin is considered formal. This approach positions the text at the left side of the page—the side where most readers tend to look first. If the justification is set at full, the newsletter will appear even more formal.
- A wide left margin is less formal. A table of contents or marginal subheads can be placed in the left margin giving the newsletter an airy, open appearance.
- Equal margins tend to create an informal look.

a paper supply company. Predesigned papers come in many colors and designs. Several have different blocks of color created on a page to help separate and organize your text.[4]

Creating Margins

After considering paper size, type, and weight, determine the margins of your newsletter pages. Margin size is linked to the number of columns needed, the formality desired, the visual elements used, and the amount of text available. Keep all margins consistent throughout your newsletter. Listed here are a few generalizations about margins in newsletters:

- A wide right margin is considered formal. This approach positions the text at the left side of the page—the side where most readers tend to look first. If the justification is set at full, the newsletter will appear even more formal.
- A wide left margin is less formal. A table of contents or marginal subheads can be placed in the left margin giving the newsletter an airy, open appearance.
- Equal margins tend to create an informal look.

[4] Keith Sutton, "Choosing Paper Styles," *Design Techniques* (2014): 8-11.

---

attention to the nameplate or headline of the newsletter, you may want to choose a bold type style and a larger type size.

Good directional flow can be achieved by using ruled lines that lead the reader's eyes through the document. Graphics elements, placed strategically throughout a newsletter, can provide a pattern for the reader's eyes to follow.

If you decide to use color in a newsletter, use it sparingly. Establish focus and directional flow by using color to highlight key information or elements in your publication.

CREATING NEWSLETTER LAYOUT

Choosing Paper Size and Type

Among the first considerations in designing a newsletter page layout are paper size and type. These decisions may be affected by the number of copies needed and the equipment available for creating, printing, and distributing the newsletters. Most newsletters are created on standard-sized, 8.5-by-11-inch paper. However, some newsletters are printed on larger sheets, such as 11 by 14 inches. Standard 8.5-by-11-inch paper is the most economical choice for printing. Another consideration is that 8.5-by-11-inch paper is easier to hold and read. In addition, standard-sized paper is cheaper to mail and fits easily in standard file folders.[3]

Choosing Paper Weight

The weight of the paper used for a newsletter is determined by the cost, the quality desired, and the graphics or photographs included. The heavier the stock, the more expensive the paper. In addition, pure white paper is more difficult to read because of glare. If possible, investigate other subtle colors. Another option is to purchase predesigned newsletter paper from

[3] Monica Alverso, "Paper Styles for Newsletters," *Design Technologies* (2014): 45-51.

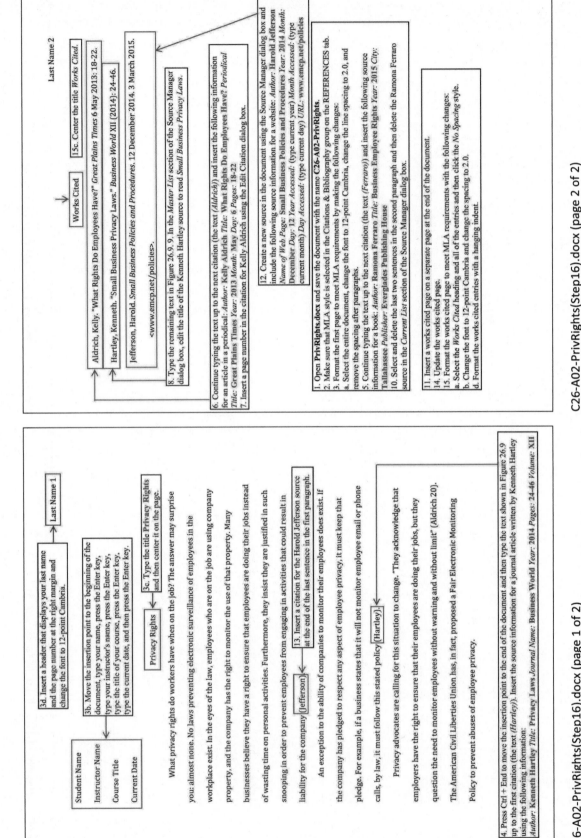

Page 1 content (left block):

Last Name 1

Student Name
Instructor Name
Course Title
Current Date

3d. Insert a header that displays your last name and the page number at the right margin and change the font to 12-point Cambria.

3b. Move the insertion point to the beginning of the document, type your name, press the Enter key, type your instructor's name, press the Enter key, type the title of your course, press the Enter key, type the current date, and then press the Enter key.

Privacy Rights

3c. Type the title Privacy Rights and then center it on the page.

What privacy rights do workers have when on the job? The answer may surprise you: almost none. No laws preventing electronic surveillance of employees in the workplace exist. In the eyes of the law, employees who are on the job are using company property, and the company has the right to monitor the use of that property. Many businesses believe they have a right to ensure that employees are doing their jobs instead of wasting time on personal activities. Furthermore, they insist they are justified in such snooping in order to prevent employees from engaging in activities that could result in liability for the company [Jefferson]

13. Insert a citation for the Harold Jefferson source at the end of the last sentence in the first paragraph.

An exception to the ability of companies to monitor their employees does exist. If the company has pledged to respect any aspect of employee privacy, it must keep that pledge. For example, if a business states that it will not monitor employee email or phone calls, by law, it must follow this stated policy [Hartley].

Privacy advocates are calling for this situation to change. "They acknowledge that employers have the right to ensure that their employees are doing their jobs, but they question the need to monitor employees without warning and without limit" (Aldrich 20). The American Civil Liberties Union has, in fact, proposed a Fair Electronic Monitoring Policy to prevent abuses of employee privacy.

4. Press Ctrl + End to move the insertion point to the end of the document and then type the text shown in Figure 26.9 up to the first citation (the text (Hartley)). Insert the source information for a journal article written by Kenneth Hartley using the following information:
Author: Kenneth Hartley *Title*: Privacy Laws *Journal Name*: **Business World** *Year*: 2014 *Pages*: 24-46 *Volume*: XII

C26-A02-PrivRights(Step16).docx (page 1 of 2)

Page 2 content (right block):

Last Name 2

Works Cited

15c. Center the title *Works Cited.*

Aldrich, Kelly. "What Rights Do Employees Have?" *Great Plains Times* 6 May 2013: 18-22.

Hartley, Kenneth. "Small Business Privacy Laws." *Business World* XII (2014): 24-46.

Jefferson, Harold. *Small Business Policies and Procedures.* 12 December 2014. 3 March 2015. <www.emcp.net/policies>.

8. Type the remaining text in Figure 26.9. 9. In the *Master List* section of the Source Manager dialog box, edit the title of the Kenneth Hartley source to read *Small Business Privacy Laws.*

6. Continue typing the text up to the next citation (the text (Aldrich)) and insert the following information for an article in a periodical: *Author*: Kelly Aldrich *Title*: What Rights Do Employees Have? *Periodical Title*: Great Plains Times *Year*: 2013 *Month*: May *Day*: 6 *Pages*: 18-22
7. Insert a page number in the citation for Kelly Aldrich using the Edit Citation dialog box.

12. Create a new source in the document using the Source Manager dialog box and include the following source information for a website: *Author*: Harold Jefferson *Name of Web Page*: Small Business Policies and Procedures *Year*: 2014 *Month*: December *Day*: 12 *Year Accessed*: (type current year) *Month Accessed*: (type current month) *Day Accessed*: (type current day) *URL*: www.emcp.net/policies

1. Open **PrivRights.docx** and save the document with the name **C26-A02-PrivRights.**
2. Make sure that MLA style is selected in the Citations & Bibliography group on the REFERENCES tab.
3. Format the first page to meet MLA requirements by making the following changes:
a. Select the entire document, change the font to 12-point Cambria, change the line spacing to 2.0, and remove the spacing after paragraphs.
5. Continue typing the text up to the next citation (the text (Ferraro)) and insert the following source information for a book: *Author*: Ramona Ferraro *Title*: Business Employee Rights *Year*: 2015 *City*: Tallahassee *Publisher*: Everglades Publishing House
10. Select and delete the last two sentences in the second paragraph and then delete the Ramona Ferraro source in the *Current List* section of the Source Manager dialog box.

11. Insert a works cited page on a separate page at the end of the document.
14. Update the works cited page.
15. Format the works cited page to meet MLA requirements with the following changes:
a. Select the *Works Cited* heading and all of the entries and then click the *No Spacing* style.
b. Change the font to 12-point Cambria and change the spacing to 2.0.
d. Format the works cited entries with a hanging indent.

C26-A02-PrivRights(Step16).docx (page 2 of 2)

18. Format the sources list to meet APA requirements by changing the title to *References*, selecting the references, and formatting the references using these specifications: change the font to 12-point Cambria, change the spacing after paragraphs to 0, and change the line spacing to 2.0.

References

Aldrich, K. (2013, May 6). What Rights Do Employees Have? *Great Plains Times*, pp. 18–22.

Hartley, K. (2014). Small Business Privacy Laws. *Business World, XII*, 24–46.

Jefferson, H. (2014, December 12). *Small Business Policies and Procedures*. Retrieved March 3, 2015, from www.emcp.net/policies

17. Change the document and sources list from MLA to APA style.
19. Save the document, print page 2, and then close C26-A02-PrivRights.docx.

C26-A02-PrivRights(Step19).docx

---

1. As you learned in this chapter, you can convert endnotes to footnotes. You can also convert footnotes to endnotes. Open C26-E01-InterfaceApps.docx and save the document with the name C26-A03-InterfaceApps.

NATURAL INTERFACE APPLICATIONS

Creating a more natural interface between human and machine is the goal in a major area of artificial intelligence. Currently, computer users are restricted in most instances to using a mouse and keyboard for input. For output, they must gaze at a fairly static, two-dimensional screen. Speakers are used for sound, and a printer for hard copy. The user interface consists of typing, pointing, and clicking.

New speech recognition and natural-language technologies promise to change that soon.[5]

Speech Recognition

One of the most immediately applicable improvements in technology comes in the area of speech recognition. Rather than typing information in the computer, users can direct the computer with voice commands. A computer that can take dictation and perform requested actions is a real step forward in convenience and potential. Speech recognition technology has developed rather slowly, mainly because the typical PC did not have the necessary speed and capacity until very recently.[6]

Natural-Language Interface

Computers that are able communicate using spoken English or Japanese, or any of the hundreds of other languages currently in use around the world, would certainly be helpful. Computers, in the not-so-distant future, will most likely be able to read, write, speak, and understand many human languages. Language translators already exist, and they are getting better all the time.

Programmers can look forward to a human-language computer interface. With better interfaces, programmers may be able to describe what they want using natural (human) language, rather than writing programs in the highly restrictive and rather alien programming languages in use today. Natural-language interfaces are an area of artificial intelligence that is broader in scope than simple speech recognition. The goal is to have a machine that can read a set of news articles on any topic and understand what it has read. Ideally, it could then write its own report summarizing what it has learned.[7]

C26-A03-InterfaceApps.docx (page 1 of 2)

Student Name

Instructor Name

Course Title

Current Date

Developing an Information System

Identifying and assembling a team of employees with the required skills and expertise is a necessary first step in developing a new in-house information system. A management group may be involved in answering questions and providing information in the early planning phases of the project, but programmers and/or software engineers handle the design and implementation of any new system. Programmers specialize in the development of new software, while software engineers are highly skilled professionals with programming and teamwork training (Janowski).

Because of their large size, information systems require the creation of a project team. A project team usually includes a project manager, who acts as the team leader. Sometimes the project manager also functions as a systems analyst, responsible for completing the systems analysis and making design recommendations. Other project team members include software engineers and technicians. The software engineers deal with programming software, while technicians handle hardware issues. The comprehensive process software engineers initiate is called the system development life cycle (SDLC), a series of steps culminating in a completed information system.

The first step in the system development life cycle is planning. The planning step involves preparing a needs analysis and conducting feasibility studies. During this step, a company usually establishes a project team, and the team creates a project plan. "The

---

Virtual Reality

Virtual reality (VR) describes the concept of creating a realistic world within the computer. Online games with thousands of interacting players already exist. In these games people can take on a persona and move about a virtual landscape, adventuring and chatting with other players. The quality of a virtual reality system is typically characterized in terms of its *immersiveness*, which measures how real the simulated world feels and how well it can make users accept the simulated world as their own and forget about reality. With each passing year, systems are able to provide increasing levels of immersion. Called by some the "ultimate in escapism," VR is becoming increasingly common—and increasingly real.[8]

Mental Interface

Although still in the experimental phase, a number of interfaces take things a bit further than VR, and they don't require users to click a mouse, speak a word, or even lift a finger. Mental interfaces use sensors mounted around the skull to read the alpha waves given off by our brains. Thinking of the color blue could be used to move the mouse cursor to the right, or thinking of the number seven could move it to the left. The computer measures brain activity and interprets it as a command, eliminating the need to physically manipulate a mouse to move the screen cursor. While this technology has obvious applications for assisting people with disabilities, military researchers are also using it to produce a superior form of interface for pilots.[9]

---

[5] Ray Curtis, *Artificial Intelligence* (Chicago: Home Town Publishing, 2015), 45-51.
[6] Heather Clemens and Nicolas Reyes, "Integrating Speech Recognition," *Design Technologies* (2014): 24-26.
[7] Daniel Glenovich, "Language Interfaces," *Corporate Computing* (2015): 8-12.
[8] William Novak, *Virtual Reality Worlds* (San Francisco: Lilly Harris Publishers, 2013), 53-68.
[9] Kathleen Beal, "Challenges of Artificial Intelligence," *Interface Design* (2015): 10-18.

---

2. Using options at the Footnote and Endnote dialog box, make the following changes:
a. Convert the footnotes to endnotes. (After converting the footnotes to endnotes, make sure to click the *Endnotes* option at the top of the Endnote and Footnote dialog box.)
b. Change the number format to arabic numbers (1, 2, 3, . . .).
c. Change the starting number to 5.

Works Cited

Janowski, Robert. "Information System Management." *Technology: Computer Networking*

(2014): 35-41.

Mendoza, Carla. *Building Computer Networks*. Oklahoma City: Blue Field Publishing House,

2015.

Yamashita, Paul. *How is an Information System Designed?* 19 October 2013. 20 February

2015. <www.emcp.net/systemdesign>.

2b. Use the information from the works cited page to insert citations into the document. The *Janowski* citation is for a journal article, the *Mendoza* citation is for a book, and the *Yamashita* citation is for a website.

1. Open **DevelopSystem.docx** and save the document with the name **C26-A04-DevelopSystem**.
2. Format the document so it displays as shown in Figure 26.10 with the following specifications:
a. Format the document in MLA style. (For help, refer to Exercise 26.2, which includes eight parts.) Change the document font to 12-point Cambria.
c. Format the works cited page to meet MLA requirements.

C26-A04-DevelopSystem.docx (page 3 of 3)

---

project plan includes an estimate of how long the project will take to complete, an outline

of the steps involved, and a list of deliverables" (Mendoza 42). Deliverables are documents,

services, hardware, and software that must be finished and delivered by a certain time and

date.

A project is ready to move into the design stage once the project team has approved

the plan, including the budget. The design process begins with the writing of the

documentation, which covers functional and design specifications. In most cases, the

project team creates the functional specifications, describing what the system must be able

to do (Yamashita).

The project can move into the next phase, implementation, once the development

team and the systems house develop the design specification and approve the plans. This

step is where the actual work of putting the system together is completed, including

creating a prototype and completing the programming. In most cases, implementing the

new system is the longest, most difficult step in the process.

A system goes into the support stage after it has been accepted and approved. A

support contract normally allows users to contact the systems house for technical support,

training, and sometimes on-site troubleshooting. Even if the system was designed in-house,

the responsible department often operates as an independent entity—sometimes even

charging the department acquiring the system. The support stage continues until a new

information system is proposed and developed, usually years later. At that point, the

existing system is retired and no longer used.

C26-A04-DevelopSystem.docx (page 2 of 3)

Chapter 27 Assessment Annotated Model Answers

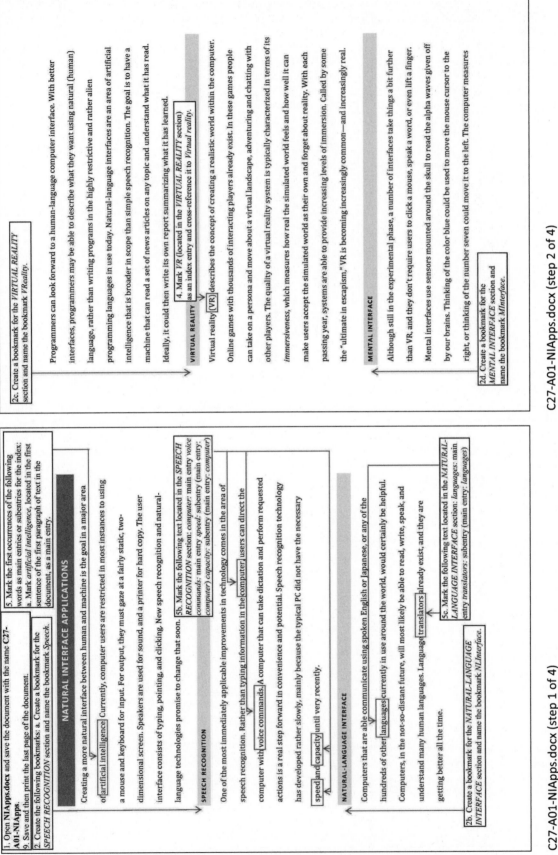

C27-A01-NIApps.docx (step 1 of 4)

1. Open **NIApps.docx** and save the document with the name C27-A01-NIApps.
9. Save and then print the last page of the document.
2. Create the following bookmarks: a. Create a bookmark for the *SPEECH RECOGNITION* section and name the bookmark *Speech.*

5. Mark the first occurrences of the following words as main entries or subentries for the index:
a. Mark *artificial intelligence*, located in the first sentence of the first paragraph of text in the document, as a main entry.

NATURAL INTERFACE APPLICATIONS

Creating a more natural interface between human and machine is the goal in a major area of artificial intelligence. Currently, computer users are restricted in most instances to using a mouse and keyboard for input. For output, they must gaze at a fairly static, two-dimensional screen. Speakers are used for sound, and a printer for hard copy. The user interface consists of typing, pointing, and clicking. New speech recognition and natural-language technologies promise to change that soon.

SPEECH RECOGNITION

5b. Mark the following text located in the *SPEECH RECOGNITION* section: *computer*: main entry *voice commands*; main entry *speed*: subentry (main entry: *computer*) *capacity*: subentry (main entry: *computer*)

One of the most immediately applicable improvements in technology comes in the area of speech recognition. Rather than typing information in the computer, users can direct the computer with voice commands. A computer that can take dictation and perform requested actions is a real step forward in convenience and potential. Speech recognition technology has developed rather slowly, mainly because the typical PC did not have the necessary speed and capacity until very recently.

NATURAL-LANGUAGE INTERFACE

Computers that are able to communicate using spoken English or Japanese, or any of the hundreds of other languages currently in use around the world, would certainly be helpful. Computers, in the not-so-distant future, will most likely be able to read, write, speak, and understand many human languages. Language translators already exist, and they are getting better all the time.

5c. Mark the following text located in the *NATURAL-LANGUAGE INTERFACE* section: *languages*: main entry *translators*: subentry (main entry: *languages*)

2b. Create a bookmark for the *NATURAL-LANGUAGE INTERFACE* section and name the bookmark *NLInterface.*

C27-A01-NIApps.docx (step 2 of 4)

2c. Create a bookmark for the *VIRTUAL REALITY* section and name the bookmark *VReality.*

Programmers can look forward to a human-language computer interface. With better interfaces, programmers may be able to describe what they want using natural (human) language, rather than writing programs in the highly restrictive and rather alien programming languages in use today. Natural-language interfaces are an area of artificial intelligence that is broader in scope than simple speech recognition. The goal is to have a machine that can read a set of news articles on any topic and understand what it has read. Ideally, it could then write its own report summarizing what it has learned.

4. Mark *VR* (located in the *VIRTUAL REALITY* section) as an index entry and cross-reference it to *Virtual reality.*

VIRTUAL REALITY

Virtual reality (VR) describes the concept of creating a realistic world within the computer. Online games with thousands of interacting players already exist. In these games people can take on a persona and move about a virtual landscape, adventuring and chatting with other players. The quality of a virtual reality system is typically characterized in terms of its *immersiveness*, which measures how real the simulated world feels and how well it can make users accept the simulated world as their own and forget about reality. With each passing year, systems are able to provide increasing levels of immersion. Called by some the "ultimate in escapism," VR is becoming increasingly common—and increasingly real.

MENTAL INTERFACE

Although still in the experimental phase, a number of interfaces take things a bit further than VR, and they don't require users to click a mouse, speak a word, or even lift a finger. Mental interfaces use sensors mounted around the skull to read the alpha waves given off by our brains. Thinking of the color blue could be used to move the mouse cursor to the right, or thinking of the number seven could move it to the left. The computer measures

2d. Create a bookmark for the *MENTAL INTERFACE* section and name the bookmark *MInterface.*

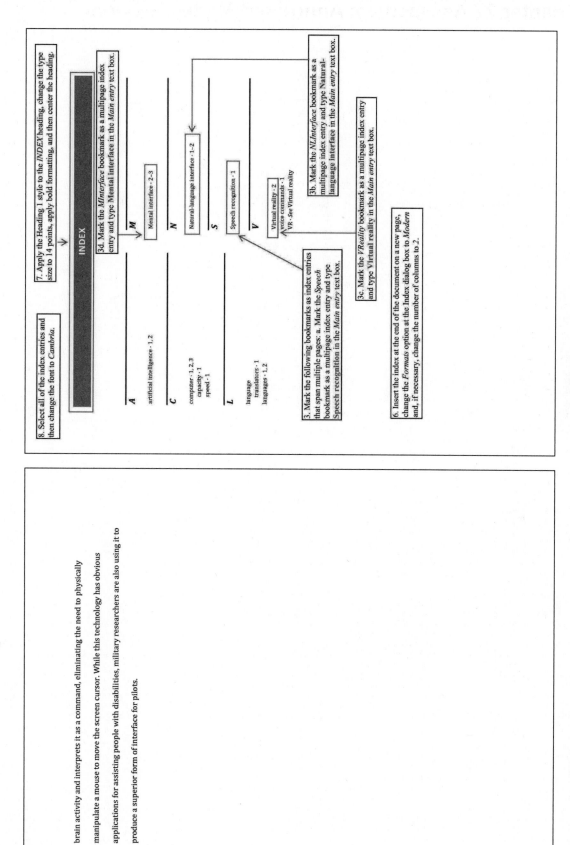

C27-A01-NIApps.docx (step 4 of 4)

C27-A01-NIApps.docx (step 3 of 4)

1. At a blank document, create the text shown in Figure 27.6 as a concordance file.

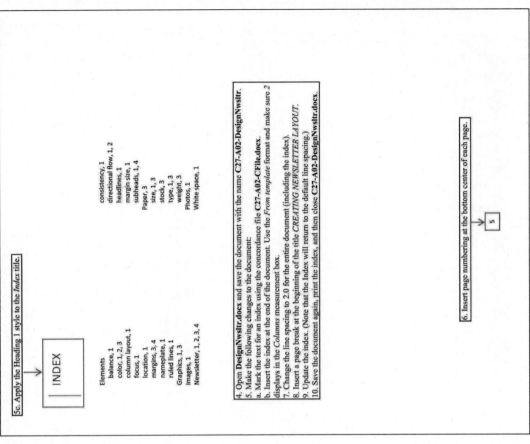

5c. Apply the Heading 1 style to the *Index* title.

INDEX

Elements	consistency, 1
balance, 1	directional flow, 1, 2
color, 1, 2, 3	headlines, 1
column layout, 1	margin size, 1
focus, 1	subheads, 1, 4
location, 1	Paper, 3
margins, 3, 4	size, 1, 3
nameplate, 1	stock, 3
ruled lines, 1	type, 1, 3
Graphics, 1, 3	weight, 3
images, 1	Photos, 1
Newsletter, 1, 2, 3, 4	White space, 1

4. Open **DesignNwsltr.docx** and save the document with the name **C27-A02-DesignNwsltr**.
5. Make the following changes to the document:
a. Mark the text for an index using the concordance file **C27-A02-CFile.docx**.
b. Insert the index at the end of the document. Use the *From template* format and make sure 2 displays in the *Columns* measurement box.
7. Change the line spacing to 2.0 for the entire document (including the index).
8. Insert a page break at the beginning of the title *CREATING NEWSLETTER LAYOUT*.
9. Update the index. (Note that the Index will return to the default line spacing.)
10. Save the document again, print the index, and then close **C27-A02-DesignNwsltr.docx**.

6. Insert page numbering at the bottom center of each page.

5

C27-A02-DesignNwsltr.docx

NEWSLETTER	Newsletter
newsletter	Newsletter
consistency	Newsletter: consistency
element	Elements
margins	Elements: margins
column layout	Elements: column layout
nameplate	Elements: nameplate
location	Elements: location
logos	Elements: logos
color	Elements: color
ruled lines	Elements: ruled lines
Focus	Elements: focus
balance	Elements: balance
graphics	Graphics
images	Images
photos	Photos
Headlines	Newsletter: headlines
subheads	Newsletter: subheads
White space	White space
directional flow	Newsletter: directional flow
paper	Paper
Size	Paper: size
type	Paper: type
weight	Paper: weight
stock	Paper: stock
margin size	Newsletter: margin size

C27-A02-CFile.docx

INDEX

1. Open **C27-A02-DesignNwsltr.docx** and save the document with the name **C27-A03- DesignNwsltr.**
2. Apply the Slice theme.
3. Display the Index dialog box, specify that you want run-in entries in one column in the *From template* format, and then close the Index dialog box. At the message asking if you want to replace the selected index, click OK.
4. Save **C27-A03-DesignNwsltr.docx.**
5. Print only the index and then close the document.

Elements: balance, 1; color, 1, 2, 3; column layout, 1; focus, 1; location, 1; margins, 4; nameplate, 1; ruled lines, 1, 2
Graphics, 1, 3
Images, 1
Newsletter, 1, 2, 3, 4: consistency, 1: directional flow, 2: headlines, 1: margin size, 1: subheads, 1, 4
Paper, 3, 4: size, 1, 3: stock, 3: type, 1, 3, 4: weight, 3, 4
Photos, 1
White space, 1

5

3b. Type INDICE and then press the Enter key. (*Indice* is the Spanish translation of the English word *Index*.)
4. Apply the Heading 1 style to the *INDICE* title and change the font to Cambria.

INDICE

A	
Alimento 2	**F**
amaranto 1	FAO 1
arroz 3	Fondo de Naciones Unidas
azúcar 2	para la Agricultura y la
frijoles 2	Alimentación 1
guisantes 2	
infusiones 2	**G**
kiwicha 1	Geografía
pan 2	América Latina 1
pastel 2	Chile 3
	Nicaragua 2

Paraguay 3	
Uruguay 3	
H	
Hierba	
Stevia 3	
S	
Salud 3	
nutritivos 1	

Before completing this assessment, check to make sure that the *Spanish (Spain)* language option is available at the Index dialog box. If it is not available, install the language. To do this, click the REVIEW tab, click the Language button in the Language group, and then click *Language Preferences* at the drop-down list. At the Word Options dialog box with *Language* selected in the left panel, click the down-pointing arrow at the right side of the *[Add additional editing languages]* option box, scroll down the drop-down list, and then click *Spanish (Spain)*. Click the Add button located to the right of the *[Add additional editing languages]* option box and then click OK to close the Word Options dialog box. (You will be instructed to restart Office.)

1. Using the *Language* option in the Index dialog box, you can create an index for a document written in Spanish. The steps for creating an index for a document written in Spanish are the same as the steps for creating a document written in English except that you need to change the *Language* option to *Spanish (Spain)*. Open **SpanishDoc.docx** and save the document with the name **C27-A04-SpanishDoc.**

2. Mark the text to include in the index using the concordance file named **SpanishCFile.docx** by completing the following steps:
a. Click the REFERENCES tab and then click the Insert Index button in the Index group.
b. At the Index dialog box, click the AutoMark button.
c. At the Open Index AutoMark File dialog box, make sure your Chapter27 folder is active and then double-click **SpanishCFile.docx** in the Content pane. (This turns on the display of nonprinting characters.)

3. Insert the index in the document by completing the following steps:
a. Position the insertion point at the end of the document and then insert a page break.
b. Click the Insert Index button in the Index group.
c. At the Index dialog box, click the down-pointing arrow at the right of the *Language* option box and then click *Spanish (Spain)* at the drop-down list.
d. At the Index dialog box, click the down-pointing arrow at the right of the *Language* option box and then click *Spanish (Spain)* at the drop-down list.
e. Click the down-pointing arrow at the right of the *Formats* option box and then click *Formal* at the drop-down list.
f. Make sure 3 displays in the *Columns* measurement box.
g. Click OK to close the dialog box.
5. Turn on the display of nonprinting characters.
6. Save **C27-A04-SpanishDoc.docx** and then print only the index page.

C27-A03-DesignNwsltr.docx

C27-A04-SpanishDoc.docx

Signature Word 2013   Model Answers   307

Computer Networks

A computer network consists of two or more computing or other devices connected by a communications medium, such as a wireless signal or a cable. A computer network provides a way to connect with others and share files and resources such as printers or an Internet connection.

In business settings, networks allow you to communicate with employees, suppliers, vendors, customers, and government agencies. Many companies have their own network, called an intranet, which is essentially a private Internet within the company's corporate "walls." Some companies also offer an extension of their internal network, called an extranet, to suppliers and customers. For example, a supplier might be allowed to access inventory information on a company's internal network to make sure the company does not run short of a vital part for its manufacturing process. In your home, networks are useful for sharing resources among members of your family. For example, using a home network, you might share one printer or fax machine among three or four computers.

The Internet is a global network made up of several networks linked together. If you consider all the applications, services, and tools the Internet allows you to access, you can begin to understand the power of networking and how it opens up a new world of sharing and functionality.

Communications Systems

A computer network is one kind of communications system. This system includes sending and receiving hardware, transmission and relay systems, common sets of standards so all the equipment can "talk" to each other, and communications software.

You use such a networked communications system whenever you send/receive IM or email messages, pay a bill online, shop at an Internet store, send a document to a shared printer at work or at home, or download a file.

The world of computer network communications systems is made up of:

- Transmission media upon which the data travels to/from its destination.
- A set of standards and network protocols (rules for how data is handled as it travels along a communications channel). Devices use these to send and receive data to and from each other.
- Hardware and software to connect to a communications pathway from the sending and receiving ends.

Blue Mountain Computer Services and Training

C27-A05-CompSystems.docx (page 1 of 4)

The first step in understanding a communications system is to learn the basics about transmission signals and transmission speeds when communicating over a network.

Types of Signals

Two types of signals are used to transmit voices and other sounds over a computer network: analog and digital. An analog signal is formed by continuous sound waves that fluctuate from high to low. Your voice is transmitted as an analog signal over traditional telephone lines at a certain frequency. A digital signal uses a discrete signal that is either high or low. In computer terms, high represents the digital bit 1, and low represents the digital bit 0. These are the only two states for digital data.

Telephone lines carry your voice using an analog signal. However, computers don't "speak" analog; rather, they use a binary system of 1s and 0s to turn analog data into digital signals. If you send data between computers using an analog medium such as a phone line, the signal has to be transformed from digital to analog (modulated) and back again to digital (demodulated) to be understood by the computer on the receiving end. The piece of hardware that sends and receives data from a transmission source such as your telephone line or cable television connection is a modem. The word modem comes from the combination of the words modulate and demodulate.

Today, most new communications technologies simply use a digital signal, saving the trouble of converting transmissions. An example of this trend is the demise in 2009 of analog television transmissions as the industry switched to digital signals. Many people were sent scrambling to either buy a more recent television set or buy a converter to convert digital transmissions back to analog to work with their older equipment. More recent computer networks, too, use a pure digital signal method of sending and receiving data over a network.

Transmission Speed

If you've ever been frustrated with how long it takes to download a file from a website, you are familiar with the fact that, in a communications system, data moves from one computer to another at different speeds. The speed of transmission is determined by a few key factors.

The first factor is the speed at which a signal can change from high to low, which is called frequency. A signal sent at a faster frequency provides faster transmission (Table 1). The other factor contributing to the speed of data transmission is bandwidth. On a computer network, the term bandwidth refers to the number of bits (pieces of data) per second that can be transmitted over a communications medium. Think of bandwidth as being like a highway. At rush hour, with the same amount of cars, a two-lane

Blue Mountain Computer Services and Training

C27-A05-CompSystems.docx (page 2 of 4)

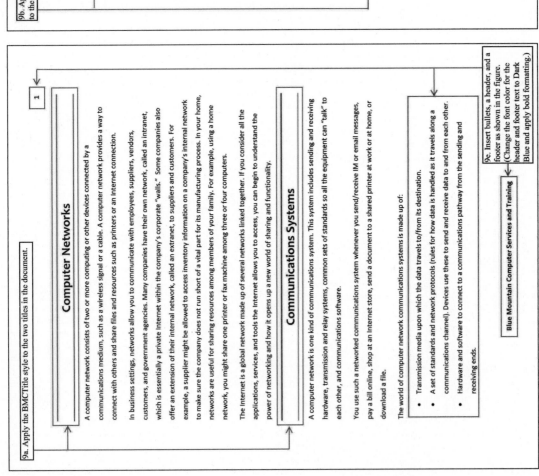

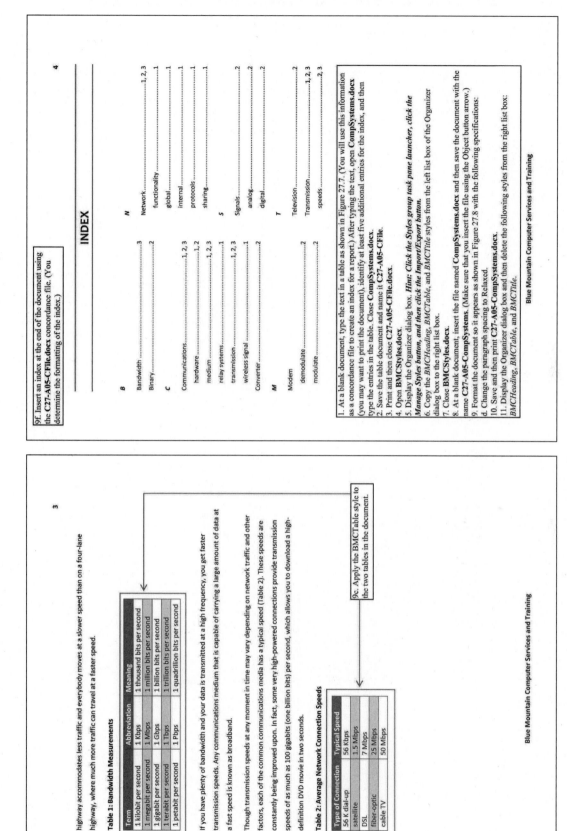

9f. Insert an index at the end of the document using the **C27-A05-CFile.docx** concordance file. (You determine the formatting of the index.)

INDEX

4

B
Bandwidth 3
Binary 2

C
Communications 1, 2, 3
hardware 1, 2
medium 1, 2, 3
relay systems 1
transmission 1, 2, 3
wireless signal 1
Converter 2

M
Modem
demodulate 2
modulate 2

N
Network 1, 2, 3
functionality 1
global 1
internal 1
protocols 1
sharing 1

S
Signals 2
analog 2
digital 2

T
Television 2
Transmission 1, 2, 3
speeds 2, 3

1. At a blank document, type the text in a table as shown in Figure 27.7. (You will use this information as a concordance file to create an index for a report.) After typing the text, open **CompSystems.docx** (you may want to print the document), identify at least five additional entries for the index, and then type the entries in the table. Close **CompSystems.docx**.
2. Save the table document and name it **C27-A05-CFile.docx**.
3. Print and then close **C27-A05-CFile.docx**.
4. Open **BMCStyles.docx**.
5. Display the Organizer dialog box. *Hint: Click the Styles group task pane launcher, click the Manage Styles button, and then click the Import/Export button.*
6. Copy the *BMCHeading, BMCTable,* and *BMCTitle* styles from the left list box of the Organizer dialog box to the right list box.
7. Close **BMCStyles.docx**.
8. At a blank document, insert the file named **CompSystems.docx** and then save the document with the name **C27-A05-CompSystems**. (Make sure that you insert the file using the Object button arrow.)
9. Format the document so it appears as shown in Figure 27.8 with the following specifications:
   d. Change the paragraph spacing to Relaxed.
10. Save and then print **C27-A05-CompSystems.docx**.
11. Display the Organizer dialog box and then delete the following styles from the right list box: *BMCHeading, BMCTable,* and *BMCTitle.*

Blue Mountain Computer Services and Training

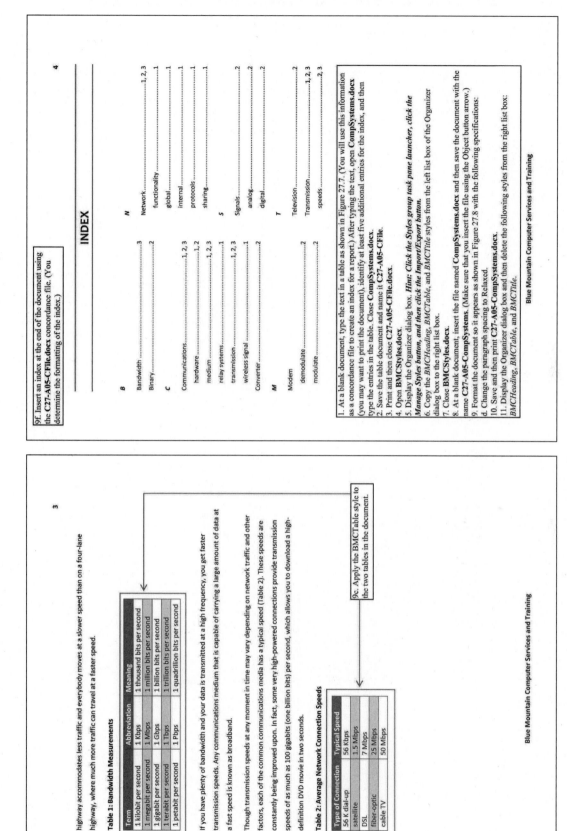

highway accommodates less traffic and everybody moves at a slower speed than on a four-lane highway, where much more traffic can travel at a faster speed.

3

Table 1: Bandwidth Measurements

Term	Abbreviation	Meaning
1 kilobit per second	1 Kbps	1 thousand bits per second
1 megabit per second	1 Mbps	1 million bits per second
1 gigabit per second	1 Gbps	1 billion bits per second
1 terabit per second	1 Tbps	1 trillion bits per second
1 petabit per second	1 Pbps	1 quadrillion bits per second

If you have plenty of bandwidth and your data is transmitted at a high frequency, you get faster transmission speeds. Any communications medium that is capable of carrying a large amount of data at a fast speed is known as broadband.

Though transmission speeds at any moment in time may vary depending on network traffic and other factors, each of the common communications media has a typical speed (Table 2). These speeds are constantly being improved upon. In fact, some very high-powered connections provide transmission speeds of as much as 100 gigabits (one billion bits) per second, which allows you to download a high-definition DVD movie in two seconds.

Table 2: Average Network Connection Speeds

Type of Connection	Typical Speed
56 K dial-up	56 Kbps
satellite	1.5 Mbps
DSL	7 Mbps
fiber-optic	25 Mbps
cable TV	50 Mbps

9c. Apply the BMCTable style to the two tables in the document.

Blue Mountain Computer Services and Training

C27-A05-CompSystems.docx (page 3 of 4)

C27-A05-CompSystems.docx (page 4 of 4)

Chapter 28 Assessment Annotated Model Answers

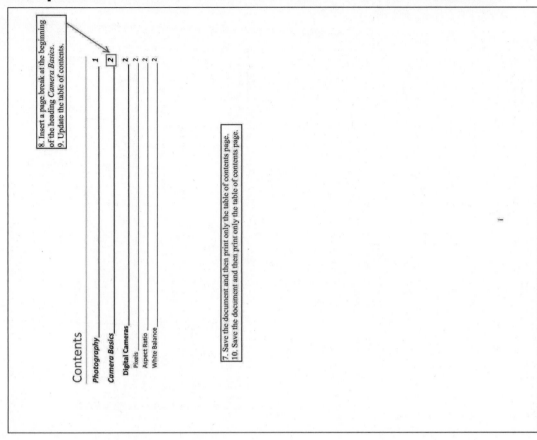

8. Insert a page break at the beginning of the heading *Camera Basics*.
9. Update the table of contents.

Contents

Photography	*1*
Camera Basics	*1*
Digital Cameras	**2**
Pixels	2
Aspect Ratio	2
White Balance	2

7. Save the document and then print only the table of contents page.
10. Save the document and then print only the table of contents page.

Contents

Photography	*1*
Camera Basics	*1*
Digital Cameras	**2**
Pixels	2
Aspect Ratio	2
White Balance	2

1. Open **PhotoRpt.docx** and save the document with the name **C28-A01-PhotoRpt**.
2. Move the insertion point to the beginning of the heading *Photography* and then insert a section break that begins a new page.
3. With the insertion point positioned below the section break, insert page numbers at the bottom centers of pages and change the beginning page number to 1.
4. Press Ctrl + Home to move the insertion point to the beginning of the document (on the blank page) and then create a table of contents with the *Automatic Table 1* option at the Table of Contents button drop-down list.
5. Display the Table of Contents dialog box, select *Distinctive* at the *Formats* option box, and make sure a 3 displays in the *Show levels* measurement box.

6. Change the page numbering format on the table of contents page to lowercase roman numerals.

i

COMPUTER INPUT DEVICES

Engineers have been especially creative in designing new ways to get information into computers. Some input methods are highly specialized and unusual, while commonly used devices often undergo redesign to improve their capabilities or to make them more ergonomic. Some commonly used input devices include keyboards, mice, trackballs, and touchpads.

KEYBOARD

A keyboard can be an external device that is battery powered or attached by means of a cable, or it can be attached to the CPU case itself, as it is for laptop computers. Most keyboards today are QWERTY keyboards, which take their name from the first six keys at the left of the first row of letters (see Figure 1). An alternative, the DVORAK keyboard, places the most commonly used keys close to the user's fingertips and speeds typing. Many keyboards have a separate numeric keypad, like that of a calculator, containing numbers and mathematical operators. All keyboards have modifier keys that enable the user to change the symbol or character that is entered when a given key is pressed. The Shift key, for example, makes a letter uppercase. Keyboards also have special cursor keys that enable the user to change the position on the screen of the cursor, a symbol that appears on the monitor to show where in a document the next change will appear. Most keyboards also have function keys, labeled F_1, F_2, F_3, and so on. These keys allow the user to issue commands by pressing a single key.

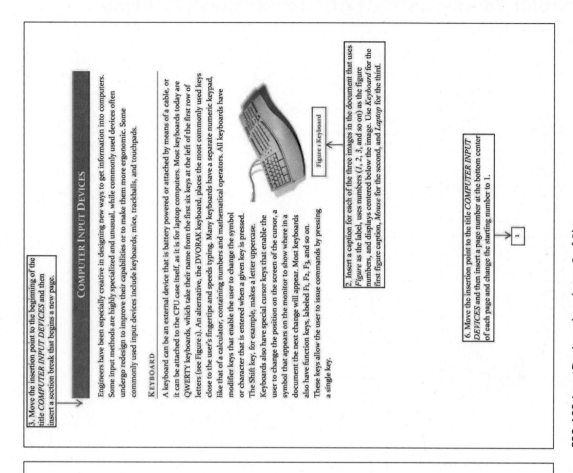

Figure 1 Keyboard

2. Insert a caption for each of the three images in the document that uses *Figure* as the label, uses numbers (*1, 2, 3*, and so on) as the figure numbers, and displays centered below the image. Use *Keyboard* for the first figure caption, *Mouse* for the second, and *Laptop* for the third.

6. Move the insertion point to the title *COMPUTER INPUT DEVICES* and then insert a page number at the bottom center of each page and change the starting number to 1.

1

---

5. Apply the Heading 1 style to the title *Table of Figures*.

TABLE OF FIGURES

4. Press Ctrl + Home, type Table of Figures, press the Enter key, and then insert a table of figures with the Formal format.

1. Open **InputDevices.docx** and save the document with the name **C28-A02-InputDevices**.
9. Update the table of figures.

7. Move the insertion point to the title *TABLE OF FIGURES* and then change the page numbering style to lowercase roman numerals.

i

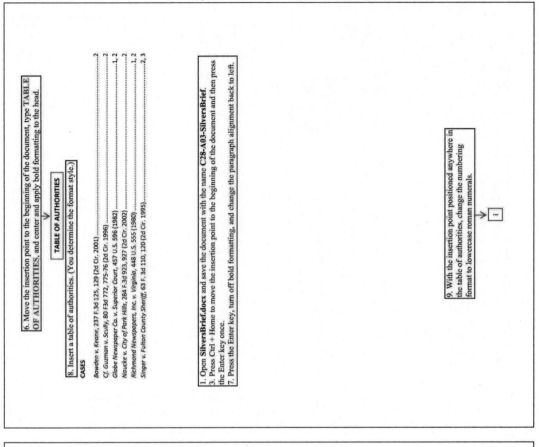

6. Move the insertion point to the beginning of the document, type TABLE OF AUTHORITIES, and center and apply bold formatting to the head.

TABLE OF AUTHORITIES

8. Insert a table of authorities. (You determine the format style.)

CASES

Bowden v. Keane, 237 F.3d 125, 129 (2d Cir. 2001) 2
Cf. Guzman v. Scully, 80 F3d 772, 775-76 (2d Cir. 1996) 2
Globe Newspaper Co. v. Superior Court, 457 U.S. 596 (1982) 1, 2
Naucke v. City of Park Hills, 284 F.3d 923, 927 (2d Cir. 2002) 2
Richmond Newspapers, Inc. v. Virginia, 448 U.S. 555 (1980) 1, 2
Singer v. Fulton County Sheriff, 63 F. 3d 110, 120 (2d Cir. 1995) 2, 3

1. Open **SilversBrief.docx** and save the document with the name **C28-A03-SilversBrief**.
3. Press Ctrl + Home to move the insertion point to the beginning of the document and then press the Enter key once.
7. Press the Enter key, turn off bold formatting, and change the paragraph alignment back to left.

9. With the insertion point positioned anywhere in the table of authorities, change the numbering format to lowercase roman numerals.

i

C28-A03-SilversBrief.docx (page 1 of 4)

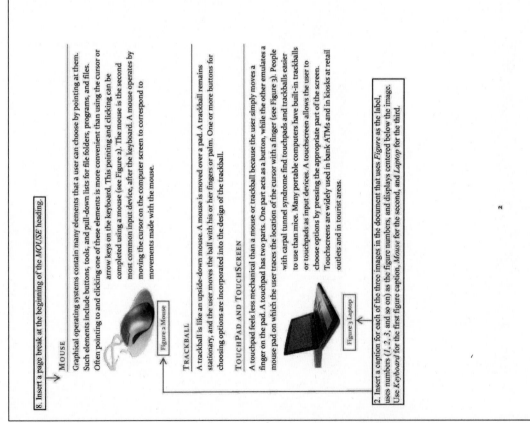

8. Insert a page break at the beginning of the *MOUSE* heading.

MOUSE

Graphical operating systems contain many elements that a user can choose by pointing at them. Such elements include buttons, tools, and pull-down lists for file folders, programs, and files. Often pointing to and clicking one of these elements is more convenient than using the cursor or arrow keys on the keyboard. This pointing and clicking can be completed using a mouse (see Figure 2). The mouse is the second most common input device, after the keyboard. A mouse operates by moving the cursor on the computer screen to correspond to movements made with the mouse.

Figure 2 Mouse

TRACKBALL

A trackball is like an upside-down mouse. A mouse is moved over a pad. A trackball remains stationary, and the user moves the ball with his or her fingers or palm. One or more buttons for choosing options are incorporated into the design of the trackball.

TOUCHPAD AND TOUCHSCREEN

A touchpad feels less mechanical than a mouse or trackball because the user simply moves a finger on the pad. A touchpad has two parts. One part acts as a button, while the other emulates a mouse pad on which the user traces the location of the cursor with a finger (see Figure 3). People with carpal tunnel syndrome find touchpads and trackballs easier to use than mice. Many portable computers have built-in trackballs or touchpads as input devices. A touchscreen allows the user to choose options by pressing the appropriate part of the screen. Touchscreens are widely used in bank ATMs and in kiosks at retail outlets and in tourist areas.

Figure 3 Laptop

2. Insert a caption for each of the three images in the document that uses *Figure* as the label, uses numbers (*1, 2, 3,* and so on) as the figure numbers, and displays centered below the image. Use *Keyboard* for the first figure caption, *Mouse* for the second, and *Laptop* for the third.

2

C28-A02-InputDevices.docx (page 3 of 3)

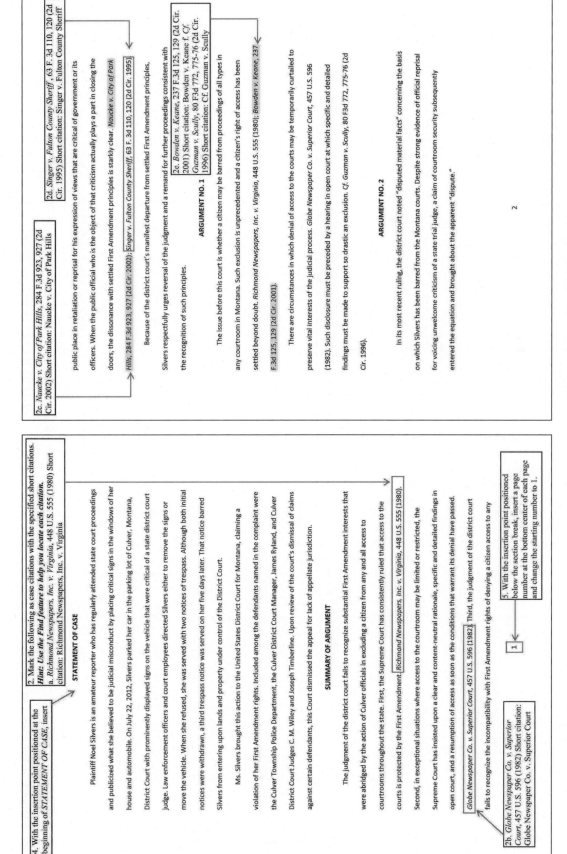

C28-A03-SilversBrief.docx (page 3 of 4)

C28-A03-SilversBrief.docx (page 2 of 4)

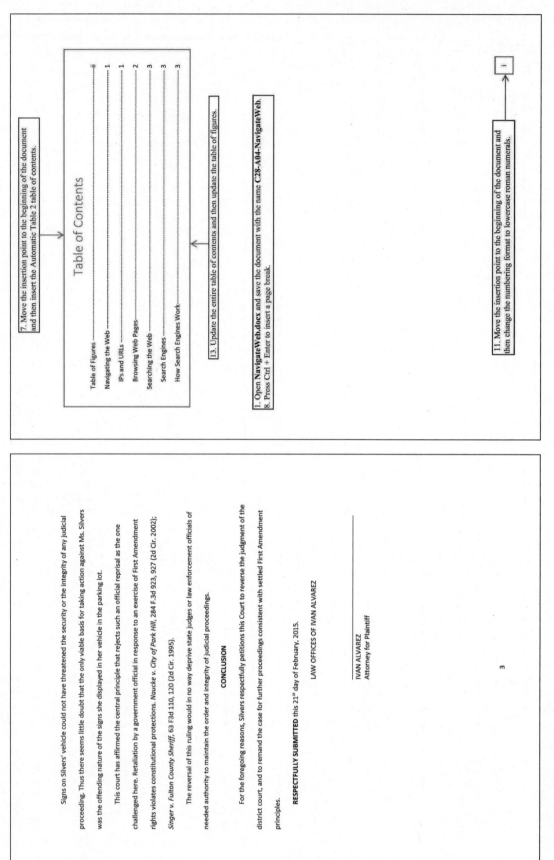

7. Move the insertion point to the beginning of the document and then insert the Automatic Table 2 table of contents.

Table of Contents

13. Update the entire table of contents and then update the table of figures.

1. Open **NavigateWeb.docx** and save the document with the name **C28-A04-NavigateWeb**.
8. Press Ctrl + Enter to insert a page break.

11. Move the insertion point to the beginning of the document and then change the numbering format to lowercase roman numerals.

i

Signs on Silvers' vehicle could not have threatened the security or the integrity of any judicial proceeding. Thus there seems little doubt that the only viable basis for taking action against Ms. Silvers was the offending nature of the signs she displayed in her vehicle in the parking lot.

This court has affirmed the central principle that rejects such an official reprisal as the one challenged here. Retaliation by a government official in response to an exercise of First Amendment rights violates constitutional protections. *Naucke v. City of Park Hill*, 284 F.3d 923, 927 (2d Cir. 2002); *Singer v. Fulton County Sheriff*, 63 F3d 110, 120 (2d Cir. 1995).

The reversal of this ruling would in no way deprive state judges or law enforcement officials of needed authority to maintain the order and integrity of judicial proceedings.

CONCLUSION

For the foregoing reasons, Silvers respectfully petitions this Court to reverse the judgment of the district court, and to remand the case for further proceedings consistent with settled First Amendment principles.

RESPECTFULLY SUBMITTED this 21st day of February, 2015.

LAW OFFICES OF IVAN ALVAREZ

IVAN ALVAREZ
Attorney for Plaintiff

3

2. Move the insertion point to the beginning of the title *Navigating the Web* and then insert a section break that begins a new page.

Navigating the Web

Since so many people create web pages, the Web should be chaotic. However, underlying systems are in place specifying how pages are organized on the Web and how they are delivered to your computer. This system involves unique addresses used to access each web page, a unique address for each computer, and browser features for locating and retrieving online content.

IPs and URLs

An *Internet Protocol (IP) address* is a series of numbers that uniquely identifies a location on the Internet. An IP address consists of four groups of numbers separated by periods. For example: 225.73.110.102. A nonprofit organization called ICANN keeps track of IP numbers around the world.

Because numbers would be difficult to remember for retrieving pages, we use a text-based address referred to as a *uniform resource locator (URL)* to go to a website. A URL, also called a *web address*, has several parts separated by a colon (:), slashes (/), and dots (.). The first part of a URL is called a *protocol* and identifies a certain way for interpreting computer information in the transmission process. *Http*, which stands for *hypertext transfer protocol*, and *ftp*, for *file transfer protocol*, are examples of protocols. Some sites use a secondary identifier for the type of site being contacted, such as *www* for *World Wide Web* site, but this is often optional.

The next part of the URL is the *domain name*, which identifies the group of servers (the domain) to which the site belongs and the particular company or organization name. A suffix, such as *.com* or *.edu*, further identifies the domain. For example, the *.com* in the URL http://www.emcp.com is a top-level domain (TLD). Several TLDs exists such as *.com*, *.net*, *.org*, *.edu*, and *.gov*. Table A provides a rundown of TLDs being used today.

Table A: Common Top-Level Domain Suffixes

Suffix	Type of Organization	Example
.biz	business site	Billboard: http://www.billboard.biz
.com	company or commercial institution	Intel: http://www.intel.com
.edu	educational institution	Harvard University: http://www.harvard.edu
.gov	government site	Internal Revenue Service: http://www.irs.gov
.int	international organizations endorsed by treaty	World Health Organization: http://www.who.int
.mil	military site	U.S. Department of Defense: http://www.defenselink.mil
.net	administrative site for ISPs	Earthlink: http://www.earthlink.net
.org	nonprofit or private organization	Red Cross: http://www.redcross.org

4. Click in any cell in the first table in the document and then use the caption feature to create the caption *Table A: Common Top-Level Domain Suffixes* and position it above the table.

3. With the insertion point below the section break, number the pages at the bottom right of each page and change the starting number to 1.

1

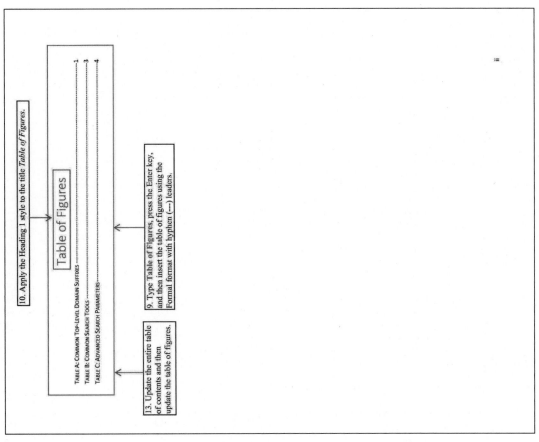

10. Apply the Heading 1 style to the title *Table of Figures*.

Table of Figures

9. Type Table of Figures, press the Enter key, and then insert the table of figures using the Formal format with hyphen (---) leaders.

13. Update the entire table of contents and then update the table of figures.

ii

Browsing Web Pages

You may already be quite comfortable with browsing the Internet, but you may not have pondered how browsers move around the Web and retrieve data. Any element of a web page (text, graphic, audio, or video) can be linked to another page using a hyperlink. A hyperlink describes a destination within a web document and can be inserted in text or a graphical object such as a company logo. Text that is linked is called *hypertext*.

A website is a series of related web pages that are linked together. You get to a website by entering the URL, such as www.amazon.com, in your browser. Every website has a starting page, called the *home page*, which is displayed when you enter the site URL. You can also enter a URL to jump to a specific page on a site, such as the Video-On-Demand page at Amazon's site, www.amazon.com/Video-On-Demand.

2

---

12. Insert a page break at the beginning of the title *Searching the Web.*

Searching the Web

A search engine, such as Google.com, Ask.com, and Yahoo.com, catalogs and indexes web pages for you. A type of search engine, called a search directory, can also catalog pages into topics such as *finance, health, news, shopping,* and so on. Search engines may seem to be free services, but in reality they are typically financed by selling advertising. Some also make money by selling information about your online activities and interests to advertisers.

Search Engines

The newest wave of search engines, including Microsoft Bing and Google Squared, not only search for content but also make choices among content to deliver more targeted results. Such search engines allow you, for example, to ask for a list of female tennis stars from 1900, on and they then assemble a table of them for you. Table B shows some common search tools with their URLs and an indication of whether they offer the ability to catalog pages in directories.

5. Click in any cell in the second table and then create the caption *Table B: Common Search Tools* and position it above the table.

Table B: Common Search Tools

Search Tool	URL	Type
Ask	www.ask.com	engine
Bing	www.bing.com	engine
Dogpile	www.dogpile.com	engine
Google	www.google.com	engine/directory
MSN	www.msn.com	engine/directory
Yahoo!	www.yahoo.com	engine/directory

How Search Engines Work

So how do search engines work? You can search for information by going to the search engine's website and typing your search text, which is comprised of one or more keywords or keyword phrases. For example, to find information about the international space station, you could type *space station* in the search engine's search text box and press the Enter key. You can narrow your search by specifying that you want to view links to certain types of results such as images, maps, or videos.

You can get more targeted search results by honing your searching technique. Effective searching is a skill that you gain through practice. For example, typing *space station* in a search engine's web page could easily return more than eighty million results. If what you really need is the cost to build the station, consider a more targeted keyword phrase like "space station cost." Search engines provide advanced search options, which you can use to include or exclude certain results. For example, you can exclude pages with certain domain suffixes (such as .com and .net) to limit your search results to educational and government sites. Table C offers some ways you can narrow your search by entering your keywords in various ways.

3

2b. Insert the table of contents as shown in Figure 28.12.

TABLE OF CONTENTS

1. Open **Networks.docx** and save the document with the name **C28-A05-Networks.**
2. Format the document so it appears as shown in Figure 28.12 with the following specifications:
c. Apply additional formatting so your document appears as shown in Figure 28.12.

2d. Insert page numbers as shown. (Change the page numbering format to lowercase roman numerals for the table of contents page and table of figures and tables page.)

i

C28-A05-Networks.docx (page 1 of 5)

---

6. Click in any cell in the third table and then create the caption *Table C: Advanced Search Parameters* and position it above the table.

Table C: Advanced Search Parameters

Item	What It Does	Example
Quotes ("")	Instruction to use exact word or words in the exact order given	"Pearl Harbor"
Minus symbol (-)	Excludes words preceded by the minus symbol from the search	jaguar –car
Wildcard (*)	Treat the asterisk as a placeholder for any possible word	*bird for bluebird, redbird, etc.
Or	Allow either one word or the other	Economy 2014 or Economy 2015

4

C28-A04-NavigateWeb.docx (page 6 of 6)

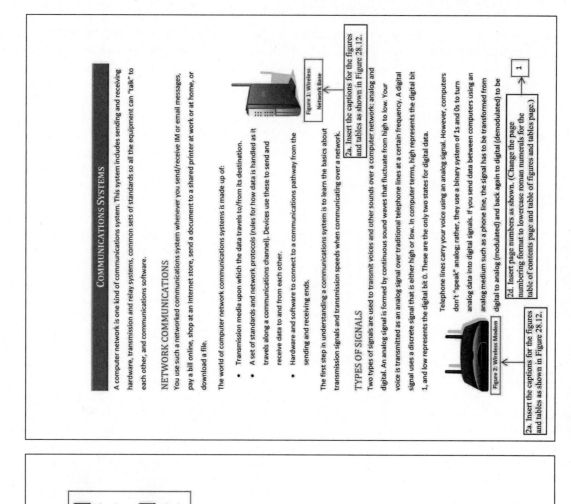

COMMUNICATIONS SYSTEMS

A computer network is one kind of communications system. This system includes sending and receiving hardware, transmission and relay systems, common sets of standards so all the equipment can "talk" to each other, and communications software.

NETWORK COMMUNICATIONS

You use such a networked communications system whenever you send/receive IM or email messages, pay a bill online, shop at an Internet store, send a document to a shared printer at work or at home, or download a file.

The world of computer network communications systems is made up of:

- Transmission media upon which the data travels to/from its destination.
- A set of standards and network protocols (rules for how data is handled as it travels along a communications channel). Devices use these to send and receive data to and from each other.
- Hardware and software to connect to a communications pathway from the sending and receiving ends.

The first step in understanding a communications system is to learn the basics about transmission signals and transmission speeds when communicating over a network.

TYPES OF SIGNALS

Two types of signals are used to transmit voices and other sounds over a computer network: analog and digital. An analog signal is formed by continuous sound waves that fluctuate from high to low. Your voice is transmitted as an analog signal over traditional telephone lines at a certain frequency. A digital signal uses a discrete signal that is either high or low. In computer terms, high represents the digital bit 1, and low represents the digital bit 0. These are the only two states for digital data.

Telephone lines carry your voice using an analog signal. However, computers don't "speak" analog; rather, they use a binary system of 1s and 0s to turn analog data into digital signals. If you send data between computers using an analog medium such as a phone line, the signal has to be transformed from digital to analog (modulated) and back again to digital (demodulated) to be

Figure 1: Wireless Network Base

2a. Insert the captions for the figures and tables as shown in Figure 28.12.

Figure 2: Wireless Modem

2a. Insert the captions for the figures and tables as shown in Figure 28.12.

2d. Insert page numbers as shown. (Change the page numbering format to lowercase roman numerals for the table of contents page and table of figures and tables page.)

1

C28-A05-Networks.docx (page 3 of 5)

FIGURES

TABLES

2 c. Insert the tables of figures and tables as shown on the second page of Figure 28.12. (You will need to create two different tables of figures: one for the figures and one for the tables.)

ii

C28-A05-Networks.docx (page 2 of 5)

Signature Word 2013   Model Answers

understood by the computer on the receiving end. The piece of hardware that sends and receives data from a transmission source such as your telephone line or cable television connection is a modem. The word modem comes from the combination of the words *modulate* and *demodulate*.

Today, most new communications technologies simply use a digital signal, saving the trouble of converting transmissions. An example of this trend is the demise in 2009 of analog television transmissions as the industry switched to digital signals. Many people were sent scrambling to either buy a newer television set or buy a converter to convert digital transmissions back to analog to work with their older equipment. Newer computer networks, too, use a pure digital signal method of sending and receiving data over a network.

TRANSMISSION SPEED

If you've ever been frustrated with how long it takes to download a file from a website, you are familiar with the fact that, in a communications system, data moves from one computer to another at different speeds. The speed of transmission is determined by a few key factors.

The first factor is the speed at which a signal can change from high to low, which is called frequency. A signal sent at a faster frequency provides faster transmission (Figure 1). The other factor contributing to the speed of data transmission is bandwidth. On a computer network, the term bandwidth refers to the number of bits (pieces of data) per second that can be transmitted over a communications medium. Think of bandwidth as being like a highway. At rush hour, with the same amount of cars, a two-lane highway accommodates less traffic and everybody moves at a slower speed than on a four-lane highway, where much more traffic can travel at a faster speed.

2a. Insert the captions for the figures and tables as shown in Figure 28.12.

Table 1: Bandwidth

Term	Abbreviation	Meaning
1 kilobit per second	1 Kbps	1 thousand bits per second
1 megabit per second	1 Mbps	1 million bits per second
1 gigabit per second	1 Gbps	1 billion bits per second
1 terabit per second	1 Tbps	1 trillion bits per second
1 petabit per second	1 Pbps	1 quadrillion bits per second

If you have plenty of bandwidth and your data is transmitted at a high frequency, you get faster transmission speeds. Any communications medium that is capable of carrying a large amount of data at a fast speed is known as broadband.

2

Though transmission speeds at any moment in time may vary depending on network traffic and other factors, each of the common communications media has a typical speed (Figure 2). These speeds are constantly being improved upon. In fact, some very high-powered connections provide transmission speeds of as much as 100 gigabits (one billion bits) per second, which allows you to download a high-definition DVD movie in two seconds.

2a. Insert the captions for the figures and tables as shown in Figure 28.12.

Table 2: Average Network Connection Speeds

Type of Connection	Typical Speed
56 K dial-up	56 Kbps
satellite	1.5 Mbps
DSL	7 Mbps
fiber-optic	25 Mbps
cable TV	50 Mbps

3

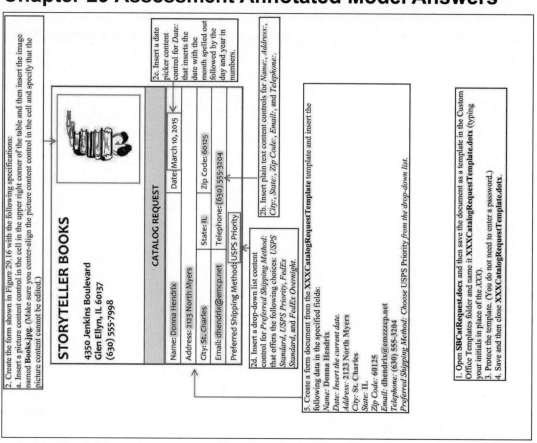

2. Create the form shown in Figure 29.16 with the following specifications:

a. Insert a picture content control in the cell in the upper right corner of the table and then insert the image named **Books.jpg**. (Make sure you center-align the picture content control in the cell and specify that the picture content cannot be edited.)

2c. Insert a date picker content control for *Date:* that inserts the date with the month spelled out followed by the day and year in numbers.

STORYTELLER BOOKS

4350 Jenkins Boulevard
Glen Ellyn, IL 60137
(630) 555-7998

CATALOG REQUEST

Name: Donna Hendrix   Date: March 10, 2015

Address: 2123 North Myers

City: St. Charles   State: IL   Zip Code: 60125

Email: dhendrix@emcp.net   Telephone: (630) 555-3204

Preferred Shipping Method: USPS Priority

2b. Insert plain text content controls for *Name:, Address:, City:, State:, Zip Code:, Email:,* and *Telephone:.*

2d. Insert a drop-down list content control for *Preferred Shipping Method:* that offers the following choices: *USPS Standard, USPS Priority, FedEx Standard,* and *FedEx Overnight.*

5. Create a form document from the **XXXCatalogRequestTemplate** template and insert the following data in the specified fields:
Name: Donna Hendrix
Date: Insert the current date.
Address: 2123 North Myers
City: St. Charles
State: IL
Zip Code: 60125
Email: dhendrix@emzzzcp.net
Telephone: (630) 555-3204
Preferred Shipping Method: Choose USPS Priority from the drop-down list.

1. Open **SBCatRequest.docx** and then save the document as a template in the Custom Office Templates folder and name it **XXXCatalogRequestTemplate.dotx** (typing your initials in place of the *XXX*).
3. Protect the template. (You do not need to enter a password.)
4. Save and then close **XXXCatalogRequestTemplate.dotx**.

C29-A02-SBHendrixCatReq.docx

1b. Insert the *Books.jpg* image using the Pictures button on the INSERT tab. Size and move the image so it displays as shown in Figure 29.15. Change the text wrapping of the image to Behind Text.

1c. Set the company name, *STORYTELLER BOOKS,* in 22-point Candara and apply bold formatting. Set the remainder of the text in 11-point Candara and apply bold formatting. Insert the book symbol at the Symbol dialog box with the *Wingdings* font selected. (The book symbol is in the first row of the symbol list box.)

STORYTELLER BOOKS

4350 Jenkins Boulevard ▢ Glen Ellyn, IL 60137 ▢ (630) 555-7998

Name: Chris Felder

Book Title: I Know Why the Caged Bird Sings   Author: Maya Angelou

Email: cfelder@emcp.net   Telephone: (630) 555-8965

Notes: I am interested in purchasing a paperback version either new or used.

1e. Insert the horizontal line by holding down the Shift key, pressing the hyphen key three times, and then pressing the Enter key.

1d. Insert a plain text content control one space after the colon for each of the following: *Name:, Book Title:, Author:, Email:, Telephone:,* and *Notes:.*

5b. Insert the following data in the specified fields: *Name:* Chris Felder *Book Title:* I Know Why the Caged Bird Sings *Author:* Maya Angelou *Email:* cfelder@emcp.net *Telephone:* (630) 555-8965 *Notes:* I am interested in purchasing a paperback version either new or used.

1. Create the form shown in Figure 29.15 with the following specifications:
a. At a blank document, click the *No Spacing* style in the Styles group on the HOME tab.
2. Protect the document and only allow filling in the form. (Do not enter a password.)
3. Save the document as a template in the Custom Office Templates folder and name it **XXXBookRequestTemplate** (using your initials in place of the *XXX*).
4. Close **XXXBookRequestTemplate.dotx**.
5. Create a form document from the **XXXBookRequestTemplate** template by completing the following steps:
a. Click the FILE tab and then click the *New* option. At the New backstage area, click the *PERSONAL* option and then click the *XXXBookRequestTemplate* thumbnail (where your initials display in place of the *XXX*).

C29-A01-SBRequest.docx

Left Document — C29-A03-FundApp.docx

1. Open **ERCFundingApp.docx** and then save the document as a template in the Custom Office Templates folder and name it **XXXERCFundAppTemplate.docx** (typing your initials in place of the XXX).
2. Enter the data in the appropriate cells and insert text and check box form fields in the template form, as shown in Figure 29.17. **Hint:** Use options in the **Legacy Tools button drop-down list.**

Evergreen Regional Center
9800 Vineville Avenue ◆ Macon, GA 31206 ◆ (478) 555-9800

Project Title: Quality Improvement Project	Date: 03/10/2015
Targeted Department: Pediatrics	Department Manager: Angela Gilmore
Required Funds: $50,000	Matching Funds: $25,000
Beginning Date: 07/01/2015	Completion Date: 06/30/2016

Check the statement(s) that best describe(s) how this proposal will meet the eligibility criteria:

☒ Improved patient care outcomes   ☒ Reduced outcome variation
☐ Cost reduction   ☒ Compliance with quality standards
☒ Improved customer relations   ☒ Increase in services

Applicant Name: Maria Alvarez	Employee Number: 321-4890
Department: Pediatrics	Extension: 4539

3. Protect the template and only allow filling in the form. (You do not need to enter a password.)
4. Save and then close **XXXERCFundAppTemplate.docx**

5. Create a form document from the **XXXERCFundAppTemplate.docx** template and insert the following data in the specified fields:
Project Title: Quality Improvement Project
Date: (Insert current date)
Targeted Department: Pediatrics
Department Manager: Angela Gilmore
Required Funds: $50,000
Matching Funds: $25,000
Beginning Date: 07/01/2015
Completion Date: 06/30/2016
Insert an "X" in each of the check boxes except Cost reduction
Applicant Name: Maria Alvarez
Employee Number: 321-4890
Department: Pediatrics
Extension: 4539

C29-A03-FundApp.docx

Right Document — C29-A04-ESpringer.docx

5. Create a form document from the **XXXWCDSFormTemplate.docx** template and insert the following data in the specified fields:
Patient Name: Ethan Mark Springer Patient Number: 4221 Address: 345 Jackson Court City: Bismarck State: nd (This text will change to uppercase when you press Tab.) Zip Code: 58506 Telephone: (701) 555-3481 Medical Insurance: (Leave the default Premiere Group.) (Leave the check mark in the Both parents check box.) Relationship: (Leave the default Mother.) Relationship: (Leave the default Father.)

WILLOW CREEK

DENTAL SERVICES

PATIENT UPDATE

Patient Name: Ethan Mark Springer	Patient Number: 4221

Address: 345 Jackson Court   City: Bismarck   State: ND   Zip Code: 58506

Telephone: (701) 555-3481

Medical Insurance   Premiere Group

Check the appropriate box identifying with whom the patient lives.

☒ Both parents   ☐ Mother
☐ Father   ☐ Other – Specify:

Guardian Information
Relationship: Mother
Name: Elizabeth Springer
Address: 345 Jackson Court, Bismarck, ND 58506
Home Telephone: (701) 555-3481
Work Telephone: (701) 555-8711

Guardian Information
Relationship: Father
Name: Chris Springer
Address: 345 Jackson Court, Bismarck, ND 58506
Home Telephone: (701) 555-3481
Work Telephone: (701) 555-0075

2a. Insert a text form field for *Patient Number:* that specifies a maximum length of 4 characters.

2b. Insert a text form field for *State:* that specifies a maximum length of 2 characters and a text format of Uppercase.

2c. Insert a text form field for *Zip Code:* that specifies a maximum length of 5 characters.

2d. Insert a text form field for *Medical Insurance:* that specifies *Premiere Group* as the default text.

2e. Insert a check box form field in the cell immediately left of *Both parents* that is checked by default.

2f. Insert a text form field for the first *Relationship:* data field that specifies *Mother* as the default text.

2g. Insert a second *Relationship:* data field that specifies *Father* as the default text.

1. Open **WCDSForm.docx** and then save the document as a template in the Custom Office Templates folder and name it **XXXWCDSFormTemplate.docx** (typing your initials in place of the XXX).
2. Enter the data in the appropriate cells and insert form fields in the form shown in Figure 29.18 with the following specifications:
h. Insert the remaining text and check box form fields as shown in Figure 29.18.
3. Protect the template and only allow filling in the form.
4. Save and then close **XXXWCDSFormTemplate.dotx.**

C29-A04-ESpringer.docx

1a. Select the name *Barrington & Gates*, the line below, and the text *Rachel Rasmussen, Associate* and then save the selected text in a custom building block in the *Quick Part* gallery named with your initials followed by *BGRR*.
8a. Click the building block content control in the top cell, click the Quick Parts button that displays at the right of the content control tab, and then click the *BGRR* building block that is preceded by your initials.

BARRINGTON & GATES

Rachel Rasmussen, Associate

Client Information

Name: Norm Peterson	Street Address: 210 West Central Avenue	
City: Boston	State: MA	Zip Code: 02108
Home Phone: (617) 555-9300	Cell Phone: (617) 555-8154	Payment Method: Cash
Employer: Boston Hall Accounting		Title: Accountant
Address: 76 Beacon Street, Suite 2001, Boston, MA 02108		Work Phone: (617) 555-8117

Referred by:

☐ Employee	☒ Friend	☐ Lawyer referral service
☐ Yellow Pages	☐ Internet	☐ Other: Click here to enter text.

8. Create a form document from the **XXXBGClientInfo.dotx** template with the following specifications:
b. Fill in each text content control by clicking the text *Click here to enter text* and then typing text of your choosing. Click only one of the check box content controls in the *Referred by* section.

1b. Select the name *Barrington & Gates*, the line below, and the text *Gerald Castello, Associate* and then save the selected text in a custom building block in the *Quick Part* gallery named with your initials followed by *BGGC*.
5a. Click the building block content control in the top cell, click the Quick Parts button that displays at the right of the content control tab, and then click the *BGGC* building block that is preceded by your initials.

BARRINGTON & GATES

Gerald Castello, Associate

Client Information

Name: Sam Malone	Street Address: 400 West Broad Street, Apt 601	
City: Boston	State: MA	Zip Code: 02108
Home Phone: (617) 555-5003	Cell Phone: (617) 555-5574	Payment Method: Check
Employer: Cheers Bar and Grill		Title: Bartender
Address: 84 Beacon Street		Work Phone: (617) 555-9605

Referred by:

☐ Employee	☐ Friend	☐ Lawyer referral service
☒ Yellow Pages	☐ Internet	☐ Other: Click here to enter text.

5. Create a document from the **XXXBGClientInfo.dotx** template with the following specifications:
b. Fill in each text content control by clicking the text *Click here to enter text* and then typing text of your choosing. Click only one of the check box content controls in the *Referred by* section.

3b. Insert a check box (using the Check Box Content Control button) in the cell immediately left of each of the following cell entries: *Employee, Friend, Lawyer referral service, Yellow Pages, Internet,* and *Other*.

1. The Controls group on the DEVELOPER tab contains additional buttons you can use when creating a form. In addition to the Legacy Tools check box form field, you can insert a check box with the Check Box Content Control. Use the Building Block Gallery Content Control button to insert a content control for inserting building blocks in a form. Experiment with the Check Box Content Control button and Building Block Gallery Content Control button to determine how to use them in a form and then open **BGBuildingBlocks.docx** and create the following building blocks:
c. Close **BGBuildingBlocks.docx**.
2. Open **BGClientInfo.docx** and then save the document as a template in the Custom Office Templates folder with the name **XXXBGClientInfo.dotx** (typing your initials in place of the *XXX*).
3. Add the following form fields to the form:
a. Make the top cell active and then insert the building block gallery content control.
4. Because your template contains the building block gallery content control, you cannot protect it and only allow filling in the form. Doing this would keep you from being able to use the building block content control. Save and then close **XXXBGClientInfo.dotx**.
6. Save the completed form document with the name **C29-A05-GC-Client**.

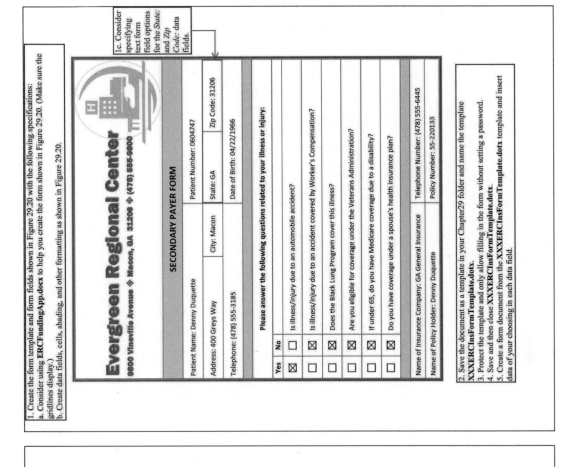

Evergreen Regional Center

9800 Vineville Avenue ◆ Macon, GA 31206 ◆ (478) 555-9800

SECONDARY PAYER FORM

Patient Name: Denny Duquette

Patient Number: 0604747

Address: 400 Greys Way

City: Macon

State: GA

Zip Code: 31206

Telephone: (478) 555-3185

Date of Birth: 04/22/1966

Please answer the following questions related to your illness or injury:

Yes	No	
☒	☐	Is Illness/injury due to an automobile accident?
☐	☒	Is illness/injury due to an accident covered by Worker's Compensation?
☐	☒	Does the Black Lung Program cover this illness?
☐	☒	Are you eligible for coverage under the Veterans Administration?
☐	☒	If under 65, do you have Medicare coverage due to a disability?
☐	☒	Do you have coverage under a spouse's health insurance plan?

Name of Insurance Company: GA General Insurance

Telephone Number: (478) 555-6445

Name of Policy Holder: Denny Duquette

Policy Number: 55-220133

1. Create the form template and form fields shown in Figure 29.20 with the following specifications:
a. Consider using **ERCFundingApp.docx** to help you create the form shown in Figure 29.20. (Make sure the gridlines display.)
b. Create data fields, cells, shading, and other formatting as shown in Figure 29.20.

1c. Consider specifying text form field options for the *State:* and *Zip Code:* data fields.

2. Save the document as a template in your Chapter29 folder and name the template **XXXERCInsFormTemplate.dotx**.
3. Protect the template and only allow filling in the form without setting a password.
4. Save and then close **XXXERCInsFormTemplate.dotx**.
5. Create a form document from the **XXXERCInsFormTemplate.dotx** template and insert data of your choosing in each data field.

C29-A07-InsForm.docx

South Sound Aviation

8994 Airport Boulevard
Auburn, WA 98022
(425) 555-3311 OR (206) 555-9075
southsoundaviation@emcp.net

FLIGHT TRAINING APPLICATION

Date: 3/10/2015

Name: Pete Mitchell

Address: 406 Mission Avenue

City: Oceanside

State: CA

Zip Code: 92058

Email: topgun@emcp.net

Home Phone: (760) 555-2005

Cell Phone: (760) 555-8210

Desired license: Certified Flight Instructor

How did you hear about South Sound Aviation? Other

2. Insert a picture content control and insert the **SSAviation.jpg** image.

2. Insert a date picker content control and plain text content controls in the appropriate cells.

2. Insert drop-down list content controls for the two bottom rows in the table. Add the following options for the *Desired license:* drop-down list content control: *Private, Commercial, Instrument,* and *Certified Flight Instructor*. Add the following options for the *How did you hear about South Sound Aviation?* Drop-down list content control: *Internet, Business card, Referral, Brochure,* and *Other*.

1. Create the form shown in Figure 29.19 as a template and use the table feature to create the columns and rows. Apply border and shading formatting as shown in the figure. Set the company name in the font Magneto and set the remaining text in Candara. Do not set a password.
3. Protect the template and only allow filling in the form.
4. Save the document as a template in your Chapter29 folder, name the template **XXXApplicationTemplate.dotx**, and then close the document.
5. Create a form document from the **XXXApplicationTemplate** template. You determine the data to enter in each data field.

C29-A06-FlightApp.docx

Signature Word 2013   Model Answers

323

Chapter 30 Assessment Annotated Model Answers

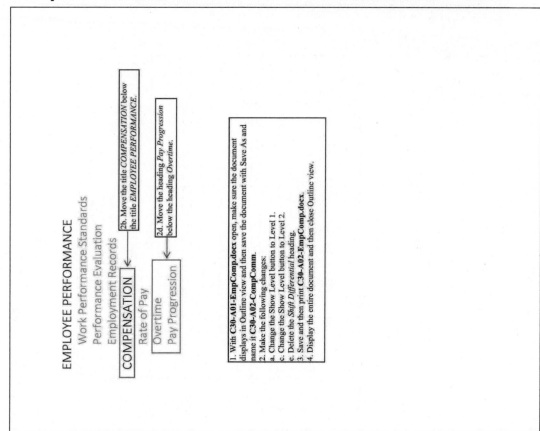

C30-A01-EmpComp.docx

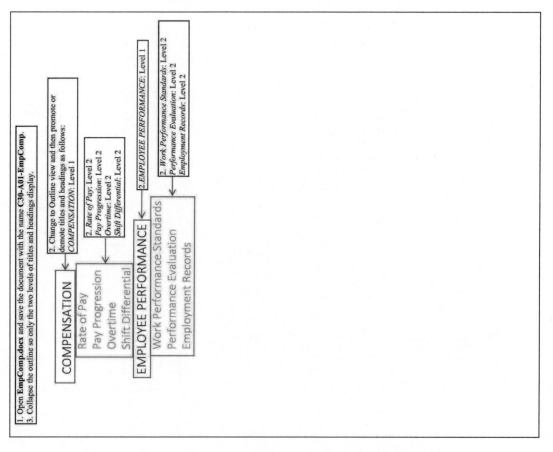

C30-A01-EmpComp.docx

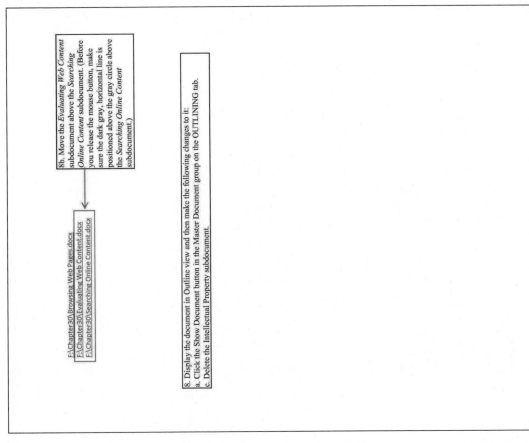

F:\Chapter30\Browsing Web Pages.docx

F:\Chapter30\Evaluating Web Content.docx
F:\Chapter30\Searching Online Content.docx

8b. Move the *Evaluating Web Content* subdocument above the *Searching Online Content* subdocument. (Before you release the mouse button, make sure the dark gray, horizontal line is positioned above the gray circle above the *Searching Online Content* subdocument.)

8. Display the document in Outline view and then make the following changes to it:
a. Click the Show Document button in the Master Document group on the OUTLINING tab.
c. Delete the Intellectual Property subdocument.

C30-A03-WebContent(Step9).docx

F:\Chapter30\Browsing Web Pages.docx

F:\Chapter30\Searching Online Content.docx

F:\Chapter30\Evaluating Web Content.docx

F:\Chapter30\Intellectual Property.docx

3. Assign to level 1 the following headings:
   Browsing Web Pages
   Searching Online Content
   Evaluating Web Content
   Intellectual Property

1. Open **WebContent.docx** and save the document with the name **C30-A03-WebContent**.
2. Change to Outline view.
3. Click the Show Document button in the Master Document group on the OUTLINING tab.
4. Create subdocuments by selecting the entire document and then clicking the Create button in the Master Document group.
5. Save and then close **C30-A03-WebContent.docx**.
6. Open **C30-A03-WebContent.docx** and then print the document. (The subdocuments will be collapsed.)

C30-A03-WebContent(Step7).docx

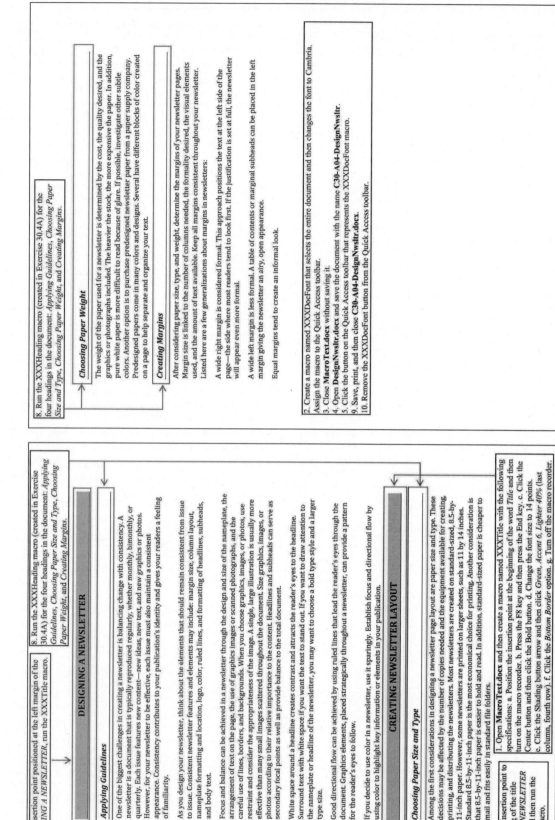

6. With the insertion point positioned at the left margin of the title *DESIGNING A NEWSLETTER*, run the XXXTitle macro.

8. Run the XXXHeading macro (created in Exercise 30.4A) for the four headings in the document: *Applying Guidelines, Choosing Paper Size and Type, Choosing Paper Weight, and Creating Margins.*

DESIGNING A NEWSLETTER

Applying Guidelines

One of the biggest challenges in creating a newsletter is balancing change with consistency. A newsletter is a document that is typically reproduced regularly, whether monthly, bimonthly, or quarterly. Each issue features new content—new ideas, new text, and new graphics or photos. However, for your newsletter to be effective, each issue must also maintain a consistent appearance. Consistency contributes to your publication's identity and gives your readers a feeling of familiarity.

As you design your newsletter, think about the elements that should remain consistent from issue to issue. Consistent newsletter features and elements may include: margin size, column layout, nameplate formatting and location, logo, color, ruled lines, and formatting of headlines, subheads, and body text.

Focus and balance can be achieved in a newsletter through the design and size of the nameplate, the arrangement of text on the page, the use of graphics images or scanned photographs, and the careful use of lines, borders, and backgrounds. When you choose graphics, images, or photos, use restraint and consider the appropriateness of the image. A single, large illustration is usually more effective than many small images scattered throughout the document. Size graphics, images, or photos according to their relative importance to the content. Headlines and subheads can serve as secondary focal points as well as provide balance to the total document.

White space around a headline creates contrast and attracts the reader's eyes to the headline. Surround text with white space if you want the text to stand out. If you want to draw attention to the nameplate or headline of the newsletter, you may want to choose a bold type style and a larger type size.

Good directional flow can be achieved by using ruled lines that lead the reader's eyes through the document. Graphics elements, placed strategically throughout a newsletter, can provide a pattern for the reader's eyes to follow.

If you decide to use color in a newsletter, use it sparingly. Establish focus and directional flow by using color to highlight key information or elements in your publication.

CREATING NEWSLETTER LAYOUT

Choosing Paper Size and Type

Among the first considerations in designing a newsletter page layout are paper size and type. These decisions may be affected by the number of copies needed and the equipment available for creating, printing, and distributing the newsletters. Most newsletters are created on standard-sized, 8.5-by-11-inch paper. However, some newsletters are printed on larger sheets, such as 11 by 14 inches. Standard 8.5-by-11-inch paper is the most economical choice for printing. Another consideration is that 8.5-by-11-inch paper is easier to fold and read. In addition, standard-sized paper is cheaper to mail and fits easily in standard file folders.

7. Move the insertion point to the beginning of the title *CREATING NEWSLETTER LAYOUT* and then run the XXXTitle macro.

1. Open **MacroText.docx** and then create a macro named XXXTitle with the following specifications: a. Position the insertion point at the beginning of the word *Title* and then turn on the macro recorder. b. Press the F8 key and then press the End key. c. Click the Center button and then click the Bold button. d. Change the font size to 14 points. e. Click the Shading button arrow and then click *Green, Accent 6, Lighter 40%* (last column, fourth row). f. Click the *Bottom Border* option. g. Turn off the macro recorder.

C30-A04-DesignNwsltr.docx (page 1 of 2)

---

8. Run the XXXHeading macro (created in Exercise 30.4A) for the four headings in the document: *Applying Guidelines, Choosing Paper Size and Type, Choosing Paper Weight, and Creating Margins.*

Choosing Paper Weight

The weight of the paper used for a newsletter is determined by the cost, the quality desired, and the graphics or photographs included. The heavier the stock, the more expensive the paper. In addition, pure white paper is more difficult to read because of glare. If possible, investigate other subtle colors. Another option is to purchase predesigned newsletter paper from a paper supply company. Predesigned papers come in many colors and designs. Several have different blocks of color created on a page to help separate and organize your text.

Creating Margins

After considering paper size, type, and weight, determine the margins of your newsletter pages. Margin size is linked to the number of columns needed, the formality desired, the visual elements used, and the amount of text available. Keep all margins consistent throughout your newsletter. Listed here are a few generalizations about margins in newsletters:

A wide right margin is considered formal. This approach positions the text at the left side of the page—the side where most readers tend to look first. If the justification is set at full, the newsletter will appear even more formal.

A wide left margin is less formal. A table of contents or marginal subheads can be placed in the left margin giving the newsletter an airy, open appearance.

Equal margins tend to create an informal look.

2. Create a macro named XXXDocFont that selects the entire document and then changes the font to Cambria. Assign the macro to the Quick Access toolbar.
3. Close **MacroText.docx** without saving it.
4. Open **DesignNwsltr.docx** and save the document with the name **C30-A04-DesignNwsltr**.
5. Click the button on the Quick Access toolbar that represents the XXXDocFont macro.
9. Save, print, and then close **C30-A04-DesignNwsltr.docx**.
10. Remove the XXXDocFont button from the Quick Access toolbar.

C30-A04-DesignNwsltr.docx (page 2 of 2)

C30-A05-PRDept.docx

1. At a blank document, run the XXXTab macro and then create the document shown in Figure 30.12. (Type the text in the first column at the second tab stop [the tab stop at 1 inch], not the left margin.)

McCORMACK FUNDS CORPORATION

Public Relations Department, Extension Numbers

Roger Maldon 129

Kimberly Holland 143

Richard Perez 317

Sharon Rawlins 211

Earl Warnberg 339

Susan Fanning 122

C30-A06-Agreement.docx

AGREEMENT BETWEEN
REINBERG MANUFACTURING AND LABOR WORKERS' UNION

Transfers and Moving Expenses

1. Employees shall be reimbursed for transfers resulting from their assignment to a location by **REINBERG MANUFACTURING** (hereinafter designated as **RM**).
2. Employees transferring to another location at their own request due to bidding or exercise of seniority shall be provided with space available transportation for self and family.
3. Employees transferring to another station to avoid furlough resulting in reduction in force shall be provided with transportation of personal effects up to 4,000 pounds at no cost to the employee.
4. Each employee requested by **RM** to be away from regular base on duty shall receive expenses.
5. **RM** will provide the **LABOR WORKERS' UNION** (hereinafter designated the **LWU**) a copy of the applicable **RM** regulations and subsequent revisions thereto.

> 4. Move the insertion point to the end of the document and then run the XXXNotSig macro and insert the following information when prompted:
> *(name 1)*: LLOYD KOVICH
> *(name 2)*: JOANNE MILNER
> *(county)*: Ramsey County

LLOYD KOVICH, President
Reinberg Manufacturing

JOANNE MILNER, President
Labor Workers' Union

STATE OF MINNESOTA)
) ss.
COUNTY OF RAMSEY)

I certify that I know or have satisfactory evidence that LLOYD KOVICH and JOANNE MILNER are the persons who appeared before me, and said persons acknowledge that they signed the foregoing Contract and acknowledged it to be their free and voluntary act for the uses and purposes therein mentioned.

NOTARY PUBLIC in and for the State of
Minnesota residing in Ramsey County

> 1. At a blank document, record a macro named XXXNotSig that includes the information shown in Figure 30.13. Click the *No Spacing* style and then set left tabs at the 0.5-inch mark, 1.5-inch mark, and 3-inch mark on the horizontal ruler. Include Fill-in fields in the macro after the places the text is in parentheses. After inserting the *(county)* Fill-in field, press the Enter key and then end the macro recording.
> 2. Close the document without saving it.
> 3. Open **Agreement.docx** and save the document with the name **C30-A06-Agreement**.

9. Open **InterfaceApplications.docx** and save the document with the name **C30-A07-InterfaceApplications.**
10. Run macros in the document by completing steps similar to those in Steps 5 through 7.

6. Run the XXXSFHTitle macro for the title of the document and run the XXXHeading macro for the three headings in the document (*Intellectual Property, Fair Use,* and *Intellectual Property Protection*).

NATURAL INTERFACE APPLICATIONS

A major area of artificial intelligence has the goal of creating a more natural interface between human and machine. Currently, computer users are restricted in most instances to using a mouse and keyboard for input. For output, they must gaze at a fairly static, two-dimensional screen. Speakers are used for sound, and a printer for hard copy. The user interface consists of typing, pointing, and clicking. New speech recognition and natural-language technologies promise to change that soon.

Speech Recognition

One of the most immediately applicable improvements comes in the area of speech recognition. Rather than typing information into the computer, users can direct it with voice commands. A computer that can take dictation and perform requested actions is a real step forward in convenience and potential. Speech recognition has developed rather slowly, mainly because the typical PC did not have the necessary speed and capacity until very recently.

Natural-Language Interface

Computers that are able to communicate using spoken English, Japanese, or any of the hundreds of other languages currently in use around the world, would certainly be helpful. In the not-so-distant future, computers will most likely be able to read, write, speak, and understand many human languages. Language translators already exist, and they are getting better all the time.

Programmers can look forward to a human-language computer interface. With better interfaces, programmers may be able to describe what they want using natural (human)

C30-A07-InterfaceApplications.docx (page 1 of 3)

---

6. Run the XXXSFHTitle macro for the title of the document and run the XXXHeading macro for the three headings in the document (*Intellectual Property, Fair Use,* and *Intellectual Property Protection*).

languages, rather than writing programs in the highly restrictive and rather alien programming languages in use today. Natural-language interfaces are an area of artificial intelligence that is broader in scope than simple speech recognition. The goal is to have a machine that can read a set of news articles on any topic and understand what it has read. Ideally, it could then write its own report summarizing what it has learned.

Virtual Reality

Virtual reality (VR) describes the concept of creating a realistic world within the computer. Online games with thousands of interacting players already exist. In these games people can take on a persona and move about a virtual landscape, adventuring and chatting with other players. The quality of a virtual reality system is typically characterized in terms of its immersiveness, which measures how real the simulated world feels and how well it can make users accept the simulated world as their own and forget about reality. With each passing year, systems are able to provide increasing levels of immersion. Called by some the "ultimate in escapism," VR is becoming increasingly common—and increasingly realistic.

Mental Interface

Although still in the experimental phase, a number of interfaces take things a bit further than VR, and they don't require users to click a mouse, speak a word, or even lift a finger. Mental interfaces use sensors mounted around the skull to read the alpha waves given off by our brains. Thinking of the color blue could be used to move the mouse cursor to the right, or thinking of the number seven could move it to the left. The computer measures brain activity and interprets it as a command, eliminating the need to physically manipulate a mouse to move the screen cursor. While this technology has obvious

C30-A07-InterfaceApplications.docx (page 2 of 3)

Page 1 of 3 (C30-A07-PropProtectIssues.docx)

6. Run the XXXSFHTitle macro for the title of the document and run the XXXHeading macro for the three headings in the document (*Intellectual Property, Fair Use,* and *Intellectual Property Protection*).

PROPERTY PROTECTION ISSUES

The ability to link computers through the Internet offers many advantages. With linked computers, we can quickly and easily communicate with other users around the world, sharing files and other data with a few simple keystrokes. The convenience provided by linking computers through the Internet also creates some drawbacks. Computer viruses can travel around the world in seconds, damaging programs and files. Hackers can enter into systems without authorization and steal or alter data. In addition, the wealth of information on the Web and the increased ease with which it can be copied have made plagiarizing easy. Plagiarism is using others' ideas and creations (their intellectual property) without permission.

All of these ethical issues revolve around property rights, the right of someone to protect and control the things he or she owns. A solid legal framework ensuring the protection of personal property exists, but computers have created many new issues that challenge conventional interpretations of these laws.

Intellectual Property

Intellectual property includes just about anything that can be created by the agency of the human mind. To encourage innovation and improvement and thus benefit society as a whole, our legal system grants patents to those who invent new and better ways of doing things. A patent awards ownership of an idea or invention to its creator for a fixed number of years. This allows the inventor the right to charge others for the use of the invention. To encourage and protect artistic and literary endeavors, authors and artists are awarded copyrights to the material they create, allowing them the right to control the use of their

---

Page 3 of 3 (C30-A07-InterfaceApplications.docx)

applications for assisting people with disabilities, military researchers are also using it to produce a superior form of interface for pilots.

C30-A07-InterfaceApplications.docx
3/12/2015
Number of Pages: 3
Student Name

7. Press Ctrl + End to move the insertion point to the end of the document and then run the XXXSFHEnd macro. At the prompt asking for your name, type your first and last names.

6. Run the XXXSFHTitle macro for the title of the document and run the XXXHeading macro for the three headings in the document (*Intellectual Property, Fair Use,* and *Intellectual Property Protection*).

works and charge others for their use. Patent and copyright violation is punishable by law, and prosecutions and convictions are frequent. The legal framework protecting intellectual property has come under constant challenge as technology has moved forward.

With the Internet, accessing and copying written works that may be protected is easy. Today, authors are increasingly dismayed to find copies of their works appearing on the Internet without their permission. The same problem occurs with graphic and artistic images on the Internet, such as photographs and artwork. Once placed on the Web, they can be copied and reused numerous times. Unauthorized copying of items appearing on websites is difficult and sometimes even technically impossible to prevent.

Fair Use

Situations exist in which using work written by others is permissible. Using another person's material without permission is permissible as long as the use is acknowledged, is for noncommercial purposes, and involves only the use of limited excerpts of protected material, such as no more than 300 words of prose and one line of poetry. Such a right is called fair use and is dealt with under the U.S. Copyright Act, Section 107. The fair use doctrine establishes that a copyrighted work, including such use by reproduction or by any other means specified by that section, for purposes such as criticism, comment, news reporting, teaching (including multiple copies for classroom use), scholarship, or research, is not an infringement of copyright.

Even under the fair use provision, describing the source of the material is important. Plagiarism may be punished by law, and in many educational institutions it can result in suspension or even expulsion.

C30-A07-PropProtectIssues.docx (page 2 of 3)

---

6. Run the XXXSFHTitle macro for the title of the document and run the XXXHeading macro for the three headings in the document (*Intellectual Property, Fair Use,* and *Intellectual Property Protection*).

Intellectual Property Protection

The problem faced by intellectual property owners in the digital age is twofold. First, new technology has presented new difficulties in interpreting previous understandings dealing with the protection of intellectual property, such as difficulties applying the fair use provision to Internet material. Second, the new technical capabilities brought about by digital technologies have greatly increased the ease with which intellectual property can be appropriated and used without authorization, making policing and protecting intellectual property very difficult. Intellectual property owners have formed new organizations to ensure the protection of their property.

C30-A07-PropProtectIssues.docx
3/12/2015
Number of Pages: 3
Student Name

7. Press Ctrl + End to move the insertion point to the end of the document and then run the XXXSFHEnd macro. At the prompt asking for your name, type your first and last names.

1. Open **SFHMacroText.docx** and then use the document to create the following macros for St. Francis Hospital:
   a. Create a macro named XXXSFHDocFormat that selects the entire document (use Ctrl + A), applies the No Spacing style (click the *No Spacing* style in the Styles group), changes the line spacing to double (press Ctrl + 2), and changes the font to Constantia.
   b. Create a macro named XXXSFHMargins that changes the top margin to 1.5 inches and the left and right margins to 1.25 inches.
   c. Create a macro named XXXSFHTitle that selects a line of text (at the beginning of the line, press the F8 key and then press the End key), changes the font size to 14 points, applies bold formatting to the text, centers the text, and then deselects the text.
   d. Create a macro named XXXSFHHeading that selects a line of text, changes the font size to 12 points, applies bold formatting to the text, applies underlining to the text, and deselects the text.
2. In this chapter, you learned how to create macros using Fill-in fields. You can also create macros using other fields from the Fields dialog box. With **SFHMacroText.docx** open, press Ctrl + End to move the insertion point to the end of the document and then create a macro named XXXSFHEnd that completes the following steps:
   a. Change the line spacing to single (press Ctrl + 1).
   b. Insert the *FileName* field.
   c. Press the Enter key and insert the *Date* field.
   d. Press the Enter key, type Number of Pages:, press the spacebar, and then insert the *NumPages* field.
   e. Press the Enter key and then insert a Fill-in field that prompts the user to type his or her name.
3. Close **SFHMacroText.docx** without saving it.
4. Open **PropProtectIssues.docx** and save the document with the name **C30-A07- PropProtectIssues.**
5. Run the XXXSFHDocFormat macro and then run the XXXSFHMargins macro.

C30-A07-PropProtectIssues.docx (page 3 of 3)

August 12, 2015

CHEF'S CHOICE

Spiedino di Mare

Shrimp and sea scallops coated with Italian bread crumbs and then grilled and topped with lemon butter sauce and served with steamed fresh vegetables.

Begin your meal with a hearty bowl of Sicilian soup, and finish it with Sogno di Cioccolata (Chocolate Dream) a rich, fudge brownie crowned with chocolate mousse, whipped cream, and chocolate sauce.

10. Open **ChefMenu02.docx** and save the document with the name **C30-A08-ChefMenu02**.
11. Press the Down Arrow key once, apply the XXXMenu macro, and type August 12, 2015 at the fill-in prompt.
12. Save, print, and then close **C30-A08-ChefMenu02.docx**.
13. Remove the XXXMenu button from the Quick Access toolbar.

---

7. Open **ChefMenu01.docx** and save the document with the name **C30-A08-ChefMenu01**.
8. Press the Down Arrow key once, apply the XXXMenu macro, and type August 11, 2015 at the fill-in prompt.

August 11, 2015

CHEF'S CHOICE

Chicken Parmesan Pasta

Herb and parmesan breaded chicken breast smothered with roasted red peppers, marinara, and bubbling mozzarella, and served on a bed of tender linguini.

Begin your meal with a fresh Caesar salad, and finish it with a delicious slice of tiramisu.

5. Press the Down Arrow key once and then apply the XXXMenu macro by clicking the button on the Quick Access toolbar that represents the macro. Type the date August 6, 2015 at the fill-in prompt. Your document should appear as shown in Figure 30.14.

August 6, 2015

WEEKLY SPECIALS

Monday – Chicken Marsala, $16.00
Mushrooms, Prosciutto, and Marsala Wine Sauce

Tuesday – Grilled Norwegian Salmon, $21.50
Fresh salmon baked in the chef's sauce of the day

Wednesday – Garlic Chicken, $16.00
Vermicelli, Grilled Asparagus

Thursday – Boneless Pork Chop Cacciatore, $16.50
Vermicelli, Marinara Sauce

Friday – Slow Roasted Prime Rib, $19.50
Onion Straws, Horseradish Cream, Lettuce, and Tomato

1. Open **MacroText.docx.**
2. Create a macro with the following specifications:
a. Name the macro XXXMenu and assign the macro to the Quick Access toolbar. (You determine the description.)
b. With insertion point at the beginning of the document, create a Fill-in field with the prompt *Type the current date.*
c. Select the entire document and then apply the following formatting:
• Change the font to 14-point Monotype Corsiva, apply bold formatting, and change the font color to Purple.
• Center the text.
• Apply Green, Accent 6, Lighter 60% paragraph shading.
• Display the Borders and Shading dialog box with the Borders tab selected, scroll down the *Style* list box and then click the third line option from the end, change the color to Purple, click the *Box* option in the *Setting* section, and then close the dialog box. d. End the recording of the macro.
3. Close **MacroText.docx** without saving it.
4. Open **Menu.docx** and save the document with the name **C30-A08-Menu.**

C30-A08-Menu.docx

Signature Word 2013   Model Answers

Unit 6 Performance Assessment Annotated Model Answers

1. Open **InterfaceApps.docx** and save the document with the name **U6-PA01- InterfaceApps.**

NATURAL INTERFACE APPLICATIONS

Creating a more natural interface between human and machine is the goal in a major area of artificial intelligence. Currently, computer users are restricted in most instances to using a mouse and keyboard for input. For output, they must gaze at a fairly static, two-dimensional screen. Speakers are used for sound, and a printer for hard copy. The user interface consists of typing, pointing, and clicking. New speech recognition and natural-language technologies promise to change that soon.

2. Create the first footnote shown in Figure U6.1 at the end of the first paragraph in the document.

Speech Recognition

One of the most immediately applicable improvements in technology comes in the area of speech recognition. Rather than typing information in the computer, users can direct the computer with voice commands. A computer that can take dictation and perform requested actions is a real step forward in convenience and potential. Speech recognition technology has developed rather slowly, mainly because the typical PC did not have the necessary speed and capacity until very recently.

3. Create the second footnote shown in Figure U6.1 at the end of the paragraph in the Speech Recognition section.

Natural-Language Interface

Computers that are able communicate using spoken English or Japanese, or any of the hundreds of other languages currently in use around the world, would certainly be helpful. Computers, in the not-so-distant future, will most likely be able to read, write, speak, and understand many human languages. Language translators already exist, and they are getting better all the time.

[1] Charles Raines and Saul Silverstein, *Computers: Natural-Language Technologies* (Newark: Mansfield & Nassen Publishing, 2015), 67-72.
[2] Theodore M. Sutton, *Computers and Communicating* (Los Angeles: Southwest Publishing House, 2014), 10-14.

U6-PA01-InterfaceApps(Step6).docx (page 1 of 3)

Programmers can look forward to a human language computer interface. With better interfaces, programmers may be able to describe what they want using natural (human) language, rather than writing programs in the highly restrictive and rather alien programming languages in use today. Natural-language interfaces are an area of artificial intelligence that is broader in scope than simple speech recognition. The goal is to have a machine that can read a set of news articles on any topic and understand what it has read. Ideally, it could then write its own report summarizing what it has learned.

Virtual Reality

Virtual reality (VR) describes the concept of creating a realistic world within the computer. Online games with thousands of interacting players already exist. In these games people can take on a persona and move about a virtual landscape, adventuring and chatting with other players. The quality of a virtual reality system is typically characterized in terms of its immersiveness, which measures how real the simulated world feels and how well it can make users accept the simulated world as their own and forget about reality. With each passing year, systems are able to provide increasing levels of immersion. Called by some the "ultimate in escapism," VR is becoming increasingly common—and increasingly real.

4. Create the third footnote shown in Figure U6.1 at the end of the paragraph in the *Virtual Reality* section.

Mental Interface

Although still in the experimental phase, a number of interfaces take things a bit further than VR, and they don't require users to click a mouse, speak a word, or even lift a finger. Mental interfaces use sensors mounted around the skull to read the alpha waves given off by our brains. Thinking of the color blue could be used to move the mouse cursor

[3] Jin Chun and Mariah Anderson, *Natural-Language Computing* (Cleveland: Hammermaster Publishing, 2015), 45-51.

U6-PA01-InterfaceApps(Step6).docx (page 2 of 3)

---

7. Select the entire document and then change the font to Constantia.
8. Select all of the footnotes and change the font to Constantia.

NATURAL INTERFACE APPLICATIONS

Creating a more natural interface between human and machine is the goal in a major area of artificial intelligence. Currently, computer users are restricted in most instances to using a mouse and keyboard for input. For output, they must gaze at a fairly static, two-dimensional screen. Speakers are used for sound, and a printer for hard copy. The user interface consists of typing, pointing, and clicking. New speech recognition and natural-language technologies promise to change that soon.[1]

Speech Recognition

One of the most immediately applicable improvements in technology comes in the area of speech recognition. Rather than typing information in the computer, users can direct the computer with voice commands. A computer that can take dictation and perform requested actions is a real step forward in convenience and potential. Speech recognition technology has developed rather slowly, mainly because the typical PC did not have the necessary speed and capacity until very recently.[2]

Natural-Language Interface

Computers that are able communicate using spoken English or Japanese, or any of the hundreds of other languages currently in use around the world, would certainly be helpful. Computers, in the not-so-distant future, will most likely be able to read, write,

---

[1] Charles Raines and Saul Silverstein, *Computers: Natural-Language Technologies* (Newark: Mansfield & Naseen Publishing, 2015), 67-72.

[2] Theodore M. Sutton, *Computers and Communicating* (Los Angeles: Southwest Publishing House, 2014), 10-14.

U6-PA01-InterfaceApps(Step10).docx (page 1 of 3)

---

to the right, or thinking of the number seven could move it to the left. The computer measures brain activity and interprets it as a command, eliminating the need to physically manipulate a mouse to move the screen cursor. While this technology has obvious applications for assisting people with disabilities, military researchers are also using it to produce a superior form of interface for pilots.[4]

5. Create the fourth footnote shown in Figure U6.1 at the end of the last paragraph in the document.

[4] Cecilia Castillo, *Computers and the Art of Virtual Reality* (Philadelphia: Old Town Press and Publishing House, 2014), 2-6.

U6-PA01-InterfaceApps(Step6).docx (page 3 of 3)

finger. Mental interfaces use sensors mounted around the skull to read the alpha waves given off by our brains. Thinking of the color blue could be used to move the mouse cursor to the right, or thinking of the number seven could move it to the left. The computer measures brain activity and interprets it as a command, eliminating the need to physically manipulate a mouse to move the screen cursor. While this technology has obvious applications for assisting people with disabilities, military researchers are also using it to produce a superior form of interface for pilots.[3]

[3] Cecilia Castillo, *Computers and the Art of Virtual Reality* (Philadelphia: Old Town Press and Publishing House, 2014), 2-6.

---

speak, and understand many human languages. Language translators already exist, and they are getting better all the time.

Programmers can look forward to a human language computer interface. With better interfaces, programmers may be able to describe what they want using natural (human) language, rather than writing programs in the highly restrictive and rather alien programming languages in use today. Natural-language interfaces are an area of artificial intelligence that is broader in scope than simple speech recognition. The goal is to have a machine that can read a set of news articles on any topic and understand what it has read. Ideally, it could then write its own report summarizing what it has learned.

Virtual Reality

Virtual reality (VR) describes the concept of creating a realistic world within the computer. Online games with thousands of interacting players already exist. In these games people can take on a persona and move about a virtual landscape, adventuring and chatting with other players. The quality of a virtual reality system is typically characterized in terms of its immersiveness, which measures how real the simulated world feels and how well it can make users accept the simulated world as their own and forget about reality. With each passing year, systems are able to provide increasing levels of immersion. Called by some the "ultimate in escapism," VR is becoming increasingly common—and increasingly real.

Mental Interface   [9. Delete the third footnote.]

Although still in the experimental phase, a number of interfaces take things a bit further than VR, and they don't require users to click a mouse, speak a word, or even lift a

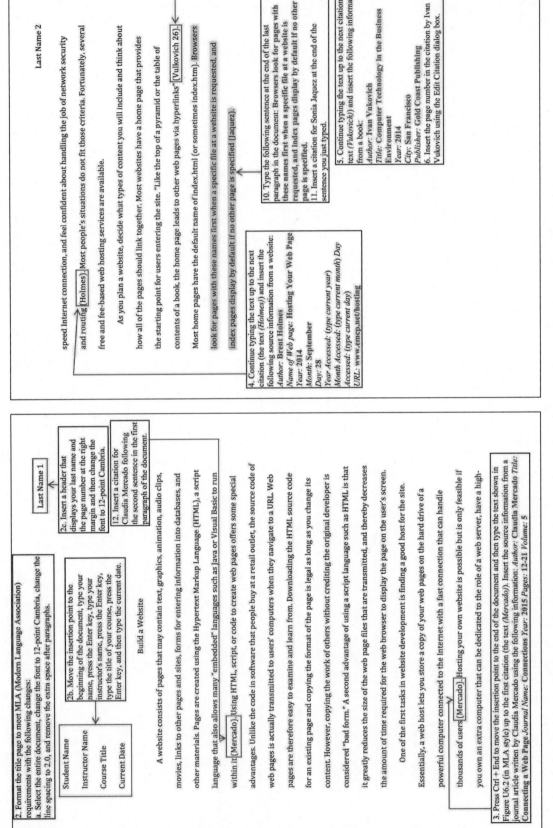

2. Format the title page to meet MLA (Modern Language Association) requirements with the following changes:
a. Select the entire document, change the font to 12-point Cambria, change the line spacing to 2.0, and remove the extra space after paragraphs.

2b. Move the insertion point to the beginning of the document, type your name, press the Enter key, type your instructor's name, press the Enter key, type the title of your course, press the Enter key, and then type the current date.

2c. Insert a header that displays your last name and the page number at the right margin and then change the font to 12-point Cambria.

Student Name

Instructor Name

Course Title

Current Date

Build a Website

A website consists of pages that may contain text, graphics, animation, audio clips, movies, links to other pages and sites, forms for entering information into databases, and other materials. Pages are created using the Hypertext Markup Language (HTML), a script language that also allows many "embedded" languages such as Java or Visual Basic to run within it [Mercado]. Using HTML, script, or code to create web pages offers some special advantages. Unlike the code in software that people buy at a retail outlet, the source code of web pages is actually transmitted to users' computers when they navigate to a URL. Web pages are therefore easy to examine and learn from. Downloading the HTML source code for an existing page and copying the format of the page is legal as long as you change its content. However, copying the work of others without crediting the original developer is considered "bad form." A second advantage of using a script language such as HTML is that it greatly reduces the size of the web page files that are transmitted, and thereby decreases the amount of time required for the web browser to display the page on the user's screen.

12. Insert a citation for Claudia Mercado following the second sentence in the first paragraph of the document.

One of the first tasks in website development is finding a good host for the site.

Essentially, a web host lets you store a copy of your web pages on the hard drive of a powerful computer connected to the Internet with a fast connection that can handle thousands of users [Mercado]. Hosting your own website is possible but is only feasible if you own an extra computer that can be dedicated to the role of a web server, have a high-

3. Press Ctrl + End to move the insertion point to the end of the document and then type the text shown in Figure U6.2 (in MLA style) up to the first citation (the text (Mercado)). Insert the source information from a journal article written by Claudia Mercado using the following information: *Author:* Claudia Mercado *Title:* Connecting a Web Page *Journal Name:* Connections *Year:* 2015 *Pages:* 12–21 *Volume:* 5

U6-PA02-BuildWebsite(Step15).docx (page 1 of 3)

speed Internet connection, and feel confident about handling the job of network security and routing [Holmes]. Most people's situations do not fit those criteria. Fortunately, several free and fee-based web hosting services are available.

As you plan a website, decide what types of content you will include and think about how all of the pages should link together. Most websites have a home page that provides the starting point for users entering the site. "Like the top of a pyramid or the table of contents of a book, the home page leads to other web pages via hyperlinks" [Vulkovich 26]. Most home pages have the default name of index.html (or sometimes index.htm). Browsers look for pages with these names first when a specific file at a website is requested, and index pages display by default if no other page is specified [Jaquez].

4. Continue typing the text up to the next citation (the text (Holmes)) and insert the following source information from a website:
Author: Brent Holmes
Name of Web page: Hosting Your Web Page
Year: 2014
Month: September
Day: 28
Year Accessed: (type current year)
Month Accessed: (type current month) *Day Accessed:* (type current day)
URL: www.emcp.net/hosting

10. Type the following sentence at the end of the last paragraph in the document: Browsers look for these names first when a specific file at a website is requested, and index pages display by default if no other page is specified.
11. Insert a citation for Sonia Jaquez at the end of the sentence you just typed.

5. Continue typing the text up to the next citation (the text (Vukovich)) and insert the following information from a book:
Author: Ivan Vukovich
Title: Computer Technology in the Business Environment
Year: 2014
City: San Francisco
Publisher: Gold Coast Publishing
6. Insert the page number in the citation by Ivan Vukovich using the Edit Citation dialog box.

U6-PA02-BuildWebsite(Step15).docx (page 2 of 3)

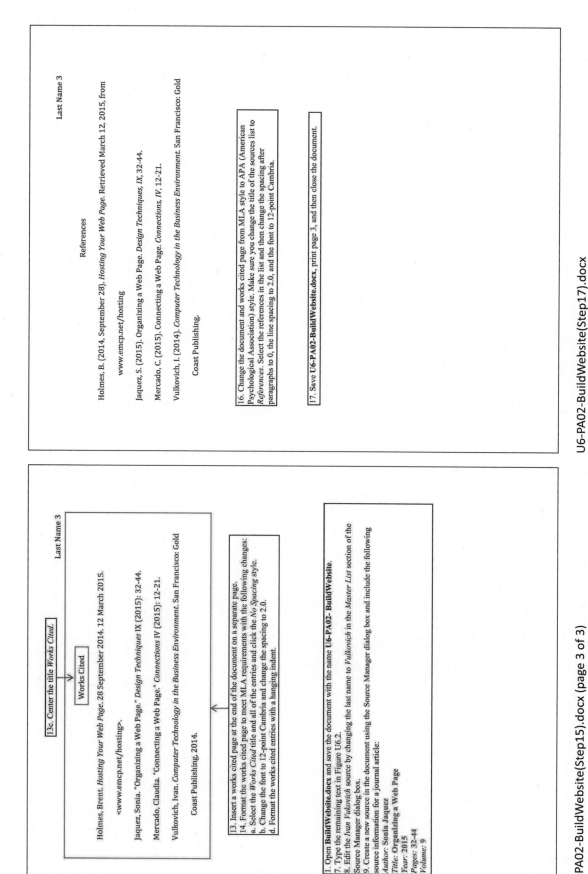

Last Name 3

References

Holmes, B. (2014, September 28). *Hosting Your Web Page.* Retrieved March 12, 2015, from

www.emcp.net/hosting

Jaquez, S. (2015). Organizing a Web Page. *Design Techniques, IX,* 32-44.

Mercado, C. (2015). Connecting a Web Page. *Connections, IV,* 12-21.

Vulkovich, I. (2014). *Computer Technology in the Business Environment.* San Francisco: Gold

Coast Publishing.

16. Change the document and works cited page from MLA style to APA (American Psychological Association) style. Make sure you change the title of the sources list to *References.* Select the references in the list and then change the spacing after paragraphs to 0, the line spacing to 2.0, and the font to 12-point Cambria.

17. Save **U6-PA02-BuildWebsite.docx**, print page 3, and then close the document.

U6-PA02-BuildWebsite(Step17).docx

Last Name 3

13c. Center the title *Works Cited.*

Works Cited

Holmes, Brent. *Hosting Your Web Page.* 28 September 2014. 12 March 2015.

<www.emcp.net/hosting>.

Jaquez, Sonia. "Organizing a Web Page." *Design Techniques* IX (2015): 32-44.

Mercado, Claudia. "Connecting a Web Page." *Connections* IV (2015): 12-21.

Vulkovich, Ivan. *Computer Technology in the Business Environment.* San Francisco: Gold

Coast Publishing, 2014.

13. Insert a works cited page at the end of the document on a separate page.
14. Format the works cited page to meet MLA requirements with the following changes:
   a. Select the *Works Cited* title and all of the entries and click the *No Spacing* style.
   b. Change the font to 12-point Cambria and change the spacing to 2.0.
   d. Format the works cited entries with a hanging indent.

1. Open **BuildWebsite.docx** and save the document with the name **U6-PA02- BuildWebsite.**
7. Type the remaining text in Figure U6.2.
8. Edit the *Ivan Vulkovich* source by changing the last name to *Vulkovich* in the *Master List* section of the Source Manager dialog box.
9. Create a new source in the document using the Source Manager dialog box and include the following source information for a journal article:
   Author: Sonia Jaquez
   Title: Organizing a Web Page
   Year: 2015
   Pages: 32-44
   Volume: 9

U6-PA02-BuildWebsite(Step15).docx (page 3 of 3)

5f. Insert a table of contents at the beginning of the document.

6. Make sure that the table of contents displays the correct page numbers. If not, update the table of contents.

TABLE OF CONTENTS

4. Open **DTPDesign.docx** and save the document with the name **U6-PA03-DTPDesign.**

5. Make the following changes to the document:

b. Change the style set to Basic (Simple).

c. Mark text for an index using the concordance file **U6-PA03-CFile.docx.**

5g. Number the table of contents page with a lowercase roman numeral.

i

U6-PA03-DTPDesign.docx (page 1 of 4)

---

1. At a blank document, create the text shown in Figure U6.3 as a concordance file.

2. Save the document with the name **U6-PA03-CFile.**

3. Print and then close **U6-PA03-CFile.docx.**

message	Message
publication	Publication
Design	Design
flyer	Flyer
letterhead	Letterhead
newsletter	Newsletter
intent	Design: intent
audience	Design: audience
layout	Design: layout
thumbnail	Thumbnail
principles	Design: principles
Focus	Design: focus
focus	Design: focus
balance	Design: balance
proportion	Design: proportion
contrast	Design: contrast
directional flow	Design: directional flow
consistency	Design: consistency
color	Design: color
White space	White space
white space	White space
Legibility	Legibility
headline	Headline
Subheads	Subheads
subheads	Subheads

U6-PA03-CFile.docx

In a text-only document, primary focus is usually created by using large or bold type for titles and headings, surrounded by enough white space to contrast with the main text. White space is the background where no text or graphics are located. The amount of white space around a focal element can enhance its appearance.

The size of a headline in proportion to surrounding text is an indicator of its importance. A headline or title set in a larger type size is easily identified and immediately informs the reader of the nature of the publication. A well-designed headline not only informs, but it attracts the reader's attention. It can play a big part in whether a reader commits to continue reading your publication. A headline/title needs to be precisely stated and easily understood.

Legibility is of utmost importance. Readers must be able to clearly see and read the individual letters in the headline/title. The impact of your headline/title as a focal element in your document is affected by your selection of an appropriate font (typeface, type size, and type style), the alignment of the text, and the horizontal and vertical white space surrounding the text.

In any type of communication, whether it be a semi-annual report, company newsletter, advertising flier, or a brochure, subheads can be used to provide a secondary focal element. A headline may be the primary focal element used to attract the reader's attention, but the subheads may be the key to luring the reader in. Subheads provide order to your text and give the reader further clues as to the content of your publication. Content divided by subheads appears more manageable to the reader's eye and lets the reader focus on a specific area of interest. Like headlines, titles and subheads need to be concise, legible, and easy to understand. Selecting an appropriate font, adjusting spacing above and below the subhead, assessing length, and choosing alignment are also important considerations.

2

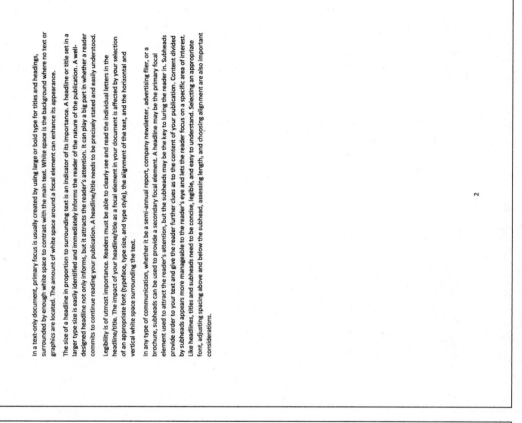

5a. Apply the Heading 1 style to the title and apply the Heading 2 style to the two headings in the report.

DESKTOP PUBLISHING DESIGN

Designing a Document

You may be asking yourself, "If the message is the most significant part of a communication, why bother with design?" A well-planned and relevant design sets your work apart from others, and it gets people to read your message. Just as people may be judged by their appearance, a publication may be judged by its design. Design also helps organize ideas so the reader can find information quickly and easily. Whether you are creating a business flier, letterhead, or newsletter, anything you create will look more attractive, professional, and convincing if you take a little extra time to design it. When designing a document, you need to consider many factors:

- What is the intent of the document?
- Who is the intended audience?
- What is the feeling the document is meant to elicit?
- What is the most important information and how can it be emphasized?
- What different types of information are to be presented and how can these elements be distinguished and kept internally consistent?
- How much space is available?
- How is the document going to be distributed?

Answering these questions will help you determine the design and layout of your communication. An important first step in planning your design and layout is to prepare a thumbnail sketch. A thumbnail is a rough sketch of the document you are attempting to create. With thumbnails, you can experiment with alternative locations for such elements as graphic images, ruled lines, columns, borders, and so on.

A good designer continually asks questions, pays attention to details, and makes well thought out decisions. Overdesigning is one of the most common problems encountered by beginning desktop publishers. Design should be used to communicate not decorate. Remember—less is better!

Although there are no hard-and-fast rules on how to arrange elements on a page, some basic design principles can be used as guidelines to help you get started. To create a visually attractive and appealing publication, some concepts to be considered are focus, balance, proportion, contrast, directional flow, consistency, and use of color.

Creating Focus

The focus on a page is an element that draws the reader's eyes. Focus is created by using elements that are large, dense, unusual, and/or surrounded by white space. Two basic design elements are used to create focus in a document:

- Titles, headlines, and subheads created in a typeface larger and bolder than the main text.
- Graphic images such as ruled lines, clip art, photographs, illustrations, logos, or images created with a draw program.

Untrained desktop publishers often create publications that are essentially typewritten documents that happen to be set in proportional type. Focus is difficult to create on a typewritten page because of the limitations of type size and positioning. With desktop publishing features, however, choice of typeface, type size, and positioning are highly flexible.

5h. Number the other pages in the report with arabic numbers and start the numbering with 1 on the page containing the report title.

1

6. Move the insertion point to the beginning of the document and then insert the Automatic Table 2 table of contents.
11. Update the table of contents.

1. Open **SoftwareCareers.docx** and save the document with the name **U6-PA04- SoftwareCareers**.

TABLE OF CONTENTS

10. Move the insertion point to the beginning of the document and then change the numbering format to lowercase roman numerals.

i

U6-PA04-SoftwareCareers.docx (page 1 of 5)

5d. Insert the index at the end of the document on a separate page.

5e. Apply the Heading 1 style to the title of the index.

INDEX

3

U6-PA03-DTPDesign.docx (page 4 of 4)

TABLES

ii

U6-PA04-SoftwareCareers.docx (page 2 of 5)

SOFTWARE DEVELOPMENT CAREERS

Software development is the creation of new software products for commercial sale. Within a software development company, this process involves a team that commonly consists of systems programmers, application programmers, multimedia developers, and quality assurance (QA) testers. These positions require a variety of skill, but each person plays an important role in getting new software products into the market for purchase by consumers or other companies. See Table 1 for a comparison of salaries in the software development area.

Table 1: Software Development Careers

Job Title	Salary*
Systems programmer	$94,000
Application programmer	$87,000
Graphic artist/multimedia developer	$62,000
Quality assurance tester	$61,000

Sources: Bureau of Labor Statistics, U.S. Department of Labor, Application Development Trends

*Based on national averages that may vary widely by region.

Systems Programming

Systems programming is a highly specialized area of software development and involves writing instructions in C++, JavaScript, or other languages to accomplish a succession of tasks. These programmers have expertise in one or more computer languages and typically must focus on the technical details rather than the human aspects of software development. A systems programmer specializes in the development of system software rather than of application software. Programming requires a high level of technical knowledge that can be gained through a computer science degree or other training.

Application Programming

The skills required for application programming are similar to those required for systems programming, but an application programmer works with application software. Application programmers may work on a project to develop new application software or on maintenance of existing application software. Similar to a systems programmer, an application programmer is typically professionally trained and usually holds a college degree in computer science. The professionals have studied techniques for software development that integrate multiple programmers working as part of a large team.

Multimedia Development

Multimedia development is the use of computers to create and enhance web content with images, sound, and movies. The job title multimedia developer includes graphic artists, digital sound editors, and animation specialists. This growing area includes individuals who have a stronger background in the arts than in computer science.

Quality Assurance

Companies that develop software also need people to test new products before they are released to the public. This testing process is called *quality assurance* (QA). QA testers carefully test each feature of a new

1

U6-PA04-SoftwareCareers.docx (page 3 of 5)

Network Administration

Network administration is another area that is integral to application development. Network administration involves the operations and maintenance of a company network, including a LAN, WAN, network segment, intranet, or interactions with the Internet. The individual responsible for these tasks is called the network administrator. On a daily basis, the network administrator must ensure that the network provides rapid response time to users, upgrade network software as needed, and set up the system so that only authorized network users have access to company programs and data. In addition, the network administrator troubleshoots particular problems with the network.

Web Administration

One type of application development is the creation of web pages. Web administration includes keeping the site working and up to date. A web administrator, sometimes called a web master, has the job of developing and maintaining a website with multiple pages. More complex websites also require programming effort if their pages need to dynamically respond to the user, such as in the case of an e-commerce site or a search engine.

3

product and record all deficiencies they uncover. A deficiency report is given to the developers so they can fix each problem before the product is released. QA testers often double as technical trainers, technical writers, or customer support specialists.

APPLICATION DEVELOPMENT CAREERS

Application development is a very large segment of IT work that uses commercial software to develop a system for a specific organization. A system could be a web page, a database, a single-user spreadsheet, or something as large as a custom information system. People working in the specific area of adapting software for use within a new system are sometimes called *programmers*, but the more accurate term is *application developer*. The major careers within the field of application development are system analyst, database administrator, network administrator, and web administrator.

Application development is highly paid and respected work that requires specialized training. Specialists in the field often work on a consulting basis, going from company to company creating new applications. Since applications are typically created for users to input data or interact with data, application developers must work closely with those who will use the application. This requires a mix of technical and interpersonal skills. The variety involved in this work makes it more interesting, but sometimes more stressful as well. Table 2 shows salary information for jobs within the application development category.

Table 2: Application Development Careers	
Job Title	Salary*
Systems analyst	$73,000
Database administrator	$72,000
Network administrator	$69,000
Web administrator	$66,000

Sources: Bureau of Labor Statistics, U.S. Department of Labor, CNN
*Based on national averages that may vary widely by region.

3. Position the insertion point in a cell in the second table and create the caption *Table 2: Application Development Careers*. (Change the paragraph spacing after to 0 points.)

Systems Analysis

Systems analysis involves gathering the requirements and developing a design for systems of distribution management, office information, management information, decision support, executive support, and factory automation. Both new information systems projects as well as modifications to existing information systems require some level of systems analysis. An individual who assesses the technical requirements and develops these types of designs is called a systems analyst.

Database Administrator

Database administration is an important part of application development since the database is at the core of a company's information system. A database administrator is responsible for the day-to-day operations of the database. This typically includes upgrading database software as needed, ensuring that the database provides rapid response time to users, integrating security strategies so only authorized users can access the database, and completing backups of the data on a regular basis.

2

U6-PA04-SoftwareCareers.docx (page 5 of 5)

U6-PA04-SoftwareCareers.docx (page 4 of 5)

342

Signature Word 2013   Model Answers

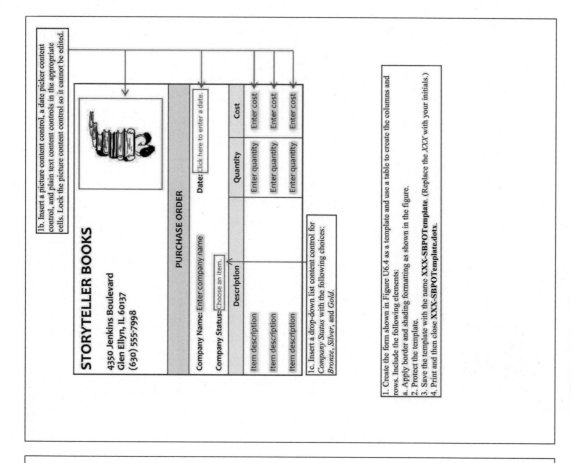

1b. Insert a picture content control, a date picker content control, and plain text content controls in the appropriate cells. Lock the picture content control so it cannot be edited.

STORYTELLER BOOKS

4350 Jenkins Boulevard
Glen Ellyn, IL 60137
(630) 555-7998

PURCHASE ORDER		
Company Name: Enter company name	**Date:** Click here to enter a date.	
Company Status: Choose an item.		
Description	**Quantity**	**Cost**
Item description	Enter quantity	Enter cost
Item description	Enter quantity	Enter cost
Item description	Enter quantity	Enter cost

1c. Insert a drop-down list content control for *Company Status* with the following choices: *Bronze, Silver,* and *Gold.*

1. Create the form shown in Figure U6.4 as a template and use a table to create the columns and rows. Include the following elements:
a. Apply border and shading formatting as shown in the figure.
2. Protect the template.
3. Save the template with the name **XXX-SBPOTemplate**. (Replace the *XXX* with your initials.)
4. Print and then close **XXX-SBPOTemplate.dotx**.

U6-PA05-SBPOTemplate.docx

STORYTELLER BOOKS

4350 Jenkins Boulevard
Glen Ellyn, IL 60137
(630) 555-7998

PURCHASE ORDER		
Company Name: John's Corner Market	**Date:** 3/12/2015	
Company Status: Gold		
Description	**Quantity**	**Cost**
Sales Insight	5	$20.50
Strategic Marketing	2	$134.50
Advertising	3	$201.00

5. Create a form document from the **XXX-SBPOTemplate** template with the following information: *Company Name:* **John's Corner Market**
Date: (*Insert current date.*)
Company Status:
Choose the Gold option.
Description: **Sales Insight**
Quantity: **5**
Cost: **$20.50**
Description: **Strategic Marketing**
Quantity: **2**
Cost: **$134.50**
Description: **Advertising**
Quantity: **3**
Cost: **$201.00**

U6-PA05-SB-JCM.docx

Top form (template):

2b. Insert a text form field for *Type of Deduction:* that specifies *Flat* as the default text.

1. Open **LAApp05.docx** and then save the document as a template and name it **XXXLAProfAppTemplate**. (Type your initials in place of the *XXX*).
2. Insert form fields in the template as shown in Figure U6.5 with the following specifications:
e. Insert the remaining text and check box form fields as shown in Figure U6.5.
3. Protect the template.

2a. Insert a text form field for *Client Number:* that specifies a maximum length of 6 characters.

2c. Insert a drop-down list form field for *Deduction Amount:* that includes the following four choices: *None, $1,000, $2,500,* and *$5,000.*

2d. Insert four check boxes in the cell in the middle of the form table as shown in Figure U6.5. **Hint: You can move the insertion point to a tab stop within a cell by pressing Ctrl + Tab.** Insert a check box form field in the cell immediately left of *AANA* that is checked by default.

LIFETIME ANNUITY COMPANY
3310 CUSHMAN STREET ✧ FAIRBANKS, AK 99705 ✧ 907-555-8875

APPLICATION FOR PROFESSIONAL LIABILITY

First Name: | Middle Name: | Last Name:

Address:

Date of Birth: | Client Number: | Current Date:

Type of Deduction: [Flat] | Deduction Amount: [None]

Check if this insurance is to be part of a program.

☒ AANA   ☐ AAOMS   ☐ APTA-PPS   ☐ None

☐ Chiropractor	☐ Medical Technician
☐ Dental Assistant	☐ Nurse
☐ Dental Hygienist	☐ Nurse Practitioner
☐ Dietitian/Nutritionist	☒ Occupational Therapist
☐ Laboratory Director	☐ Optometrist
☐ Medical Office Assistant	☐ Paramedic/EMT

APPLICANT'S SIGNATURE: DATE:

U6-PA06-XXXLAProfAppTemplate.docx

Bottom form (completed):

5. Create a form document from the **XXXLAProfAppTemplate.docx** template and then insert the following information in the specified data fields:
First Name: Rachel
Middle Name: Brianne
Last Name: Hayward
Address: 12091 South 234th Street, Fairbanks, AK 99704

LIFETIME ANNUITY COMPANY
3310 CUSHMAN STREET ✧ FAIRBANKS, AK 99705 ✧ 907-555-8875

APPLICATION FOR PROFESSIONAL LIABILITY

First Name: Rachel | Middle Name: Brianne | Last Name: Hayward

Address: 12091 South 234th Street, Fairbanks, AK 99704

Date of Birth: 01/18/1982 | Client Number: 10-541 | Current Date: 3/12/2015

Type of Deduction: Flat | Deduction Amount: $5,000

Check if this insurance is to be part of a program.

☒ AANA   ☐ AAOMS   ☒ APTA-PPS   ☐ None

☐ Chiropractor	☐ Medical Technician
☐ Dental Assistant	☐ Nurse
☐ Dental Hygienist	☐ Nurse Practitioner
☐ Dietitian/Nutritionist	☒ Occupational Therapist
☐ Laboratory Director	☐ Optometrist
☐ Medical Office Assistant	☐ Paramedic/EMT

APPLICANT'S SIGNATURE: DATE:

5. Date of Birth: 01/18/1982
Client Number: 10-541
Current Date: (Insert the current date.)
Type of Deduction: Flat
Deduction Amount: $5,000
(Leave the check mark in the AANA check box and also insert a check mark in the APTA-PPS check box.)
(Insert a check mark in the Occupational Therapist check box.)

U6-PA06-ProfAppHayward.docx

7. Make the following changes to the document:
b. Delete the Groupware subdocument.

F:\Unit06PA\Electronic Mail.docx
F:\Unit06PA\Web Browsers.docx
F:\Unit06PA\Instant Messaging Software.docx
F:\Unit06PA\Webconferencing.docx

7a. Move the Web Browsers subdocument above the Instant Messaging Software subdocument. (Before you release the mouse button, make sure the dark gray, horizontal line is positioned above the gray circle above the Instant Messaging Software subdocument.)

---

5. Save and then close U6-PA07-CommSoftware.docx.
6. Open U6-PA07-CommSoftware.docx and then print the document. (The subdocuments will be collapsed.)

F:\Unit06PA\Electronic Mail.docx
F:\Unit06PA\Instant Messaging Software.docx
F:\Unit06PA\Groupware.docx
F:\Unit06PA\Web Browsers.docx
F:\Unit06PA\Webconferencing.docx

1. Open CommSoftware.docx and save the document with the name U6-PA07-CommSoftware.
2. Display the document in Outline view and assign to level 1 the following headings:
Electronic Mail
Instant Messaging Software
Groupware
Web Browsers
Webconferencing
3. Click the Show Document button in the Master Document group in the Outlining tab.
4. Create subdocuments by selecting the entire document and then clicking the Create button in the Master Document group.

Signature Word 2013 Model Answers

---

6. With the insertion point positioned at the beginning of the title *LEASE AGREEMENT*, run the XXXAPMTitle macro.

1b. Create a macro named XXXAPMTitle that changes the font size to 14 points, applies bold formatting, centers the text, and applies Blue, Accent 1, Lighter 60% paragraph shading.

LEASE AGREEMENT

THIS LEASE AGREEMENT (hereinafter referred to as the "Agreement") made and entered into this DAY of MONTH, YEAR, by and between Lessor and Lessee.

WITNESSETH:

WHEREAS, Lessor is the owner of real property and is desirous of leasing the Premises to Lessee upon the terms and conditions as contained herein.

NOW, THEREFORE, for and in consideration of the covenants and obligations contained herein and other good and valuable consideration, the receipt and sufficiency of which is hereby acknowledged, the parties hereto agree as follows:

1. TERM. Lessor leases to Lessee and Lessee leases from Lessor the Premises.

2. RENT. The total rent for the premise is RENT due on the first day of each month less any set off for approved repairs.

3. DAMAGE DEPOSIT. Upon the due execution of this Agreement, Lessee shall deposit with Lessor the sum of DEPOSIT receipt of which is hereby acknowledged by Lessor, as security for any damage caused to the Premises during the term hereof. Such deposit shall be returned to Lessee, without interest, and less any set off for damages to the Premises upon the termination of this Agreement.

4. USE OF PREMISES. The Premises shall be used and occupied by Lessee and Lessee's immediate family, exclusively, as a private single family dwelling, and no part of the Premises shall be used at any time during the term of this Agreement by Lessee for the purpose of carrying on any business, profession, or trade of any kind, or for any purpose other than as a private single family dwelling. Lessee shall not allow any other person, other than Lessee's immediate family, to occupy the Premises.

5. CONDITION OF PREMISES. Lessee stipulates, represents, and warrants that Lessee has examined the Premises, and that they are in good order, repair, and in a safe, clean and tenantable condition.

6. ALTERATIONS AND IMPROVEMENTS. Lessee shall make no alterations or improvements on the Premises or construct any building or make any other improvements on the Premises without the prior written consent of Lessor.

7. NON-DELIVERY OF POSSESSION. In the event Lessor cannot deliver possession of the Premises to Lessee upon the commencement of the term, through no fault of Lessor or its agents, then Lessor or its agents shall have no liability, but the rental herein provided shall abate until possession is given. Lessor or its agents shall have thirty (30) days in which to give possession, and if possession is tendered within such time, Lessee agrees to accept the demised Premises and pay the rental herein provided from that date. In the event possession cannot be

U6-PA08-Lease(Step8).docx (page 1 of 2)

---

delivered within such time, through no fault of Lessor or its agents, then this Agreement and all rights hereunder shall terminate.

8. UTILITIES. Lessee shall be responsible for arranging for and paying for all utility services required on the Premises.

IN WITNESS WHEREOF the parties have reviewed the information above and certify, to the best of their knowledge, that the information provided by the signatory is true and accurate.

_____

Lessor

_____

Lessee

This document is the sole property of Azure Property Management and may not be reproduced, copied, or sold without express written consent of a legal representative of Azure Property Management.

Prepared by: Grace Hillstrand
Date: May 22, 2015

2. At a new blank document, create a macro named XXXAPMInfo that includes the information shown in Figure U6.6. Insert Fill-in fields in the macro where the text in is in parentheses.

7. Move the insertion point to the end of the document and then run the XXXAPMInfo macro. Insert the following information when prompted:
(name): Grace Hillstrand
(date): May 22, 2015

1. At a blank document, create the following macros:
a. Create a macro named XXXAPMFormat (using your initials in place of the *XXX*) that selects the entire document, changes the font to Constantia, and changes the font color to Dark Blue.
3. After recording the macros, close the documents without saving them.
4. Open **Lease.docx** and save the document with the name **U6-PA08-Lease.**
5. Run the XXXAPMFormat macro.

U6-PA08-Lease(Step8).docx (page 2 of 2)

Page 1 of 2 panel:

9. Open **REAgrmnt.docx** and save the document with the name **U6-PA08- REAgrmnt.**
10. Run the XXXAPMFormat macro.

11. With the insertion point positioned at the beginning of the title *Real Estate Sale Agreement,* run the XXXAPMTitle macro.

REAL ESTATE SALE AGREEMENT

The Buyer, BUYER, and Seller, SELLER, hereby agree that SELLER will sell and BUYER will buy the following property, with such improvements as are located thereon, and is described as follows: All that tract of land lying and being in Land Lot _____ of the _____ District, Section _____ of _____ County, and being known as Address: _____ City: _____ State: _____ Zip: _____, together with all light fixtures, electrical, mechanical, plumbing, air-conditioning, and any other systems or fixtures as are attached thereto; all plants, trees, and shrubbery now a part thereof, together with all the improvements thereon, and all appurtenances thereto, all being hereinafter collectively referred to as the "Property." The full legal description of said Property is the same as is recorded with the Clerk of the Superior Court of the County in which the Property is located and is made a part of this Agreement by reference.

SELLER will sell and BUYER will buy upon the following terms and conditions, as completed or marked. On any conflict of terms or conditions, that which is added will supersede that which is printed or marked. It is understood that the Property will be bought by Warranty Deed, with covenants, restrictions, and easements of record.

Financing: The balance due to SELLER will be evidenced by a negotiable Promissory Note of Borrower, secured by a Mortgage or Deed to Secure Debt on the Property and delivered by BUYER to SELLER dated the date of closing.

New financing: If BUYER does not obtain the required financing, the earnest money deposit shall be forfeited to SELLER as liquidated damages. BUYER will make application for financing within five days of the date of acceptance of the Agreement and in a timely manner furnish any and all credit, employment, financial and other information required by the lender.

Closing costs: BUYER will pay all closing costs to include; Recording Fees, Intangibles Tax, Credit Reports, Funding Fees, Loan Origination Fee, Document Preparation Fee, Loan Insurance Premium, Title Insurance Policy, Attorney's Fees, Courier Fees, Overnight Fee, Appraisal Fee, Survey, Transfer Tax, Satisfaction and Recording Fees, Wood Destroying Organism Report and any other costs associated with the funding or closing of this Agreement.

Prorations: All taxes, rentals, condominium or association fees, monthly mortgage insurance premiums and interest on loans will be prorated as of the date of closing.

Title insurance: Within five (5) days of this Agreement SELLER will deliver to BUYER or closing attorney; Title insurance commitment for an owner's policy in the amount of the purchase price. Any expense of securing title, including but not limited to legal fees, discharge of liens and recording fees will be paid by SELLER.

Survey: Within ten (10) days of acceptance of this Agreement, BUYER or closing attorney may, at BUYER's expense, obtain a new staked survey showing any improvements now existing thereon and certified to BUYER, lender and the title insurer.

Default and attorney's fees: Should BUYER elect not to fulfill obligations under this Agreement, all earnest monies will be retained by SELLER as liquidated damages and fund settlement of any

U6-PA08-REAgrmnt(Step13).docx (page 1 of 2)

Page 2 of 2 panel:

claim, whereupon BUYER and SELLER will be relieved of all obligations under this Agreement. If SELLER defaults under this agreement, the BUYER may seek specific performance in return of the earnest money deposit. In connection with any litigation arising out of this Agreement, the prevailing party shall be entitled to recover all costs including reasonable attorney's fees.

IN WITNESS WHEREOF, all of the parties hereto affix their hands and seals this _____ day of _____, 20_____.

This document is the sole property of Azure Property Management and may not be reproduced, copied, or sold without express written consent of a legal representative of Azure Property Management.

Prepared by: Grace Hillstrand
Date: May 29, 2015

12. Move the insertion point to the end of the document and then run the XXXAPMInfo macro. Insert the following information when prompted: *(name):* Grace Hillstrand *(date):* May 29, 2015

U6-PA08-REAgrmnt(Step13).docx (page 2 of 2)

Table of Contents

1

U6-PA09–BDHandbook.docx (page 2 of 8)

Brennan Distributors

EMPLOYEE HANDBOOK

Student Name

U6-PA09-BDHandbook.docx (page 1 of 8)

- Insert a page break before each centered title (except the first title, *Introduction*).

Probationary Periods

Acceptance by an applicant of an offer of employment by an appointing authority and their mutual agreement to the date of hire is known as an appointment.

Types of Appointment

New Hire: When you initially accept an appointment, you are considered a new hire. As a new hire, you will be required to serve a probationary period of either six months or one year.

Reemployment: Reemployment is a type of appointment that does not result in a break in service. The following are types of reemployment:

1. Military reemployment: Any remaining portion of a probationary period must be completed upon return to the company.

2. Reemployment of a permanent employee who has been laid off: Completion of a new probationary period is required if you are reemployed in a different class or in a different department.

3. Reemployment due to reclassification of a position to a lower class.

4. Reemployment of seasonal employees.

5. Reemployment due to a permanent disability arising from an injury sustained at work.

Further information on this subject can be obtained by contacting your personnel representative or a representative in the human resources department.

Reinstatement: If you have resigned from company service as a permanent employee in good standing, you may be reinstated to the same or a similar class within a two-year period following termination.

The probationary period following reinstatement may be waived, but you will not be eligible to compete in promotional examinations until you have completed six months of permanent service. You cannot be reinstated to a position that is at grade 20 or above if the position is allocated at a higher grade level than the position you held at the time of termination.

Reappointment: You may be reappointed to a class that you formerly held or to a comparable class if you meet the current minimum qualifications and receive the appointing authority's approval. If you are a probationary employee, you must complete a new probationary period. You cannot be reappointed to a position at grade 20 or above if the position is allocated at a higher level than the position you formerly held.

Demotion: An employee may request or accept a demotion to a position in a class with a lower grade level if the employee meets the minimum qualifications and if the appointing authority approves. You may not demote through non-competitive means to a position at grade 20 or higher. If the position is allocated to a higher grade level than the position you currently hold.

Promotion: Promotion is advancement to a vacant position in a class that has a higher grade than the class previously held. As an employee of the company, you may compete in recruitments for promotional openings when you have served six months (full-time equivalent) of consecutive service. When you accept a promotion, you will be required to serve a trial period of either six months or one year. If you fail to attain permanent status in a vacant position to which you were promoted, you shall be restored to your former position.

2

U6-PA09-BDHandbook.docx (page 4 of 8)

Introduction

This employee handbook has been prepared to give you general information about the work environment and some of the rules and policies under which we operate. Periodically, you may receive updated information concerning changes in policy. This handbook is not a contract guaranteeing employment for any specific duration. Although we hope that your employment relationship with us will be long term, you or Brennan Distributors (BD) may terminate this relationship at any time, for any reason, with or without cause or notice. This is an at-will relationship that remains in full force and effect, notwithstanding any statements to the contrary made by any BD employees or representatives or set forth in any other document.

- Insert appropriate page numbering in the document.

1

U6-PA09-BDHandbook.docx (page 3 of 8)

349

• Insert a page break before each centered title (except the first title, *Introduction*).

Employee Performance

Work Performance Standards

Work performance standards are written statements of the results and/or behavior expected of an employee when his or her job elements are satisfactorily performed under existing working conditions. Each employee in a permanent position must be provided with a current set of work performance standards for his or her position.

Performance Evaluation

If you are serving a six-month (full-time equivalent) probationary period, your supervisor will evaluate your performance at the end of the second and fifth months. If you are completing a one-year (full-time equivalent) probationary period, your evaluations will be conducted at the end of the third, seventh, and eleventh months. You will receive a copy of each performance report. Once you have attained permanent status, your performance will be evaluated annually during the month prior to your pay progression date.

Each evaluation will include a discussion between you and your supervisor to review and clarify goals and methods to achieve them. The evaluation will also include a written report of your progress in the job. Evaluations will be made with reference to established work performance standards.

Employment Records

Your official personnel file is maintained in the human resources department. The human resources department maintains a working file with copies of the documentation in your specific department. Your file includes personnel action documents, mandatory employment forms, your performance evaluations, and documentation of disciplinary action. Your file may include letters of commendation, training certificates, or other work relation documents that you or your supervisor has requested to be included in your file.

3

• Insert a page break before each centered title (except the first title, *Introduction*).

Compensation

Rate of Pay

The compensation schedule for employees consists of pay ranges for each grade. Within each grade are ten steps. As an employee of the company, your pay will be set at one of the steps within the grade for the class to which you are appointed. Your pay is further determined by the compensation schedule applicable to your participation in the company's retirement system.

Direct Deposit Option

You have the option to forward your paycheck directly to a checking or savings account in a bank of your choice. The company payroll center representative can provide you with a direct deposit authorization card.

Pay Progression

You will receive a merit salary increase annually on your pay progression date if your last performance evaluation was standard or better, and you have not reached the top step in your grade. The maximum merit salary increase is an adjustment of one step annually.

If your date of promotion coincides with your pay progression date, the merit salary increase will be computed first and the promotional increase applied to your new pay rate. If you continue to do satisfactory work, you will remain eligible for annual merit salary increases until you have reached the maximum step within your grade. In addition to merit salary increases, your salary may be adjusted by general salary increases granted by the company.

Overtime

Under state law, overtime is any time worked in excess of eight hours a day, eight hours in a 16-hour period or 40 hours in a week. Employees who choose and are approved for variable/innovative workday schedules earn overtime after 40 hours in a week.

Cash payment is the principal method of compensation for overtime. Payments are computed based on the employee/employer-paid salary schedule. Agreements may be reached with your employer to provide for compensatory time off in lieu of cash payments. Compensatory time must be taken within a reasonable time after accrual or at the direction of the appointing authority. If you request compensatory time off and give at least two weeks' notice, it cannot be unreasonably denied.

Longevity Pay

When you have completed eight years of continuous service and have standard or better performance, you will be entitled to longevity pay based on a longevity chart. Eligible full-time or part-time employees who work less than full-time for a portion of the 6-month qualifying period are entitled to a prorated amount based on the semi-annual payment. Longevity payments are issued in July and December.

Payment for Holidays

Nonexempt employees are entitled to receive payment for eleven holidays per year when they are in "paid status" during any portion of the shift immediately preceding the holiday. In addition, a nonexempt employee who works on a holiday is entitled to earn time and one-half cash payment or time and one-half compensatory time for the hours worked on the holiday. Exempt employees who work on a holiday do not receive additional compensation, but may have their schedule adjusted during the week in which the holiday occurs or in a subsequent week to recognize the holiday or additional time worked.

Shift Differential

Shift differential is an adjustment in pay equivalent to an additional 5 percent of an employee's normal rate of pay. To qualify, a nonexempt employee must work in a unit requiring multiple shifts in a 24-hour

4

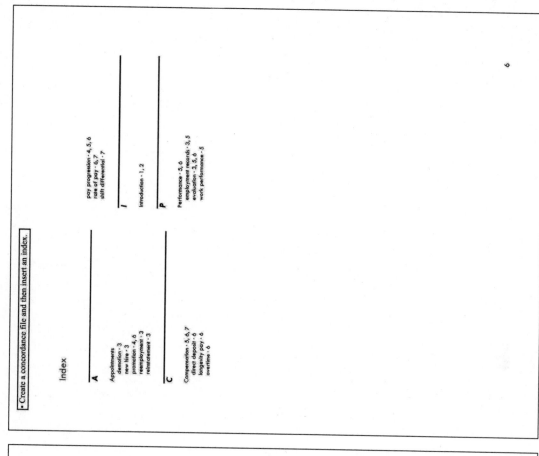

- Create a concordance file and then insert an index.

Index

A

Appointments
demotion · 3
new hire · 3
promotion · 4, 6
reemployment · 3
reinstatement · 3

C

Compensation · 5, 6, 7
direct deposit · 6
longevity pay · 6
overtime · 6

pay progression · 4, 5, 6
rate of pay · 6, 7
shift differential · 7

I

Introduction · 1, 2

P

Performance · 5, 6
employment records · 3, 5
evaluation · 3, 5, 6
work performance · 5

6

period and be assigned to a period of work of at least 8 hours of which at least four hours fall between 6:00 p.m. and 7:00 a.m. Employees working a qualifying shift that is reduced due to daylight savings time will still receive shift differential pay for that shift.

5

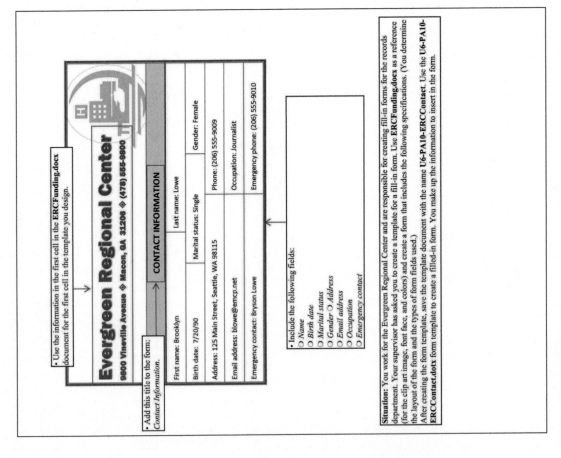

- Add this title to the form: *Contact Information.*

- Use the information in the first cell in the **ERCFunding.docx** document for the first cell in the template you design.

Evergreen Regional Center

9800 Vineville Avenue ◇ Macon, GA 31206 ◇ (478) 555-9800

CONTACT INFORMATION		
First name: Brooklyn	Last name: Lowe	
Birth date: 7/20/90	Marital status: Single	Gender: Female
Address: 125 Main Street, Seattle, WA 98115	Phone: (206) 555-9009	
Email address: blowe@emcp.net	Occupation: Journalist	
Emergency contact: Bryson Lowe	Emergency phone: (206) 555-9010	

- Include the following fields:
  - ○ *Name*
  - ○ *Birth date*
  - ○ *Marital status*
  - ○ *Gender* ○ *Address*
  - ○ *Email address*
  - ○ *Occupation*
  - ○ *Emergency contact*

Situation: You work for the Evergreen Regional Center and are responsible for creating fill-in forms for the records department. Your supervisor has asked you to create a template for a fill-in form. Use **ERCFunding.docx** as a reference (for the clip art image, font face, and colors) and create a form that includes the following specifications. (You determine the layout of the form and the types of form fields used.)
After creating the form template, save the template document with the name **U6-PA10-ERCContact**. Use the **U6-PA10-ERCContact.dotx** form template to create a filled-in form. You make up the information to insert in the form.

U6-PA10-ERCContactInfo.docx

Grading Rubrics

The following are suggested rubrics. Instructors should feel free to customize these rubrics to suit their grading standards and/or to adjust the point values.

*Suggested Scoring Distribution
  Above average: student completes 80% or more of task
  Average: student completes 70 to 79% of task
  Below average: student completes 69% or less of task

Chapter 1. Creating, Printing, and Editing Documents

Applying Your Skills

Assessment 1.1 – Type a Document

Step	Task	Criterion	Value	Score*
1	Typing	Typed paragraph. Used WordWrap.	8	
1	Spelling and Punctuation	Corrected errors highlighted by the spelling checker. Correctly used only one space after end-of-sentence punctuation.	8	
2-3	Saving and Printing	Saved document with specified name and printed document.	4	
		TOTAL POINTS FOR THIS EXERCISE	**20**	

Assessment 1.2 – Edit a Document Containing Proofreaders' Marks

Step	Task	Criterion	Value	Score*
1-2	Opening and Saving	Opened correct document. Completed Save As and saved with specified name.	2	
3	Editing	Completed four deletions (and some replacements that went with them), one change of case from uppercase to lowercase, two separate insert actions, and one instance of joining two paragraphs.	10	
3	Spelling	Though not instructed, corrected all typographical errors in document.	6	
4	Saving and Printing	Saved document and printed document.	2	
		TOTAL POINTS FOR THIS EXERCISE	**20**	

Assessment 1.3 – Edit a Document Containing Proofreaders' Marks

Step	Task	Criterion	Value	Score*
1-2	Opening and Saving	Opened correct document. Completed Save As with specified name.	2	
3	Editing	Completed 13 deletions (and some replacements that went with them), two separate insert actions, and two instances of joining two paragraphs.	10	
3	Spelling	Though not instructed, corrected all typographical errors in document.	6	
4	Saving and Printing	Saved document and printed document.	2	
		TOTAL POINTS FOR THIS EXERCISE	**20**	

Expanding Your Skills

Assessment 1.4 – Compose a Document on Saving a Document

Step	Task	Criterion	Value	Score*
1	Composing	Composed a paragraph about when to use Save As and included the advantages of Save As.	12	
1	Spelling	Though not instructed, corrected all typographical errors in document.	6	
2-3	Saving and Printing	Saved document with specified name and printed document.	2	
		TOTAL POINTS FOR THIS EXERCISE	**20**	

Assessment 1.5 – Use Help to Learn About and Then Create a Document Describing Keyboard Shortcuts

Step	Task	Criterion	Value	Score*
1-4	Using Help	Used Microsoft Word Help to obtain information about keyboard shortcuts.	8	
5	Creating	Created a document describing four keyboard shortcuts found in Microsoft Word Help.	12	
5	Spelling	Though not instructed, corrected all typographical and grammatical errors in document.	8	
6-7	Saving and Printing	Saved document with specified name and printed document.	2	
		TOTAL POINTS FOR THIS EXERCISE	**30**	

Achieving Signature Status

Assessment 1.6 – Create a Cover Letter

Step	Task	Criterion	Value	Score*
1	Style	Correctly selected the No Spacing style thumbnail in the Styles group on the HOME tab.	4	
2	Typing	Pressed the Enter key six times before typing date in letter. Typed the personal business letter as instructed including the current date and replaced the *Student Name* text with their first and last names.	10	
2	Formatting	Correctly formatted the document as a personal business letter as referenced in Appendix B.	4	
2	Spelling	Though not instructed, corrected all typographical errors in document.	10	
3-4	Saving and Printing	Saved document with specified name and printed document.	2	
		TOTAL POINTS FOR THIS EXERCISE	**30**	

Chapter 2. Formatting Characters

Applying Your Skills

Assessment 2.1 – Create and Format a Utility Program Document

Step	Task	Criterion	Value	Score*
1	Typing	Typed document shown in Figure 2.5. Used WordWrap.	10	
2	Formatting	Bolded and underlined title; italicized *utility program* in first paragraph; bolded the five utility programs.	6	
3-4	Saving and Printing	Saved document with specified name and printed document.	2	
5	Formatting	Changed font of entire document to 12-point Cambria.	2	
6	Formatting	Removed underlining in title and changed to uppercase.	2	
7	Formatting	Removed bold in utility programs (five instances) and replaced with underlining. Did not underline the colon after each utility program.	4	
8-11	Hiding text and redisplaying text	Selected text and hid text (two instances). Displayed nonprinting characters and redisplayed the hidden text *Backup Utility:* and sentence following it. Turned off nonprinting characters.	2	
12	Saving and Printing	Saved document with specified name and printed document.	2	
		TOTAL POINTS FOR THIS EXERCISE	30	

Assessment 2.2 – Format a Memo

Step	Task	Criterion	Value	Score*
1-2	Opening and Saving	Opened correct file. Saved the memo with specified name.	2	
3-4	Formatting	Removed underlining from two book titles and applied italics.	6	
5	Formatting	Bolded the memo headings.	4	
6	Typing	Replaced *XX* initials with own initials. Changed document name after initials as specified.	2	
7	Formatting	Changed font of entire document to Cambria.	4	
8	Saving and Printing	Saved document and printed document.	2	
		TOTAL POINTS FOR THIS EXERCISE	20	

Assessment 2.3 – Format a Training Announcement

Step	Task	Criterion	Value	Score*
1-2	Opening and Saving	Opened correct file. Saved the document with specified name.	2	
3-4	Formatting	Selected entire document and changed the font to 16-point Candara and the font color to Red.	8	

Step	Task	Criterion	Value	Score*
5	Formatting	Selected title and changed the font size to 20 and applied the Fill - Black, Text 1, Outline - Background 1, Hard Shadow - Accent 1 text effect.	8	
6	Saving and Printing	Saved document and printed document.	2	
		TOTAL POINTS FOR THIS EXERCISE	**20**	

Assessment 2.4 – Apply Styles, a Style Set, and a Theme to a Document

Step	Task	Criterion	Value	Score*
1-2	Opening and Saving	Opened correct file. Saved the document with specified name.	2	
3	Formatting	Applied Heading 1 style to the title.	2	
4	Formatting	Applied Heading 2 style to five headings in the document.	6	
5-9	Formatting	Changed paragraph spacing to Compact. Applied the Basic (Stylish) style set and the Integral theme. Changed the theme colors to Violet II and the theme fonts to Candara.	5	
10	Formatting	Selected title, changed the font color to Dark Blue, and applied bold formatting.	3	
11	Saving and Printing	Saved document and printed document.	2	
		TOTAL POINTS FOR THIS EXERCISE	**20**	

Expanding Your Skills

Assessment 2.5 – Create and Format a Memo

Steps	Task	Criterion	Value	Score*
1	Typing	Typed document.	4	
1	Formatting and Spelling	Correctly formatted document as a memo. Corrected all spelling and typographical errors.	4	
1	Formatting	Italicized text; inserted superscript (3 instances); inserted subscript (3 instances).	6	
2	Formatting	Changed font of entire memo to 12-point Constantia. Realigned headings as needed.	4	
3-4	Saving and Printing	Saved document with specified name and printed document.	2	
		TOTAL POINTS FOR THIS EXERCISE	**20**	

Assessment 2.6 – Research Text Effect Button

Step	Task	Criterion	Value	Score*
1	**Researching and Typing**	Researched the four options for Text Effects (*Outline, Shadow, Reflection* and *Glow*). Typed a memo to instructor describing the options. Applied a minimum of three effects to the words *Text Effects and Typography Button Options*.	10	
1	**Formatting and Editing**	Correctly formatted memo. Corrected all spelling, typographical, and grammatical errors.	8	
2-3	**Saving and Printing**	Saved document with specified name and printed document.	2	
		TOTAL POINTS FOR THIS EXERCISE	20	

Achieving Signature Status

Assessment 2.7 – Type and Format Text on Writing a Cover Letter

Step	Task	Criterion	Value	Score*
1	**Typing**	Typed document correctly. Used WordWrap.	8	
1	**Editing**	Corrected all spelling and typographical errors.	8	
1	**Formatting**	Applied font and text effects including bold and italics as illustrated. Used 11-point Constantia font.	12	
2-3	**Saving and Printing**	Saved document with specified name and printed document.	2	
		TOTAL POINTS FOR THIS EXERCISE	30	

Assessment 2.8 – Type a Business Letter

Step	Task	Criterion	Value	Score*
1	**Opening and Saving**	Opened correct file. Saved file with specified name.	4	
2	**Formatting**	Applied No Spacing style in Styles group.	2	
2	**Typing**	Typed document correctly. Used WordWrap.	10	
2	**Formatting**	Typed document as a block style business letter. Added reference initials as instructed.	4	
2	**Spelling and Editing**	Corrected spelling and typographical errors.	8	
3-4	**Saving and Printing**	Saved document with specified name and printed document.	2	
		TOTAL POINTS FOR THIS EXERCISE	30	

Chapter 3. Aligning and Indenting Paragraphs

Applying Your Skills

Assessment 3.1 – Apply Alignment and Spacing Formatting to a Document

Step	Task	Criterion	Value	Score*
1	**Typing**	Applied the No Spacing style. Typed text and corrected typographical errors.	6	
1	**Formatting**	Centered first five lines of text. Right aligned last two lines of text. Changed font of centered text to 18-point Constantia bold. Changed font of right aligned text to 10-point Constantia bold. Increased paragraph spacing after each line of centered text by 12 points.	12	
2-3	**Saving and Printing**	Saved file with specified name. Printed document.	2	
		TOTAL POINTS FOR THIS EXERCISE	**20**	

Assessment 3.2 – Apply Character and Paragraph Formatting to a Document

Step	Task	Criterion	Value	Score*
1-2	**Opening and Saving**	Opened correct file. Saved file with specified file name.	2	
3-7	**Formatting**	Changed line spacing to 1.0. Applied numbering format to five lines of text. Applied bullet formatting to paragraphs 2 through 5. Indented right margin of paragraphs 2 through 5 to 0.5 inch. Changed style set to Shaded. Centered title.	10	
8	**Saving and Printing**	Saved file with specified name. Printed document.	2	
9-12	**Formatting**	Changed document line spacing to 1.15. Justified first paragraph of text below title to the end of the document. Deleted paragraph numbered as 4. Applied bullet formatting to the four lines of numbered text.	4	
13-14	**Saving and Printing**	Saved document. Printed document.	2	
		TOTAL POINTS FOR THIS EXERCISE	**20**	

Assessment 3.3 – Create and Format a Bibliography

Step	Task	Criterion	Value	Score*
1	**Typing**	Typed bibliography as illustrated. Used WordWrap within each paragraph. Corrected typographical errors.	10	
1	**Formatting**	Applied No Spacing style. Changed line spacing to double. Centered, bolded, and italicized as indicated. Created hanging indents. Changed alignment to justified.	18	
2-3	**Saving and Printing**	Saved document with specified name. Printed document.	2	
		TOTAL POINTS FOR THIS EXERCISE	**30**	

Assessment 3.4 – Apply Character and Paragraph Formatting to a Travel Document

Step	Task	Criterion	Value	Score*
1-2	**Opening and Saving**	Opened correct file. Saved file as specified.	2	
3	**Typing**	Typed text for Photo Opportunities at end of document as illustrated. Corrected typographical errors.	6	
4	**Formatting**	Added 6 points of spacing after all paragraphs in the document.	2	
5-6	**Formatting**	Applied 16-point Constantia font and Gradient Fill - Blue, Accent 1, Reflection text effect to title. Applied 12-point Constantia font and Gradient Fill - Blue, Accent 1, Reflection text effect to three headings in document.	6	
7	**Formatting**	Applied bullet formatting to paragraphs 2 through 5 in *Rainy Day Activities* section.	4	
8	**Formatting**	Applied bullets to the text in the *Kauai Sights* section.	2	
9	**Typing**	Typed text between paragraphs 2 and 3 in the *Kauai Sights* section. Corrected typographical errors.	4	
10	**Formatting**	Increased left paragraph indent to 2.1 inch in the bulleted text below the *Photo Opportunities* heading.	2	
11	**Saving and Printing**	Saved document. Printed document.	2	
		TOTAL POINTS FOR THIS EXERCISE	30	

Expanding Your Skills

Assessment 3.5 – Insert Symbol Bullets

Step	Task	Criterion	Value	Score*
1-2	**Opening and Saving**	After experimenting with creating symbol bullets, opened correct file. Saved file as specified.	2	
3	**Applying Bullets**	Applied a new symbol bullet to paragraphs of text in the document. (Symbols will vary.)	4	
4	**Typing**	At the end of the document, typed explanation of steps to inserting new symbol bullet. Numbered the steps. Corrected typographical and grammatical errors.	12	
5	**Saving and Printing**	Saved document. Printed document.	2	
		TOTAL POINTS FOR THIS EXERCISE	20	

Achieving Signature Status

Assessment 3.6 – Format a Document on Resume Strategies

Step	Task	Criterion	Value	Score*
1	Opening and Saving	Opened correct file. Saved file as specified.	2	
2	Formatting	Applied character and paragraph formatting as specified including bolding, numbering, italicizing, and centering.	16	
3	Saving and Printing	Saved document. Printed document.	2	
		TOTAL POINTS FOR THIS EXERCISE	**20**	

Assessment 3.7 – Type a Business Letter

Step	Task	Criterion	Value	Score*
1	Opening and Saving	Opened the letterhead file. Saved file as specified.	2	
2	Typing	Typed document. Used WordWrap. Corrected typographical errors.	18	
2	Formatting	Using illustration as guide, inserted bullets. Inserted bulleted paragraphs 0.5 inch from right margin. Justified paragraphs in the body of letter.	6	
2	Typing	Replaced XX reference initials with your own initials.	2	
3	Saving and Printing	Saved document. Printed document.	2	
		TOTAL POINTS FOR THIS EXERCISE	**30**	

Chapter 4. Customizing Paragraphs

Applying Your Skills

Assessment 4.1 – Format an Abbreviations Document

Step	Task	Criterion	Value	Score*
1	Opening and Saving	Opened correct file. Saved file with specified name.	2	
2	Typing	Typed four lines of text below R.N. Registered Nurse text. Used correct tab stops. Corrected typographical errors.	2	
3-5	Formatting	Applied Heading 1 style to title. Applied Heading 2 style to two headings. Changed style set to Lines (Simple). Applied Frame theme.	3	
6	Changing Tabs	In the *Personal Names* section, changed the 1-inch tab stop to 0.5 inch. Changed the 3.5-inch left tab to 1.5 inch.	3	

Step	Task	Criterion	Value	Score*
7	Formatting and Changing Tabs	Text was sorted alphabetically in the *Academic*, *Professional*, and *Religious Designations*. Changed the 1-inch left tab to 0.5 inch. Changed the 3.5-inch left tab to 1.5 inch.	3	
8	Formatting	Centered the title.	1	
9	Adding Border and Applying Shading	Added top border to *Abbreviations* with same color as bottom border. Applied shading of choice.	2	
10	Applying Shading	Applied shading to two other headings.	2	
11	Saving and Printing	Saved document. Printed document.	2	
		TOTAL POINTS FOR THIS EXERCISE	**20**	

Assessment 4.2 – Type and Format a Table of Contents

Step	Task	Criterion	Value	Score*
1	Typing	Typed document. Corrected typographical errors.	4	
1	Formatting	Set font to 11-point Cambria. Applied bold and centered title. Before typing text, set left tabs at 1 inch and 1.5 inch. Set right tab with dot leaders at 5.5 inch.	4	
2-3	Saving and Printing	Saved document as specified. Printed document.	2	
4	Changing Tabs	Deleted 1.5-inch left tab and set left tab at 0.5 inch. Moved the 5.5-inch right tab to 6-inch mark.	4	
5	Applying Borders and Shading	Applied paragraph borders. Applied shading of choice.	4	
6	Saving and Printing	Saved document. Printed document.	2	
		TOTAL POINTS FOR THIS EXERCISE	**20**	

Assessment 4.3 – Type an Employee List

Step	Task	Criterion	Value	Score*
1	Typing	Typed document. Corrected typographical errors.	6	
1	Formatting	Used *No Spacing* style. Changed font to 12-point Candara. Applied bold to title, subtitle, and column headings. Set and used left tab for first column, center tab for second column, and right tab for third column. Applied shading as illustrated.	12	
2-3	Saving and Printing	Saved file with specified name. Printed document.	2	
		TOTAL POINTS FOR THIS EXERCISE	**20**	

Assessment 4.4 – Format a Beta Testing Agreement

Step	Task	Criterion	Value	Score*
1	Opening and Saving	Opened correct file. Saved file with specified name.	2	
2	Deleting	Deleted paragraph beginning with *Licensee agrees that Software includes...*	3	
3	Moving Paragraphs	Moved paragraph beginning with *This Agreement shall be governed, construed and...* above paragraph *In consideration of the mutual covenants...*	3	
4-10	Opening and Copying	Opened correct file. Copied the first, second, third, and fifth paragraphs. Closed file.	4	
11-14	Pasting	Used the Clipboard task pane and pasted paragraph beginning with *Licensee shall comply with...* above paragraph *In consideration of the mutual....* Pasted paragraph beginning with *This Agreement constitutes the entire...* above *Stylus Enterprises:.* Pasted paragraph beginning with *IN WITNESS WHEREOF, parties hereto...* above Stylus Enterprises:.	5	
15	Clearing Clipboard task pane	Cleared items from Clipboard task pane.	1	
16	Saving and Printing	Saved file. Printed document.	2	
		TOTAL POINTS FOR THIS EXERCISE	**20**	

Expanding Your Skills

Assessment 4.5 – Write a Letter on Changing the Paste Options Default

Step	Task	Criterion	Value	Score*
1	Changing Default Paste Options	Experimented and learned how to change the default paste options when pasting text within and between documents from the default Keep Source Formatting to Merge Formatting.	8	
2	Typing	Composed and typed a personal business letter to instructor including information on three buttons displayed in the Paste Options button gallery and steps on how to change the default for pasting within and between documents. Corrected typographical and grammatical errors.	20	
3-4	Saving and Printing	Saved file with specified name. Printed document.	2	
		TOTAL POINTS FOR THIS EXERCISE	**30**	

Achieving Signature Status

Assessment 4.6 – Create an Open House Notice

Step	Task	Criterion	Value	Score*
1	**Formatting**	Changed font to Candara, line spacing to single, and spacing after paragraphs to 4 points.	6	
1	**Typing and Formatting**	After pressing the Enter key once, typed text; applied character and paragraph formatting and set tabs including a right tab with leaders. Pressed Enter key three times after the last line. Corrected typographical errors.	12	
1	**Formatting**	Selected text from the beginning of the document to the blank line below last line of type and applied border as indicated using the third option from bottom in the Styles list, a Blue color in the *Standard Colors* section, and a width of 4 1/2 pt. Applied the Green, Accent 6, Lighter 80% paragraph shading to the text.	8	
1	**Copying**	After completing formatting, copied and pasted box two times in document.	2	
2-3	**Saving and Printing**	Saved file with specified name. Printed document.	2	
		TOTAL POINTS FOR THIS EXERCISE	30	

Assessment 4.7 – Create and Format a Table of Contents

Step	Task	Criterion	Value	Score*
1	**Formatting**	After pressing Enter once, changed spacing after paragraphs to 0 points and pressed Enter again.	2	
1	**Typing**	Typed title and subtitle, pressed Enter three times, and changed spacing after paragraphs to 8 points.	4	
1	**Formatting**	Set tabs including right leader tab.	4	
1	**Typing**	Typed table of contents correctly. Used tabs. Corrected typographical errors.	12	
1	**Formatting**	Applied borders and shading as indicated.	6	
2-3	**Saving and Printing**	Saved file with specified name. Printed document.	2	
		TOTAL POINTS FOR THIS EXERCISE	30	

Chapter 5. Proofing Documents

Applying Your Skills

Assessment 5.1 – Complete a Spelling and Grammar Check and Format a Style Document on Numbers

Step	Task	Criterion	Value	Score*
1	**Opening and Saving**	Opened correct file. Saved file with specified name.	2	
2	**Spelling and Grammar Check**	Completed spelling and grammar check on document.	4	
3	**Displaying Word Count**	Total number of words, paragraphs, and lines were identified at the end of the document.	3	
4	**Formatting**	Applied Heading 1 style to title. Applied Heading 2 style to two headings.	3	
4	**Formatting**	Changed style set to Basic (Elegant).	2	
4	**Applying Bullets**	Selected indented text in the section *Time Expressions* and applied bullets. Selected indented text in the section *Dates* and applied bullets.	4	
5	**Saving and Printing**	Saved file. Printed document.	2	
		TOTAL POINTS FOR THIS EXERCISE	**20**	

Assessment 5.2 – Complete a Spelling and Grammar Check and Proofread a Document

Step	Task	Criterion	Value	Score*
1	**Opening and Saving**	Opened correct file. Saved file with specified name.	2	
2	**Spelling and Grammar Check**	Completed spelling and grammar check on document.	4	
3	**Proofreading and Editing**	Proofread document. Corrected changes not found in spelling and grammar check.	7	
4	**Sorting**	Sorted numbered paragraphs in ascending order (lowest to highest).	5	
5	**Using Thesaurus**	Replaced word *circumstances* with *situations* in last paragraph	2	
6	**Using Thesaurus**	Replaced word *tasks* with *responsibilities* in last paragraph	2	
7	**Formatting**	Applied Title style to title. Applied Heading 1 style to two headings.	3	
7	**Formatting**	Changed style set to Centered. Applied Dividend theme. Changed theme colors to Orange.	3	
8	**Saving and Printing**	Saved file. Printed document.	2	
		TOTAL POINTS FOR THIS EXERCISE	**30**	

Assessment 5.3 – Create and Format a Document Featuring Translated Terms

Step	Task	Criterion	Value	Score*
1	**Translating**	Translated seven words to Spanish and French.	4	
2	**Typing**	Typed English words followed by Spanish and French translations.	8	
2	**Formatting**	Set text in columns. Applied formatting to enhance visual appeal.	6	
3-4	**Saving and Printing**	Saved file with specified file name. Printed document.	2	
		TOTAL POINTS FOR THIS EXERCISE	**20**	

Expanding Your Skills

Assessment 5.4 – Write and Translate Steps for Customizing the Grammar Check

Step	Task	Criterion	Value	Score*
1-2	**Proofreading and Typing**	Displayed Proofing in Word options. After experimenting with options in each section, typed a paragraph briefly describing the options. Corrected typographical errors.	10	
3	**Typing**	Typed appropriate title.	2	
4	**Translating**	Translated entire document into a language other than French or Spanish.	4	
5	**Copying**	Copied translated text from website to document.	2	
6-7	**Saving and Printing**	Saved file with specified name. Printed document.	2	
		TOTAL POINTS FOR THIS EXERCISE	**20**	

Achieving Signature Status

Assessment 5.5 – Format a Document on Resume Writing

Step	Task	Criterion	Value	Score*
1	**Opening and Saving**	Opened correct file. Saved document with specified name.	2	
2	**Spelling and Grammar Check**	Completed spelling and grammar check.	4	
2	**Formatting**	Applied character and paragraph formatting as illustrated.	6	
3	**Proofreading and Editing**	Proofread document. Corrected errors not found in check.	6	
4	**Saving and Printing**	Saved file. Printed document.	2	
		TOTAL POINTS FOR THIS EXERCISE	**20**	

Assessment 5.6 – Type a Business Letter

Step	Task	Criterion	Value	Score*
1	**Opening and Saving**	Opened correct file. Saved document with specified name.	2	
2	**Typing**	Typed business letter. Used WordWrap. Inserted appropriate reference initials.	14	
2	**Formatting**	Added four bullets as illustrated. Justified alignment of body of letter.	4	
3	**Spelling and Grammar Check**	Completed spelling and grammar check.	4	
3	**Proofreading and Editing**	Proofread document. Corrected errors not found in check.	4	
4	**Saving and Printing**	Saved file. Printed document.	2	
		TOTAL POINTS FOR THIS EXERCISE	**30**	

Unit 1. Preparing Documents

Assessing Proficiencies

Assessment U1.1 – Format an Online Shopping Document

Step	Task	Criterion	Value	Score*
1	**Opening and Saving**	Opened correct file. Saved document with specified name.	2	
2	**Formatting**	Changed font of entire document to 12-point Cambria.	2	
3	**Formatting**	Applied 14-point Calibri bold formatting to two titles and three headings.	5	
4	**Formatting**	Centered two titles.	2	
5	**Formatting**	Applied bullet formatting to paragraphs 2 through 5 in the *Advantages of Online Shopping* section.	4	
6	**Formatting**	Applied bold formatting to first sentence of each bulleted paragraph.	2	
7	**Sorting**	Sorted in ascending order the numbered paragraphs in the *Online Shopping Safety Tips* section.	3	
8	**Formatting**	Applied hanging indents to paragraphs below the *REFERENCES* title.	4	
9	**Formatting**	Applied Gold, Accent 4, Lighter 80% paragraph shading and bottom border line to the two titles.	2	
10	**Formatting**	Added 18 points of spacing before the *REFERENCES* title.	2	
11	**Saving and Printing**	Saved file. Printed document.	2	
		TOTAL POINTS FOR THIS EXERCISE	**30**	

Assessment U1.2 – Format a Corporate Report

Step	Task	Criterion	Value	Score*
1	**Opening and Saving**	Opened correct file. Saved document with specified name.	2	
2	**Formatting**	Changed bullets in the section *Compensation Philosophy* to custom bullets of their choice.	4	
2	**Formatting**	Applied Heading 1 style to title. Applied Emphasis style to the headings *Compensation Philosophy* and *Competitive Compensation*.	4	
2	**Formatting**	Changed style set to Shaded. Applied Dividend theme. Applied Blue theme colors.	6	
2	**Formatting**	Centered title.	2	
3	**Saving and Printing**	Saved file. Printed document.	2	
		TOTAL POINTS FOR THIS EXERCISE	**20**	

Assessment U1.3 – Create, Format, and Copy a Training Announcement

Step	Task	Criterion	Value	Score*
1	**Formatting and Typing**	Applied No Spacing style; pressed Enter key once. Typed text and pressed Enter key four times after last line of text. Corrected typographical errors.	4	
1	**Formatting**	Centered first five lines of text. Right aligned last two lines of text.	4	
1	**Formatting**	Changed centered text to 16-point Candara. Changed font color to Dark Blue. Changed right-aligned text to 10-point Candara. Changed font color to Dark Blue.	4	
1	**Formatting**	Selected from first blank line at beginning of document through one blank line below the right-aligned text and applied a thick-thin paragraph border. Changed the border color to Blue, Accent 1, Darker 25%. Applied Green, Accent 6, Lighter 80% shading.	4	
1	**Copying and Pasting**	Copied the text (including borders and shading) and pasted it two times in the document. Three announcements fit on one page and are evenly distributed.	2	
2-3	**Saving and Printing**	Saved document with specified name. Printed document.	2	
		TOTAL POINTS FOR THIS EXERCISE	**20**	

Assessment U1.4 – Format a Software Document

Step	Task	Criterion	Value	Score*
1	Opening and Saving	Opened correct file. Saved document with specified name.	2	
2	Formatting	Selected entire document and changed spacing after paragraphs to 0 points, changed line spacing to 1.5, and changed font to 12-point Constantia.	4	
3	Formatting	Indented paragraphs beginning with bold text 0.5 inch from left and right margins.	4	
4-5	Formatting	Changed title font to 14-point Constantia bold. Centered title. Applied Orange, Accent 2, Lighter 80% paragraph shading to title.	6	
6	Formatting	Inserted double border line above title and single border below title.	2	
7	Saving and Printing	Saved file. Printed document.	2	
		TOTAL POINTS FOR THIS EXERCISE	**20**	

Assessment U1.5 – Format a Travel Document

Step	Task	Criterion	Value	Score*
1	Opening and Saving	Opened correct file. Saved file with specified name.	2	
2	Typing	Typed *Special Highlights* section below last line of text in document. Corrected typographical errors.	4	
3	Formatting	Added 6 points of spacing after paragraphs to entire document.	2	
4-7	Formatting	Applied Heading 1 style to title. Applied Heading 2 style to two headings. Changed style set to Lines (Stylish). Applied Wood Type theme.	3	
8	Numbering	Selected text in *Fast Facts* section and applied paragraph numbering.	2	
9	Inserting Text	Inserted text between paragraphs 3 and 4. Corrected typographical errors.	3	
10	Formatting	Bolded words and colon at beginning of six numbered paragraphs.	2	
11	Saving and Printing	Saved file. Printed document.	2	
		TOTAL POINTS FOR THIS EXERCISE	**20**	

Assessment U1.6 – Set Tabs and Create a Training Costs Document

Step	Task	Criterion	Value	Score*
1	Setting Tabs and Typing	Set left tab for first column and right tabs for second and third columns. Typed text and corrected typographical errors.	8	
2	Formatting	Changed font size of title and subtitle to 14 points.	2	
2	Formatting	Applied Dark Blue paragraph shading to title. Applied Gold, Accent 4, Lighter 80% paragraph shading to subtitle.	4	

Step	Task	Criterion	Value	Score*
2	**Formatting**	With insertion point at end of document on the line below the text, applied Dark Blue paragraph shading.	4	
3-4	**Saving and Printing**	Saved file with specified name. Printed document.	2	
		TOTAL POINTS FOR THIS EXERCISE	**20**	

Assessment U1.7 – Set Tabs and Create a Vacation Packages Document

Step	Task	Criterion	Value	Score*
1	**Setting Tabs and Typing**	Set left tab for first column. Set right tab with leaders for second column. Typed text as instructed. Corrected typographical errors.	10	
2	**Formatting**	Applied Heading 1 style to title. Applied Heading 2 style to three headings.	4	
2	**Formatting**	Changed style set to Lines (Stylish).	2	
2	**Formatting**	Changed theme fonts to Arial.	2	
2	**Formatting**	Centered title. Inserted a top single-line border. Applied Blue-Gray, Text 2, Lighter 80% paragraph shading. Changed spacing from title text to top paragraph border to 3 points. Changed spacing from title text to bottom border to 4 points.	8	
2	**Formatting**	Changed paragraph spacing before the three headings to 12 points and after to 6 points.	2	
3-4	**Saving and Printing**	Saved file with specified name. Printed document.	2	
		TOTAL POINTS FOR THIS EXERCISE	**30**	

Assessment U1.8 – Customize Grammar Checking and Check Spelling and Grammar in a Document

Step	Task	Criterion	Value	Score*
1	**Opening and Saving**	Opened correct file. Saved document with specified name.	2	
2	**Changing Word Options**	In the *Proofing* section of Word Options, changed *Writing Style* to *Grammar & Style*.	2	
3	**Checking Spelling and Grammar**	Completed a spelling and grammar check on entire document.	2	
4	**Proofreading**	Proofread document. Made necessary corrections.	4	
5	**Formatting**	Applied formatting to enhance visual appeal of document.	6	
6	**Changing Word Options**	In the *Proofing* section of Word Options, changed *Writing Style* to *Grammar Only*.	2	
7	**Saving and Printing**	Saved file. Printed document.	2	
		TOTAL POINTS FOR THIS EXERCISE	**20**	

Assessment U1.9 – Format Resume Formats

Step	Task	Criterion	Value	Score*
1	**Typing**	Typed document. Corrected typographical errors.	8	
1	**Formatting**	Applied character and paragraph formatting as illustrated.	10	
2-3	**Saving and Printing**	Saved document with specified name. Printed document.	2	
		TOTAL POINTS FOR THIS EXERCISE	**20**	

Assessment U1.10 – Format a Job Announcement

Step	Task	Criterion	Value	Score*
1	**Opening and Saving**	Opened correct file. Saved document with specified name.	2	
2	**Formatting**	Applied formatting as illustrated. Changed spacing from text in title to top and bottom paragraph borders to 4 points with measurements at Border and Shading Options dialog box.	16	
3	**Saving and Printing**	Saved file. Printed document.	2	
		TOTAL POINTS FOR THIS EXERCISE	**20**	

Creating Original Documents

Assessment U1.11 – Create and Format an Announcement

Step	Task	Criterion	Value	Score*
1	**Typing**	Based on information provided, created an announcement about the appointment of the new corporate president. Added title to document.	14	
1	**Checking Spelling and Grammar**	Although not instructed, performed spelling and grammar check. Corrected typographical errors.	6	
1	**Formatting**	Applied formatting to enhance visual appeal of document.	8	
2-3	**Saving and Printing**	Saved file with specified name. Printed document.	2	
		TOTAL POINTS FOR THIS EXERCISE	**30**	

Assessment U1.12 – Create and Format a Word Commands Document

Step	Task	Criterion	Value	Score*
1	**Typing**	Based on information provided, created a summary of some Word commands to be used in a training class.	14	
1	**Checking Spelling and Grammar**	Although not instructed, performed spelling and grammar check. Corrected typographical errors.	6	
1	**Formatting**	Applied formatting to enhance visual appeal of document.	8	

Step	Task	Criterion	Value	Score*
2-3	**Saving and Printing**	Saved file with specified name. Printed document.	2	
		TOTAL POINTS FOR THIS EXERCISE	**30**	

Assessment U1.13 – Prepare a Memo Illustrating Font Use

Step	Task	Criterion	Value	Score*
1	**Typing**	Based on information provided, created a memo describing the use of two handwriting fonts, two decorative fonts, and two plain fonts.	14	
1	**Checking Spelling and Grammar**	Although not instructed, performed spelling and grammar check. Corrected typographical errors.	4	
1	**Formatting**	Used correct formatting for memo.	4	
1	**Formatting**	When describing font, set text with font being described.	6	
2-3	**Saving and Printing**	Saved file with specified name. Printed document.	2	
		TOTAL POINTS FOR THIS EXERCISE	**30**	

Chapter 6. Formatting Pages

Applying Your Skills

Assessment 6.1 – Apply Formatting to a Computers in Industry Report

Step	Task	Criterion	Value	Score*
1	**Opening and Saving**	Opened correct file. Saved file with specified name.	2	
2-4	**Formatting**	Applied Heading 1 to titles *COMPUTERS IN INDUSTRY* and *REFERENCES*. Applied Heading 2 to headings in report. Changed style set to Centered.	4	
5	**Formatting**	Applied hanging indents to paragraphs below *REFERENCES* title.	4	
6	**Formatting**	Changed top, left, and right margins to 1.25 inches.	4	
7	**Hyphenating**	Manually hyphenated text in document. Did not hyphenate proper nouns.	4	
8	**Watermark**	Inserted SAMPLE 1 watermark.	3	
9	**Formatting**	Inserted a double-line page border in Blue color with a weight of 1 ½ points.	3	
10	**Formatting**	Changed top, left, bottom, and right measurements to 31 points in the Border and Shading Options dialog box.	4	
11	**Saving and Printing**	Saved file. Printed document.	2	
		TOTAL POINTS FOR THIS EXERCISE	**30**	

Assessment 6.2 – Apply Formatting to a Data Security Training Notice

Step	Task	Criterion	Value	Score*
1	**Opening and Saving**	Opened correct file. Saved file with specified name.	2	
2	**Formatting**	Changed font for entire document to 12-point Candara.	2	
3	**Formatting**	Set title font to 14-point Candara bold. Centered title.	2	
4	**Formatting**	Changed page orientation to landscape.	3	
5	**Formatting**	Changed left and right margins to 1.8 inches and top margin to 2.3 inches.	3	
6	**Watermark**	Inserted ASAP 1 watermark.	2	
7	**Formatting**	Inserted a page border using third option in the *Style* list box and changed border color to Dark Red with entire page border visible. If necessary changed measurements in Border and Shading Options to 31 points.	4	
8	**Saving and Printing**	Saved file. Printed document.	2	
		TOTAL POINTS FOR THIS EXERCISE	20	

Assessment 6.3 – Apply Formatting to an Interface Applications Report

Step	Task	Criterion	Value	Score*
1	**Opening and Saving**	Opened correct file. Saved file with specified name.	2	
2	**Formatting**	Changed top margin to 1.5 inches.	2	
3	**Formatting**	Formatted text from first paragraph to end of document into two columns with 0.6 inch spacing and a line between columns.	4	
4	**Formatting**	Balanced columns on second page.	2	
5	**Hyphenating**	Manually hyphenated text in document.	4	
6	**Formatting**	Inserted a page border using first star images and changed line width to 10 points.	4	
7	**Saving and Printing**	Saved file. Printed document.	2	
		TOTAL POINTS FOR THIS EXERCISE	20	

Expanding Your Skills

Assessment 6.4 – Apply a Picture Watermark

Step	Task	Criterion	Value	Score*
1	**Opening and Saving**	Opened correct file. Saved file with specified name.	2	
2-4	**Inserting Custom Watermark**	Set Watermark to *Custom Watermark*. Followed instructions to insert picture as watermark. Inserted BG picture as watermark.	4	

Step	Task	Criterion	Value	Score*
5	**Typing**	Inserted initials in place of *XX* at the end of the letter.	2	
6	**Saving and Printing**	Saved file. Printed document.	2	
		TOTAL POINTS FOR THIS EXERCISE	**10**	

Achieving Signature Status

Assessment 6.5 – Create and Format an Announcement

Step	Task	Criterion	Value	Score*
1	**Typing**	Typed document. Corrected typographical errors.	6	
1	**Formatting**	Set text to Constantia. Changed to landscape orientation. Changed left and right margins to 2 inches. Set left tab and right tab with leaders. Inserted watermark as illustrated. Inserted page border. Changed border color to Dark Red and text to Dark Blue.	10	
2	**Formatting**	Changed top, left, bottom, and right measurements to 31 points. (if necessary to ensure printing of entire page border).	2	
3-4	**Saving and Printing**	Saved file. Printed document.	2	
		TOTAL POINTS FOR THIS EXERCISE	**20**	

Assessment 6.6 – Format a Report on Delivering a Presentation

Step	Task	Criterion	Value	Score*
1	**Opening and Saving**	Opened correct file. Saved file with specified name.	2	
2	**Formatting**	Changed top margin to 1.25 inches.	2	
3	**Formatting**	Applied bold and italic to text and inserted bullets as illustrated.	4	
4	**Formatting**	Set text from first paragraph to end of document to two columns with a line between columns.	4	
5	**Formatting**	Applied paragraph shading and border to title as illustrated.	2	
6	**Formatting**	Applied page border. Changed page border color to Blue, Accent 5, Darker 50%.	2	
7	**Formatting**	Changed top, left, bottom, and right measurements to 31 points. (if necessary to ensure printing of entire page border).	2	
8	**Saving and Printing**	Saved file. Printed document.	2	
		TOTAL POINTS FOR THIS EXERCISE	**20**	

Chapter 7. Customizing Page Formatting

Applying Your Skills

Assessment 7.1 – Format and Insert a Cover Page in a Document

Step	Task	Criterion	Value	Score*
1	Opening and Saving	Opened correct file. Saved file with specified name.	2	
2	Formatting	Applied Heading 1 to title. Applied Heading 2 to headings.	3	
3-5	Formatting	Changed style set to Casual. Changed theme to Basis. Changed theme colors to Blue Warm.	3	
6	Formatting	Centered title.	2	
7	Inserting Page Break	Inserted page break at beginning of *Using Visual Aids* heading.	2	
8	Inserting Cover Page	Inserted Slice (Light) cover page at beginning of document.	2	
8	Inserting Text and Deleting Placeholders	In *DOCUMENT TITLE* placeholder, typed Computer Manuals. In *Document Subtitle* placeholder, typed Strategies for Reading Computer Manuals. Deleted *School* placeholder. Typed first and last names in *Course title* placeholder.	10	
9	Inserting Page Numbering	With insertion point on title of main document (not cover page), inserted Thin Line page numbering, bottom of pages.	4	
10	Saving and Printing	Saved file. Printed document.	2	
	TOTAL POINTS FOR THIS EXERCISE		30	

Assessment 7.2 – Format and Insert a Header and Footer in a Report

Step	Task	Criterion	Value	Score*
1	Opening and Saving	Opened correct file. Saved file with specified name.	2	
2	Formatting	Changed top margin to 1.25 inches.	1	
3	Formatting	Changed theme to Banded.	2	
4	Inserting Page Break	Inserted page break at beginning of *Indicate Titles* heading.	2	
5	Inserting Header	Inserted Retrospect header at beginning of document. In the *DOCUMENT TITLE* placeholder, typed Quotation Marks. In the *DATE* placeholder, selected Today button.	4	
6	Inserting Footer	Inserted Retrospect footer and typed first and last names at the left side of the footer.	2	
7	Saving and Printing	Saved file. Printed document.	1	
8	Removing Header and Footer	Removed header and footer.	2	

Step	Task	Criterion	Value	Score*
9	**Inserting Header**	Inserted Facet (Odd Page) header.	4	
10	**Inserting Footer**	Inserted Ion (Dark) footer. In the *DOCUMENT TITLE* placeholder, typed Quotation Marks. At the right side of the footer, typed first and last names.	4	
10	**Formatting**	Applied bold formatting and changed the font size to 10 points in the footer.	2	
11	**Inserting Watermark**	Inserted DRAFT 1 watermark.	2	
15	**Saving and Printing**	Saved file. Printed document.	2	
		TOTAL POINTS FOR THIS EXERCISE	**30**	

Assessment 7.3 – Find and Replace Text in a Real Estate Agreement

Step	Task	Criterion	Value	Score*
1	**Opening and Saving**	Opened correct file. Saved file with specified name.	2	
2-4	**Finding and Replacing**	Found all occurrences of BUYER (matching case) and replaced with Craig Metzner. Found all occurrences of SELLER (matching case) and replaced with Carol Winters. Found all word forms of *buy* and replaced with *purchase*.	10	
5	**Inserting Page Break**	Inserted page break at the beginning of the paragraph that begins *Default and attorney's fees:*.	2	
6	**Inserting Page Numbers**	Inserted Bold Numbers 2 page numbers at the bottom of each page.	4	
7	**Saving and Printing**	Saved file. Printed document.	2	
		TOTAL POINTS FOR THIS EXERCISE	**20**	

Assessment 7.4 – Create a Notice Using Click and Type

Step	Task	Criterion	Value	Score*
1	**Typing**	Using Click and Type feature, typed document (5 centered lines and 2 right-aligned lines). Corrected typographical errors.	10	
2-4	**Formatting**	Changed centered text to 16-point Candara bold in Dark Blue. Changed right-aligned text to 12-point Candara bold in Dark Blue. Changed vertical alignment to Center.	8	
5-6	**Saving and Printing**	Saved file with specified name. Printed document.	2	
		TOTAL POINTS FOR THIS EXERCISE	**20**	

Assessment 7.5 – Insert a Header, Footer, and Cover Page from Office.com

Step	Task	Criterion	Value	Score*
1	Opening and Saving	Opened correct file. Saved file with specified name.	2	
2	Formatting	Changed top margin to 1.25 inches. Applied Title style to the title, Heading 1 style to the subtitle, and Heading 2 style to the three headings.	5	
3	Inserting a Header	Inserted a header from Office.com (student choice).	2	
4	Inserting a Footer	Inserted a footer from Office.com (student choice).	2	
5	Inserting Cover Page	Inserted cover page from the Office.com option. Inserted appropriate text. Deleted any placeholders not pertinent to document.	7	
6	Printing and Saving	Saved file. Printed document.	2	
		TOTAL POINTS FOR THIS EXERCISE	**20**	

Achieving Signature Status

Assessment 7.6 – Format a Resume

Step	Task	Criterion	Value	Score*
1	Opening and Saving	Opened correct file. Saved file with specified name.	2	
2	Formatting	Applied Heading 1 style to title. Applied Heading 2 style to headings. Changed style set to Lines (Stylish). Changed theme colors to Blue Green. Inserted Banded cover page and inserted text into placeholders and deleted necessary placeholders to look like cover page in the figure. Inserted Ion (Dark) header and footer. Applied other formatting as necessary.	16	
3	Saving and Printing	Saved file. Printed document.	2	
		TOTAL POINTS FOR THIS EXERCISE	**20**	

Chapter 8. Inserting Elements and Navigating in a Document

Applying Your Skills

Assessment 8.1 – Apply Headers and Footers to Employee Orientation Documents

Step	Task	Criterion	Value	Score*
1	Opening and Saving	Opened correct file. Saved file with specified name.	2	
2	Inserting File	Inserted EmpPerf.docx file at end of document.	2	

Step	Task	Criterion	Value	Score*
3-5	Typing	Typed Séverin Technologies® at end of document. Used Shift + Enter and inserted current date. Used Shift + Enter and inserted current time.	2	
6	Formatting	Created a drop cap with first letter of first paragraph. Specified drop cap dropped two lines.	2	
7	Formatting	Inserted page break at beginning of title EMPLOYEE PERFORMANCE on second page. Applied Heading 1 style to two titles in document. Applied Heading 2 style to four headings. Changed style set to Black & White (Capitalized). Applied the Frame theme. Changed theme colors to Blue Green. Centered two titles. Inserted Integral header and typed Employee Handbook in the [DOCUMENT TITLE] placeholder. Inserted the Integral footer and typed first and last names in the [author] placeholder. Inserted a page break at the beginning of the title *EMPLOYEE PERFORMANCE*.	10	
8	Saving and Printing	Saved file. Printed document.	2	
		TOTAL POINTS FOR THIS EXERCISE	**20**	

Assessment 8.2 – Format and Navigate in Corporate Report Documents

Step	Task	Criterion	Value	Score*
1	Opening and Saving	Opened correct file. Saved file with specified name.	2	
2	Inserting file	Inserted **CompRep.docx** file at end of document.	2	
3	Formatting	Inserted a page break at the beginning of the heading *Compensation Committee Report*. Applied the Minimalist style set. Inserted the Austin footer.	6	
4-8	Inserting Bookmarks	Turned on display of bookmarks. Moved insertion point to end of third paragraph (beginning with *The audit committee selects…*) and inserted bookmark named *Audit*. Moved to end of first paragraph in *Fees to Independent Auditor* section (after Excel Worksheet) and inserted bookmark named *Audit_Fees*. Moved insertion point to end of last paragraph of text in document and inserted bookmark named *Compensation*. Navigated in document using bookmarks.	10	

Step	Task	Criterion	Value	Score*
9-12	Inserting Hyperlink	Moved insertion point to end of first paragraph in the *Committee Responsibilities* section and inserted hyperlink to *Audit_Fees* bookmark. Selected text (Excel Worksheet) at end of first paragraph in the *Fees to Independent Auditor* section and inserted a hyperlink to the Excel file named *ExcelAuditorFees.xlsx* (located in Chapter08 folder on storage medium). Clicked (Excel Worksheet) hyperlink and printed Excel worksheet. Closed Excel program without saving workbook.	8	
13	Saving and Printing	Saved file. Printed document.	2	
		TOTAL POINTS FOR THIS EXERCISE	**30**	

Expanding Your Skills

Assessment 8.3 – Customize Drop Cap Options

Step	Task	Criterion	Value	Score*
1	Opening and Saving	Opened correct file. Saved file with specified name.	2	
2-3	Creating Drop Cap	Created drop cap for letter below title and each heading in document. Dropped cap within the text. Changed drop cap font to Castellar. Dropped the cap two lines. Changed the Distance from text to 0.1 inch. Changed font color to Orange, Accent 6, Darker 50%.	12	
4	Saving and Printing	Saved file. Printed document.	2	
5	Typing	Created and typed memo describing steps to create drop caps. Corrected typographical and grammatical errors.	12	
6-7	Saving and Printing	Saved file with specified name. Printed document.	2	
		TOTAL POINTS FOR THIS EXERCISE	**30**	

Assessment 8.4 – Determine Symbol Keyboard Shortcuts and Write a Letter

Step	Task	Criterion	Value	Score*
1	Opening and Saving	Opened letterhead file. Saved file with specified name.	2	
2-3	Typing and Proofreading	Typed letter describing steps to insert symbol from Symbol dialog box and how to insert symbols using keyboard shortcuts (symbols listed in exercise). Addressed block-style business letter to name provided. Corrected typographical and grammatical errors.	16	
4	Saving and Printing	Saved file. Printed document.	2	
		TOTAL POINTS FOR THIS EXERCISE	**20**	

Assessment 8.5 – Create and Format a Document on Resumes for Career Changers

Step	Task	Criterion	Value	Score*
1	**Typing and Inserting**	Typed document as illustrated. Inserted bullets from **Questions.docx** file. Corrected typographical errors.	10	
1	**Formatting**	Applied character formatting as illustrated. Applied Heading 1 style to title. Applied Heading 3 style to headings. Changed Quick Styles set to Shaded. Applied Wisp theme and changed theme colors to Violet II. Inserted Retrospect footer.	8	
1	**Creating Hyperlinks**	Selected text: *Top-ten Growth Industries*. Created hyperlink to the Excel **EmpGrowth.xlsx** file. Selected text: *Employment Trends*. Created hyperlink to PowerPoint **EmpTrends.pptx** file.	4	
1	**Formatting**	Applied additional formatting to ensure document appears as illustrated.	4	
2-3	**Checking Hyperlinks**	Clicked hyperlink to display the **EmpGrowth.xlsx** workbook. Exited Excel without saving. Clicked hyperlink to display the **EmpTrends.pptx** presentation. Advanced each slide. Exited PowerPoint without saving.	2	
4-5	**Saving and Printing**	Saved file with specified name. Printed document.	2	
		TOTAL POINTS FOR THIS EXERCISE	30	

Chapter 9. Maintaining Documents

Applying Your Skills

Assessment 9.1 – Create a Folder and Copy and Rename Documents

Step	Task	Criterion	Value	Score*
1	**Creating Folder**	Created new folder named *CheckingTools* within Chapter09 folder.	2	
2	**Copying Files**	Copied (not cut) all documents beginning with *SpellCheck* and *GrammarCheck* into CheckingTools folder.	4	
3-4	**Renaming Files**	Renamed **SpellCheck01.docx** to **VacationAdventures.docx** in CheckingTools folder. Renamed **GrammarCheck01.docx** to **NaturalInterfaces.docx**.	6	
5	**Using Print Screen**	Used Print Screen key to capture an image of the Open dialog box, closed Open dialog box, inserted file in blank document, printed document, closed without saving.	4	
6-7	**Opening Folder and Deleting Folder**	Opened Chapter09 folder. Deleted CheckingTools folder and all documents within it.	4	
		TOTAL POINTS FOR THIS EXERCISE	20	

Assessment 9.2 – Save a Document in Different Formats

Step	Task	Criterion	Value	Score*
1	Opening and Saving	Opened correct file. Saved file with specified name.	2	
2	Formatting	Applied Heading 2 style to *LEASE AGREEMENT* title. Changed style set to Centered. Applied the Wisp theme.	6	
3	Saving and Printing	Saved file with specified name. Printed document.	2	
4-5	Saving and Closing	Saved file in the Word 97-2003 format with specific name. Closed document.	2	
6-7	Opening and Saving	Opened the correct file. Saved document in plain-text format with specified name.	2	
8	Opening, Saving, and Closing	Opened the correct file. Saved document as a PDF file with specified name. Closed PDF file.	2	
9	Opening and Formatting	Opened PDF file in Word. Formatted document with Candara font.	2	
10	Saving, Printing, and Closing	Saved correct file. Printed document. Closed all files.	2	
	TOTAL POINTS FOR THIS EXERCISE		20	

Assessment 9.3 – Use a Template to Create a Fax Document

Step	Task	Criterion	Value	Score*
1	Opening Template	Opened Fax (Equity theme) template.	2	
1	Typing	Inserted text in specified fields. Corrected typographical errors.	16	
2-3	Saving and Printing	Saved fax document with specified name. Printed document.	2	
	TOTAL POINTS FOR THIS EXERCISE		20	

Expanding Your Skills

Assessment 9.4 – Create a Calendar and Write a Memo

Step	Task	Criterion	Value	Score*
1	Creating Calendar	Used calendar template and created calendar.	4	
2-4	Printing, Saving, and Closing	Printed first page of calendar. Saved file with specified name. Closed calendar.	2	
5	Typing and Formatting	Typed memo explaining steps used to create calendar. Corrected typographical and grammatical errors. Formatted memo.	12	
6-7	Saving and Printing	Saved memo with specified name. Printed memo.	2	
	TOTAL POINTS FOR THIS EXERCISE		20	

Achieving Signature Status

Assessment 9.5 – Create a Folder and Save Documents in Different Formats

Step	Task	Criterion	Value	Score*
1	**Creating Folders and Saving**	Created new folder named *FileFormats*. Opened documents from Chapter09 folder on storage medium and saved into FileFormats folder with four file formats as illustrated.	14	
2	**Printing**	Opened FileFormats folder and changed view to Details. Used Print Screen key to capture image of Open dialog box. Pasted image into document, printed document, and closed without saving.	6	
	TOTAL POINTS FOR THIS EXERCISE		20	

Assessment 9.6 – Create an Invitation

Step	Task	Criterion	Value	Score*
1	**Opening Template**	Selected company annual picnic invitation flyer in the Office.com Templates section.	2	
1	**Editing**	Edited information as illustrated. Corrected typographical errors.	10	
1	**Inserting Page Border**	Used page border (as illustrated) with border style third from bottom in the *Style* list box. Changed width to 4 ½ points. Changed color to Blue, Accent 1.	6	
2-3	**Saving and Printing**	Saved invitation with specified name. Printed document.	2	
	TOTAL POINTS FOR THIS EXERCISE		20	

Chapter 10. Managing and Printing Documents

Applying Your Skills

Assessment 10.1 – Arrange Documents

Step	Task	Criterion	Value	Score*
1-10	**Opening, Arranging, and Restoring**	Opened correct files. Made documents active. Arranged windows. Minimized documents. Restored documents. Maximized documents.	4	
11-12	**Opening and Saving**	Saved document with specified name. Opened document.	4	
13	**Viewing**	Viewed documents side by side.	2	
14-15	**Formatting**	Scrolled through documents simultaneously. Changed formatting (font, font size, and shading) to match **Hardware.docx** file. Closed **Hardware.docx** file.	8	
16	**Saving and Printing**	Saved file. Printed document.	2	
	TOTAL POINTS FOR THIS EXERCISE		20	

Assessment 10.2 – Create an Envelope

Step	Task	Criterion	Value	Score*
1	**Creating Envelope**	Created envelope as illustrated. Corrected typographical errors.	8	
2-3	**Saving and Printing**	Saved envelope with specified name. Printed envelope.	2	
		TOTAL POINTS FOR THIS EXERCISE	**10**	

Assessment 10.3 – Create Mailing Labels

Step	Task	Criterion	Value	Score*
1	**Creating Labels**	Created mailing labels with text as specified. Corrected typographical errors.	8	
2-4	**Saving, Printing, and Closing**	Saved file with specified name. Printed document. Closed blank document.	2	
		TOTAL POINTS FOR THIS EXERCISE	**10**	

Expanding Your Skills

Assessment 10.4 – Create and Format Labels

Step	Task	Criterion	Value	Score*
1-3	**Creating Labels**	Selected Labels tab. Typed name and address as specified in the Address text box. Clicked New Document button.	2	
4	**Formatting**	Selected all labels. Changed Left Indent marker to 0.5-inch marker on Ruler. Deselected text.	2	
5	**Formatting**	Vertically centered text in each label. Selected all labels and selected Align Center Left button in Alignment group in Table Tools Layout tab. Deselected text.	4	
6-7	**Saving and Printing**	Saved label document with specified name. Printed labels.	2	
		TOTAL POINTS FOR THIS EXERCISE	**10**	

Achieving Signature Status

Assessment 10.5 – Create Custom Labels

Step	Task	Criterion	Value	Score*
1	**Typing**	Typed company name and address one time as specified. Corrected typographical errors.	4	
1	**Formatting**	Set text in 14-point Harlow Solid Italic. Set "S" in *Southland* and "*A*" in *Aviation* to 20-point size. Changed font color to Blue.	6	
1	**Creating Labels**	Selected company name and address and created label by selecting New Document. Used Avery US Letter label, product number 5160.	6	
1	**Formatting**	Centered all names and addresses in each label.	2	
2-3	**Saving and Printing**	Saved completed labels document with specified name. Printed document.	2	
		TOTAL POINTS FOR THIS EXERCISE	**20**	

Assessment 10.6 – Create Personal Labels

Step	Task	Criterion	Value	Score*
1	**Typing and Formatting**	Typed name and address in blank document. Applied formatting to enhance visual appeal of label (font, font size, and color).	12	
2	**Creating Labels**	Created labels. Selected label vendor and product number of choice.	6	
3-4	**Saving and Printing**	Saved label document with specified name. Printed document.	2	
		TOTAL POINTS FOR THIS EXERCISE	20	

Unit 2. Formatting and Managing Documents

Assessing Proficiencies

Assessment U2.1 – Format a Corporate Report

Step	Task	Criterion	Value	Score*
1	**Opening and Saving**	Opened correct file. Saved document with specified name.	2	
2	**Inserting File**	At beginning of the heading *Manufacturing*, inserted **R&D.docx** file.	2	
3-5	**Formatting**	Applied Heading 1 style to title. Applied Heading 2 style to headings. Changed style set to Basic (Stylish). Centered title *TERRA ENERGY CORPORATION*. Applied Frame theme. Changed theme colors to Blue II.	10	
6-9	**Formatting**	Inserted continuous section break at beginning of first paragraph beginning with *Terra Energy Corporation is a*... Formatted text below section break into two columns. Balanced columns on second page. Created drop cap with first letter of first word *Terra* in first paragraph of text. Made drop cap two lines in height.	6	
10	**Hyphenating**	Manually hyphenated words in document.	2	
11	**Page Numbering**	Inserted page numbering at bottom center of each page.	2	
12	**Inserting Cover Page**	Inserted Motion cover page. Typed appropriate text in text placeholders.	4	
13	**Saving and Printing**	Saved file. Printed document.	2	
		TOTAL POINTS FOR THIS EXERCISE	30	

Assessment U2.2 – Create and Format an Announcement

Step	Task	Criterion	Value	Score*
1	Typing	Used Click and Type feature and typed document as illustrated (five centered lines and two right-aligned lines). Corrected typographical errors.	4	
2-4	Formatting	Changed font of centered text to 20-point Cambria and font color to Orange, Accent 2, Darker 50%. Changed font of right-aligned text to 14-point Cambria and font color to Orange, Accent 2, Darker 50%. Changed vertical alignment of text to Center.	6	
5	Inserting Page Border	Inserted page border using the first double-line option in the *Style* list box. Changed width to 2 ¼ points and font color to Dark Blue.	4	
6-7	Saving and Printing	Saved file with specified name. Printed document.	2	
8	Formatting	Changed page orientation to landscape.	2	
9	Saving and Printing	Saved file. Printed document.	2	
		TOTAL POINTS FOR THIS EXERCISE	20	

Assessment U2.3 – Format a Computer Security Report

Step	Task	Criterion	Value	Score*
1	Opening and Saving	Opened correct file. Saved document with specified name.	2	
2	Formatting	Changed style set to Centered. Applied Dividend theme. Inserted Retrospect footer with first and last names at the left side of footer.	4	
3	Typing	At end of paragraph in the *Types of Viruses* section typed (Pie Chart).	2	
4-8	Bookmarks	Displayed bookmarks. Inserted bookmark named *Types* following a space after (Pie Chart) in the *Types of Viruses* section. Inserted bookmark named *Effects* at end of first paragraph in the *Methods of Virus Operation* section. Inserted bookmark named *Infection* at end of the second paragraph in the *Methods of Virus Operation* section. Navigated in document using bookmarks.	6	
9-10	Inserting Hyperlink	Inserted hyperlink to the *Effects* bookmark at end of the first paragraph in the section. Selected text *(Pie Chart)* and inserted hyperlink to Excel named **Viruses.xlsx** located in the Unit02PA folder on storage medium.	6	
11	Printing Hyperlink	Clicked (Pie Chart) hyperlink and printed Excel worksheet. Closed Excel program.	4	
12	Inserting Watermark	Inserted DRAFT1 watermark in document.	2	
13	Saving and Printing	Saved file. Printed document.	2	
		TOTAL POINTS FOR THIS EXERCISE	30	

Assessment U2.4 – Create a Business Letter Using a Template

Step	Task	Criterion	Value	Score*
1	**Opening Template**	Opened Letter (Equity theme) template.	2	
1	**Typing**	Typed information in specified fields. Corrected typographical errors.	6	
2	**Formatting**	Selected salutation text and removed bold formatting.	2	
3	**Deleting and Inserting Text**	Deleted three paragraphs of text in body of letter. Inserted **AnnualMtg.docx**. Removed blank space above complimentary close.	6	
4	**Typing**	Typed information in the specified fields (*Closing* and *Sender title*).	2	
5-6	**Saving and Printing**	Saved file with specified name. Printed document.	2	
		TOTAL POINTS FOR THIS EXERCISE	20	

Assessment U2.5 – Format an Employment Appointments Document

Step	Task	Criterion	Value	Score*
1	**Opening and Saving**	Opened correct file. Saved file with specified name.	2	
2	**Formatting**	Changed top, left, and right margins to 1.25 inches.	3	
3-5	**Formatting**	Applied Heading 1 style to title. Applied Heading 2 style to heading. Changed style set to Minimalist. Applied Slice theme.	5	
5-8	**Inserting**	Inserted page break at beginning of text *Reappointment*. Inserted current date and time at end of document. Inserted Austin header and typed document title: **Employee Handbook**. Inserted Austin footer.	8	
9	**Saving and Printing**	Saved file. Printed document.	2	
		TOTAL POINTS FOR THIS EXERCISE	20	

Assessment U2.6 – Create an Envelope

Step	Task	Criterion	Value	Score*
1	**Creating and Typing**	Created envelope. Typed text. Corrected typographical errors.	8	
2-3	**Saving and Printing**	Saved file with specified name. Printed envelope.	2	
		TOTAL POINTS FOR THIS EXERCISE	10	

Assessment U2.7 – Create Mailing Labels

Step	Task	Criterion	Value	Score*
1	Creating and Typing	Created mailing labels. Typed name and address for Dr. Erin Sutton as specified. Selected label vendor and product of choice.	8	
2-3	Saving and Printing	Saved file with specified file name. Printed labels.	2	
		TOTAL POINTS FOR THIS EXERCISE	**10**	

Assessment U2.8 – Format a Report

Step	Task	Criterion	Value	Score*
1	Opening and Saving	Opened correct file. Saved file with specified file name.	2	
2	Formatting	Changed top margin to 1.5 inch. Set text in 12-point Cambria. Set title text in 16-point Cambria. Set text in two columns with a line between columns as illustrated.	8	
2	Formatting	Applied bullets as illustrated. Decreased indent so bullets display at left margin. Applied Blue II theme colors.	4	
2	Formatting	Inserted Ion (Dark) header and footer.	4	
2	Formatting	Applied other character and paragraph formatting as illustrated.	6	
2	Hyphenating	Manually hyphenated text in report.	4	
3	Saving and Printing	Saved file. Printed document.	2	
		TOTAL POINTS FOR THIS EXERCISE	**30**	

Assessment U2.9 – Prepare a Gift Certificate

Step	Task	Criterion	Value	Score*
1	Creating	Used Gift Certificate template in Gift Certificate option in Office.com Templates section.	4	
1	Typing	Typed appropriate information. Corrected typographical errors.	6	
1	Formatting	Changed font size to 28 and color to Dark Blue in all three certificates for company name. Deleted text: *Cut along dotted line* above each certificate.	8	
2-3	Saving and Printing	Saved file with specified name. Printed document.	2	
		TOTAL POINTS FOR THIS EXERCISE	**20**	

Creating Original Documents

Assessment U2.10 – Format a Computer Guidelines Company Document

Step	Task	Criterion	Value	Score*
1	**Opening and Saving**	Opened correct file. Saved file with specified name.	2	
2	**Formatting**	Formatted document by applying and/or inserting at least: a style set, heading style, header, footer, and/or page numbers, and a cover page.	8	
3	**Saving and Printing**	Saved file. Printed document.	1	
4	**Typing**	Used Word letter template. Composed and typed letter with explanation of formatting and reasons why formatting was selected. Corrected typographical and grammatical errors.	8	
5	**Saving and Printing**	Saved file with specified name. Printed document.	1	
		TOTAL POINTS FOR THIS EXERCISE	**20**	

Assessment U2.11 – Create a Calendar Using a Calendar Template

Step	Task	Criterion	Value	Score*
1	**Downloading Template**	Downloaded calendar template for the current year.	2	
2	**Typing**	Typed data on vacation days in appropriate weeks/months on calendar.	5	
3	**Saving**	Saved file with specified name.	1	
4	**Printing**	Printed only pages containing months of June, July, and August.	2	
		TOTAL POINTS FOR THIS EXERCISE	**10**	

Assessment U2.12 – Research and Prepare a Netiquette Report

Step	Task	Criterion	Value	Score*
1	**Researching**	Searched the Internet (or another source) for information on "rules of netiquette." Used at least two sources.	6	
2	**Typing**	Created a document describing netiquette rules. Used own words (did not copy and paste). Corrected typographical and grammatical errors.	12	
3	**Formatting**	Applied formatting to enhance visual appeal.	8	
4	**Citing References**	Typed web addresses for sites used as references.	2	
5	**Saving and Printing**	Saved file with specified name. Printed document.	2	
		TOTAL POINTS FOR THIS EXERCISE	**30**	

Chapter 11. Inserting Images

Applying Your Skills

Assessment 11.1 – Create a Flyer with a Picture and Text

Step	Task	Criterion	Value	Score*
1	Typing	Pressed Enter key three times. Typed text. Pressed Enter key and typed phone number.	2	
2	Inserting Picture	Used Ctrl + Home and inserted **Ocean.jpg** picture.	4	
2	Formatting	Changed position to Position in Top Center with Square Text Wrapping. Changed text wrapping to Behind Text. Changed width to 4.5 inches. Corrected Brightness to -20% and Contrast to +20%.	8	
3	Formatting	Changed text font to 26-point Script MT Bold. Changed text color to White. Centered text.	4	
4-5	Saving and Printing	Saved file with specified name. Printed document.	2	
		TOTAL POINTS FOR THIS EXERCISE	**20**	

Assessment 11.2 – Insert and Format a Clip Art Image

Step	Task	Criterion	Value	Score*
1	Opening and Saving	Opened correct file. Saved document with specified name.	2	
2	Inserting Image	Inserted *cornucopia* clip art image.	4	
2	Formatting	Formatted the clip art image to 1.4 inches in height. Changed the Brightness to 0% (Normal) and Contrast to 20%. Positioned the clip art image to Middle Right with Square Text Wrapping. Applied the Offset Diagonal Bottom Left picture effect shadow.	12	
3	Saving and Printing	Saved file. Printed document.	2	
		TOTAL POINTS FOR THIS EXERCISE	**20**	

Assessment 11.3 – Insert and Format a Clip Art Image in a Data Security Training Notice

Step	Task	Criterion	Value	Score*
1	Opening and Saving	Opened correct file. Saved file with specified name.	2	
2	Inserting Clip Art	After searching "computer" and "padlock icon", inserted clip art image as illustrated.	2	
3	Formatting Picture	Rotated image by flipping it horizontally.	2	

Step	Task	Criterion	Value	Score*
4-7	Formatting	Applied *Light Gradient – Accent 6* option and selected *Offset Diagonal Right* Shadow option. Selected *Tight Reflection, touching* option in the *Reflections Variations* section. Changed text wrapping to Square. Changed shape height measurement to 1.3 inches. In Position tab, changed horizontal absolute position to 6.2 inches to the right of the left margin and vertical absolute position to 2.2 inches below the page.	12	
8	Saving and Printing	Saved file. Printed document.	2	
		TOTAL POINTS FOR THIS EXERCISE	**20**	

Assessment 11.4 – Insert, Ungroup, and Recolor a Clip Art Image in a Vacation Document

Step	Task	Criterion	Value	Score*
1	Opening and Saving	Opened correct file. Saved file with specified name.	2	
2	Inserting image	Used the words *illustrations of sunglasses, mountains and the sun* and inserted clip art image as illustrated.	4	
2	Formatting	Changed text wrapping to Square. Changed shape height measurement to 2.3 inches. Ungrouped clip art image. Recolored individual components using the Green shape fill color to the mountains, and the Blue shape fill color to the water shapes. Positioned image in Middle Right with Square Text Wrapping.	8	
3	Saving and Printing	Saved file. Printed document.	2	
		TOTAL POINTS FOR THIS EXERCISE	**20**	

Assessment 11.5 – Create and Format a Cycle SmartArt Graphic

Step	Task	Criterion	Value	Score*
1	Creating SmartArt	Selected Basic Radial cycle graphic. Added a shape. Applied Polished SmartArt style. Changed colors to Colorful Range – Accent Colors 3 to 4. Changed height of SmartArt diagram to 5.5 inches and width to 6.5 inches.	12	
1	Typing	Typed text in shapes as illustrated.	6	
2-3	Saving and Printing	Saved file with specified name. Printed document.	2	
		TOTAL POINTS FOR THIS EXERCISE	**20**	

Assessment 11.6 – Create and Format a SmartArt Organizational Chart

Step	Task	Criterion	Value	Score*
1	Creating Organizational Chart	Selected Hierarchy organizational chart. Selected top text box and inserted shape above. Selected top right text box and added shape below. Applied Colorful Range – Accent Colors 3 to 4 option. Increased height to 4.5 inches and width to 6.5 inches.	12	
1	Typing	Typed text in each text box as illustrated.	4	
1	Formatting	Positioned organizational chart in middle of page.	2	
2-3	Saving and Printing	Saved file with specified name. Printed document.	2	
		TOTAL POINTS FOR THIS EXERCISE	**20**	

Expanding Your Skills

Assessment 11.7 – Create a Flyer

Step	Task	Criterion	Value	Score*
1	Typing	Typed text as illustrated. Corrected typographical errors.	3	
1	Formatting	Set text font to Comic Sans MS. Adjusted font size appropriately.	3	
1	Inserting Borders	Inserted and formatted paragraph borders with the first double-line style and Dark Red color and page borders with first thick-thin line style and Dark Red color.	4	
1	Inserting Picture	Inserted **Pug.jpg** picture.	2	
1	Formatting	Removed and kept background so picture displays as illustrated.	4	
1	Formatting	Changed text wrapping for picture to Behind Text. Sized and positioned picture as illustrated.	6	
1	Formatting	Made changes to document. Document same as illustrated.	4	
2	Changing Borders	Increased measurements at Border and Shading Option so entire page border will print.	2	
3-4	Saving and Printing	Saved file with specified name. Printed document.	2	
		TOTAL POINTS FOR THIS EXERCISE	**30**	

Assessment 11.8 – Ungroup and Recolor a Clip Art Image

Step	Task	Criterion	Value	Score*
1	**Inserting Clip Art Image**	Opened blank document. Opened **TECLogo.docx** file. Copied clip art image from document. Pasted clip art image into blank document.	4	
1	**Formatting**	Flipped clip art image, ungrouped image, recolored components as illustrated.	10	
1	**Typing**	Typed text as illustrated. Corrected typographical errors.	12	
1	**Formatting**	Set title in Copperplate Gothic bold. Changed formatting as illustrated.	2	
2-4	**Saving and Printing**	Saved file with specified name. Printed document. Closed **TECLogo.docx** without saving changes.	2	
		TOTAL POINTS FOR THIS EXERCISE	30	

Assessment 11.9 – Create and Format a SmartArt Graphic

Step	Task	Criterion	Value	Score*
1	**Creating SmartArt**	Used Pyramid List Diagram. Applied Inset SmartArt style. Changed color Colorful Range – Accent Colors 5 to 6). Applied Light Green shape fill color to bottom shape, Light Blue fill color to middle shape, and Red fill color to top shape.	14	
1	**Typing**	Typed text as illustrated. Corrected typographical errors.	4	
2-3	**Saving and Printing**	Saved file with specified name. Printed document.	2	
		TOTAL POINTS FOR THIS EXERCISE	20	

Chapter 12. Inserting Shapes, WordArt, and Advanced Character Formatting

Applying Your Skills

Assessment 12.1 – Create a Screenshot

Step	Task	Criterion	Value	Score*
1	**Opening**	Opened correct files.	2	
2	**Typing**	Typed the current date in DATE: heading. Typed instructor's name in TO: heading, and typed student's name in FROM: heading. Corrected typographical errors.	6	
3	**Inserting Screenshot**	Inserted screenshot of specified file at the bottom of the **ImagesMemo.docx** document.	2	
4	**Formatting**	Changed text wrapping of screenshot image to Tight and changed the height to 2.3 inches.	2	

Step	Task	Criterion	Value	Score*
5-7	**Opening and Inserting a Screenshot**	Opened correct file. Inserted screenshot of specified file at the bottom of the **ImagesMemo.docx** document.	2	
8	**Formatting**	Changed text wrapping of screenshot image to Tight and changed the height to 2.3 inches.	2	
9	**Typing**	Typed reference initials, then used Shift + Enter, followed by the specified file name.	2	
10-12	**Saving and Printing**	Saved document with specified name. Printed document.	2	
		TOTAL POINTS FOR THIS EXERCISE	**20**	

Assessment 12.2 – Create a Letterhead with Text and a Drawn Line

Step	Task	Criterion	Value	Score*
1	**Typing**	Typed text and corrected typographical errors.	2	
1	**Formatting**	Changed font to 56-point Freestyle Script bold. Changed font color to Blue. Centered text.	4	
2	**Formatting**	Changed Text Fill to *Medium Gradient – Accent 1*. Changed Text Outline a Dark Blue *Solid line*. Changed *Shadow* effect to *Offset Diagonal Bottom Right*. Changed *3-D Format* to Top *Bevel, Circle*.	6	
3	**Inserting and Formatting**	Added a line below the text. Used Line option from Shapes. Applied Intense Line – Accent 1 shape style. Changed Shape outline color to Blue. Applied the Offset Bottom shadow effect.	6	
4-5	**Saving and Printing**	Saved the file with specified name. Printed document.	2	
		TOTAL POINTS FOR THIS EXERCISE	**20**	

Assessment 12.3 – Create an Announcement with a Shape and Text Box

Step	Task	Criterion	Value	Score*
1	**Formatting**	Used Bevel shape. Changed height to 3.3 inches and width to 5.7 inches. Change shape style to Subtle Effect – Gold, Accent 4. Applied Offset Diagonal Top Right shadow effect. Applied Orange, 8 pt glow, Accent color 2 glow effect. Changed position of text box to Position in Top Center with Square Text Wrapping.	10	
2	**Typing**	Typed text inside shape as illustrated. Corrected typographical errors.	2	
2	**Formatting**	Changed text font to 36-point Monotype Corsiva bold. Changed font color to Orange, Accent 2, Darker 50%.	6	
3-4	**Saving and Printing**	Saved file with specified name. Printed document.	2	
		TOTAL POINTS FOR THIS EXERCISE	**20**	

Assessment 12.4 –Insert a Pull Quote Text Box and WordArt in a Document

Step	Task	Criterion	Value	Score*
1	**Opening and Saving**	Opened correct file. Saved file with specified name.	2	
2	**Inserting and Typing**	Inserted Sidebar Quote text box. Typed text in text box as illustrated. Corrected typographical errors.	10	
3-4	**Formatting**	Changed shape width of the text box to 2.6 inches. Changed position to Position in Middle Left with Square Text Wrapping.	4	
5	**Formatting**	Applied WordArt to the title. Applied the style Fill-Black, Text 1, Outline – Background 1, Hard Shadow – Accent 1. Applied Blue text fill color. Applied Green, 5 pt glow, Accent color 6 glow text effect in the *Glow Variations section*. Applied Perspective Below 3-D rotation text effect in the *Perspective* section. Changed the height to 1 inch and the width to 6.5 inches.	12	
6	**Saving and Printing**	Saved file. Printed document.	2	
		TOTAL POINTS FOR THIS EXERCISE	30	

Assessment 12.5 – Create a Flyer with Shapes and a Text Box

Step	Task	Criterion	Value	Score*
1	**Creating Arrow**	Used Curved Right Arrow shape. Changed height of arrow to 4.8 inches and width of arrow to 3 inches. Applied Moderate Effect – Orange, Access 2 shape style. Changed shape outline color to Dark Blue.	6	
2-4	**Copying and Formatting**	Copied arrow shape to the right. Flipped arrow horizontally and vertically. Moved right arrow up slightly as illustrated.	4	
5	**Drawing Text Box**	Drew text box between arrows with height of 1.3 inches and width of 4 inches. Changed shape outline to No Outline.	2	
6-7	**Typing and Formatting**	Typed text. Corrected typographical errors. Centered paragraph alignment. Changed font to 28-point Franklin Gothic Heavy. Changed font color to Dark Blue. Positioned text box between arrows as illustrated.	6	
8-9	**Saving and Printing**	Saved file with specified name. Printed document.	2	
		TOTAL POINTS FOR THIS EXERCISE	20	

Assessment 12.6 – Apply Character Spacing and OpenType Features

Step	Task	Criterion	Value	Score*
1	**Opening and Saving**	Opened correct file. Saved file with specified name.	2	
2	**Typing and Formatting**	Selected quote text beginning with *"In every community there is work to be done…"* and changed stylistic set to 4.	4	
3-4	**Formatting**	Changed scale to 90% and spacing to Expanded to two headings.	4	
5-6	**Formatting**	Changed number spacing to Tabular to numbers in specified sections.	4	
7	**Formatting**	Use the Advanced tab in the Font dialog box to apply the *Use Contextual Alternates* option.	4	
8	**Saving and Printing**	Saved file with specific name. Printed document.	2	
		TOTAL POINTS FOR THIS EXERCISE	**20**	

Expanding Your Skills

Assessment 12.7 – Edit a Drawn Line

Step	Task	Criterion	Value	Score*
1	**Opening and Saving**	Opened correct file. Saved file with specified name.	1	
2-3	**Formatting**	Selected horizontal line. Used Format Shape dialog box to customize shape. Changed line color to Blue, Accent 1, Lighter 40%. Selected Line Style and changed line style width to 4 points. Changed beginning and ending arrow style to Diamond Arrow.	4	
4	**Formatting**	Selected Glow effects. Selected Dark Blue color. Changed size to 3 point.	4	
5	**Saving and Printing**	Saved file. Printed document.	1	
		TOTAL POINTS FOR THIS EXERCISE	**10**	

Assessment 12.8 – Format and Insert WordArt Text in a Travel Document

Step	Task	Criterion	Value	Score*
1	**Opening and Saving**	Opened correct file. Saved file with specified name.	2	
2	**Formatting**	Applied bulleted list formatting to the paragraphs below the *Fast Facts* heading.	2	
3	**Formatting**	Changed left and right margins to 1.5 inches.	2	
4	**Inserting and Formatting WordArt**	Inserted WordArt text, Ski Resorts. Used Gradient Fill – Blue, Accent 1, Reflection WordArt Style.	4	

Step	Task	Criterion	Value	Score*
5	**Formatting WordArt Text Box Border**	Changed gradient fill direction to Linear Up. Applied Offset Diagonal Top Left shadow effect. Applied Blue shadow color. Applied *Tight Reflections, touching* reflection. Applied the 3-D Slope bevel format.	10	
6	**Formatting WordArt Text Box**	Changed height to 1 inch and width to 5.5 inches. Changed position to Position in Top Center with Square Text Wrapping. Applied Square transform text effect.	8	
7	**Saving and Printing**	Saved file. Printed document.	2	
		TOTAL POINTS FOR THIS EXERCISE	30	

Achieving Signature Status

Assessment 12.9 – Create an Announcement

Step	Task	Criterion	Value	Score*
1	**Typing**	Typed text as illustrated. Corrected typographical errors.	8	
1	**Inserting WordArt and Formatting**	Inserted WordArt as illustrated. Used Fill – Blue, Accent 1, Outline – Background 1, Hard Shadow – Accent 1 WordArt Style. Applied Dark Blue text fill color and Blue text outline. Applied Inside Diagonal Top Left shadow text effect. Applied Subtle Effect – Blue, Accent 1 shape style. Applied Offset Top shadow shape effect. Applied Square transform text effect.	10	
2	**Inserting and Formatting Clip Art**	Inserted *caduceus* clip art image. Changed text wrapping to Tight. Changed clip art image color to Blue, Accent color 1 Light. Corrected Brightness to -20% and Contrast to + 40%. Sized and moved clip art image as illustrated.	4	
3	**Formatting**	Changed font to Candara. Applied character and page formatting as illustrated.	4	
4	**Formatting**	If necessary, increased measurement to ensure printing of entire page border.	2	
5-6	**Saving and Printing**	Saved file with specified name. Printed document.	2	
		TOTAL POINTS FOR THIS EXERCISE	30	

Assessment 12.10 – Insert Screenshots in a Memo

Step	Task	Criterion	Value	Score*
1	Opening and Saving	Opened correct file. Saved file with specified name.	1	
2	Inserting Screenshots	Inserted screenshot of **FirstAidAnnounce** document. Inserted screenshot of document created in Assessment 12.10 as second screenshot. Adjusted zoom to ensure entire announcement page is displayed.	6	
2	Editing	Though not instructed, changed reference initials to own initials.	1	
3	Saving and Printing	Saved file. Printed document.	2	
		TOTAL POINTS FOR THIS EXERCISE	**10**	

Chapter 13. Creating Tables

Applying Your Skills

Assessment 13.1 – Create and Format a Table in a Letter

Step	Task	Criterion	Value	Score*
1	Opening and Saving	Opened correct file. Saved file with specified name.	2	
2	Creating Table	Created three column, eight row table at blank line between the two paragraphs. Typed text as illustrated. Corrected typographical errors.	8	
2	Formatting Table	Applied center, bold, and italic to text in first row. Applied bold to text in cells in first column below heading. Applied blue fill to first row (Blue, Accent 5, Darker 50%). Applied green fill to second, fourth, sixth, and eighth rows (Green, Accent 6, Lighter 80%). Applied blue fill to third, fifth, and seventh row (Blue, Accent 1, Lighter 80%).	8	
3	Saving and Printing	Saved file. Printed document.	2	
		TOTAL POINTS FOR THIS EXERCISE	**20**	

Assessment 13.2 – Create and Format a Tour Package Table

Step	Task	Criterion	Value	Score*
1	Typing and Formatting	Typed title in 16-point bold size.	4	
1	Creating and Typing Table	Created three column and five row table below the title. Typed text in cells as illustrated. Corrected typographical errors.	8	
1	Formatting	Applied Grid Table 4 – Accent 1 table style. Removed check mark from *First Column* check box.	4	
2-3	Saving and Printing	Saved file with specified name. Printed document.	2	
		TOTAL POINTS FOR THIS EXERCISE	**20**	

Assessment 13.3 – Format a Contacts List Table

Step	Task	Criterion	Value	Score*
1	**Opening and Saving**	Opened correct file. Saved file with specified name.	2	
2	**Formatting**	Selected entire table and changed font to Candara.	2	
3	**Formatting**	Applied Grid Table 2 – Accent 4 table style. Removed check mark from *First Column* check box in Table Style Options. If necessary, added check mark to Header Row check box.	6	
4	**Formatting**	Applied first thick-thin line style border and Dark Blue border color. Clicked the *Box* option.	6	
5	**Formatting**	Applied the *Double solid lines*, ½ pt border style to bottom of first row.	2	
6	**Saving and Printing**	Saved file. Printed document.	2	
		TOTAL POINTS FOR THIS EXERCISE	20	

Expanding Your Skills

Assessment 13.4 – Draw and Format an Employment Information Table

Step	Task	Criterion	Value	Score*
1	**Typing**	Typed title as illustrated followed by one Enter.	1	
1	**Drawing Table**	Drew table with three columns and seven rows.	3	
1	**Typing**	Typed text as illustrated. Corrected typographical errors.	6	
2	**Formatting**	Applied formatting to enhance visual appeal of table.	8	
3	**Saving and Printing**	Saved file with specified name. Printed document.	2	
		TOTAL POINTS FOR THIS EXERCISE	20	

Assessment 13.5 – Create a Monthly Calendar with a Quick Table

Step	Task	Criterion	Value	Score*
1	**Creating Table**	Used Quick Table to create a monthly calendar for the next month.	4	
2	**Formatting**	Applied additional formatting to enhance visual appeal of calendar.	4	
3-4	**Saving and Printing**	Saved file with specified name. Printed document.	2	
		TOTAL POINTS FOR THIS EXERCISE	10	

Assessment 13.6 – Create and Format Tables

Step	Task	Criterion	Value	Score*
1	**Typing and Creating Tables**	Typed headings as illustrated. Created first table with five columns and seven rows. Created second table with five columns and four rows. Typed text as illustrated. Corrected typographical errors.	12	
1	**Formatting**	Chose the *AutoFit to contents* option. Applied Grid Table 3 – Accent 5 table style to both tables. Removed check marks from *Header Row* and *First Column* check boxes in Table Style Options group. Vertically centered text on page.	6	
2	**Saving and Printing**	Saved file with specified name. Printed document.	2	
		TOTAL POINTS FOR THIS EXERCISE	20	

Chapter 14. Enhancing Tables

Applying Your Skills

Assessment 14.1 – Create and Format a Supply Request Form Table

Step	Task	Criterion	Value	Score*
1	**Creating a Table**	Created table with five columns and eight rows. Inserted three additional rows in table.	2	
1	**Formatting**	Merged cells in first row.	2	
1	**Typing**	Typed text in cells as illustrated. Corrected typographical errors.	2	
1	**Formatting**	Changed row height in first row to 0.58 inch. Selected text in first row and changed font size to 22 points. Selected rows 2 through 11 and changed row height to 0.3 inch. Applied Grid Table 4 - Accent 5 table style. Removed check mark from First Column option in Table Style Options group. Changed alignment of text in first row to Center. Changed alignment of text in second row to Center and applied bold formatting.	12	
2-3	**Saving and Printing**	Saved file with specified name. Printed document.	2	
		TOTAL POINTS FOR THIS EXERCISE	20	

Assessment 14.2 – Format a Transportation Services Table

Step	Task	Criterion	Value	Score*
1	**Opening and Saving**	Opened correct file. Saved file with specified name.	2	
2	**Formatting**	Deleted row beginning with *City Travel 24-hour customer service.*	2	
2	**Inserting Rows and Typing**	With insertion point in *Edgewood City Transit* cell, inserted four rows above. Typed text as illustrated. Corrected typographical errors.	4	

Step	Task	Criterion	Value	Score*
2	Formatting	Selected cells with text *Railway information, Status hotline,* and *Travel information* and changed left cell margin measurement to 0.3 inch. Selected two cells below *City Travel Card* and changed left cell margin measurement to 0.3 inch. Selected these cells below *Edgewood City* transit and changed left cell margin measurement to 0.3 inch. Selected three cells below *Mainline Bus* and changed left cell margin measurement to 0.3 inch.	6	
2	Inserting, Formatting, and Typing	Inserted column at left of first column. Merged cells in new column. Typed text: Edgewood Area Transportation Services. Changed text direction as illustrated. Changed alignment to Center. Changed font size to 18. Changed width of first column to 1 inch.	8	
2	Formatting	Changed width of second column to 2.2 inches. Changed width of third column to 1.1 inch. Applied bold and italic as illustrated. Applied shading to cells as illustrated: Dark Blue for first column and Gold, Accent 4, Lighter 80% to the first row and Blue, Accent 5, Lighter 80% for other cells.	4	
3	Formatting	Centered table between left and right margins.	2	
4	Saving and Printing	Saved file. Printed document.	2	
		TOTAL POINTS FOR THIS EXERCISE	30	

Assessment 14.3 – Create and Format a Training Costs Table

Step	Task	Criterion	Value	Score*
1	Creating and Formatting a Table	Created table with two columns and seven rows. Merged cells in top row. Changed alignment to Center.	2	
1	Typing	Typed text in cells as illustrated. Corrected typographical errors.	4	
1	Formatting	Top right-aligned cells containing money amounts and blank cell (cells B2 through B7). Applied AutoFit to contents of cells. Applied Grid Table 5 Dark – Accent 6 table style. Changed font size for text in cell A1 to 14 points. Changed spacing between cells to 0.02 inch.	8	
2	Inserting Formula	Inserted SUM formula in cell B7 for cells B2 through B6. Inserted dollar sign before number inserted by formula.	2	
3-4	Saving and Printing	Saved file with specified name. Printed document.	2	
		TOTAL POINTS FOR THIS EXERCISE	20	

Assessment 14.4 – Insert Formulas and Format a Training Department Table

Step	Task	Criterion	Value	Score*
1	Opening and Saving	Opened correct file. Saved with specified name.	2	
2	Inserting Formula	Inserted formulas below the *Average* heading that calculate averages of numbers in modules columns. Changed Number format to 0 at Formula dialog box.	6	
3	Editing	Changed number in B6 from 78 to 90. Changed number in B7 from 76 to 90. Recalculated averages in cells E6 and E7.	6	
4	Formatting	Applied Grid Table 2 – Accent 4 table style. Removed check mark from *First Column* check box in Table Style Options.	4	
5	Saving and Printing	Saved file. Printed document.	2	
		TOTAL POINTS FOR THIS EXERCISE	**20**	

Assessment 14.5 – Insert Formulas and Format a Financial Analysis Table

Step	Task	Criterion	Value	Score*
1	Opening and Saving	Opened correct file. Saved file with specified name.	2	
2-5	Inserting Formulas	Inserted SUM formula in cell B13 for cells B6 through B12. Inserted SUM formula in cell C13 for cells C6 through C12. Inserted formula in cell B14 that subtracts amount in B13 from amount in B4. (=B4-B13). Inserted formula in cell C14 that subtracts amount in C13 from amount in C4. (=C4-C13).	10	
6-7	Formatting	Applied Grid Table 4 – Accent 2 table style. Removed check mark from First Column check box in Table Style Options. Selected top two rows in table and changed alignment to Center.	6	
8	Saving and Printing	Saved file. Printed document.	2	
		TOTAL POINTS FOR THIS EXERCISE	**20**	

Expanding Your Skills

Assessment 14.6 – Insert an Average Formula

Step	Task	Criterion	Value	Score*
1	Opening and Saving	Opened correct file. Saved file with specified name.	2	
2-3	Inserting Formulas	Added Average formula in empty cell below 67% and repeated last function (F4) in the remaining empty cells in Average column.	4	
4	Formatting	Changed spacing between cells to 0.01 inch.	2	
5	Saving and Printing	Saved file. Printed document.	2	
		TOTAL POINTS FOR THIS EXERCISE	**10**	

Assessment 14.7 – Insert a Table in a Document and Repeat a Header Row

Step	Task	Criterion	Value	Score*
1	Opening and Saving	Opened correct file. Saved file with specified name.	2	
2	Inserting File	Inserted correct file at the beginning of second paragraph in letter.	2	
3	Displaying	Displayed first row in table at top of table on second page as header row.	3	
4	Replacing	Replaced XX reference initials with own initials.	1	
5	Saving and Printing	Saved file. Printed document.	2	
		TOTAL POINTS FOR THIS EXERCISE	**10**	

Achieving Signature Status

Assessment 14.8 – Create a Cover Letter Containing a Table

Step	Task	Criterion	Value	Score*
1	Typing	Typed letter as illustrated. Corrected typographical errors.	10	
1	Creating a Table	Created table as illustrated. Typed text as illustrated. Corrected typographical errors.	10	
1	Formatting	Formatted table as illustrated.	8	
2-3	Saving and Printing	Saved file with specified name. Printed document.	2	
		TOTAL POINTS FOR THIS EXERCISE	**30**	

Chapter 15. Creating Charts

Applying Your Skills

Assessment 15.1 – Create and Format a Column Chart

Step	Task	Criterion	Value	Score*
1	Typing and Creating a Chart	Typed text. Corrected typographical errors. Created 3-D clustered column chart.	4	
1	Formatting	Inserted data table with legend keys. Removed legend. Selected chart title text and typed Sales by State. Applied Style 11 chart style and Color 4 color option. Inserted Primary Major Vertical gridlines.	5	
1	Filtering	Filtered sales to display only for Florida and Georgia.	2	
2-3	Saving and Printing	Saved file with specified name. Printed document.	2	
4	Removing Filters	Removed filters so data for all four states displays.	2	
5-7	Formatting	Changed chart type to clustered bar chart. Switched the Row/Columns in the chart. Removed axes from the chart.	3	

Step	Task	Criterion	Value	Score*
8	Saving and Printing	Saved document with specified name. Printed document.	2	
		TOTAL POINTS FOR THIS EXERCISE	**20**	

Assessment 15.2 – Create and Format a Pie Chart

Step	Task	Criterion	Value	Score*
1	Typing	Typed data. Corrected typographical errors.	2	
1	Creating a Chart and Formatting	Created pie chart. Applied Layout 4 quick layout. Applied Style 9 chart style. Typed chart title text *DEPARTMENT EXPENSES* and applied Subtle Effect – Blue, Accent 1 shape style. Applied the 3-D Format Circle top bevel effect. Changed position of chart to Position in Middle Center with Square Text Wrapping.	10	
2-3	Saving and Printing	Saved file with specified name. Printed document.	2	
4	Editing Data	Changed data in Excel worksheet. Changed *Salaries* percentage from 67% to 62%. Changed *Travel* percentage from 15% to 17%. Changed *Equipment* percentage from 11% to 14%.	4	
5	Saving and Printing	Saved file. Printed document.	2	
		TOTAL POINTS FOR THIS EXERCISE	**20**	

Assessment 15.3 – Create and Format a Bar Chart

Step	Task	Criterion	Value	Score*
1	Typing	Typed data. Corrected typographical errors.	4	
1	Creating a Chart and Formatting	Created 3-D Clustered Bar. Removed legend. Inserted Primary Minor Vertical gridlines. Applied Dark Red shape fill color and Light Blue shape outline color to the *"Sales in Millions" Series*. Applied Dark Blue text fill color to the chart area. Changed height of chart to 4.5 inches and width to 6.5 inches.	14	
2-3	Saving and Printing	Saved file with specified name. Printed document.	2	
		TOTAL POINTS FOR THIS EXERCISE	**20**	

Assessment 15.4 – Create and Format a Line Chart

Step	Task	Criterion	Value	Score*
1	Typing and Creating a Chart	Typed data. Corrected typographical errors. Created a line chart.	10	

Step	Task	Criterion	Value	Score*
2-3	Formatting	Selected Line with Markers line chart type. Selected Switch Row/Column button. Applied Style 11 chart style. Removed chart title. Applied gradient fill. Applied Fill – Black, Text 1, Shadow WordArt style to chart area. Changed the absolute height to 2.5 inches and absolute width to 5 inches. Changed wrapping style to Top and bottom and changed distance from text bottom to 0.2 inches. Changed the horizontal alignment of chart to center and the vertical absolute position to 4.8 inches below top margin.	18	
4	Saving and Printing	Saved file with specified name. Printed document.	2	
		TOTAL POINTS FOR THIS EXERCISE	30	

Expanding Your Skills

Assessment 15.5 – Create and Format a Chart

Step	Task	Criterion	Value	Score*
1	Typing and Creating a Chart	Typed data. Corrected typographical errors. Created chart and selected chart type.	2	
1	Formatting	Selected design, layout, and format of chart and chart elements.(Chart selection/design will vary.) Inserted *Taxes* as chart title.	16	
2-3	Saving and Printing	Saved file with specified name. Printed document.	2	
		TOTAL POINTS FOR THIS EXERCISE	20	

Assessment 15.6 – Type a Business Letter Containing a Column Chart

Step	Task	Criterion	Value	Score*
1	Opening and Saving	Opened correct file. Saved file with specific name.	2	
2	Typing	Typed letter as illustrated. Corrected typographical errors.	8	
2	Inserting and Formatting	Inserted chart. Applied Style 5 to the chart. Changed color to Color 2. Changed font size of title to 12 points. Sized and positioned chart as illustrated. Inserted initials in place of *XX*.	8	
3	Saving and Printing	Saved file. Printed document.	2	
		TOTAL POINTS FOR THIS EXERCISE	20	

Achieving Signature Status

Assessment 15.7 – Create and Format a Pie Chart

Step	Task	Criterion	Value	Score*
1	Opening and Saving	Opened correct file. Saved file with specified name.	2	
2	Creating Chart	Created pie chart with data provided.	6	

Step	Task	Criterion	Value	Score*
2	Formatting	Used Pie in 3-D pie chart option. Removed legend. Inserted Data Callout data labels. Changed text fill color to black. Applied bold formatting to text. Changed font size of title to 28 points. Removed shape outline from chart. Increased size of chart and positioned it in the middle of the page.	10	
3	Saving and Printing	Saved file. Printed document.	2	
		TOTAL POINTS FOR THIS EXERCISE	**20**	

Unit 3. Performance Assessments

Assessing Proficiencies

Assessment U3.1 – Create a Flyer with WordArt and a Clip Art Image

Step	Task	Criterion	Value	Score*
1	Typing	Typed WordArt text as illustrated. Corrected typographical errors.	2	
1	Formatting	Used Fill – White, Outline – Accent 1, Shadow. Increased width to 6.5 inches and height to 1 inch. Applied Deflate text effect transform shape. Changed text fill color to Green, Accent 6, Lighter 40%.	5	
1	Typing	Typed text as illustrated. Corrected typographical errors.	2	
1	Formatting	Used 22-point Calibri and bold. Centered text.	5	
1	Inserting	Inserted *Eiffel Tower Paris* clip art image shown. Changed wrapping style to Square. Changed height and width to 2.2 inches. Positioned and sized image as illustrated.	4	
2-3	Saving and Printing	Saved file with specified name. Printed document.	2	
		TOTAL POINTS FOR THIS EXERCISE	**20**	

Assessment U3.2 – Create and Format an Organizational Chart

Step	Task	Criterion	Value	Score*
1	Creating	Used SmartArt to create organizational chart. Corrected typographical errors.	10	
1	Formatting	Changed color to Colorful Range – Accent Colors 4 to 5. Applied Metallic Scene SmartArt style.	8	
2-3	Saving and Printing	Saved file with specified name. Printed document.	2	
		TOTAL POINTS FOR THIS EXERCISE	**20**	

Signature Word 2013 Grading Rubrics

Assessment U3.3 – Create and Format a SmartArt Cycle Graphic

Step	Task	Criterion	Value	Score*
1	**Creating**	Created cycle diagram. Used Basic Radial SmartArt graphic. Inserted two additional shapes. Turned on **bold**. Typed text in shapes as illustrated.	8	
1	**Formatting**	Changed color to Colorful Range – Accent Colors 4 to 5. Applied Cartoon SmartArt style. Increased height to 4.5 inches and width to 6.5 inches. Positioned chart in middle of the page. Change text fill color to Black, Text 1.	10	
2-3	**Saving and Printing**	Saved file with specified name. Printed document.	2	
		TOTAL POINTS FOR THIS EXERCISE	**20**	

Assessment U3.4 – Create and Format a Training Announcement

Step	Task	Criterion	Value	Score*
1	**Creating and Formatting**	Used Bevel shape. Applied Moderate Effect – Green, Accent 6 style. Change shape outline to Dark Blue. Applied Offset Diagonal Top Left shadow to shape. Changed shape height to 2.8 inches and width to 6 inches. Changed position to Middle Center with Square Text Wrapping.	10	
1	**Typing and Formatting**	Typed text as illustrated inside bevel shape. Set text to 20-point Candara bold. Changed font color to Dark Blue.	8	
2-3	**Saving and Printing**	Saved file with specified name. Printed document.	2	
		TOTAL POINTS FOR THIS EXERCISE	**20**	

Assessment U3.5 – Create an Announcement with a Picture and Text

Step	Task	Criterion	Value	Score*
1	**Inserting**	Inserted **River** picture from Unit03PA folder.	2	
2-6	**Formatting**	Cropped out portion of trees at left and right and portion of hill at the top. Changed Brightness: 0% (Normal) Contrast: +20%. Changed position to Top Center with Square Text Wrapping. Wrapped picture behind text.	7	
7	**Inserting Text**	Typed Riverside Apartments on first line. Typed 1-888-555-8800 on second line.	2	
7	**Formatting Text**	Changed font size to 22-point Constantia and applied bold. Change font color to White, Background 1. Changed alignment to Center.	7	
8-9	**Saving and Printing**	Saved file with specified name. Printed document.	2	
		TOTAL POINTS FOR THIS EXERCISE	**20**	

Assessment U3.6 – Format a Photography Report

Step	Task	Criterion	Value	Score*
1	**Opening and Saving**	Opened correct file. Saved file with specified name.	2	
2	**Formatting**	Used *Photography* text to create WordArt with Fill – Black, Text 1, Shadow option. Changed height to .7 inches and width to 4 inches. Changed position to Top Center with Square Text Wrapping. Changed text wrapping to Top and Bottom. Applied Square transform text effect in *Warp* section.	6	
3	**Inserting Text Box and Formatting**	Inserted Motion Quote text box and positioned in the Middle Center with Square Text Wrapping. Typed *Photography, as a powerful medium…"* in the text box. Changed text to 11 points and applied bold formatting. Changed the width of text box to 3.1 inches.	7	
4	**Formatting**	Selected quote at bottom of document. Changed character spacing to Expanded by 0.3 points. Turned on kerning for fonts 16 points and above. Changed *Stylistic sets* option to 4.	3	
5	**Saving and Printing**	Saved file. Printed document.	2	
		TOTAL POINTS FOR THIS EXERCISE	20	

Assessment U3.7 – Create and Format a Table

Step	Task	Criterion	Value	Score*
1	**Creating Table**	Created table with 3 columns and 10 rows.	4	
1	**Formatting**	Merged and centered cells in row 1. Merged and centered cells in row 2.	4	
1	**Typing**	Typed text as illustrated.	2	
1	**Formatting**	Changed height of row 1 to 0.7 inch. Changed height of row 2 to 0.4 inch. Changed heights of remaining rows to 0.3 inch. Changed font size to 16 points for first row text. Aligned, centered, and applied bold to text in first three rows. Applied shading for first and third rows: Green, Accent 6, Lighter 40%. Applied shading for second row: Gold, Accent 4, Lighter 80%.	8	
2-3	**Saving and Printing**	Saved file with specified name. Printed document.	2	
		TOTAL POINTS FOR THIS EXERCISE	20	

Assessment U3.8 – Format a Travel Table

Step	Task	Criterion	Value	Score*
1	**Opening and Saving**	Opened correct file. Saved file with specified name.	2	

Step	Task	Criterion	Value	Score*
2	Formatting	Changed font of entire table to 12-point Candara. Applied Grid Table 4 – Accent 4 table style. Removed check mark from *First Column* option. Aligned and centered text in first three rows. Increased font size of text in first row to 18 points. Applied bold to text in rows 2 and 3. Increased height of rows 1 and 2 slightly as illustrated. Centered text in row 3. Centered cells in columns below the headings *Length* and *Estimated Cost*.	7	
3	Saving and Printing	Saved file. Printed document.	2	
4	Opening and Saving	Opened correct file. Saved document with specified name.	2	
5	Copying	Selected and copied table and blank line below table. Pasted copy of table at the beginning of second paragraph in letter.	2	
6-7	Formatting	Deleted first row of table. Change alignment of table to Center.	2	
8	Typing	Replaced XX initials with own initials.	1	
9-10	Saving and Printing	Saved filed. Printed document.	2	
		TOTAL POINTS FOR THIS EXERCISE	20	

Assessment U3.9 – Calculate Averages in a Table

Step	Task	Criterion	Value	Score*
1	Opening and Saving	Opened correct file. Saved file with specified name.	2	
2	Inserting Formulas	Inserted formulas in appropriate cells. Calculated averages of quizzes. Changed *Number Format* to 0.	8	
3-5	Formatting	Applied AutoFit to contents of table. Applied table style of choice. Applied formatting to improve visual appeal of table.	8	
6	Saving and Printing	Saved file. Printed document.	2	
		TOTAL POINTS FOR THIS EXERCISE	20	

Assessment U3.10 – Calculate Quantities and Totals in a Table

Step	Task	Criterion	Value	Score*
1	Opening and Saving	Opened correct file. Saved file with specified name.	1	
2	Inserting Formulas	Inserted formulas in appropriate cells multiplying quantity by unit price. Inserted formula in bottom cell of fourth column totaling amounts of cells above.	8	
3	Saving and Printing	Saved file. Printed document.	1	
		TOTAL POINTS FOR THIS EXERCISE	10	

Assessment U3.11 – Create and Format a Column Chart

Step	Task	Criterion	Value	Score*
1	**Creating Chart**	Created column chart. Typed text. Corrected typographical errors.	4	
1	**Formatting**	Changed chart type to 3-D Clustered Column. Applied Layout 3 chart layout. Applied Style 5 chart style. Changed chart title to *2015 Sales*. Inserted data table with legend keys. Selected chart area and applied Subtle Effect – Green, Accent 6 shape style and applied Offset Bottom shadow shape effect. Applied Dark Red shape fill to the *Second Half* series. Changed chart height to 4 inches and width to 6.25 inches. Positioned chart in middle of page with square text wrapping.	20	
2-3	**Saving and Printing**	Saved file with specified name. Printed document.	2	
4	**Editing**	Changed data in Excel worksheet. Changed amount in cell C2 from $285,450 to $302,500. Changed amount in cell C4 from $180,210 to $190,150.	2	
5	**Saving and Printing**	Saved file. Printed document.	2	
		TOTAL POINTS FOR THIS EXERCISE	**30**	

Assessment U3.12 – Create and Format a Pie Chart

Step	Task	Criterion	Value	Score*
1	**Creating Chart**	Typed text. Corrected typographical errors. Created pie chart.	4	
1	**Formatting**	Applied Layout 6 chart layout. Applied Style 3 chart style. Changed chart title to *District Expenditures*. Moved legend to left side of chart. Applied Gold, Accent 4, Lighter 80% shape fill and applied Gray-50%, 11 pt glow, Accent color 3 glow shape effect to chart area. Applied Blue shape outline color to legend. Applied WordArt style Fill – Blue, Accent 1, Outline – Background 1, Hard Shadow – Accent to chart title. Moved data labels to inside ends of pie "pieces". Centered legend between left edge of chart border and pie. Positioned chart centered at top of page with square text wrapping.	24	
2-3	**Saving and Printing**	Saved file with specified file name. Printed document.	2	
		TOTAL POINTS FOR THIS EXERCISE	**30**	

Creating Original Documents

Assessment U3.13 – Write Steps Describing How to Use SmartArt

Step	Task	Criterion	Value	Score*
1	Creating and Typing	Typed document describing SmartArt feature and types of diagrams a user can create with it. Provided specific steps describing how to create an organizational chart using Organization Chart graphic. Provided specific steps describing how to create a Radial Cycle graphic. Corrected typographical and grammatical errors.	28	
2	Saving and Printing	Saved file with specified name. Printed document.	2	
		TOTAL POINTS FOR THIS EXERCISE	30	

Assessment U3.14 – Create an Expenditures Table

Step	Task	Criterion	Value	Score*
1	Creating Table	Created table. Typed text. Corrected typographical errors.	8	
2	Formatting	Formatted table to enhance visual appeal of table.	10	
3	Saving and Printing	Saved file with specified name. Printed document.	2	
		TOTAL POINTS FOR THIS EXERCISE	20	

Assessment U3.15 – Create a Column Chart

Step	Task	Criterion	Value	Score*
1	Creating Chart	Using information from U3.14, created column chart.	8	
2	Formatting	Formatted chart to enhance visual appeal.	10	
3	Saving and Printing	Saved file with specified name. Printed document.	2	
		TOTAL POINTS FOR THIS EXERCISE	20	

Assessment U3.16 – Create a Store Letterhead

Step	Task	Criterion	Value	Score*
1	Typing	Typed text. Corrected typographical errors.	2	
2	Inserting	Inserted appropriate clip art image.	2	
3	Formatting	Formatted letterhead using features to enhance visual appeal.	4	
4	Saving and Printing	Saved file with specified name. Printed document	2	
		TOTAL POINTS FOR THIS EXERCISE	10	

Chapter 16. Merging Documents

Applying Your Skills

Assessment 16.1 – Create a Data Source File

Step	Task	Criterion	Value	Score*
1	Creating and Saving	Create a document. Saved file with specified name.	1	
2	Customizing Data Source	Deleted specified fields. Added a custom field named *Cell Phone*.	4	
3-6	Typing	Created source document. Typed names and addresses. Corrected typographical errors.	14	
7	Saving	Saved data source file with specified name.	1	
	TOTAL POINTS FOR THIS EXERCISE		**20**	

Assessment 16.2 – Create a Main Document and Merge with a Data Source File

Step	Task	Criterion	Value	Score*
1	Opening and Saving	Opened correct file. Saved file with specified name.	1	
2	Using Data Source	Chose correct source document to be used in the merge.	1	
3-4	Inserting Fields	Inserted *AddressBlock* field before the first paragraph. Inserted the *GreetingLine* field after the *AddressBlock* field.	4	
5	Inserting Fields and Text	Inserted the appropriated fields and typed text. Corrected typographical errors.	10	
6	Merging	Merged main document with data source document.	1	
7-9	Printing and Saving	Saved merged letters. Printed merged letters. Saved main document.	3	
	TOTAL POINTS FOR THIS EXERCISE		**20**	

Assessment 16.3 –Create an Envelope Main Document and Merge with a Data Source File

Step	Task	Criterion	Value	Score*
1	Creating	Created envelope main document using the standard size 10 envelope.	3	
2	Selecting Data Source	Selected correct data source file.	1	
3	Inserting Field	Inserted *AddressBlock* field in appropriate location in document.	2	
4	Merging	Merged envelope main document with data source.	2	
5-7	Saving and Printing	Saved merged envelopes with specified name. Printed envelopes. Closed main document without saving.	2	
	TOTAL POINTS FOR THIS EXERCISE		**10**	

Assessment 16.4 –Create a Label Main Document and Merge with a Data Source File

Step	Task	Criterion	Value	Score*
1	Creating Mailing Labels	Used *Avery US Letter 5160 Easy Peel Address Labels* option in the Mail Merge feature to create mailing labels.	8	
2	Selecting Data Source	Selected the correct data source to be used in the mail merge.	2	
3	Inserting Field	Inserted *AddressBlock* field.	2	
4	Updating Fields	Updated labels.	1	
5	Merging	Merged label main document with all records in the data source.	3	
6	Formatting	Selected document and applied the No Spacing style.	2	
7-9	Saving and Printing	Saved merged labels with specified name. Printed labels. Closed label main document without saving.	2	
		TOTAL POINTS FOR THIS EXERCISE	**20**	

Assessment 16.5 – Edit a Data Source File

Step	Task	Criterion	Value	Score*
1	Opening and Saving	Opened correct main document file. Saved main document with specified name.	2	
2	Editing	Edited data source file. Changed *Cardoza* to *Cordova*. Changed address for Mr. Daryl Gillette to *9843 22nd Southwest* and changed ZIP code to *94102*. Deleted record for Mr. Lucas Yarborough. Inserted two new records.	6	
3	Inserting	In main document, inserted sentence at beginning of third paragraph with Fill-in field for (*vacation*): Last summer we booked a fabulous (vacation) for you and your entire family.	6	
4-6	Inserting	Immediately below document name, typed: Letter followed by a space and inserted a Merge Record # field. Entered twice and inserted an If…Then…Else…field with specifications as illustrated. Changed file name below reference initials as illustrated.	6	
7	Merging	Merged main document with data source file. Typed text for each record as illustrated.	8	
8-10	Saving and Printing	Saved merged document with specified name. Printed letters. Saved main document.	2	
		TOTAL POINTS FOR THIS EXERCISE	**30**	

Assessment 16.6 – Use the Mail Merge Wizard to Create Envelopes

Step	Task	Criterion	Value	Score*
1	**Using Mail Merge Wizard**	Used Mail Merge wizard to merge records from correct data source with envelope main document.	6	
2-4	**Saving, Printing, and Closing**	Saved merged envelopes with specified name. Printed only first two envelopes. Closed documents without saving.	4	
		TOTAL POINTS FOR THIS EXERCISE	**10**	

Expanding Your Skills

Assessment 16.7 – Create a Client Directory

Step	Task	Criterion	Value	Score*
1	**Copying File**	Copied specified file and inserted into same folder. Renamed copied file with specified name.	2	
2	**Creating a Directory Main Document**	Created a directory main document and specified correct file as data source file.	4	
3	**Adding Field**	Added a new field named *Telephone* in the data source file.	2	
4	**Typing Data**	Typed telephone numbers in specified fields.	2	
5	**Adding Records**	Added four records to data source in appropriate fields.	2	
6	**Setting Tabs**	At blank document, set left tab at 1-inch mark and 4-inch mark.	2	
7	**Inserting Fields**	Inserted fields as instructed.	2	
8	**Merging**	Merged directory main document with data source.	2	
9	**Inserting**	Inserted headings in bold as instructed.	2	
10-11	**Saving and Printing**	Saved directory with specified name. Printed directory.	2	
12	**Converting to Table**	Converted text to table.	2	
13	**Formatting**	Deleted first column (empty). Applied autofit to table contents. Applied table style (styles will vary). Made other formatting changes to enhance the display of table.	4	
14-15	**Saving and Printing**	Saved directory. Printed directory. Closed directory main document without saving.	2	
		TOTAL POINTS FOR THIS EXERCISE	**30**	

Assessment 16.8 – Merge Specific Records

Step	Task	Criterion	Value	Score*
1	**Opening and Saving**	Opened correct file. Saved file with specified name.	1	
2	**Data Source**	Identified file as data source file.	6	
3-4	**Inserting Fields**	Inserted appropriate fields in letter main document. Changed file name below reference initials at bottom of page with specified name.	6	

Step	Task	Criterion	Value	Score*
5	Merging	Merged only records 8 through 11.	6	
6-8	Saving and Printing	Saved merged letters document with specified name. Printed document. Saved and closed main document.	1	
		TOTAL POINTS FOR THIS EXERCISE	**20**	

Assessment 16.9 – Merge Labels with an Excel Worksheet

Step	Task	Criterion	Value	Score*
1a	Selecting Labels Option	Opened correct file. Saved file with specified name. Changed *Label vendors* to *Avery US Letter* and selected the *42395 EcoFriendly Name Badges* option.	2	
1b	Creating Data Source	Named data source file with correct name. Specified workbook at data source.	2	
1c	Inserting Fields	Inserted the specified fields.	8	
1d	Merging	Updated labels and merged the documents.	2	
2	Formatting	Changed font size to 20 and center aligned.	4	
3-5	Saving and Printing	Saved the merged document. Printed document. Closed main document without saving.	2	
		TOTAL POINTS FOR THIS EXERCISE	**20**	

Achieving Signature Status

Assessment 16.10 – Create and Merge a Data Source and Main Document

Step	Task	Criterion	Value	Score*
1	Opening and Saving	Opened correct file. Saved file with specified name.	2	
2	Creating Data Source	Created data source file. Corrected typographical errors. Named data source file with correct name.	4	
3	Preparing Main Document	Prepared main document. Inserted current date at beginning of letter. Inserted individual fields for inside address. Inserted appropriate greeting line field. Typed appropriate complimentary close. Typed own first and last name in complimentary close. Typed own initials and document name in appropriate location.	6	
3	Typing	Typed letter. Corrected typographical errors.	6	
3	Inserting	Inserted Merge Record # field near bottom of letter. Inserted If…Then…Else field at beginning of last paragraph in letter (*As a valued client…*). Specified *City* field name option box, typed Peoria in *Compare to* text box, and typed two sentences as illustrated in the *Insert this text* text box.	4	
4	Proofreading	Checked for errors. Corrected typographical errors.	4	
5-7	Merging, Saving, and Printing	Completed merge. Saved merged letters with specified name. Printed letters. Saved main document.	4	
		TOTAL POINTS FOR THIS EXERCISE	**30**	

Chapter 17. Managing Lists

Applying Your Skills

Assessment 17.1 – Insert Custom Bullets and Numbering in a Technology Document

Step	Task	Criterion	Value	Score*
1	**Opening and Saving**	Opened correct file. Saved file with specified name.	2	
2	**Formatting**	Changed style set to Lines (Simple). Changed theme to Frame.	2	
3	**Inserting Bullets**	Selected questions below *Technology Information Questions* heading and inserted check mark bullets.	3	
4	**Creating Bullets**	Created a computer disc symbol bullet in 14-point font size. Applied symbol bullet to eight paragraphs of text below *Technology Timeline: Storage Devices and Media* heading.	4	
5-6	**Applying Multilevel List Numbering**	Selected paragraphs below *Information Systems* and *Commerce* heading, selected Multilevel List button, and clicked middle option in top row of *List Library* section. Applied same multilevel list numbering to paragraphs of text below the *Internet* heading.	4	
7	**Saving and Printing**	Saved file. Printed document.	2	
8	**Defining Multilevel List**	Selected paragraphs of text below *Information Systems and Commerce* heading. Defined new multilevel list: Level 1 inserted Arabic numbers followed by a period and aligned at 0 inch and indented at 0.25 inch. Level 2 inserted capital letters followed by a period and aligned at 0.25 inch and indented at 0.5 inch. Level 3 inserted Arabic numbers followed by right parenthesis and aligned at 0.5 inch and indented 0.75 inch.	9	
9	**Applying Multilevel List**	Applied new multilevel list to paragraphs of text below Internet heading.	2	
10	**Saving and Printing**	Saved file. Printed document.	2	
	TOTAL POINTS FOR THIS EXERCISE		30	

Assessment 17.2 – Type a Corporate Report Document That Contains Special Characters

Step	Task	Criterion	Value	Score*
1	**Typing**	Typed text as illustrated. Inserted nonbreaking hyphens in corporate names. Inserted en dashes in the money amount ($20 – 25 million). Inserted time (in the Department Meetings section). Inserted em dashes around *an important indicator of current demand.* Inserted the trademark and copyright symbols correctly. Inserted nonbreaking spaces within keyboard shortcuts. Corrected typographical errors.	18	

Step	Task	Criterion	Value	Score*
2-3	Saving and Printing	Saved file with specified name. Printed document.	2	
		TOTAL POINTS FOR THIS EXERCISE	**20**	

Expanding Your Skills

Assessment 17.3 – Create and Insert a Picture Bullet in a Document

Step	Task	Criterion	Value	Score*
1	Typing	Typed text. Corrected typographical errors.	6	
1	Formatting	Changed left and right margins to 1.5 inches. Set text in 36-point Angsana New (or similar typeface).	2	
1	Inserting Picture Bullet	Inserted picture bullet **WhiteHorse.jpg** located in Chapter17 folder. Applied bullet as illustrated.	4	
1	Formatting	Applied Green, Accent 6, Darker 25% shading to title. Changed title text font color to White, Background 1. Applied bold formatting. Made other formatting changes so document appears as illustrated.	4	
1	Inserting Page Border	Inserted page border and changed color to Green, Accent 6, Darker 25%	2	
2-3	Saving and Printing	Saved file with specified name. Printed document.	2	
		TOTAL POINTS FOR THIS EXERCISE	**20**	

Achieving Signature Status

Assessment 17.4 – Type a Business Letter

Step	Task	Criterion	Value	Score*
1	Opening and Saving	Opened correct letterhead file. Saved file with specified name.	2	
2	Typing	Typed text as block style business letter. Inserted current date in place of (Current Date). Inserted appropriate symbols as illustrated. Inserted nonbreaking space between words: *Mont* and *Tremblant* in company name. Inserted en dash between times in third column. Typed first and last name in place of (Student Name). Corrected typographical errors.	18	
2	Formatting	Formatted table as illustrated. Applied Grid Table 2 - Accent 3 table style and centered table. Made other changes in table to appear as illustrated.	8	
3	Saving and Printing	Saved file. Printed document.	2	
		TOTAL POINTS FOR THIS EXERCISE	**30**	

Chapter 18. Sorting and Selecting; Finding and Replacing Data

Applying Your Skills

Assessment 18.1 – Sort Text in a McCormack Funds Document

Step	Task	Criterion	Value	Score*
1	**Opening and Saving**	Opened correct file. Saved file with specified name.	1	
2	**Sorting Lines**	Sorted nine lines below *Executive Team* heading in ascending alphabetic order by last name.	6	
3	**Sorting Columns**	Sorted columns below the *New Employees* heading alphabetically by last name in first column.	6	
4	**Sorting Columns**	Sorted by *Salesperson* column in table in ascending order.	6	
5	**Saving and Printing**	Saved file. Printed document.	1	
		TOTAL POINTS FOR THIS EXERCISE	**20**	

Assessment 18.2 – Sort Text in a Health Services Document

Step	Task	Criterion	Value	Score*
1	**Opening and Saving**	Opened correct file. Saved file with specified document name.	1	
2	**Sorting**	Sorted columns of text below *Rhodes Health Services* title by clinic name in ascending order.	6	
3	**Sorting**	Sorted columns of text below *Executive Team* heading by last name in ascending order.	6	
4	**Sorting**	Sorted by *Second Half Expenses* column in the table in descending order.	6	
5	**Saving and Printing**	Saved file. Printed document.	1	
		TOTAL POINTS FOR THIS EXERCISE	**20**	

Assessment 18.3 – Create Labels for Key Life Customers

Step	Task	Criterion	Value	Score*
1	**Copying**	Copied correct file. Renamed copied file.	4	
2	**Creating Mail Labels**	Used Mail Merge to create mailing labels with Avery US Letter 5360 label product. Used existing data source for labels.	7	
3	**Sorting**	Sorted records by ZIP code in ascending order and then by last name in ascending order. Saved labels document with specified name.	7	
4-6	**Printing and Closing**	Saved labels. Printed labels. Closed labels main document without saving.	2	
		TOTAL POINTS FOR THIS EXERCISE	**20**	

Assessment 18.4 – Create Labels for Key Life Boston Customers

Step	Task	Criterion	Value	Score*
1	Creating Labels	Created mailing labels with Avery US Letter 5360 label product. Used existing data source file.	4	
2-3	Sorting and Saving	Selected only those customers living in Boston. Completed mail merge and saved labels document with specified name.	4	
4-5	Printing and Closing	Printed Boston labels. Closed labels main document without saving.	2	
		TOTAL POINTS FOR THIS EXERCISE	**10**	

Assessment 18.5 – Finding and Replacing Formatting and Special Characters and Using Wildcard Characters

Step	Task	Criterion	Value	Score*
1	Opening and Saving	Opened correct file. Saved file with specified document name.	1	
2-3	Finding and Replacing	Replaced text set in +*Body* font with Constantia. Replaced text set in Candara and bold formatting with Corbel and bold formatting	4	
4-6	Finding and Replacing	Replaced all section breaks with nothing. Replaced all em dashes with a colon followed by a space. Replaced all occurrences of *Ne?land?Davis* with *Newland-Davis*.	3	
7	Saving and Printing	Save document. Printed document.	2	
		TOTAL POINTS FOR THIS EXERCISE	**10**	

Expanding Your Skills

Assessment 18.6 – Create Name Tag Labels for Contacts in New York

Step	Task	Criterion	Value	Score*
1-2	Creating Name Badges	Used Mail Merge. Selected *Avery US Letter, 45395 EcoFriendly Name Badges*.	2	
3-5	Typing and Naming Data Source	Clicked Select New Recipients button. Used *Type a New List*. Created and customized data source file. Typed information in appropriate fields for 14 records. Named data source file with specified name.	10	
6-7	Inserting Fields	Inserted fields in first label as illustrated. Updated labels.	4	
8	Sorting	Sorted by company name in ascending order. Filtered by state of New York.	4	
9	Merging	Merged with name tag labels.	4	
10	Formatting	Selected entire table. Applied Grid Table 3 - Accent 3 table style. Changed alignment to Align Center. Changed font to 16-point Lucida Calligraphy bold.	4	
11-13	Saving, Printing, and Closing	Saved name tags label document with specified name. Printed name tags. Closed main document without saving.	2	
		TOTAL POINTS FOR THIS EXERCISE	**30**	

Assessment 187.7 – Create a Contacts Table

Step	Task	Criterion	Value	Score*
1	**Opening and Saving**	Opened correct file. Saved with specified name.	2	
2	**Sorting**	Sorted text in ascending order by state and then by company name.	10	
3	**Converting to Table**	Converted text to table. Split table as illustrated.	6	
4	**Formatting**	Applied formatting to table as illustrated.	10	
5	**Saving and Printing**	Saved file. Printed document.	2	
	TOTAL POINTS FOR THIS EXERCISE		**30**	

Chapter 19. Managing Page Numbers, Headers, and Footers

Applying Your Skills

Assessment 19.1 – Insert and Customize Page Numbering in a Computer Report

Step	Task	Criterion	Value	Score*
1	**Opening and Saving**	Opened correct file. Saved file with specified name.	2	
2	**Formatting**	Applied Heading 1 style to two titles. Applied Heading 2 style to five headings. Inserted section break/new page at beginning of title *Security Risks*. Changed style set to Centered. Applied chapter multilevel list numbering. Inserted chapter numbering at bottom center of each page in both sections of document.	16	
3	**Saving and Printing**	Saved file. Printed document.	2	
	TOTAL POINTS FOR THIS EXERCISE		**20**	

Assessment 19.2 – Create Odd and Even Page Footers in a Robot Report

Step	Task	Criterion	Value	Score*
1	**Opening and Saving**	Opened correct file. Saved file with specified name.	2	
2	**Formatting**	Applied Heading 2 style to title *ROBOTS AS ANDROIDS*. Applied Heading 3 styles to five headings. Changed style set Lines (Distinctive). Changed paragraph spacing to Relaxed. Centered title. Kept heading, *Navigation*, together with paragraph below.	2	
3	**Creating Odd Page Footer**	Inserted odd page footer with current date at left margin (month spelled out). Inserted clip art image related to robots in middle of footer. Changed height of robot image to approximately 0.6 inch and applied *Behind Text* text wrapping. At right margin typed: **Page** and page number.	7	

Step	Task	Criterion	Value	Score*
4	Creating Even Page Footer	Inserted even page footer with Page and page number typed at left margin. Inserted same robot image in middle of footer. At right margin, inserted current date in same format as odd page footer.	7	
5	Saving and Printing	Saved file. Printed document.	2	
		TOTAL POINTS FOR THIS EXERCISE	**20**	

Assessment 19.3 – Create and Edit Footers in a Software Report

Step	Task	Criterion	Value	Score*
1	Opening and Saving	Opened correct file. Saved file with specified name.	2	
2	Formatting	Inserted a section break/new page at beginning of title CHAPTER 2: *GRAPHICS AND MULTIMEDIA SOFTWARE*.	2	
3	Creating Footer	Created footer for first section: *Chapter 1* at left margin; Page number in middle; student first and last name at right margin.	8	
4-5	Editing Footer	In second section, changed *Chapter 1* to *Chapter 2*. Began page numbering in second section with number 1.	6	
6-7	Printing and Saving	Printed page one of section one and page one of section two. Saved file.	2	
		TOTAL POINTS FOR THIS EXERCISE	**20**	

Expanding Your Skills

Assessment 19.4 – Insert a Horizontal Line in a Footer in an Online Shopping Report

Step	Task	Criterion	Value	Score*
1	Opening and Saving	Opened correct file. Saved file with specified name.	2	
2	Editing	Kept heading *Online Superstores* together with paragraph below.	2	
3-6	Creating Footer	Created footer with horizontal line followed by current date (tabbed once). Lines will vary. Applied bold formatting and Dark Blue font color to the date. Closed footer pane.	6	
7-9	Creating Header	Used Quick Parts to create header with author document property. If necessary, replaced with student first and last name. Tabbed twice after author placeholder. Inserted FileName as field.	8	
10-11	Saving and Printing	With document active, saved file. Printed document.	2	
		TOTAL POINTS FOR THIS EXERCISE	**20**	

Assessment 19.5 – Format a Document with Headers, Footers, and Page Numbers

Step	Task	Criterion	Value	Score*
1	**Opening and Saving**	Opened correct file. Saved file with specified name.	2	
2	**Formatting**	Inserted section break/new page at beginning of title, *Online Content*. Inserted section break/new page at beginning of title, *E-Commerce*. Applied chapter multilevel list numbering.	2	
2-3	**Inserting Headers and Footers and Reviewing**	At beginning of document created an odd page header with student name at left margin and current date at right margin. Inserted border below text. Created an even page header with current date at left and student name at right margin. Inserted a border line below text. Created odd page footer with page numbering at bottom right margin of each page and included chapter page numbering. Inserted a border line above page number from left to right margin. Created an even page footer with page numbering at bottom left margin of each page and included chapter page numbering. Inserted a border line above page numbering. At chapter 1 title, changed page numbering to include the chapter number. At chapter 2 title, changed page number to start with 1 and included chapter number. At chapter 3 title, changed page number to start at 1 and included chapter number. Reviewed document for all changes.	24	
4-7	**Saving and Printing**	Saved file. Printed only first page of sections 1, 2, and 3.	2	
		TOTAL POINTS FOR THIS EXERCISE	30	

Chapter 20. Managing Shared Documents

Applying Your Skills

Assessment 20.1 – Insert Comments and Track Changes in a Computer Virus and Security Report

Step	Task	Criterion	Value	Score*
1	**Opening and Saving**	Opened correct file. Saved file with specified name.	1	
2	**Deleting Comments**	Deleted comment.	1	
3-5	**Inserting Comments**	Inserted comment at end of first paragraph in *IPs and URLs* section. Inserted comment at end of third paragraph in *IPs and URLs* section. Inserted comment at end of last paragraph in document.	6	
11	**Saving and Printing**	Saved file. Printed only the comments.	2	
		TOTAL POINTS FOR THIS EXERCISE	10	

Assessment 20.2 – Track Changes in a Viruses Report

Step	Task	Criterion	Value	Score*
1	**Opening and Saving**	Opened correct file. Saved file with specified name.	2	
2	**Editing with Tracking On**	With tracking on, edited first sentence of document. Inserted word (computer's) in last sentence of first paragraph. Deleted word (real) in second sentence of *TYPES OF VIRUSES* section and replaced with: **significant**. Deleted last sentence in *Methods of Virus Operation* section. Turned off tracking.	6	
3	**Changing User Name**	In Word Options, changed User Name to Stacey Phillips and Initials to SP.	1	
4	**Editing with Tracking On**	With tracking on, deleted words (or cracker) in seventh sentence in *Types of Viruses* section. Deleted word (garner) in first sentence in *CHAPTER 2: SECURITY RISKS* section and replaced with: **generate**. Moved *Employee Theft* section below *Cracking Software for Copying* section. Turned off tracking.	6	
5	**Changing User Name**	Changed User name back to original name. Changed Initials back to original initials.	1	
6	**Printing with Markups**	Printed document showing markups.	1	
7	**Accepting Changes**	Accepted all changes in document except moving *EMPLOYEE THEFT* section below *CRACKING SOFTWARE FOR COPYING* section.	2	
8	**Saving and Printing**	Saved file. Printed document.	1	
		TOTAL POINTS FOR THIS EXERCISE	20	

Assessment 20.3 – Compare Documents

Step	Task	Criterion	Value	Score*
1	**Comparing Documents and Inserting Changes**	Compared two documents. Inserted changes in new document.	8	
2-3	**Saving and Printing Markups**	Saved compared document with specified file name. Printed list of markups only (not document).	2	
4	**Rejecting Changes**	Rejected changes made to bulleted text and changes made to last paragraph in *Disaster Recovery Plan*. Accepted all other changes.	6	
5	**Numbering Pages**	Inserted page numbers at bottom center of each page.	2	
6	**Saving and Printing**	Saved file. Printed document.	2	
		TOTAL POINTS FOR THIS EXERCISE	20	

Assessment 20.4 – Combine Documents

Step	Task	Criterion	Value	Score*
1-2	**Opening and Saving**	Opened correct file. Saved file with specified name. Closed document.	2	
3-5	**Combining Documents**	Combined original document with revised document. Accepted all changes. Saved document.	4	
6	**Combining Documents**	Combined original document with revised documents.	4	
7	**Printing List of Markups**	Printed list of markups only.	4	
8	**Accepting Changes**	Accepted all changes in document.	4	
9	**Saving and Printing**	Saved file. Printed only the document.	2	
		TOTAL POINTS FOR THIS EXERCISE	**20**	

Assessment 20.5 – Link an Excel Chart with a Word Document

Step	Task	Criterion	Value	Score*
1-3	**Opening and Saving**	Opened correct Word document. Saved file with specified name. Opened correct Excel file. Saved file with specified name.	2	
4	**Linking**	Linked Excel chart to the end of the Word document	2	
5	**Saving and Printing**	Saved Word document. Printed Word document.	1	
6	**Editing**	Changed amounts in cells **F3** and **E4**.	2	
7	**Saving**	Saved Excel file.	1	
8-9	**Opening, Saving, and Printing**	Opened Word document. Updated changes. Saved document. Printed document.	2	
		TOTAL POINTS FOR THIS EXERCISE	**10**	

Expanding Your Skills

Assessment 20.6 –Track Changes Made to a Table

Step	Task	Criterion	Value	Score*
1	**Opening and Saving**	Opened correct file. Saved file with specified name.	2	
2	**Customizing Track Changes Options**	Changed color for inserted cells to Light Purple. Changed color for deleted cells to Light Green.	4	
3	**Editing Track Changes**	Turned on Track Changes. Inserted a new row at beginning of table and merged cells in the new row. Typed **Mobile Bay Products** in merged cell. Deleted the *Barclay, Kurt* row. Inserted a new row below *Tanaka, Diana* and typed **Caswell, Martin** in first cell; **$495,678** in second cell; and **$475,850** in third cell. Turned off Track Changes.	8	

Step	Task	Criterion	Value	Score*
4	**Saving and Printing**	Saved file. Printed document with markups.	2	
5-6	**Accepting Changes**	Accepted all changes. At Track Changes Option returned inserted cells color back to Light Blue and deleted cells color back to Pink.	2	
7	**Saving and Printing**	Saved document and printed document.	2	
		TOTAL POINTS FOR THIS EXERCISE	20	

Achieving Signature Status

Assessment 20.7 –Track Changes in an Employee Performance Document

Step	Task	Criterion	Value	Score*
1	**Opening and Saving**	Opened correct file. Saved file with specified name.	2	
2	**Editing and Tracking**	Turned on Track Changes. Made changes as illustrated.	9	
3	**Printing Markups**	Printed list of markups only.	2	
4	**Accepting Changes**	Accepted all changes.	1	
5	**Saving and Printing**	Saved file. Printed document.	2	
6-7	**Combining Documents and Accepting Changes**	Combined original document with revised document. Accepted all changes.	2	
8	**Saving and Printing**	Saved file. Printed document.	2	
		TOTAL POINTS FOR THIS EXERCISE	20	

Unit 4. Performance Assessments

Assessing Proficiencies

Assessment U4.1 – Use Mail Merge to Create Letters to Customers

Step	Task	Criterion	Value	Score*
1	**Opening and Saving**	Open correct document. Saved files with specified name.	1	
2-3	**Using Mail Merge**	Used Mail Merge to prepare six letters with information provided. Corrected typographical errors.	15	
4	**Saving Files**	Saved data source file with specified name. Saved merged document with specified name. Saved merged letters with specified name.	2	
4-5	**Printing and Saving**	Printed merged letters. Saved and closed main document.	2	
		TOTAL POINTS FOR THIS EXERCISE	20	

Assessment U4.2 – Use Mail Merge to Create Envelopes

Step	Task	Criterion	Value	Score*
1-2	**Preparing Envelopes**	Used Mail Merge feature to prepare envelopes. Used correct file as data source document.	6	
3-5	**Saving and Printing**	Saved merged envelopes with specified name. Printed envelopes. Closed main document without saving.	4	
		TOTAL POINTS FOR THIS EXERCISE	10	

Assessment U4.3 – Edit the Data Source and Main Document and Merge Letters

Step	Task	Criterion	Value	Score*
1	**Opening and Saving**	Opened correct file. Saved main document with specified name.	2	
2	**Editing**	Edited data source file with four changes.	8	
3	**Inserting Text**	Inserted sentence at end of third paragraph in body of letter of main document. Included fill-in fields as illustrated.	2	
4	**Saving**	Saved main document.	1	
5	**Merging Records**	Merged records. Typed text in fields.	6	
6-8	**Saving and Printing**	Saved merged document with specified name. Printed letters. Saved and closed main document.	1	
		TOTAL POINTS FOR THIS EXERCISE	20	

Assessment U4.4 – Use Mail Merge to Create Labels

Step	Task	Criterion	Value	Score*
1-3	**Creating Mail Labels**	Used Mail Merge to create mailing labels with Avery US Letter 5360 Mailing Labels. Used correct data source. Filtered records. Selected customers living in Grand Rapids. Completed merge. Saved labels document with specified name.	8	
4-5	**Printing and Closing**	Printed labels. Closed labels main document without saving.	2	
		TOTAL POINTS FOR THIS EXERCISE	10	

Assessment U4.5 – Use Mail Merge to Create a Directory

Step	Task	Criterion	Value	Score*
1-2	**Creating Directory**	Used Mail Merge to create directory. Used correct data source file. Included customer title, first and last names at left margin; street address at tab stop; and city, state, and zip code at second tab stop. Created heading for each column.	10	
3	**Converting to Table**	Converted text to table. Formatted table to enhance visual appeal.	8	
4-6	**Saving and Printing**	Saved document with specified name. Printed and closed files without saving.	2	
		TOTAL POINTS FOR THIS EXERCISE	20	

Assessment U4.6 – Sort Data in Columns and a Table

Step	Task	Criterion	Value	Score*
1	**Opening and Saving**	Opened correct file. Saved file with specified name.	2	
2-3	**Sorting**	Sorted columns below *CONTACTS* title in ascending order by last name. Sorted amounts *in Home Equity Loans* column in descending order.	6	
4	**Saving and Printing**	Saved file. Printed document.	2	
		TOTAL POINTS FOR THIS EXERCISE	**10**	

Assessment U4.7 – Create and Apply Custom Bullets and a Multilevel List

Step	Task	Criterion	Value	Score*
1	**Opening and Saving**	Opened correct file. Saved file with specified name.	2	
2-4	**Formatting**	Applied Title style to title *Mobile Bay Products*. Applied Heading 1 style to headings *Stock Awards* and *Employee Stock Plan*. Changed style set to Centered.	4	
5	**Defining Picture Bullets**	Selected bulleted paragraphs. Defined new picture bullet with the image of a globe with blue grid lines and a black background.	4	
6-7	**Formatting**	Applied multilevel list to text below *Employee Stock Plan*. Defined new multilevel list. Inserted capital letters followed by period for level 2 and inserted Arabic numbers followed by periods for level 3.	8	
8	**Saving and Printing**	Saved file. Printed document.	2	
		TOTAL POINTS FOR THIS EXERCISE	**20**	

Assessment U4.8 – Keep Text Together and Insert Footers in a Report

Step	Task	Criterion	Value	Score*
1	**Opening and Saving**	Opened correct file. Saved file with specified name.	2	
2-3	**Formatting**	Kept heading *Self-Replicating Robots* with *paragraph* of text below. Kept heading *REFERENCES* with paragraph of text below.	2	
4-5	**Inserting Footers**	Inserted odd page footer with title at left margin and page number at right margin. Inserted even page footer with page number at left margin and document title at right margin.	4	
6	**Saving and Printing**	Saved file. Printed document.	2	
		TOTAL POINTS FOR THIS EXERCISE	**10**	

Assessment U4.9 –Insert Headers and Footers in Different Sections of a Document

Step	Task	Criterion	Value	Score*
1	**Opening and Saving**	Opened correct file. Saved file with specified name.	2	
2-5	**Formatting**	Inserted section break/new page at title *SOFTWARE PRICING.* Applied Title style to two titles. Applied Heading 1 style to six headings. Changed style set to Centered. Applied Depth theme and changed theme fonts to Blue II.	14	
6	**Creating Header**	Created header with current date at right margin in both sections of document.	4	
7	**Creating Footer**	Created footer for first section that prints *Software Delivery* at left margin, page number in middle, and student's first and last names at right margin.	4	
8	**Editing Footer**	Edited footer in second section to *Software Pricing* (instead of *Software Delivery*).	4	
9	**Saving and Printing**	Saved file. Printed document.	2	
		TOTAL POINTS FOR THIS EXERCISE	30	

Assessment U4.10 – Insert Comments and Track Changes in a Document

Step	Task	Criterion	Value	Score*
1	**Opening and Saving**	Opened correct file. Saved file with specified name.	2	
2-3	**Inserting Text**	Inserted comment at end of first paragraph. Inserted comment at end of first paragraph *in Online Shopping Venues* section.	6	
4-5	**Tracking**	At end of last sentence in second paragraph deleted words: *and most are eliminating paper tickets altogether* (including comma before and). Edited heading *Advantages of Online Shopping* to *Online Shopping Advantages.* Applied bold to first sentence of each bulleted paragraph on first page. Turned off tracking.	6	
6	**Editing**	In Word Options, changed User name to **Colleen Burton** and Initials to **CB**.	2	
7	**Tracking**	In first paragraph of *Online Shopping Advantages* deleted: *the following.* Inserted bulleted text between third and fourth bulleted paragraphs on second page: **Keep thorough records of all transactions.** Turned off tracking.	6	
8	**Printing**	Printed document with all markups.	2	
9-10	**Editing and Accepting Changes**	In Word Options, changed user name back to original name and initials back to original initials. Accepted all changes except the change deleting words: *and most are eliminating paper tickets altogether.*	4	
11	**Saving and Printing**	Saved file. Printed document.	2	
		TOTAL POINTS FOR THIS EXERCISE	30	

Step	Task	Criterion	Value	Score*
1-2	**Opening and Saving**	Opened correct file. Saved file with specified name. Closed file.	2	
3-5	**Combining, Saving, and Printing**	Combined correct files (original and revised). Saved file. Printed document showing markups.	6	
6-7	**Accepting and Making Changes**	Accepted all changes to document. Changed style set to Basic (Stylist). Applied Wisp theme. Applied Red theme colors. Inserted the Austin footer.	10	
8	**Saving and Printing**	Saved file. Printed document.	2	
		TOTAL POINTS FOR THIS EXERCISE	**20**	

Creating Original Documents

Assessment U4.12 – Use Mail Merge to Create Letters to Volunteers

Step	Task	Criterion	Value	Score*
1	**Creating Main Document**	Used Mail Merge to compose letter with information provided. Corrected typographical and grammatical errors. Saved main document with specified name.	18	
2	**Creating Data Source**	Created data source with information provided. Corrected typographical errors. Saved data source file with specified name.	6	
3	**Merging and Saving**	Merged main document with records in data source file. Saved merged document with specified name.	4	
4	**Printing and Saving**	Printed letters. Saved and closed main document.	2	
		TOTAL POINTS FOR THIS EXERCISE	**30**	

Chapter 21. Inserting and Customizing Quick Parts

Applying Your Skills

Assessment 21.1 – Inserting Building Blocks and Fields in a Report

Step	Task	Criterion	Value	Score*
1	**Opening and Saving**	Opened correct file. Saved file with specified name.	2	
2	**Formatting**	Changed spacing after paragraphs to 6 points for entire document. Inserted page break at beginning of document. Applied Heading 1 style to two titles. Applied Heading 2 style to three headings in document. Changed theme to Banded. Changed theme colors to Red. Applied hanging indent to paragraphs of text below the title *REFERENCES*. Indented second paragraph *in Fair Use* section 0.5 inch from left and right margin.	12	

Step	Task	Criterion	Value	Score*
3-5	**Inserting Table of Contents**	Inserted *Automatic Table 2* table of contents building block at beginning of document. Applied Heading 1 style to *TABLE OF CONTENTS* title. Inserted *Banded* header building block. In *DOCUMENT TITLE* placeholder, typed: **property protection issues**.	4	
6-7	**Inserting Footer**	Inserted *Banded* footer building block. Double-clicked in document.	2	
8-9	**Inserting Cover Page**	At beginning of document, inserted *Banded* cover page building block. Applied 28-point font size to the *PROPERTY PROTECTION ISSUES* title. Typed student's first and last names above the *[COMPANY NAME]* placeholder. In *[COMPANY NAME]* placeholder, typed: **barrington & gates**. Deleted the *[Company address]* placeholder. Inserted a field for file name at end of document.	8	
10	**Saving and Printing**	Saved file. Printed document.	2	
		TOTAL POINTS FOR THIS EXERCISE	30	

Assessment 21.2 – Create Building Blocks and Prepare an Agreement

Step	Task	Criterion	Value	Score*
1-2	**Saving new Template**	Saved new template.	2	
3-9	**Opening File and Naming Building Block**	Selected text and saved building block with specified name. Closed file without saving.	6	
10-14	**Typing and Inserting Quick Part**	At blank document, typed text as illustrated. Corrected typographical errors. Selected text and saved building block with specified name. *Inserted Quick Part* gallery. Inserted *Auto Text* gallery. Closed document without saving.	6	
15-16	**Creating Agreement**	Created document as illustrated. Inserted custom building blocks and a file.	10	
17-18	**Saving and Printing**	Saved completed agreement with specified name. Printed document and closed file.	2	
19-22	**Print Screen**	At blank document, clicked AutoText button on Quick Access toolbar, pressed Print Screen, and clicked in document to remove drop-down list. Pasted screen capture in document. Printed document and closed without saving.	2	
23	**Removing Buttons from Quick Access Toolbar**	Removed Quick Parts button and AutoText button from Quick Access toolbar.	2	
		TOTAL POINTS FOR THIS EXERCISE	30	

Expanding Your Skills

Assessment 21.3 – Insert Document Properties and Fields in a Report

Step	Task	Criterion	Value	Score*
1-3	Opening and Saving	Opened correct file. Saved file with specified name.	2	
4	Inserting Fields	Inserted fields as instructed.	4	
5	Printing	Printed only last page of document.	1	
6-8	Deleting and Inserting	Deleted third reference in *REFERENCES* section. With insertion point at end of document, updated file size numbers. Updated number of words (F9).	2	
9-10	Printing and Saving	Printed only last page of document. Saved file.	1	
		TOTAL POINTS FOR THIS EXERCISE	**10**	

Assessment 21.4 –Insert an Equation Building Block

Step	Task	Criterion	Value	Score*
1-3	Explaining Process of Inserting an Equation Building Block	Typed list of steps followed to insert an equation Building Block.	8	
4	Saving and Printing	Saved file. Printed document.	2	
		TOTAL POINTS FOR THIS EXERCISE	**10**	

Achieving Signature Status

Assessment 21.5 – Create Custom Building Blocks

Step	Task	Criterion	Value	Score*
1	Opening document	Opened a blank document based on template created in Assessment 21.2.	2	
2	Inserting document	Inserted specified document into current document.	2	
3-4	Selecting Text, Naming Building Block, and Removing Document	Selected and saved selected text in custom building block, named building block with specified name. Removed document.	6	
5-10	Naming Building Block	At blank document selected *No Spacing* style. Typed complimentary closing with information provided. With text selected, saved text in custom building block in *AutoText* gallery with specified name. Deleted all of text in document.	4	

Step	Task	Criterion	Value	Score*
11-13	**Naming Building Block**	At blank document selected *No Spacing* style. Typed paragraph with information provided. Corrected typographical errors. With text selected, saved text in custom building block in *AutoText* gallery with specified name. Closed document without saving.	4	
14-15	**Creating Business Letter**	At blank document selected *No Spacing* style. Inserted building blocks for letterhead, footer, first paragraph of text, and complimentary close. Typed additional text as illustrated. Corrected typographical errors.	4	
16-17	**Saving and Printing**	Saved completed letter with specified name. Printed and closed document.	2	
18-21	**Printing Screen and Printing**	At blank document, clicked Quick Parts button, pointed to *Auto Text*, pressed Print Screen, and clicked in document to remove drop-down list. Pasted screen capture in document. Printed document and closed without saving.	4	
22	**Deleting Template**	Deleted template.	2	
	TOTAL POINTS FOR THIS EXERCISE		30	

Chapter 22. Customizing AutoCorrect and Word Options

Applying Your Skills

Assessment 22.1 – Insert and Format Text in a Medical Plan Document

Step	Task	Criterion	Value	Score*
1	**Opening and Saving**	Opened correct file. Saved file with specified name.	2	
2	**Adding Text to AutoCorrect**	Added text to AutoCorrect: *kl* replaced with *Key Life Health Plan* *m* replaced with *medical*	4	
3	**Typing**	Typed text as illustrated. Corrected typographical errors.	10	
4	**Formatting**	Applied Heading 1 style to title. Applied Heading 2 style to four headings. Changed style set to Lines (Simple). Changed theme to Frame.	3	
5-6	**Inserting Header and Footer**	Inserted *Ion (Dark)* header building block. Inserted *Ion (Dark)* footer building block. Typed **Key Life Health Plan** in *[DOCUMENT TITLE]*. Typed student's first and last names at the right side of footer.	4	
7	**Formatting**	Decreased value of footer distance to 0.3 inch.	2	
8-10	**Inserting Fields**	At end of document, inserted *FileName* field. Inserted *PrintDate* field.	2	
10-12	**Saving, Printing, Deleting**	Saved file. Printed document. Deleted two entries added in AutoCorrect. Closed file.	3	
	TOTAL POINTS FOR THIS EXERCISE		30	

Assessment 22.2 – Create a Vacation Document with AutoCorrect and Special Symbols

Step	Task	Criterion	Value	Score*
1	**Adding to AutoCorrect**	Added two words and one symbol to AutoCorrect.	6	
2	**Typing**	Typed text as illustrated. Used AutoCorrect as illustrated. Corrected typographical errors.	10	
3-4	**Saving and Printing**	Saved file with specified name. Printed document.	2	
5	**Deleting AutoCorrect Entries**	Deleted three entries added to AutoCorrect.	2	
		TOTAL POINTS FOR THIS EXERCISE	**20**	

Assessment 22.3 – Create a Custom Tab and Group

Step	Task	Criterion	Value	Score*
1	**Creating New Tab**	Created new tab with specifications as instructed.	2	
2-4	**Opening Recent File**	Used new tab to open recent file.	1	
5	**Saving as Word 97-2003 file**	Saved file as Word 97-2003 file. Closed document.	2	
6-8	**Printing**	Opened correct file. Sent document to printer. Closed document.	1	
9-12	**Opening and Using Quick Access Toolbar**	Opened two blank documents. Inserted screen clipping.	2	
13	**Printing**	Printed document with screen clipping. Closed without saving.	1	
14	**Resetting Ribbon**	Reset ribbon back to default.	1	
		TOTAL POINTS FOR THIS EXERCISE	**10**	

Expanding Your Skills

Assessment 22.4 – Create a Report on Word Options and Customization Features

Step	Task	Criterion	Value	Score*
1-3	**Creating Report**	After determining how to change Word options, created report describing steps to: change Office Theme Dark Gray; change minutes for saving AutoRecover information to 5 minutes; change number of recent documents displayed at Open backstage area to 15. Added information describing how to add track changes and caps lock notification. Corrected typographical and grammatical errors.	14	
4	**Formatting**	Formatted document to improve visual appeal.	4	
5-6	**Saving and Printing**	Saved file with specified name. Printed document.	2	
		TOTAL POINTS FOR THIS EXERCISE	**20**	

Assessment 22.5 – Create a Resume Document with AutoCorrect Text

Step	Task	Criterion	Value	Score*
1	**Creating and Formatting Document**	Created document. Created AutoCorrect entries. Set body text in 11-point Constantia. Changed title to 26-point Constantia. Changed font color to dark blue. Inserted page border, paragraph border, and paragraph shading as illustrated. Inserted clip art as illustrated. Formatted clip art text wrapping to Tight, flipped image horizontally, and changed color to Blue, Accent color 1 Light. Corrected typographical errors.	10	
2-3	**Saving and Printing**	Saved file with specified name. Printed document.	2	
4-9	**Using Screen Captures**	Displayed entries created (one at a time). Used screen capture feature and pasted to blank document. Fit all screen capture images by decreasing size of each image.	6	
10-11	**Saving and Printing**	Saved file with specified name. Printed document.	2	
		TOTAL POINTS FOR THIS EXERCISE	**20**	

Chapter 23. Customizing Themes

Applying Your Skills

Assessment 23.1 – Create and Apply Custom Themes to a Medical Plans Document

Step	Task	Criterion	Value	Score*
1	**Creating Custom Theme Colors**	Created custom theme colors. Changed Accent 1 color to Dark Red. Changed Accent 5 color to Gold, Accent 4, Darker 50%.	2	
2	**Creating Custom Theme fonts**	Created custom theme font with specified name that changed the heading and body fonts.	2	
3-5	**Creating Custom Theme Effect**	Selected *Top Shadow* in Theme Effects. Saved custom theme with specified name. Closed document without saving.	2	
6	**Opening and Saving**	Opened correct file. Saved file with specified name.	2	
7-9	**Formatting**	Changed style set to Lines (Simple). Inserted title, **Key Life Health Plan** at beginning of document. Applied Heading 1 style to title. Applied Heading 2 style to three headings. Inserted correct file at end of document. Applied custom theme.	10	
10	**Saving and Printing**	Saved file. Printed document.	2	
		TOTAL POINTS FOR THIS EXERCISE	**20**	

Assessment 23.2 – Create and Apply Custom Themes to Real Photography Document

Step	Task	Criterion	Value	Score*
1	**Creating Custom Theme Colors**	Created custom theme colors. Changed Text/ Background – Dark 2 color to Orange, Accent 2, Darker 50%. Changed Accent 1 color to custom color. Typed 0 in *Red* text box, 140 in *Green* text box, and 0 in *Blue* text box.	8	
2	**Creating Custom Theme Font**	Created custom theme font with specified name. Changed Heading font to Harrington.	4	
3-5	**Creating Custom Theme Effects**	Selected *Grunge Texture* in Theme Effects. Saved custom theme with specified name. Closed document without saving changes.	2	
6	**Opening and Saving**	Opened correct file. Saved file with specified name.	2	
7	**Applying Custom Theme**	Applied custom theme to document.	2	
8	**Saving and Printing**	Saved file. Printed document.	2	
		TOTAL POINTS FOR THIS EXERCISE	20	

Expanding Your Skills

Assessment 23.3 – Explore and Apply Themes

Step	Task	Criterion	Value	Score*
1	**Opening and Saving**	Opened correct file. Saved file with specified name.	2	
2-5	**Applying Theme**	Applied the Droplet theme to document. Determined heading font and body font. Determined title font color and heading font color.	4	
6	**Inserting**	At end of document, typed: **Theme name:**. Typed name of theme applied. On next line typed: **Heading and body font:**. Typed name of font. On next line typed: **Title font color:**. Typed title font color name. On next line typed: **Heading font color:**. Typed heading font color name.	4	
7	**Saving and Printing**	Saved file with specified name. Printed document.	2	
8	**Applying Different Theme**	Applied Organic theme to document. Determined heading and body font, title font color, and heading font color. Changed information at bottom of document with new theme information.	6	
9	**Saving and Printing**	Saved file. Printed document.	2	
		TOTAL POINTS FOR THIS EXERCISE	20	

Assessment 23.4 – Create and Apply a Custom Theme

Step	Task	Criterion	Value	Score*
1	Opening and Saving	Opened correct file. Saved file with specified name.	2	
2-5	Applying and Creating Custom Themes	Created custom theme colors. Created custom theme fonts. Applied Riblet theme effect to SmartArt graphic. Saved custom theme colors and fonts and Riblet theme effect with specified custom theme.	6	
6	Saving and Printing	Saved file. Printed document.	2	
7-8	Opening and Applying Custom Theme	Opened correct file. Saved file with specified name. Applied custom theme to document.	2	
9	Saving and Printing	Saved file. Printed document.	2	
10	Inserting Screen Captures	At blank document, inserted screen captures of the three custom themes. Resized images to fit all three screen capture images on one page.	2	
11-12	Saving and Printing	Saved file with specified name. Printed document.	2	
13	Deleting Custom Themes	Deleted custom color theme, custom font theme, and custom themes.	2	
		TOTAL POINTS FOR THIS EXERCISE	**20**	

Chapter 24. Creating and Managing Styles

Applying Your Skills

Assessment 24.1 – Create and Apply Styles to a Committee Report

Step	Task	Criterion	Value	Score*
1	Opening and Saving	Opened correct file. Saved file with specified name.	1	
2-3	Creating Styles	Created style based on formatting of *Kodiak Title* text. Named style with specified name. At end of document, created new style from formatting. Named style with specified name. Changed left and right indent to 0.5 inch and spacing after to 12 points. Clicked Italic button. Changed font color to Dark Blue. Inserted blue, single-line, top border and blue, single-line, bottom border.	6	
4	Creating Style	Created style. Named style with specified name. Changed font Copperplate Gothic Bold. Changed font color to Blue.	2	
5-6	Saving	Saved styles as Quick Styles set with specified name. Saved document.	2	
7	Opening and Saving	Opened correct report. Saved document with specified name.	1	

Step	Task	Criterion	Value	Score*
8-11	Applying Styles	Changed to Quick Styles set created. Applied XXKodiakTitle style to two titles. Applied XXKodiakHeading style to four headings. Applied XXKodiak Quote style to second paragraph of text (begins *Assist the company's board of directors...*). XX replaced with student's initials.	6	
12-13	Editing Styles	Edited XXKodiakTitle. Changed font color to Dark Blue and underlined text. Edited XXKodiakHeading style by changing font color to Dark Blue.	4	
14-17	Applying Styles and Saving	Displayed Styles in alphabetical order. Selected bulleted text in *Committee Responsibilities* section and applied Block Text style. Changed font color to Dark Blue. Selected bulleted text in *Compensation Philosophy* section and applied Block Text style. Changed font color to Dark Blue. Saved modified styles as Quick Styles set with same name.	4	
18	Saving and Printing	Saved file. Printed document.	2	
20	Deleting contents	Deleted contents of document (except the header).	1	
20-21	Saving and Closing	Saved document as template with specified name. Closed template.	1	
		TOTAL POINTS FOR THIS EXERCISE	30	

Assessment 24.2 – Create and Apply Multilevel List and Table Styles

Step	Task	Criterion	Value	Score*
1	Opening	Opened correct file.	1	
2-3	Creating Style	Created style with specified name. Applied formatting at Define New List Style dialog box. For first level numbering, changed font to Cambria, turned on bold, and changed font color to dark Blue. For second level numbering, specified snowflake symbol as bullet, turned on bold, and changed font color to Dark Blue. Deleted contents (except for header).	5	
4-5	Saving Template and Closing	Saved the template. Closed template.	2	
6-7	Inserting File	Opened a document based on template. Inserted correct document into current document.	2	
8-12	Applying Styles	Changed Quick Styles set to XXKodiak. Applied XXKodiak Title style to title, *Kodiak Annual Meeting*. Applied XXKodiak Heading style to two headings in document. Applied XXKMList multilevel list style to text below the *Finance Department Agenda* heading and to text below *Research Department Agenda* heading.	5	
13-14	Saving and Printing	Saved file. Printed document.	1	

Step	Task	Criterion	Value	Score*
15-16	**Opening and Creating New Style**	Opened correct template. Created New Style. In Name text box, typed XXKMTable. Changed Style type to *Table*. Changed font of entire table to 12-point Cambria in Dark Blue. Selected *All Borders* and changed border color to Blue. For header row, changed font size to 12, turned on bold, changed font color to White, Background 1 and applied fill color of Blue, Accent 1, Darker 25%. For odd banded rows, applied fill color of Blue, Accent 1, Lighter 80%.	2	
17	**Saving**	Saved template with specified name. Closed template.	1	
18	**Inserting**	At blank document, deleted XXXKodiak style set.	1	
		TOTAL POINTS FOR THIS EXERCISE	**20**	

Assessment 24.3 – Organize Styles

Step	Task	Criterion	Value	Score*
1-2	**Opening File**	Opened correct file.	1	
3-4	**Copying Styles**	Opened template. Displayed Organizer dialog box. Copied XXList and XXTable styles. Saved template.	2	
5-6	**Inserting and Saving**	Opened document based on template. Inserted correct file at blank document. Saved file with specified name.	2	
7-9	**Applying Styles**	Applied XXKodiakTitle style to title, *Quarterly Sales*. Applied XXKodiakHeading style to four headings in document. Applied XXKMTable style to four tables in document.	5	
10	**Saving and Printing**	Saved file. Printed document.	2	
11	**Closing**	Closed file without saving.	5	
		TOTAL POINTS FOR THIS EXERCISE	**20**	

Expanding Your Skills

Assessment 24.4 – Modify a Predesigned Table Style

Step	Task	Criterion	Value	Score*
1-2	**Opening and Saving**	After experimenting with modifying table styles, closed document. Opened correct file. Saved file with specified name.	2	
3-4	**Modifying Table Style**	While in any cell on top table, clicked Table Tools Design tab. Modified List Table 1– Accent 1 table style. Changed name to *XXNSSTable*. Changed font to Candara for whole table. Changed alignment to Align Center. Changed table alignment to Center. Changed header row fill color to Blue, Accent 1, Lighter 60%. Changed first column alignment to Align Center Left and turned off bold. For odd banded rows, changed fill color to Green, Accent 6, Lighter 80%. For even banded rows, changed fill color to Blue, Accent 1, Lighter 80%.	12	

Step	Task	Criterion	Value	Score*
5	**Applying Table Style**	After modifying table style, applied table style to four tables in document.	4	
6	**Saving and Printing**	Saved file. Printed document.	2	
		TOTAL POINTS FOR THIS EXERCISE	20	

Achieving Signature Status

Assessment 24.5 – Design, Apply, and Organize Styles

Step	Task	Criterion	Value	Score*
1	**Opening and Saving**	Opened correct letterhead file. Saved file with specified name.	1	
2-4	**Creating Styles**	Formatted and named styles in letterhead. Saved styles in Quick Styles set with specified name. Saved and closed document.	3	
5	**Opening and Saving**	Opened correct file. Saved with specified name.	1	
6-9	**Applying Styles**	Applied XXXRphoto style set. Applied title style to text: *Photography, Camera Basics*, and *Digital Cameras*. Applied heading style to text: *Pixels, Aspect Ratio*, and *White Balance*. Applied quote style to first and last paragraphs in document.	3	
10	**Saving and Printing**	Saved file. Printed document. Deleted all report content.	2	
11-12	**Saving a Template**	Saved correct document as a template. Closed template.	1	
13	**Creating Document**	Typed note to instructor describing the three styles created including name of styles and formatting applied to each style. Corrected typographical and grammatical errors. Saved file with specified name. Printed and closed document.	5	
14-15	**Creating and Copying Table Style**	At blank document, created table style for Real Photography. Copied table style to template. Saved document with specified name. Closed document.	4	
16-19	**Applying Style**	At blank document, inserted correct file. Applied title style to text: *July Weekly Invoices*. Applied heading style to four headings. Applied table style to four tables. Saved document with specified name.	6	
20-21	**Printing**	Checked to ensure tables fit on one page. Printed and closed document.	2	
22	**Deleting Quick Styles Set**	At blank document, deleted style set recently created.	2	
		TOTAL POINTS FOR THIS EXERCISE	30	

Chapter 25. Protecting, Preparing, and Sharing Documents

Applying Your Skills

Assessment 25.1 – Restrict Formatting and Editing of a Writing Report

Step	Task	Criterion	Value	Score*
1	Opening and Saving	Opened correct file. Saved file with specified name.	2	
2-3	Restricting Formatting and Enforcing Protection	Restricted formatting to Heading 2 and Heading 3 styles. Enforced protection. Included password: *writing*.	6	
4-7	Applying Headings	Displayed Restrict Formatting and Editing task pane. Clicked <u>Available styles</u> hyperlink. Applied Heading 2 style to title THE *WRITING PROCESS* AND *REFERENCES* ADVANTAGE. Applied Heading 3 style to seven headings in document. Closed Styles pane. Closed Restrict Formatting and Editing task pane.	10	
8-9	Saving and Printing	Saved document. Printed only page one. Closed document.	2	
		TOTAL POINTS FOR THIS EXERCISE	**20**	

Assessment 25.2 – Restrict Editing to Comments in a Software Life Cycle Document

Step	Task	Criterion	Value	Score*
1	Opening and Saving	Opened correct file. Saved file with specified name.	2	
2	Restricting Editing	Restricted editing to only comments. Enforced protection (password not included). Saved and closed file.	2	
3-6	Inserting Comments	Inserted comment at end of first paragraph of text in document. Inserted comment at end of paragraph in *Design* section. Inserted comment at end of paragraph in *Testing* section. Closed Reviewing pane and Restrict Editing task pane.	4	
7-8	Printing Comments and Saving	Printed only the comments. Saved and closed file.	2	
		TOTAL POINTS FOR THIS EXERCISE	**10**	

Assessment 25.3 – Insert Document Properties, Check Accessibility and Compatibility, and Save a Presentation Document in a Different Format

Step	Task	Criterion	Value	Score*
1	Opening and Saving	Opened correct file. Saved document with specified name.	2	

Step	Task	Criterion	Value	Score*
2	**Formatting**	Applied Heading 1 style to title: *Delivering a How-To Presentation*. Applied Heading 2 style to three headings in document. Changed style set to Centered. Applied View theme and changed theme colors to Green. Changed color of clip art image to Green, Accent color 1 Light	6	
3	**Typing**	Typed information in specified text boxes in the document information panel.	4	
4	**Creating Custom Properties**	Created custom properties as instructed. After creating custom properties, captured image of screen.	4	
5	**Inserting Screen Capture and Printing**	Closed document information panel. Inserted screen capture image. Printed document. Closed document without saving.	2	
6	**Saving and Printing**	Saved file. Printed only document properties.	2	
7	**Running Accessibility Checker and Creating Alternate Text**	Ran accessibility checker. Created alternate text for clip art image and SmartArt graphic. Closed accessibility checker.	4	
8	**Saving and Printing**	Saved file. Printed document.	2	
9-10	**Running Compatibility Checker and Saving**	Ran compatibility checker to determine features not supported by earlier versions of Word. Saved document in Word 97-2003 Document (*.doc) format with specified name.	2	
11	**Saving and Printing**	Saved file. Printed document.	2	
		TOTAL POINTS FOR THIS EXERCISE	30	

Expanding Your Skills

Assessment 25.4 – Create a Document on Inserting and Removing a Signature

Step	Task	Criterion	Value	Score*
1-2	**Researching, Typing, and Formatting a Memo**	Typed a memo to instructor with information on inserting and removing a signature. The document included the following information: An appropriate title, How to create a signature line in Word, How to sign a signature line in Word, How to remove a signature from Word, How to add an invisible digital signature in Word. Applied formatting to enhance appearance of document. Corrected typographical and grammatical errors.	18	
3-4	**Saving and Printing**	Saved memo with specified name. Printed memo.	2	
		TOTAL POINTS FOR THIS EXERCISE	20	

Assessment 25.5 – Format, Insert Document Properties, Check Compatibility, and Save a Document in a Different Format

Step	Task	Criterion	Value	Score*
1	Opening and Saving	Opened correct file. Saved file with specified name.	2	
2	Formatting	Formatted document as illustrated. Applied Lines (Stylish) style set. Applied Dividend theme. Inserted Integral footer. Typed first and last name in [Author] placeholder. Inserted SmartArt Continuous Cycle diagram. Changed colors to Colorful – Accent Colors. Applied Metallic Scene style. Recolored clip art image as illustrated. Made other changes as illustrated.	10	
3	Typing	Typed text in specified text boxes.	4	
4	Adding Properties	Added properties at Properties dialog box with Custom tab. Added *Client* property: **Stylus Enterprises**. Added *Department* property: **Development Department**. Added *Document number* property: **24**. Created screen capture. Closed Properties dialog box. At blank document, pasted screen capture image. Printed document. Closed document without saving.	4	
5	Saving and Printing	With correct document opened, saved document. Printed only the document properties.	2	
6-8	Removing Hidden Text and Running Checker	Removed hidden text. Ran accessibility checker and created alternate text for clip art image. Saved document.	4	
9-10	Running Checker and Saving	Ran compatibility checker to determine features not supported by earlier versions of Word. Saved document in Word 97-2003 Document (*.doc) format.	2	
11	Saving and Printing	Saved file in .docx format. Printed document.	2	
	TOTAL POINTS FOR THIS EXERCISE		30	

Unit 5. Performance Assessments

Assessing Proficiencies

Assessment U5.1 – Format and Insert Fields in a Report

Step	Task	Criterion	Value	Score*
1	Opening and Saving	Opened correct file. Saved file with specified name.	1	
2	Inserting	At beginning of document, inserted page break.	1	
3-6	Formatting	Applied Heading 1 style to title in document. Applied Heading 2 style to seven headings in document. Changed style set to Lines (Stylish). Changed paragraph spacing to Double. Applied Blue Warm theme.	10	

Step	Task	Criterion	Value	Score*
7	Moving	Moved *Population* chart below paragraph of text in *Population* section.	2	
8-11	Inserting	Inserted Filigree footer building block. At beginning of document, inserted the *Automatic Table 1* table of contents building block. At end of document, inserted a field inserting file name followed by Enter. Inserted a field inserting current date and time.	4	
12	Saving and Printing	Saved file. Printed document.	2	
		TOTAL POINTS FOR THIS EXERCISE	**20**	

Assessment U5.2 – Create Building Blocks and Prepare a Business Letter

Step	Task	Criterion	Value	Score*
1-3	Opening and Saving	Opened correct file. Selected entire document and saved text in custom building block in *Quick Part* gallery. Named building block with specified name. Closed document.	4	
4-6	Opening and Saving	Opened correct file. Selected entire document and saved text in custom building block in *Quick Part* gallery. Named building block with specified name. Closed document.	2	
7-10	Typing and Saving	At blank document, applied *No Spacing* style in Styles group. Typed text as illustrated. Corrected typographical errors. Selected entire document and saved text in custom building block in *Quick Part* gallery. Named building block with specified name. Saved custom building blocks as a Quick Parts button. Closed document without saving.	4	
11	Typing	At blank document, applied *No Spacing* style. Created business letter. Inserted as page header specific custom building block. Typed date, inside address, and first paragraph as illustrated. Inserted custom building block as instructed. Typed remaining text in letter. Corrected typographical errors. Inserted as page footer the specified custom building block.	14	
12-13	Saving and Printing	Saved completed letter with specified name. Printed and closed letter.	2	
14-16	Opening and Capturing Quick Parts	Opened blank document. Screen captured Quick Parts. Pasted screen capture in document.	2	
17-18	Printing and Saving	Printed document. Closed without saving. Removed Quick Parts button and deleted custom building blocks.	2	
		TOTAL POINTS FOR THIS EXERCISE	**30**	

Assessment U5.3 – Create and Apply Custom Themes and AutoCorrect Entries to a Rental Form

Step	Task	Criterion	Value	Score*
1-4	**Creating Custom Themes**	Created custom theme colors. Changed Text/Background – Dark 2 color to Orange, Accent 2, Darker 50%. Changed Accent 1 color to Green, Accent 6, Darker 25%. Created custom theme fonts. Applied Verdana to headings and Cambria to body text. Saved custom theme with specified name. Closed document without saving changes.	4	
5	**Opening and Saving**	Opened correct file. Saved file with specified name.	2	
6	**Searching and Replacing**	Searched for all occurrences of *trc* and replaced with *Tennison Rental Company*.	2	
7	**Using AutoCorrect**	Inserted *trc* in Replace and inserted *Tennison Rental Company* in With text box. Inserted *cera* in Replace text box and inserted *Construction Equipment Rental Agreement* in With text box.	2	
8	**Typing**	At blank line above heading *Further Assurances*, typed text as illustrated. Corrected typographical errors. Used Numbering feature to number paragraphs with lowercase letter followed by right parenthesis.	10	
9-13	**Formatting**	Applied Heading 1 style to title. Applied Heading 2 style to headings. Applied custom theme to document. Inserted building block inserting *SAMPLE* as watermark. Inserted *Semaphore* footer. Centered title. Changed spacing after title to 12 pt.	4	
14	**Saving and Printing**	Saved file. Printed document.	2	
15	**Saving Theme**	At blank screen, Saved Current Theme. Used Print Screen key for screen capture. Canceled and closed dialog box. Pasted screen capture in document. Printed and closed document without saving.	2	
16	**Deleting Themes and AutoCorrect**	Deleted custom themes, custom theme colors, and custom theme fonts. Deleted *trc* and *cera* AutoCorrect entries.	2	
	TOTAL POINTS FOR THIS EXERCISE		30	

Assessment U5.4 – Create and Apply Building Blocks and Styles to a Business Conduct Report

Step	Task	Criterion	Value	Score*
1	**Opening**	Opened correct file.	2	
2-4	**Creating Custom Building Blocks**	Selected clip art image and text. Saved in custom building block. Selected horizontal line, address, and telephone number and saved in custom building block. Inserted custom building blocks in Quick Part gallery as Quick Parts button.	6	

Step	Task	Criterion	Value	Score*
5-9	**Creating Styles**	Selected *Title* text and created style. Selected *Heading 1* text and created style. Created *Heading 2* text and created style. Saved styles as Quick Styles set with specified name. Closed file without saving changes.	6	
10	**Opening and Saving**	Opened correct document. Saved file with specified name.	2	
11-15	**Applying Custom Styles**	Changed style set to *Tennison*. Applied custom title style to title. Applied custom Heading 1 style to headings in all uppercase letters. Applied custom Heading 2 styles to headings with only first letter in uppercase. Inserted *TRCHeader* building block as header. Inserted *TRCFooter* building block as footer. Saved file. Printed and closed document.	10	
16	**Creating Screen Captures**	Created screen captures of Style Set and Quick Parts. Pasted both screen captures. If necessary, decreased size of screen captures to ensure both captures displayed on one page. Printed document and closed without saving it.	2	
17-18	**Deleting**	Deleted building blocks created for assignment. Removed Quick Parts button. Deleted custom Quick Styles set named *Tennison*.	2	
		TOTAL POINTS FOR THIS EXERCISE	30	

Assessment U5.5 – Format a Report with Styles

Step	Task	Criterion	Value	Score*
1-2	**Creating Tab**	Inserted new tab after View tab. Renamed tab. Renamed custom group. Changed Choose commands from option to All Commands. Added commands. Closed Word Options dialog box. Closed document without saving.	4	
3-5	**Opening and Copying**	Opened correct file. Copied Styles as instructed. Closed organizer. Closed file.	4	
6	**Opening and Saving**	Opened correct file. Saved file with specified name.	2	
7	**Applying Styles**	Applied NSSTitle style to title. Applied NSSHeading1 style to three headings. Applied NSSTable style to three tables.	4	
8	**Inserting**	Inserted document property as instructed.	4	
9	**Inserting Footer**	Inserted footer as instructed.	3	
10	**Saving and Printing**	Saved file. Printed document.	2	
11	**Modifying Styles**	Modified font color of NSSHeading1 style to Dark Blue. Modified NSSTable style aligning table at left and applied Blue, Accent 1, Lighter 80% shading to even banded rows.	4	
12	**Saving and Printing**	Saved file. Printed document.	2	

Step	Task	Criterion	Value	Score*
13-14	**Resetting Ribbon**	Reset ribbon. Closed document without saving.	1	
		TOTAL POINTS FOR THIS EXERCISE	**30**	

Assessment U5.6 – Restrict Formatting in a Report

Step	Task	Criterion	Value	Score*
1	**Opening and Saving**	Opened correct file. Saved file with specified name.	2	
2-4	**Restricting and Enforcing Protection**	Restricted formatting to Heading 1 and Heading 2 styles. Enforced protection and included password: *report*. Saved and closed file.	8	
5-9	**Formatting**	Opened correct file. Clicked Available styles hyperlink in Restrict Editing task pane. Applied Heading 1 style to title of report. Applied Heading 2 style to four headings. Closed Styles task pane. Closed Restrict Editing task pane.	8	
10-11	**Saving and Printing**	Saved file. Printed only page one.	2	
		TOTAL POINTS FOR THIS EXERCISE	**20**	

Assessment U5.7 – Insert Document Properties and Save a Document in a Previous Version of Word

Step	Task	Criterion	Value	Score*
1	**Opening and Saving**	Opened correct file. Saved file with specified name.	2	
2	**Formatting**	Applied Heading 1 style to three headings in document. Changed style set to Centered. Applied Blue II theme colors.	4	
3	**Inserting**	Inserted correct file at end of document.	2	
4-5	**Typing**	Typed information as illustrated in specified text boxes. Closed document information panel.	4	
6	**Saving and Printing**	Saved file. Printed only document properties.	2	
7-8	**Inspecting, Removing Hidden Text, Saving, and Printing**	Inspected document and removed hidden text. Saved file. Printed document.	2	
9	**Running Compatibility Checker**	Ran compatibility checker to determine features not supported by earlier versions of Word.	2	
10-11	**Saving and Printing**	Saved document in Word 97-2003 Document (*.doc) format with specified name. Saved file with .docx format. Printed file.	2	
		TOTAL POINTS FOR THIS EXERCISE	**20**	

Creating Original Documents

Assessment U5.8 – Design and Apply Building Blocks

Step	Task	Criterion	Value	Score*
1	**Creating Letterhead**	Created letterhead including company name, address, telephone number, and clip art image or other elements to add visual interest. Saved letterhead with specified name. Created building block.	4	
2-5	**Creating Building Blocks**	Created building block footer with specified information. Created complimentary close building block with specified information. Created client name and address building block with specified information. Created client name and address building block with specified information.	10	
6	**Creating Letter**	Created letter to Jake Montoya including date and building blocks. Formatted business letter using default Microsoft spacing. Inserted correct file.	6	
7	**Saving and Printing**	Saved file with specified name. Printed and closed letter.	2	
8	**Creating Letter**	Created similar letter to Claudia Sanborn.	6	
9-10	**Saving and Printing**	Saved file with specified name. Printed letter.	2	
		TOTAL POINTS FOR THIS EXERCISE	30	

Assessment U5.9 – Create AutoCorrect Entries and Format an Agreement Document

Step	Task	Criterion	Value	Score*
1	**Creating AutoCorrect**	Created AutoCorrect entries as instructed.	4	
2	**Opening and Typing**	Opened correct file. Typed text as illustrated. Corrected typographical errors.	8	
3	**Inserting**	Inserted date printed field and file name field at end of document. Inserted footer building block as footer. Inserted cover page.	8	
4	**Formatting**	Added or applied other enhancements to improve visual appeal of document.	6	
5	**Saving and Printing**	Saved file with specified name. Printed and closed document.	2	
6	**Deleting**	Deleted building blocks and AutoCorrect entries created for exercise.	2	
		TOTAL POINTS FOR THIS EXERCISE	30	

Chapter 26. Inserting Endnotes, Footnotes, and References

Applying Your Skills

Assessment 26.1 – Insert Footnotes in a Designing Newsletter Report

Step	Task	Criterion	Value	Score*
1	Opening and Saving	Opened correct file. Saved with specified name.	2	
2-6	Creating Footnotes	Created five footnotes as illustrated and inserted in correct locations.	10	
7	Saving and Printing	Saved file. Printed document.	2	
8-9	Formatting	Changed font to Constantia for entire document. Changed font for all footnotes to Constantia.	2	
10	Deleting	Deleted third footnote.	2	
11	Saving and Printing	Saved file. Printed document.	2	
		TOTAL POINTS FOR THIS EXERCISE	**20**	

Assessment 26.2 – Insert Sources and Citations in a Privacy Rights Report

Step	Task	Criterion	Value	Score*
1	Opening and Saving	Opened correct file. Saved with specified file name.	2	
2-3	Formatting MLA Style	Formatted title page as MLA style. Changed entire document font to 12-point Cambria and line spacing to 2.0. Removed spacing after paragraphs. At beginning of document, on separate lines typed student's name, instructor's name, title of course, current date (followed by Enter). Typed and centered the title *Privacy Rights*. Inserted header with student's last name and page number at the right margin with font changed to 12-point Cambria.	2	
4-7	Typing Citations	Typed text as illustrated for three citations. Corrected typographical errors. Inserted page number in Kelly Aldrich citation using Edit Citations.	4	
8	Typing	Typed remaining text as illustrated. Corrected typographical errors.	6	
9-10	Editing	Edited Kenneth Hartley source title. Deleted last two sentences in second paragraph. Deleted Ramona Ferraro source.	2	
11	Inserting Works Cited Page	Inserted a works cited page at end of document on separate page.	2	
12	Creating Source	Created new source with specified information.	2	
13-14	Inserting and Updating	Inserted citation for Harold Jefferson at end of last sentence in first paragraph. Updated works cited page.	2	

Step	Task	Criterion	Value	Score*
15	Formatting	Formatted works cited page for MLA requirements. Selected *Works Cited* Heading and all entries and applied *No Spacing* style. Changed font to 12-point Cambria. Changed spacing to 2.0. Centered title *Works Cited*. Formatted entries with a hanging indent.	3	
16	Saving and Printing	Saved file. Printed document.	1	
17	Changing to APA Style	Changed document and works cited page from MLA to APA style.	1	
18	Formatting	Changed title to *References*. Changed font to 12-point Cambria. Changed spacing after paragraphs to 0. Changed line spacing to 2.0.	2	
19	Saving and Printing	Saved file. Printed page 2.	1	
		TOTAL POINTS FOR THIS EXERCISE	30	

Expanding Your Skills

Assessment 26.3 – Customize Footnotes/Endnotes

Step	Task	Criterion	Value	Score*
1	Opening and Saving	Opened correct file. Saved file with specified name.	2	
2	Editing	Converted footnotes to endnotes. Changed number format to Arabic numbers (1, 2, 3…). Changed starting number to 5.	6	
5	Saving and Printing	Saved file. Printed document.	2	
		TOTAL POINTS FOR THIS EXERCISE	10	

Achieving Signature Status

Assessment 26.4 – Format a Report in MLA Style

Step	Task	Criterion	Value	Score*
1	Opening and Saving	Opened correct file. Saved with specified name.	2	
2	Formatting	Changed document font to 12-point Cambria. Inserted citations into document and used information from works cited page. Formatted works cited page to meet MLA requirements.	16	
3	Saving and Printing	Saved filed. Printed document.	2	
		TOTAL POINTS FOR THIS EXERCISE	20	

Chapter 27. Creating Indexes

Applying Your Skills

Assessment 27.1 – Create an Index for a Natural Interface Report

Step	Task	Criterion	Value	Score*
1	Opening and Saving	Opened correct file. Saved file with specified name.	2	
2	Creating Bookmarks	Created four bookmarks as illustrated.	4	
3	Marking Bookmarks	Marked four bookmarks as index entries that span pages as illustrated.	4	
4	Indexing and Cross Referencing	Marked *VR* as index entry and cross reference VR to *Virtual reality*.	2	
5	Marking as Main Entries	Marked first occurrence of specified words as main entries or subentries for index as illustrated.	6	
6-7	Inserting Index and Formatting	Inserted index at end of document on separate page. Changed Formats option to *Modern*. Changed number of columns to *2*. Applied Heading 1 style to *INDEX* heading. Changed heading font to 14 points. Applied bold formatting and centered heading.	8	
8	Formatting	Selected all index entries and changed font to *Cambria*.	2	
9-10	Saving and Printing	Saved file. Printed last page of document. Closed document.	2	
		TOTAL POINTS FOR THIS EXERCISE	**30**	

Assessment 27.2 – Create an Index Using a Concordance File

Step	Task	Criterion	Value	Score*
1	Typing	Typed text as shown as concordance file.	6	
2-3	Saving and Printing	Saved file with specified name. Printed and closed document.	2	
4	Opening and Saving	Opened correct file. Saved file with specified name.	2	
5	Editing and Formatting	Marked text for an index using concordance file. Inserted index at end of document. Used *From Template* format. Formatted to two columns. Applied Heading 1 style to *Index* title.	4	
6-9	Formatting	Numbered pages at bottom center of each page. Changed line spacing to 2.0 for entire document (including the index). Inserted page break at beginning of title *CREATING NEWSLETTER LAYOUT*. Updated index.	4	
10	Saving and Printing	Saved document. Printed index.	2	
		TOTAL POINTS FOR THIS EXERCISE	**20**	

Expanding Your Skills

Assessment 27.3 – Customize an Index

Step	Task	Criterion	Value	Score*
1	Opening and Saving	Opened corrected file. Saved with specified name.	2	
2	Formatting	Applied Slice theme.	2	
3	Formatting Index	Displayed Index dialog box. Changed to *From template* format. Specified run-in entries in one column. Closed Index dialog box. Replaced selected index.	4	
4-5	Saving and Printing	Saved file. Printed index only. Closed document.	2	
		TOTAL POINTS FOR THIS EXERCISE	**10**	

Assessment 27.4 – Create an Index for a Spanish Document

Step	Task	Criterion	Value	Score*
0	Ensuring Spanish language option is available	Ensured that Spanish language option is available.	1	
1	Changing Language Option to Spanish, Opening and Saving Document	Changed language option to Spanish. Opened and saved corrected file.	4	
2	Marking Text	Marked text to include index using the specified concordance file.	6	
3	Inserting Index	Inserted index as specified.	4	
4	Applying Heading Style	Applied Heading 1 style to *INDICE* title and changed font to Cambria.	2	
5	Turning off Display of Nonprinting Characters	Turned off display of nonprinting characters.	1	
6	Saving and Printing	Saved file. Printed index only.	2	
		TOTAL POINTS FOR THIS EXERCISE	**20**	

Achieving Signature Status

Assessment 27.5 – Format a Report and Create an Index

Step	Task	Criterion	Value	Score*
1-3	Typing, Saving, and Printing	Typed text in table. Corrected typographical errors. Opened correct file. Typed at least five additional entries in table. Closed file. Saved table document with specified name. Printed and closed document.	10	
4-7	Opening and Copying	Opened correct file. Displayed Organizer dialog box. Copied *BMCHeading*, *BMCTable*, and *BMCTitle* from left list box to right list box. Closed file.	6	

Step	Task	Criterion	Value	Score*
8	**Inserting and Saving**	At blank document, inserted file and saved document with specified name.	2	
9	**Formatting Document**	Applied BMCTitle style to two titles. Applied BMCHeading to headings in document. Applied BMCTable style to two tables. Modified table style as illustrated. Changed paragraph spacing to Relaxed. Inserted bullets, header, and footer as illustrated. Changed font color for header and footer to Dark Blue. Inserted index at end of document using concordance file.	8	
10	**Saving and Printing**	Saved file. Printed document.	2	
11-12	**Deleting Styles**	Displayed Organizer dialog box and deleted styles from right list box: *BMCHeading*, *BMCTable*, and *BMCTitle*.	2	
		TOTAL POINTS FOR THIS EXERCISE	30	

Chapter 28. Creating Specialized Tables

Applying Your Skills

Assessment 28.1 – Create and Update a Table of Contents for a Photography Report

Step	Task	Criterion	Value	Score*
1	**Opening and Saving**	Opened correct file. Saved file with specified name.	2	
2	**Inserting Section Break**	Inserted next page section break at the beginning of heading *Photography*.	2	
3	**Inserting Page Numbers**	Inserted page numbering at bottom center of page starting with number 1.	2	
4-6	**Inserting**	Inserted a table of contents at beginning of document with Automatic Table 1 option. Applied *Distinctive* format and displayed level 3. On table of contents page, changed page numbering style to lowercase roman numerals.	8	
7	**Saving and Printing**	Saved file. Printed only the table of contents page.	2	
8-9	**Inserting and Updating**	Inserted a page break at beginning of heading *Camera Basics*. Updated table of contents.	2	
10-11	**Saving and Printing**	Saved file. Printed only table of contents page. Closed document.	2	
		TOTAL POINTS FOR THIS EXERCISE	20	

Assessment 28.2 – Insert a Captions and a Table of Figures in a Report

Step	Task	Criterion	Value	Score*
1	Opening and Saving	Opened correct file. Saved file with specified name.	2	
2	Inserting Captions	Inserted captions for each of the three images. Used *Figure* as label and Arabic numbers as figure numbers. Displayed centered below image.	3	
3	Inserting	Inserted a next page section break at the beginning of title *COMPUTER INPUT DEVICES*.	2	
4-5	Inserting and Formatting	At the beginning of the document, inserted a table of figures with Formal format. Typed **Table of Figures**. Applied Heading 1 style to the title *Table of Figures*.	5	
6-7	Inserting and Formatting	At the beginning of *COMPUTER INPUT DEVICES* title, inserted page numbering at bottom center of each page with starting number at 1. At the beginning of *TABLE OF FIGURES* title changed page numbering style to lowercase roman numerals.	4	
8-9	Inserting Page Breaks and Updating	Inserted page break at beginning of *MOUSE* heading. Updated table of figures.	2	
10	Saving and Printing	Saved file. Printed document.	2	
		TOTAL POINTS FOR THIS EXERCISE	20	

Assessment 28.3 – Create a Table of Authorities for a Legal Brief

Step	Task	Criterion	Value	Score*
1	Opening and Saving	Opened correct file. Saved file with specified name.	2	
2	Marking Citations	Marked six case citations with specified short citations.	6	
3-5	Formatting	Added one Enter at beginning of document. At beginning of *STATEMENT OF CASE* inserted a section break/new page. Inserted page numbering (below section break) at bottom center of each page. Changed starting number to 1.	4	
6-7	Editing	Typed **TABLE OF AUTHORITIES** at beginning of document centered and bold followed by one Enter. Turned off bold and changed paragraph alignment to left.	2	
8-9	Inserting	Inserted table of authorities (format will vary). Changed numbering format to lowercase roman numerals.	4	
10	Saving and Printing	Saved file. Printed document.	2	
		TOTAL POINTS FOR THIS EXERCISE	20	

Expanding Your Skills

Assessment 28.4 – Create a Table of Contents and a Table of Figures

Step	Task	Criterion	Value	Score*
1	Opening and Saving	Opened correct file. Saved file with specified name.	2	
2-3	Inserting	Inserted section break/new page at beginning of title *Navigating the Web*. Below section break, inserted numbered pages at bottom right of each page. Changed starting number to 1.	4	
4-6	Creating Captions	Used caption feature to create caption above first table: *Table A: Common Top-Level Domain Suffixes*. Created caption above second table: *Table B: Common Search Tools*. Created caption above third table: *Table C: Advanced Search Parameters*.	4	
7-9	Inserting	At beginning of document, inserted Automatic Table 2 table of contents. Inserted page break. Typed: **Table of Figures**. Pressed Enter. Inserted table of figures using Formal format with hyphen (---) leaders.	4	
10-13	Formatting	Applied Heading 1 style to *Table of Figures*. At beginning of document, changed numbering format to lowercase roman numerals. Inserted page break at beginning of title *Searching the Web*. Updated entire table of contents and table of figures.	4	
14	Saving and Printing	Saved file. Printed document.	2	
		TOTAL POINTS FOR THIS EXERCISE	**20**	

Achieving Signature Status

Assessment 28.5 – Create a Table of Contents, a Table of Figures, and a Table of Tables

Step	Task	Criterion	Value	Score*
1	Opening and Saving	Opened correct file. Saved file with specified name.	2	
2	Formatting	Applied Medium Shading 2 – Accent 2 table style to two tables. Removed check mark from First Column check box.	4	
2	Inserting	Inserted captions for the figures and tables as illustrated. Inserted table of contents as illustrated. Inserted table for figures and table for tables as illustrated. Inserted page numbering as illustrated.	8	
2	Formatting	Applied necessary formatting so document appears as illustrated.	4	
3	Saving and Printing	Saved file. Printed document.	2	
		TOTAL POINTS FOR THIS EXERCISE	**20**	

Chapter 29. Creating Forms

Applying Your Skills

Assessment 29.1 – Create and Fill in a Book Order Form

Step	Task	Criterion	Value	Score*
1	**Creating Form**	Created form as template. Applied *No Spacing* style. Inserted Books.jpg image. Sized and moved image as illustrated. Changed text wrapping to Behind Text. Set company name in 22-point Candara bold. Set remainder of text in 11-point Candara bold. Inserted book symbol with Wingdings font selected. Inserted plain text content controls one space after colon (from Name: to Notes:). Inserted horizontal line.	10	
2-4	**Protecting and Saving**	Protected template (no password). Saved template with specified name. Closed document.	2	
5	**Creating Form Document**	Opened correct template. Inserted data in specified fields.	6	
6-7	**Saving and Printing**	Saved document with specified name. Printed document.	2	
		TOTAL POINTS FOR THIS EXERCISE	**20**	

Assessment 29.2 – Create and Fill in a Catalog Request Form

Step	Task	Criterion	Value	Score*
1	**Opening and Saving Document**	Opened and saved document as a template.	2	
2	**Creating Form**	Created form as template. Inserted picture content control in cell in upper right corner of table and inserted **Books.jpg** image. Inserted plain text content controls as illustrated (from *Name*: to *Telephone*: excluded Date). Inserted a date picker content control for *Date*: that inserted date with month spelled out followed by day and year in numbers. Inserted drop-down list content control for *Preferred Shipping Method*: (included four shipping methods).	10	
3-4	**Protecting and Saving**	Protected template (no password). Saved template with specified name. Closed file.	2	
5	**Creating Form Document**	Opened correct template. Inserted data in specified fields as illustrated.	4	
6-7	**Saving and Printing**	Saved document with specified name. Printed document.	2	
		TOTAL POINTS FOR THIS EXERCISE	**20**	

Assessment 29.3 – Create and Fill in an Application Form

Step	Task	Criterion	Value	Score*
1	**Opening and Saving Document**	Opened and saved document as template.	2	
2	**Creating Form**	Created form as template. Inserted Legacy tools text and check box form fields as illustrated.	10	
3-4	**Protecting and Saving**	Protected template (no password). Saved template with specified name.	2	
5	**Creating Form Document**	Opened correct template. Inserted data in specified fields as illustrated.	4	
6-7	**Saving and Printing**	Saved document with specified name. Printed document.	2	
		TOTAL POINTS FOR THIS EXERCISE	**20**	

Assessment 29.4 – Create and Fill in a Patient Update Form

Step	Task	Criterion	Value	Score*
1	**Opening and Saving Document**	Opened and saved document as a template.	2	
2	**Creating Form and Inserting**	Created form as template. Inserted Legacy tools form fields (8) as illustrated with correct specifications.	16	
3-4	**Protecting and Saving**	Protected template. Saved template with specified name.	2	
5	**Creating Form Document**	Created form document from correct template. Inserted data in specified fields.	8	
6-7	**Saving and Printing**	Saved document with specified name. Printed document.	2	
		TOTAL POINTS FOR THIS EXERCISE	**30**	

Expanding Your Skills

Assessment 29.5 – Create a Client Information Form that Includes Building Block Gallery Content Controls

Step	Task	Criterion	Value	Score*
1	**Opening and Creating Building Blocks**	Opened correct file. Created two building blocks. Closed document.	4	
2	**Opening and Saving Document**	Opened and saved document as a template.	2	
3	**Inserting**	Added form fields to form as specified.	6	
4	**Saving**	Saved template (without protecting it) with specified name. Closed template.	2	
5	**Creating Form Document**	Opened correct template. Clicked specific building block content control and building block gallery content control as illustrated. Filled in each text content controls. Clicked only one check box content controls in *Referred by* section.	6	

Step	Task	Criterion	Value	Score*
6-7	Saving and Printing	Saved completed form document with specific name. Printed and closed document.	2	
8	Creating Form Document	Created form document from correct template including building block content control, building block gallery content control, and text content controls. Clicked only one check box content controls in *Referred by* section.	6	
9-10	Saving and Printing	Saved completed form document with specified name. Printed document.	2	
		TOTAL POINTS FOR THIS EXERCISE	30	

Achieving Signature Status

Assessment 29.6 – Create and Fill in an Application Form

Step	Task	Criterion	Value	Score*
1	Creating Form	As illustrated, created form as template. Used Table feature to create columns and rows. Applied border and shading formatting. Set company name in Magneto and set remaining text in Candara.	10	
2	Inserting	Inserted picture content control and inserted correct image. Inserted a date picker content control and plain text content controls in appropriate cells. Included drop-down choices in two drop-down list content controls.	10	
3-4	Protecting and Saving	Protected template. Saved template with specified name.	4	
5	Creating Form Document	Created form document from correct template. (Data will vary.	4	
6-7	Saving and Printing	Saved document with specified name. Printed document.	2	
		TOTAL POINTS FOR THIS EXERCISE	30	

Assessment 29.7 – Create and Fill in a Secondary Payer Form

Step	Task	Criterion	Value	Score*
1	Creating Form Template	Created form as illustrated. Created data fields, cells, shading, and other formatting as illustrated. Specified text form field options for *State:* and *Zip Code:* data fields (suggested).	16	
2-4	Protecting and Saving	Protected template. Saved template with specified name.	4	
5	Creating Form	Created form from template. Inserted data in each data field. (Data will vary.)	8	
6-7	Saving and Printing	Saved document with specified name. Printed document.	2	
		TOTAL POINTS FOR THIS EXERCISE	30	

Chapter 30. Using Outline View and Formatting with Macros

Applying Your Skills

Assessment 30.1 – Assign Levels in Outline View

Step	Task	Criterion	Value	Score*
1	Opening and Saving	Opened correct file. Saved document with specified name.	2	
2	Assigning Levels	Promoted and demoted titles and headings: *COMPENSATION:* (Level 1), *Rate of Pay:* (Level 2), *Pay Progression:* (Level 2), *Overtime:* (Level 2), *Shift Differential:* (Level 2) *EMPLOYEE PERFORMANCE:* (Level 1), *Work Performance Standards* (Level 2), *Performance Evaluation* (Level 2), *Employment Records:* (Level 2).	14	
3	Collapsing Outline	Collapsed outline. Only two levels displayed.	2	
4	Saving and Printing	Saved file. Printed (Only collapsed outline will print.)	2	
		TOTAL POINTS FOR THIS EXERCISE	**20**	

Assessment 30.2 – Move and Delete Headings in a Collapsed Outline

Step	Task	Criterion	Value	Score*
1	Opening and Saving	Opened correct file (from Assessment 30.1). Displayed in Outline view. Saved document with specified file name – Save As.	2	
2	Editing	Changed Show Level button to Level 1. Moved *COMPENSATION* title below title *EMPLOYEE PERFORMANCE*. Changed Show Level button to Level 2. Moved heading *Pay Progression* below the heading *Overtime*. Deleted *Overtime* heading.	4	
3	Saving and Printing	Saved file. Printed document.	2	
4-5	Displaying and Saving	Displayed entire document and closed Outline view. Saved document.	2	
		TOTAL POINTS FOR THIS EXERCISE	**10**	

Assessment 30.3 – Create and Arrange a Master Document

Step	Task	Criterion	Value	Score*
1	Opening and Saving	Opened correct file. Saved file with specified name.	2	
2-3	Assigning Levels	Changed to Outline view. Assigned headings to level 1: *Browsing Web Pages, Searching Online Content, Evaluating Web Content, Intellectual Property*.	6	

Step	Task	Criterion	Value	Score*
4-5	**Creating Subdocuments**	Used Show Document button. Created subdocuments, by selecting entire document and clicking Create button.	4	
6	**Saving**	Saved file. Closed file.	2	
7	**Opening and Printing**	Opened correct file. Printed document (subdocuments are collapsed).	2	
8	**Editing**	Moved subdocument *Evaluating Web Content* above subdocument *Searching Online Content.* Deleted subdocument Intellectual Property.	2	
9	**Saving and Printing**	Saved file. Printed document.	2	
		TOTAL POINTS FOR THIS EXERCISE	20	

Assessment 30.4 – Record and Run Formatting Macros

Step	Task	Criterion	Value	Score*
1	**Opening**	Opened correct file.	1	
1	**Creating Macro**	Created macro named XXXTitle as specified. With insertion point at beginning of *Title*, turned on macro recorder. Pressed F8 and End key. Clicked Center button; clicked Bold button. Changed font size to 14. Clicked Shading button arrow. Clicked Green, Accent 6, Lighter 40%. Clicked *Bottom Border* option. Turned off macro recorder.	6	
2	**Creating Macro**	Created macro named XXXDocFont. Selected entire document. Changed font to Cambria. Assigned macro to Quick Access toolbar.	4	
3	**Closing**	Closed file without saving.	1	
4	**Opening and Saving**	Opened correct file. Saved with specified name.	2	
5-8	**Running Macros**	Ran four macros: XXXDocFont macro, XXXTitle macro (at left margin of *DESIGNING A NEWSLETTER* title), XXXTitle macro (at beginning of *CREATING NEWSLETTER LAYOUT* title), and XXXHeading macro (four headings in document).	4	
9	**Saving and Printing**	Saved file. Printed and closed file.	1	
10	**Removing Button**	Removed XXXDocFont button from Quick Access toolbar.	1	
		TOTAL POINTS FOR THIS EXERCISE	20	

Assessment 30.5 – Record and Run a Macro that Sets Tabs

Step	Task	Criterion	Value	Score*
1	**Running Macro and Creating**	Ran XXXTab macro. Created document as illustrated. Typed text in first column at second tab stop (1 inch) not left margin. Corrected typographical errors.	6	
2	**Saving**	Saved completed document with specified name.	2	
3	**Printing**	Printed document.	2	
		TOTAL POINTS FOR THIS EXERCISE	**10**	

Assessment 30.6 – Record and Run a Macro with Fill-in Fields

Step	Task	Criterion	Value	Score*
1-2	**Recording Macro**	At blank document, set *No Spacing* style. Recorded macro named XXXNotSig. Includes information as illustrated. Set left tabs at 0.5-inch mark, 1.5-inch mark, and 3-inch mark on Ruler. Included Fill-In fields in macro (text in parentheses). Inserted (county) Fill-in field, pressed Enter, and ended macro recording. Closed document without saving.	6	
3	**Opening and Saving**	Opened correct document. Saved file with specified name.	1	
4	**Running Macros**	Ran XXXNotSig macro at end of document. Typed information when prompted: (*name 1*) = **LLOYD KOVICH**, (*name 2*) = **JOANNE MILNER**, (*county*) = **Ramsey County**	2	
5	**Saving and Printing**	Saved file. Printed document.	1	
		TOTAL POINTS FOR THIS EXERCISE	**10**	

Expanding Your Skills

Assessment 30.7 – Create and Run a Macro with Fields

Step	Task	Criterion	Value	Score*
1	**Opening File and Creating Macros**	Opened correct file. Created macro. XXXSFHDocFormat that selects entire document (Ctrl + A), applies No Spacing style, changes line spacing to double (Ctrl + 2), and changes font to Constantia. Created macro XXXSFHMargins that changes top margin to 1.5 inches and left/right margins to 1.25 inches. Created macro XXXSFHTitle that selects line of text, changes font to 14, turns on bold, centers text, and deselects text. Created macro XXXSFHHeading that selects line of text, changes font to 12, turns on bold, turns on underline, and deselects text.	10	
2-3	**Creating Macro**	With correct file opened, created XXXSFHEnd macro that changes line spacing to single (Ctrl + 1), inserts *FileName* field, inserts *Date* field, types **Number of Pages**: and inserts *NumPages* field. Pressed Enter and inserted Fill-in field prompting user to type his or her name. Closed file without saving it.	4	

Step	Task	Criterion	Value	Score*
4	**Opening and Saving**	Opened correct file. Saved document with specified name.	2	
5-7	**Running Macros**	Ran XXXSFHDocFormat macro and XXXSFHMargins macro. Ran XXXTitle macro for title. Ran XXXHeading macro for three headings in document. Ran XXXSFHEnd macro (at end of document). When prompted typed first and last names.	4	
8	**Saving and Printing**	Saved file. Printed and closed document.	2	
9	**Opening and Saving**	Opened correct file. Saved document with specified name.	2	
10	**Running Macros**	Ran macros similar to steps 5-7.	4	
11	**Saving and Printing**	Saved file. Printed document.	2	
		TOTAL POINTS FOR THIS EXERCISE	**30**	

Achieving Signature Status

Assessment 30.8 – Create and Run a Menu Formatting Macro

Step	Task	Criterion	Value	Score*
1-3	**Creating Macro**	Opened correct file. Created XXXMenu macro and assigned to Quick Access toolbar. Created Fill-in field with prompt: *Type the current date.* Applied formatting to entire document: changed font to 14-point Monotype Corsiva and font color to Purple; centered text; applied Green, Accent 6, Lighter 60% paragraph shading; displayed Borders and Shading, changed color to Purple clicked *Box* option in *Setting* section, and closed dialog box. Ended recording of macro. Closed document without saving.	10	
4	**Opening and Saving**	Opened correct file. Saved document with specified name.	1	
5	**Running Macro**	Pressed Down Arrow key once and applied XXXMenu macro. Typed date: **August 6, 2015** at fill-in prompt. Document should appear as illustrated.	1	
6	**Saving and Printing**	Saved file. Printed and closed document.	1	
7	**Opening and Saving**	Opened correct file. Saved document with specified name.	1	
8	**Running Macro**	Pressed Down Arrow key once and applied XXXMenu macro. Typed date: **August 11, 2015** at fill-in prompt.	1	
9	**Saving and Printing**	Saved file. Printed and closed document with specified name.	1	
10	**Opening and Saving**	Opened correct file. Saved document with specified name.	1	

Step	Task	Criterion	Value	Score*
11	Running Macro	Pressed Down Arrow key once and applied XXXMenu macro. Typed date: **August 12, 2015** at fill-in prompt.	1	
12	Saving and Printing	Saved file. Printed and closed document with specified name.	1	
13	Removing Button	Removed XXXMenu button from Quick Access toolbar.	1	
		TOTAL POINTS FOR THIS EXERCISE	20	

Unit 6. Performance Assessments

Assessing Proficiencies

Assessment U6.1 – Insert Footnotes in a Report

Step	Task	Criterion	Value	Score*
1	Opening and Saving	Opened correct file. Saved with specified name.	2	
2-5	Creating Footnotes	Created four footnotes as illustrated (end of first paragraph, end of paragraph in *Speech Recognition* section, end of paragraph in *Virtual Reality* section, and end of last paragraph in document).	8	
6	Saving and Printing	Saved file. Printed document.	2	
7-8	Editing	Selected entire document and changed font to Constantia. Selected all footnotes and changed font to Constantia.	4	
9	Deleting	Deleted third footnote.	2	
10	Saving and Printing	Saved file. Printed document.	2	
		TOTAL POINTS FOR THIS EXERCISE	20	

Assessment U6.2 – Create Citations and Prepare a Works Cited Page for a Report

Step	Task	Criterion	Value	Score*
1	Opening and Saving	Opened correct file. Saved with specified file name.	2	
2	Formatting and Typing	Formatted title page to MLA style. Selected entire document and changed font to 12-point Cambria, line spacing to 2.0, and removed spacing after paragraphs. At beginning of document, typed name, instructor's name, title of course, and current date as specified. Inserted header with last name and page number at right margin. Changed font to 12-point Cambria.	4	
3-8	Typing and Editing	At end of document, typed text as specified in MLA style including citations. Edited as specified. Corrected typographical errors.	8	
9	Creating New Source	Created new source for journal article as specified.	2	

Step	Task	Criterion	Value	Score*
10	**Typing**	Typed text at end of document as specified. Corrected typographical errors.	4	
11-12	**Inserting Citations**	Inserted citations as instructed.	2	
13	**Inserting Works Cited Page**	Inserted works cited page at end of document on a separate page.	2	
14	**Formatting**	Formatted works cited page to meet MLA requirements. Selected *Works Cited* title and all entries and changed to *No Spacing* style. Changed font to 12-point Cambria and spacing to 2.0. Centered title *Works Cited*. Used hanging indents on works cited entries.	2	
15	**Saving and Printing**	Saved file. Printed document.	1	
16	**Applying Style**	Changed document and works cited page from MLA style to APA style. Changed title to *References*. Selected references and changed spacing after paragraphs to 0. Changed line spacing to 2. Changed font to 12-point Cambria.	2	
17	**Saving and Printing**	Saved file. Printed page 3.	1	
	TOTAL POINTS FOR THIS EXERCISE		30	

Assessment U6.3 – Create an Index and Table of Contents for a Report

Step	Task	Criterion	Value	Score*
1	**Typing Concordance File**	Created text as concordance file. Corrected typographical errors.	8	
2-3	**Saving and Printing**	Saved file with specified name. Printed and closed document.	1	
4	**Opening and Saving**	Opened correct file. Saved file with specified name.	1	
5-6	**Formatting**	Applied Heading 1 style to title. Applied Heading 2 style to two headings. Changed style set to Basic (Simple). Marked text for index using specified file. Compiled index at end of document. Applied Heading 1 style to title of index. Inserted table of contents at beginning of document. Numbered table of contents page with lowercase roman numeral. Numbered other pages in report with Arabic numbers. Started numbering with 1 on page containing the report title. If necessary, updated table of contents to display correct page numbers.	8	
7	**Saving and Printing**	Saved file. Printed document.	2	
	TOTAL POINTS FOR THIS EXERCISE		20	

Assessment U6.4 – Create Captions and Insert a Table of Figures in a Report

Step	Task	Criterion	Value	Score*
1	**Opening and Saving**	Opened correct file. Saved file with specified name.	2	
2-3	**Creating Captions**	Created captions above table 1 and table 2. Changed paragraph spacing after to 0 pt.	4	
4-10	**Inserting and Formatting**	Inserted section break/new page at beginning of document. Below section break, numbered pages at bottom center of each page and changed starting page number to 1. At beginning of document inserted Automatic Table 2 table of contents. Inserted page break. Typed: **Tables**. Inserted table of figures (Formal format). Applied Heading 1 style to title: *Tables*. At beginning of document, changed numbering format to lowercase roman numerals.	10	
11	**Updating**	Updated table of contents.	2	
12	**Saving and Printing**	Saved file. Printed document.	2	
		TOTAL POINTS FOR THIS EXERCISE	20	

Assessment U6.5 – Create and Fill in a Purchase Order Form

Step	Task	Criterion	Value	Score*
1	**Creating Form**	Created form as template as illustrated. Used table to create columns and rows. Applied border and shading as illustrated. Inserted picture content control, date picker content control, plain text content controls in appropriate cells. Locked picture content control. Inserted drop-down list content control for *Company Status* with choices: *Bronze*, *Silver*, and *Gold*.	18	
2-3	**Protecting and Saving**	Protected template. Saved template with specified name.	2	
4	**Printing**	Printed and closed template.	2	
5	**Creating Form Document**	Created form document from correct template. Typed information as specified.	6	
6-7	**Saving and Printing**	Saved document with specific name. Printed document.	2	
TOTAL POINTS FOR THIS EXERCISE			30	

Assessment U6.6 – Create and Fill in an Insurance Application Form

Step	Task	Criterion	Value	Score*
1-2	**Creating Template and Inserting Form Fields**	Opened correct file. Saved as template. Inserted form fields in template as illustrated.	18	
3-4	**Protecting and Saving**	Protected template. Saved template with specified name. Printed template. Closed template.	4	

Step	Task	Criterion	Value	Score*
5	**Creating Form Document**	Created form document from correct template. Inserted information in specified data fields.	6	
6-7	**Saving and Printing**	Saved document with specified file name. Printed document.	2	
		TOTAL POINTS FOR THIS EXERCISE	**30**	

Assessment U6.7 – Create Subdocuments

Step	Task	Criterion	Value	Score*
1	**Opening and Saving**	Opened correct file. Saved document with specified name.	2	
2	**Formatting**	In Outline view, assigned level 1 to headings: *Electronic Mail, Instant Messaging Software, Groupware, Web Browsers, Webconferencing.*	6	
3-4	**Creating Subdocuments**	Clicked Show Document button. Created subdocuments by selecting entire document. Clicked Create button.	2	
5	**Saving**	Saved file with specified name. Closed file.	2	
6	**Opening and Printing**	Opened correct file. Printed document (subdocuments will be collapsed).	2	
7	**Editing**	Moved subdocument Web Browsers above subdocument Instant Messaging Software. Deleted subdocument Groupware.	4	
8	**Saving and Printing**	Saved file. Printed document.	2	
		TOTAL POINTS FOR THIS EXERCISE	**20**	

Assessment U6.8 – Create and Run Macros

Step	Task	Criterion	Value	Score*
1	**Creating Macros**	Created macro XXXAPMFormat that selects document, changes font to Constantia, and changes font color to Dark Blue. Created macro XXXAPMTitle that changes font to 14, turns on bold, centers text, and applies Blue, Accent 1, Lighter 60% paragraph shading.	8	
2	**Creating Macro**	Created macro XXXAPMInfo with information Illustrated.	2	
3	**Closing**	After recording macros, close documents without saving.	1	
4	**Opening and Saving**	Opened correct file. Saved with specified name.	1	
5-7	**Running Macros**	Ran XXXAPMFormat macro. Ran XXXAPMTitle macro at beginning of title. Ran XXXAPMInfo macro at the end of document. Inserted information provided.	2	
8	**Saving and Printing**	Saved file. Printed and closed document.	1	

Step	Task	Criterion	Value	Score*
9	Opening and Saving	Opened correct file. Saved document with specified name.	2	
10-12	Running Macros	Ran XXXAPMFormat macro. Ran XXXAPMTitle macro at beginning of title. Ran XXXAPMInfo macro at end of document. Inserted information provided.	2	
13	Saving and Printing	Saved file. Printed document.	1	
		TOTAL POINTS FOR THIS EXERCISE	20	

Creating Original Documents

Assessment U6.9 – Format an Employee Handbook

Step	Task	Criterion	Value	Score*
1	Opening and Saving	Opened correct file. Saved file with specified name.	2	
2	Formatting	Inserted page breaks before each centered title (except first title). Applied heading styles to titles and headings. Selected and changed style set of choice. Applied theme for ease of reading. Inserted table of contents. Created concordance file and inserted an index. Inserted appropriate page numbering. Added elements to improve visual appeal of document.	16	
3	Saving and Printing	Saved file. Printed document.	2	
		TOTAL POINTS FOR THIS EXERCISE	20	

Assessment U6.10 – Create a Contact Information Form

Step	Task	Criterion	Value	Score*
1	Creating Form Template	Created form template (used **ERCFunding** as reference). Student determined layout of form and types of form fields used (field names provided). Corrected typographical errors.	10	
2	Saving	Saved template with specified name.	1	
3	Creating Form	Used correct form template to create fill-in form. Provided information to insert in form.	8	
4	Saving and Printing	Saved completed form document with specified name. Printed document.	1	
		TOTAL POINTS FOR THIS EXERCISE	20	

Supplemental Assessments

Unit 1 Instructions

Assessment 1

1. At a blank document, click the *No Spacing* style in the Styles group on the HOME tab and then type the text exactly as shown below in correct memo format using default Word spacing (see Appendix C).

    a. Apply italic and bold formatting as indicated in the text below.

    b. Use the current year in the *DATE:* heading.

    c. Indent the second paragraph 0.5 inch from the left and right margins, as shown.

2. Select the entire document and change the font to 12-point Cambria.

3. Apply bold and italic formatting to the *TO:* heading (including the colon). Repeat the bold and italic formatting on the *FROM:*, *DATE:*, and *SUBJECT:* headings. Make sure the headings remain aligned.

4. Complete a spelling and grammar check on the document. Proofread the document and make any necessary corrections.

5. Save the document and name it **U01-SA01**.

6. Print and then close **U01-SA01.docx**.

TO: Computer Science Faculty; FROM: Your Name; DATE: October 23, 20xx; SUBJECT: Web Design Course

At last week's Southern Computer Technology conference, I met Jean Edmonds; she is from Plains Community College wear they added a Web design course to their curriculum last year. I received a letter from her last week in which she shared some information regarding their success.

> The interest in the class has been phenomenal. We advertised the course in our college schedule and sent brochures to all college students. Thirty people registered for the course during the first week, and the coarse was closed the second week. Student evaluations, completed last semester, were very favorable. The instructor for the course is using the textbook *Web Design Applications* by Cliff A. Green.

I plan on contacting Jean before we attend the National Computer Technology conference. I want to ask her any questions our department personnel might have so we can discuss them at the conference. Please gather your thoughts and **send me any questions you have by October 27** so I can send Jean a letter in time for our meeting.

We will continue our discussion regarding the introduction of a Web design course at our next department meeting, Monday, November 14.

xx

U01-SA01.docx

Assessment 2

1. Open the document named **ECCLtrhd.docx** (located in the **SA-StudentDataFiles** folder) and save the document with the name **U01-SA02**.

2. Click *No Spacing* style in the Styles group on the HOME tab.

3. Change the font to Constantia.

4. Type the business letter shown below in correct block style format (see Appendix D).

   a. Insert today's date.

   b. Add an appropriate salutation and closing; use your name as the sender.

   c. Insert your choice of bullets before each item in the bulleted list.

   d. Research Web design elements on the Internet. Prepare two additional questions about elements that might be taught and then add them to the bulleted list.

   e. Change the alignment to justified for all paragraphs in the body of the letter.

5. Find a synonym for the word *concerning* in the fourth sentence of the first paragraph.

6. Save, print, and then close **U01-SA02.docx**.

Please send a letter with the following text to: Ms. Jean Edmonds; Computer Science Department; Plains Community College; 432 Main Street; Lincoln, NE 68521

Thank you for sharing the information regarding your new Web design course. The members of my department were encouraged by your success when I shared the details with them. In our discussion, I asked them for additional ideas that you and I might discuss at the upcoming National Computer Technology conference. Below is a list of additional questions they asked concerning implementing the Web design course. I thought it might be helpful for you to know what type of information we were seeking before our meeting.

- What is the format of the course meetings?
- How many sections will you offer in the future?

I look forward to continuing our discussion next week at the conference. Let's plan on meeting Wednesday after the opening session in the lobby of the conference center. Please call me at (206) 555-1538 if you would like to meet at a different time and place.

Assessment 3

1. At a blank document, change the font to 24-point Candara.

2. Type the text shown below, using the current year for the date.

   Attention!
   New Course: Web Design Basics will be offered Spring 20xx
   For more information, please contact:
   Your Name
   Computer Science Department

3. Apply formatting as indicated below:

   a. Center-align the text.

   b. Apply bold formatting to the first line of text.

   c. Add an extra line space between the first and second lines.

   d. Apply the small caps font effect to the new course name, *Web Design Basics*.

   e. Apply a border and shading of your choosing around the text.

4. Translate the first line, *Attention!*, into Spanish and place the Spanish text on the blank line below the English text. Type the Spanish text without any accents or special symbols.

5. Make any other adjustments necessary to enhance the appearance of the announcement.

6. Save the document and name it **U01-SA03**.

7. Print and then close **U01-SA03.docx**.

Assessment 4

1. Open **SmokeDetectors.docx** (located in the **SA-StudentDataFiles** folder) and save the document with the name **U01-SA04**.

2. Apply the Heading 2 style to the title of the document and then center the title.

3. Apply the Heading 3 style to the headings in the document.

4. Change the style set to Lines (Stylish).

5. Change the theme to Parallax.

6. Change the line spacing to 1.0 for the entire document.

7. Change the line spacing of the bulleted list to 1.5.

8. Change the bulleted list to a numbered list.

9. In the first paragraph below the *Placing Smoke Alarms* heading, find an appropriate synonym for the word *usually* and for the word *typically*.

10. Move the insertion point to the end of the document, press the Enter key once, and then change the alignment to Align Right.

11. Type your name, press Shift + Enter, and then insert today's date.

12. Save, print, and then close **U01-SA04.docx**.

Assessment 5

1. At a blank document, change the style to No Spacing.

2. Set a left tab at 1 inch, a right tab with dot leaders at 3.5 inches, and a right tab with dot leaders at 5.5 inches.

3. Type the following information, centering the title and subtitle as shown and making sure to tab before typing the first column of text:

Everest Technologies
Independent Auditor Fees

Item	2014	2015
Audit fees	$935,245	$754,230
Audit-related fees	10,590	12,540
Tax fees	21,315	17,443
All other fees	14,326	10,328
Total	$981,476	$794,541

4. Set the title in 20-point Tahoma bold and set the subtitle in 14-point Tahoma bold.

5. Select the column headings (*Item*, *2014*, and *2015*), display the Tabs dialog box, and then remove the leaders from the right tab set at 3.5 inches and remove the leaders from the right tab set at 5.5 inches.

6. Set the column headings in bold and italics.

7. Select the six lines of tabbed text and then apply a single-line, 1-point border around the outside of the selected text and apply Orange, Accent 2, Lighter 80% shading.

8. Save the document and name it **U01-SA05**.

9. Print and then close **U01-SA05.docx**.

Unit 1 Grading Rubrics

The following are suggested rubrics. Instructors should feel free to customize the rubrics to suit their grading standards and/or to adjust the point values.

*Suggested Scoring Distribution
Above average: student completes 80% or more of task
Average: student completes 70 to 79% of task
Below average: student completes 69% or less of task

Assessment 1

Step	Task	Criterion	Value	Score*
1	**Typing and formatting**	Clicked *No Spacing* style and typed text as instructed. Applied bold and italic formatting to text as indicated, and indented second paragraph 0.5 inch from left and right margins.	6	
2	**Formatting**	Selected entire document and changed font to 12-point Cambria.	4	
3	**Formatting**	Applied bold and italic formatting to *TO:*, *FROM:*, *DATE:*, and *SUBJECT:* headings.	4	
4	**Editing**	Completed a spelling and grammar check. Proofread the document and corrected errors.	4	
5-6	**Saving and printing**	Saved, printed, and closed document.	2	
		TOTAL POINTS FOR THIS EXERCISE	20	

Assessment 2

Step	Task	Criterion	Value	Score*
1	**Opening and saving**	Opened and saved document.	2	
2-3	**Formatting**	Clicked *No Spacing* style and changed font to Constantia.	4	
4	**Typing and researching**	Correctly typed text, inserted date, added salutation and closing with own name as sender, inserted bullets, prepared and included two additional questions in bulleted list, and changed alignment to justified for paragraphs in body of letter.	8	
5	**Using Synonym feature**	Replaced *concerning* with synonym.	4	
6	**Saving and printing**	Saved, printed, and closed document.	2	
		TOTAL POINTS FOR THIS EXERCISE	**20**	

Assessment 3

Step	Task	Criterion	Value	Score*
1	**Formatting**	Changed font to 24-point Candara.	2	
2	**Typing**	Correctly typed text as indicated.	5	
3	**Formatting**	Correctly applied formatting as instructed.	5	
4	**Translating from English to Spanish**	Translated first line into Spanish and inserted it on second line.	4	
5	**Formatting**	Made other adjustments to create a visually attractive announcement.	2	
6-7	**Saving and printing**	Saved, printed, and closed document.	2	
		TOTAL POINTS FOR THIS EXERCISE	**20**	

Assessment 4

Step	Task	Criterion	Value	Score*
1	**Opening and saving**	Opened and saved document.	2	
2-5	**Formatting**	Applied Heading 2 and Heading 3 styles, changed style set to Lines (Stylish), applied Parallax theme, and changed line spacing of entire document to 1.0.	5	
6-7	**Formatting**	Changed bulleted list spacing to 1.5 and changed bulleted list to numbered list.	4	
8	**Using Synonym feature**	Found appropriate synonyms for *usually* and *typically*.	3	

Step	Task	Criterion	Value	Score*
9-10	Typing	Added line to end of document, changed alignment, and entered name and date as instructed.	4	
11	Saving and printing	Saved, printed, and closed document.	2	
		TOTAL POINTS FOR THIS EXERCISE	**20**	

Assessment 5

Step	Task	Criterion	Value	Score*
1-2	Formatting	Clicked *No Spacing style* and set tabs as indicated.	6	
3	Typing	Typed information and set tabs as instructed.	4	
4	Formatting	Set title in 20-point Tahoma bold and set subtitle in 14-point Tahoma bold.	2	
5	Formatting	Selected column headings and then removed leaders from tabs as instructed.	4	
6	Formatting	Set column headings in bold and italics.	2	
7	Adding borders and shading	Added correct border and shading.	5	
8-9	Saving and printing	Saved, printed, and closed document.	2	
		TOTAL POINTS FOR THIS EXERCISE	**25**	

Unit 1 Model Answers

U01-SA01.docx

TO: Computer Science Faculty

FROM: Student Name

DATE: October 23, 2015

SUBJECT: Web Design Course

At last week's Southern Computer Technology conference, I met Jean Edmonds; she is from Plains Community College where they added a Web design course to their curriculum last year. I received a letter from her last week in which she shared some information regarding their success.

The interest in the class has been phenomenal. We advertised the course in our college schedule and sent brochures to all college students. Thirty people registered for the course during the first week, and the course was closed the second week. Student evaluations, completed last semester, were very favorable. The instructor for the course is using the textbook *Web Design Applications* by Cliff A. Green.

I plan on contacting Jean before we attend the National Computer Technology conference. I want to ask her any questions our department personnel might have so we can discuss them at the conference. Please gather your thoughts and **send me any questions you have by October 27** so I can send Jean a letter in time for our meeting.

We will continue our discussion regarding the introduction of a Web design course at our next department meeting, Monday, November 14.

xx
U01-SA01.docx

U01-SA02.docx

Evergreen Community College

June 8, 2015

Ms. Jean Edmonds
Computer Science Department
Plains Community College
432 Main Street
Lincoln, NE 68521

Dear Ms. Edmonds:

Thank you for sharing the information regarding your new Web design course. The members of my department were encouraged by your success when I shared the details with them. In our discussion, I asked them for additional ideas that you and I might discuss at the upcoming National Computer Technology conference. Below is a list of additional questions they asked regarding implementing the Web design course. I thought it might be helpful for you to know what type of information we were seeking before our meeting.

- What is the format of the course meetings?
- How many sections will you offer in the future?
- Do you include form validation in your course?
- Do you include page stretching in your course?

I look forward to continuing our discussion next week at the conference. Let's plan on meeting Wednesday after the opening session in the lobby of the conference center. Please call me at (206) 555-1538 if you would like to meet at a different time and place.

Sincerely,

Student Name
U01-SA02.docx

1500 South Alameda Avenue □ Seattle, Washington 98211 □ (206) 555-1500

HOME SAFETY: SMOKE ALARMS

Smoke alarms are one of the simplest and most efficient ways of protecting a home and household members from severe injury or death caused by a home fire. The U.S. Department of Housing and Urban Development (HUD) estimates that a home fire occurs every 66 seconds in the United States. The National Fire Protection Association (NFPA) estimates that having a functioning home smoke alarm in the home reduces by 50 percent the chances of dying from a fire. Unfortunately, approximately one-third of all smoke alarms placed in homes do not function properly.

Types of Smoke Alarms

The two common types of smoke alarms are ionization and photoelectric. An ionization detector is the most common and uses ionization sensors to detect smoke. Ionization detectors are very sensitive and are designed to detect hot and fast-moving fires that produce minimal smoke. Photoelectric detectors detect the presence of visible particulars in the air. Inside the detector a light emitting diode (LED) directs a narrow beam of infrared light across the detection chamber. When smoke or particles enter the chamber, the infrared light beam is scattered. When a preset amount of light is detected, the detector alarm sounds. Photoelectric detectors are not as sensitive as ionization detectors and are designed to detect cool or slow-moving fires that produce a lot of smoke.

Placing Smoke Alarms

For existing homes, smoke alarms generally are required on every habitable level and within the vicinity of all bedrooms. In new construction, the minimum requirements are much greater. All smoke alarms must be interconnected and hooked directly to the electrical wiring and are required inside each bedroom. Smoke alarms are normally not placed in kitchens and bathrooms since the steam may set them off.

Where a smoke alarm is positioned in a home varies depending on the size and layout of the home and where household members sleep at night. Since the primary job of the smoke alarm is to wake up sleeping people, a smoke alarm should be positioned as close as possible to the bedrooms or other places where people frequently sleep. If sleeping areas are separated, each area should have its own detector.

If a person generally sleeps with the bedroom door closed or smokes in bed, a smoke alarm should be placed in the bedroom. A closed bedroom door may offer some protection from fire and smoke coming from outside the room but a smoke alarm outside the bedroom may be difficult to hear. In a multiple-level home with bedrooms upstairs, a smoke alarm should be placed near the top of the stairs. If the home contains a basement, a smoke alarm should be placed on the basement ceiling near the steps to the rest of the house. A smoke alarm should not be placed within six inches of where a wall and ceiling meet or near heating and cooling ducts. Smoke alarms placed in these locations may not receive the flow of smoke required to activate the alarm.

Developing an Escape Plan

Someone in every household should develop an escape plan in case of fire and practice the plan with all members of the home. When developing an escape plan, consider the following:

1. Draw a floor plan of the home that identifies at least two methods of escape from every room.

2. Practice evacuating the home while blindfolded since the amount of smoke generated by a house fire will impair vision.

3. Practice staying low to the ground while escaping.

Attention!
Atencion!

New Course: WEB DESIGN BASICS will be offered
Spring 2015

For more information, please contact:

Student Name

Computer Science Department

Everest Technologies
Independent Auditor Fees

Item	2014	2015
Audit fees	$935,245	$754,230
Audit-related fees	10,590	12,540
Tax fees	21,315	17,443
All other fees	14,326	10,328
Total	$981,476	$794,541

---

4. Practice stopping, dropping to the ground, and rolling in case clothing catches on fire.

5. Identify a safe meeting place outside the home.

6. Practice alerting other members of the household.

Safety Tips

Along with the development of an escape plan, a member of the household should post emergency telephone numbers near the telephone. However, in the case of a home fire, household members should leave the house first and then place the emergency call from a safe location. A person in a multiple-level home should purchase collapsible ladders and have each household member practice using them. A-B-C type fire extinguishers should be available in the home and each household member should know how to use them. Combustible materials should not be stored in closed areas or near a heat source.

When cooking in the home, keep the stove area clean and clear of combustibles such as bags and boxes and other appliances. If a fire does occur in the kitchen, put a lid over the burning pan or use a fire extinguisher. Never pour water on grease fires.

Have a certified electrician check all electrical wiring in the house and replace any frayed or cracked wiring. Make sure no wiring is located under rugs, over nails, or in high traffic areas and do not overload outlets or extension cords. All outlets should have cover plates and no wiring should be exposed. A homeowner should only purchase appliances and electrical devices that have a label indicating that they have been inspected by a testing laboratory such as Underwriter's Laboratories (UL) or Factory Mutual (FM).

For additional safe tips, contact the local fire department, the Office of the State Fire Commissioner, or a chapter of the American Red Cross.

Taking Care of Smoke Alarms

A member of the household should establish a system for monitoring and taking care of all smoke alarms in the home. Smoke alarms require regular testing and battery and lamp replacements.

Monthly Testing: Once a month, a member of the household should test all smoke alarms in the home. To test an ionization detector, hold a burning candle approximately six inches under the detector. To test a photoelectric detector, extinguish the candle flame and let visible smoke draft into the detector. The smoke alarm's alarm should sound within twenty seconds. Some detectors have a more refined test system that simulates the presence of smoke. Check the smoke alarm package to determine if the smoke alarm has this feature.

Cleaning Detectors: Dust and cobwebs can interfere with the operation of a smoke alarm so detectors should be cleaned on a regular basis and according to the manufacturer's instructions. Do not remove the detector's cover and use a standard vacuum cleaner hose and attachment when cleaning the detector.

Replacing Batteries and Lamps: If the battery power is running low in a smoke alarm, the detector emits a low-power warning sound. When this happens, remove the battery and replace it with a new one. Replace batteries according to the manufacturer's instructions. Replace batteries immediately when moving into a new home. A photoelectric detector contains a lamp that needs to be replaced on a periodic basis. Keep a supply of replacement lamps on hand to replace in the detector as needed.

Student Name
June 8, 2015

Unit 2 Instructions

Assessment 1

1. At a blank document, change the font to 12-point Cambria.

2. Type the title text shown below, centered and bolded.

3. Press the Enter key after typing the title, turn off bold, change to left alignment, and then set the following tabs:

   a. Set a left tab at the 0.5-inch mark.

   b. Set a left tab with dot leaders at the 2.75-inch mark.

   c. Set a right tab with dot leaders at the 6.0-inch mark.

4. Type the columns of text using the tabs you set; be sure to press the Tab key before typing each entry in the first column.

5. Select the title and the columns of text and then change the line spacing to 1.5.

6. Insert a footer using the Blank predesigned footer and then type the following footer text in the *[Type here]* placeholder: ***Registration materials must be turned in by November 4 so final room arrangements can be made.**

7. Select the footer text you just typed and then change the font to 10-point Cambria bold.

8. Save the document and name it **U02-SA01**.

9. Print and then close **U02-SA01.docx**.

Training Schedule and Costs*
Independent Auditor Fees
Supervising Others . . . . .November 11, 9 a.m. to 3 p.m.. . . . .$199
Document Preparation . . . . . . .November 18, 9 a.m. to 12 noon. $115
Proofreading Techniques. . . . . . .November 18, 1 p.m. to 4 p.m. $89
Utilizing the Internet. . . . . November 20, 10 a.m. to 12 noon $75
Ethics in Business . . . . .November 25, 1 p.m. to 5 p.m. $75

Assessment 2

1. Open **CompSections1&2.docx** (located in the **SA-StudentDataFiles** folder) and save the document with the name **U02-SA02.**

2. Move the insertion point to the end of the document and then insert the document named **CompSection3.docx** (located in the **SA-StudentDataFiles** folder) into the **U02-SA02.docx** document.

3. Select the entire document and then change the font to 12-point Cambria.

4. Select all section titles and change the formatting to 14-point Candara bold. Select all headings and change the formatting to 12-point Candara bold italic.

5. Insert the Retrospect predesigned header. Insert your name as the document title and the current date in the date placeholder.

6. Check page breaks in the document and, if necessary, insert your own page break(s).

7. Save, print and then close **U02-SA02.docx**.

Assessment 3

1. Open **SecurityTraining.docx** (located in the **SA-StudentDataFiles** folder) and save the document with the name **U02-SA03**.

2. Apply 20-point Corbel bold formatting to the title and center the title.

3. Move the last sentence in the first paragraph to the end of the last paragraph of text in the document.

4. Type this sentence at the end of the first paragraph in the document: **This event has been planned in response to several requests from our various departments, so please add these dates to your calendars.**

5. Create a drop cap for the first letter of the first paragraph.

6. Indent the first line of paragraphs two through four 0.25 inches.

7. Select the name *Jessie Levigne* located in the last paragraph of text and replace it with Chloë Valérien.

8. Move the insertion point to the blank line at the end of the document, press the Enter key, and then type the following text centered and set in 16-point Corbel bold: **Dates to Remember**.

9. Type the three workshop dates (with the days but without the times) below the *Dates to Remember* heading, format the dates in 11-point Calibri bold, and center the dates. *Hint: Read the document text to find the workshop dates.*

10. Change the page orientation to Landscape.

11. Change the vertical alignment of the text on the page to Center.

12. Insert the ASAP 1 watermark.

13. Insert an art page border of your choosing.

14. Save, print, and then close **U02-SA03.docx**.

Assessment 4

1. Using the Internet, research three of your favorite vacation spots.

2. Write a memo to your instructor (refer to Appendix C) introducing him or her to your favorite vacation destinations; include a short paragraph about each.

3. After typing the three paragraphs about your favorite vacation destinations, press the Enter key once, and then insert two tabs (you determine the location and type of tabs). Create a list of the vacation locations by typing the vacation locations at the first tab and the Web addresses at the second tab.

4. Add a footer using the Blank predesigned footer that reads **Information for Planning Your Next Vacation.**

5. Save the document and name it **U02-SA04**.

6. Proofread, save, print, and then close **U02-SA04.docx**.

Assessment 5

1. Open **CompCommunications.docx** (located in the **SA-StudentDataFiles** folder) and save the document with the name **U02-SA05**.

2. Insert a Next Page section break at the beginning of the heading *REFERENCES* located toward the end of the document.

3. Move the insertion point to the right of the period that ends the second paragraph in the *Home Entertainment* section, press the Enter key once, and then insert the document named **CompSecurity.docx** (located in the **SA-StudentDataFiles** folder).

4. Apply the Heading 1 style to the following titles: *COMPUTERS IN COMMUNICATIONS, COMPUTERS IN ENTERTAINMENT, UNAUTHORIZED ACCESS, INFORMATION THEFT*, and *REFERENCES*.

5. Apply the Heading 2 style to the headings (beginning with *Telecommunications* and ending with *Data Browsing*) in the document.

6. Change the style set to Lines (Stylish) and change the theme colors to Blue.

7. Insert the Austin header in the document. Type **Computer Technology** as the title of the header. Apply bold formatting to the header text.

8. Insert page numbering at the bottom of each page using the Accent Bar 1 option.

9. Move the insertion point to the beginning of the title *COMPUTERS IN COMMUNICATIONS* located at the beginning of the document and then insert the Semaphore cover page. Insert the current date in the *[DATE]* placeholder, type **Information Technology** in the *[DOCUMENT SUBTITLE]* placeholder, insert your school's name in the *[COMPANY NAME]* placeholder, and insert your name in the Author tab. Delete the *[Company address]* placeholder.

10. Select the second paragraph below the heading *Television and Film* and then indent the paragraph from the left and right margins 0.5 inches.

11. Select the four references that display below the *REFERENCES* heading and then apply a hanging indent to the four selected paragraphs of text.

12. Print, save, and close **U02-SA05.docx**.

Assessment 6

1. Open **SmokeDetectors.docx** (located in the **SA-StudentDataFiles** folder) and save the document with the name **U02-SA06**.

2. Format the text from the beginning of the first paragraph to the end of the document into two columns with 0.5 inch spacing and a line between columns.

3. Manually hyphenate the text in the document. Select the title, change the font size to 16 points, insert a double-line top and bottom border, and apply *Green, Accent 6, Lighter 60%* shading.

4. For each headings that appears on a separate line (beginning with *Types of Smoke Alarms* and ending with *Taking Care of Smoke Alarms*), change the font size to 12 points and apply *Gold, Accent 4, Lighter 80%* shading and a single line bottom border.

5. Balance the columns on the third page.

6. Save, print, and then close **U02-SA06.docx**.

Unit 2 Grading Rubrics

The following are suggested rubrics. Instructors should feel free to customize the rubrics to suit their grading standards and/or to adjust the point values.

Suggested Scoring Distribution
  Above average: student completes 80% or more of task
  Average: student completes 70 to 79% of task
  Below average: student completes 69% or less of task

Assessment 1

Step	Task	Criterion	Value	Score*
1	Formatting	Changed font to 12-point Cambria.	2	
2	Typing and formatting	Typed title text centered and set in bold.	2	
3-4	Formatting	Set tabs and then type tabbed text as instructed.	8	
5	Formatting	Changed line spacing to 1.5.	2	
6	Inserting footer	Inserted footer using Blank predesigned footer and typed footer text.	4	
7	Formatting	Selected footer text and changed font to 10-point Cambria bold.	1	
8-9	Saving and printing	Saved, printed, and closed document.	1	
		TOTAL POINTS FOR THIS EXERCISE	20	

Assessment 2

Step	Task	Criterion	Value	Score*
1	Opening and saving	Opened and saved document.	1	
2	Inserting file	Inserted file in document.	4	
3	Formatting	Changed font for entire document to 12-point Cambria.	3	
4	Formatting	Changed section titles to 14-point Candara bold and headings to 12-point Candara bold italic.	4	
5	Formatting	Inserted Retrospect predesigned header and typed student name and current date in header placeholders.	5	
6	Formatting	Inserted page break(s) as needed.	2	
7	Saving and printing	Saved, printed, and closed document.	1	
		TOTAL POINTS FOR THIS EXERCISE	20	

Assessment 3

Step	Task	Criterion	Value	Score*
1	**Opening and saving**	Opened and saved document.	1	
2	**Formatting**	Centered title and applied 20-point Corbel bold formatting to title.	2	
3	**Formatting**	Moved last sentence in first paragraph to end of last paragraph of text.	2	
4	**Formatting**	Typed sentence at end of first paragraph.	2	
5	**Creating drop cap**	Created drop cap for first letter of first paragraph.	4	
6	**Formatting**	Indented first line of second through fourth paragraphs 0.25 inches.	3	
7	**Inserting symbols**	Replaced name *Jessie Levigne* with *Chloë Valérien*.	3	
8	**Formatting and typing**	Moved insertion point to blank line at end of document, pressed Enter, and then typed new text centered and set in 16-point Corbel bold.	2	
9	**Formatting and typing**	Typed workshop dates (with days and without times) and set dates in 11-point Calibri bold.	3	
10	**Changing page orientation**	Changed orientation to Landscape.	3	
11	**Vertically centering text**	Vertically centered text on the page.	3	
12	**Inserting watermark**	Inserted ASAP 1 watermark.	3	
13	**Inserting page border**	Inserted art page border.	3	
14	**Saving and printing**	Saved, printed, and closed document.	1	
		TOTAL POINTS FOR THIS EXERCISE	**35**	

Assessment 4

Step	Task	Criterion	Value	Score*
1	**Researching**	Researched (obtained information on) three favorite vacation spots on Internet.	6	
2	**Creating and typing**	Wrote a memo to instructor containing a paragraph on each vacation spot.	6	
3	**Creating, typing, and formatting**	Created tabs and typed vacation locations and Web addresses.	5	
4	**Inserting footer**	Inserted Blank predesigned footer and typed text in footer.	2	
5-6	**Saving and printing**	Saved, proofread, printed, and closed document.	1	
		TOTAL POINTS FOR THIS EXERCISE	**20**	

Assessment 5

Step	Task	Criterion	Value	Score*
1	**Opening and saving**	Opened and saved document.	1	
2	**Inserting section break**	Inserted Next Page section break at beginning the *REFERENCES* heading.	2	
3	**Inserting file**	Inserted file into current document where indicated.	3	
4-6	**Formatting**	Applied Heading 1 and Heading 2 styles, changed the style set to Lines (Stylish), and changed theme colors to Blue.	5	
7	**Inserting header**	Inserted Austin header and typed text in placeholders as indicated.	4	
8	**Inserting page numbers**	Inserted page numbers on bottom of pages using Accent Bar 1 option.	4	
9	**Inserting cover page**	Inserted Semaphore cover page and typed text in placeholders as indicated.	5	
10	**Formatting**	Indented second paragraph of text below *Television and Film* heading 0.5 inches from left and right margins.	3	
11	**Formatting**	Applied hanging indents to four paragraphs of text below the *REFERENCES* heading.	2	
12	**Saving and printing**	Saved, printed, and closed document.	1	
		TOTAL POINTS FOR THIS EXERCISE	30	

Assessment 6

Step	Task	Criterion	Value	Score*
1	**Opening and saving**	Opened and saved document.	1	
2	**Creating and formatting columns**	Formatted text into two columns with 0.5 spacing and a line between.	6	
3	**Hyphenating**	Manually hyphened text in document.	5	
4-5	**Formatting borders and shading**	Applied font size, borders, and shading to title and headings.	5	
6	**Formatting**	Balanced columns on third page.	2	
7	**Saving and printing**	Saved, printed, and closed document.	1	
		TOTAL POINTS FOR THIS EXERCISE	20	

Unit 2 Model Answers

SECTION 1: UNAUTHORIZED ACCESS

Like uncharted wilderness, the Internet lacks borders. This inherent openness is what makes the Internet so valuable and yet so vulnerable. Over its short life, the Internet has grown so quickly that the legal system has not been able to keep pace. The security risks posed by networks and the Internet can be grouped into three categories: unauthorized access, information theft, and denial of service.

Hackers, individuals who gain access to computers and networks illegally, are responsible for most cases of unauthorized access. Hackers tend to exploit sites and programs that have poor security measures in place. However, they also gain access to more challenging sites by using sophisticated programs and strategies. Many hackers claim they hack merely because they like the challenge of trying to defeat security measures. They rarely have a more malicious motive, and they generally do not aim to destroy or damage the sites that they invade. In fact, hackers dislike being identified with those who seek to cause damage. They refer to hackers with malicious or criminal intent as crackers.

User IDs and Passwords

To gain entry over the Internet to a secure computer system, most hackers focus on finding a working user ID and password combination. User IDs are easy to come by and are generally not secure information. Sending an e-mail, for example, displays the sender's user ID in the return address, making it very public. The only missing element is the password. Hackers know from experience which passwords are common; they have programs that generate thousands of likely passwords and they try them systematically over a period of hours or days.

System Backdoors

Programmers can sometimes inadvertently aid hackers by providing unintentional entrance to networks and information systems. One such unintentional entrance is a system "backdoor," which is a user ID and password that provides the highest level of authorization. Programmers innocently create a "backdoor" in the early days of system development to allow other programmers and team members to access the system to fix problems. Through negligence or by design, the user ID and password are sometimes left behind in the final version of the system. People who know about them can then enter the system, bypassing the security perhaps years later when the backdoor has been forgotten.

Spoofing

A sophisticated way to break into a network via the Internet involves spoofing, which is the process of fooling another computer by pretending to send information from a legitimate source. It works by altering the address that the system automatically puts on every message sent. The address is changed to one that the receiving computer is programmed to accept as a trusted source of information.

U02-SA02.docx (page 1 of 4)

Training Schedule and Costs*

Supervising Others .... November 11, 9 a.m. to 3 p.m. $199

Document Preparation .... November 18, 9 a.m. to 12 noon $115

Proofreading Techniques .... November 18, 1 p.m. to 4 p.m. $89

Utilizing the Internet .... November 20, 10 a.m. to 12 noon $75

Ethics in Business .... November 25, 1 p.m. to 5 p.m. $75

*Registration materials must be turned in by November 4 so final room arrangements can be made.

U02-SA01.docx

SECTION 3: COMPUTER VIRUSES

One of the most familiar risks to computer security is the computer virus. A computer virus is a program that is written by a hacker or cracker and designed to perform some kind of trick upon an unsuspecting victim's computer. In some cases, the trick is mild, such as drawing an offensive image on the screen or changing all of the characters in a document to another language. In other cases, the trick is much more severe, such as reformatting the hard drive and erasing all the data or damaging the motherboard so that it cannot operate properly.

Types of Viruses

Viruses can be categorized by their effects which include nuisance, data destruction, espionage, and hardware destruction. A nuisance virus usually does no real damage; it is just an inconvenience. In contrast, a data-destructive virus is designed to destroy data—the installed programs, documents, databases, and saved e-mails that form the heart of a personal computer and are the most difficult component of a computer to replace. The Espionage viruses are designed to bypass security by creating a backdoor into a system. These viruses do no damage but allow a hacker or cracker to enter the system later for the purpose of stealing data or spying on the work of a competitor. Very rarely, a virus is created that attempts to damage the hardware of the computer system itself. Called hardware-destructive viruses, these bits of programming can weaken or destroy chips, drives, and other components.

Methods of Virus Operation

Viruses operate and are transmitted in a variety of ways. Typically, an e-mail virus is transmitted as an attachment to a message sent over the Internet. E-mail viruses require the victim to click on the attachment to cause the virus to execute. Another common mode of virus transmission is via a macro, which is a small subprogram that allows users to customize and automate certain functions. A macro virus is written specifically for one program, which then becomes infected when it opens a file with the virus stored in one of its macros. Another method of virus transmission involves the boot sector of a floppy disk or hard disk, which contains a variety of information, including how the disk is organized and whether it is capable of loading an operating system. When a disk is left in a drive and the computer reboots, the operating system automatically reads the boot sector to learn about that disk and to attempt to start any operating system on it. A boot sector virus is designed to alter the boot sector of a disk so that whenever the operating system reads the boot sector, the computer automatically becomes infected.

The Trojan horse virus is hidden inside another legitimate program or data file and is transmitted with the other program or file; a stealth virus is designed to hide itself from detection software. Polymorphic viruses also are designed to avoid detection by antivirus software. They alter themselves so antivirus software that works by examining familiar

---

Spyware

Spyware is a type of software that allows an intruder to spy upon someone else's computer. This alarming technology takes advantage of loopholes in the computer's security systems and allows a stranger to witness and record another person's every mouse click or keystroke on the monitor as it occurs. The spy can record activities and gain access to passwords and credit card information. Spyware generally requires the user to install it on the machine that is being spied upon, so it is highly unlikely that random strangers on the Internet could simply begin watching your computer. In the workplace, however, someone might be able to install the software without the victim's knowledge. Disguised as an e-mail greeting, for example, the program can operate like a virus that gets the unwary user to install the spyware unknowingly.

SECTION 2: INFORMATION THEFT

Information can be a company's most valuable possession. Stealing corporate information, a crime included in the category of industrial espionage, is unfortunately both easy to do and difficult to detect. This is due in part to the invisible nature of software and data. If a cracker breaks into a company network and manages to download the company database from the network onto a disk, there is no visible sign to the company that anything is amiss. The original database is still in place, working the same way it always has.

Wireless Device Security

The growing number of wireless devices has created a new opportunity for data theft. Wireless devices such as cameras, Web phones, networked computers, PDAs, and input and output peripherals are inherently less secure than wired devices. Security is quite lax, and in some cases nonexistent, in new wireless technologies for handheld computers and cell phone systems. In a rush to match competition, manufacturers have tended to sacrifice security to move a product to the marketplace faster. Already, viruses are appearing in e-mails for cell phones and PDAs. With little protection available for these new systems, hackers and spies are enjoying a free hand with the new technology. One of the few available security protocols for wireless networks is Wired Equivalent Privacy (WEP), developed in conjunction with the standard for wireless local area networks. Newer versions of WEP with enhanced security features make it more difficult for hackers to intercept and modify data transmissions sent by radio waves or infrared signals.

Data Browsing

Data browsing is a less damaging form of information theft that involves an invasion of privacy. Workers in many organizations have access to networked databases that contain private information about people. Accessing this information without an official reason is against the law. The IRS had a particularly large problem with data browsing in the late 1990s. Some employees were fired and the rest were given specialized training in appropriate conduct.

DATA SECURITY TRAINING

The technical support team is preparing three workshops focusing on protecting and securing company data. This event has been planned in response to several requests from our various departments, so please add these dates to your calendars.

The first workshop, scheduled for Tuesday, April 7, from 9:00 to 11:30 a.m., will cover backing up crucial data. Participants will be briefed on the company's new rotating backup process, which involves backing up data from specific departments on specific days of the week.

The second workshop, scheduled for Wednesday, April 15, from 1:30 to 3:00 p.m., will focus on disaster recovery plan formulation and will include data backup procedures, remote backup locations, and redundant systems.

The third and final workshop, scheduled for Thursday, April 23, from 3:00 to 5:30 p.m., will focus on data security and cover data encryption. Participants will learn about encryption schemes designed to scramble information before transferring it electronically.

For more information or to sign up for a workshop, please contact Chloë Valérien at extension 5560. The workshops are open to all employees; however participants must obtain approval from their immediate supervisor.

Dates to Remember

Tuesday, April 7

Wednesday, April 15

Thursday, April 23

U02-SA03.docx

STUDENT NAME   06/18/2015

patterns cannot detect them. Polymorphic viruses alter themselves randomly as they move from computer to computer, making detection more difficult. Multipartite viruses alter their form of attack. They get their name from their ability to attack in several different ways. They may first infect the boot sector, and then later move on to become a Trojan horse type by infecting a disk file. These viruses are more sophisticated than other computer viruses, and therefore are more difficult to guard against. Yet another type of virus is the logic bomb, which generally sits quietly dormant waiting for a specific event or set of conditions to occur. One famous logic bomb was the widely publicized Michelangelo virus, which infected personal computers and caused them to display a message on the artist's birthday.

U02-SA02.docx (page 4 of 4)

JUNE 18, 2015

COMPUTER TECHNOLOGY

INFORMATION TECHNOLOGY

STUDENT NAME
STUDENT'S SCHOOL NAME

U02-SA05.docx (page 1 of 6)

TO: Instructor Name

FROM: Student Name

DATE: June 18, 2015

SUBJECT: Favorite Vacation Spots

One of my favorite vacation spots is Mackinac Island. Mackinac Island has an "all natural" theme park image. Visitors are able to enjoy a horse and buggy ride around the island or bicycle or roller blade around the island or enjoy the pedestrian walk around the island. Since Mackinac is surrounded by water, it has escaped the vast changes of time. Families enjoy exploring the historic, natural beauty of Mackinac Island State Park, honored by National Geographic as one of the ten finest in America.

Another wonderful vacation spot that lives up to its name is Paradise, Michigan. Paradise, Michigan invites you to explore the shores of Lake Superior, the Tahquamenon River, the Tahquamenon Falls, Whitefish Bay, Whitefish Point, and various rivers and streams. There is an overabundance of water filled recreation and attractions during all our marvelous seasons. Boat, fish, swim, waterski, canoe, and kayak during our summer season.

My final favorite place to vacation is Sault Ste. Marie, which is better known as "the Soo." The Soo is another unspoiled area where the shorelines and wilderness are a refreshing retreat from the hustle and bustle of society. The Soo Locks are a marvel to enjoy and are the busiest locks in the world. While in the Soo, you can go see Tahquamenon Falls, the second largest waterfall east of the Mississippi River, and enjoy the splendor of the Northern Lights as well!

Mackinac Island	www.xxxxxxx.com
Paradise, Michigan	www.xxxxxxx.com
Sault Ste. Marie	www.xxxxxxx.com

sn

U02-SA04.docx

Information for Planning Your Next Vacation

U02-SA04.docx

COMPUTERS IN COMMUNICATIONS

Computers were originally stand-alone devices, incapable of communicating with other computers. This changed in the 1970s and 1980s when the development of special telecommunications hardware and software led to the creation of the first private networks, allowing connected computers to exchange data. Exchanged data took the form of requests for information, replies to requests for information, or instructions on how to run programs stored on the network.

The ability to link computers enables users to communicate and work together efficiently and effectively. Linked computers have become central to the communications industry. They play a vital role in telecommunications, publishing, and news services.

Telecommunications

The industry that provides for communication across distances is called telecommunications. The telephone industry uses computers to switch and route phone calls automatically over telephone lines. In addition to the spoken word, many other kinds of information move over such lines, including faxes and computer data. Data can be sent from computer to computer over telephone lines using a device known as a modem. One kind of data frequently sent by modem is electronic mail, or email, which can be sent from person to person via the Internet or an online service. A more recent innovation in telecommunications is teleconferencing, which allows people in various locations to see and hear one another and thus hold virtual meetings.

Publishing

Just twenty years ago, book manuscripts were typeset mechanically on a typesetting machine and then reproduced on a printing press. Now, anyone who has access to a computer and either a modem or a printer can undertake what has come to be known as electronic publishing. Writers and editors use word processing applications to produce text. Artists and designers use drawing and painting applications to created original graphics, or they use inexpensive scanners to digitize illustrations and photographs (turn them into computer-readable files). Typesetters use personal computers to combine text, illustrations, and photographs. Publishers typically send computer-generated files to printers for production of the film and plates from which books and magazines are printed.

News Services

News providers rely on reporters located worldwide. Reporters use email to send, or upload, their stories to wire services. Increasingly, individuals get daily news reports from online services. News can also be accessed from specific providers, such as the *New York Times* or *U.S.A. Today*, via the Internet. One of the most popular Internet sites provides continuously updated weather reports.

COMPUTERS IN ENTERTAINMENT

Possibilities in the television and film industries have soared with computer technology, especially in production. Computer games have captured the public imagination and created enormous growth in the computer game market.

Television and Film

Many of the spectacular graphics and special effects seen on television and in movies today are created with computers. The original *Star Wars* films, for example, relied heavily on hand-constructed models and hand-drawn graphics. Twenty years after the first release of the films, they were re-released with many new special effects, including futuristic cityscape backgrounds, new alien creatures, and new sounds that were created on computers and added to the films by means of computerized video editing. In an article on special effects, Jaclyn McFadden, an industry expert talked about the evolution of computer simulation.

The film *Jurassic Park* brought computer simulation to a new level by combining puppetry and computer animation to simulate realistic looking dinosaurs. *Toy Story*, released in 1996, was the first wholly computer-animated commercial movie.

Software products are available that automatically format scripts of various kinds. Industry analysts predict that the improvements in computer technology will continue to enhance and improve the visual appeal of television and film media.

Home Entertainment

The advent of powerful desktop personal computers has led to the production of home computer games that rival those of arcade machines in complexity. In the 1970s, computer games such as Pong and Pac-Man captured the public's imagination. Since then, there has been enormous growth in the computer game market. Manufacturers such as Sega and Nintendo produce such games as well as small computer game systems for home use. Typical arcade-style computer games include simulations of boxing, warfare, racing, skiing, and flight.

Other computer games make use of television or of small, independent, hand-held devices. Games are now able to take advantage of three-dimensional graphics that create virtual environments.

UNAUTHORIZED ACCESS

Like uncharted wilderness, the Internet lacks borders. This inherent openness is what makes the Internet so valuable and yet so vulnerable. Over its short life, the Internet has grown so quickly that the legal system has not been able to keep pace. The security risks posed by networks and the Internet can be grouped into three categories: unauthorized access, information theft, and denial of service.

Hackers, individuals who gain access to computers and networks illegally, are responsible for most cases of unauthorized access. Hackers tend to exploit sites and programs that have poor security measures in place. However, they also gain access to more challenging sites by using sophisticated programs and strategies. Many hackers claim they hack merely because they like the challenge of trying to defeat security measures. They rarely have a more malicious motive, and they generally do not aim to destroy or damage the sites that they invade. In fact, hackers dislike being identified with those who seek to cause damage. They refer to hackers with malicious or criminal intent as *crackers*.

User IDs and Passwords

To gain entry over the Internet to a secure computer system, most hackers focus on finding a working user ID and password combination. User IDs are easy to come by and are generally not secure information. Sending an email, for example, displays the sender's user ID in the return address, making it very public. The only

Wired Equivalent Privacy (WEP), developed in conjunction with the standard for wireless local area networks. Newer versions of WEP with enhanced security features make it more difficult for hackers to intercept and modify data transmissions sent by radio waves or infrared signals.

Data Browsing

Data browsing is a less damaging form of information theft that involves an invasion of privacy. Workers in many organizations have access to networked databases that contain private information about people. Accessing this information without an official reason is against the law. The IRS had a particularly large problem with data browsing in the late 1990s. Some employees were fired and the rest were given specialized training in appropriate conduct.

---

missing element is the password. Hackers know from experience which passwords are common; they have programs that generate thousands of likely passwords and they try them systematically over a period of hours or days.

System Backdoors

Programmers can sometimes inadvertently aid hackers by providing unintentional entrance to networks and information systems. One such unintentional entrance is a system "backdoor," which is a user ID and password that provides the highest level of authorization. Programmers innocently create a "backdoor" in the early days of system development to allow other programmers and team members to access the system to fix problems. Through negligence or by design, the user ID and password are sometimes left behind in the final version of the system. People who know about them can then enter the system, bypassing the security perhaps years later, when the backdoor has been forgotten.

Spoofing

A sophisticated way to break into a network via the Internet involves spoofing, which is the process of fooling another computer by pretending to send information from a legitimate source. It works by altering the address that the system automatically puts on every message sent. The address is changed to one that the receiving computer is programmed to accept as a trusted source of information.

Spyware

Spyware is a type of software that allows an intruder to spy upon someone else's computer. This alarming technology takes advantage of loopholes in the computer's security systems and allows a stranger to witness and record another person's every mouse click or keystroke on the monitor as it occurs. The spy can record activities and gain access to passwords and credit card information. Spyware generally requires the user to install it on the machine that is being spied upon, so it is highly unlikely that random strangers on the Internet could simply begin watching your computer. In the workplace, however, someone might be able to install the software without the victim's knowledge. Disguised as an email greeting, for example, the program can operate like a virus that gets the unwary user to install the spyware unknowingly.

INFORMATION THEFT

Information can be a company's most valuable possession. Stealing corporate information, a crime included in the category of industrial espionage, is unfortunately both easy to do and difficult to detect. This is due in part to the invisible nature of software and data. If a cracker breaks into a company network and manages to download the company database from the network onto a disk, there is no visible sign to the company that anything is amiss. The original database is still in place, working the same way it always has.

Wireless Device Security

The growing number of wireless devices has created a new opportunity for data theft. Wireless devices such as cameras, Web phones, networked computers, PDAs, and input and output peripherals are inherently less secure than wired devices. Security is quite lax, and in some cases nonexistent, in new wireless technologies for handheld computers and cell phone systems. In a rush to match competition, manufacturers have tended to sacrifice security to move a product to the marketplace faster. Already, viruses are appearing in emails for cell phones and PDAs. With little protection available for these new systems, hackers and spies are enjoying a free hand with the new technology. One of the few available security protocols for wireless networks is

HOME SAFETY: SMOKE ALARMS

Smoke alarms are one of the simplest and most efficient ways of protecting a home and household members from severe injury or death caused by a home fire. The U.S. Department of Housing and Urban Development (HUD) estimates that a home fire occurs every 66 seconds in the United States. The National Fire Protection Association (NFPA) estimates that having a functioning home smoke alarm in the home reduces by 50 percent the chances of dying from a fire. Unfortunately, approximately one-third of all smoke alarms placed in homes do not function properly.

Types of Smoke Alarms

The two common types of smoke alarms are ionization and photoelectric. An ionization detector is the most common and uses ionization sensors to detect smoke. Ionization detectors are very sensitive and are designed to detect hot and fast-moving fires that produce minimal smoke. Photoelectric detectors detect the presence of visible particulars in the air. Inside the detector a light emitting diode (LED) directs a narrow beam of infrared light across the detection chamber. When smoke or particles enter the chamber, the infrared light beam is scattered. When a preset amount of light is detected, the detector alarm sounds. Photoelectric detectors are not as sensitive as ionization detectors and are designed to detect cool or slow-moving fires that produce a lot of smoke.

Placing Smoke Alarms

For existing homes, smoke alarms usually are required on every habitable level and within the vicinity of all bedrooms. In new construction, the minimum requirements are much greater. All smoke alarms must be interconnected and hooked directly to the electrical wiring and are required inside each bedroom. Smoke alarms are typically not placed in kitchens and bathrooms since the steam may set them off.

Where a smoke alarm is positioned in a home varies depending on the size and layout of the home and where household members sleep at night. Since the primary job of the smoke alarm is to wake up sleeping people, a smoke alarm should be positioned as close as possible to the bedrooms or other places where people frequently sleep. If sleeping areas are separated, each area should have its own detector.

If a person generally sleeps with the bedroom door closed or smokes in bed, a smoke alarm should be placed in the bedroom. A closed bedroom door may offer some protection from fire and smoke coming from outside the room but a smoke alarm outside the bedroom may be difficult to hear. In a multiple-level home with bedrooms upstairs, a smoke alarm should be placed near the top of the stairs. If the home contains a basement, a smoke alarm should be placed on the basement ceiling near the steps to the rest of the house. A smoke alarm should not be placed within six inches of where a wall and ceiling meet or near heating and cooling ducts. Smoke alarms placed in these locations may not receive the flow of smoke required to activate the alarm.

Developing an Escape Plan

Someone in every household should develop an escape plan in case of fire and practice the plan with all members of the home. When developing an escape plan, consider the following:

- Draw a floor plan of the home that identifies at least two methods of escape from every room.

Computer Technology

REFERENCES

Fuller, F. & Larson, B. (2014). *Computers: understanding technology* (pp. 121-125). St. Paul, MN: Paradigm Publishing.

McFadden, J. M. (2013). *The art of special effects* (pp. 45-48). Los Angeles: Richardson-Dryers Publishing House.

North, J. & Amundsen, R. (2015). *Computer gaming*. Cleveland, OH: Blue Horizon Publishers.

Ziebel, K. M. & Weisenburg, H. L. (2013). *Computers and publishing*. Seattle, WA: Greenlake Publishing House.

5 | Page

according to the manufacturer's instructions. Replace batteries immediately when moving into a new home. A photoelectric detector contains a lamp that needs to be replaced on a periodic basis. Keep a supply of replacement lamps on hand to replace in the detector as needed.

- Practice evacuating the home while blindfolded since the amount of smoke generated by a house fire will impair vision.

- Practice staying low to the ground while escaping.

- Practice stopping, dropping to the ground, and rolling in case clothing catches on fire.

- Identify a safe meeting place outside the home.

- Practice alerting other members of the household.

Safety Tips

Along with the development of an escape plan, a member of the household should post emergency telephone numbers near the telephone. However, in the case of a home fire, household members should leave the house first and then place the emergency call from a safe location. A person in a multiple-level home should purchase collapsible ladders and have each household member practice using them. A-B-C type fire extinguishers should be available in the home and each household member should know how to use them. Combustible materials should not be stored in closed areas or near a heat source.

When cooking in the home, keep the stove area clean and clear of combustibles such as bags and boxes and other appliances. If a fire does occur in the kitchen, put a lid over the burning pan or use a fire extinguisher. Never pour water on grease fires.

Have a certified electrician check all electrical wiring in the house and replace any frayed or cracked wiring. Make sure no wiring is located under rugs, over nails, or in high traffic areas and do not overload outlets or extension cords.

All outlets should have cover plates and no wiring should be exposed. A homeowner should only purchase appliances and electrical devices that have a label indicating that they have been inspected by a testing laboratory such as Underwriter's Laboratories (UL) or Factory Mutual (FM).

For additional safe tips, contact the local fire department, the Office of the State Fire Commissioner, or a chapter of the American Red Cross.

Taking Care of Smoke Alarms

A member of the household should establish a system for monitoring and taking care of all smoke alarms in the home. Smoke alarms require regular testing and battery and lamp replacements.

Monthly Testing: Once a month, a member of the household should test all smoke alarms in the home. To test an ionization detector, hold a burning candle approximately six inches under the detector. To test a photoelectric detector, extinguish the candle flame and let visible smoke draft into the detector. The smoke alarm's alarm should sound within twenty seconds. Some detectors have a more refined test system that simulates the presence of smoke. Check the smoke alarm package to determine if the smoke alarm has this feature.

Cleaning Detectors: Dust and cobwebs can interfere with the operation of a smoke alarm so detectors should be cleaned on a regular basis and according to the manufacturer's instructions. Do not remove the detector's cover and use a standard vacuum cleaner hose and attachment when cleaning the detector.

Replacing Batteries and Lamps: If the battery power is running low in a smoke alarm, the detector emits a low-power warning sound. When this happens, remove the battery and replace it with a new one. Replace batteries

Unit 3 Instructions

Assessment 1

1. At a blank document, create your own letterhead using the following guidelines:

    a. Change the top margin to 0.5 inch.

    b. Use your name and address in the letterhead document and include at least the following elements in the letterhead: a drawn shape or shapes, a drawn line, and WordArt or a clip art image. Apply formatting to the elements in your letterhead to make it visually appealing.

    c. Your letterhead should not be more than 1.5 inches tall.

2. Save the document and name it **U03-SA01**.

3. Print and then close **U03-SA01.docx**.

Assessment 2

1. At a blank document, create a SmartArt graphic using the Basic Chevron Process graphic.

2. Add a shape to the SmartArt graphic and then type the following text in the specified shapes:

    a. Type **Design** in the first shape (at the left side).

    b. Type **Develop** in the second shape.

    c. Type **Test** in the third shape.

    d. Type **Revise** in the fourth shape.

3. Make the following changes to the SmartArt graphic:

    a. Make sure the entire SmartArt graphic is selected (not a shape in the graphic) and then change the SmartArt style to Brick Scene.

    b. Change the colors to Colorful Range - Accent Colors 5 to 6.

    c. Change the text fill color to Yellow.

    d. Apply the Orange, 8 pt glow, Accent color 2 glow text effect.

    e. Change the position of the graphic to Position in Top Center with Square Text Wrapping.

4. Save the document and name it **U03-SA02**.

5. Print and then close **U03-SA02.docx**.

Assessment 3

1. At a blank document, create a table with three columns and ten rows as shown below with the following specifications:

    a. Merge cells A1 through C1 as shown below.

    b. Merge cells A2 through C2 as shown below.

    c. Change the row height of row 1 to 0.6 inch, the row height of row 2 to 0.4 inch, and the row height of the remaining rows to 0.3 inch.

    d. Type the text in cells as shown in the table below.

2. Change the font size of the text in the first row to 18 points.

3. Change the font size of the text in the second row to 14 points.

4. Align center and bold the text in the first three rows.

5. Apply Green, Accent 6, Lighter 40% shading to the first and third rows.

6. Apply Green, Accent 6, Lighter 80% shading to the second row.

7. Save the document and name it **U03-SA03**.

8. Print and then close **U03-SA03.docx**.

COLEMAN DEVELOPMENT CORPORATION		
Community Development Committee Members		
Name and Title	**Company**	**Current Address**

Assessment 4

1. At a blank document, type **Screenshots** and then press the Enter key five times.

2. Select *Screenshots* and then create WordArt with the text using the Fill - White, Outline - Accent 1, Shadow option.

3. Make the following changes to the WordArt:

   a. Apply the Green, Accent 6, Lighter 40% text fill.

   b. Change the text outline color to Light Blue.

   c. Change the position of the WordArt to Position in Top Center with Square Text Wrapping.

   d. Select the *Screenshots* WordArt text and then change the point size to 48 points.

4. Save the document and name it **U03-SA04**.

5. Open **U03-SA02.docx** and then make **U03-SA04.docx** the active document.

6. Move the insertion point to the end of the document and then change the paragraph alignment to Center.

7. Insert a screenshot of the screen containing the **U03-SA02.docx** document.

8. Make **U03-SA02.docx** the active document and then close the document.

9. With **U03-SA04.docx** the active document, move the insertion point below the screenshot image.

10. Open **U03-SA03.docx**.

11. Make **U03-SA04.docx** the active document and then make a screenshot clipping of just the table in the **U03-SA03.docx** document.

12. Make **U03-SA03.docx** the active document and then close the document.

13. Save, print, and then close **U03-SA04.docx**.

Assessment 5

1. At a blank document, change the page orientation to landscape, change the left margin to 1.5 inches, and change the vertical alignment of the text on the page to Center.

2. Type the text shown below.

3. Select the text you just typed, change the font to 24-point Copperplate Gothic Bold in Dark Blue color, and then change the line spacing to 2.0.

4. Insert an appropriate clip art image using the word *finance* to find an image. Change the text wrapping for the clip art image to Tight, position the image at the right side of the text, and then size the image so it fills the area between the lines of text and the right margin. Make other adjustments to improve the visual display of the clip art image.

5. Save the document and name it **U03-SA05**.

6. Print and then close **U03-SA05.docx**.

Financial Planning
October 23, 2015
Miller Auditorium
2:00 p.m. to 4:30 p.m.

Assessment 6

1. At a blank document, use the text shown in the table below to create a pie chart using the 3-D Pie chart type option.

2. After creating the pie chart, make the following changes to the chart:

   a. Apply the Layout 1 chart layout.

   b. Apply the Style 8 chart style.

   c. Apply the Subtle Effect - Gold, Accent 4 shape style.

   d. Change the position of the chart to Position in Middle Center with Square Text Wrapping.

   e. Change the font size of the title *Employees* to 24 points.

3. Save the document and name it **U03-SA06**.

4. Print and then close **U03-SA06.docx**.

	Employees
Full-time	52%
Part-time	24%
Exempt	15%
Temporary	9%

Unit 3 Grading Rubrics

The following are suggested rubrics. Instructors should feel free to customize the rubrics to suit their grading standards and/or to adjust the point values.

*Suggested Scoring Distribution
  Above average: student completes 80% or more of task
  Average: student completes 70 to 79% of task
  Below average: student completes 69% or less of task

Assessment 1

Step	Task	Criterion	Value	Score*
1	**Creating and formatting**	Created letterhead with a top margin of 0.5 inch and included at least a drawn shape, a drawn line, and WordArt or a clip art image. Included name and address in letterhead.	9	
2-3	**Saving and printing**	Saved, printed, and closed document.	1	
		TOTAL POINTS FOR THIS EXERCISE	10	

Assessment 2

Step	Task	Criterion	Value	Score*
1	**Creating SmartArt**	Created SmartArt graphic using Basic Chevron Process diagram.	6	
2	**Formatting SmartArt**	Added shape to SmartArt graphic and typed text in shapes.	3	
3	**Modifying SmartArt**	Changed SmartArt style, colors, text fill color, text effect, and position.	5	
4-5	**Saving and printing**	Saved, printed, and closed document.	1	
		TOTAL POINTS FOR THIS EXERCISE	15	

Assessment 3

Step	Task	Criterion	Value	Score*
1	**Creating and modifying a table**	Created table with three columns and ten rows. Merged cells, changed row heights, and typed text in table.	9	
2-6	**Formatting**	Changed text font size and alignment, applied bold formatting, and applied shading to rows.	5	
7-8	**Saving and printing**	Saved, printed, and closed document.	1	
		TOTAL POINTS FOR THIS EXERCISE	15	

Assessment 4

Step	Task	Criterion	Value	Score*
1-2	**Creating WordArt**	Typed text and then created WordArt with text.	6	
3	**Modifying WordArt**	Changed WordArt text fill, text outline color, position, and text point size.	5	
4-5	**Saving and opening**	Saved document, opened previously created document, and made other document active.	2	
6	**Formatting**	Changed paragraph alignment.	1	
7	**Inserting screenshot**	Inserted screenshot of U03-SA02.docx document screen.	6	
8-10	**Closing and opening**	Closed document and opened previously created document.	2	
11	**Inserting screenshot clipping**	Inserted screenshot clipping of table in U03-SA03.docx.	6	
12	**Closing**	Made document active and then closed document.	1	
13	**Saving and printing**	Saved, printed, and closed document.	1	
		TOTAL POINTS FOR THIS EXERCISE	30	

Assessment 5

Step	Task	Criterion	Value	Score*
1	**Formatting**	Changed page orientation, left margin, and vertical alignment.	5	
2-3	**Typing and formatting**	Typed text and then changed font, font size, font color, and line spacing.	3	
4	**Inserting and formatting clip art image**	Inserted clip art image and changed text wrapping, position, size, and other formatting of image to improve visual display.	6	
5-6	**Saving and printing**	Saved, printed, and closed document.	1	
		TOTAL POINTS FOR THIS EXERCISE	15	

Assessment 6

Step	Task	Criterion	Value	Score*
1	**Creating pie chart**	Created pie chart using 3-D Pie chart type option.	7	
2	**Formatting chart**	Changed chart layout, chart style, and shape style; changed chart position; and changed font size of chart title.	7	
3-4	**Saving and printing**	Saved, printed, and closed document.	1	
		TOTAL POINTS FOR THIS EXERCISE	15	

Unit 3 Model Answers

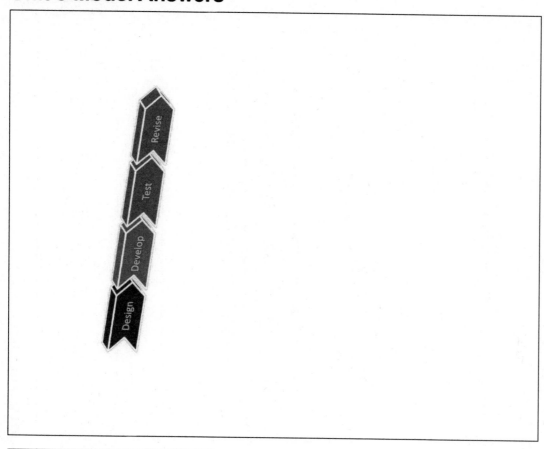

STUDENT NAME
123 MAIN STREET
MIDTOWN, CA 94203

(Note: The letterhead students create will vary from what is shown here.)

U03-SA02.docx

U03-SA01.docx

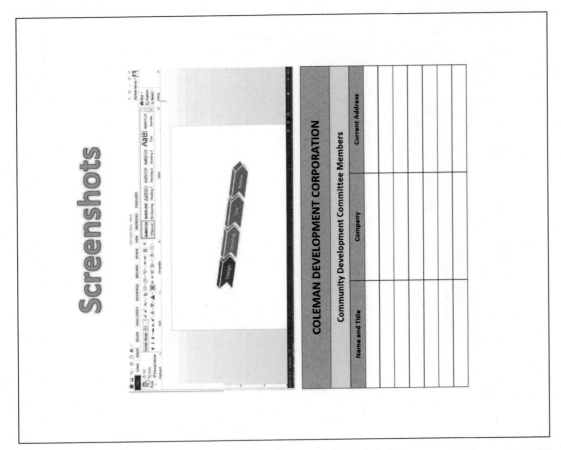

U03-SA04.docx

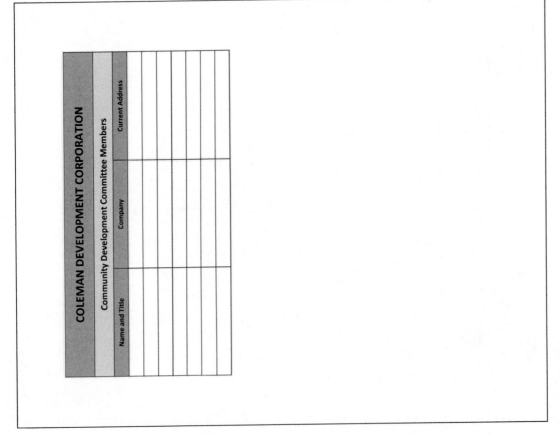

U03-SA03.docx

Signature Word 2013 Supplemental Assessments

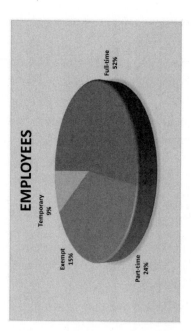

FINANCIAL PLANNING

OCTOBER 23, 2015

MILLER AUDITORIUM

2:00 P.M. TO 4:30 P.M.

Unit 4 Instructions

Assessment 1

1. Open **CCCLtrhd.docx** (located in the **SA-StudentDataFiles** folder) and then save the document with Save As and name it **U04-SA01-MD**.

2. Look at the information shown in Figure SA-U4.1 and SA-Figure U4.2 below. Use the Mail Merge feature to prepare five letters using the information shown in the figures. Name the data source file **U04-SA01-DS**.

3. Prepare the main document as a business letter (see Appendix D in your textbook) using the information shown in Figure SA-U4.1 with the following specifications:

   a. Choose the No Spacing style.

   b. Insert the current date at the beginning of the letter.

   c. Insert the appropriate greeting line field and change the comma in the greeting line to a colon.

   d. Format the table with the following specification: AutoFit the columns in the table; apply the White, Background 1, Darker 15% shading to the first column in the table; and center the table horizontally.

   e. Type the appropriate complimentary close and type your first and last names in the complimentary close.

   f. Type your initials and the document name in the appropriate location in the letter.

   g. Save the **U04-SA01-MD.docx** main document.

4. Before merging the letters, check for errors.

5. Complete the merge and insert the following fill-in information for each letter:

   Record 1 = check in

   Record 2 = course check points

   Record 3 = finish-line photos

   Record 4 = clean up

   Record 5 = concessions

6. Save the merged letters document and name it **U04-SA01-CCCLtrs**.

7. Print and then close **U04-SA01-CCCLtrs.docx**.

8. Save and then close **U04-SA01-MD.docx**.

Figure SA-U4.1

Mr. Mason Mitchell 2350 Seven Pines Drive Creve Coeur, MO 63141	Ms. Courtney Cerulo 11250 Holtwood Street Chesterfield, MO 63017	Mr. Todd Baum 3290 Button Court Creve Coeur, MO 63141
Mr. Jack Clark 130 Rascal Way St. Louis, MO 63146	Mrs. Janice Shafer 3203 Emerald Drive Creve Coeur, MO 63141	

Figure SA-U4.2

Thank you for volunteering to help at this year's Park Rescue Run to be held at Creve Coeur Park on Saturday, October 24. Below you will find a tentative schedule for the day's events. You are scheduled to help with (insert fill-in field for the assignment); please arrive at the appropriate location 15 minutes before the assignment begins.

7:30 a.m.	Runners check in, concessions open
8:00 a.m.	Course check points assigned
8:15 a.m.	Race begins
11:00 a.m.	Finish-line photos begin
12:30 p.m. to 3:00 p.m.	Barbeque and games
3:30 p.m.	Clean up

Please encourage your friends and neighbors to participate in this event; the proceeds will be used to enhance the park that everyone enjoys. Each runner will receive a t-shirt, and all volunteers will receive a cap commemorating their participation.

Assessment 2

1. Use the Mail Merge feature to create mailing labels with the Avery US Letter 5810 Address Labels product. Use the data source file **U04-SA01-DS.mdb** that you created in Assessment 1 for the labels.

2. Display the Mail Merge Recipients dialog box, sort the records in ascending order by zip code, and select all recipients *except* Mrs. Janice Shafer.

3. Complete the merge and then save the labels document with the name **U04-SA02-Labels**.

4. Print and then close **U04-SA02-Labels.docx**.

5. Close the labels main document without saving it.

Assessment 3

1. At a blank document, click the No Spacing style, and then create the document shown below with the following specifications:

   a. Change the font to 11-point Cambria.

   b. Center and bold the title as shown.

   c. Choose your own tab settings for the text in columns.

   d. When typing the text for each row, be sure to press the Tab key before typing the first column of text.

2. Select the columns of text and change the line spacing to 1.5.

3. Sort the columns in ascending order by the course title (Field 2).

4. Move the insertion point immediately right of the title and insert the following comment: *Registration materials must be turned in by November 2 so final room arrangements can be made.* Select the comment text and then change the font to 11-point Cambria.

5. Save the document and name it **U04-SA03**.

6. Print and then close **U04-SA03.docx**.

<table>
<tr><td colspan="3" align="center">Training Schedule and Costs</td></tr>
</table>

Training Schedule and Costs

Supervising Others . . . . November 16, 9 a.m. to 3 p.m. $199

Document Preparation . . . . .November 23, 9 a.m. to noon $115

Proofreading Techniques. . . . . . . November 23, 1 p.m. to 4 p.m. $89

Utilizing the Internet. . . . . November 25, 10 a.m. to noon $75

Ethics in Business . . . . November 25, 1 p.m. to 5 p.m. $140

Assessment 4

1. Open **CompAdvantage.docx** (located in the **SA-StudentDataFiles** folder) and then save the document with Save As and name it **U04-SA04**.

2. Select the entire document, change the font to 11-point Cambria, and change the line spacing to single.

3. Set the title in 14-point Cambria bold and center the title. Move the insertion point immediately right of the title and then press the Enter key once.

4. Move the insertion point to the left margin of the first paragraph of text in the document and then insert a continuous section break.

5. Format the body of the document into two columns with a line between.

6. Add 6 points of spacing before and 3 points of spacing after each of the headings in the document (*Speed*, *Accuracy*, *Versatility*, *Storage*, and *Communications*).

7. Move the insertion point immediately right of the period that ends the paragraph of text below the *Storage* heading, press the Enter key twice, and then insert the table shown below. Autofit the contents of the table, apply the Grid Table 4 - Accent 5 table style, and remove the check mark from the *First Column* check box. Horizontally center the table.

8. Balance the columns of text on the last page (page 2).

9. Select the table and then apply the Keep with next feature.

10. Create a footer with the following specifications:

    a. Change the font to 10-point Cambria bold and then type **The Computer Advantage** at the left margin.

    b. Press the Tab key to move the insertion point to the center tab in the footer and then insert a clip art image of a computer. Change the width of the computer image to 0.5 inch.

    c. Insert page numbering at the right margin of the footer.

11. Save, print, and then close **U04-SA04.docx**.

Popular Storage Devices
CDs and DVDs
External hard drives
Portable USB drives
Online websites

Assessment 5

1. Open **WritingProcess.docx** (located in the **SA-StudentDataFiles** folder) and save the document with the name **U04-SA05**.

2. Insert a next page section break at the beginning of the title *EDITING AND PROOFREADING* located on page 3.

3. Apply chapter multilevel list numbering.

4. Move the insertion point to the beginning of the document and then create an odd page header that prints *Writing and Editing* at the left margin and your name at the right margin. Create an even page header that prints your name at the left margin and *Writing and Editing* at the right margin.

5. Create an odd page footer that inserts page numbering at the bottom right margin of each page and includes chapter page numbering. Create an even page footer that inserts page numbering at the bottom left margin of each page and includes chapter page numbering.

6. Move the insertion point to the chapter 2 title and then change the page numbering so its starts with 1 and includes chapter page numbering.

7. Move the insertion point to the end of the sentence below the chapter 1 title and then insert the comment **Review the company's procedures manual and determine if it includes specific information on writing and formatting business correspondence.**

8. Move the insertion point to the end of the paragraph below the *Define Your Purpose* heading and then insert the comment **Provide several examples of company correspondence.**

9. Turn on track changes and then make the following changes:

    a. Add this bulleted item to the end of the bulleted list in the *Identify Your Reader* section: **How is the reader likely to feel about my message?**

    b. Delete the bulleted item *Causes leading to some effect* that displays in the second group of bulleted items in the *Select Your Information and Plan How to Organize It* section.

    c. Delete the second paragraph of text below the heading *Make Strong Paragraphs Your Building Blocks*.

10. Save the document and then print the document with markups.

11. Accept all of the changes.

12. Save, print, and then close **U04-SA05.docx**.

Unit 4 Grading Rubrics

The following are suggested rubrics. Instructors should feel free to customize the rubrics to suit their grading standards and/or to adjust the point values.

*Suggested Scoring Distribution
Above average: student completes 80% or more of task
Average: student completes 70 to 79% of task
Below average: student completes 69% or less of task

Assessment 1

Step	Task	Criterion	Value	Score*
1	**Opening and saving**	Opened and saved document.	1	
2	**Creating data source file**	Created data source file for merging.	10	
3	**Creating main document**	Created main document in business letter format including typing text, inserting fields, creating and formatting table, and inserting Fill-in field.	10	

Step	Task	Criterion	Value	Score*
4-5	**Checking for errors and merging documents**	Checked main document for errors, merged main document with data source file, and typed appropriate text in Fill-in field for each record.	8	
6-8	**Printing and saving**	Saved, printed, and closed the documents.	1	
		TOTAL POINTS FOR THIS EXERCISE	30	

Assessment 2

Step	Task	Criterion	Value	Score*
1	**Creating labels main document**	Created labels main document and used existing data source file.	5	
2	**Sorting**	Sorted contents of **U04-SA01-DS.mdb** by zip code and selected all records *except* Mrs. Janice Shafer.	6	
3	**Merging and saving**	Merged labels main document with data source and then saved merged labels document.	3	
4-5	**Printing and closing**	Printed labels document and then closed documents.	1	
		TOTAL POINTS FOR THIS EXERCISE	15	

Assessment 3

Step	Task	Criterion	Value	Score*
1	**Formatting and typing**	Applied No Spacing style, changed font to 11-point Cambria, centered and bolded title, set tabs, and typed text.	8	
2	**Formatting**	Changed line spacing of columns to 1.5.	1	
3	**Sorting columns**	Sorted course titles in ascending order.	5	
4	**Inserting comment**	Inserted comment and then selected and applied 11-point Cambria to comment text.	5	
5-6	**Saving and printing**	Saved, printed, and closed document.	1	
		TOTAL POINTS FOR THIS EXERCISE	20	

Assessment 4

Step	Task	Criterion	Value	Score*
1	**Opening and saving**	Opened and saved document.	1	
2-4	**Formatting**	Changed font for entire document to 11-point Cambria, changed line spacing to single, changed font size of title text to 14 points and bolded and centered title, and inserted a continuous section break.	4	

Step	Task	Criterion	Value	Score*
5	**Formatting**	Formatted body of document into two columns with line between.	6	
6	**Formatting**	Applied 6 points of spacing before and 3 points of spacing after each heading in document.	3	
7	**Creating and formatting table**	Inserted table in document and applied formatting so table displayed as shown in instructions.	8	
8	**Formatting**	Balanced columns of text on second page.	2	
9	**Formatting**	Applied Keep with text feature to table.	3	
10	**Inserting footer**	Inserted footer that printed *The Computer Advantage* at left margin, inserted clip art image of computer at center of footer, and inserted page number at right margin of footer.	7	
11	**Saving and printing**	Saved, printed, and closed document.	1	
		TOTAL POINTS FOR THIS EXERCISE	35	

Assessment 5

Step	Task	Criterion	Value	Score*
1	**Opening and saving**	Opened and saved document.	1	
2	**Formatting**	Inserted next page section break.	1	
3	**Applying multilevel list numbering**	Applied chapter multilevel list numbering.	4	
4	**Creating headers**	Created odd page header and even page header.	7	
5	**Creating footers**	Created odd page footer and even page footer.	7	
6	**Inserting and formatting page numbering**	Inserted page numbering at bottom right margin of each page that included chapter page numbering.	6	
7-8	**Inserting comments**	Inserted comments in document.	4	
9	**Tracking changes**	Turned on track changes and made edits to document.	3	
10	**Saving and printing**	Saved document and then printed document with markups.	3	
11	**Accepting changes**	Accepted all tracked changes.	3	
12	**Saving and printing**	Saved, printed, and closed document.	1	
		TOTAL POINTS FOR THIS EXERCISE	40	

Unit 4 Model Answers

CITY OF CREVE COEUR

Current Date

Mr. Mason Mitchell
2350 Seven Pines Drive
Creve Coeur, MO 63141

Dear Mr. Mitchell:

Thank you for volunteering to help at this year's Park Rescue Run to be held at Creve Coeur Park on Saturday, October 24. Below you will find a tentative schedule for the day's events. You are scheduled to help with check in; please arrive at the appropriate location 15 minutes before the assignment begins.

7:30 a.m.	Runners check in, concessions open
8:00 a.m.	Course check points assigned
8:15 a.m.	Race begins
11:00 a.m.	Finish-line photos begin
12:30 p.m. to 3:00 p.m.	Barbeque and games
3:30 p.m.	Clean up

Please encourage your friends and neighbors to participate in this event; the proceeds will be used to enhance the park that everyone enjoys. Each runner will receive a t-shirt, and all volunteers will receive a cap commemorating their participation.

Very truly yours,

Student Name

SN
U04-SA01-MD.docx

CITY OF CREVE COEUR

Current Date

Ms. Courtney Cerulo
11250 Holtwood Street
Chesterfield, MO 63017

Dear Ms. Cerulo:

Thank you for volunteering to help at this year's Park Rescue Run to be held at Creve Coeur Park on Saturday, October 24. Below you will find a tentative schedule for the day's events. You are scheduled to help with course check points; please arrive at the appropriate location 15 minutes before the assignment begins.

7:30 a.m.	Runners check in, concessions open
8:00 a.m.	Course check points assigned
8:15 a.m.	Race begins
11:00 a.m.	Finish-line photos begin
12:30 p.m. to 3:00 p.m.	Barbeque and games
3:30 p.m.	Clean up

Please encourage your friends and neighbors to participate in this event; the proceeds will be used to enhance the park that everyone enjoys. Each runner will receive a t-shirt, and all volunteers will receive a cap commemorating their participation.

Very truly yours,

Student Name

SN
U04-SA01-MD.docx

CITY OF CREVE COEUR

Current Date

Mr. Todd Baum
3290 Button Court
Creve Coeur, MO 63141

Dear Mr. Baum:

Thank you for volunteering to help at this year's Park Rescue Run to be held at Creve Coeur Park on Saturday, October 24. Below you will find a tentative schedule for the day's events. You are scheduled to help with finish-line photos; please arrive at the appropriate location 15 minutes before the assignment begins.

7:30 a.m.	Runners check in, concessions open
8:00 a.m.	Course check points assigned
8:15 a.m.	Race begins
11:00 a.m.	Finish-line photos begin
12:30 p.m. to 3:00 p.m.	Barbeque and games
3:30 p.m.	Clean up

Please encourage your friends and neighbors to participate in this event; the proceeds will be used to enhance the park that everyone enjoys. Each runner will receive a t-shirt, and all volunteers will receive a cap commemorating their participation.

Very truly yours,

Student Name

SN
U04-SA01-MD.docx

CITY OF CREVE COEUR

Current Date

Mr. Jack Clark
130 Rascal Way
St. Louis, MO 63146

Dear Mr. Clark:

Thank you for volunteering to help at this year's Park Rescue Run to be held at Creve Coeur Park on Saturday, October 24. Below you will find a tentative schedule for the day's events. You are scheduled to help with clean up; please arrive at the appropriate location 15 minutes before the assignment begins.

7:30 a.m.	Runners check in, concessions open
8:00 a.m.	Course check points assigned
8:15 a.m.	Race begins
11:00 a.m.	Finish-line photos begin
12:30 p.m. to 3:00 p.m.	Barbeque and games
3:30 p.m.	Clean up

Please encourage your friends and neighbors to participate in this event; the proceeds will be used to enhance the park that everyone enjoys. Each runner will receive a t-shirt, and all volunteers will receive a cap commemorating their participation.

Very truly yours,

Student Name

SN
U04-SA01-MD.docx

Left letter (U04-SA01-CCCltrs.docx)

CITY OF CREVE COEUR

Current Date

Mrs. Janice Shafer
3203 Emerald Drive
Creve Coeur, MO 63141

Dear Mrs. Shafer:

Thank you for volunteering to help at this year's Park Rescue Run to be held at Creve Coeur Park on Saturday, October 24. Below you will find a tentative schedule for the day's events. You are scheduled to help with concessions; please arrive at the appropriate location 15 minutes before the assignment begins.

7:30 a.m.	Runners check in, concessions open
8:00 a.m.	Course check points assigned
8:15 a.m.	Race begins
11:00 a.m.	Finish-line photos begin
12:30 p.m. to 3:00 p.m.	Barbeque and games
3:30 p.m.	Clean up

Please encourage your friends and neighbors to participate in this event; the proceeds will be used to enhance the park that everyone enjoys. Each runner will receive a t-shirt, and all volunteers will receive a cap commemorating their participation.

Very truly yours,

Student Name

SN
U04-SA01-MD.docx

Right letter (U04-SA01-MD.docx)

CITY OF CREVE COEUR

Current Date

«AddressBlock»

«GreetingLine»

Thank you for volunteering to help at this year's Park Rescue Run to be held at Creve Coeur Park on Saturday, October 24. Below you will find a tentative schedule for the day's events. You are scheduled to help with concessions; please arrive at the appropriate location 15 minutes before the assignment begins.

7:30 a.m.	Runners check in, concessions open
8:00 a.m.	Course check points assigned
8:15 a.m.	Race begins
11:00 a.m.	Finish-line photos begin
12:30 p.m. to 3:00 p.m.	Barbeque and games
3:30 p.m.	Clean up

Please encourage your friends and neighbors to participate in this event; the proceeds will be used to enhance the park that everyone enjoys. Each runner will receive a t-shirt, and all volunteers will receive a cap commemorating their participation.

Very truly yours,

Student Name

SN
U04-SA01-MD.docx

Training Schedule and Costs

Document Preparation .... November 23, 9 a.m. to noon $115
Ethics in Business .... November 25, 1 p.m. to 5 p.m. $140
Proofreading Techniques .... November 23, 1 p.m. to 4 p.m. $89
Supervising Others .... November 16, 9 a.m. to 3 p.m. $199
Utilizing the Internet .... November 25, 10 a.m. to noon $75

U04-SA03.docx

Ms. Courtney Cerulo
11250 Holtwood Street
Chesterfield, MO 63017

Mr. Jack Clark
130 Rascal Way
St. Louis, MO 63146

Mr. Todd Baum
3290 Button Court
Creve Coeur, MO 63141

Mr. Mason Mitchell
2350 Seven Pines Drive
Creve Coeur, MO 63141

U04-SA02-Labels.docx

THE COMPUTER ADVANTAGE

Before the early 1980s, computers were unknown to the average person. Many people had never even seen a computer, let alone used one. The few computers that existed were relatively large, bulky devices confined to secure computer centers in corporate or government facilities. Referred to as mainframes, these computers were maintenance intensive, requiring special climate-controlled conditions and several full-time operators for each machine. Because early mainframes were expensive and difficult to operate, usage was restricted to computer programmers and scientists, who used them to perform complex operations, such as processing payrolls and designing sophisticated military weaponry.

Beginning in the early 1980s, the computer world changed dramatically with the introduction of microcomputers, also called personal computers (PCs). These relatively small computers were considerably more affordable and much easier to use than their mainframe ancestors. Within a few years, ownership of personal computers became widespread in the workplace, and today, the personal computer is a standard appliance in homes and schools.

Today's computers come in a variety of shapes and size and differ significantly in computing capability, price, and speed. Whatever their size, cost, or power, all computers offer advantages over manual technologies in the areas of speed, accuracy, versatility, storage capabilities, and communications capabilities.

Speed

Computers operate with lightening-like speed, and processing speeds are increasing as computer manufacturers introduce new and improved models. Contemporary personal computers are capable of executing billions of program instructions in one second. Some larger computers, such as supercomputers, can execute trillions of instructions per second, a rate important for processing huge amounts of data involved in forecasting weather, monitoring space shuttle flights, and managing other data-intensive applications.

Accuracy

People sometimes blame human errors and mistakes on a computer. In truth, if a computer user enters correct data and uses accurate programs, computers are extremely accurate. A popular expression among computers professionals is "garbage in—garbage out" (GIGO), which means that if inaccurate programs and/or data are entered into a computer for processing, the resulting output will also be inaccurate. The computer user is responsible for entering data correctly and making certain that programs are correct.

Versatility

Computers are perhaps the most versatile of all machines or devices. They can perform a variety of personal, business, and scientific applications. Families use computers for entertainment, communications, budgeting, online shopping, completing homework assignments, playing games, and listening to music. Banks conduct money transfers, account withdrawals, and the payment of checks via computer. Retailers use computers to process sales transactions and to check on the availability of products. Manufacturers can manage their entire production, warehousing, and selling processes with computerized systems. Schools access computers for keeping records, conducting distance learning classes, scheduling events, and analyzing budgets. Universities, government agencies, hospitals, and scientific organizations conduct life-enhancing research using computers. Perhaps the most ambitious such computer-based scientific research of all time is the Human Genome Project. Completed in April of 2003, this program was more than two years ahead of schedule and at a cost considerably lower than originally forecast. This project

---

represented an international effort the sequence three billion DNA (deoxyribonucleic acid) letters in the human genome, which is the collection of gene types that comprise every person. Scientists from all over the world can now access the genome database and use the information to research ways to improve human health and fight disease.

Storage

Storage is a defining computer characteristic and is one of the features that revolutionized early computing, for it made computers incredibly flexible. A computer is capable of accepting and storing programs and data. Once stored in the computer, a user can access a program again and again to process different data. Computers can store huge amounts of data in comparably tiny physical spaces. For example, one compact disk can store about 109,000 pages of magazine text, and the capacities of internal storage devices are many times larger.

Popular Storage Devices
CDs and DVDs
External hard drives
Portable USB drives
Online websites

Communications

Most modern computers contain special equipment and programs that allow them to communicate with other computers through telephone lines, cable connections, and satellites. A structure in which computers are linked together using special programs and equipment is a network. Newer communications technologies allow users to exchange information over wireless networks using wireless devices such as personal digital assistants (PDAs), notebook computers, cell phones, and pagers.

A network can be relatively small or quite large. A local area network (LAN) is one confined to a relatively small geographical area, such as a building, factory, or college campus. A wide area network (WAN) spans a large geographical area and might connect a company's manufacturing plants dispersed throughout North America. Constant, quick connections along with other computer technologies have helped boost productivity for manufacturers.

CHAPTER 1 THE WRITING PROCESS

To write clear and concise business correspondence, consider the following points[sx1].

Define Your Purpose

Knowing your purpose for writing is the foundation for any written project. Before you begin writing an email, letter, or other document, ask yourself what you are trying to accomplish and the purpose for writing[sx2].

Identify Your Reader

As you define your purpose, you will need to develop a good picture of the person who will be reading your document. Ask yourself:

- Who is my reader?
- What do I know about my reader that will help determine the best approach?
- Is the audience one person or a group?
- Is my reader a coworker, a subordinate, a superior, or a customer?
- How is the reader likely to feel about my message?

Select Your Information and Plan How to Organize It

Once you have defined your purpose and identified your reader, decide what information you will include. Ask yourself questions such as:

- What does my reader want or need to know?
- What information should I include?
- What information will help my reader respond positively?
- What information should I not include?

To answer these questions, you may find spending a few minutes listing all of the information you *could* include in your document helpful. You may also find writing a rough draft of your document helpful. Write the draft quickly, including any information that comes to you. Once you have it all on paper, you can work with it, deciding what to include and what to leave out.

When you have decided what information to include, consider how you will organize that information. Ask yourself the order in which to organize the information to accomplish your purpose. You could organize your information:

- Most important to least important
- Least important to most important
- Cause leading to some effect
- An effect followed by its causes
- Chronological (first occurrence to last)
- Problem followed by proposed solutions
- Response to several questions in the order in which the questions were asked

1-1

- Steps in a process (first step to last)
- Proposal or request followed by reasons

However you organize your ideas, think about your document as having a beginning, a middle, and an end, each with its own purpose. The following is true whether you are writing several paragraphs or a single paragraph.

Beginning

- Introduces main idea or subject
- Gets reader's attention
- Establishes positive tone

Middle

- Contains more detailed information and support for main idea
- Leads reader logically to the conclusion intended by the writer

End

- States writer's conclusion and action reader should take
- Maintains (or reestablishes) positive tone

Write Your First Draft Quickly and Plan to Edit

A first draft is rarely a final draft, even for the best writers; therefore, write something to get you started. Let your purpose, reader, and organizational plan guide you, but do not let them stifle you. Keep going even if you occasionally lose your focus. Once you have a full draft, you can add or delete information, reorganize, and edit sentences.

Make Strong Paragraphs Your Building Blocks

Most of your written business communication will be too complex to be conveyed in a single sentence. Letters and even simple informal messages often (though not always) require that you state a general idea and follow with more information about that idea: support for the idea, reasons, examples, explanations, further discussion, and so on.

~~If you include one main idea in each paragraph, you can move your reader through complicated information idea by idea — paragraph by paragraph — until you believe your reader can draw a logical conclusion.~~

Occasionally, a good paragraph is a single sentence. More often a good paragraph is a group of sentences that focus on one main idea. This focus on a single idea is called *unity*. Good paragraphs also help the reader understand relationships between ideas (from paragraph to paragraph) and between ideas and their supporting details. This clarity of relationships is called *coherence*. Both unity and coherence improve when a paragraph begins with a sentence that states or implies the main idea.

Remember, good paragraphs:

- Build a clear document
- Focus on a single idea (unity)

1-2

- State the main idea as directly as possible
- Support the main idea with any needed details
- Help the reader understand relationships (coherence)

Use the Active Voice

Use the active voice most of the time. Active-voice sentences use fewer words and are more direct than passive-voice sentences. For example:

Passive voice: The policy statement was written by your manager.

Active voice: Your manager wrote the policy statement.

In the active-voice sentence, the subject (*manager*) is the person who performed the action (*wrote*). This structure allows the active-voice sentence to omit two weak words that serve only to lengthen it: *was* and *by*.

Although the active voice is more direct and efficient, the passive voice is useful at times. Use the passive voice when:

- Your writing is so formal or impersonal that you must avoid names and pronouns, as in formal reports
- Active-voice options sound awkward or forced
- You want to improve sentence variety
- You wish to deemphasize the subject of the sentence

1-3

U04-SA05(Step10).docx (page 3 of 5)

U04-SA05(Step10).docx (page 4 of 5)

CHAPTER 1 THE WRITING PROCESS

To write clear and concise business correspondence, consider the following points.

Define Your Purpose

Knowing your purpose for writing is the foundation for any written project. Before you begin writing an email, letter, or other document, ask yourself what you are trying to accomplish and the purpose for writing.

Identify Your Reader

As you define your purpose, you will need to develop a good picture of the person who will be reading your document. Ask yourself:

- Who is my reader?
- What do I know about my reader that will help determine the best approach?
- Is the audience one person or a group?
- Is my reader a coworker, a subordinate, a superior, or a customer?
- How is the reader likely to feel about my message?

Select Your Information and Plan How to Organize It

Once you have defined your purpose and identified your reader, decide what information you will include. Ask yourself questions such as:

- What does my reader want or need to know?
- What information should I include?
- What information will help my reader respond positively?
- What information should I not include?

To answer these questions, you may find spending a few minutes listing all of the information you *could* include in your document helpful. You may also find writing a rough draft of your document helpful. Write the draft quickly, including any information that comes to you. Once you have it all on paper, you can work with it, deciding what to include and what to leave out.

When you have decided what information to include, consider how you will organize that information. Ask yourself the order in which to organize the information to accomplish your purpose. You could organize your information:

- Most important to least important
- Least important to most important
- An effect followed by its causes
- Chronological (first occurrence to last)
- Problem followed by proposed solutions
- Response to several questions in the order in which the questions were asked
- Steps in a process (first step to last)
- Proposal or request followed by reasons

CHAPTER 2 EDITING AND PROOFREADING

Editing and proofreading are the final steps in producing a document that communicates effectively. Although the processes are closely related and are sometimes handled simultaneously, a few important distinctions exist. Editing usually involves checking and revising content as well as style. That means checking to see that the document's organization is logical, that sentence meaning is clear, and that the most effective words are used. Editing in this sense is typically handled by the writer. If you are asked to edit another's work, know your limits before you begin. You may not be able to change another person's work as extensively as you would your own because you cannot know the writer's preferences, particularly if that person is your boss.

Proofreading involves checking a document's mechanics, including errors in punctuation, capitalization, spelling, grammar, and format. Proofreading can also involve comparing a printed document against an edited manuscript, making sure that you have made all indicated changes. Because it is the final stage before a document reaches its audience, proofreading should be completed as thoroughly as possible.

Edit Information

Once you have a full first draft of your document, reconsider your purpose and your reader. Ask questions such as:

- Does the document include all of the important information?
- Have I said too much? Can I cut any information?
- Have I said too little? Can I add information to improve the communication with the reader?
- Have I used the best words? Are they the right level of formality? Does each word contribute to my meaning?

Edit Organization

Once you have all of the information you need, consider how you have organized it. Ask yourself questions such as:

- Will the reader be able to identify early in the document my purpose for writing?
- Is the information presented in a logical order?
- Does the order of the information help the reader see connections among my ideas?
- Does the order of the information lead the reader to the conclusion I intend?
- Do I provide a clear and positive conclusion?
- If I want a response, will my reader know exactly what I want?

However you organize your ideas, think about your document as having a beginning, a middle, and an end, each with its own purpose. The following is true whether you are writing several paragraphs or a single paragraph.

Beginning

- Introduces main idea or subject
- Gets reader's attention
- Establishes positive tone

Middle

- Contains more detailed information and support for main idea
- Leads reader logically to the conclusion intended by the writer

End

- States writer's conclusion and action reader should take
- Maintains (or reestablishes) positive tone

Write Your First Draft Quickly and Plan to Edit

A first draft is rarely a final draft, even for the best writers; therefore, write something to get you started. Let your purpose, reader, and organizational plan guide you, but do not let them stifle you. Keep going even if you occasionally lose your focus. Once you have a full draft, you can add or delete information, reorganize, and edit sentences.

Make Strong Paragraphs Your Building Blocks

Most of your written business communication will be too complex to be conveyed in a single sentence. Letters and even simple informal messages often (though not always) require that you state a general idea and follow with more information about that idea: support for the idea, reasons, examples, explanations, further discussion, and so on.

Occasionally, a good paragraph is a single sentence. More often a good paragraph is a group of sentences that focus on one main idea. This focus on a single idea is called *unity*. Good paragraphs also help the reader understand relationships between ideas (from paragraph to paragraph) and between ideas and their supporting details. This clarity of relationships is called *coherence*. Both unity and coherence improve when a paragraph begins with a sentence that states or implies the main idea.

Remember, good paragraphs:

- Build a clear document
- Focus on a single idea (unity)
- State the main idea as directly as possible
- Support the main idea with any needed details
- Help the reader understand relationships (coherence)

Use the Active Voice

Use the active voice most of the time. Active-voice sentences use fewer words and are more direct than passive-voice sentences. For example:

Passive voice: The policy statement *was written* by your manager.

Active voice: Your *manager wrote* the policy statement.

In the active-voice sentence, the subject (*manager*) is the person who performed the action (*wrote*). This structure allows the active-voice sentence to omit two weak words that serve only to lengthen it: *was* and *by*.

Although the active voice is more direct and efficient, the passive voice is useful at times. Use the passive voice when:

- Your writing is so formal or impersonal that you must avoid names and pronouns, as in formal reports
- Active-voice options sound awkward or forced
- You want to improve sentence variety
- You wish to deemphasize the subject of the sentence

CHAPTER 2 EDITING AND PROOFREADING

Editing and proofreading are the final steps in producing a document that communicates effectively. Although the processes are closely related and are sometimes handled simultaneously, a few important distinctions exist. Editing usually involves checking and revising content as well as style. That means checking to see that the document's organization is logical, that sentence meaning is clear, and that the most effective words are used. Editing in this sense is typically handled by the writer. If you are asked to edit another's work, know your limits before you begin. You may not be able to change another person's work as extensively as you would your own because you cannot know the writer's preferences, particularly if that person is your boss.

Proofreading involves checking a document's mechanics, including errors in punctuation, capitalization, spelling, grammar, and format. Proofreading can also involve comparing a printed document against an edited manuscript, making sure that you have made all indicated changes. Because it is the final stage before a document reaches its audience, proofreading should be completed as thoroughly as possible.

Edit Information

Once you have a full first draft of your document, reconsider your purpose and your reader. Ask questions such as:

- Does the document include all of the important information?
- Have I said too much? Can I cut any information?
- Have I said too little? Can I add information to improve the communication with the reader?
- Have I used the best words? Are they the right level of formality? Does each word contribute to my meaning?

Edit Organization

Once you have all of the information you need, consider how you have organized it. Ask yourself questions such as:

- Will the reader be able to identify early in the document my purpose for writing?
- Is the information presented in a logical order?
- Does the order of the information help the reader see connections among my ideas?
- Does the order of the information lead the reader to the conclusion I intend?
- Do I provide a clear and positive conclusion?
- If I want a response, will my reader know exactly what I want?

2-1

Unit 5 Instructions

Assessment 1

1. At a blank document, add the following text to AutoCorrect:

    a. Type **Cf** in the *Replace* text box and type **Cardiff** in the *With* text box.

    b. Type **Sn** in the *Replace* text box and type **Snowdonia** in the *With* text box.

    c. Type **BB** in the *Replace* text box and type **Brecon Beacons** in the *With* text box.

    d. Type the pound currency symbol (£) in the *With* text box and type **pd** in the *Replace* text box.

2. Apply the No Spacing style and then type the text shown below.

3. Save the document and name it **U05-SA01**.

4. Print and then close **U05-SA01.docx**.

5. Delete the *BB*, *Cf*, *pd*, and *Sn* AutoCorrect entries.

WELSH TOUR

Join the Welsh Tour and explore the beautiful country of Wales. The tour includes stunning mountain scenery, impressive coastal vistas, magnificent castles and fortresses, and the pristine and pastoral lowlands. During this six-day tour, you will visit Cf, Sn, BB, and Conwy Castle.

Highlights

- Cf, capital city of Wales
- Tintern Abbey, inspiration to William Wordsworth
- Hike the BB
- Conwy Castle, built by Edward I to contain the Welsh
- Sn National Park

Adult price	Student price
$459	$419
£825	£690

WELSH MINI-TOUR

This three-day adventure includes the best of Welsh (Cf, BB, coastlines, and castles) and includes breakfast and accommodations in the Black Mountains, an area of outstanding natural beauty.

Highlights

- Cf, capital city of Wales
- Hike the BB
- Tintern Abbey, inspiration to William Wordsworth

Adult price	Student price
$329	$299
£550	£470

Assessment 2

1. Open **TECHandbook.docx** (located in the **SA-StudentDataFiles** folder) and then save the document with Save As and name it **U05-SA02**.

2. Move the insertion point to the blank line below the paragraph of text on the first page and then insert a page break. (This creates a blank page 2.)

3. Move the insertion point to the beginning of the title *Section 1: General Information* (located on the third page) and then insert a continuous section break.

4. Move the insertion point to the beginning of the document and then insert the Integral footer. Select the author placeholder and then type **Terra Energy Corporation Employee Handbook**.

5. With the insertion point at the beginning of the document, change the format of page numbers to lowercase roman numerals.

6. Move the insertion point to the end of the title *Section 1: General Information* and then format the page numbers to start with number 1 (in arabic numbers).

7. Move the insertion point to the beginning of page 2 (the blank page) and then insert the Automatic Table 2 table of contents building block.

8. Move the insertion point to the beginning of the document and then insert the Banded cover page. Type **EMPLOYEE HANDBOOK** in the *[DOCUMENT NAME]* placeholder; type **Terra Energy Corporation** in the *[COMPANY NAME]* placeholder; and then delete the *[Company address]* placeholder.

9. Save, print, and then close **U05-SA02.docx**

Assessment 3

1. At a blank document, create custom theme colors named *SuppU5CustomColors* followed by your initials that make the following color changes:

   a. Change the Text/Background - Dark 1 color to White, Text 1.

   b. Change the Accent 1 color to Blue.

   c. Change the Accent 2 color to Dark Blue.

   d. Change the Accent 3 color to Dark Red.

2. Create custom theme fonts named *SuppU5CustomFonts* followed by your initials that change the Heading font to Copperplate Gothic Bold.

3. Click the Theme Effects button and then click *Glossy* at the drop-down gallery.

4. Save the custom theme and name it *SuppU5CustomTheme* followed by your initials. ***Hint: Do this with the* Save Current Theme *option at the Themes drop-down gallery.***

5. Close the document without saving the changes.

6. Open **DevelopSystem.docx** (located in the **SA-StudentDataFiles** folder) and then save the document with Save As and name it **U05-SA03**.

7. Apply your SuppU5CustomThemeXX theme to the document.

8. Insert a page break at the beginning of the heading *SUPPORT STAGE*.

9. Save, print, and then close **U05-SA03.docx**.

10. At a blank document, use the Print Screen key to make a screen capture of the Theme Colors drop-down gallery (make sure your custom theme colors display), a screen capture of the Theme Fonts drop-down gallery (make sure your custom theme fonts display), and a screen capture of the Themes button drop-down gallery. Insert all three screen captures on the same page. (You will need to size the images.)

11. Save the document and name it **U05-SA03-ScreenImages**.

12. Print and then close **U05-SA03-ScreenImages.docx**.

13. At a blank document, delete the custom color theme you created, the custom font theme, and the custom theme.

Assessment 4

1. Open **CommunicationSkills.docx** (located in the **SA-StudentDataFiles** folder) and then save the document with Save As and name it **U05-SA04**.

2. Apply the Intense Emphasis style to the headings *Communicating on the Job, Questions to Ask Yourself*, and *How to Demonstrate Skills on Resume*.

3. Display the document information panel and then type the following information in the specified text boxes:

    a. Author = (Type your name)

    b. Title = **Communication Skills**

    c. Subject = **Supplemental Assessment 4**

    d. Keywords = **communicate, job, resume**

    e. Category = **Resume**

    f. Status = **Final**

    g. Comments = **This document describes how to demonstrate communication skills on a resume.**

4. Display the Properties dialog box with the Custom tab selected and then add the following properties:

    a. Add the *Client* property with the text **Apex Employment**.

    b. Add the *Department* property with the text **Employment Department**.

    c. Before closing the Properties dialog box, press Alt + Print Screen to make a screen capture of the Properties dialog box.

    d. Close the Properties dialog box.

    e. At the document, close the document information panel, press Ctrl + N to insert a blank document, and then paste your screen image.

    f. Save the document and name it **U05-SA04-ScreenImage**.

    g. Print and then close the document.

5. At the **U05-SA04.docx** document, save the document and then print only the document properties.

6. Inspect the document and remove any hidden text.

7. Run the accessibility checker and then create alternate text for the clip art image on the first page.

8. Save **U05-SA04.docx**.

9. Save **U05-SA04.docx** with Save As and name it **U05-SA04-Comments**.

10. Display the Restrict Editing task pane, restrict editing to only comments, and then start enforcing the protection (do not include a password).

11. Insert the following comment at the end of the paragraph below the title: **Examples are needed to help the reader understand the concept.**

12. Insert the following comment at the end of the last paragraph in the *Communicating on the Job* section: **Provide audio files of business conversations.**

13. Print only the comments.

14. Save and then close **U05-SA04-Comments.docx**.

Assessment 5

1. Open **CompTechnology.docx** (located in the **SA-StudentDataFiles** folder) and then save the document with Save As and name it **U05-SA05**.

2. With the insertion point positioned at the beginning of the title *COMPUTERS IN COMMUNICATIONS*, create a style named *Title1* that changes the font to 14-point Tahoma bold, changes the font color to Dark Blue, changes the text to center alignment, inserts a bottom border line (½ point width), and applies Blue, Accent 1, Lighter 60% paragraph shading.

3. Apply the Title1 style to the two other titles (*COMPUTERS IN ENTERTAINMENT* and *REFERENCES*).

4. Move the insertion point to the beginning of the heading *Telecommunications* and then create a style named *Title2* that changes the font to 11-point Tahoma bold, turns on italics, changes the font color to Dark Blue, inserts a bottom border line (½ point width), and applies Blue, Accent 1, Lighter 80% paragraph shading.

5. Apply the Title2 style to the remaining headings (*Publishing, News Services, Television and Film,* and *Home Entertainment*).

6. Insert page breaks before the titles *COMPUTERS IN ENTERTAINMENT* and *REFERENCES*.

7. Apply hanging indent format to the four references.

8. Insert page numbering at the bottom center of each page.

9. Save and then print **U05-SA05.docx**.

10. Move the insertion point to the beginning of the document and then press the Print Screen key.

11. Close **U05-SA05.docx**.

12. Press Ctrl + N to display a blank document and then click the Paste button to paste the screen image in the document.

13. Save the document and name it **U05-SA05-ScreenImage**.

14. Print and then close **U05-SA05-ScreenImage.docx**.

Unit 5 Grading Rubrics

The following are suggested rubrics. Instructors should feel free to customize the rubrics to suit their grading standards and/or to adjust the point values.

*Suggested Scoring Distribution
Above average: student completes 80% or more of task
Average: student completes 70 to 79% of task
Below average: student completes 69% or less of task

Assessment 1

Step	Task	Criterion	Value	Score*
1	**Creating AutoCorrect entries**	Created four AutoCorrect entries.	8	
2	**Formatting and typing**	Applied No Spacing style and then typed text as indicated using AutoCorrect to insert some text.	7	

Step	Task	Criterion	Value	Score*
3-4	**Printing and saving**	Saved, printed, and closed document.	1	
5	**Deleting AutoCorrect entries**	Deleted four AutoCorrect entries entered in Step 1.	4	
		TOTAL POINTS FOR THIS EXERCISE	20	

Assessment 2

Step	Task	Criterion	Value	Score*
1	**Opening and saving**	Opened and saved document.	1	
2-3	**Formatting**	Inserted page break and inserted a continuous section break.	2	
4	**Inserting footer**	Inserted Integral predesigned footer and typed text in author placeholder.	4	
5-6	**Formatting**	Changed page number format to lowercase roman numerals.	4	
7	**Inserting building block**	Inserted Automatic Table 2 table of contents building block.	4	
8	**Inserting cover page**	Inserted Banded predesigned cover page and typed text in placeholders as directed.	4	
9	**Saving and printing**	Saved, printed, and closed document.	1	
		TOTAL POINTS FOR THIS EXERCISE	20	

Assessment 3

Step	Task	Criterion	Value	Score*
1	**Creating custom theme colors**	Created and named custom theme colors.	5	
2	**Creating custom theme font**	Created and named custom theme fonts.	4	
3	**Creating custom theme effects**	Applied Glossy theme effect.	2	
4	**Saving a custom theme**	Saved and named custom theme.	4	
5-6	**Closing and opening**	Closed, opened, named, and saved document.	2	
7	**Applying custom theme**	Applied custom theme.	2	
8	**Formatting**	Inserted a page break at the beginning of SUPPORT STAGE heading.	1	
9	**Saving and printing**	Saved, printed, and closed document.	1	

Step	Task	Criterion	Value	Score*
10-12	**Creating a document**	Used Print Screen key to create screen image of Theme Colors button drop-down gallery, Theme Fonts button drop-down gallery, and Save Current Theme dialog box, all with custom items displayed. Pasted screen images in one page of document and then saved, printed, and closed document.	6	
13	**Deleting custom theme**	Deleted custom color theme, custom font theme, and custom theme.	3	
	TOTAL POINTS FOR THIS EXERCISE		30	

Assessment 4

Step	Task	Criterion	Value	Score*
1	**Opening and saving**	Opened and saved document.	1	
2	**Applying a style**	Applied Intense Emphasis style to headings.	3	
3	**Typing data at document information panel.**	Entered specific text at document information panel.	4	
4	**Creating custom properties**	Created Client property and Department property at Properties dialog box with Custom tab selected.	5	
5	**Saving and printing**	Saved document and then printed only document properties.	3	
6	**Inspecting document**	Inspected document and removed hidden text.	3	
7	**Running accessibility checker**	Ran accessibility checker and then created alternate text for clip art image.	5	
8-9	**Saving**	Saved document and then saved document with new name.	2	
10	**Restricting formatting**	Restricted formatting to only comments.	4	
11-12	**Inserting comments**	Inserted comments in document.	2	
13	**Printing**	Printed only comments.	2	
14	**Saving and closing**	Saved and then closed document.	1	
	TOTAL POINTS FOR THIS EXERCISE		35	

Assessment 5

Step	Task	Criterion	Value	Score*
1	**Opening and saving**	Opened and saved document.	1	
2	**Creating a style**	Created style named *Title1* that changed font to 14-point Tahoma bold, changed font color to Dark Blue, changed text to center alignment, inserted bottom border line, and applied paragraph shading.	10	

Step	Task	Criterion	Value	Score*
3	**Applying a style**	Applied Title1 style to titles in document.	3	
4	**Creating a style**	Created style named *Title2* that changed font to 11-point Tahoma bold, turned on italics, changed font color to Dark Blue, inserted bottom border line, and applied paragraph shading.	10	
5	**Applying a style**	Applied Title2 style to headings in document.	3	
6-8	**Formatting**	Inserted page breaks, applied hanging indent formatting, and inserted page numbering.	3	
9	**Saving and printing**	Saved and printed document.	1	
10-14	**Creating a document**	Used Print Screen key to create screen image, pasted screen image in blank document, and then saved, printed, and closed document.	4	
		TOTAL POINTS FOR THIS EXERCISE	35	

Unit 5 Model Answers

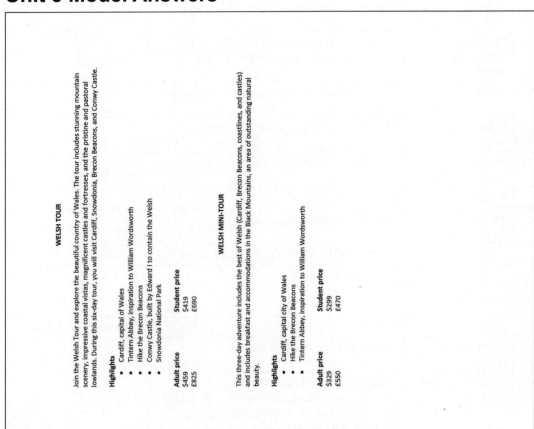

U05-SA01.docx

Terra Energy Corporation

Employee Handbook

This employee handbook has been prepared to give you general information about some of the work rules, work environment, and policies under which we operate. Periodically, you may receive updated information concerning changes in policy. This handbook is not a contract guaranteeing employment for any specific duration. Although we hope that your employment relationship with us will be long term, you or Terra Energy Corporation (TEC) may terminate this relationship at any time, for any reason, with or without cause or notice. This is an at-will relationship that remains in full force and effect, notwithstanding any statements to the contrary made by any TEC employees or representatives, or set forth in any other document.

TERRA ENERGY CORPORATION EMPLOYEE HANDBOOK

i

U05-SA02.docx (page 2 of 8)

EMPLOYEE HANDBOOK

Terra Energy Corporation Employee Handbook
TERRA ENERGY CORPORATION

U05-SA02.docx (page 1 of 8)

Table of Contents

U05-SA02.docx (page 3 of 8)

Section 1: General Information

New Employee Orientation

The Terra Energy Corporation New Employee Orientation Program is designed to welcome new employees into the spirit and culture of TEC, to clearly establish health care performance expectations, and to set the stage for success. New personnel are encouraged to begin their jobs with the monthly orientation in order to be introduced to the overall operations of TEC.

During your first few days of employment, you will participate in an orientation program conducted by several representatives of TEC. During this program, you will receive important information regarding the performance requirements of your position, basic TEC policies, your compensation package, as well as benefits and safety programs, plus other information necessary to acquaint you with your job and TEC. You will also be asked to complete all designated forms and appropriate federal, state, and local tax forms. During the orientation, you will be required to present information establishing your identity and your eligibility to work in the United States in accordance with applicable federal law. You will not be allowed to begin working unless this information has been provided.

Medical Screenings

As part of the TEC employment procedures, an applicant is required to undergo a post-offer, pre-employment medical screening and an alcohol and drug test. Any offer of employment that an applicant receives from TEC is contingent upon, among other things, satisfactory completion of screening and a determination by TEC that the applicant is capable of performing the essential functions of the position that has been offered, with or without reasonable accommodations.

As a condition of continued employment, employees may also be required to undergo periodic medical examinations, and/or alcohol and drug screening, at times specified by the TEC. In connection with these examinations, employees are required to provide TEC with access to their medical records, if requested. TEC receives a full medical report from its examining physicians regarding the applicant's or employee's state of health. All company-required pre-employment and alcohol and drug screenings are paid in full by TEC.

All drivers will be required to participate in random drug screening. This screening will take place every six months and/or more often if deemed necessary by an TEC management representative. Other OMA employees may be asked at any time to participate in this random drug screening.

Licensure

Persons being considered for employment whose occupations are regulated by a state licensing board must present proof of licensure before beginning work. Employees are responsible for renewing their licenses when necessary and ensuring that licenses are kept current. An employee who fails to present or maintain a valid license as requested will not be allowed to work.

U05-SA02.docx (page 4 of 8)

- **Newsletter:** TEC publishes a monthly newsletter providing information on new hires, benefit updates, and the latest health care news.
- **Bulletins board postings:** Bulletin boards are located throughout the clinic and provide information to keep employees up to date on announcements and clinic news.

Employer Communication

TEC supervisors, department leaders, and other management representatives maintain open and constructive communication in the following ways:

- **Department and unit meetings:** Departments and units meet to communicate goals and objectives and to discuss workplace issues of interest to employees. Employees should check with supervisors to obtain a schedule of the meetings.
- **Management meetings:** All levels of management routinely hold meetings to communicate information and discuss matters of importance.

Section 3: Employment Categories

Employee Categories

Throughout this handbook, you will see references to several employee categories with which you should become familiar. The categories include the following:

- **Exempt:** Refers to those employees excluded from the overtime provisions of the Fair Labor Standards Act. The professional clinical staff is considered exempt. The introductory period for exempt employees is 90 days.
- **Non-exempt:** Refers to those positions eligible for overtime pay if more than 40 hours are worked during a work week. The introductory period for non-exempt employees is 90 days.

Category Definitions

- **Probationary:** All persons newly hired or rehired are considered probationary employees until the completion of 90 calendar days of employment.
- **Regular full time:** A regular full-time employee is one who is employed on a regular basis on a schedule of 30 to 40 hours per week. Regular full-time employees are fully eligible for all benefits.
- **Regular part time:** Employees scheduled for 20 or more hours per week are eligible for employee benefits on a prorated basis in relation to their scheduled hours worked, up to 40.
- **Non-benefit eligible part time:** Employees scheduled to work less than 20 hours may be terminated without notice or cause.
- **Temporary full time:** A temporary full-time employee is one who is employed on a schedule of 40 hours per week for a limited period of time and is so informed at the time of hire.

TERRA ENERGY CORPORATION EMPLOYEE HANDBOOK 3

Introductory Period

All new employees and current employees promoted or transferred to a new position shall be on a 90-day probationary period starting on their first day worked. This period may be extended if additional time is required in order to completely assess an employee's performance. This period gives both TEC and the employee time to assess their new relationship and performance. During this period, an employee may not be eligible for all benefits.

Identification Badges

As a vital part of our security program, an identification badge containing your name and photo will be issued to you as you begin employment. If your identification badge is lost or stolen, you must pay for a replacement. You are required to wear your identification badge in clear view at all times while on duty.

Upon termination of employment, you must return your identification badge to a Human Resources Department representative.

Security

All vehicles, lockers, desks, offices, and containers that are TEC property, as well as briefcases, backpacks, parcels, and other personal belongings of employees, are subject to inspection and search by TEC or their designated agents.

Performance Review

All TEC employees will be evaluated at periodic intervals based on his/her job description and not less than annually. A performance appraisal is intended to document and maintain satisfactory performance of an individual employee by providing a means of measuring an employee's effectiveness on the job, identifying areas where an employee is in need of training or improving, and maintaining a high level of motivation through feedback and the setting of specific goals on the basis of the feedback.

Employees are responsible for working with their supervisors on an ongoing basis to develop and maintain a clear performance plan defining various performance expectations and their relative priority.

Section 2: Communication

Employee Communication

Effective communication is essential to provide the best patient care, maintain productivity, sustain morale, and foster constructive employee relations. Employee communications in the TEC environment include the following:

- **Employee/supervisor meetings:** Questions and concerns relating to job activities should first be presented to supervisors. Communication between the supervisor and the employee should be ongoing and address concerns, duties, and expectations. Supervisors can help employees achieve their professional goals by providing career development information.

TERRA ENERGY CORPORATION EMPLOYEE HANDBOOK 2

- **Temporary part time:** A temporary part-time employee is one who is employed on a schedule of less than 30 hours per week for a limited period of time and is so informed at the time of hire.
- **Per visit:** Per-visit employees are hired to work on a per diem basis for an undetermined period of time. Per-visit employees can be terminated without notice or cause.

Section 4: Employee Compensation

Pay Range

A pay range is established for each of the organization's jobs and these ranges are internally equitable as well as externally competitive when compared with the rates paid by other employers for comparable jobs. Each employee whose performance is "proficient" or better will receive a rate of pay that falls within the pay range that has been established for his/her job.

Compensation Procedures

The position of each employee's salary within the range that has been established for his or her job will be determined primarily by the employee's relevant experience and job performance. TEC compensation programs are designed and administered in such a way as to comply with all applicable laws and to provide fair and equitable treatment for all employees.

Regular pay procedures: All TEC employees are normally paid on Fridays on a bi-weekly basis. If a scheduled payday falls on a company observed holiday, you will usually be paid on the day preceding the holiday. All required deductions, such as federal, state, and local taxes, and all authorized voluntary deductions, such as health insurance contributions, will be withheld automatically from your paycheck. All documentation of work completed must be submitted by those staff members providing direct patient care.

Merit increases: The purpose of merit increases is to recognize and reward employee performance over a designated period of time, and a minimum of once a year.

Acting pay: Acting pay may be granted when an employee is temporarily assigned, for a period of at least one week or more, to assume a substantial portion of the responsibilities of a job with a higher pay range.

On-call pay: Since some employees are required to be available for work on an on-call basis, special rates for on-call hours will be paid to non-exempt employees. Your supervisor will notify you of proper procedures if you are required to work on-call.

Bonus pay: Bonus pay is additional compensation paid to an employee, or group of employees, in addition to their normal rate of pay. Bonus pay may be granted only under limited circumstances.

Market adjustments: Market adjustments to salary ranges may occur outside of the annual salary planning cycle when market demand has resulted in an increased rate of pay for a particular job or job category.

Reductions in pay: For a variety of reasons, an employee may be reassigned to a job that has a lower pay range than the job they had previously held. In such cases, reduction in pay guidelines will apply.

TERRA ENERGY CORPORATION EMPLOYEE HANDBOOK 4

Shift differentials: Employees receive shift differential pay for all hours worked if they work a minimum of six consecutive hours during a shift where a differential applies.

Weekend differential: An employee who works four or more consecutive hours during a designated weekend period is entitled to receive a weekend differential for all hours worked on that shift. For the purposes of this policy, the weekend is defined as beginning 11:00 p.m. Friday and ending 7:00 a.m. Monday.

TERRA ENERGY CORPORATION EMPLOYEE HANDBOOK 5

Identifying and assembling a team of employees with the required skills and expertise is a necessary first step in developing a new in-house information system. A management group may be involved in answering questions and providing information in the early planning phases of the project, but programmers and/or software engineers handle the design and implementation of any new system.

Programmers specialize in the development of new software, while software engineers are highly skilled professionals with programming and teamwork training. Their organized, professional application of the software development process is called software engineering.

PROJECT TEAM

Because of their large size, information systems require the creation of a project team. A project team usually includes a project manager, who acts as the team leader. Sometimes the project manager also functions as a systems analyst, responsible for completing the systems analysis and making design recommendations. Other project team members include software engineers and technicians. The software engineers deal with programming software, while technicians handle hardware issues. The comprehensive process software engineers initiate is called the system development life cycle (SDLC), a series of steps culminating in a completed information system.

PROJECT PLAN

The first step in the system development cycle is planning. The planning step involves preparing a needs analysis and conducting feasibility studies. During this step, a company usually establishes a project team and the team creates a project plan. The project plan includes an estimate of how long the project will take to complete, an outline of the steps involved, and a list of deliverables. Deliverables are documents, services, hardware, and software that must be finished and delivered by a certain time and date.

DESIGNING THE SYSTEM

A project is ready to move into the design stage once the project team has approved the plan, including the budget. The design process begins with the writing of the documentation, which covers functional and design specifications. In most cases, the project team creates the functional specifications, describing what the system must be able to do.

IMPLEMENTATION

The project can move into the next phase, implementation, once the development team and the systems house develop the design specification and approve the plans. This step is where the actual work of putting the system together is completed, including creating a prototype and completing the programming. In most cases, implementing the new system is the longest, most difficult step in the process.

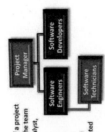

U05-SA03.docx (page 1 of 2)

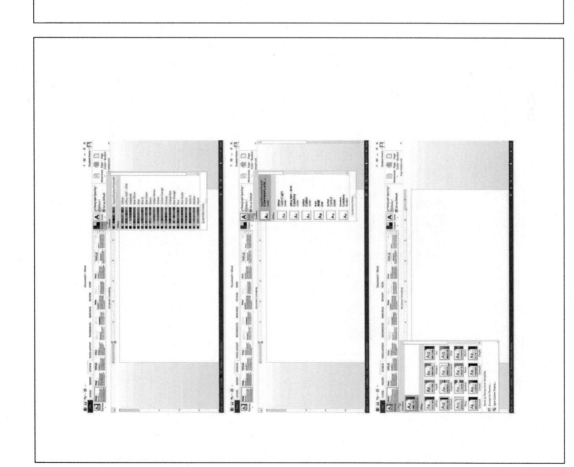

U05-SA03-ScreenImages.docx

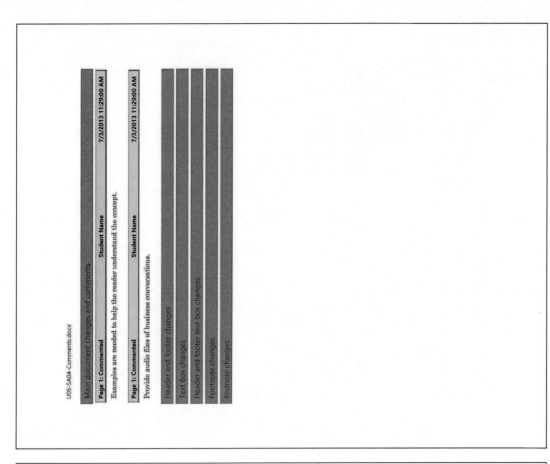

U05-SA04-Comments.docx

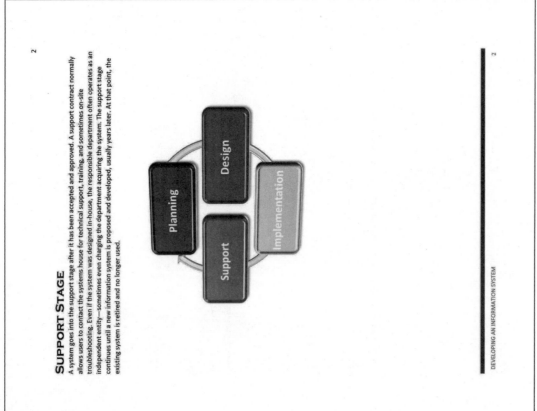

U05-SA03.docx (page 2 of 2)

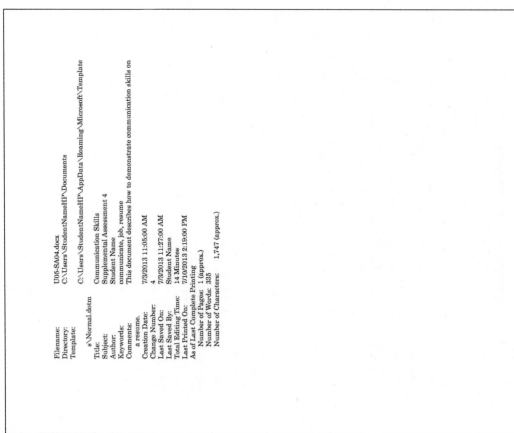

Filename: U05-SA04.docx
Directory: C:\Users\StudentNameHP\Documents
Template: C:\Users\StudentNameHP\AppData\Roaming\Microsoft\Template
                   s\Normal.dotm
Title: Communication Skills
Subject: Supplemental Assessment 4
Author: Student Name
Keywords: communicate, job, resume
Comments: This document describes how to demonstrate communication skills on
                   a resume.
Creation Date: 7/3/2013 11:05:00 AM
Change Number: 4
Last Saved On: 7/3/2013 11:27:00 AM
Last Saved By: Student Name
Total Editing Time: 14 Minutes
Last Printed On: 7/10/2013 2:19:00 PM
As of Last Complete Printing
   Number of Pages: 1 (approx.)
   Number of Words: 335
   Number of Characters: 1,747 (approx.)

U05-SA04.docx

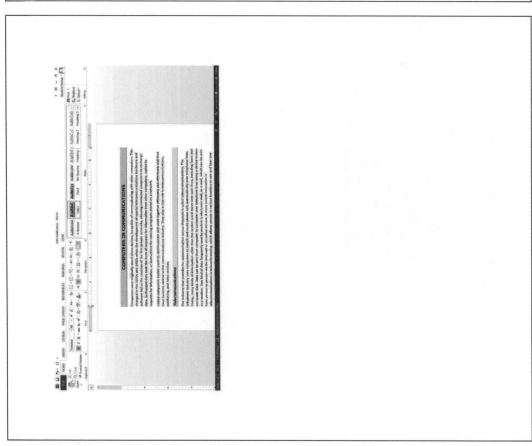

U05-SA04-ScreenImage.docx

COMPUTERS IN COMMUNICATIONS

Computers were originally stand-alone devices, incapable of communicating with other computers. This changed in the 1970s and 1980s when the development of special telecommunications hardware and software led to the creation of the first private networks, allowing connected computers to exchange data. Exchanged data took the form of requests for information from other computers, replies to requests for information, or instructions for running programs stored on a network.

Linked computers enable users to communicate and work together efficiently and effectively and thus have become central to the communications industry. They play a vital role in telecommunications, publishing, and news services.

Telecommunications

The industry that provides for communication across distances is called telecommunications. The telephone industry uses computers to switch and route phone calls automatically over telephone lines. Today, many kinds of information other than the spoken word move over such lines, including faxes and computer data. Data can be sent from computer to computer over telephone lines using a device known as a modem. One kind of data frequently sent by modem is electronic mail, or e-mail, which can be sent from person to person via the Internet or an online service. A more recent innovation in telecommunications is teleconferencing, which allows people in various locations to see and hear one another and thus hold virtual meetings.

Publishing

Just twenty years ago, book manuscripts were typeset mechanically or on a typesetting machine and then reproduced on a printing press. Now anyone who has access to a computer and either a modem or a printer can undertake what has come to be known as electronic publishing. Writers and editors use word processing applications to produce text. Artists and designers use drawing and painting applications to create original graphics, and they use inexpensive scanners to digitize illustrations and photographs, or turn them into computer-readable files. Typesetters use personal computers to combine text, illustrations, and photographs. Publishers typically send computer-generated files to printers for production of the film and plates from which books and magazines are printed.

News Services

News providers rely on reporters located worldwide. Reporters use e-mail to send, or upload, their stories to wire services. Increasingly, individuals get daily news reports from online services. News can also be accessed from specific providers, such as the *New York Times* or *U.S.A. Today*, via the Internet. One of the most popular Internet sites provides continuously updated weather reports.

1

U05-SA05.docx (page 1 of 3)

U05-SA05-ScreenImage.docx

REFERENCES

Fuller, Floyd and Brian Larson. (2015) *Computers: Understanding Technology* (pp. 121-125). St. Paul, MN: Paradigm Publishing.

McFadden, Jaclyn M. (2014) *The Art of Special Effects* (pp. 45-48). Los Angeles, CA: Richardson-Dryers Publishing House.

North, Jordan and Raymond Amundsen. (2013) *Computer Gaming.* Cleveland, OH: Blue Horizon Publishers.

Ziebel, Karina M. and Heather L. Weisenburg. (2014) *Computers and Publishing.* Seattle, WA: Greenlake Publishing House.

3

COMPUTERS IN ENTERTAINMENT

Possibilities in the television and film industries have soared with computer technology, especially in production. Computer games have captured the public imagination and created enormous growth in the computer game market.

Television and Film

Many of the spectacular graphics and special effects seen on television and in movies today are created with computers. The original *Star Wars* films, for example, relied heavily on hand-constructed models and hand-drawn graphics. Twenty years after the first release of the films, they were re-released with many new special effects, including futuristic cityscape backgrounds, new alien creatures, and new sounds that were created on computers and added to the films by means of computerized video editing. In an article on special effects, Jaclyn McFadden, an industry expert talked about the evolution of computer simulation.

The film *Jurassic Park* brought computer simulation to a new level by combining puppetry and computer animation to simulate realistic looking dinosaurs. *Toy Story*, released in 1996, was the first wholly computer-animated commercial movie.

Software products are available that automatically format scripts of various kinds. Industry analysts predict that the improvements in computer technology will continue to enhance and improve the visual appeal of television and film media.

Home Entertainment

In the 1970s, computer games such as Pong and Pac-Man captured the public's imagination. Since then, there has been enormous growth in the computer game market. The advent of powerful desktop personal computers has led to the production of home computer games that rival those of arcade machines in complexity. Manufacturers such as Sega and Nintendo produce large, complex, video arcade games as well as small computer game systems for home use.

Typical arcade-style computer games include simulations of boxing, warfare, racing, skiing, and flight. Other computer games make use of television or of small, independent, hand-held devices. Games are now able to take advantage of three-dimensional graphics that create virtual environments.

2

Unit 6 Instructions

Assessment 1

1. Open **CompEntertainment.docx** (located in the **SA-StudentDataFiles** folder) and then save the document with Save As and name it **U06-SA01**.

2. Change the style set to Centered.

3. Number the pages at the bottom center of each page *except* the first page.

4. Insert the following footnote at the end of the paragraph in the *Telecommunications* section: **Tony Waller, "Design Principles," Network Designs (2015): 19-22.**

5. Insert the following footnote at the end of the paragraph in the *Publishing* section: **Juanita Jackson, Publishing (Seattle: Walker Publications, 2014), 90-110.**

6. Insert the following footnote at the end of the second paragraph in the *Home Entertainment* section: **Bill Fortner, "Gaming News," Home Computing (2015): 44-47.**

7. Save, print, and then close **U06-SA01.docx**.

Assessment 2

1. Open **CompChapters.docx** (located in the **SA-StudentDataFiles** folder) and then save the document with Save As and name it **U06-SA02**.

2. Insert a continuous section break at the beginning of the title *CHAPTER 1: COMPUTER VIRUSES*.

3. With the insertion point positioned after the section break, insert page numbering at the bottom center of each page and change the starting number to *1*.

4. Move the insertion point to the beginning of the document and then create a table of contents with the Automatic Table 1 option.

5. In the table of contents page, change the page numbering style to lowercase Roman numerals.

6. Mark all occurrences of the following entries for an index:

   a. viruses = main entry

   b. security risks = main entry

   c. hacker = main entry

   d. cracker = main entry

   e. Polymorphic = subentry (main entry = viruses)

   f. Multipartite = subentry (main entry = viruses)

   g. logic bomb = subentry (main entry = viruses)

   h. Trojan horse = subentry (main entry = viruses)

   i. Michelangelo = subentry (main entry = viruses)

7. Move the insertion point to the end of the document, insert a page break, type INDEX, and then press the Enter key.

8. Generate the index in one column in the format of your choosing.

9. Apply the Heading 1 style to the title *INDEX*.

10. Update the entire table of contents. (Make sure you update the entire table and not just page numbers.)

11. Save, print, and then close **U06-SA02.docx**.

Assessment 3

1. At a blank document, click the No Spacing style and then type the following text centered (press the Enter key twice after typing the last line of text):

Specialty Enterprises
Annual Picnic and Golf Tournament
August 22, 2015
Sunbrook Golf Club

2. Select the text *Specialty Enterprises* and then format the text as WordArt. Change the position of the WordArt to Position in Top Center with Square Text Wrapping and then change the text wrapping to Top and Bottom. Apply additional formatting to enhance the appearance of the WordArt.

3. Move the insertion point to the end of the document and then create a table (you determine the number of columns and row) that contains the following information and questions with the appropriate form fields:

   a. Name

   b. Department

   c. Are you planning on attending the picnic? (Include yes or no check boxes.)

   d. How many will be attending?

   e. What will you bring to accompany our main dish? (Create a drop-down list with these choices: *hot dish*, *cold dish*, *dessert*, and *paper products*.)

   f. Will you be playing in the golf tournament? (Include yes or no check boxes.)

   g. If yes, list the people in your group. (Create four form fields for names.)

4. Make additional formatting changes to enhance the document.

5. Insert the Filigree predesigned footer.

6. Protect the template so users can only fill in the form. (Do not include a password.)

7. Save the document as a template and name it **U06-SA03-PicnicForm**.

8. Close **U06-SA03-PicnicForm.dotx**.

9. Create a new document using the **U06-SA03-PicnicForm.dotx** template. Fill out the form for Max Walters from Accounting. He will be coming to the picnic with his wife and three children, they will bring a dessert, and Max will be playing golf with June Walters and Joan Roth.

10. Save the document and name it **U06-SA03**.

11. Print and then close **U06-SA03.docx**.

Assessment 4

1. Create an Employee Data form by opening a blank document and inserting a 4 × 8 table. Merge cells as shown below and then type the information shown below (centering the title as shown):

L & N Employee Data			
First name:		Last name:	
Address:			
City:		State:	ZIP:
Phone:	Birthday:	Employment date:	
Spouse's name:		Spouse's birthday:	
Child #1's name:		Child #2's name:	
Department:		Vacation time:	

2. Insert form fields for each of the labels (all entries except the title) in the table with the following specifications:

   a. Insert a text form field for *State:* that specifies a maximum length of 2 characters and a text format of Uppercase.

   b. Insert a text form field for *ZIP:* that specifies a maximum length of 5.

   c. Insert a drop-down form field for *Department:* that includes the following choices in the order listed: *HR*, *IT*, *CL*, *PK*, *SL*, and *DT*.

   d. Insert a drop-down form field for *Vacation time:* that includes the following choices in the order listed: *1 week*, *2 weeks*, and *3 weeks*.

3. Make the following changes to the table:

   a. Apply the Grid Table 4 - Accent 1 table style to the table and remove the check mark from the *First Column* check box in the Table Style Options group on the TABLE TOOLS DESIGN tab.

   b. Select the entire table and then change the row height to 0.5 inch.

   c. Change the alignment for the first row to Align Center and change the alignment for the remaining cells to Align Center Left.

   d. Change the font size for the title, *L & N Employee Data*, to 18 points.

4. Restrict editing to allow only filling in forms and do not include a password.

5. Save the document as a template and name it **U06-SA04-EmpDataForm**.

6. Print the **U06-SA04-EmpDataForm.dotx** template and then close the template.

7. Create a form document from the **U06-SA04-EmpDataForm.dotx** template. You determine the data to enter in each data field.

8. Save the document with the name **U06-SA04**.

9. Print and then close **U06-SA04.docx**.

Assessment 5

1. Open **HandbookSections.docx** and then save the document with Save As and name it **U06-SA05**.

2. Display the document in Outline view and use the Promote to Heading 1 button in the Outline Tools group to promote the following titles to level 1:

   GENERAL INFORMATION
   COMMUNICATION
   EMPLOYMENT CATEGORIES
   EMPLOYEE COMPENSATION

3. Click the Show Document button in the Master Document group on the OUTLINING tab.

4. Create subdocuments by selecting from the *GENERAL INFORMATION* heading to the end of the document and then clicking the Create button in the Master Document group. ***Note: If an extra bullet displays at the end of the document, position the insertion point to the right of the bullet and then press the Backspace key two times.***

5. Save and then close **U06-SA05.docx**.

6. Open **U06-SA05.docx** and then print the document. (The subdocuments will be collapsed.)

7. Make the following changes to the document:

   a. Display the document in Outline view.

   b. Move the EMPLOYEE COMPENSATION subdocument above the COMMUNICATION subdocument. (Make sure the dark gray, horizontal line is positioned above the gray circle above the COMMUNICATION subdocument before you release the mouse button.)

   c. Delete the EMPLOYEE CATEGORIES subdocument.

8. Save, print, and then close **U06-SA05.docx**.

Unit 6 Grading Rubrics

The following are suggested rubrics. Instructors should feel free to customize the rubrics to suit their grading standards and/or to adjust the point values.

*Suggested Scoring Distribution
Above average: student completes 80% or more of task
Average: student completes 70 to 79% of task
Below average: student completes 69% or less of task

Assessment 1

Step	Task	Criterion	Value	Score*
1	**Opening and saving**	Opened and saved document.	1	
2-3	**Formatting**	Changed style set to Centered, numbered pages at bottom center of each page except first page.	5	
4-6	**Inserting footnotes**	Inserted three footnotes.	8	
7	**Saving and printing**	Saved, printed, and closed document.	1	
		TOTAL POINTS FOR THIS EXERCISE	15	

Assessment 2

Step	Task	Criterion	Value	Score*
1	Opening and saving	Opened and saved document.	1	
2-3	Formatting	Inserted page break, inserted continuous section break, and inserted page numbering starting with number *1* at bottom center of each page after section break.	3	
4-5	Creating table of contents	Created table of contents using Automatic Table 1 option and changed page numbering style for table of contents page.	6	
6	Marking index entries	Marked occurrences of specified text in document for an index.	10	
7	Formatting	Inserted page break and typed *INDEX* title.	4	
8	Generating and formatting index	Generated one-column index and applied formatting of own choice.	5	
9	Formatting	Applied Heading 1 style to *INDEX* title.	2	
10	Updating table of contents	Updated entire table of contents, not just page numbers.	3	
11	Saving and printing	Saved, printed, and closed document.	1	
		TOTAL POINTS FOR THIS EXERCISE	**35**	

Assessment 3

Step	Task	Criterion	Value	Score*
1	Typing	Typed specified text.	2	
2	Creating WordArt	Created WordArt with *Specialty Enterprises* text and then modified WordArt.	4	
3	Creating table with form fields	Created table that included text and form fields for fill-in form.	10	
4-5	Formatting	Made additional formatting changes to enhance document (students' choice) and inserted Filigree predesigned footer.	4	
6	Restricting and protecting	Restricted editing of document to only filling in form and started protection.	5	
7-8	Saving as template	Saved document as template and then closed document.	4	
9	Opening and filling in form	Created new document using template and then filled in form.	5	
10-11	Saving and printing	Saved, printed, and closed document.	1	
		TOTAL POINTS FOR THIS EXERCISE	**35**	

Assessment 4

Step	Task	Criterion	Value	Score*
1	Creating table and typing	Created 4 x 8 table, merged cells, typed text, and centered title.	9	
2	Inserting form fields	Inserted form fields in table.	8	
3	Formatting	Applied Grid Table 4 - Accent 1 table style to table, changed row height of all rows to 0.5 inch, changed alignment as instructed, and changed font size for title.	2	
4	Restricting and protecting	Restricted editing of document to only filling in the form and started protection without including password.	5	
5	Saving as template	Saved document as template.	4	
6	Printing and then closing	Printed and closed document.	1	
7	Opening and filling in form	Created new document using template and then filled in form using own choice of data.	5	
8-9	Saving and printing	Saved, printed, and closed document.	1	
		TOTAL POINTS FOR THIS EXERCISE	35	

Assessment 5

Step	Task	Criterion	Value	Score*
1	Opening and saving	Opened and saved document.	1	
2	Assigning levels in Outline view	Changed to Outline view and then assigned titles to level 1.	5	
3-4	Creating subdocuments	Created subdocuments.	4	
5-6	Saving, closing, and opening	Saved and closed document and then opened and printed document.	1	
7	Modifying document	Moved subdocument in document to another location and deleted subdocument.	3	
8	Saving and printing	Saved, printed, and closed document.	1	
		TOTAL POINTS FOR THIS EXERCISE	15	

Unit 6 Model Answers

COMPUTERS IN COMMUNICATIONS

Computers were originally stand-alone devices, incapable of communicating with other computers. This changed in the 1970s and 1980s when the development of special telecommunications hardware and software led to the creation of the first private networks, allowing connected computers to exchange data. Exchanged data took the form of requests for information from other computers, replies to requests for information, or instructions for running programs stored on a network.

Linked computers enable users to communicate and work together efficiently and effectively and thus have become central to the communications industry. They play a vital role in telecommunications, publishing, and news services.

Telecommunications

The industry that provides for communication across distances is called telecommunications. The telephone industry uses computers to switch and route phone calls automatically over telephone lines. Today, many kinds of information other than the spoken word move over such lines, including faxes and computer data. Data can be sent from computer to computer over telephone lines using a device known as a modem. One kind of data frequently sent by modem is electronic mail, or e-mail, which can be sent from person to person via the Internet or an online service. A more recent innovation in telecommunications is teleconferencing, which allows people in various locations to see and hear one another and thus hold virtual meetings.[1]

Publishing

Just twenty years ago, book manuscripts were typeset mechanically or on a typesetting machine and then reproduced on a printing press. Now anyone who has access to a computer and either a modem or a printer can undertake what has come to be known as electronic publishing. Writers and editors use word processing applications to produce text. Artists and designers use drawing and painting applications to create original graphics, and they use inexpensive scanners to digitize illustrations and photographs, or turn them into computer-readable files. Typesetters use personal computers to combine text, illustrations, and photographs. Publishers typically send computer-generated files to printers for production of the film and plates from which books and magazines are printed.[2]

News Services

News providers rely on reporters located worldwide. Reporters use e-mail to send, or upload, their stories to wire services. Increasingly, individuals get daily news reports from online services. News can also be accessed from specific providers, such as the *New York Times* or *U.S.A. Today*, via the Internet. One of the most popular Internet sites provides continuously updated weather reports.

COMPUTERS IN ENTERTAINMENT

Possibilities in the television and film industries have soared with computer technology, especially in production. Computer games have captured the public imagination and created enormous growth in the computer game market.

[1] Tony Waller, "Design Principles," *Network Designs* (2015): 19-22.
[2] Juanita Jackson, *Publishing* (Seattle: Walker Publications, 2014), 90-110.

Television and Film

Many of the spectacular graphics and special effects seen on television and in movies today are created with computers. The original *Star Wars* films, for example, relied heavily on hand-constructed models and hand-drawn graphics. Twenty years after the first release of the films, they were re-released with many new special effects, including futuristic cityscape backgrounds, new alien creatures, and new sounds that were created on computers and added to the films by means of computerized video editing. In an article on special effects, Jaclyn McFadden, an industry expert talked about the evolution of computer simulation.

The film *Jurassic Park* brought computer simulation to a new level by combining puppetry and computer animation to simulate realistic looking dinosaurs. *Toy Story*, released in 1996, was the first wholly computer-animated commercial movie.

Software products are available that automatically format scripts of various kinds. Industry analysts predict that the improvements in computer technology will continue to enhance and improve the visual appeal of television and film media.

Home Entertainment

In the 1970s, computer games such as Pong and Pac-Man captured the public's imagination. Since then, there has been enormous growth in the computer game market. The advent of powerful desktop personal computers has led to the production of home computer games that rival those of arcade machines in complexity. Manufacturers such as Sega and Nintendo produce large, complex, video arcade games as well as small computer game systems for home use.

Typical arcade-style computer games include simulations of boxing, warfare, racing, skiing, and flight. Other computer games make use of television or of small, independent, hand-held devices. Games are now able to take advantage of three-dimensional graphics that create virtual environments.[3]

[3] Bill Fortner, "Gaming News," *Home Computing* (2015): 44-47.

2

Contents

1

CHAPTER 1: COMPUTER VIRUSES

One of the most familiar forms of risk to computer security is the computer virus. A computer virus is a program written by a hacker or a cracker, designed to perform some kind of trick upon an unsuspecting victim's computer. In some cases, the trick performed is mild, such as drawing an offensive image on the victim's screen or changing all of the characters in a document to another language. Sometimes the trick is much more severe, such as reformatting the hard drive and erasing all the data or damaging the motherboard so that it cannot operate properly.

Types of Viruses

Viruses can be categorized by their effects, which include being a nuisance, destroying data, facilitating espionage, and destroying hardware. A nuisance virus usually does no real damage but is an inconvenience. The most difficult part of a computer to replace is the data on the hard drive. The installed programs, documents, databases, and saved e-mails form the heart of a personal computer. A data-destructive virus is designed to destroy this data. Some viruses are designed to create a backdoor into a system to bypass security. Called espionage viruses, they do no damage but allow a hacker or cracker to enter the system later for the purpose of stealing data or spying on the work of the competitor. Very rarely, a virus is created to damage the hardware of the computer system itself. Called hardware-destructive viruses, these bits of programming can weaken or destroy chips, drives, and other components.

Methods of Virus Operation

Viruses operate and are transmitted in a variety of ways. An e-mail virus is normally transmitted as an attachment to a message sent over the Internet. E-mail viruses require the victim to click on the attachment, which causes the virus to execute. Another common mode of virus transmission is via a macro, a small subprogram that allows users to customize and automate certain functions. A macro virus is written specifically for one program, which then becomes infected when it opens a file with the virus stored in its macros. The boot sector of a floppy disk or hard disk contains a variety of information, including how the disk is organized and whether it is capable of loading an operating system. When a disk is left in a drive and the computer reboots, the operating system automatically reads the boot sector to learn about that disk and to attempt to start any operating system on it. A boot sector virus is designed to alter the boot sector of a disk so that whenever the operating system reads the boot sector, the computer will automatically become infected.

Other types of viruses and methods of infection include the Trojan horse virus, which hides inside another legitimate program or data file, and the stealth virus, which is designed to hide itself from detection software. Polymorphic viruses alter themselves to prevent detection by antivirus software, which operates by examining familiar patterns. Polymorphic viruses alter themselves randomly as they move from computer to computer, making detection more difficult. Multipartite viruses alter their form of attack. Their name reflects their ability to attack in several different ways. They may first infect the boot sector and then later act like a Trojan horse virus by infecting a disk file. These viruses are more sophisticated and therefore more difficult to guard against. Another type of virus is the logic bomb, which generally sits quietly dormant waiting for a specific event or set of conditions to occur. A well- known example of a logic bomb was the widely publicized Michelangelo virus, which infected personal computers and caused them to display a message on the artist's birthday.

1

CHAPTER 2: SECURITY RISKS

Although hackers, crackers, and viruses garner the most attention as security risks, companies face a variety of other dangers to their hardware and software systems. Principally, these risks involve types of system failure, employee theft, and the cracking of software for copying.

Systems Failure

A fundamental element in making sure that computer systems operate properly is protecting the electrical power that runs them. Power interruptions such as blackouts and brownouts have very adverse effects on computers. An inexpensive type of power strip called a surge protector can guard against power fluctuations and can also serve as an extension cord and splitter. A much more vigorous power protection system is an uninterruptible power supply (UPS), which provides a battery backup. Similar in nature to a power strip but much bulkier and a bit more expensive, a UPS provides steady, spike-free power and keeps a computer running during a blackout.

Employee Theft

Although accurate estimates are difficult to pinpoint, businesses certainly lose millions of dollars a year in stolen computer hardware and software. In large organizations, such theft often goes unnoticed or unreported. Someone takes a hard drive or a scanner home for legitimate use, then leaves the job sometime later and keeps the machine. Sometimes, employees take components to add to their home PC systems, or thieves break into businesses and haul away computers. Such thefts cost far more than the price of the stolen computers because they also involve the cost of replacing the lost data, the cost of time lost while the machines are gone, and the cost of installing new machines and training people to use them.

Cracking Software for Copying

A common goal of hackers is to crack a software protection scheme. A crack is a method of circumventing a security scheme that prevents a user from copying a program. A common protection scheme for software is to require the installation CD to be resident in the drive whenever the program runs. Making copies of the CD with a burner, however, easily fools this protection scheme. Some game companies are taking an extra step to make duplication difficult by scrambling some of the data on the original CDs, which CD burners will automatically correct when copying. When the copied and corrected CD is used, the software checks for the scrambled track information. If the error is not found, the software will not run.

2

U06-SA02.docx (page 3 of 4)

INDEX

3

U06-SA02.docx (page 4 of 4)

L & N Employee Data

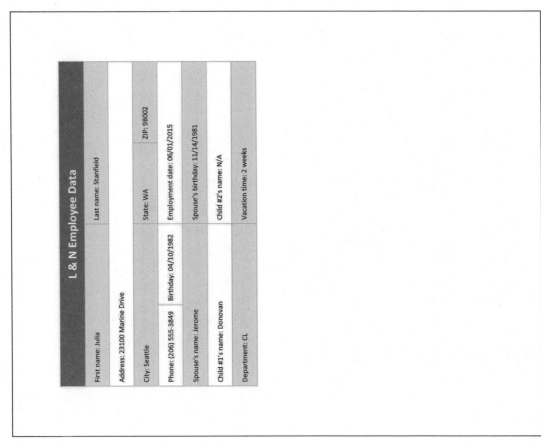

First name: Julia		Last name: Stanfield	
Address: 23100 Marine Drive			
City: Seattle		State: WA	ZIP: 98002
Phone: (206) 555-3849	Birthday: 04/10/1982	Employment date: 06/01/2015	
Spouse's name: Jerome		Spouse's birthday: 11/14/1981	
Child #1's name: Donovan		Child #2's name: N/A	
Department: CL		Vacation time: 2 weeks	

Specialty Enterprises

Annual Picnic and Golf Tournament
August 22, 2015
Sunbrook Golf Club

Name: Max Walters	Department: Accounting

Are you planning on attending the picnic? ☒ Yes ☐ No How many will be attending? 5

What will you bring to accompany our main dish? dessert

Will you be playing in the golf tournament? ☒ Yes ☐ No
If yes, list the people in your group: Max Walters, June Walters, Joan Roth,

EMPLOYEE HANDBOOK

This employee handbook is to be provided to each new employee of Terra Energy Corporation (TEC) during employee orientation. Each section of this handbook will be discussed and reviewed during the orientation.

GENERAL INFORMATION

New Employee Orientation

The Terra Energy Corporation New Employee Orientation Program is designed to welcome new employees into the spirit and culture of TEC, to clearly establish health care performance expectations, and to set the stage for success. New personnel are encouraged to begin their jobs with the monthly orientation in order to be introduced to the overall operations of TEC.

During your first few days of employment, you will participate in an orientation program conducted by several representatives of TEC. During this program, you will receive important information regarding the performance requirements of your position, basic TEC policies, your compensation package, as well as benefits and safety programs, plus other information necessary to acquaint you with your job and TEC. You will also be asked to complete all designated forms and appropriate federal, state, and local tax forms. During the orientation, you will be required to present information establishing your identity and your eligibility to work in the United States in accordance with applicable federal law. You will not be allowed to begin working unless this information has been provided.

Medical Screenings

As part of the TEC employment procedures, an applicant is required to undergo a post-offer, pre-employment medical screening and an alcohol and drug test. Any offer of employment that an applicant receives from TEC is contingent upon, among other things, satisfactory completion of screening and a determination by TEC that the applicant is capable of performing the essential functions of the position that has been offered, with or without reasonable accommodations.

As a condition of continued employment, employees may also be required to undergo periodic medical examinations, and/or alcohol and drug screening, at times specified by the TEC. In connection with these examinations, employees are required to provide TEC with access to their medical records, if requested. TEC receives a full medical report from its examining physicians regarding the applicant's or employee's state of health. All company-required pre-employment and alcohol and drug screenings are paid in full by TEC.

All drivers will be required to participate in random drug screening. This screening will take place every six months and/or more often if deemed necessary by an TEC management representative. Other OMA employees may be asked at any time to participate in this random drug screening.

Licensure

Persons being considered for employment whose occupations are regulated by a state licensing board must present proof of licensure before beginning work. Employees are responsible for renewing their licenses when necessary and ensuring that licenses are kept current. An employee who fails to present or maintain a valid license as requested will not be allowed to work.

Introductory Period

All new employees and current employees promoted or transferred to a new position shall be on a 90-day probationary period starting on their first day worked. This period may be extended if additional time is required in order to completely assess an employee's performance. This period gives both TEC and the employee time to assess their new relationship and performance. During this period, an employee may not be eligible for all benefits.

Identification Badges

As a vital part of our security program, an identification badge containing your name and photo will be issued to you as you begin employment. If your identification badge is lost or stolen, you must pay for a replacement. You are required to wear your identification badge in clear view at all times while on duty.

Upon termination of employment, you must return your identification badge to a Human Resources Department representative.

Security

All vehicles, lockers, desks, offices, and containers that are TEC property, as well as briefcases, backpacks, parcels, and other personal belongings of employees, are subject to inspection and search by TEC or their designated agents.

Performance Review

All TEC employees will be evaluated at periodic intervals based on his/her job description and not less than annually. A performance appraisal is intended to document and maintain satisfactory performance of an individual employee by providing a means of measuring an employee's effectiveness on the job, identifying areas where an employee is in need of training or improving, and maintaining a high level of motivation through feedback and the setting of specific goals on the basis of the feedback.

Employees are responsible for working with their supervisors on an ongoing basis to develop and maintain a clear performance plan defining various performance expectations and their relative priority.

COMMUNICATION

Employee Communication

Effective communication is essential to provide the best patient care, maintain productivity, sustain morale, and foster constructive employee relations. Employee communications in the TEC environment include the following:

- **Employee/supervisor meetings:** Questions and concerns relating to job activities should first be presented to supervisors. Communication between the supervisor and the employee should be ongoing and address concerns, duties, and expectations. Supervisors can help employees achieve their professional goals by providing career development information.
- **Newsletter:** TEC publishes a monthly newsletter providing information on new hires, benefit updates, and the latest health care news.
- **Bulletin board postings:** Bulletin boards are located throughout the clinic and provide information to keep employees up to date on announcements and clinic news.

Employer Communication

TEC supervisors, department leaders, and other management representatives maintain open and constructive communication in the following ways:

The position of each employee's salary within the range that has been established for his or her job will be determined primarily by the employee's relevant experience and job performance. TEC compensation programs are designed and administered in such a way as to comply with all applicable laws and to provide fair and equitable treatment for all employees.

- **Regular pay procedures:** All TEC employees are normally paid on Fridays on a bi-weekly basis. If a scheduled payday falls on a company observed holiday, you will usually be paid on the day preceding the holiday. All required deductions, such as federal, state, and local taxes, and all authorized voluntary deductions, such as health insurance contributions, will be withheld automatically from your paycheck. All documentation of work completed must be submitted by those staff members providing direct patient care.
- **Merit increases:** The purpose of merit increases is to recognize and reward employee performance over a designated period of time, and a minimum of once a year.
- **Acting pay:** Acting pay may be granted when an employee is temporarily assigned, for a period of at least one week or more, to assume a substantial portion of the responsibilities of a job with a higher pay range.
- **On-call pay:** Since some employees are required to be available for work on an on-call basis, special rates for on-call hours will be paid to non-exempt employees. Your supervisor will notify you of proper procedures if you are required to work on-call.
- **Bonus pay:** Bonus pay is additional compensation paid to an employee, or group of employees, in addition to their normal rate of pay. Bonus pay may be granted only under limited circumstances.
- **Market adjustments:** Market adjustments to salary ranges may occur outside of the annual salary planning cycle when market demand has resulted in an increased rate of pay for a particular job or job category.
- **Reductions in pay:** For a variety of reasons, an employee may be reassigned to a job that has a lower pay range than the job they had previously held. In such cases, reduction in pay guidelines will apply.
- **Shift differentials:** Employees receive shift differential pay for all hours worked if they work a minimum of six consecutive hours during a shift where a differential applies.
- **Weekend differential:** An employee who works four or more consecutive hours during a designated weekend period is entitled to receive a weekend differential for all hours worked on that shift. For the purposes of this policy, the weekend is defined as beginning 11:00 p.m. Friday and ending 7:00 a.m. Monday.

- **Department and unit meetings:** Departments and units meet to communicate goals and objectives and to discuss workplace issues of interest to employees. Employees should check with supervisors to obtain a schedule of the meetings.
- **Management meetings:** All levels of management routinely hold meetings to communicate information and discuss matters of importance.

EMPLOYMENT CATEGORIES

Employee Categories

Throughout this handbook, you will see references to several employee categories with which you should become familiar. The categories include the following:

- **Exempt:** Refers to those employees excluded from the overtime provisions of the Fair Labor Standards Act. The professional clinical staff is considered exempt. The introductory period for exempt employees is 90 days.
- **Non-exempt:** Refers to those positions eligible for overtime pay if more than 40 hours are worked during a work week. The introductory period for non-exempt employees is 90 days.

Category Definitions

- **Probationary:** All persons newly hired or rehired are considered probationary employees until the completion of 90 calendar days of employment.
- **Regular full time:** A regular full-time employee is one who is employed on a regular basis on a schedule of 30 to 40 hours per week. Regular full-time employees are fully eligible for all benefits.
- **Regular part time:** Employees scheduled for 20 or more hours per week are eligible for employee benefits on a prorated basis in relation to their scheduled hours worked, up to 40.
- **Non-benefit eligible part time:** Employees scheduled to work less than 20 hours may be terminated without notice or cause.
- **Temporary full time:** A temporary full-time employee is one who is employed on a schedule of 40 hours per week for a limited period of time and is so informed at the time of hire.
- **Temporary part time:** A temporary part-time employee is one who is employed on a schedule of less than 30 hours per week for a limited period of time and is so informed at the time of hire.
- **Per visit:** Per-visit employees are hired to work on a per diem basis for an undetermined period of time. Per-visit employees can be terminated without notice or cause.

EMPLOYEE COMPENSATION

Pay Range

A pay range is established for each of the organization's jobs and these ranges are internally equitable as well as externally competitive when compared with the rates paid by other employers for comparable jobs. Each employee whose performance is "proficient" or better will receive a rate of pay that falls within the pay range that has been established for his/her job.

Compensation Procedures

EMPLOYEE HANDBOOK

This employee handbook is to be provided to each new employee of Terra Energy Corporation (TEC) during employee orientation. Each section of this handbook will be discussed and reviewed during the orientation.

J:\IRC_Signature\SupplementalActivities\GENERAL INFORMATION.docx
J:\IRC_Signature\SupplementalActivities\EMPLOYEE COMPENSATION.docx
J:\IRC_Signature\SupplementalActivities\COMMUNICATION.docx

EMPLOYEE HANDBOOK

This employee handbook is to be provided to each new employee of Terra Energy Corporation (TEC) during employee orientation. Each section of this handbook will be discussed and reviewed during the orientation.

J:\IRC_Signature\SupplementalActivities\GENERAL INFORMATION.docx
J:\IRC_Signature\SupplementalActivities\COMMUNICATION.docx
J:\IRC_Signature\SupplementalActivities\EMPLOYMENT CATEGORIES.docx
J:\IRC_Signature\SupplementalActivities\EMPLOYEE COMPENSATION.docx